TRIPLE SHOT DOUBLE-PUMP NO WHIP

Zits

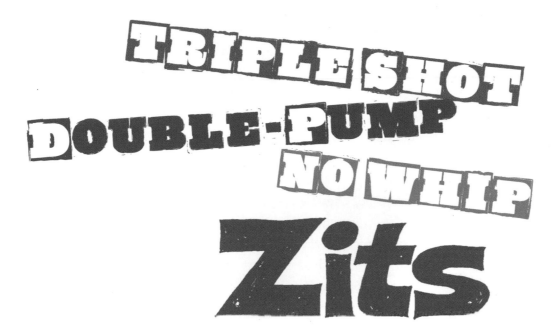

Also By Jerry Scott and Jim Borgman

Zits: Sketchbook 1

Growth Spurt: Zits Sketchbook 2

Don't Roll Your Eyes at Me, Young Man!: Zits Sketchbook 3

Are We an "Us"?: Zits Sketchbook 4

Zits Unzipped: Zits Sketchbook 5

Busted!: Zits Sketchbook 6

Road Trip: Zits Sketchbook 7

Teenage Tales: Zits Sketchbook No. 8

Thrashed: Zits Sketchbook No. 9

Pimp My Lunch: Zits Sketchbook No. 10

Are We Out of the Driveway Yet?: Zits Sketchbook No. 11

Rude, Crude, and Tattooed: Zits Sketchbook No. 12

Jeremy and Mom

Pierced

Lust and Other Uses for Spare Hormones

Jeremy & Dad

You're Making That Face Again

Drive!

Zombie Parents

Treasuries

Humongous Zits

Big Honkin' Zits

Zits: Supersized

Random Zits

Crack of Noon

Alternative Zits

My Bad

Sunday Brunch

Gift Book

A Zits Guide to Living with Your Teenager

TRIPLE SHOT DOUBLE-PUMP NO WHIP Zits

A ZITS® Treasury by Jerry Scott and Jim Borgman

Andrews McMeel
Publishing

Kansas City • Sydney • London

Zits® is syndicated internationally by King Features Syndicate, Inc. For information, write King Features Syndicate, Inc., 300 West Fifty-Seventh Street, New York, New York 10019.

Andrews McMeel Publishing, LLC
an Andrews McMeel Universal company
1130 Walnut Street, Kansas City, Missouri 64106

www.andrewsmcmeel.com

14 15 16 17 18 SDB 11 10 9 8 7 6 5 4 3

ISBN: 978-1-4494-2310-0

Library of Congress Control Number: 2012945462

ATTENTION: SCHOOLS AND BUSINESSES
Andrews McMeel books are available at quantity discounts with bulk purchase for educational, business, or sales promotional use. For information, please e-mail the Andrews McMeel Publishing Special Sales Department: specialsales@amuniversal.com.

To Big Sky Cafe,
where caffeine and comics converge
—JS

To The Laughing Goat, Awakenings, Lookout Joe's,
New Moon Bakery, and Buffalo Bill's Coffee Shop
—JB

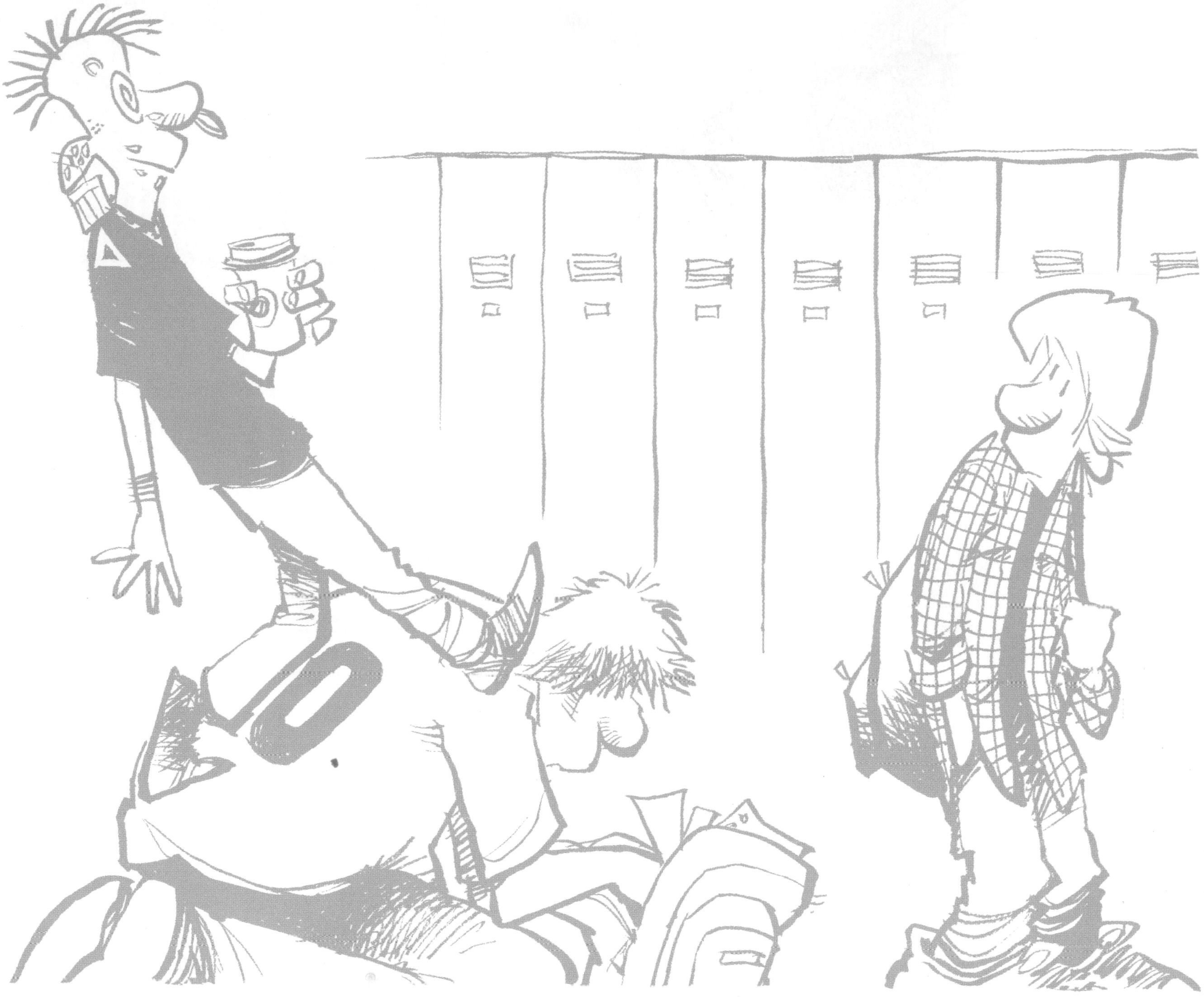

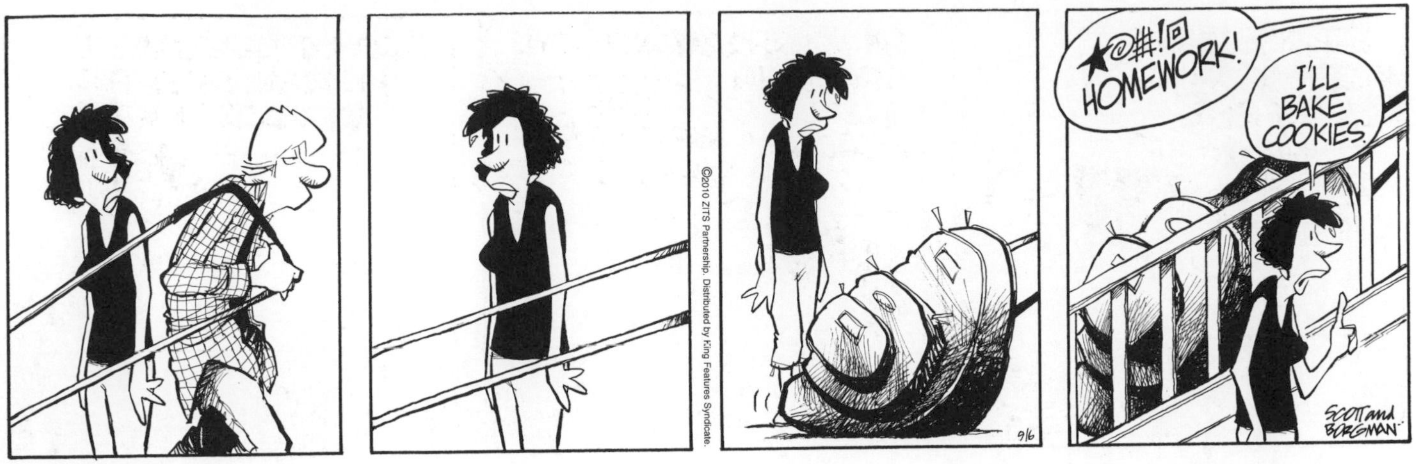
©2010 ZITS Partnership. Distributed by King Features Syndicate.
★@#!◙ HOMEWORK!
I'LL BAKE COOKIES.
9/6
SCOTT and BORGMAN

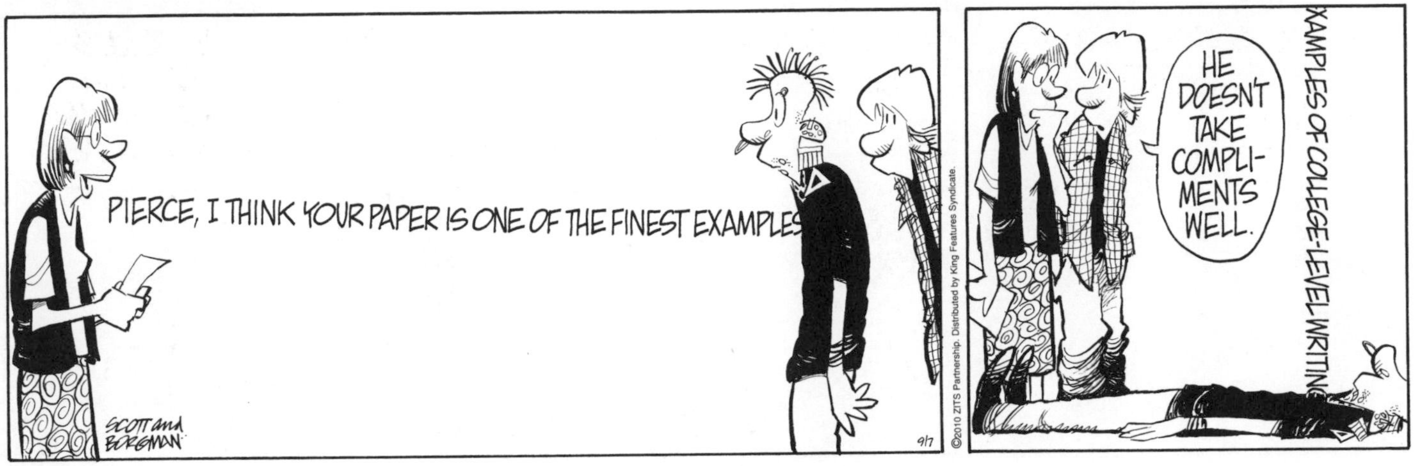
PIERCE, I THINK YOUR PAPER IS ONE OF THE FINEST EXAMPLES
SCOTT and BORGMAN
9/7
©2010 ZITS Partnership. Distributed by King Features Syndicate.
XAMPLES OF COLLEGE-LEVEL WRITING
HE DOESN'T TAKE COMPLIMENTS WELL.

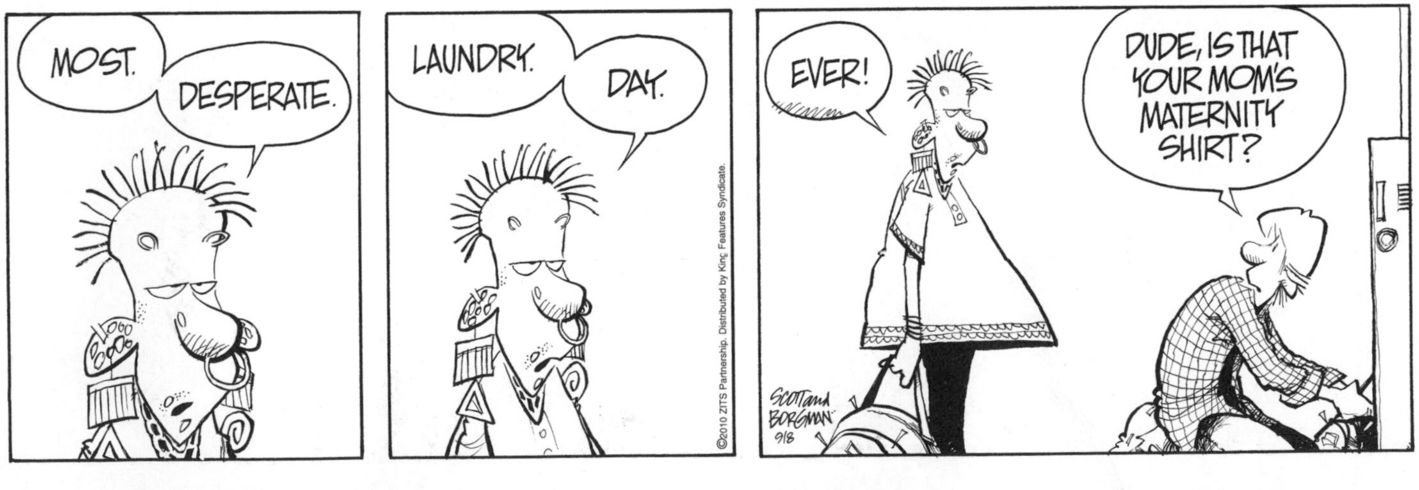
MOST.
DESPERATE.
LAUNDRY.
DAY.
©2010 ZITS Partnership. Distributed by King Features Syndicate.
EVER!
DUDE, IS THAT YOUR MOM'S MATERNITY SHIRT?
SCOTT and BORGMAN
9/8

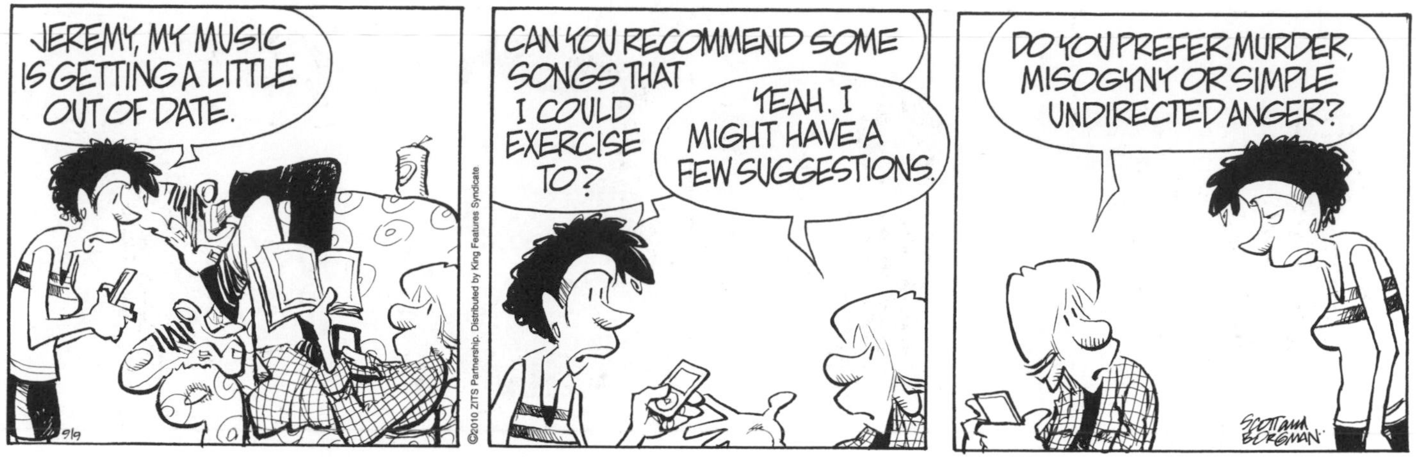
JEREMY, MY MUSIC IS GETTING A LITTLE OUT OF DATE.
9/9
©2010 ZITS Partnership. Distributed by King Features Syndicate
CAN YOU RECOMMEND SOME SONGS THAT I COULD EXERCISE TO?
YEAH. I MIGHT HAVE A FEW SUGGESTIONS.
DO YOU PREFER MURDER, MISOGYNY OR SIMPLE UNDIRECTED ANGER?
SCOTT and BORGMAN

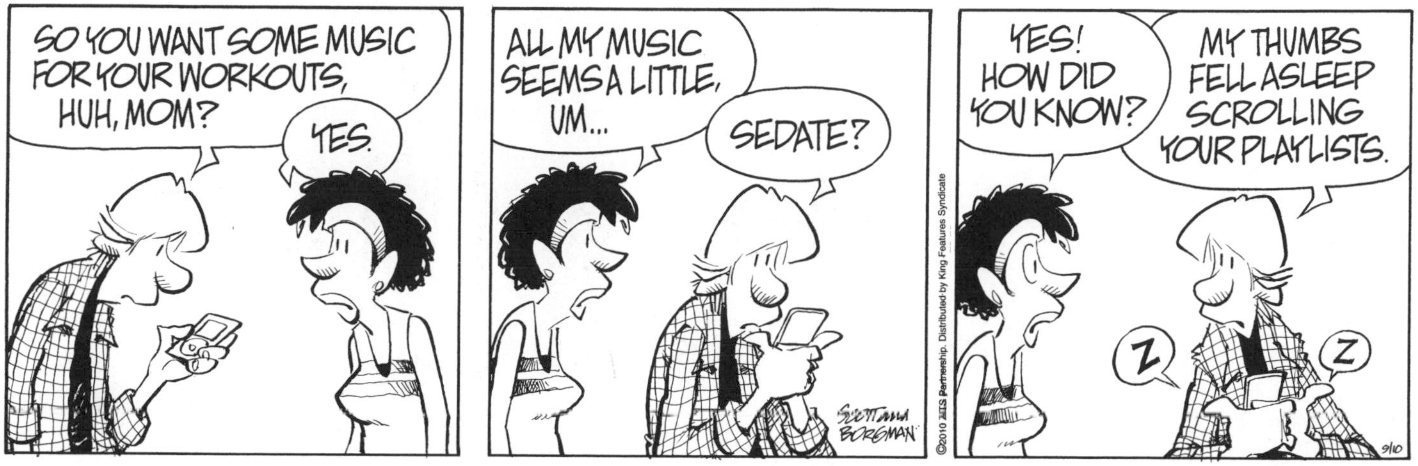
SO YOU WANT SOME MUSIC FOR YOUR WORKOUTS, HUH, MOM?
YES.
ALL MY MUSIC SEEMS A LITTLE, UM...
SEDATE?
SCOTT and BORGMAN
©2010 ZITS Partnership. Distributed by King Features Syndicate
YES! HOW DID YOU KNOW?
MY THUMBS FELL ASLEEP SCROLLING YOUR PLAYLISTS.
Z
Z
9/10

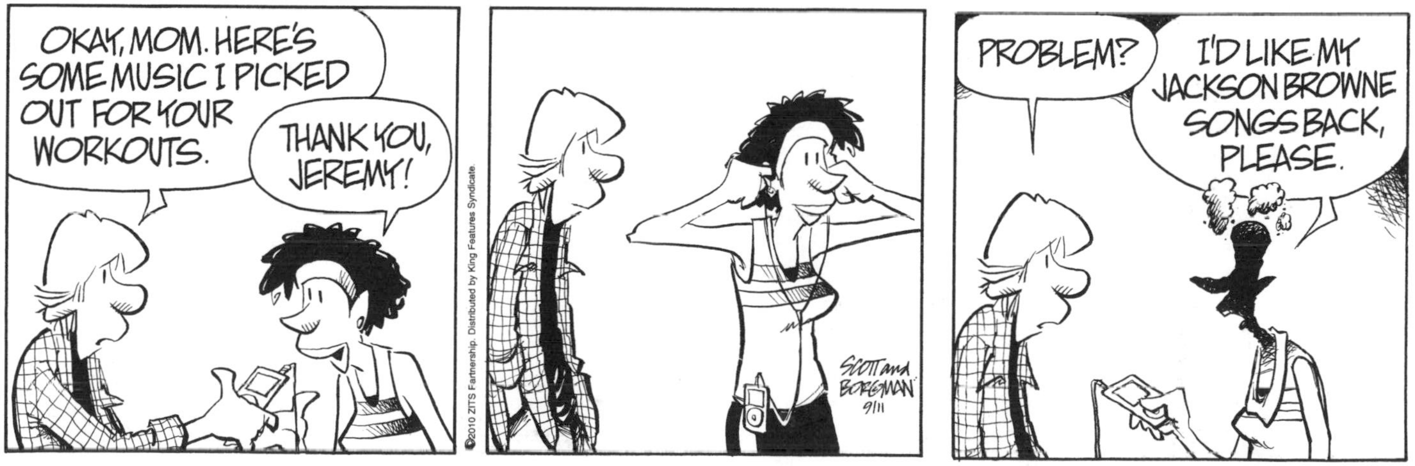
OKAY, MOM. HERE'S SOME MUSIC I PICKED OUT FOR YOUR WORKOUTS.
THANK YOU, JEREMY!
©2010 ZITS Partnership. Distributed by King Features Syndicate.
SCOTT and BORGMAN
9/11
PROBLEM?
I'D LIKE MY JACKSON BROWNE SONGS BACK, PLEASE.

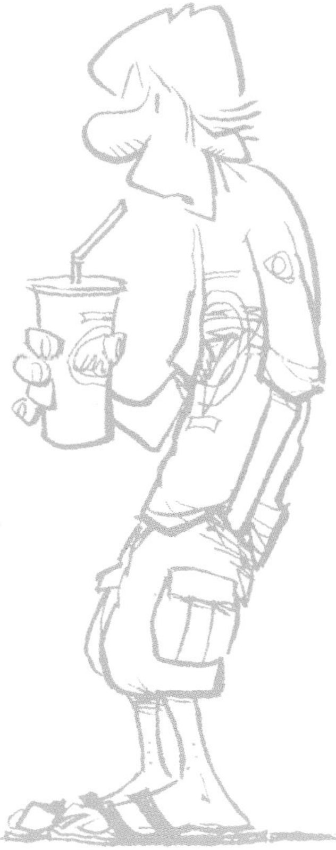

Zits

by JERRY SCOTT and JIM BORGMAN

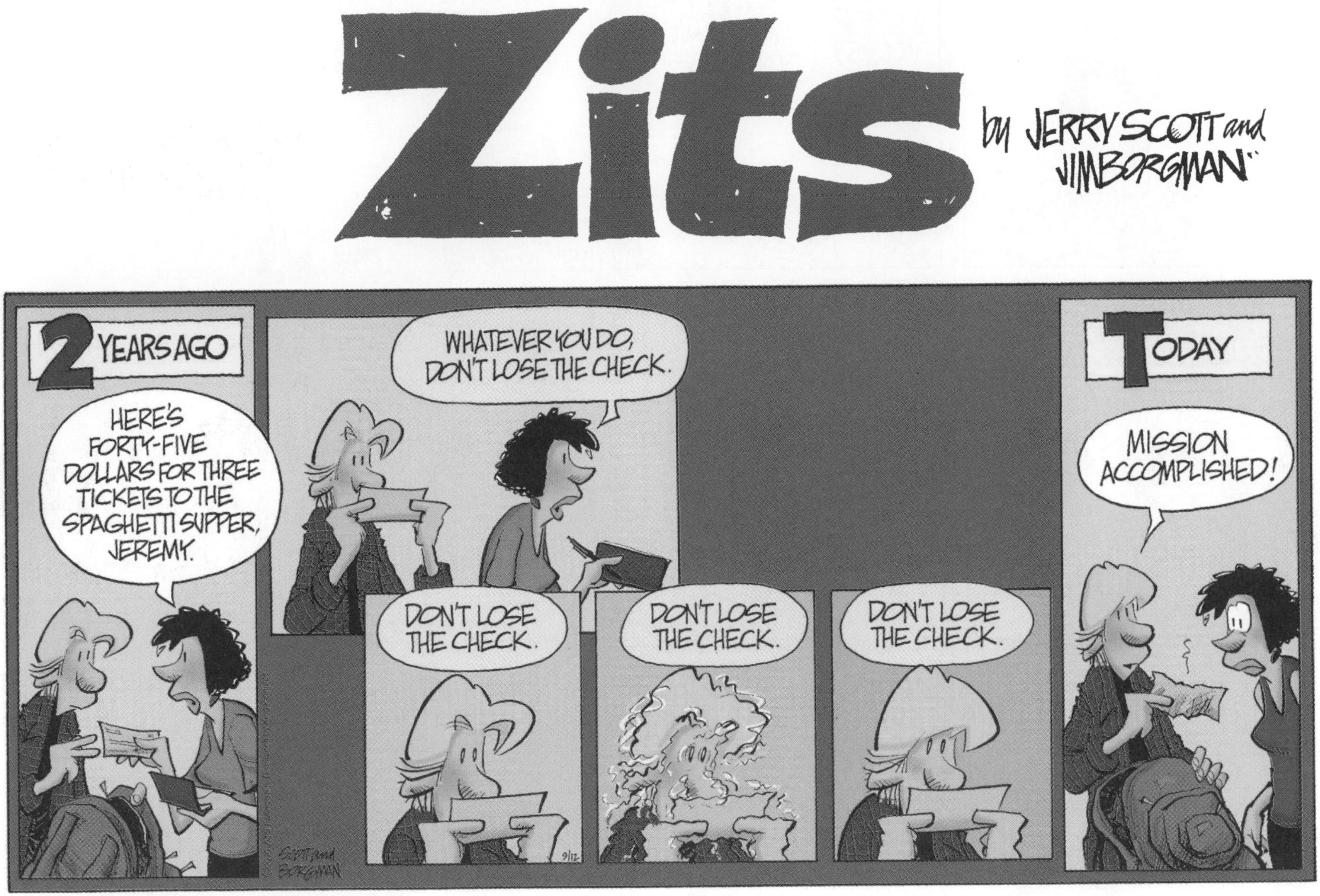

2 YEARS AGO
HERE'S FORTY-FIVE DOLLARS FOR THREE TICKETS TO THE SPAGHETTI SUPPER, JEREMY.
WHATEVER YOU DO, DON'T LOSE THE CHECK.
DON'T LOSE THE CHECK.
DON'T LOSE THE CHECK.
DON'T LOSE THE CHECK.
TODAY
MISSION ACCOMPLISHED!

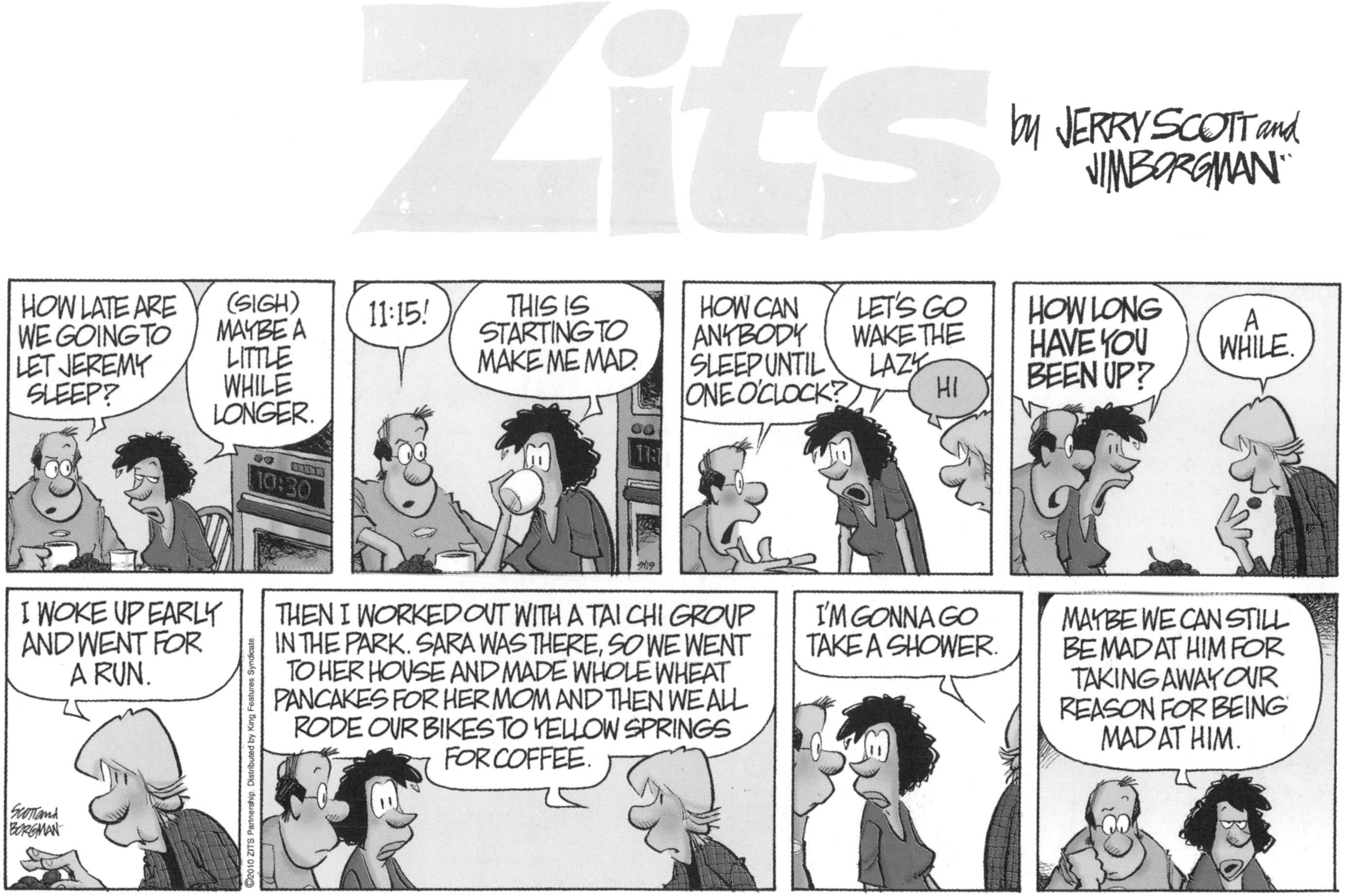
Zits
by JERRY SCOTT and JIM BORGMAN
HOW LATE ARE WE GOING TO LET JEREMY SLEEP?
(SIGH) MAYBE A LITTLE WHILE LONGER.
10:30
11:15!
THIS IS STARTING TO MAKE ME MAD.
HOW CAN ANYBODY SLEEP UNTIL ONE O'CLOCK?
LET'S GO WAKE THE LAZY
HI
HOW LONG HAVE YOU BEEN UP?
A WHILE.
I WOKE UP EARLY AND WENT FOR A RUN.
SCOTT and BORGMAN
©2010 ZITS Partnership. Distributed by King Features Syndicate.
THEN I WORKED OUT WITH A TAI CHI GROUP IN THE PARK. SARA WAS THERE, SO WE WENT TO HER HOUSE AND MADE WHOLE WHEAT PANCAKES FOR HER MOM AND THEN WE ALL RODE OUR BIKES TO YELLOW SPRINGS FOR COFFEE.
I'M GONNA GO TAKE A SHOWER.
MAYBE WE CAN STILL BE MAD AT HIM FOR TAKING AWAY OUR REASON FOR BEING MAD AT HIM.

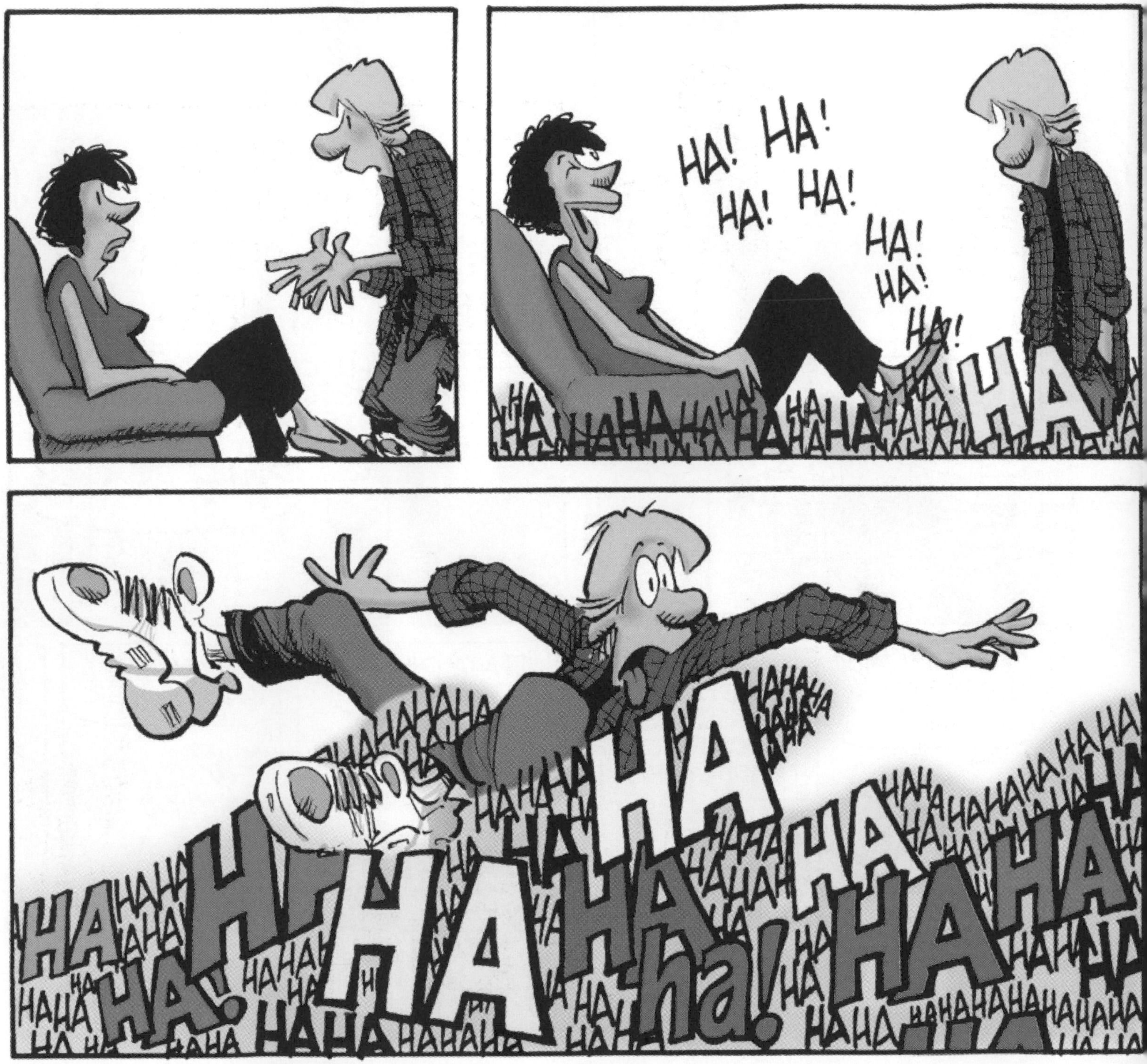
HA! HA!
HA! HA!
HA!
HA!
HA!

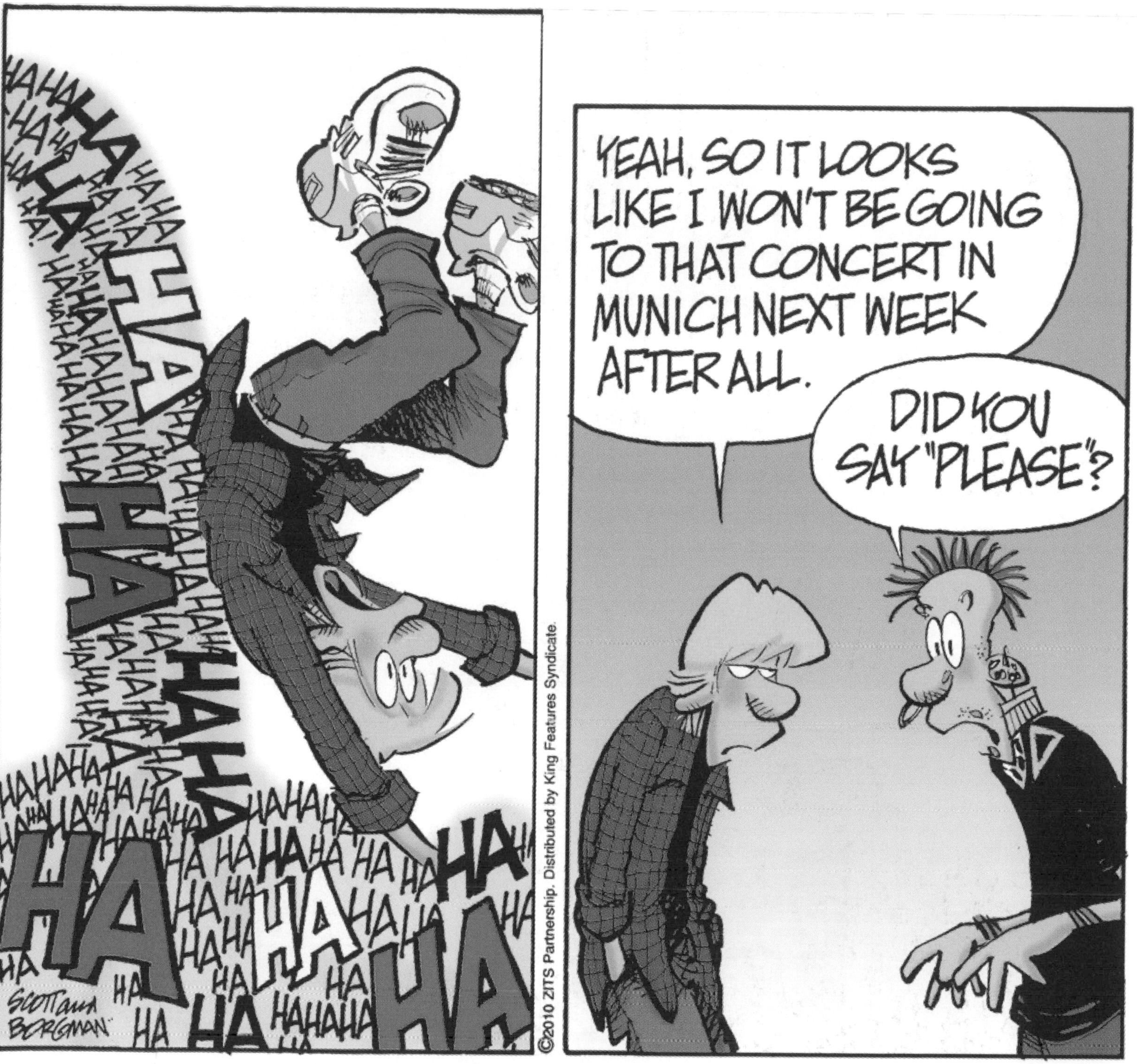
HA HA HA HA HA HA HA HA HA HA HA HA HA HA HA HA HA HA HA HA
SCOTT AND BORGMAN
YEAH, SO IT LOOKS LIKE I WON'T BE GOING TO THAT CONCERT IN MUNICH NEXT WEEK AFTER ALL.
DID YOU SAY "PLEASE"?

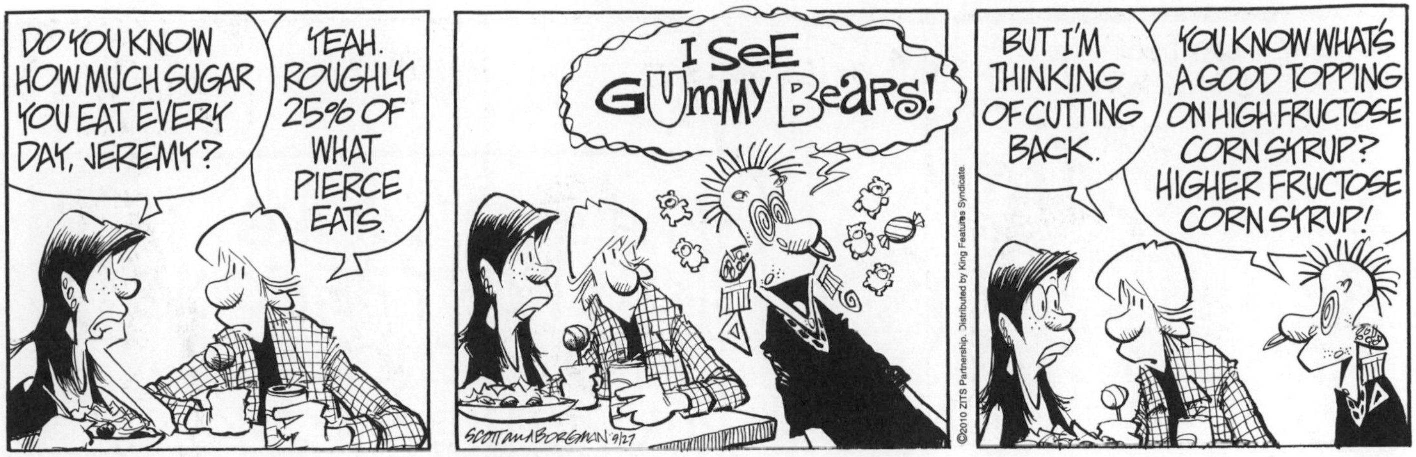
DO YOU KNOW HOW MUCH SUGAR YOU EAT EVERY DAY, JEREMY?
YEAH. ROUGHLY 25% OF WHAT PIERCE EATS.
I SEE GUMMY BEARS!
SCOTT AND BORGMAN 9/27
BUT I'M THINKING OF CUTTING BACK.
YOU KNOW WHAT'S A GOOD TOPPING ON HIGH FRUCTOSE CORN SYRUP? HIGHER FRUCTOSE CORN SYRUP!
©2010 ZITS Partnership. Distributed by King Features Syndicate.

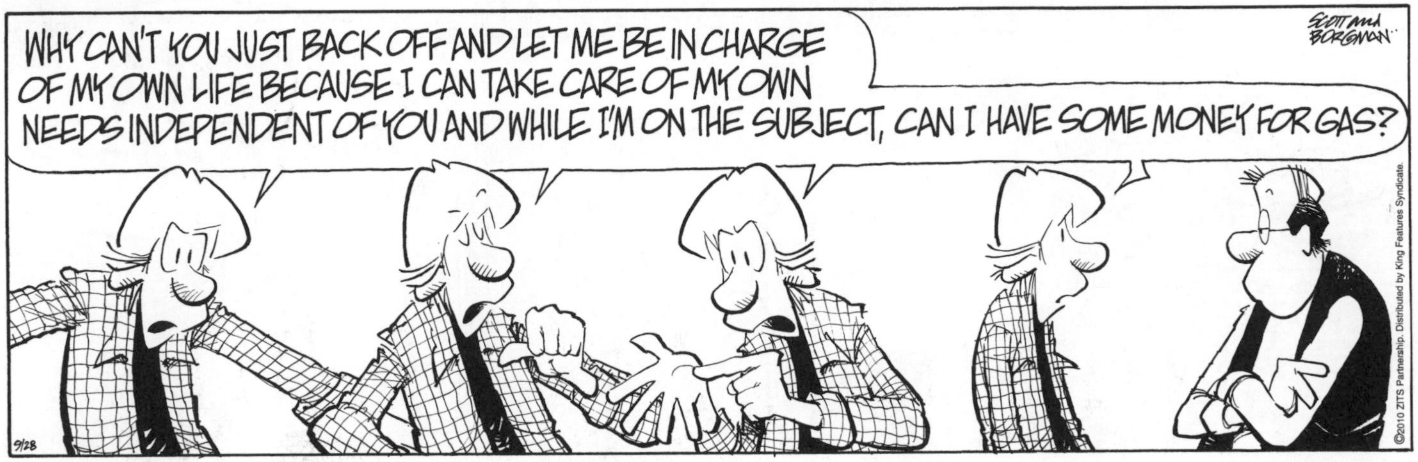
SCOTT AND BORGMAN
WHY CAN'T YOU JUST BACK OFF AND LET ME BE IN CHARGE OF MY OWN LIFE BECAUSE I CAN TAKE CARE OF MY OWN NEEDS INDEPENDENT OF YOU AND WHILE I'M ON THE SUBJECT, CAN I HAVE SOME MONEY FOR GAS?
9/28
©2010 ZITS Partnership. Distributed by King Features Syndicate.

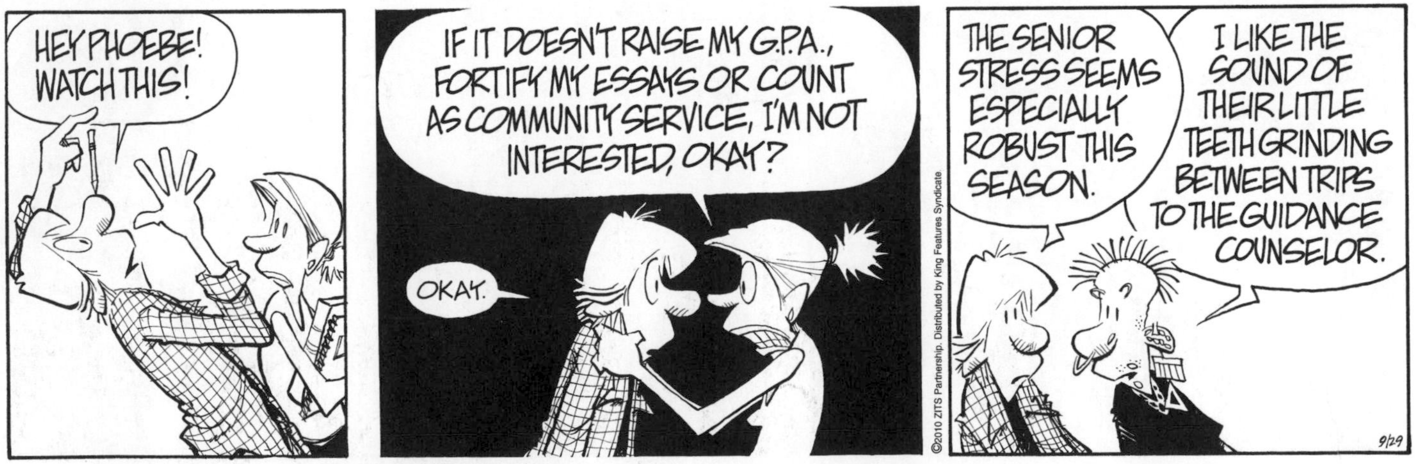
HEY PHOEBE! WATCH THIS!
IF IT DOESN'T RAISE MY G.P.A., FORTIFY MY ESSAYS OR COUNT AS COMMUNITY SERVICE, I'M NOT INTERESTED, OKAY?
OKAY.
©2010 ZITS Partnership. Distributed by King Features Syndicate
THE SENIOR STRESS SEEMS ESPECIALLY ROBUST THIS SEASON.
I LIKE THE SOUND OF THEIR LITTLE TEETH GRINDING BETWEEN TRIPS TO THE GUIDANCE COUNSELOR.
9/29

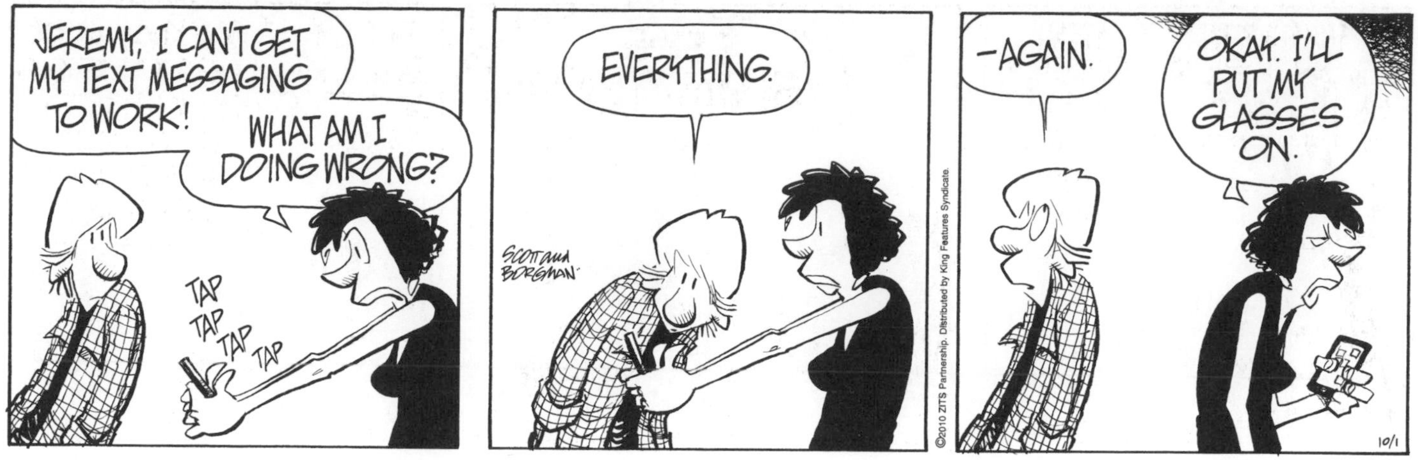
JEREMY, I CAN'T GET MY TEXT MESSAGING TO WORK!
WHAT AM I DOING WRONG?
TAP TAP TAP TAP
EVERYTHING.
-AGAIN.
OKAY. I'LL PUT MY GLASSES ON.
©2010 ZITS Partnership. Distributed by King Features Syndicate.
10/1

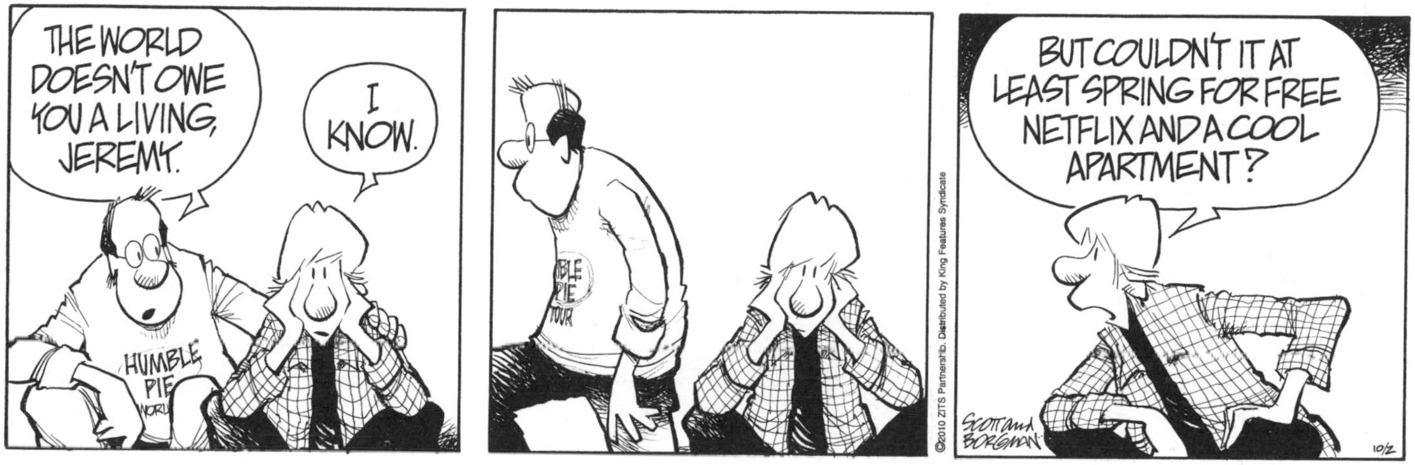
THE WORLD DOESN'T OWE YOU A LIVING, JEREMY.
I KNOW.
BUT COULDN'T IT AT LEAST SPRING FOR FREE NETFLIX AND A COOL APARTMENT?
©2010 ZITS Partnership. Distributed by King Features Syndicate
10/2

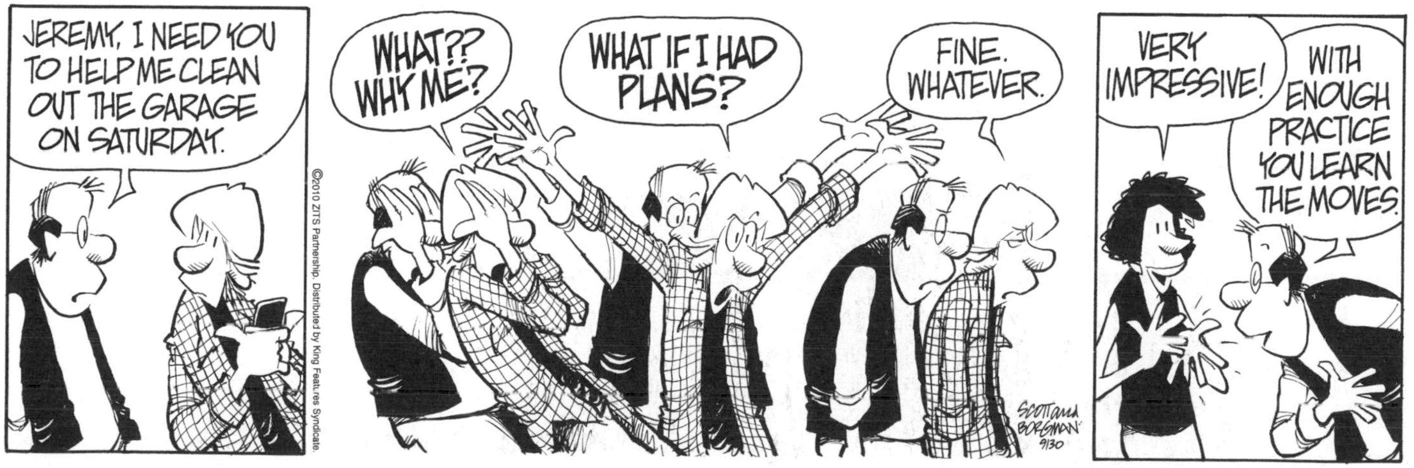
JEREMY, I NEED YOU TO HELP ME CLEAN OUT THE GARAGE ON SATURDAY.
WHAT?? WHY ME?
WHAT IF I HAD PLANS?
FINE. WHATEVER.
VERY IMPRESSIVE!
WITH ENOUGH PRACTICE YOU LEARN THE MOVES.
©2010 ZITS Partnership. Distributed by King Features Syndicate.
9/30

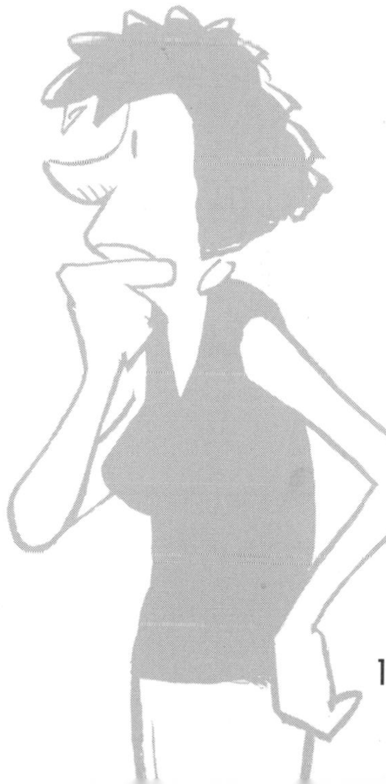

Zits

by JERRY SCOTT and JIM BORGMAN

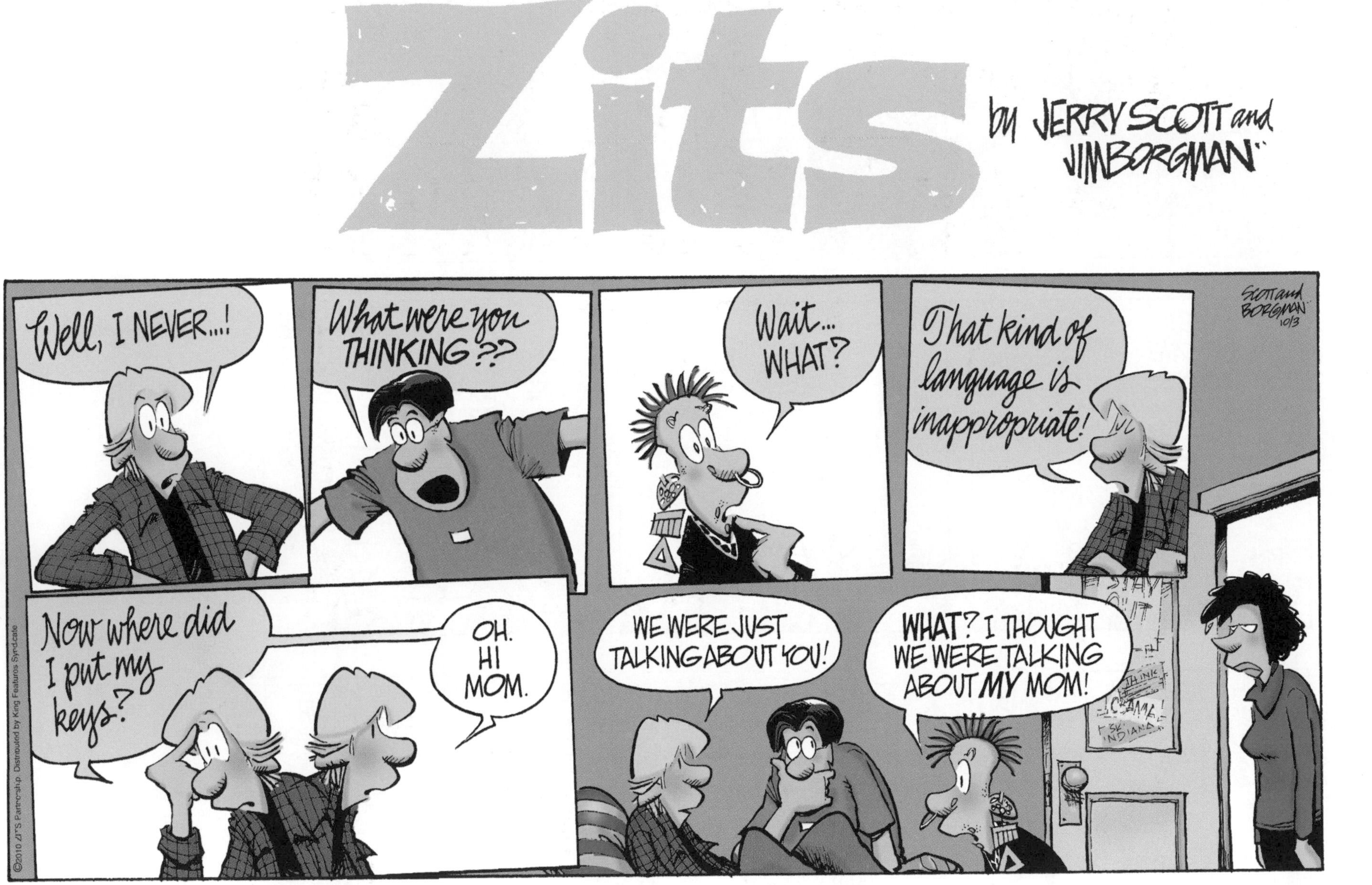
Well, I NEVER...!
What were you THINKING ??
Wait... WHAT?
That kind of language is inappropriate!
SCOTT and BORGMAN 10/3
Now where did I put my keys?
OH. HI MOM.
WE WERE JUST TALKING ABOUT YOU!
WHAT? I THOUGHT WE WERE TALKING ABOUT MY MOM!
©2010 ZITS Partnership. Distributed by King Features Syndicate

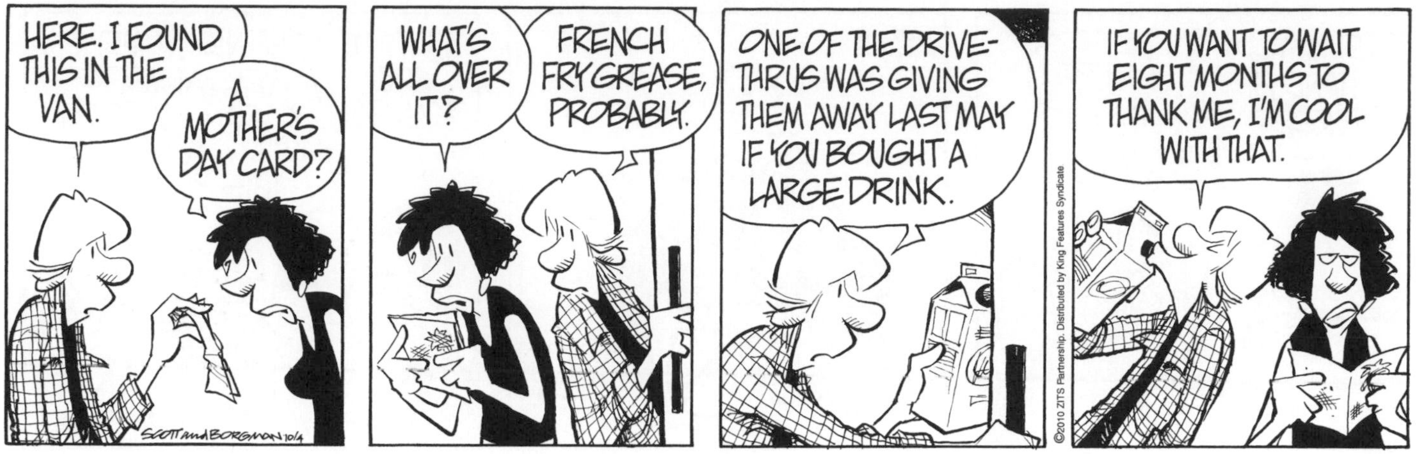
HERE. I FOUND THIS IN THE VAN.
A MOTHER'S DAY CARD?
WHAT'S ALL OVER IT?
FRENCH FRY GREASE, PROBABLY.
ONE OF THE DRIVE-THRUS WAS GIVING THEM AWAY LAST MAY IF YOU BOUGHT A LARGE DRINK.
IF YOU WANT TO WAIT EIGHT MONTHS TO THANK ME, I'M COOL WITH THAT.
SCOTT and BORGMAN 10/4
©2010 ZITS Partnership. Distributed by King Features Syndicate

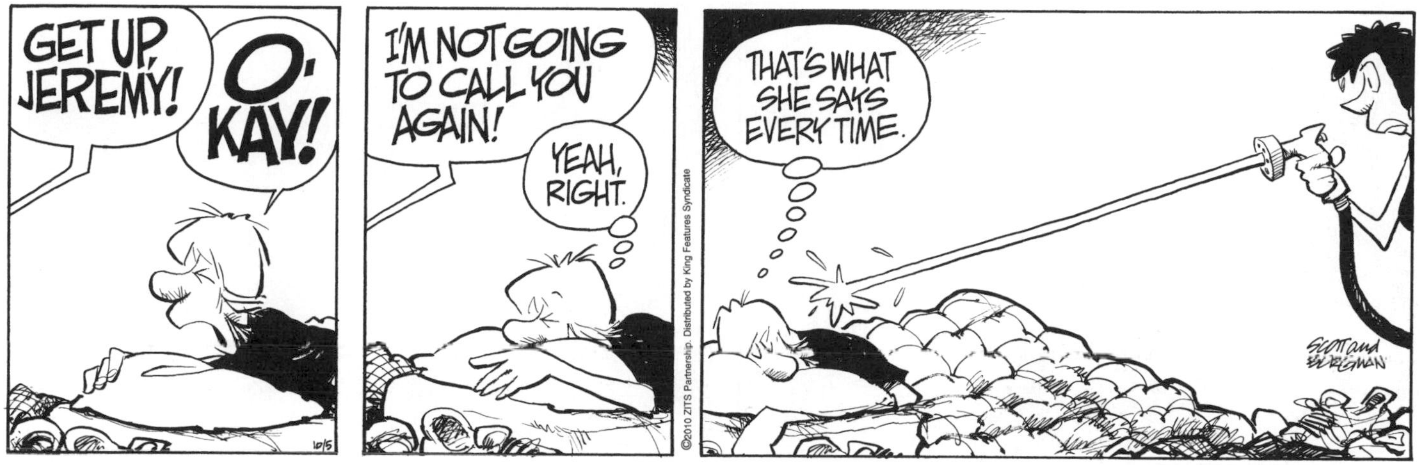
GET UP, JEREMY!
O-KAY!
I'M NOT GOING TO CALL YOU AGAIN!
YEAH, RIGHT.
THAT'S WHAT SHE SAYS EVERY TIME.
SCOTT and BORGMAN
10/5
©2010 ZITS Partnership. Distributed by King Features Syndicate

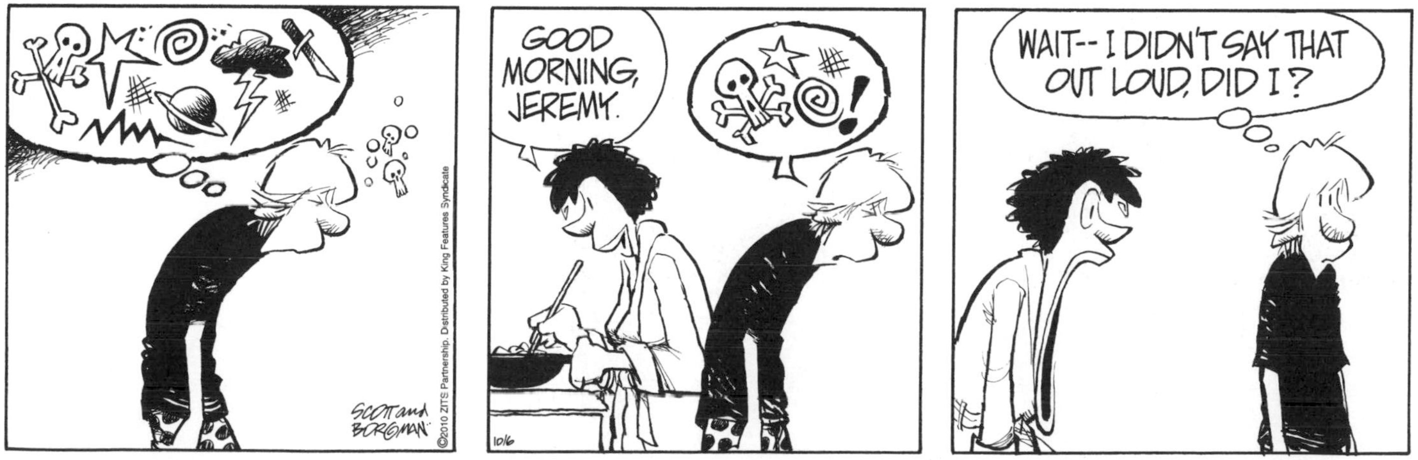
GOOD MORNING, JEREMY.
WAIT-- I DIDN'T SAY THAT OUT LOUD, DID I?
SCOTT and BORGMAN
10/6
©2010 ZITS Partnership. Distributed by King Features Syndicate

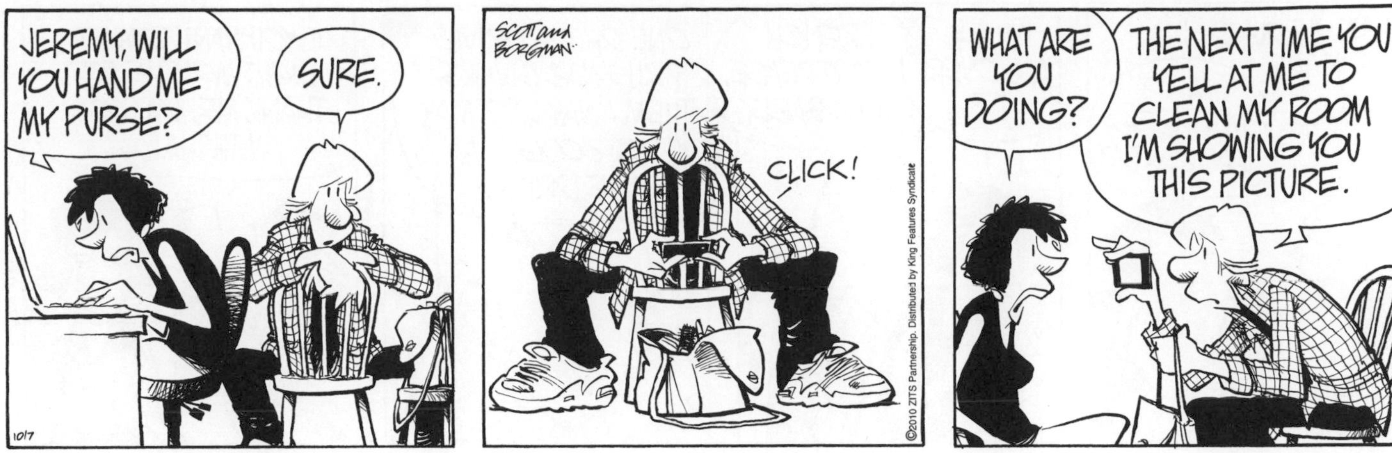
JEREMY, WILL YOU HAND ME MY PURSE?
SURE.
10/7
SCOTT and BORGMAN
CLICK!
©2010 ZITS Partnership. Distributed by King Features Syndicate
WHAT ARE YOU DOING?
THE NEXT TIME YOU YELL AT ME TO CLEAN MY ROOM I'M SHOWING YOU THIS PICTURE.

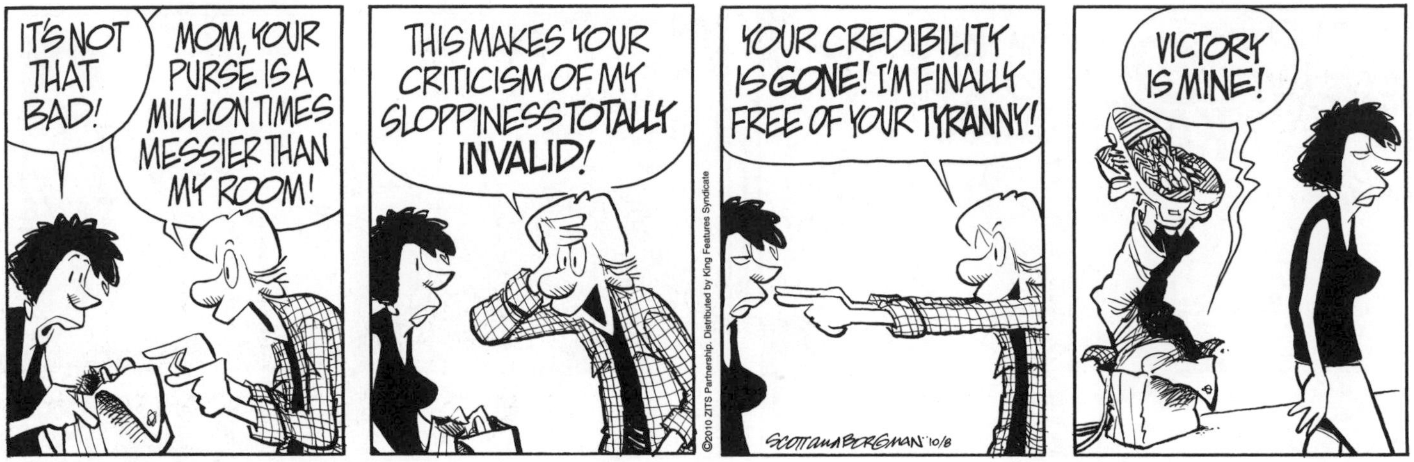
IT'S NOT THAT BAD!
MOM, YOUR PURSE IS A MILLION TIMES MESSIER THAN MY ROOM!
THIS MAKES YOUR CRITICISM OF MY SLOPPINESS TOTALLY INVALID!
©2010 ZITS Partnership. Distributed by King Features Syndicate
YOUR CREDIBILITY IS GONE! I'M FINALLY FREE OF YOUR TYRANNY!
SCOTT and BORGMAN 10/8
VICTORY IS MINE!

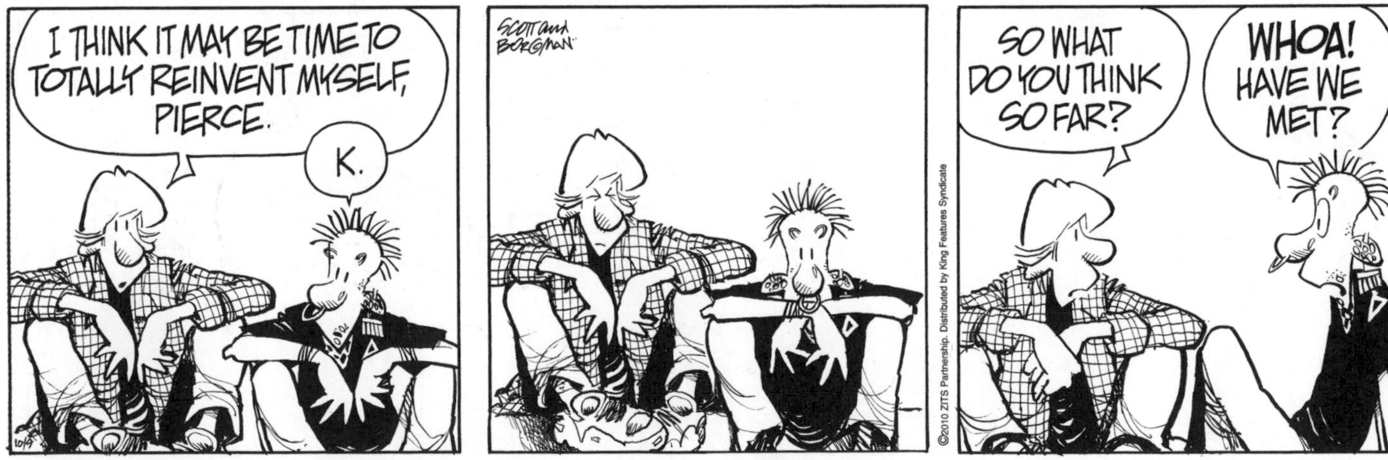
I THINK IT MAY BE TIME TO TOTALLY REINVENT MYSELF, PIERCE.
K.
10/9
SCOTT and BORGMAN
©2010 ZITS Partnership. Distributed by King Features Syndicate
SO WHAT DO YOU THINK SO FAR?
WHOA! HAVE WE MET?

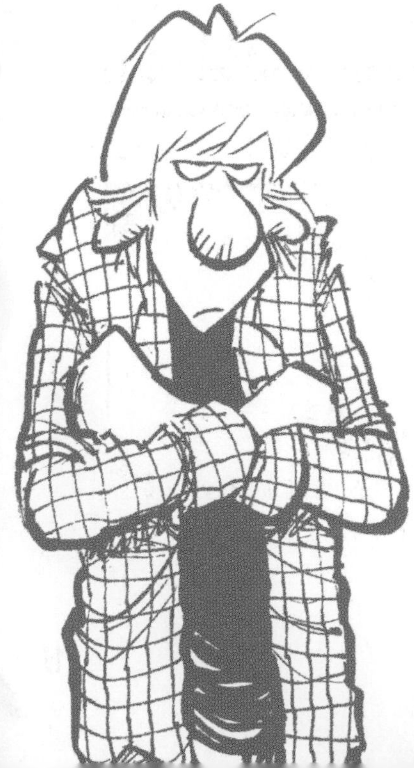

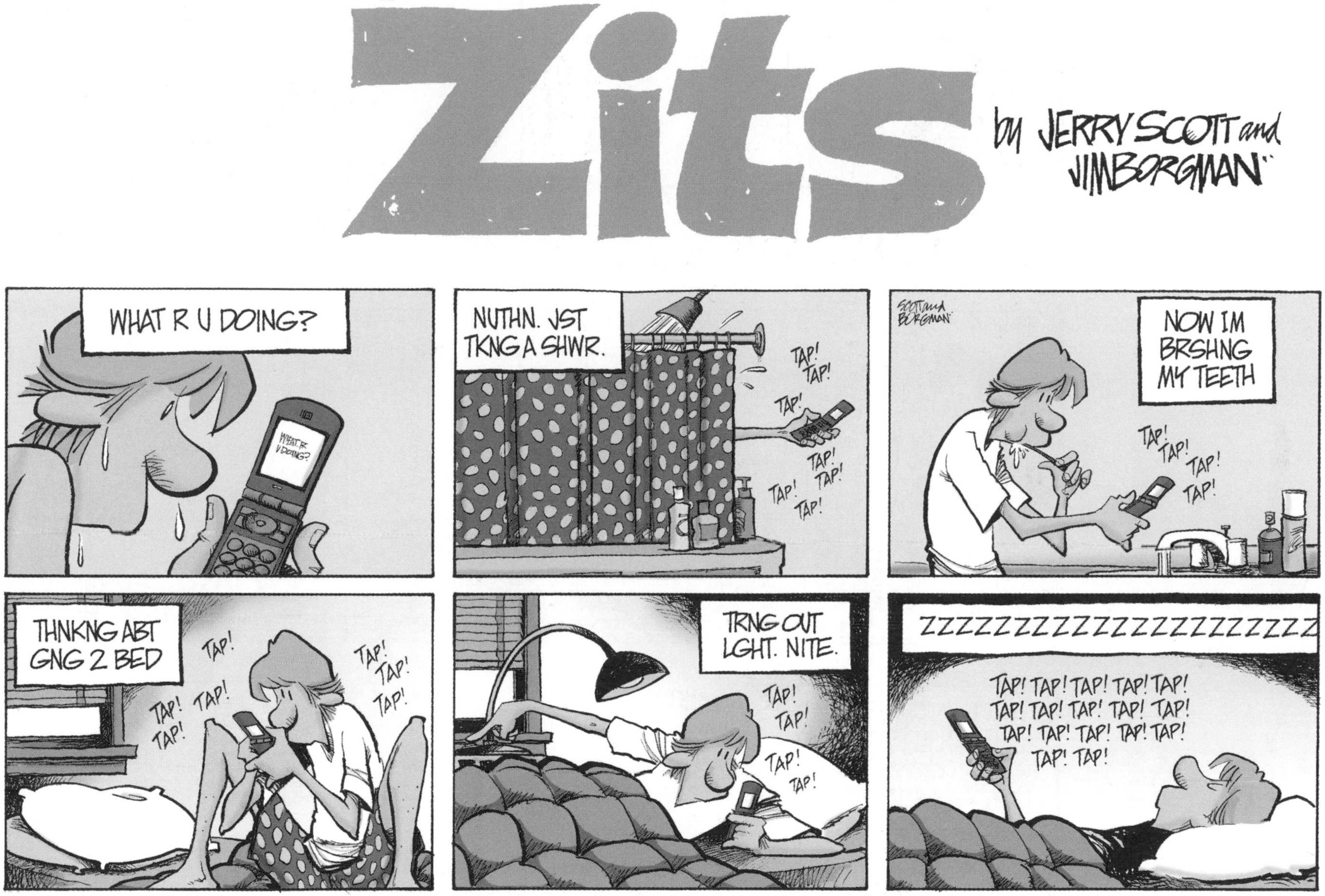
Zits
by JERRY SCOTT and JIM BORGMAN
WHAT R U DOING?
WHAT R U DOING?
NUTHN. JST TKNG A SHWR.
TAP! TAP!
TAP!
TAP! TAP!
TAP!
TAP!
SCOTT and BORGMAN
NOW IM BRSHNG MY TEETH
TAP! TAP! TAP! TAP!
THNKNG ABT GNG 2 BED
TAP!
TAP! TAP!
TAP!
TAP! TAP! TAP!
TRNG OUT LGHT. NITE.
TAP! TAP!
TAP! TAP!
ZZZZZZZZZZZZZZZZZZZZZZZ
TAP! TAP! TAP! TAP! TAP!
TAP! TAP! TAP! TAP! TAP!
TAP! TAP! TAP! TAP! TAP!
TAP! TAP!

No need to call your ophthalmologist. This Sunday strip was intentionally colored in shades of pink as part of an organized effort by cartoonists to recognize and support National Breast Cancer Awareness Month.

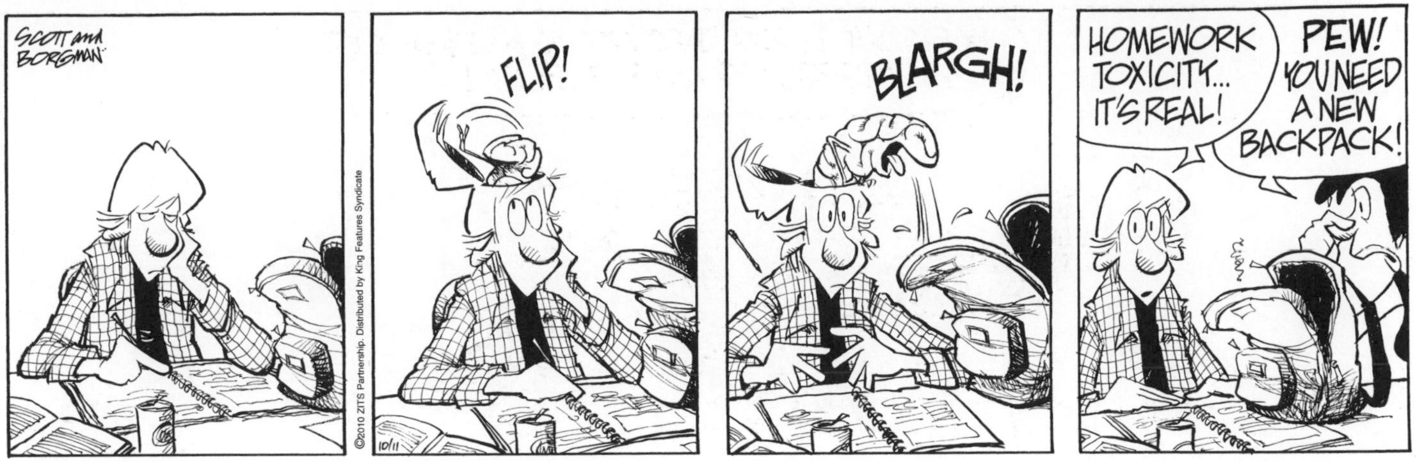
SCOTT and BORGMAN
©2010 ZITS Partnership. Distributed by King Features Syndicate
10/11
FLIP!
BLARGH!
HOMEWORK TOXICITY... IT'S REAL!
PEW! YOU NEED A NEW BACKPACK!

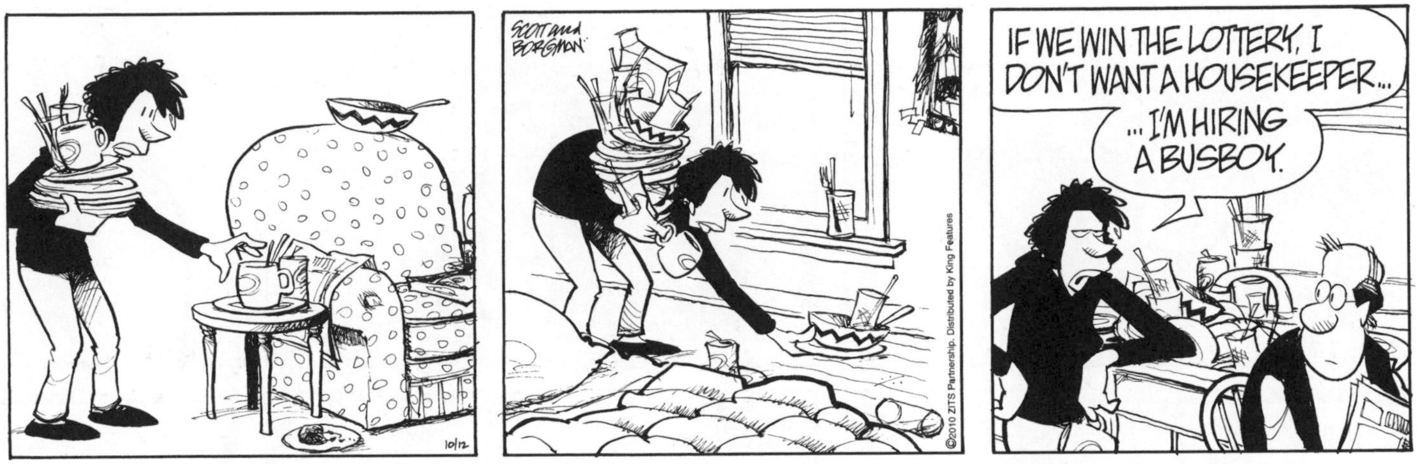
10/12
SCOTT and BORGMAN
©2010 ZITS Partnership. Distributed by King Features
IF WE WIN THE LOTTERY, I DON'T WANT A HOUSEKEEPER...
...I'M HIRING A BUSBOY.

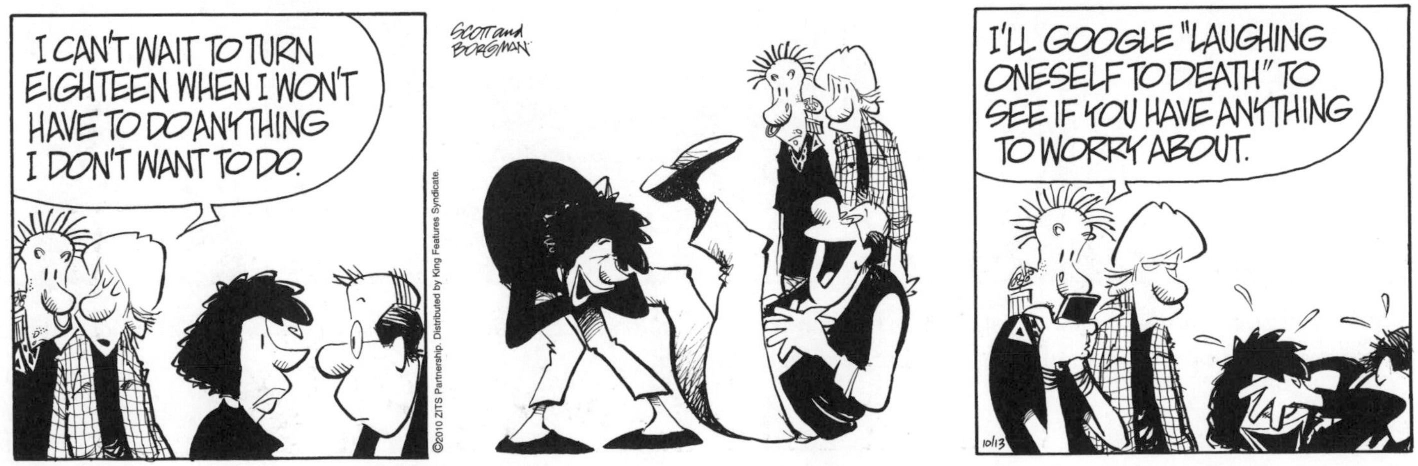
I CAN'T WAIT TO TURN EIGHTEEN WHEN I WON'T HAVE TO DO ANYTHING I DON'T WANT TO DO.
©2010 ZITS Partnership. Distributed by King Features Syndicate.
SCOTT and BORGMAN
I'LL GOOGLE "LAUGHING ONESELF TO DEATH" TO SEE IF YOU HAVE ANYTHING TO WORRY ABOUT.
10/13

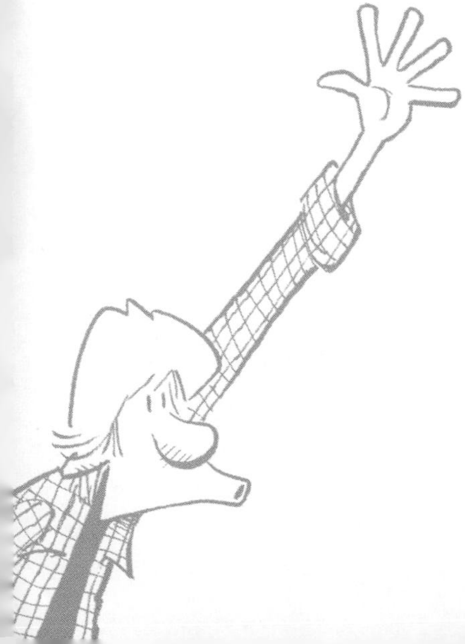

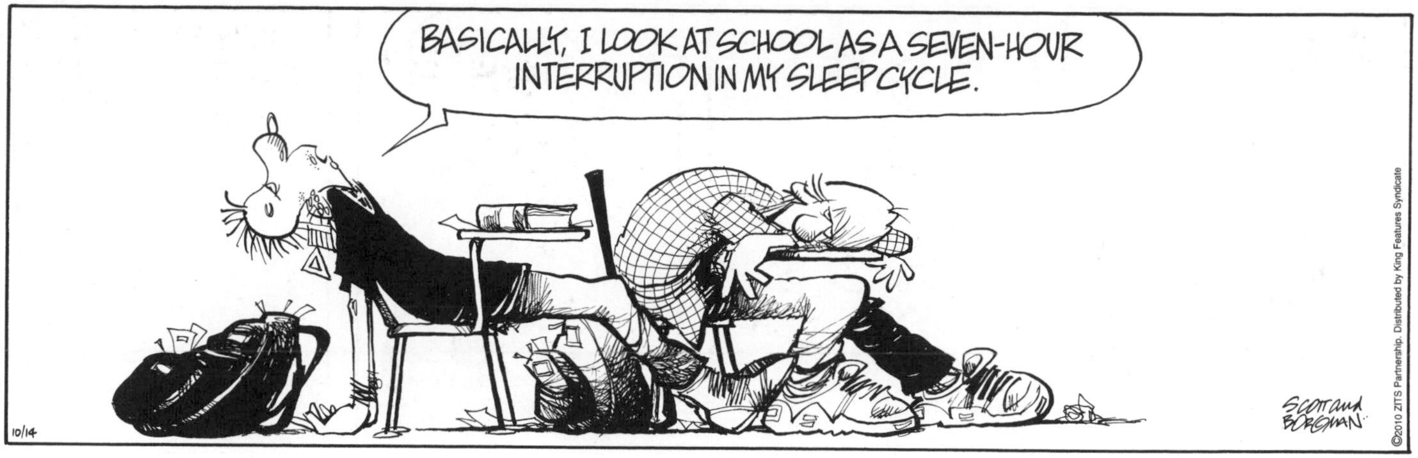
BASICALLY, I LOOK AT SCHOOL AS A SEVEN-HOUR INTERRUPTION IN MY SLEEP CYCLE.
10/14
SCOTT and BORGMAN
©2010 ZITS Partnership. Distributed by King Features Syndicate

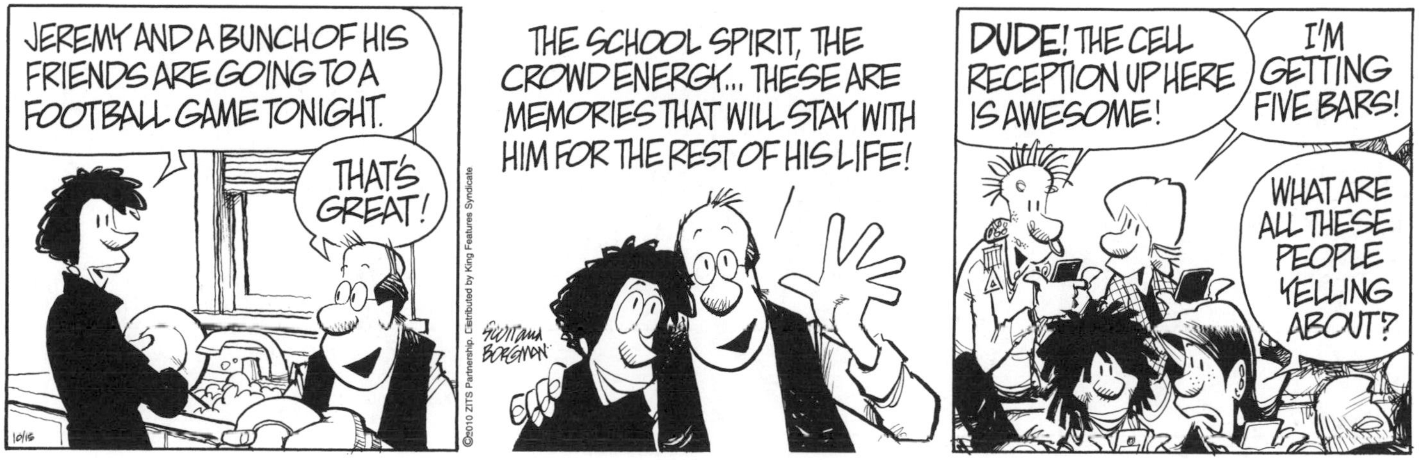
JEREMY AND A BUNCH OF HIS FRIENDS ARE GOING TO A FOOTBALL GAME TONIGHT.
THAT'S GREAT!
THE SCHOOL SPIRIT, THE CROWD ENERGY... THESE ARE MEMORIES THAT WILL STAY WITH HIM FOR THE REST OF HIS LIFE!
DUDE! THE CELL RECEPTION UP HERE IS AWESOME!
I'M GETTING FIVE BARS!
WHAT ARE ALL THESE PEOPLE YELLING ABOUT?
10/15
SCOTT and BORGMAN
©2010 ZITS Partnership. Distributed by King Features Syndicate

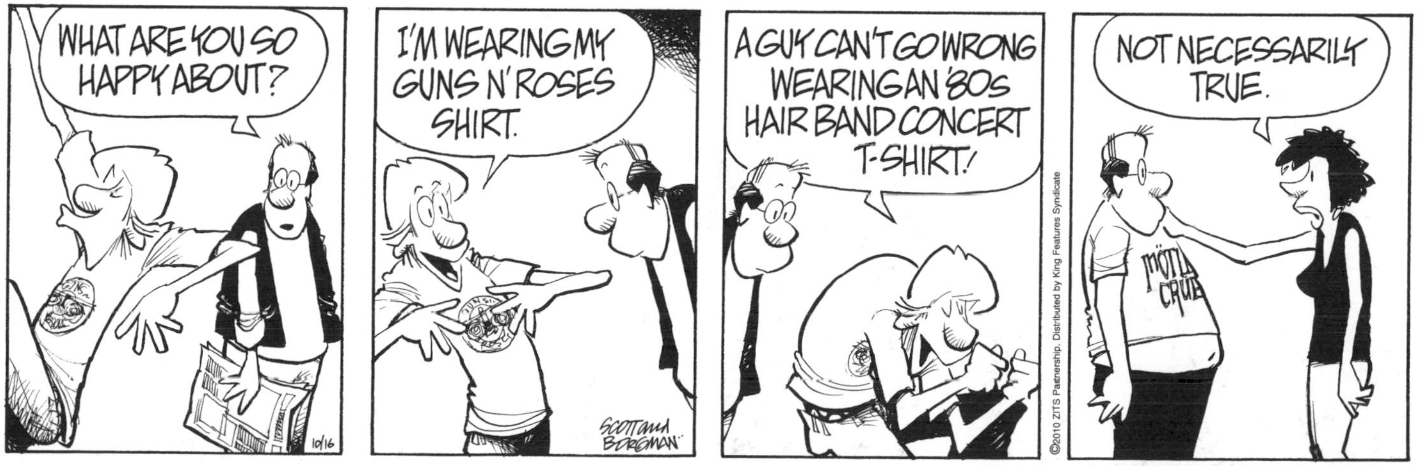
WHAT ARE YOU SO HAPPY ABOUT?
I'M WEARING MY GUNS N' ROSES SHIRT.
A GUY CAN'T GO WRONG WEARING AN '80s HAIR BAND CONCERT T-SHIRT!
NOT NECESSARILY TRUE.
MÖTLEY CRÜE
10/16
SCOTT and BORGMAN
©2010 ZITS Partnership. Distributed by King Features Syndicate

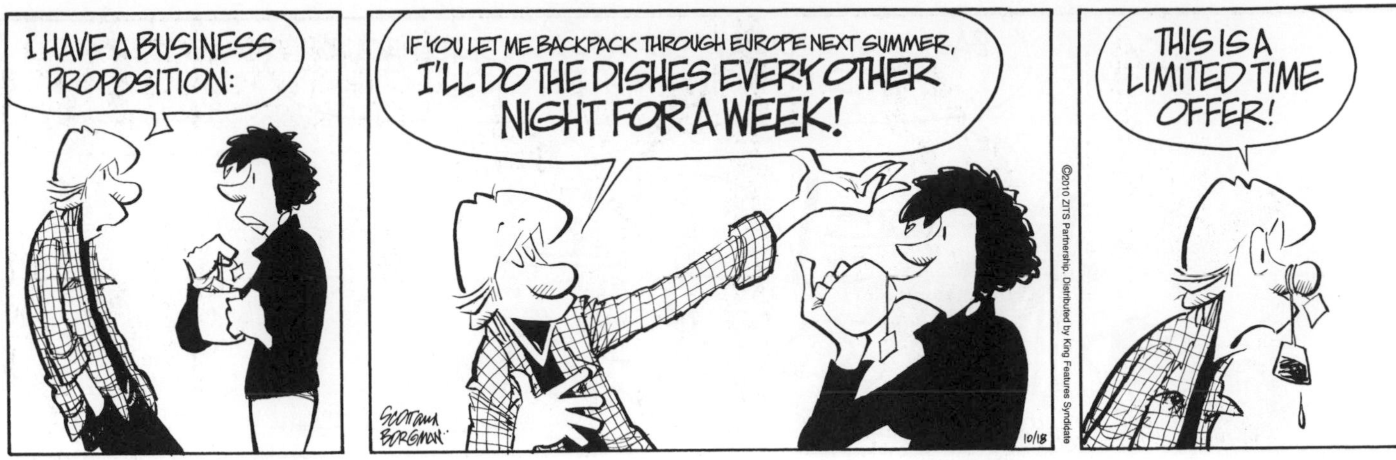
I HAVE A BUSINESS PROPOSITION:
IF YOU LET ME BACKPACK THROUGH EUROPE NEXT SUMMER, I'LL DO THE DISHES EVERY OTHER NIGHT FOR A WEEK!
THIS IS A LIMITED TIME OFFER!
©2010 ZITS Partnership. Distributed by King Features Syndicate

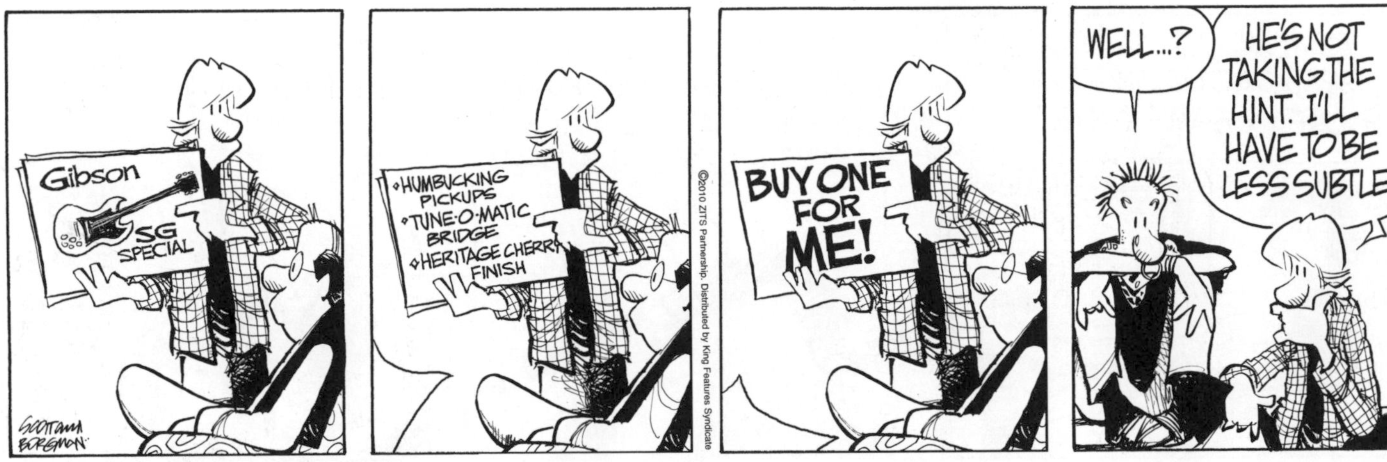
Gibson
SG SPECIAL
◇HUMBUCKING PICKUPS
◇TUNE-O-MATIC BRIDGE
◇HERITAGE CHERRY FINISH
BUY ONE FOR ME!
WELL...?
HE'S NOT TAKING THE HINT. I'LL HAVE TO BE LESS SUBTLE.
©2010 ZITS Partnership. Distributed by King Features Syndicate

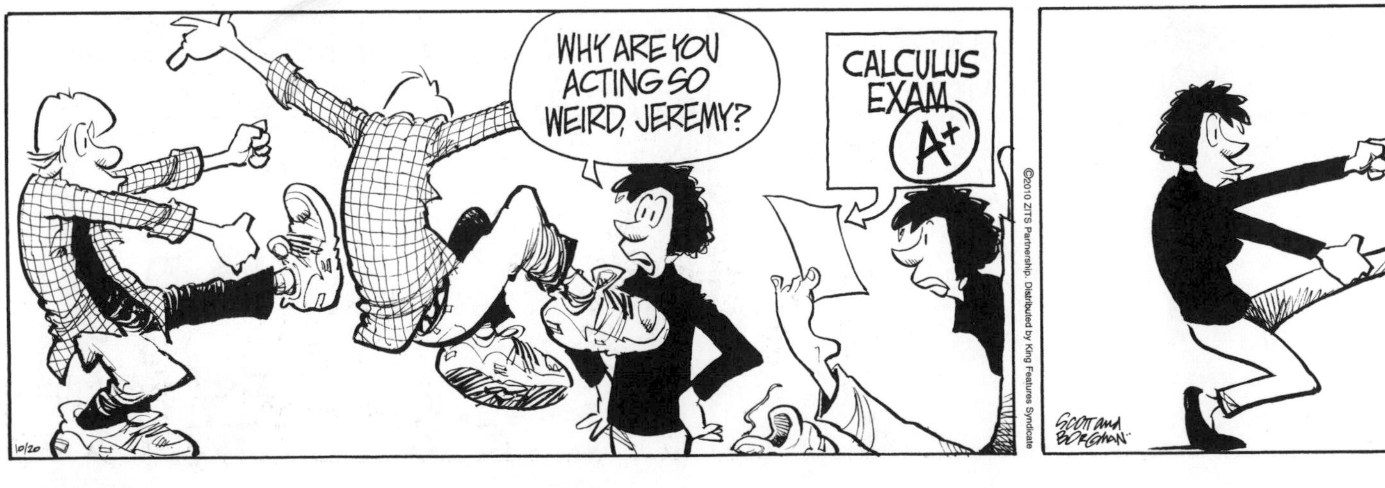
WHY ARE YOU ACTING SO WEIRD, JEREMY?
CALCULUS EXAM
A+
©2010 ZITS Partnership. Distributed by King Features Syndicate

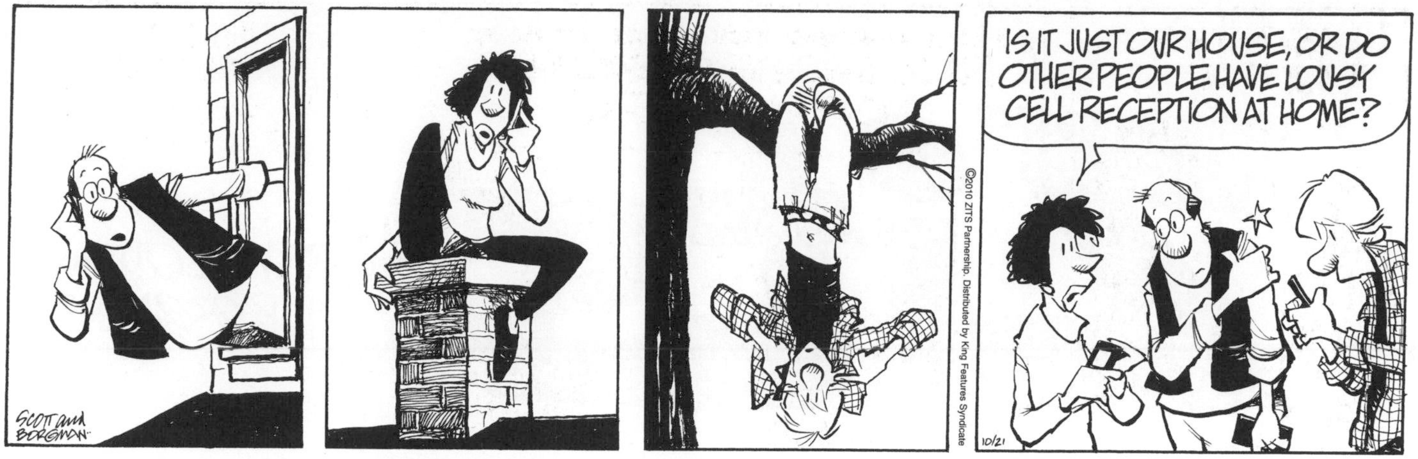
SCOTT and BORGMAN
©2010 ZITS Partnership. Distributed by King Features Syndicate
IS IT JUST OUR HOUSE, OR DO OTHER PEOPLE HAVE LOUSY CELL RECEPTION AT HOME?
10/21

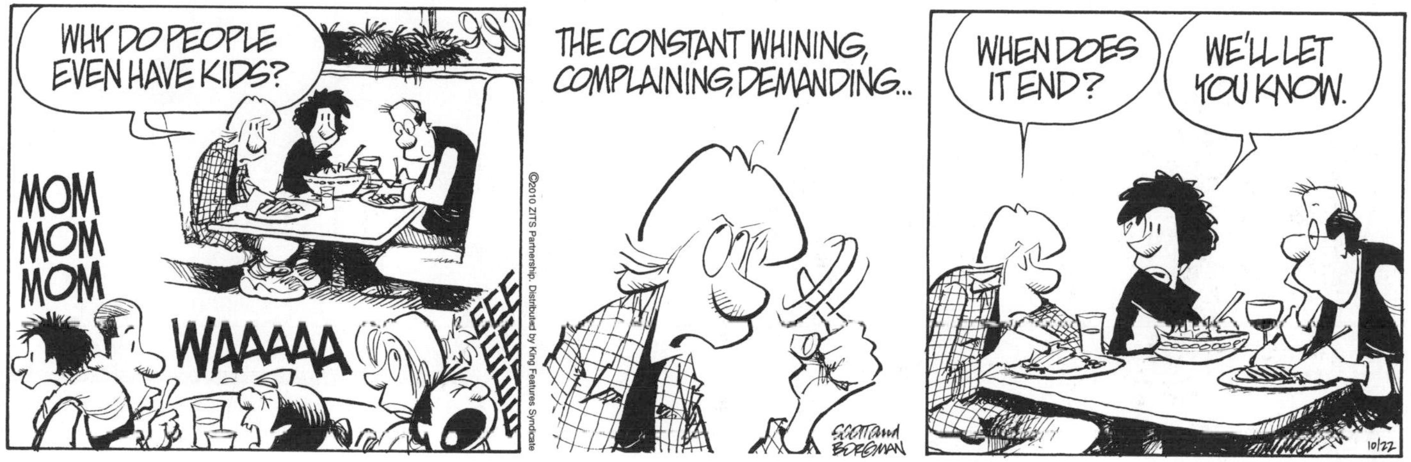
WHY DO PEOPLE EVEN HAVE KIDS?
MOM MOM MOM
WAAAAA
EEEEEEE
©2010 ZITS Partnership. Distributed by King Features Syndicate
THE CONSTANT WHINING, COMPLAINING, DEMANDING...
SCOTT and BORGMAN
WHEN DOES IT END?
WE'LL LET YOU KNOW.
10/22

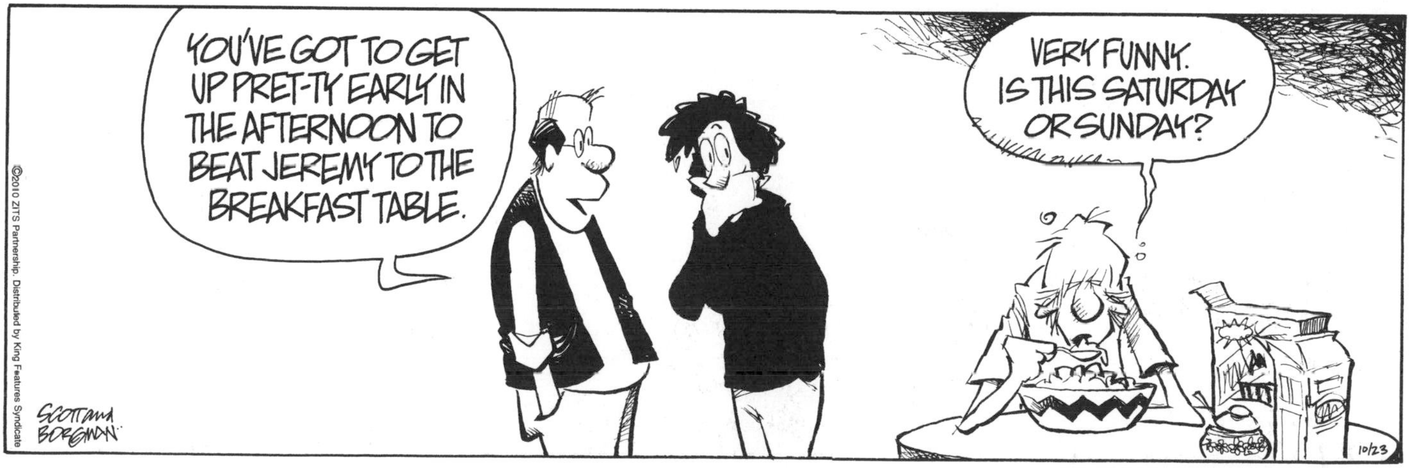
©2010 ZITS Partnership. Distributed by King Features Syndicate
YOU'VE GOT TO GET UP PRET-TY EARLY IN THE AFTERNOON TO BEAT JEREMY TO THE BREAKFAST TABLE.
VERY FUNNY. IS THIS SATURDAY OR SUNDAY?
SCOTT and BORGMAN
10/23

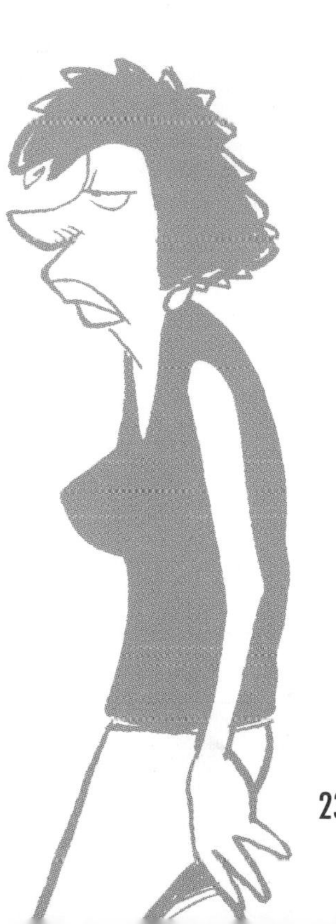

Zits

by JERRY SCOTT and JIM BORGMAN

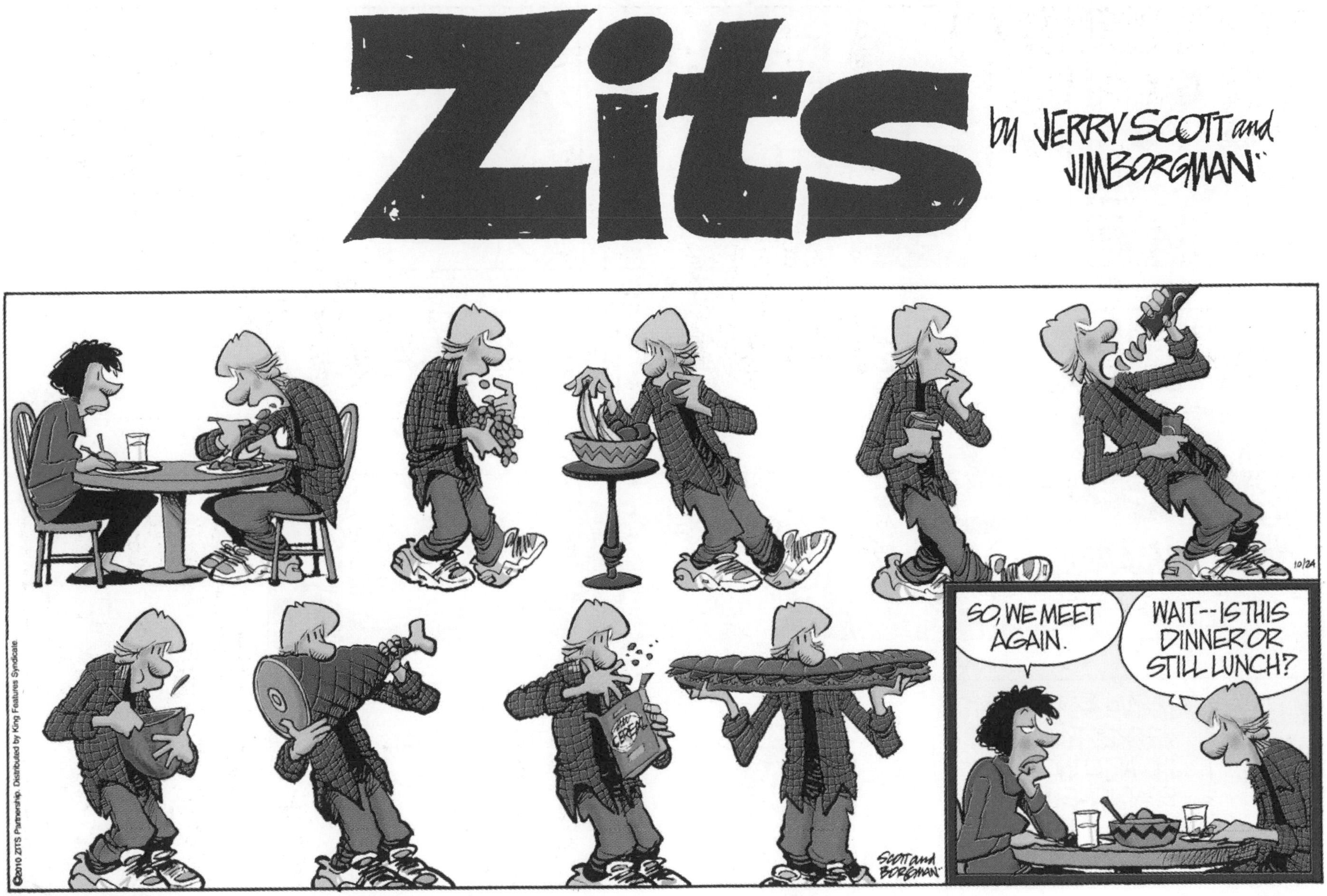
10/24
SO, WE MEET AGAIN.
WAIT--IS THIS DINNER OR STILL LUNCH?
CEREAL
SCOTT and BORGMAN
©2010 ZITS Partnership. Distributed by King Features Syndicate.

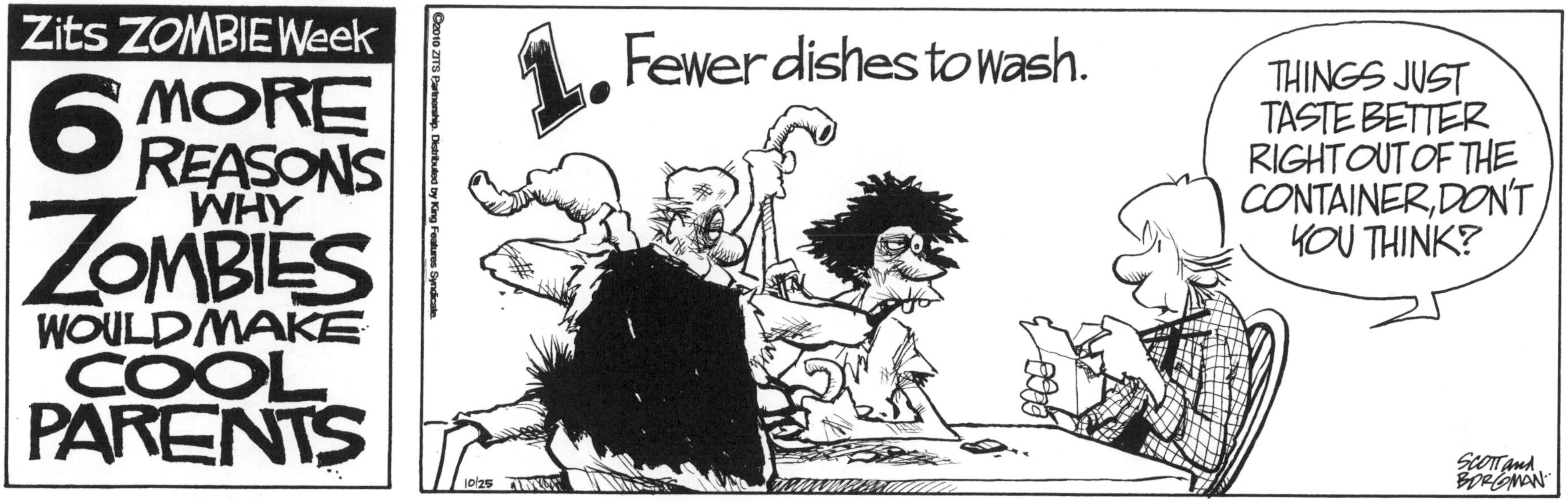
Zits ZOMBIE Week
6 MORE REASONS WHY ZOMBIES WOULD MAKE COOL PARENTS
©2010 ZITS Partnership. Distributed by King Features Syndicate.
1. Fewer dishes to wash.
THINGS JUST TASTE BETTER RIGHT OUT OF THE CONTAINER, DON'T YOU THINK?
10/25
SCOTT and BORGMAN

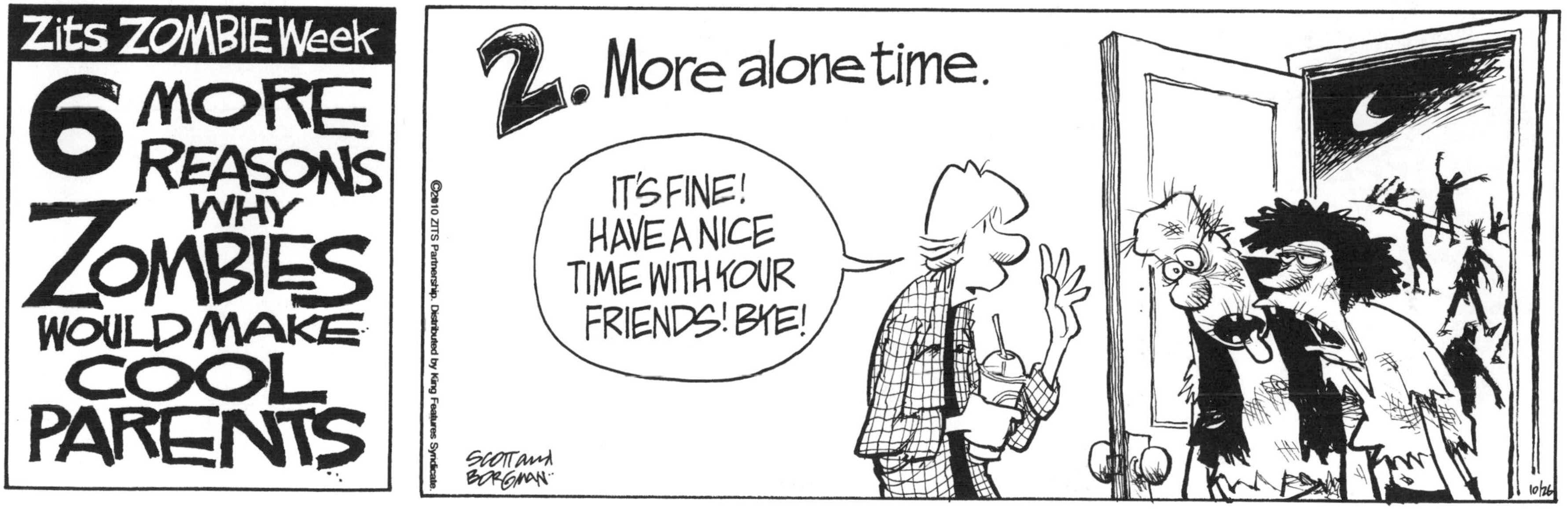
Zits ZOMBIE Week
6 MORE REASONS WHY ZOMBIES WOULD MAKE COOL PARENTS
©2010 ZITS Partnership. Distributed by King Features Syndicate.
2. More alone time.
IT'S FINE! HAVE A NICE TIME WITH YOUR FRIENDS! BYE!
SCOTT and BORGMAN
10/26

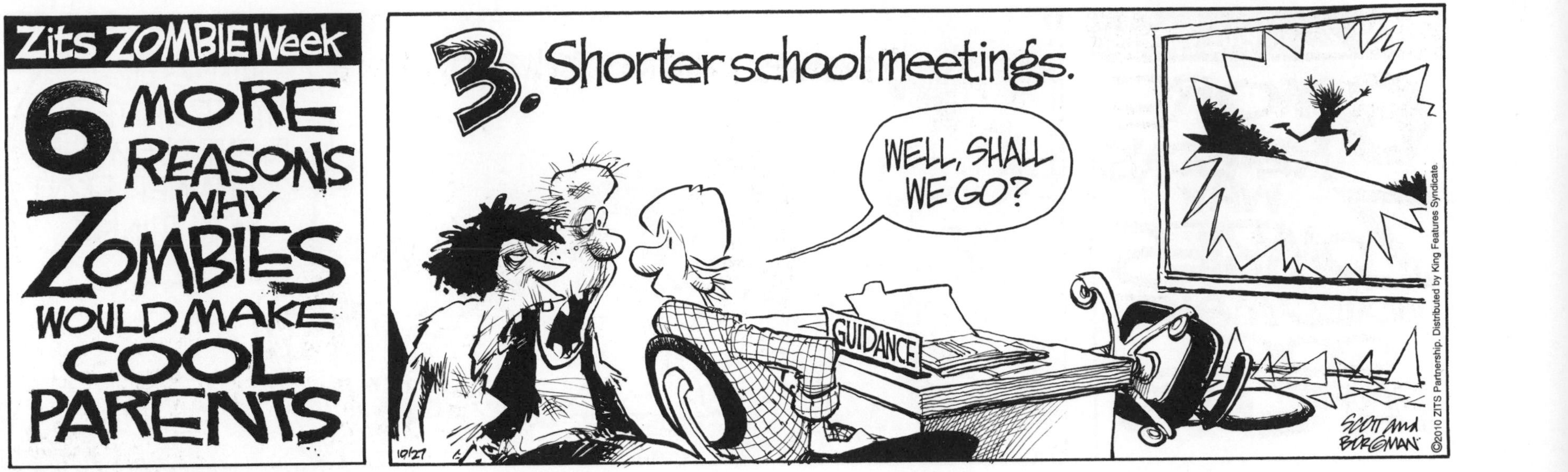
Zits ZOMBIE Week
6 MORE REASONS WHY ZOMBIES WOULD MAKE COOL PARENTS
3. Shorter school meetings.
WELL, SHALL WE GO?
GUIDANCE
10/27
SCOTT and BORGMAN
©2010 ZITS Partnership. Distributed by King Features Syndicate.

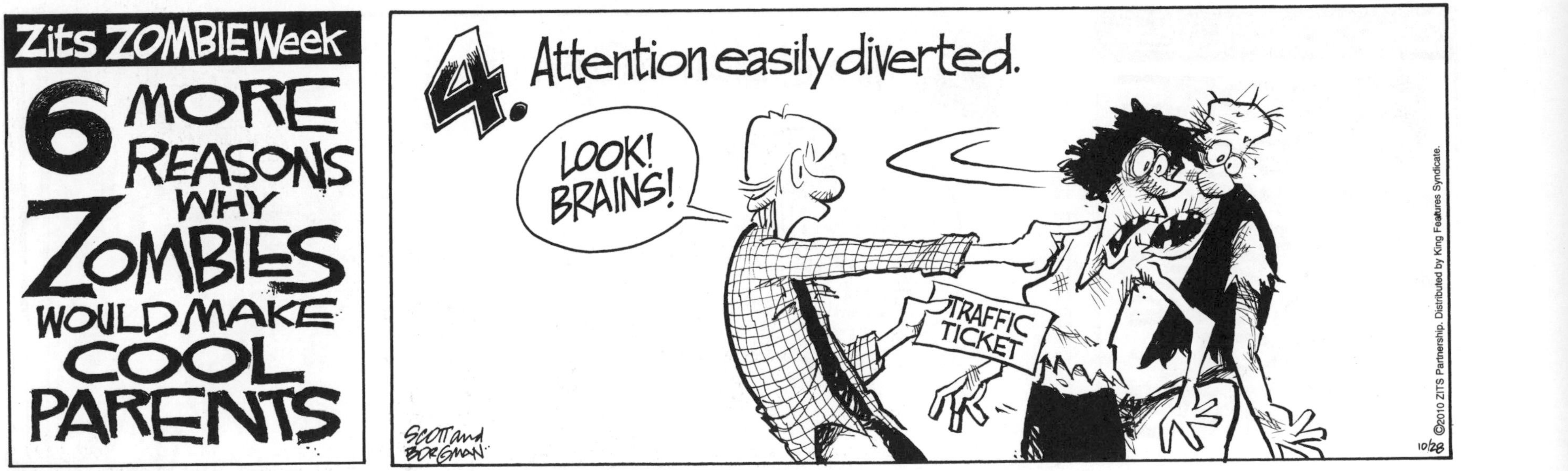
Zits ZOMBIE Week
6 MORE REASONS WHY ZOMBIES WOULD MAKE COOL PARENTS
4. Attention easily diverted.
LOOK! BRAINS!
TRAFFIC TICKET
SCOTT and BORGMAN
©2010 ZITS Partnership. Distributed by King Features Syndicate.
10/28

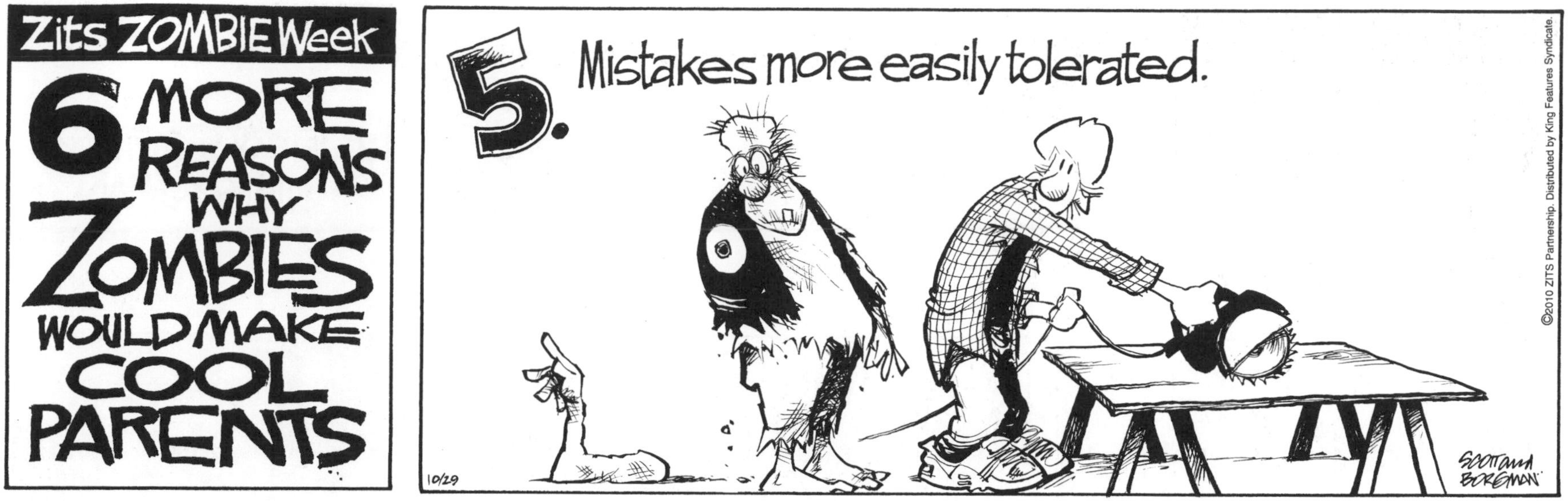
Zits ZOMBIE Week
6 MORE REASONS WHY ZOMBIES WOULD MAKE COOL PARENTS
5. Mistakes more easily tolerated.
©2010 ZITS Partnership. Distributed by King Features Syndicate.
10/29
SCOTT and BORGMAN

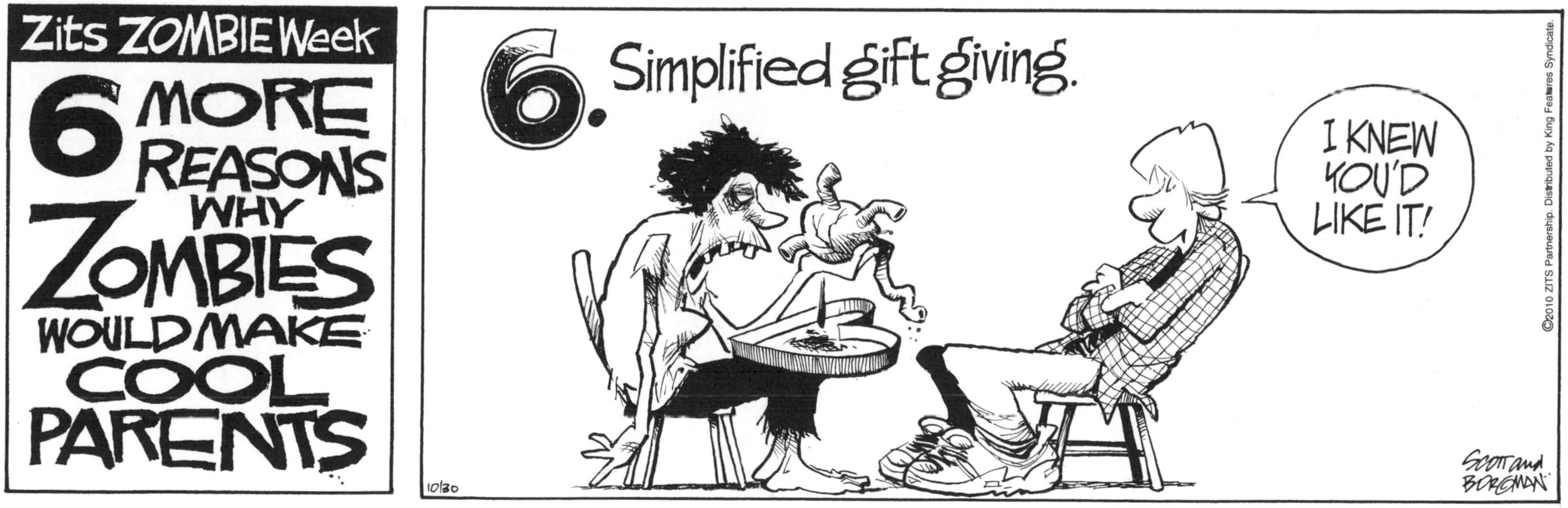
Zits ZOMBIE Week
6 MORE REASONS WHY ZOMBIES WOULD MAKE COOL PARENTS
6. Simplified gift giving.
I KNEW YOU'D LIKE IT!
©2010 ZITS Partnership. Distributed by King Features Syndicate.
10/30
SCOTT and BORGMAN

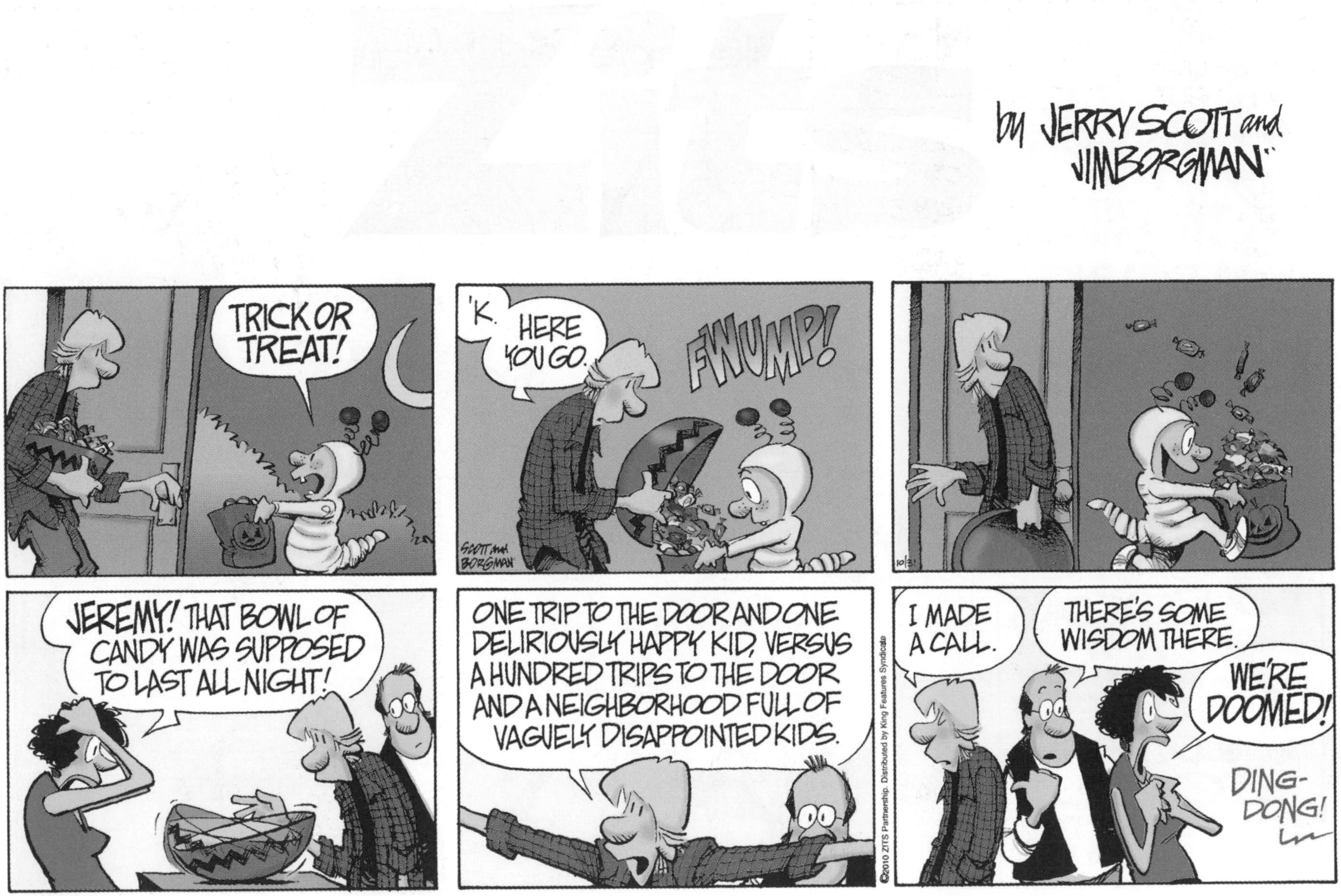
Zits
by JERRY SCOTT and JIM BORGMAN
TRICK OR TREAT!
'K.
HERE YOU GO.
FWUMP!
SCOTT and BORGMAN
JEREMY! THAT BOWL OF CANDY WAS SUPPOSED TO LAST ALL NIGHT!
ONE TRIP TO THE DOOR AND ONE DELIRIOUSLY HAPPY KID, VERSUS A HUNDRED TRIPS TO THE DOOR AND A NEIGHBORHOOD FULL OF VAGUELY DISAPPOINTED KIDS.
©2010 ZITS Partnership. Distributed by King Features Syndicate
I MADE A CALL.
THERE'S SOME WISDOM THERE.
WE'RE DOOMED!
DING-DONG!

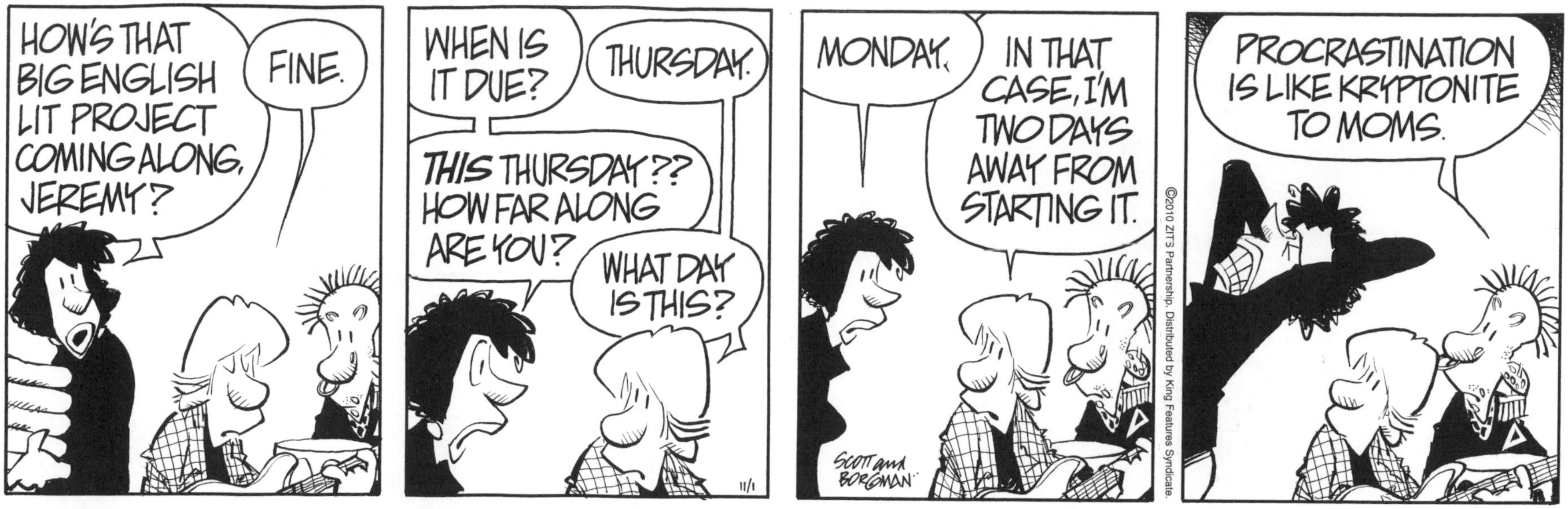
HOW'S THAT BIG ENGLISH LIT PROJECT COMING ALONG, JEREMY?
FINE.
WHEN IS IT DUE?
THURSDAY.
THIS THURSDAY?? HOW FAR ALONG ARE YOU?
WHAT DAY IS THIS?
MONDAY.
IN THAT CASE, I'M TWO DAYS AWAY FROM STARTING IT.
PROCRASTINATION IS LIKE KRYPTONITE TO MOMS.
SCOTT AND BORGMAN
11/1
©2010 ZITS Partnership. Distributed by King Features Syndicate.

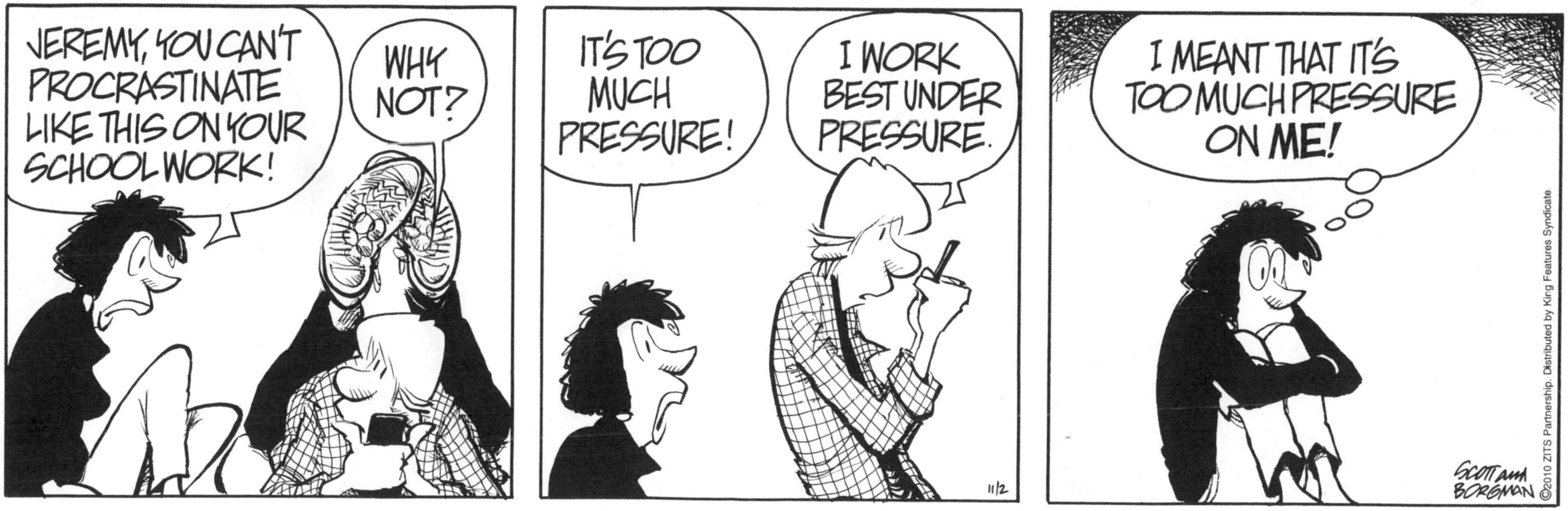
JEREMY, YOU CAN'T PROCRASTINATE LIKE THIS ON YOUR SCHOOLWORK!
WHY NOT?
IT'S TOO MUCH PRESSURE!
I WORK BEST UNDER PRESSURE.
I MEANT THAT IT'S TOO MUCH PRESSURE ON ME!
SCOTT AND BORGMAN
11/2
©2010 ZITS Partnership. Distributed by King Features Syndicate.

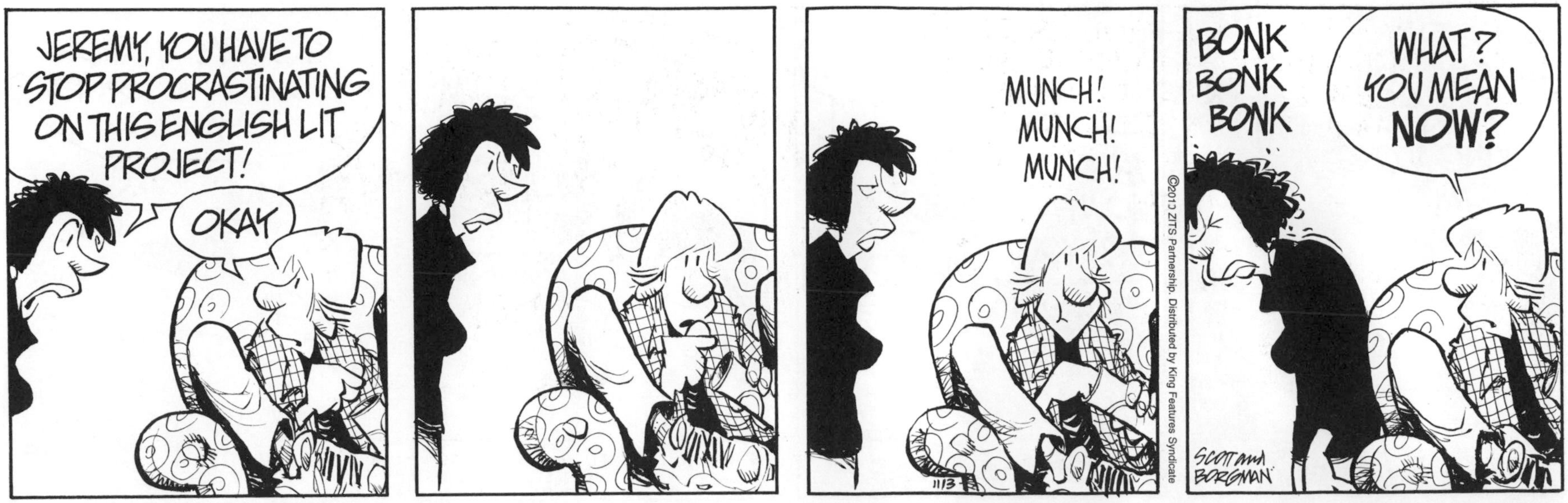
JEREMY, YOU HAVE TO STOP PROCRASTINATING ON THIS ENGLISH LIT PROJECT!
OKAY
MUNCH! MUNCH! MUNCH!
BONK BONK BONK
WHAT? YOU MEAN NOW?
©2010 ZITS Partnership. Distributed by King Features Syndicate
SCOTT AND BORGMAN

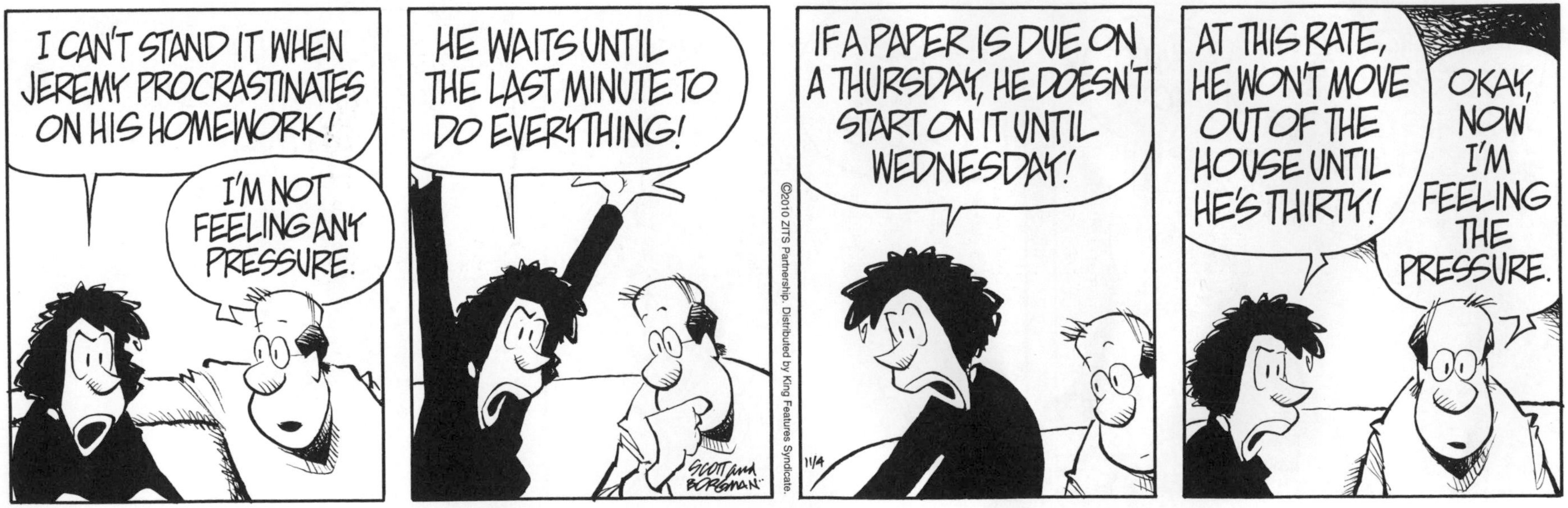
I CAN'T STAND IT WHEN JEREMY PROCRASTINATES ON HIS HOMEWORK!
I'M NOT FEELING ANY PRESSURE.
HE WAITS UNTIL THE LAST MINUTE TO DO EVERYTHING!
SCOTT AND BORGMAN
©2010 ZITS Partnership. Distributed by King Features Syndicate.
IF A PAPER IS DUE ON A THURSDAY, HE DOESN'T START ON IT UNTIL WEDNESDAY!
AT THIS RATE, HE WON'T MOVE OUT OF THE HOUSE UNTIL HE'S THIRTY!
OKAY, NOW I'M FEELING THE PRESSURE.

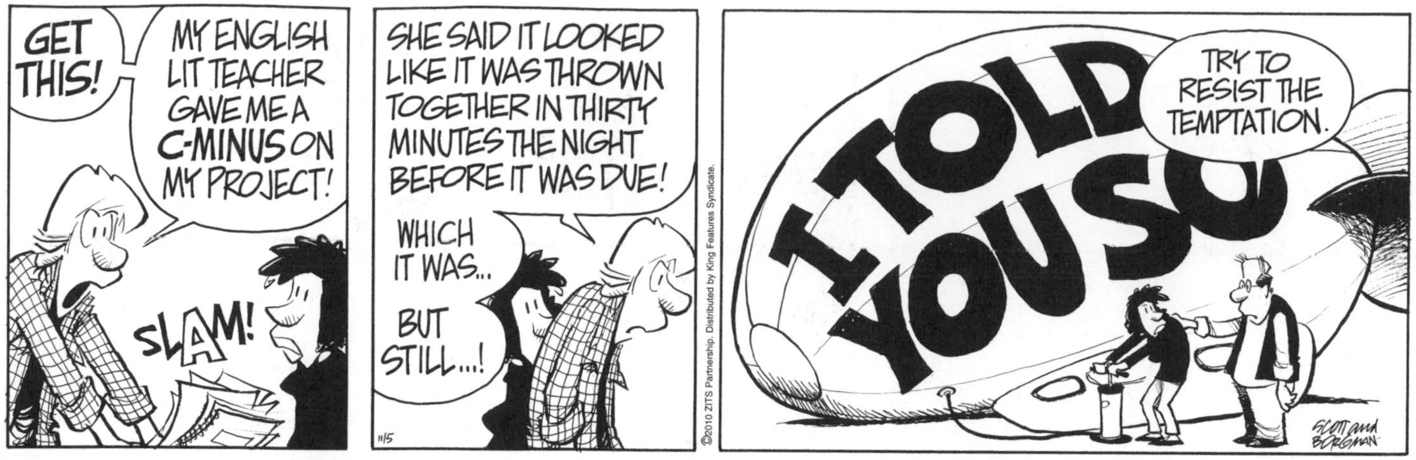
GET THIS!
MY ENGLISH LIT TEACHER GAVE ME A C-MINUS ON MY PROJECT!
SLAM!
SHE SAID IT LOOKED LIKE IT WAS THROWN TOGETHER IN THIRTY MINUTES THE NIGHT BEFORE IT WAS DUE!
WHICH IT WAS...
BUT STILL...!
I TOLD YOU SO
TRY TO RESIST THE TEMPTATION.
SCOTT AND BORGMAN
©2010 ZITS Partnership. Distributed by King Features Syndicate.

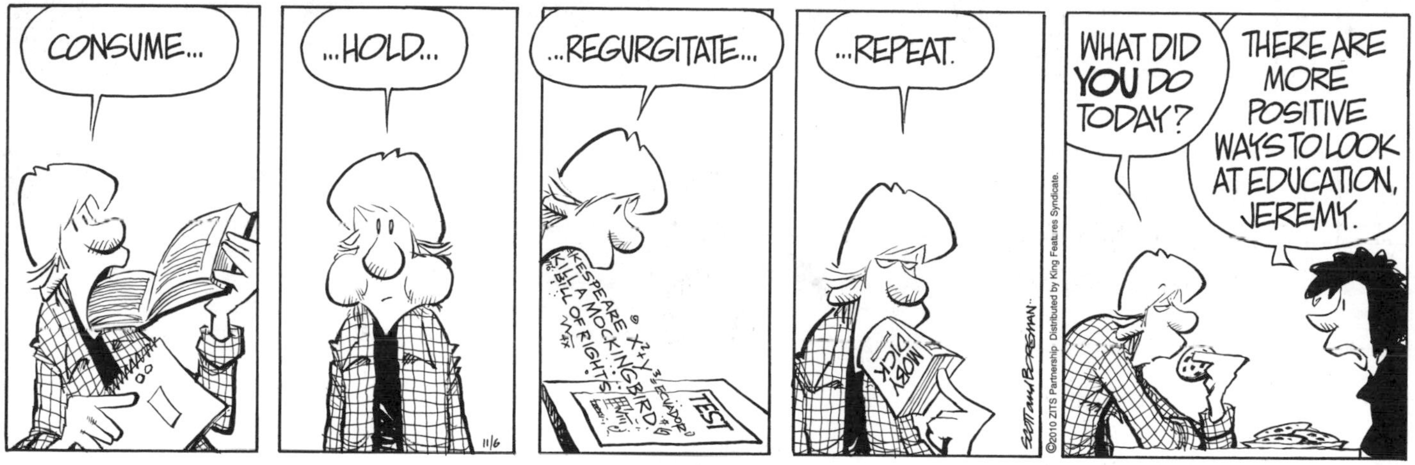
CONSUME...
...HOLD...
...REGURGITATE...
TEST
...REPEAT.
MOBY DICK
SCOTT AND BORGMAN
©2010 ZITS Partnership. Distributed by King Features Syndicate.
WHAT DID YOU DO TODAY?
THERE ARE MORE POSITIVE WAYS TO LOOK AT EDUCATION, JEREMY.

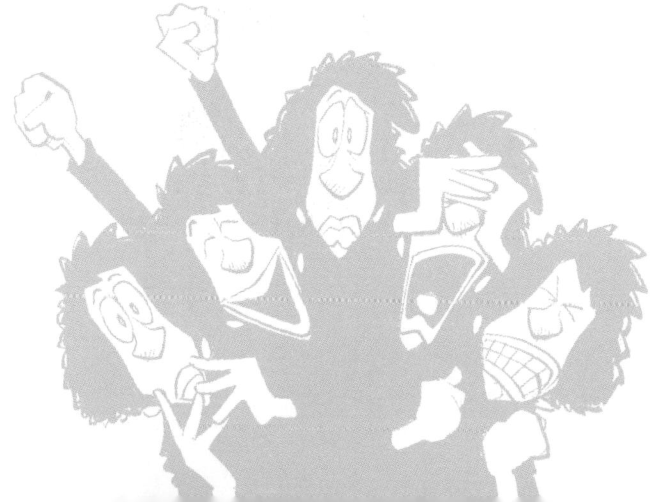

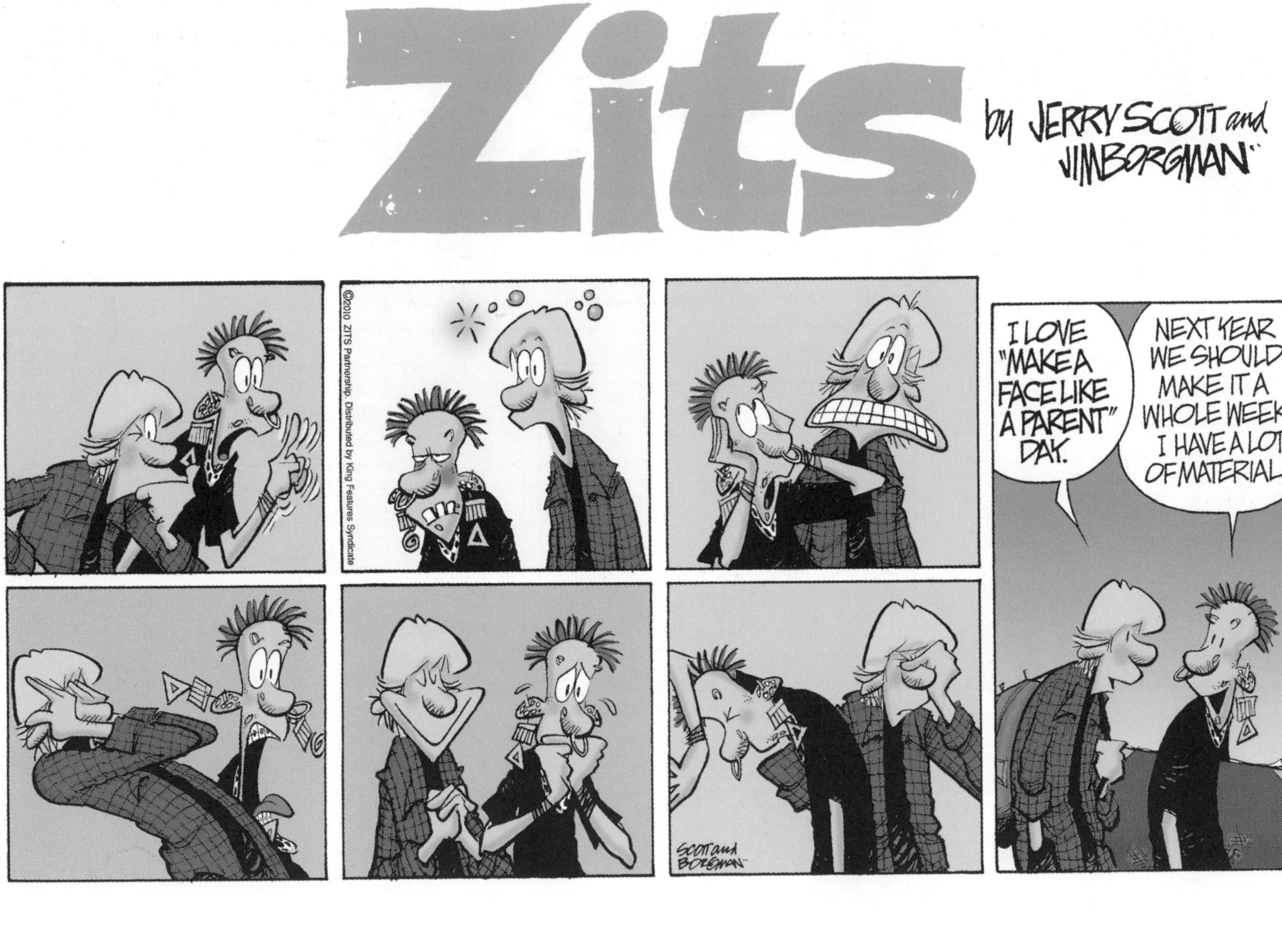
Zits
by JERRY SCOTT and JIM BORGMAN
©2010 ZITS Partnership. Distributed by King Features Syndicate
I LOVE "MAKE A FACE LIKE A PARENT" DAY.
NEXT YEAR WE SHOULD MAKE IT A WHOLE WEEK... I HAVE A LOT OF MATERIAL.
SCOTT and BORGMAN
11/7

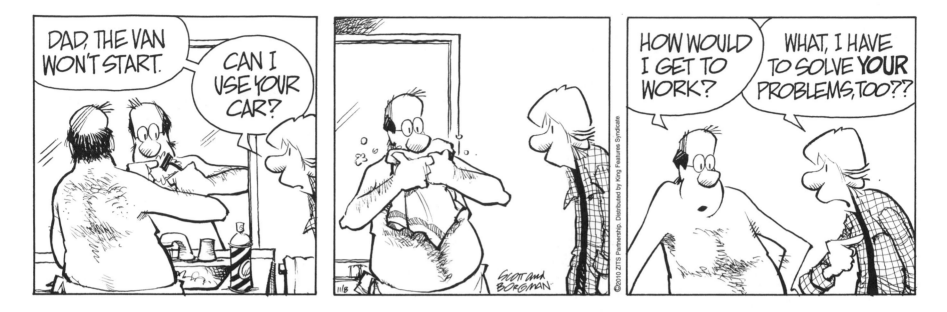

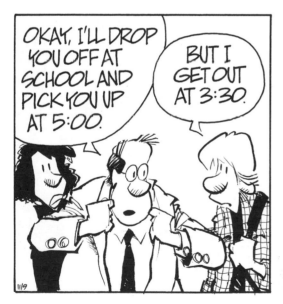

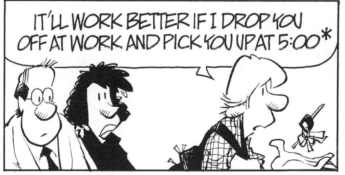

DAD, THE VAN WON'T START.
CAN I USE YOUR CAR?
11/8
SCOTT AND BORGMAN
©2010 ZITS Partnership. Distributed by King Features Syndicate.
HOW WOULD I GET TO WORK?
WHAT, I HAVE TO SOLVE **YOUR** PROBLEMS, TOO??

OKAY, I'LL DROP YOU OFF AT SCHOOL AND PICK YOU UP AT 5:00.
BUT I GET OUT AT 3:30.
11/9
IT'LL WORK BETTER IF I DROP YOU OFF AT WORK AND PICK YOU UP AT 5:00*
*5:00 IS AGREED TO MEAN 5:00 SOMEWHERE IN, BUT NOT LIMITED TO THE CONTIGUOUS UNITED STATES, CANADA, CENTRAL AND SOUTH AMERICAS OR ANY CONTINENT BORDERED BY AN OCEAN OR HAVING A VOWEL IN ITS NAME, PLUS OR MINUS 45 MINUTES.
DID YOU JUST HEAR AN ASTERISK?
YOU DIDN'T?
SCOTT AND BORGMAN
©2010 ZITS Partnership. Distributed by King Features Syndicate.

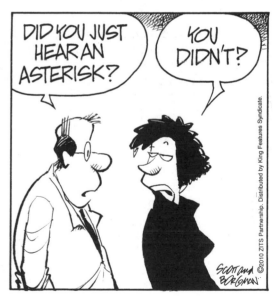

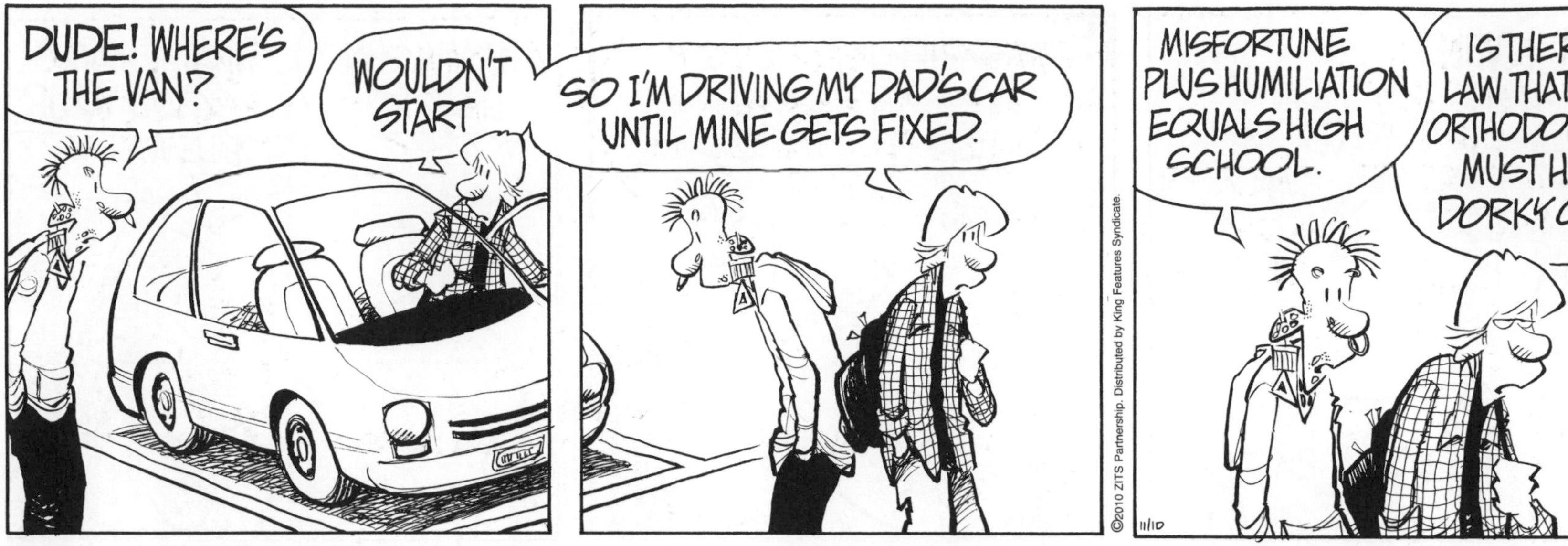
DUDE! WHERE'S THE VAN?
WOULDN'T START
SO I'M DRIVING MY DAD'S CAR UNTIL MINE GETS FIXED.
MISFORTUNE PLUS HUMILIATION EQUALS HIGH SCHOOL.
IS THERE A LAW THAT SAYS ORTHODONTISTS MUST HAVE DORKY CARS?
©2010 ZITS Partnership. Distributed by King Features Syndicate.
11/10
SCOTT and BORGMAN

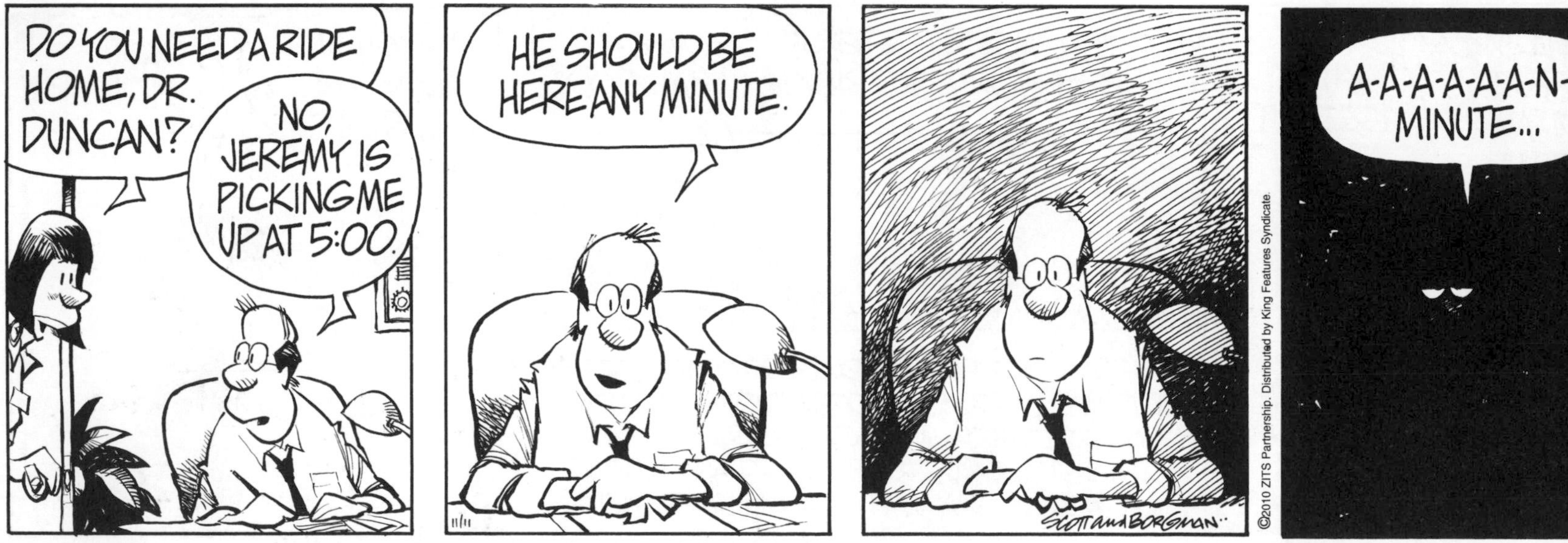
DO YOU NEED A RIDE HOME, DR. DUNCAN?
NO, JEREMY IS PICKING ME UP AT 5:00.
HE SHOULD BE HERE ANY MINUTE.
A-A-A-A-A-A-N-Y MINUTE...
11/11
SCOTT and BORGMAN
©2010 ZITS Partnership. Distributed by King Features Syndicate.

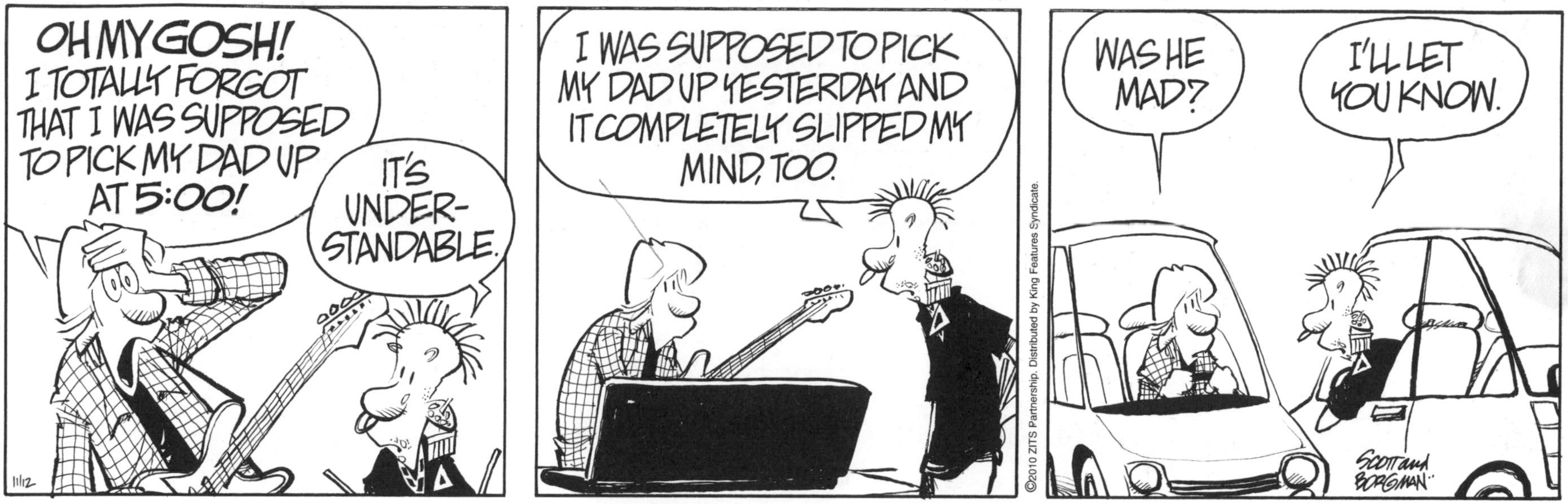
OH MY GOSH! I TOTALLY FORGOT THAT I WAS SUPPOSED TO PICK MY DAD UP AT 5:00!
IT'S UNDER-STANDABLE.
I WAS SUPPOSED TO PICK MY DAD UP YESTERDAY AND IT COMPLETELY SLIPPED MY MIND, TOO.
WAS HE MAD?
I'LL LET YOU KNOW.
©2010 ZITS Partnership. Distributed by King Features Syndicate.
SCOTT and BORGMAN
11/12

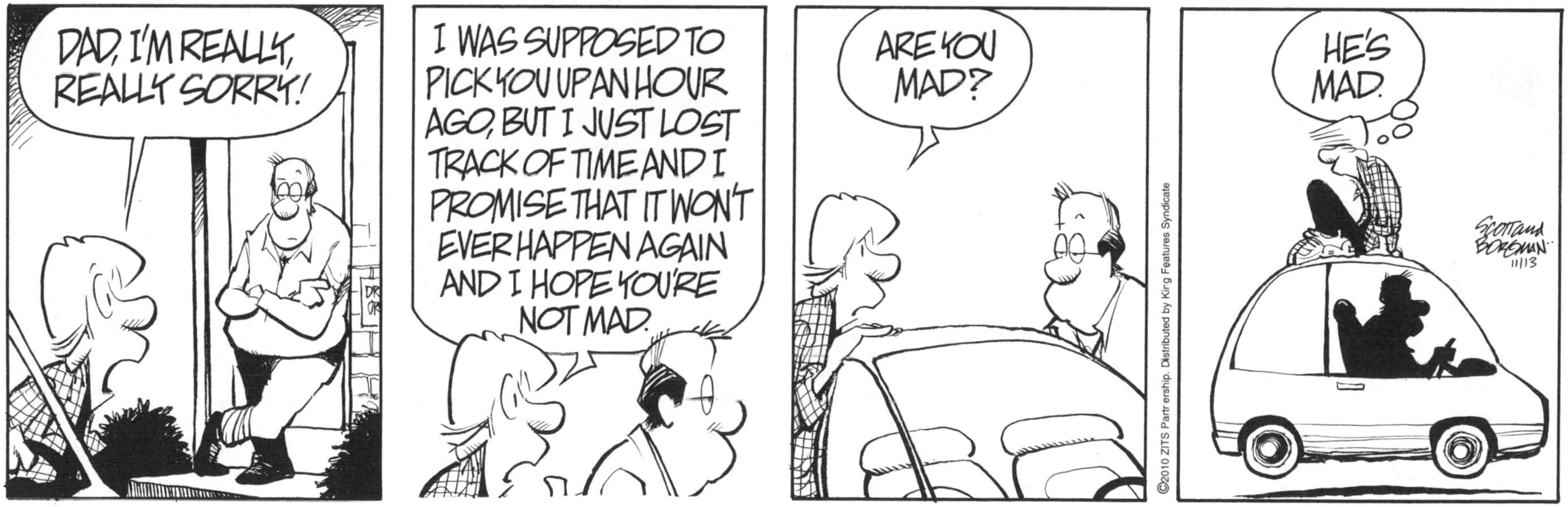
DAD, I'M REALLY, REALLY SORRY!
I WAS SUPPOSED TO PICK YOU UP AN HOUR AGO, BUT I JUST LOST TRACK OF TIME AND I PROMISE THAT IT WON'T EVER HAPPEN AGAIN AND I HOPE YOU'RE NOT MAD.
ARE YOU MAD?
HE'S MAD.
©2010 ZITS Partnership. Distributed by King Features Syndicate
SCOTT and BORGMAN
11/13

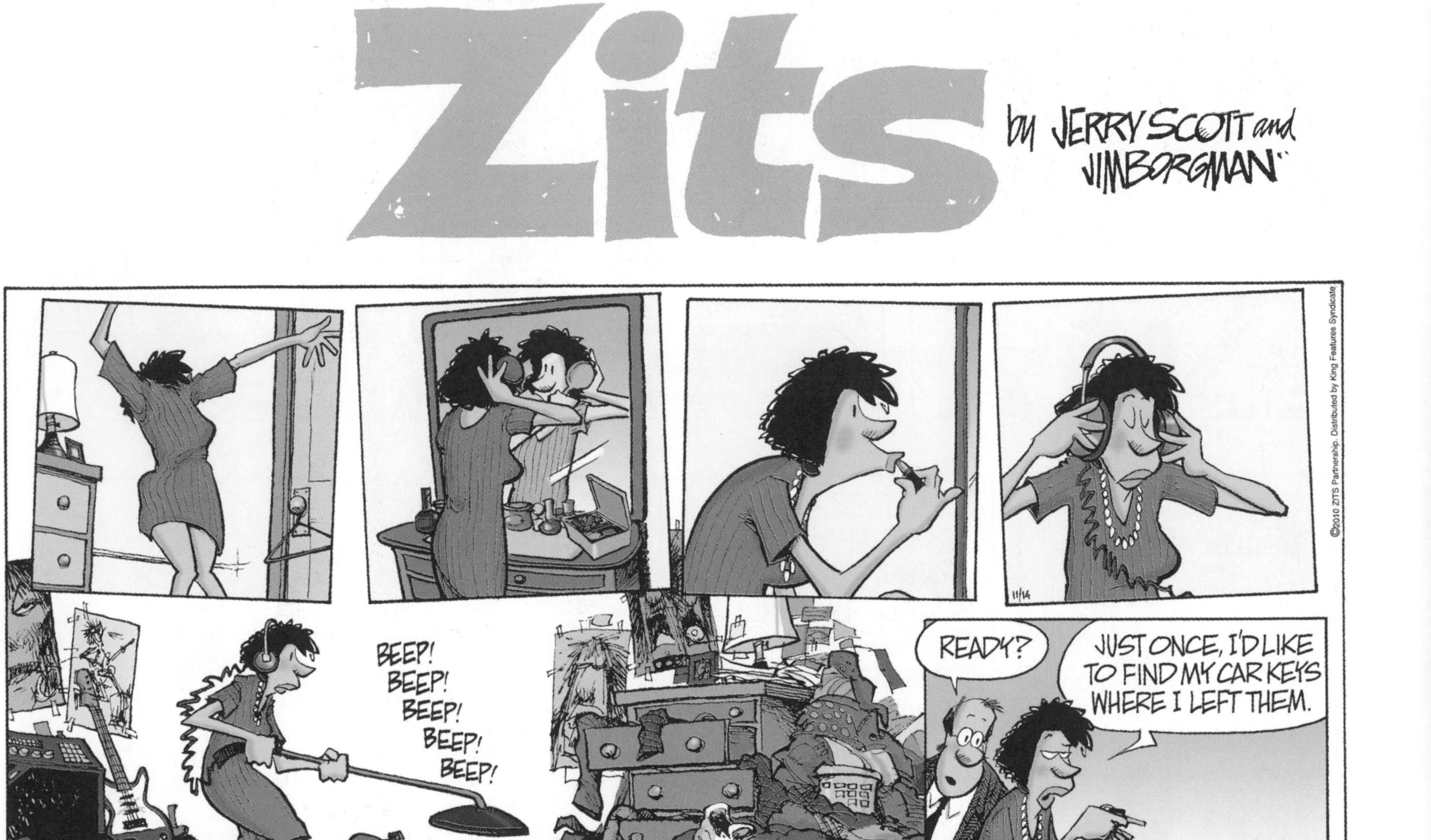
Zits
by JERRY SCOTT and JIM BORGMAN
©2010 ZITS Partnership. Distributed by King Features Syndicate
BEEP! BEEP! BEEP! BEEP! BEEP!
READY?
JUST ONCE, I'D LIKE TO FIND MY CAR KEYS WHERE I LEFT THEM.
SCOTT and BORGMAN

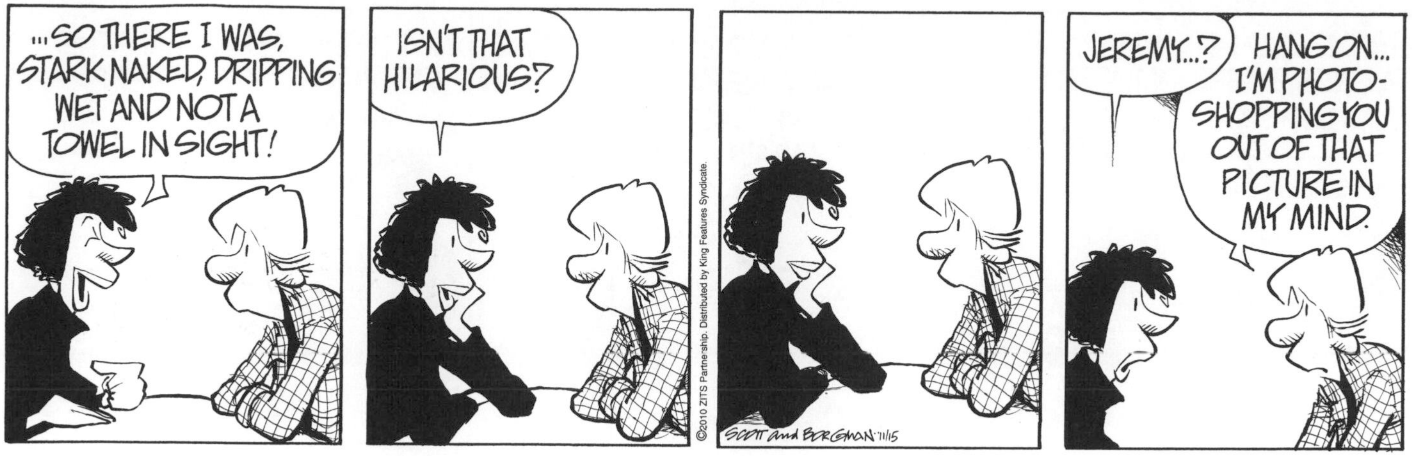
...SO THERE I WAS, STARK NAKED, DRIPPING WET AND NOT A TOWEL IN SIGHT!
ISN'T THAT HILARIOUS?
©2010 ZITS Partnership. Distributed by King Features Syndicate.
SCOTT and BORGMAN 11/15
JEREMY...?
HANG ON... I'M PHOTO-SHOPPING YOU OUT OF THAT PICTURE IN MY MIND.

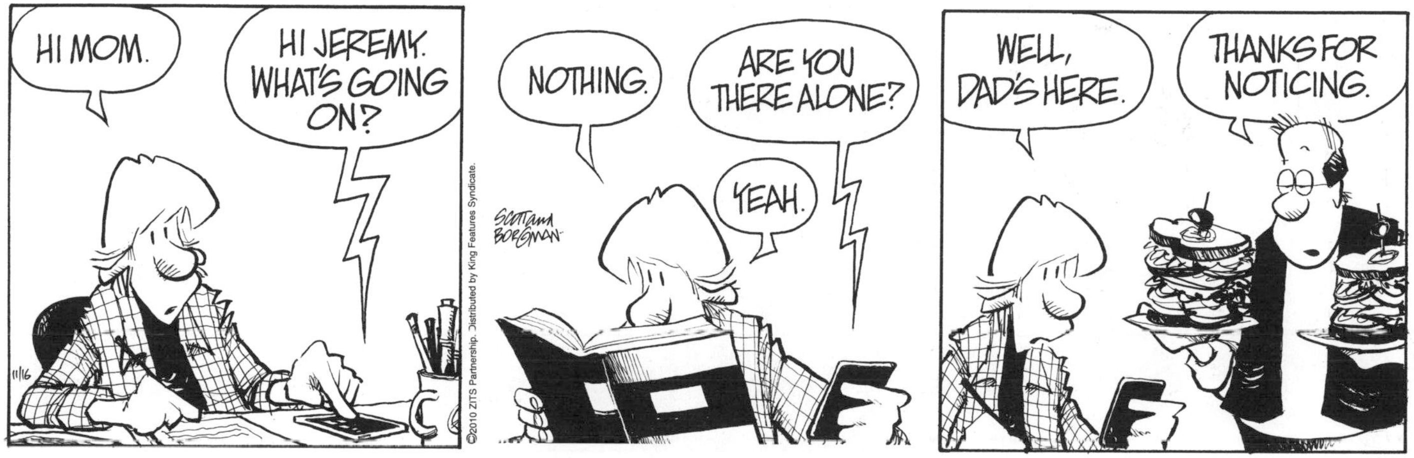
HI MOM.
HI JEREMY. WHAT'S GOING ON?
11/16
©2010 ZITS Partnership. Distributed by King Features Syndicate.
SCOTT and BORGMAN
NOTHING.
ARE YOU THERE ALONE?
YEAH.
WELL, DAD'S HERE.
THANKS FOR NOTICING.

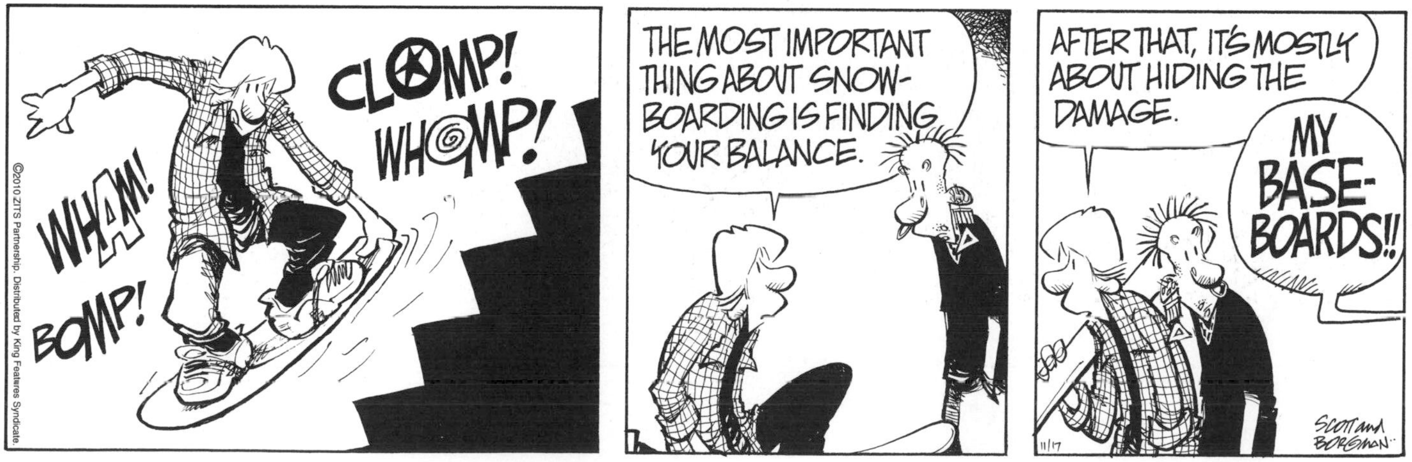
CLOMP! WHOMP!
WHAM! BOMP!
©2010 ZITS Partnership. Distributed by King Features Syndicate.
THE MOST IMPORTANT THING ABOUT SNOW-BOARDING IS FINDING YOUR BALANCE.
AFTER THAT, IT'S MOSTLY ABOUT HIDING THE DAMAGE.
MY BASE-BOARDS!!
11/17
SCOTT and BORGMAN

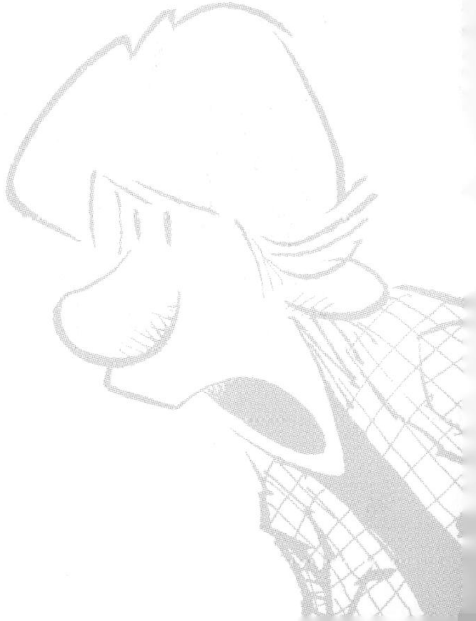

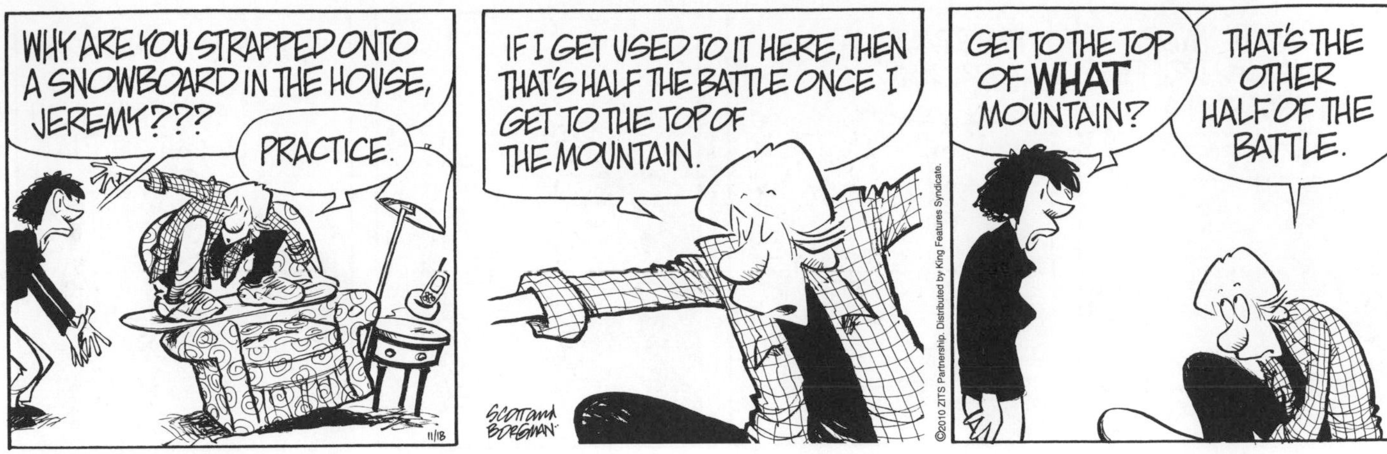
WHY ARE YOU STRAPPED ONTO A SNOWBOARD IN THE HOUSE, JEREMY???
PRACTICE.
IF I GET USED TO IT HERE, THEN THAT'S HALF THE BATTLE ONCE I GET TO THE TOP OF THE MOUNTAIN.
GET TO THE TOP OF WHAT MOUNTAIN?
THAT'S THE OTHER HALF OF THE BATTLE.
©2010 ZITS Partnership. Distributed by King Features Syndicate.

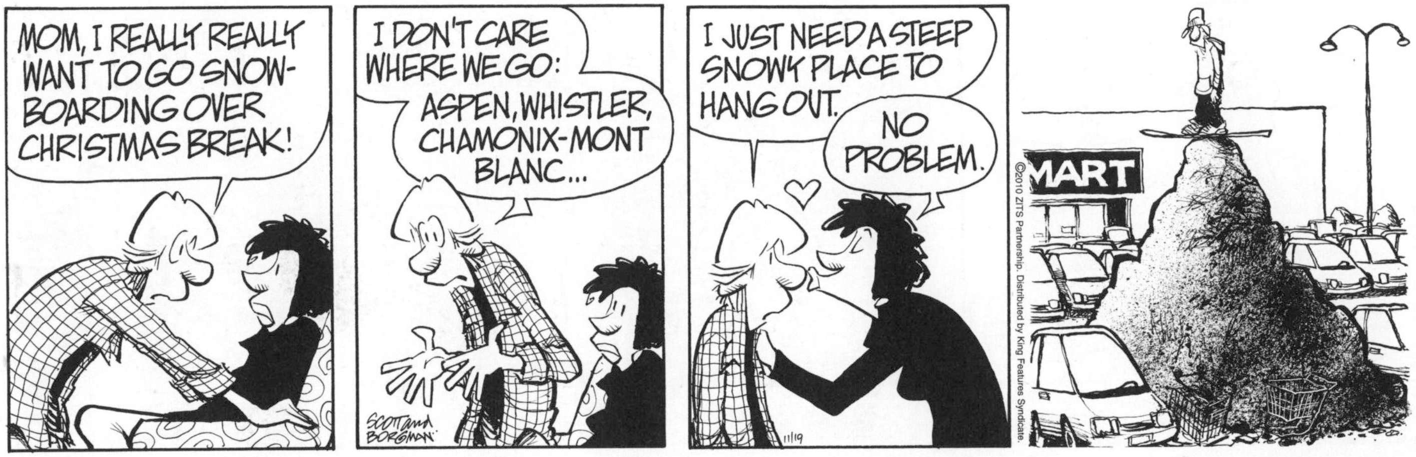
MOM, I REALLY REALLY WANT TO GO SNOW-BOARDING OVER CHRISTMAS BREAK!
I DON'T CARE WHERE WE GO:
ASPEN, WHISTLER, CHAMONIX-MONT BLANC...
I JUST NEED A STEEP SNOWY PLACE TO HANG OUT.
NO PROBLEM.
MART
©2010 ZITS Partnership. Distributed by King Features Syndicate.

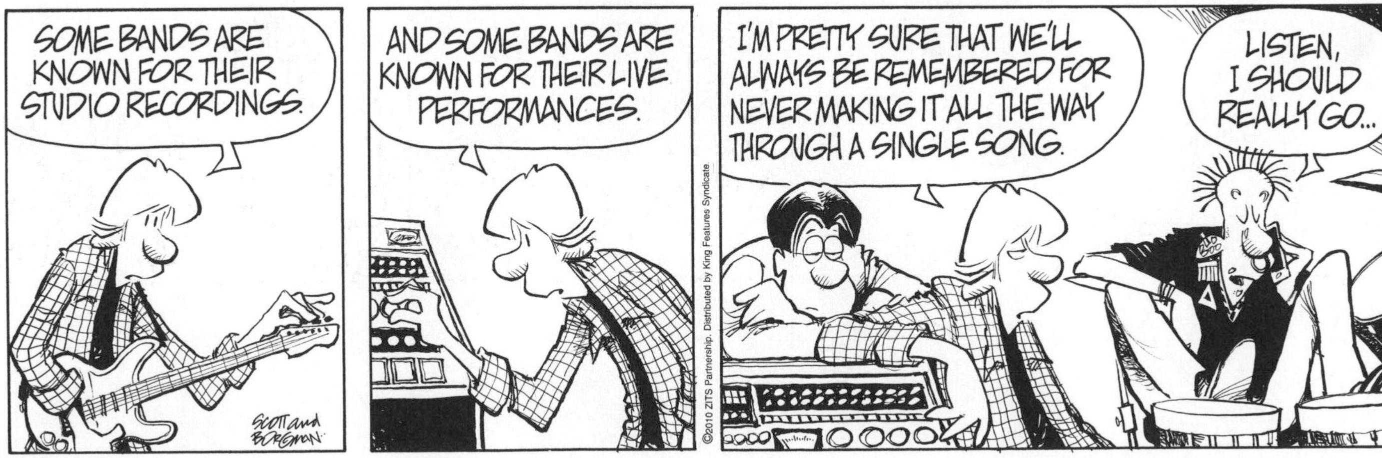
SOME BANDS ARE KNOWN FOR THEIR STUDIO RECORDINGS.
AND SOME BANDS ARE KNOWN FOR THEIR LIVE PERFORMANCES.
I'M PRETTY SURE THAT WE'LL ALWAYS BE REMEMBERED FOR NEVER MAKING IT ALL THE WAY THROUGH A SINGLE SONG.
LISTEN, I SHOULD REALLY GO...
©2010 ZITS Partnership. Distributed by King Features Syndicate.

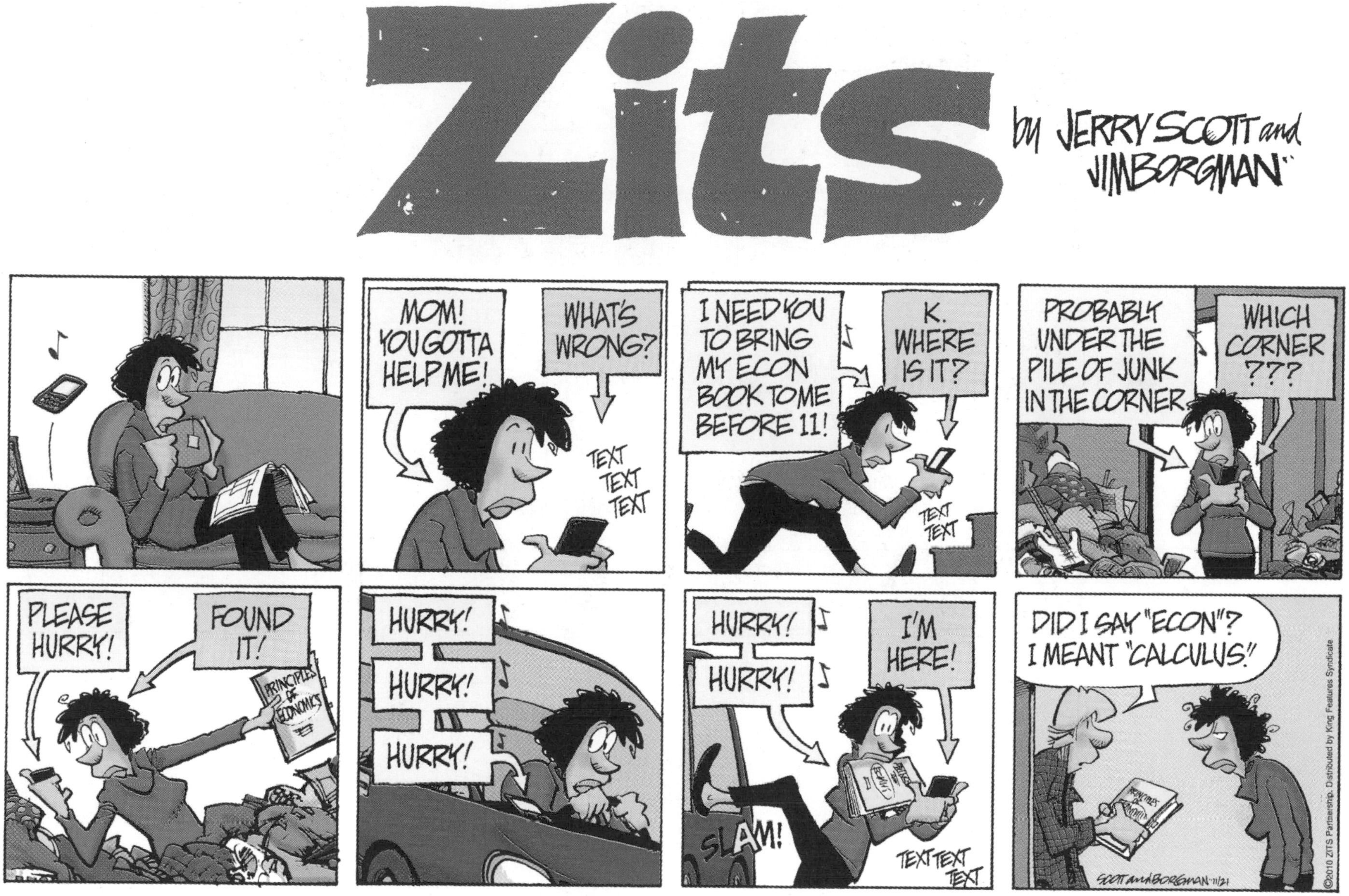

Zits
by JERRY SCOTT and JIM BORGMAN
MOM! YOU GOTTA HELP ME!
WHAT'S WRONG?
TEXT TEXT TEXT
I NEED YOU TO BRING MY ECON BOOK TO ME BEFORE 11!
K. WHERE IS IT?
TEXT TEXT
PROBABLY UNDER THE PILE OF JUNK IN THE CORNER
WHICH CORNER ???
PLEASE HURRY!
FOUND IT!
PRINCIPLES OF ECONOMICS
HURRY!
HURRY!
HURRY!
HURRY!
HURRY!
I'M HERE!
SLAM!
TEXT TEXT TEXT
DID I SAY "ECON"? I MEANT "CALCULUS."
SCOTT AND BORGMAN 11/21
©2010 ZITS Partnership. Distributed by King Features Syndicate

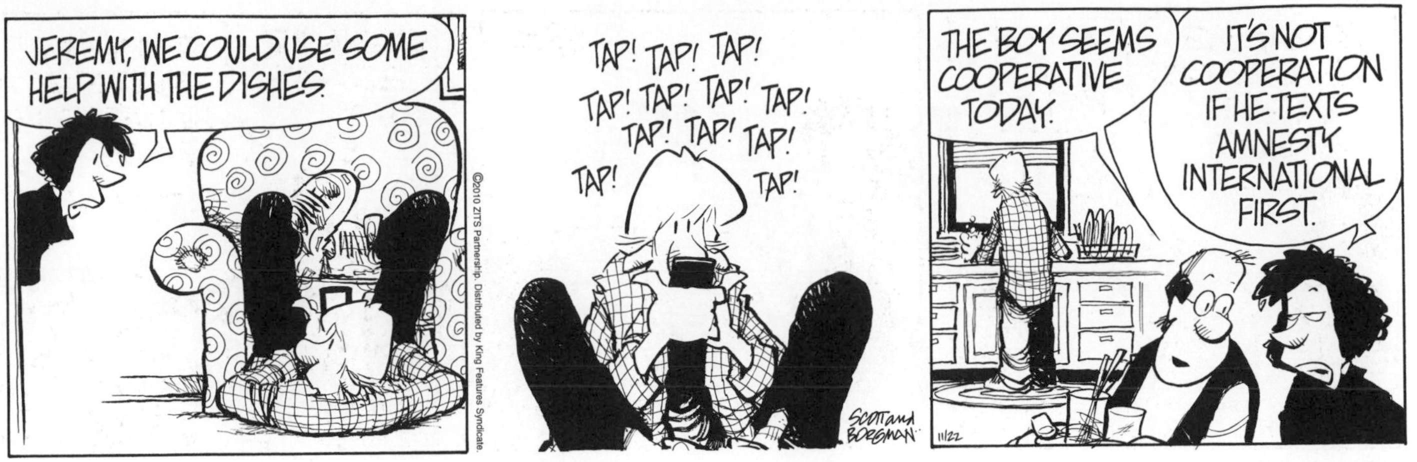
JEREMY, WE COULD USE SOME HELP WITH THE DISHES.
©2010 ZITS Partnership. Distributed by King Features Syndicate.
TAP! TAP! TAP! TAP! TAP! TAP! TAP! TAP! TAP! TAP! TAP! TAP!
SCOTT and BORGMAN
11/22
THE BOY SEEMS COOPERATIVE TODAY.
IT'S NOT COOPERATION IF HE TEXTS AMNESTY INTERNATIONAL FIRST.

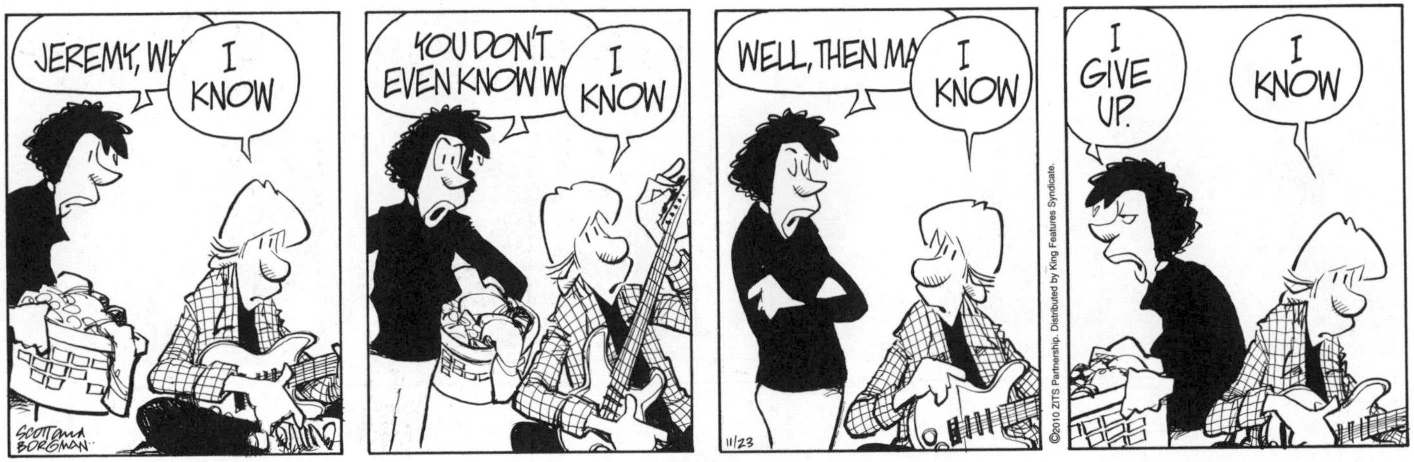
JEREMY, WH
I KNOW
SCOTT and BORGMAN
YOU DON'T EVEN KNOW W
I KNOW
WELL, THEN MA
I KNOW
11/23
©2010 ZITS Partnership. Distributed by King Features Syndicate.
I GIVE UP.
I KNOW

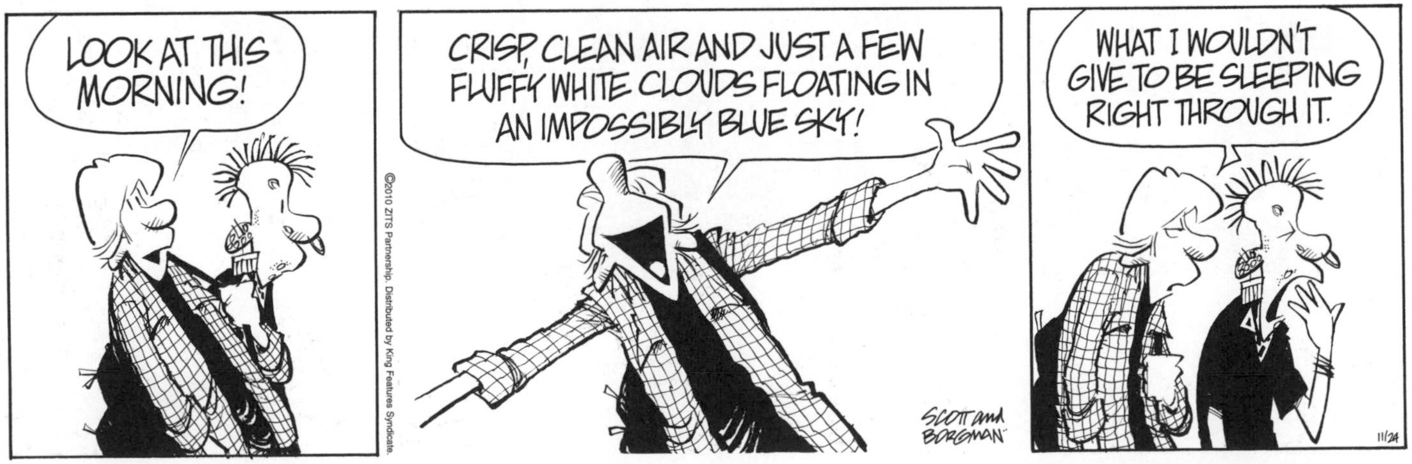
LOOK AT THIS MORNING!
©2010 ZITS Partnership. Distributed by King Features Syndicate.
CRISP, CLEAN AIR AND JUST A FEW FLUFFY WHITE CLOUDS FLOATING IN AN IMPOSSIBLY BLUE SKY!
SCOTT and BORGMAN
WHAT I WOULDN'T GIVE TO BE SLEEPING RIGHT THROUGH IT.
11/24

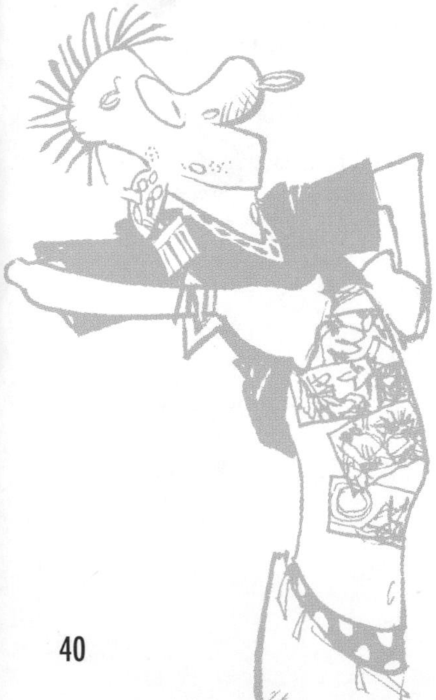

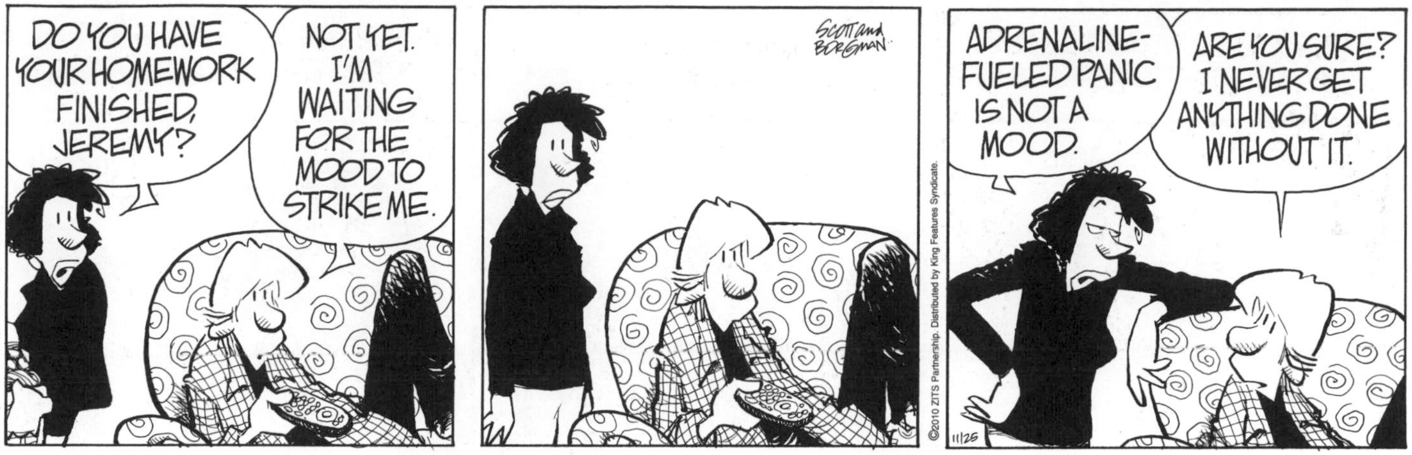
DO YOU HAVE YOUR HOMEWORK FINISHED, JEREMY?
NOT YET. I'M WAITING FOR THE MOOD TO STRIKE ME.
SCOTT and BORGMAN
ADRENALINE-FUELED PANIC IS NOT A MOOD.
ARE YOU SURE? I NEVER GET ANYTHING DONE WITHOUT IT.
©2010 ZITS Partnership. Distributed by King Features Syndicate.
11/25

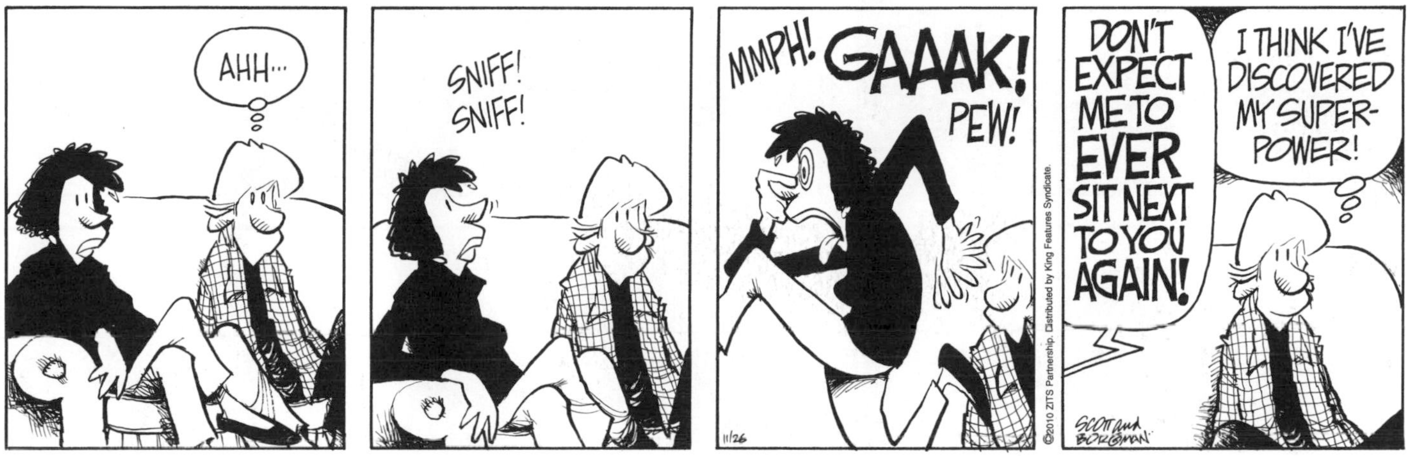
AHH...
SNIFF! SNIFF!
MMPH! GAAAK! PEW!
11/26
DON'T EXPECT ME TO EVER SIT NEXT TO YOU AGAIN!
I THINK I'VE DISCOVERED MY SUPER-POWER!
©2010 ZITS Partnership. Distributed by King Features Syndicate.
SCOTT and BORGMAN

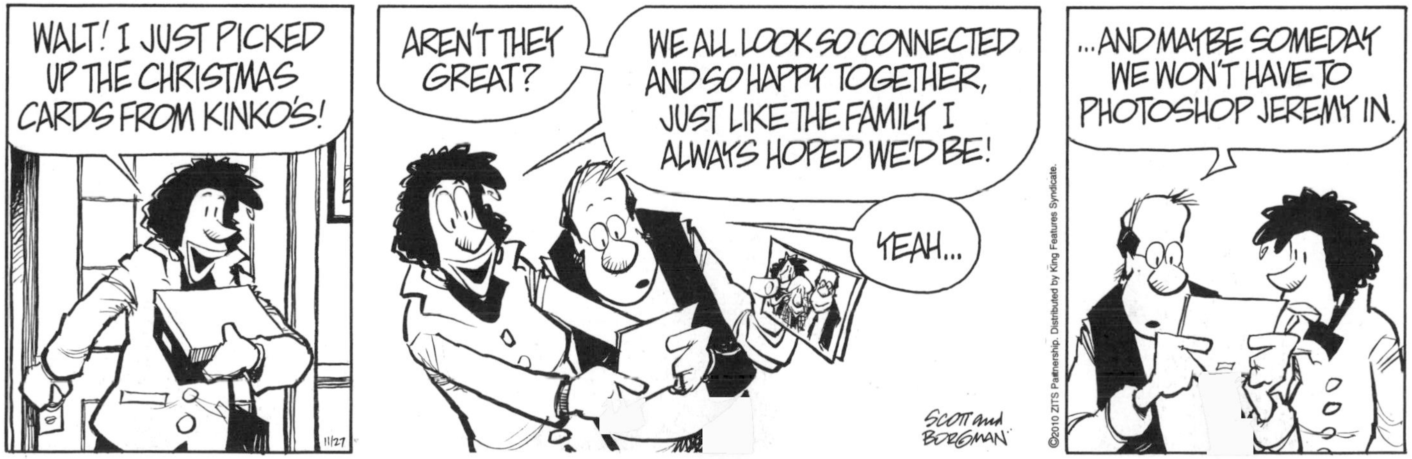
WALT! I JUST PICKED UP THE CHRISTMAS CARDS FROM KINKO'S!
11/27
AREN'T THEY GREAT?
WE ALL LOOK SO CONNECTED AND SO HAPPY TOGETHER, JUST LIKE THE FAMILY I ALWAYS HOPED WE'D BE!
YEAH...
SCOTT and BORGMAN
©2010 ZITS Partnership. Distributed by King Features Syndicate.
...AND MAYBE SOMEDAY WE WON'T HAVE TO PHOTOSHOP JEREMY IN.

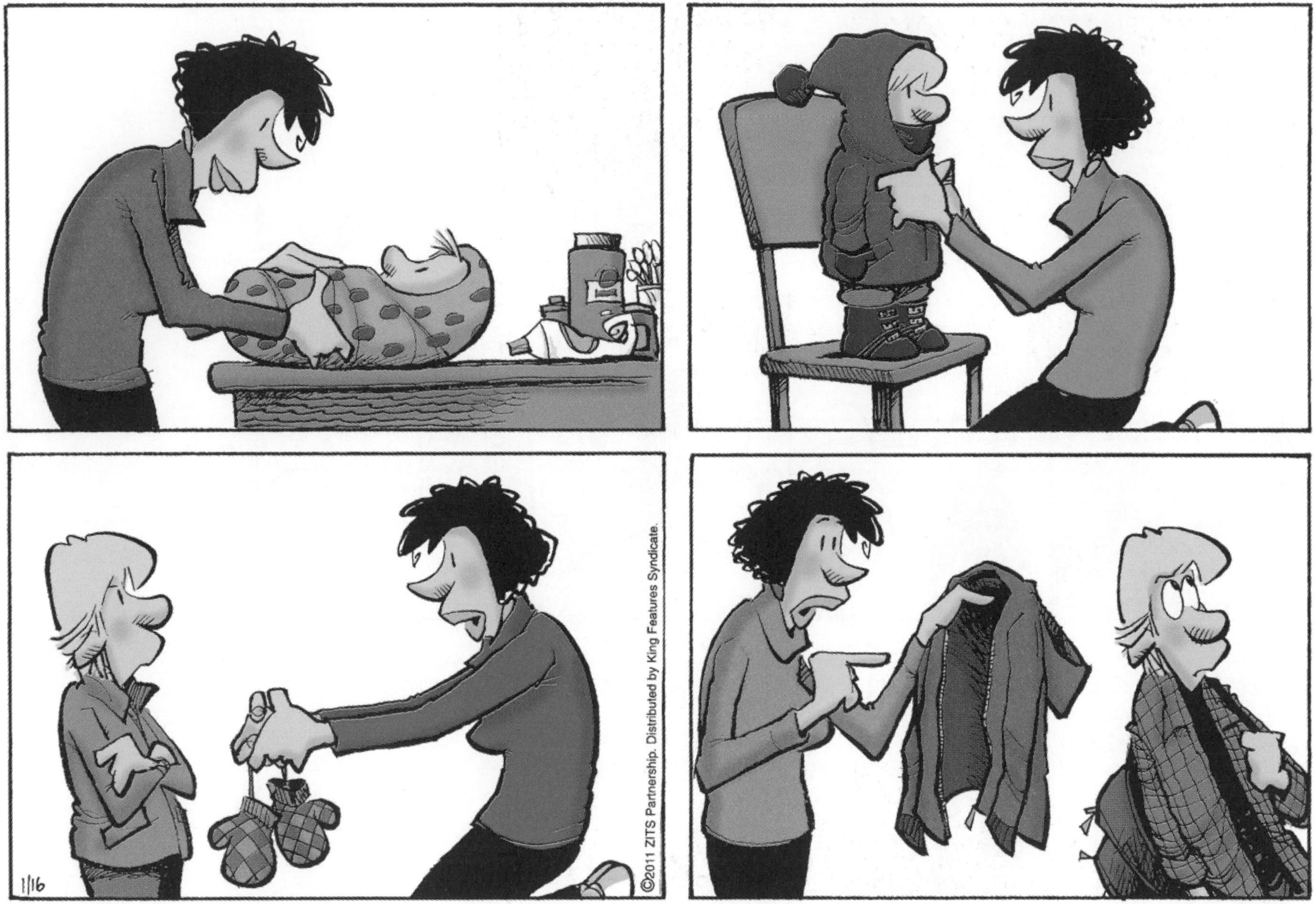
1/16
©2011 ZITS Partnership. Distributed by King Features Syndicate.

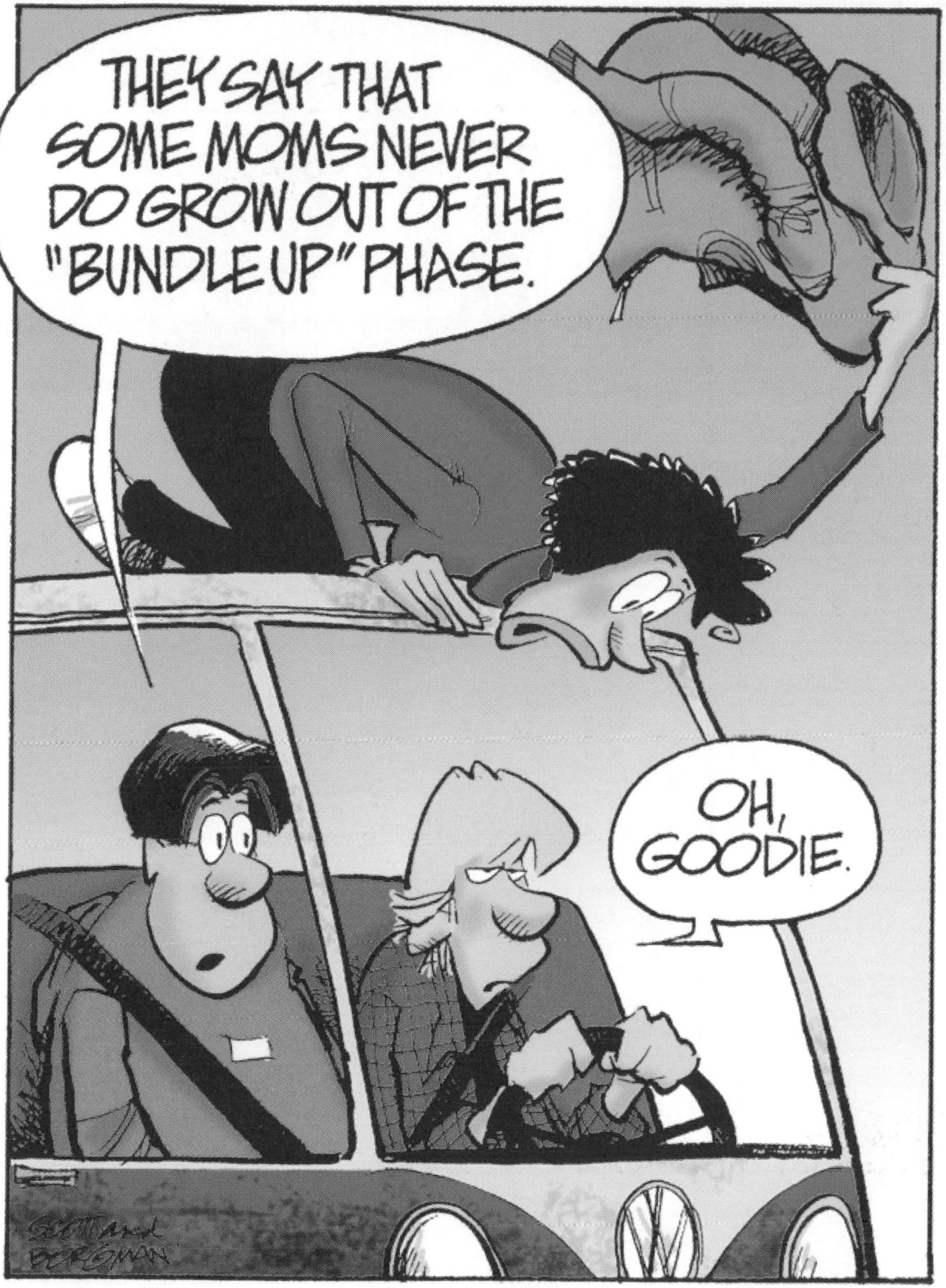
THEY SAY THAT SOME MOMS NEVER DO GROW OUT OF THE "BUNDLE UP" PHASE.
OH, GOODIE.
SCOTT and BORGMAN

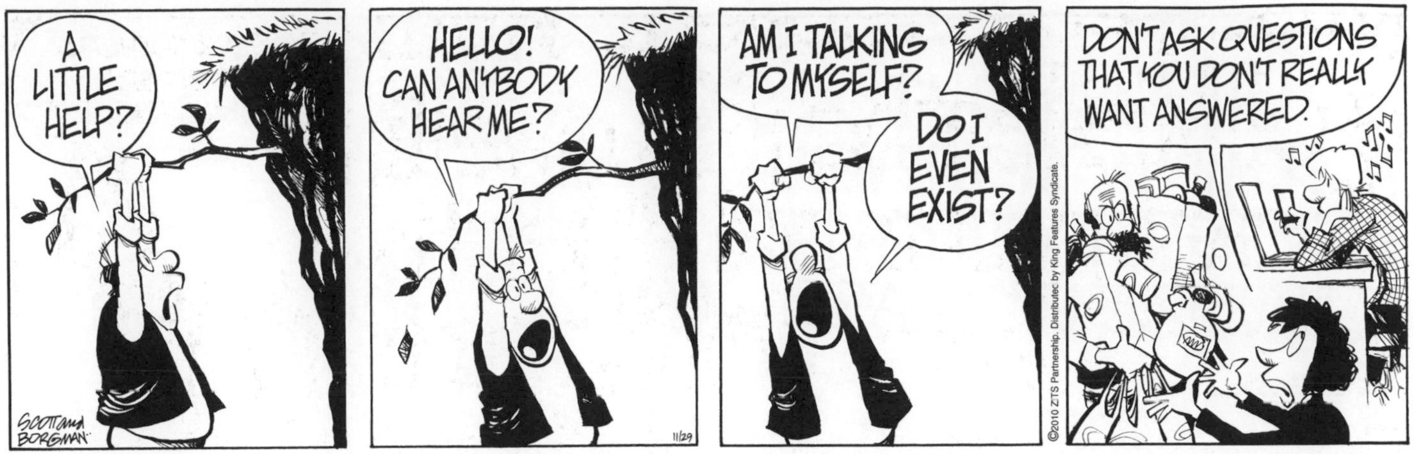
A LITTLE HELP?
SCOTT and BORGMAN
HELLO! CAN ANYBODY HEAR ME?
11/29
AM I TALKING TO MYSELF?
DO I EVEN EXIST?
©2010 ZITS Partnership. Distributed by King Features Syndicate.
DON'T ASK QUESTIONS THAT YOU DON'T REALLY WANT ANSWERED.

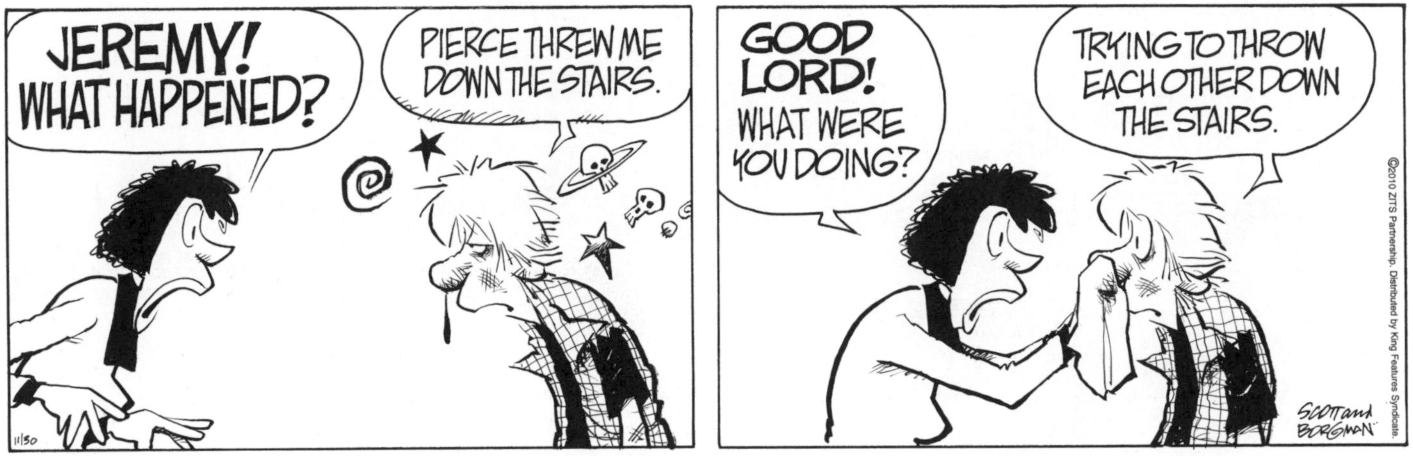
JEREMY! WHAT HAPPENED?
PIERCE THREW ME DOWN THE STAIRS.
11/30
GOOD LORD! WHAT WERE YOU DOING?
TRYING TO THROW EACH OTHER DOWN THE STAIRS.
SCOTT and BORGMAN
©2010 ZITS Partnership. Distributed by King Features Syndicate.

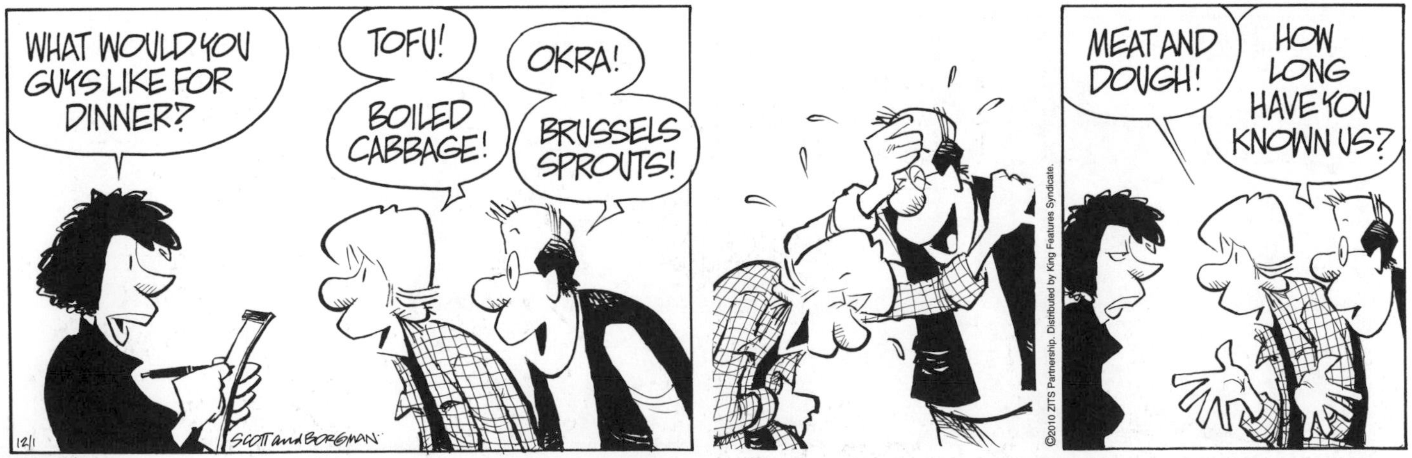
WHAT WOULD YOU GUYS LIKE FOR DINNER?
TOFU!
OKRA!
BOILED CABBAGE!
BRUSSELS SPROUTS!
12/1
SCOTT and BORGMAN
©2010 ZITS Partnership. Distributed by King Features Syndicate.
MEAT AND DOUGH!
HOW LONG HAVE YOU KNOWN US?

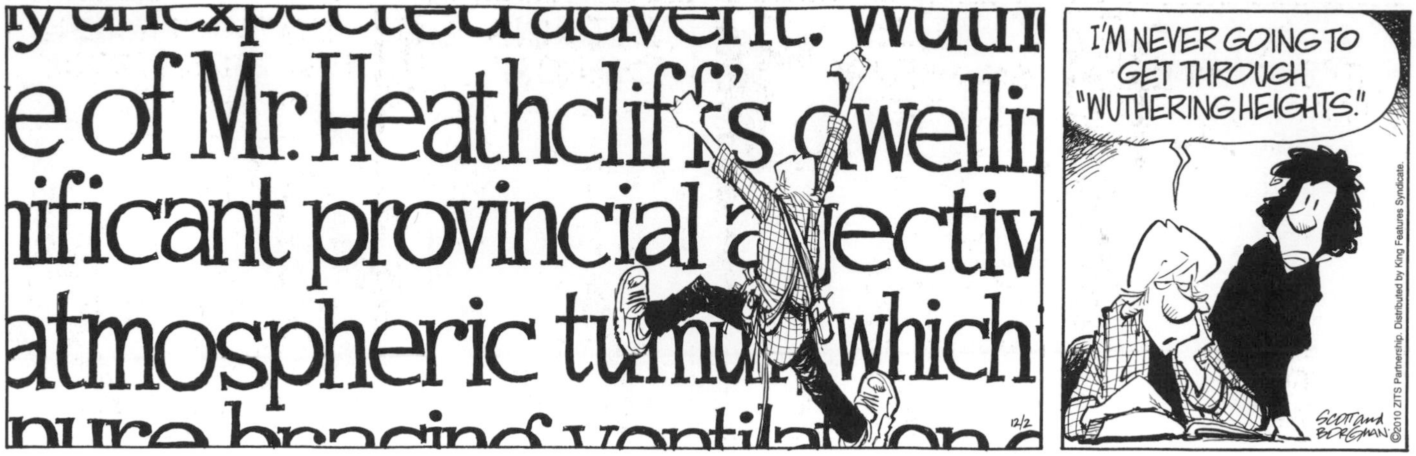
I'M NEVER GOING TO GET THROUGH "WUTHERING HEIGHTS."
SCOTT and BORGMAN
©2010 ZITS Partnership. Distributed by King Features Syndicate.

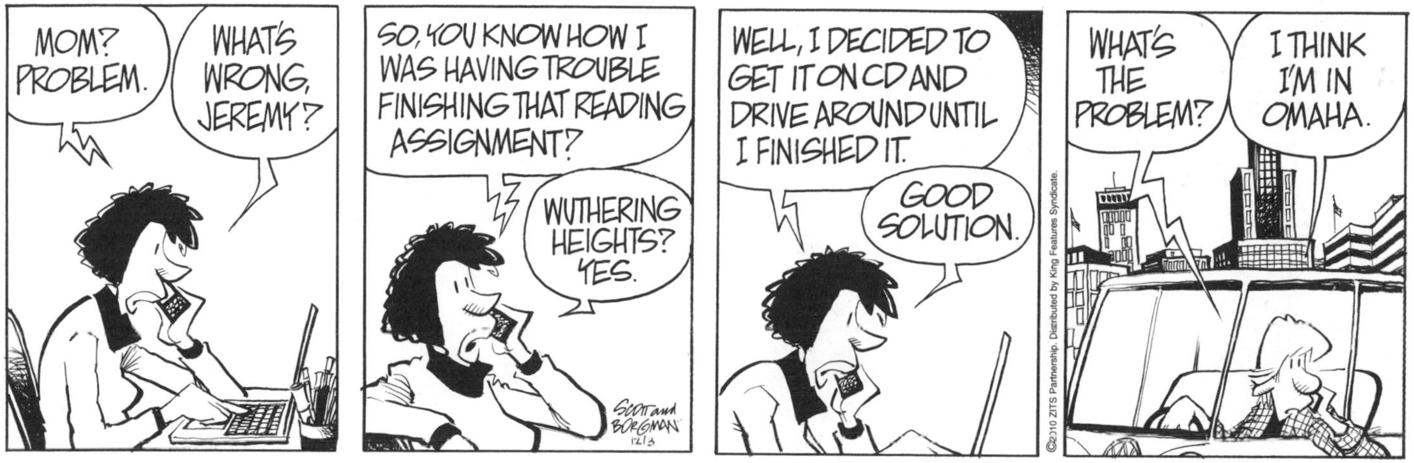
MOM? PROBLEM.
WHAT'S WRONG, JEREMY?
SO, YOU KNOW HOW I WAS HAVING TROUBLE FINISHING THAT READING ASSIGNMENT?
WUTHERING HEIGHTS? YES.
SCOTT and BORGMAN
WELL, I DECIDED TO GET IT ON CD AND DRIVE AROUND UNTIL I FINISHED IT.
GOOD SOLUTION.
©2010 ZITS Partnership. Distributed by King Features Syndicate.
WHAT'S THE PROBLEM?
I THINK I'M IN OMAHA.

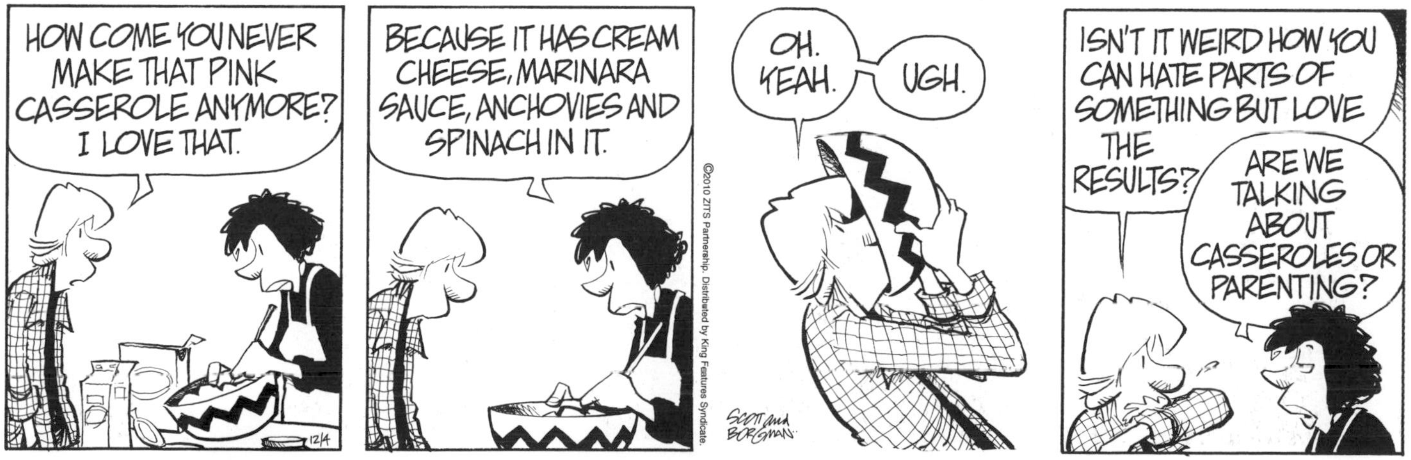
HOW COME YOU NEVER MAKE THAT PINK CASSEROLE ANYMORE? I LOVE THAT.
BECAUSE IT HAS CREAM CHEESE, MARINARA SAUCE, ANCHOVIES AND SPINACH IN IT.
©2010 ZITS Partnership. Distributed by King Features Syndicate.
OH. YEAH.
UGH.
SCOTT and BORGMAN
ISN'T IT WEIRD HOW YOU CAN HATE PARTS OF SOMETHING BUT LOVE THE RESULTS?
ARE WE TALKING ABOUT CASSEROLES OR PARENTING?

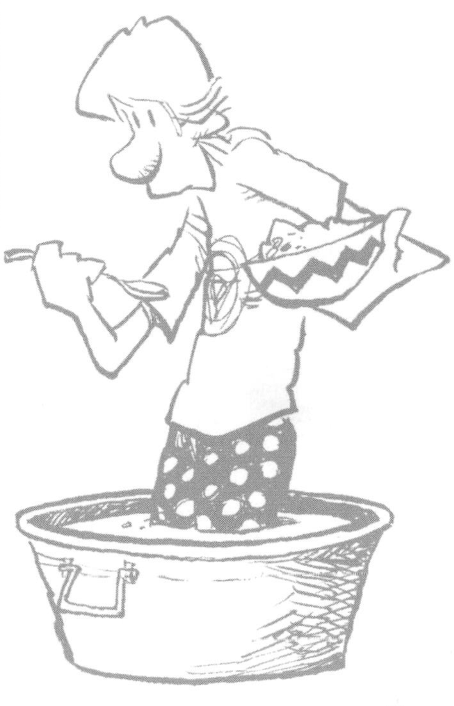

Zits

by JERRY SCOTT and JIM BORGMAN

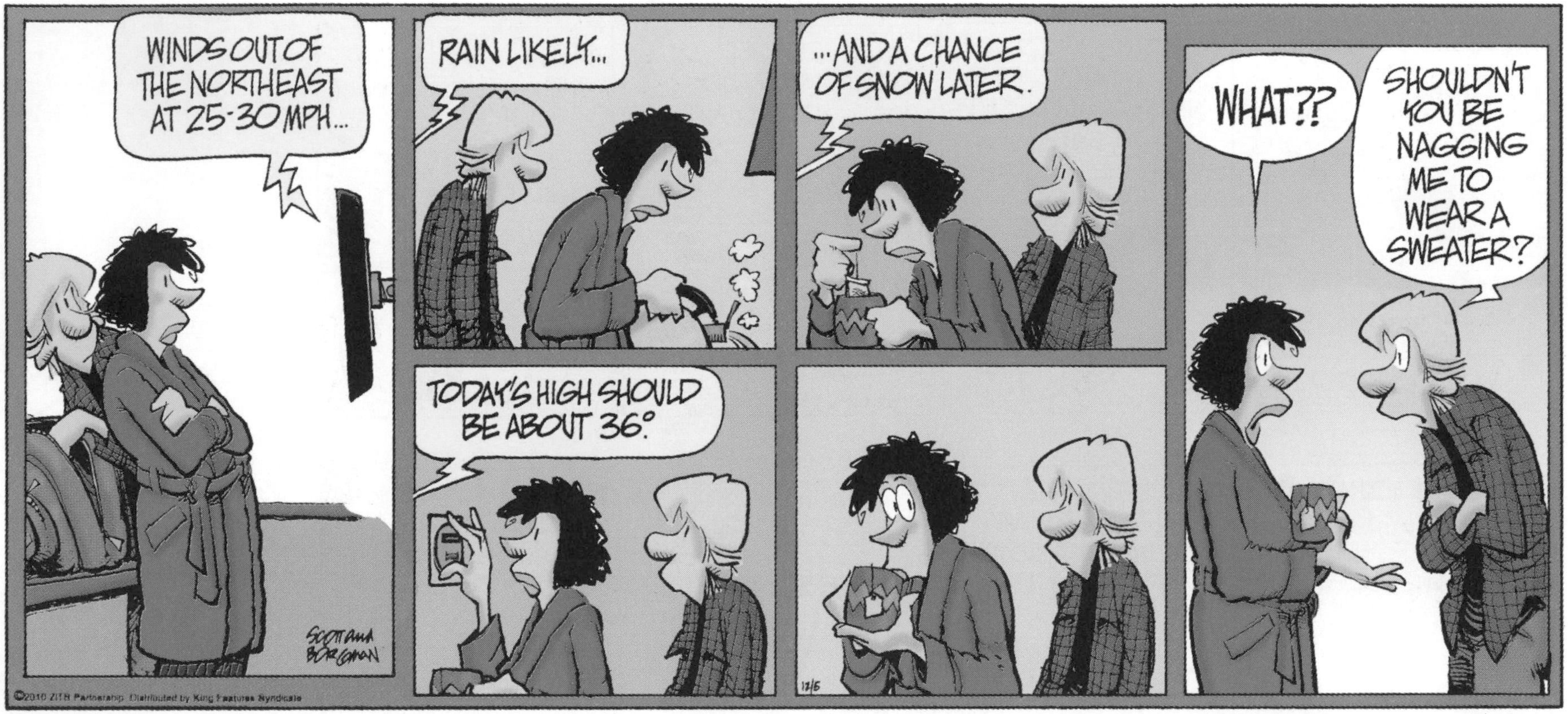
WINDS OUT OF THE NORTHEAST AT 25-30 MPH...
SCOTT and BORGMAN
RAIN LIKELY...
...AND A CHANCE OF SNOW LATER.
TODAY'S HIGH SHOULD BE ABOUT 36°.
12/5
WHAT??
SHOULDN'T YOU BE NAGGING ME TO WEAR A SWEATER?
©2010 ZITS Partnership. Distributed by King Features Syndicate

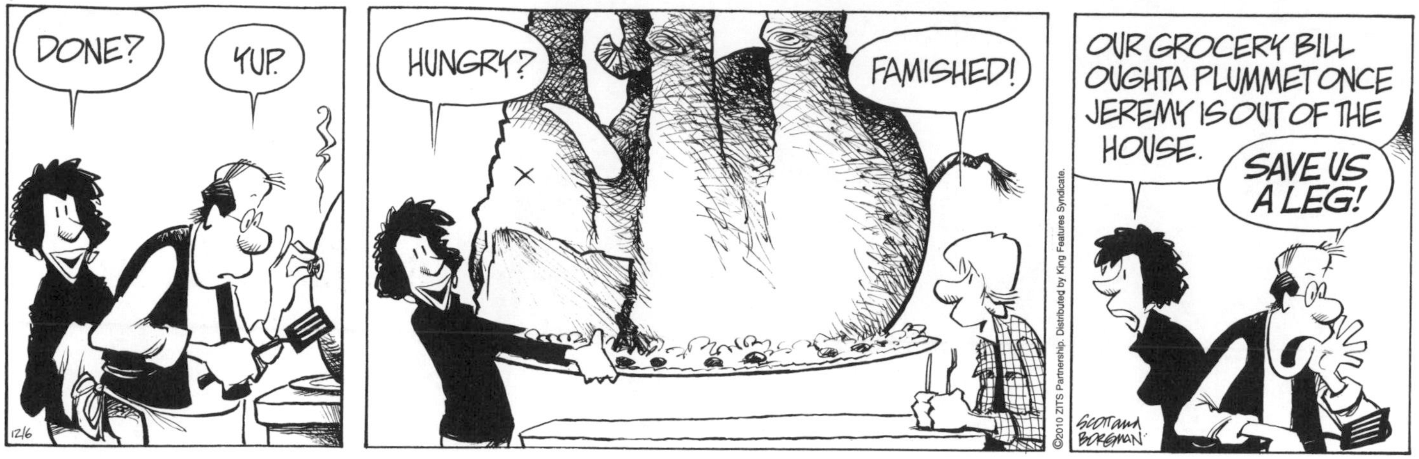

DONE?
YUP.
12/6
HUNGRY?
FAMISHED!
OUR GROCERY BILL OUGHTA PLUMMET ONCE JEREMY IS OUT OF THE HOUSE.
SAVE US A LEG!
©2010 ZITS Partnership. Distributed by King Features Syndicate.
SCOTT AND BORGMAN

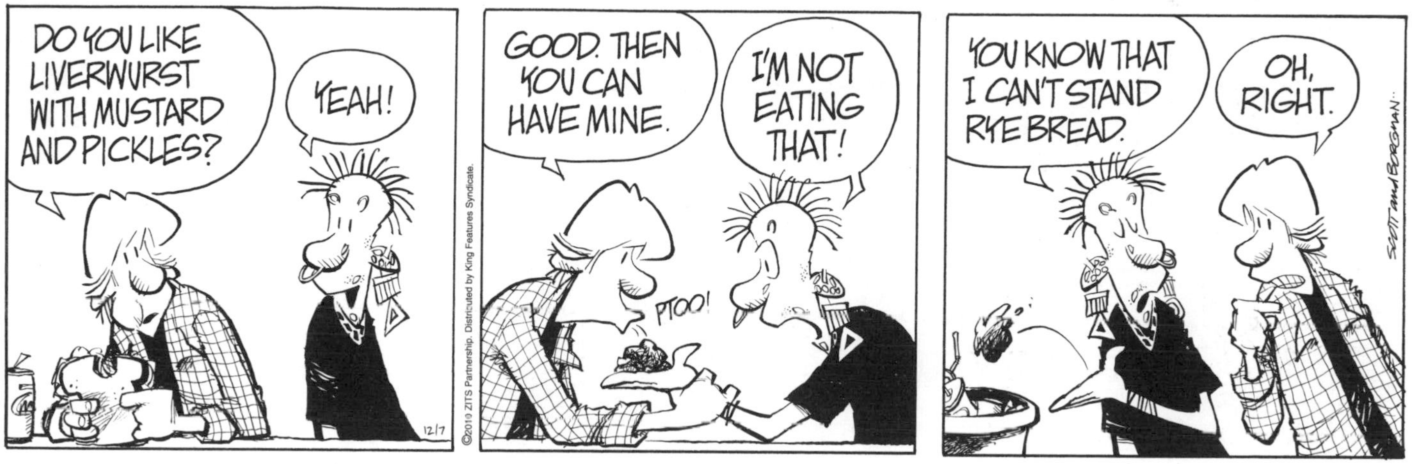

DO YOU LIKE LIVERWURST WITH MUSTARD AND PICKLES?
YEAH!
12/7
©2010 ZITS Partnership. Distributed by King Features Syndicate.
GOOD. THEN YOU CAN HAVE MINE.
I'M NOT EATING THAT!
PTOO!
YOU KNOW THAT I CAN'T STAND RYE BREAD.
OH, RIGHT.
SCOTT AND BORGMAN

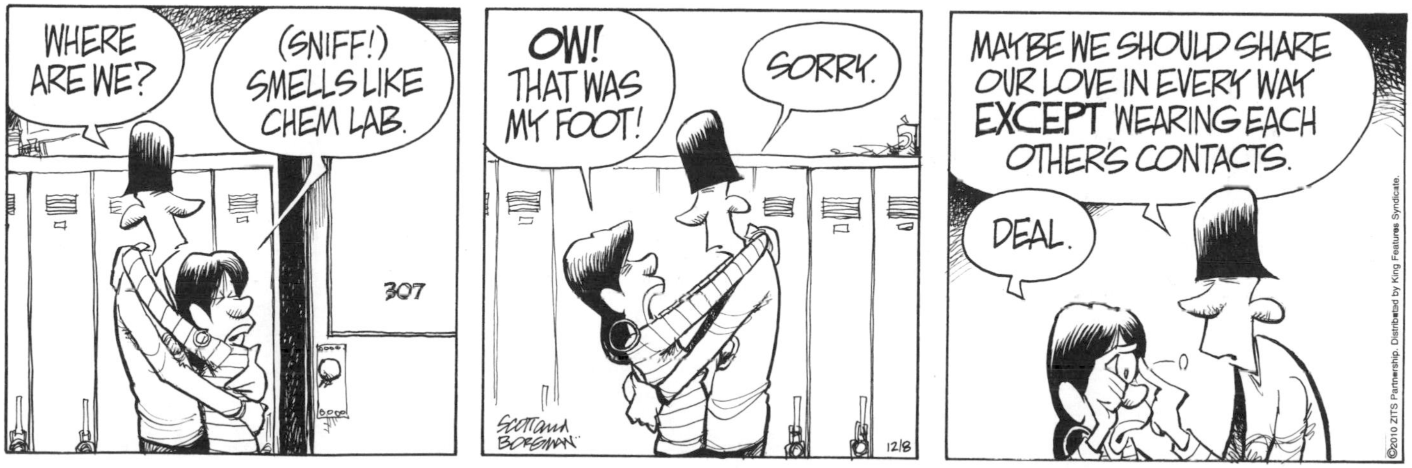

WHERE ARE WE?
(SNIFF!) SMELLS LIKE CHEM LAB.
307
OW! THAT WAS MY FOOT!
SORRY.
SCOTT AND BORGMAN
12/8
MAYBE WE SHOULD SHARE OUR LOVE IN EVERY WAY EXCEPT WEARING EACH OTHER'S CONTACTS.
DEAL.
©2010 ZITS Partnership. Distributed by King Features Syndicate.

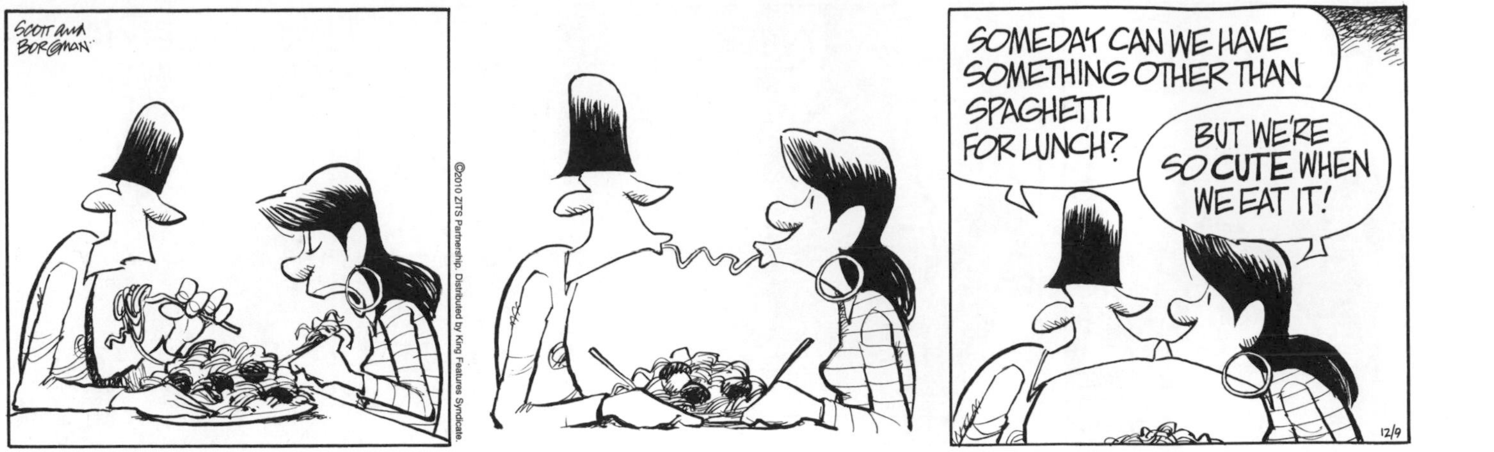
SCOTT and BORGMAN
©2010 ZITS Partnership. Distributed by King Features Syndicate.
SOMEDAY CAN WE HAVE SOMETHING OTHER THAN SPAGHETTI FOR LUNCH?
BUT WE'RE SO **CUTE** WHEN WE EAT IT!
12/9

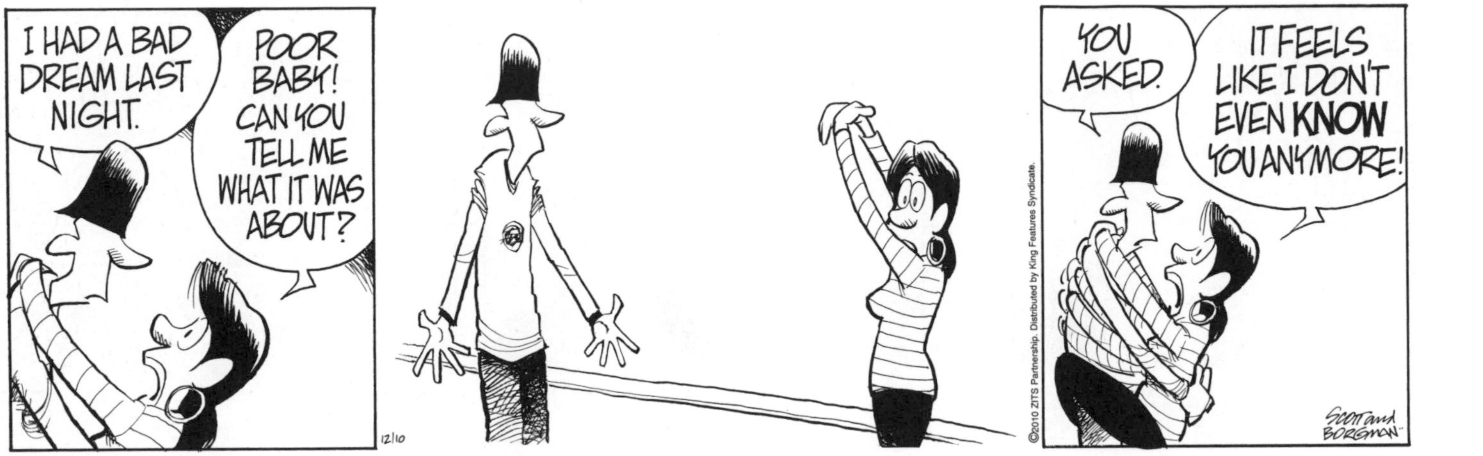
I HAD A BAD DREAM LAST NIGHT.
POOR BABY! CAN YOU TELL ME WHAT IT WAS ABOUT?
12/10
©2010 ZITS Partnership. Distributed by King Features Syndicate.
YOU ASKED.
IT FEELS LIKE I DON'T EVEN **KNOW** YOU ANYMORE!
SCOTT and BORGMAN

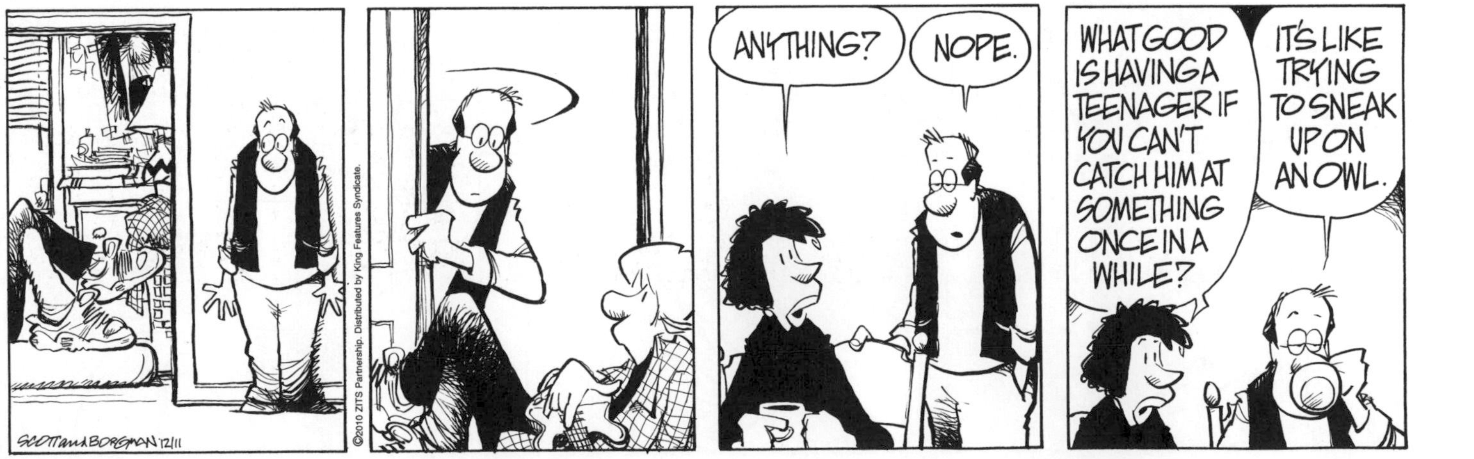
SCOTT and BORGMAN 12/11
©2010 ZITS Partnership. Distributed by King Features Syndicate.
ANYTHING?
NOPE.
WHAT GOOD IS HAVING A TEENAGER IF YOU CAN'T CATCH HIM AT SOMETHING ONCE IN A WHILE?
IT'S LIKE TRYING TO SNEAK UP ON AN OWL.

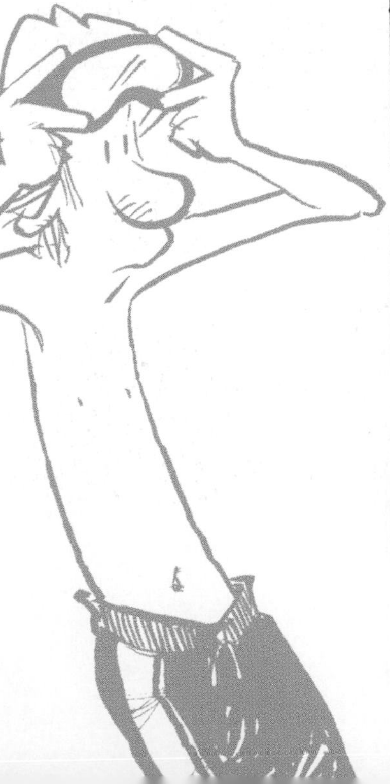

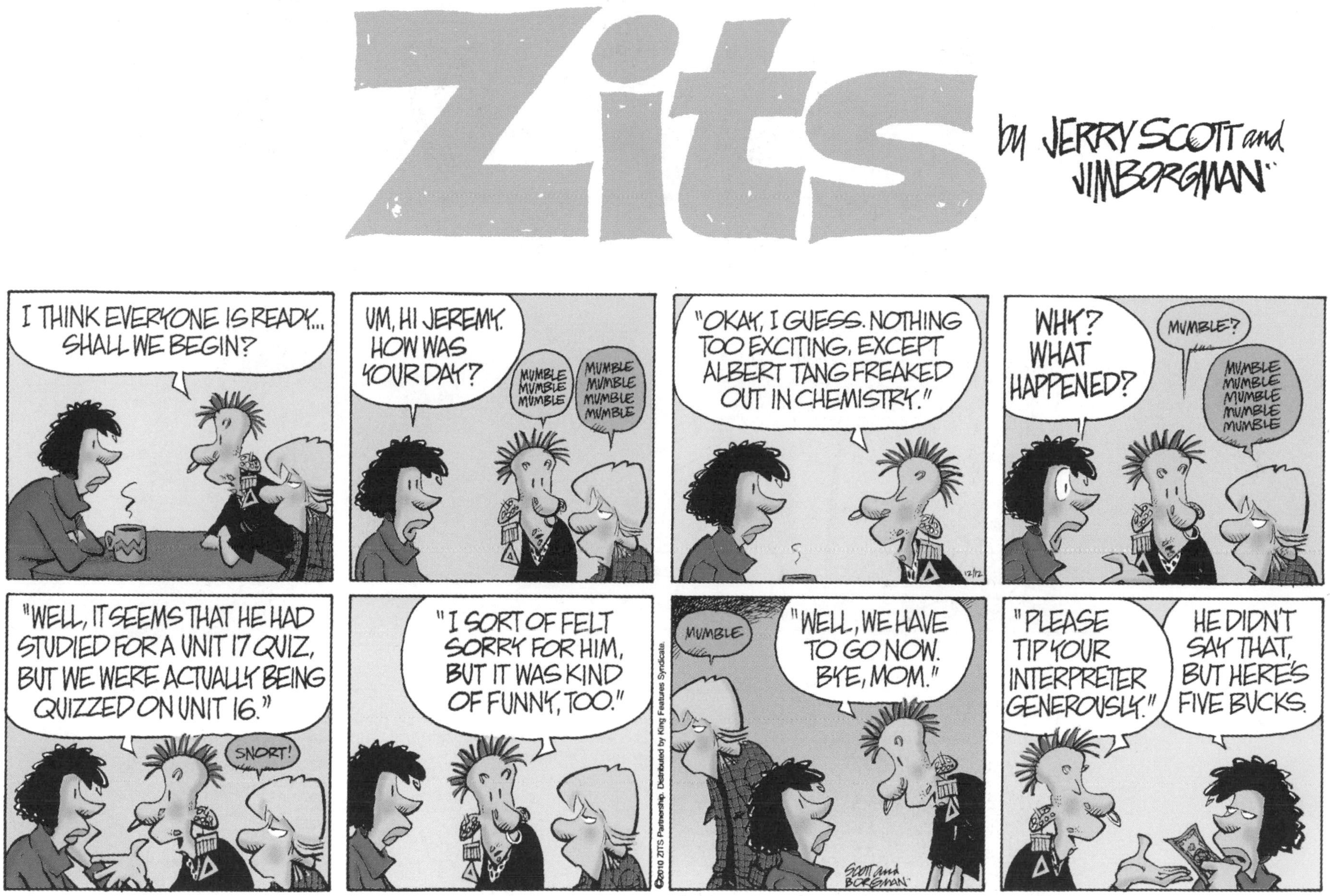
Zits
by JERRY SCOTT and JIM BORGMAN
I THINK EVERYONE IS READY... SHALL WE BEGIN?
UM, HI JEREMY. HOW WAS YOUR DAY?
MUMBLE MUMBLE MUMBLE
MUMBLE MUMBLE MUMBLE MUMBLE
"OKAY, I GUESS. NOTHING TOO EXCITING, EXCEPT ALBERT TANG FREAKED OUT IN CHEMISTRY."
12/12
WHY? WHAT HAPPENED?
MUMBLE?
MUMBLE MUMBLE MUMBLE MUMBLE MUMBLE
"WELL, IT SEEMS THAT HE HAD STUDIED FOR A UNIT 17 QUIZ, BUT WE WERE ACTUALLY BEING QUIZZED ON UNIT 16."
SNORT!
"I SORT OF FELT SORRY FOR HIM, BUT IT WAS KIND OF FUNNY, TOO."
©2010 ZITS Partnership. Distributed by King Features Syndicate.
MUMBLE
"WELL, WE HAVE TO GO NOW. BYE, MOM."
SCOTT and BORGMAN
"PLEASE TIP YOUR INTERPRETER GENEROUSLY."
HE DIDN'T SAY THAT, BUT HERE'S FIVE BUCKS.

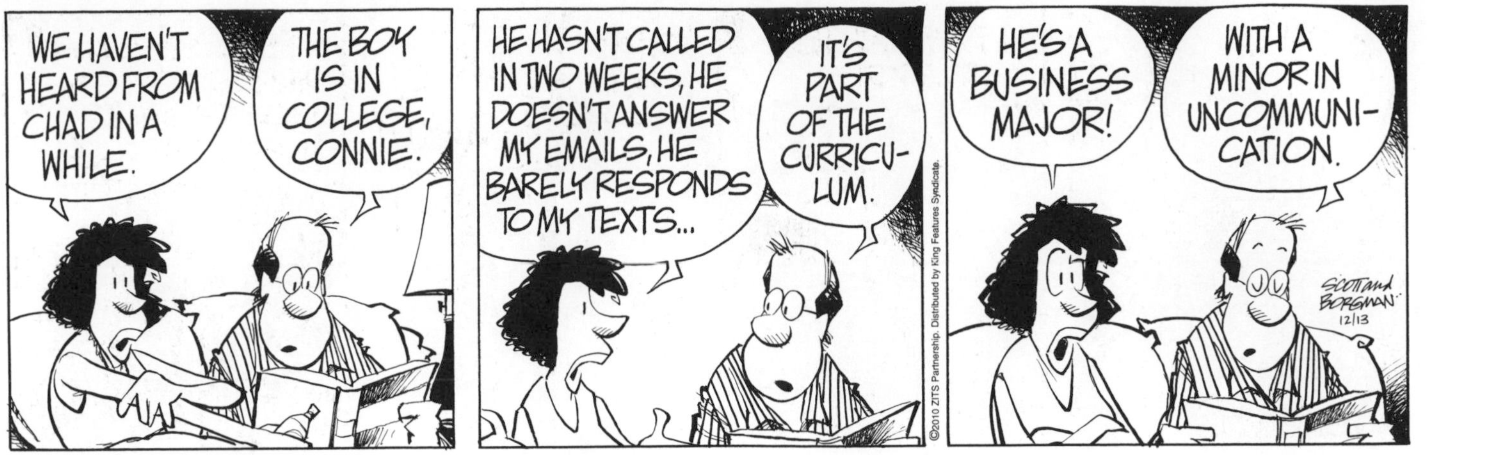
WE HAVEN'T HEARD FROM CHAD IN A WHILE.
THE BOY IS IN COLLEGE, CONNIE.
HE HASN'T CALLED IN TWO WEEKS, HE DOESN'T ANSWER MY EMAILS, HE BARELY RESPONDS TO MY TEXTS...
IT'S PART OF THE CURRICULUM.
©2010 ZITS Partnership. Distributed by King Features Syndicate.
HE'S A BUSINESS MAJOR!
WITH A MINOR IN UNCOMMUNICATION.
SCOTT and BORGMAN 12/13

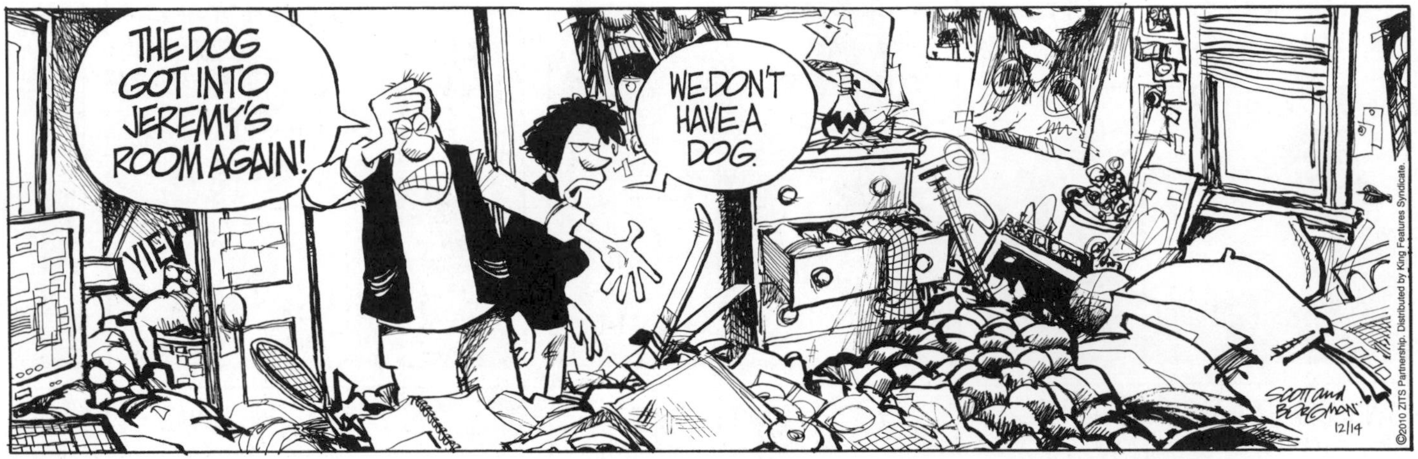
THE DOG GOT INTO JEREMY'S ROOM AGAIN!
WE DON'T HAVE A DOG.
SCOTT and BORGMAN 12/14
©2010 ZITS Partnership. Distributed by King Features Syndicate.

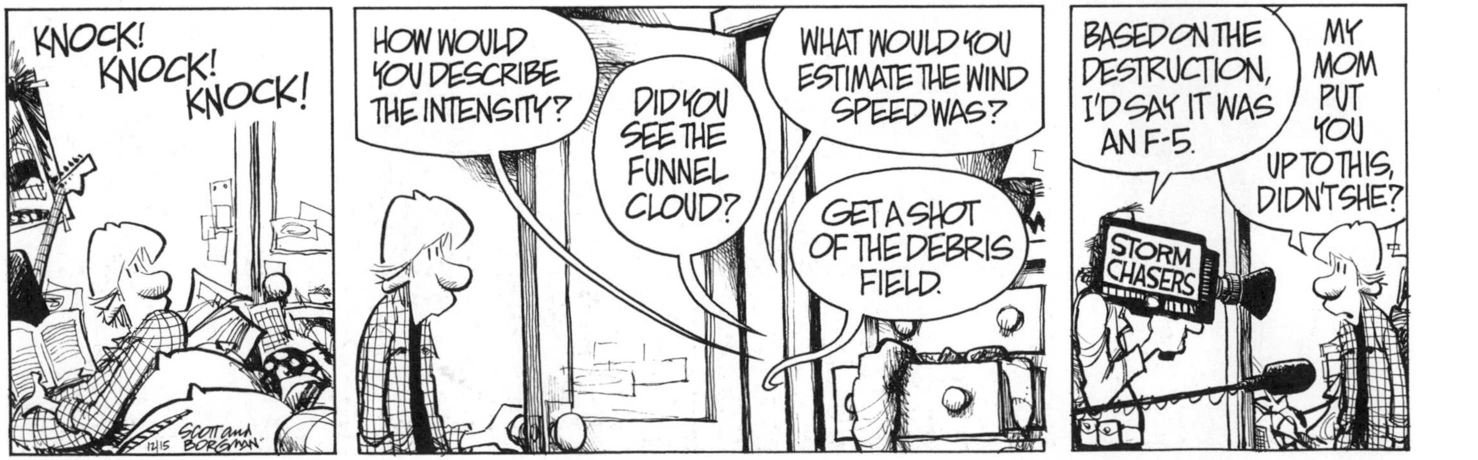
KNOCK! KNOCK! KNOCK!
12/15 SCOTT and BORGMAN
HOW WOULD YOU DESCRIBE THE INTENSITY?
DID YOU SEE THE FUNNEL CLOUD?
WHAT WOULD YOU ESTIMATE THE WIND SPEED WAS?
GET A SHOT OF THE DEBRIS FIELD.
BASED ON THE DESTRUCTION, I'D SAY IT WAS AN F-5.
MY MOM PUT YOU UP TO THIS, DIDN'T SHE?
STORM CHASERS

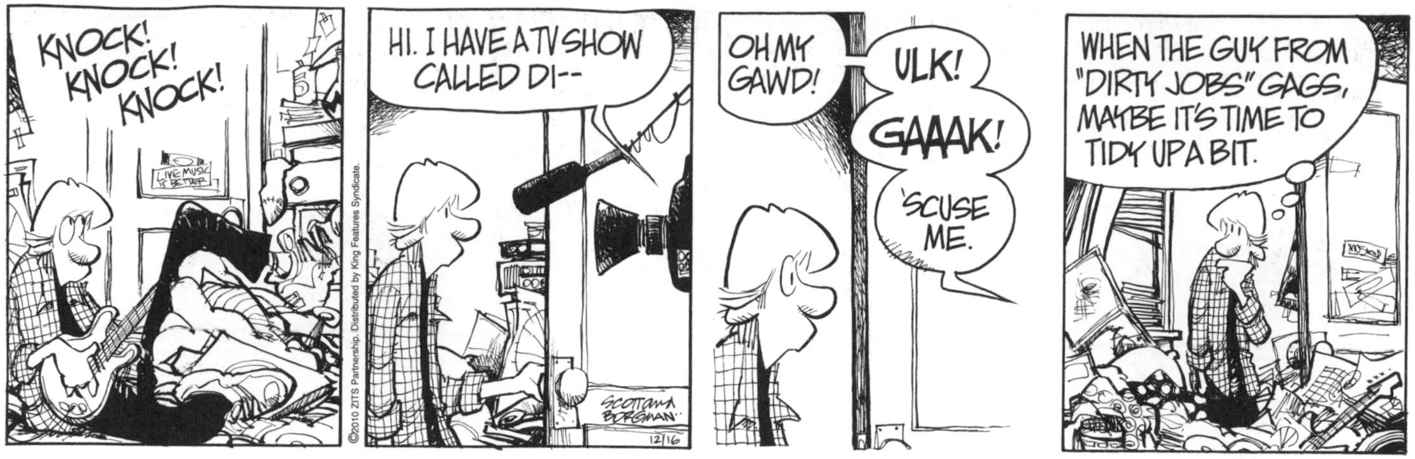
KNOCK! KNOCK! KNOCK!
LIVE MUSIC IS BETTER
©2010 ZITS Partnership. Distributed by King Features Syndicate.
HI. I HAVE A TV SHOW CALLED DI--
SCOTT and BORGMAN
12/16
OH MY GAWD!
ULK!
GAAAK!
'SCUSE ME.
WHEN THE GUY FROM "DIRTY JOBS" GAGS, MAYBE IT'S TIME TO TIDY UP A BIT.

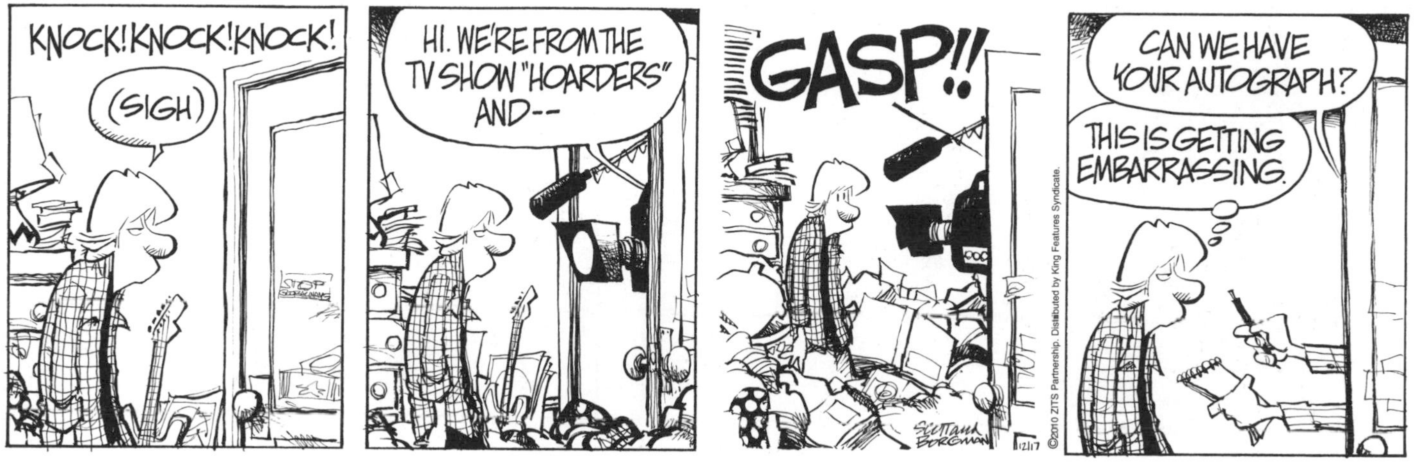
KNOCK! KNOCK! KNOCK!
(SIGH)
STOP
HI. WE'RE FROM THE TV SHOW "HOARDERS" AND--
GASP!!
SCOTT and BORGMAN
12/17
©2010 ZITS Partnership. Distributed by King Features Syndicate.
CAN WE HAVE YOUR AUTOGRAPH?
THIS IS GETTING EMBARRASSING.

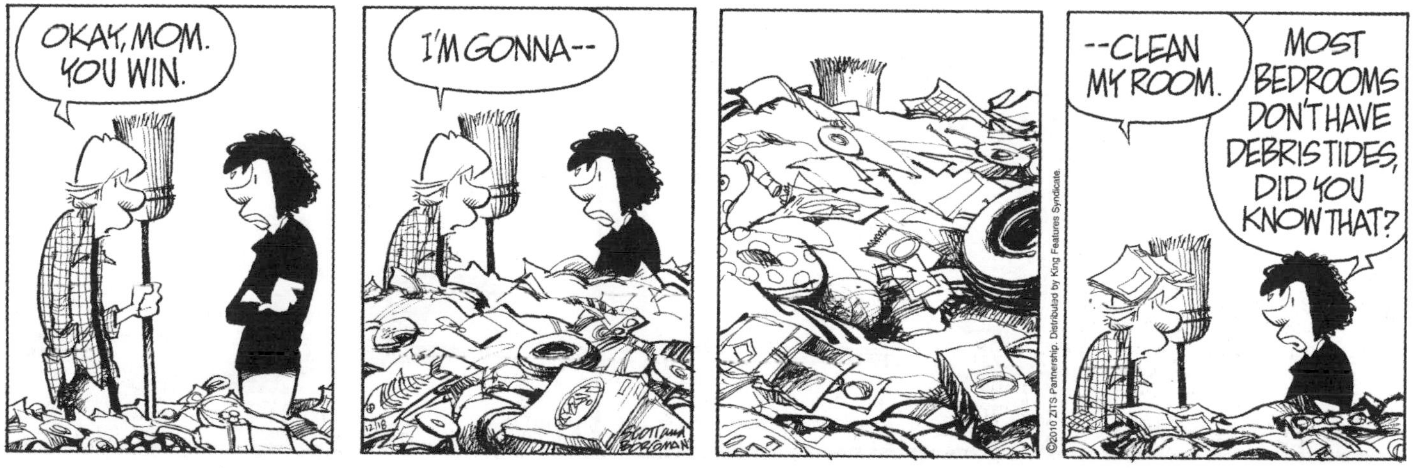
OKAY, MOM. YOU WIN.
I'M GONNA--
12/18
SCOTT and BORGMAN
©2010 ZITS Partnership. Distributed by King Features Syndicate.
--CLEAN MY ROOM.
MOST BEDROOMS DON'T HAVE DEBRIS TIDES, DID YOU KNOW THAT?

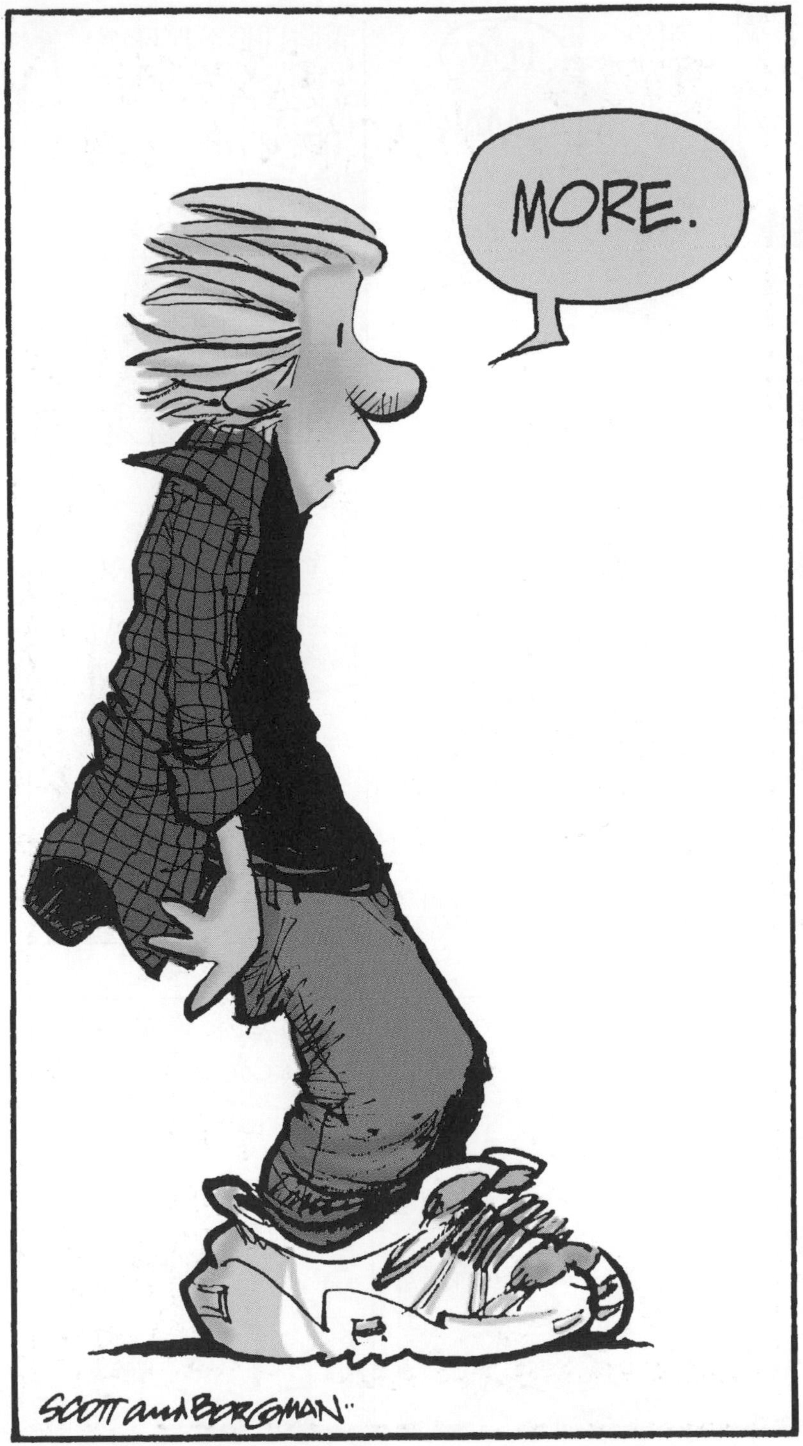
MORE.
SCOTT and BORGMAN

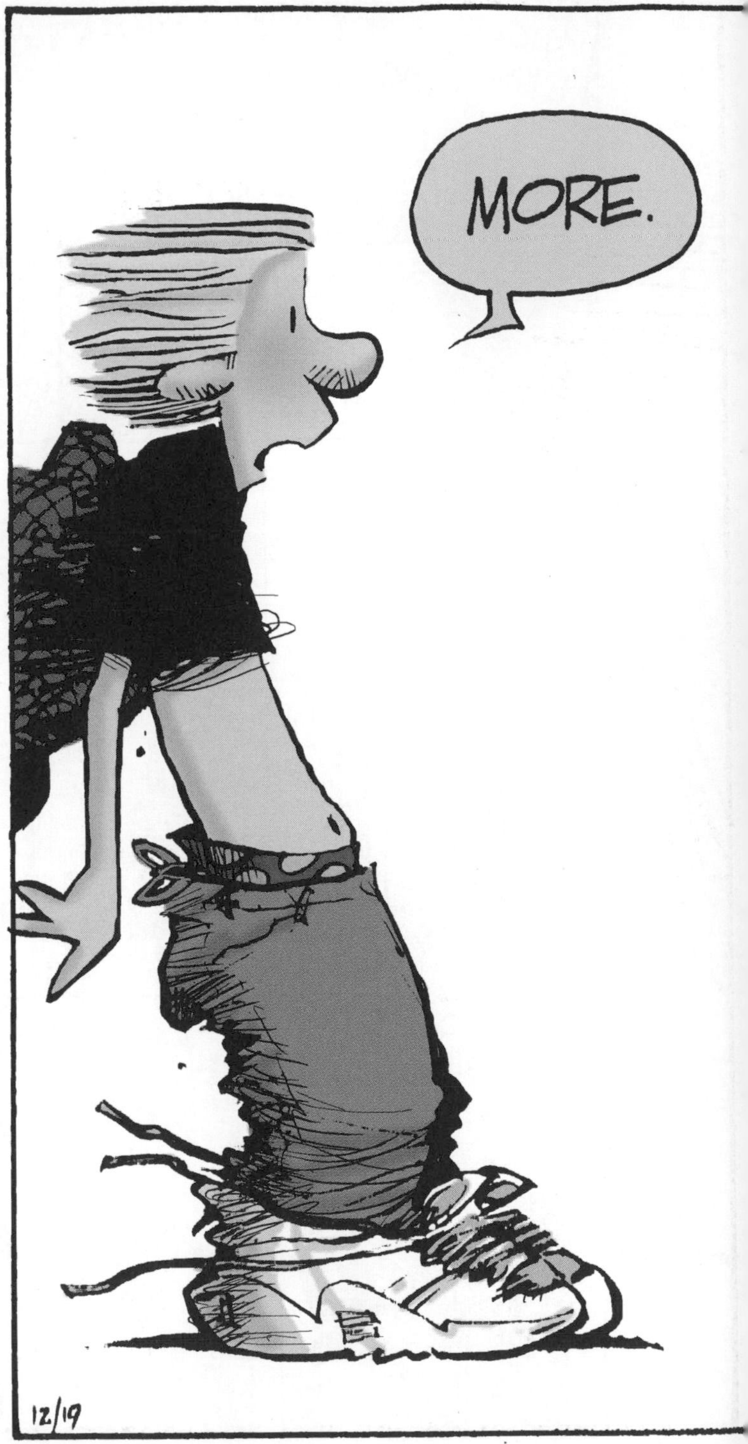
MORE.
12/19

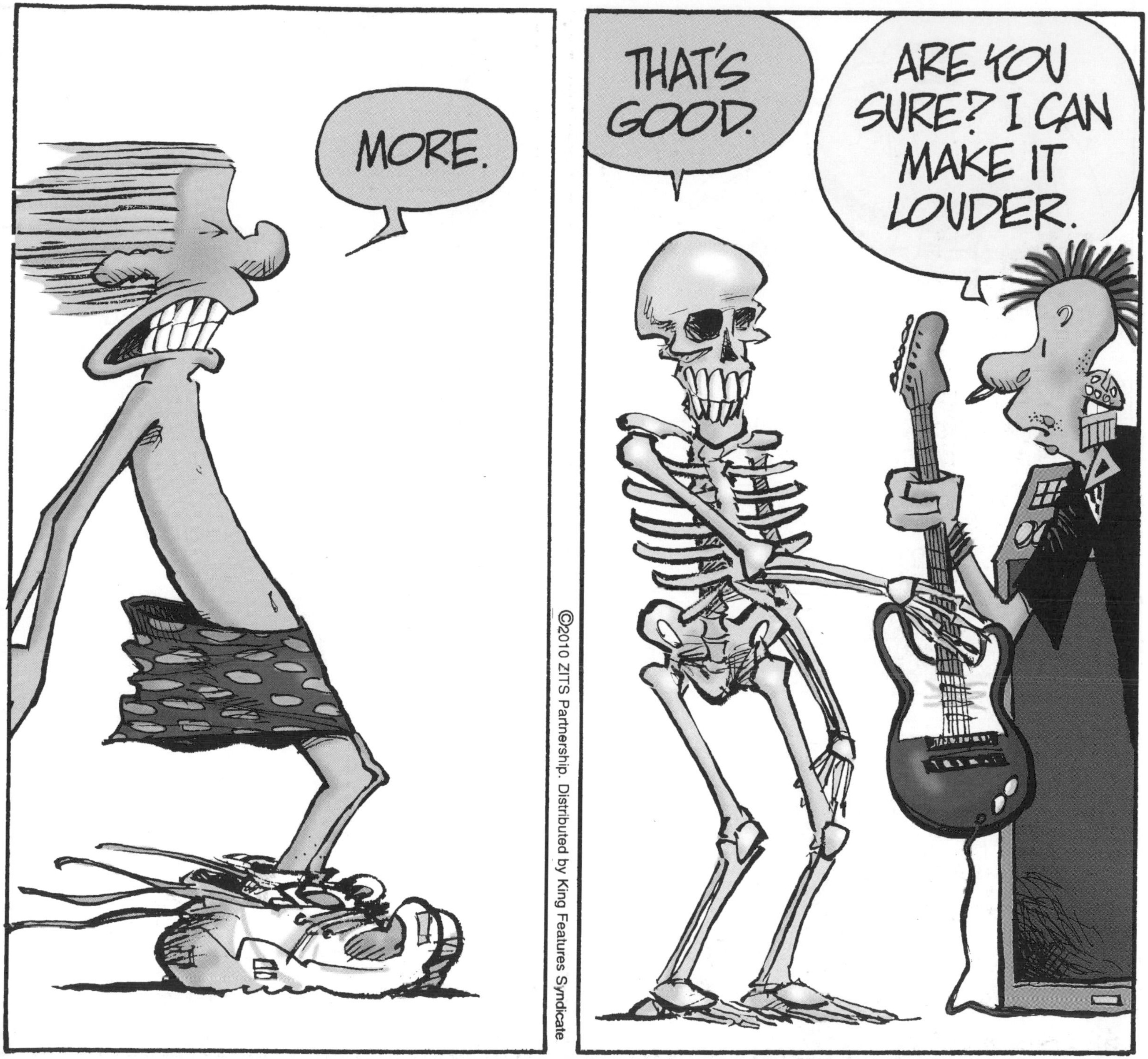
MORE.
THAT'S GOOD.
ARE YOU SURE? I CAN MAKE IT LOUDER.

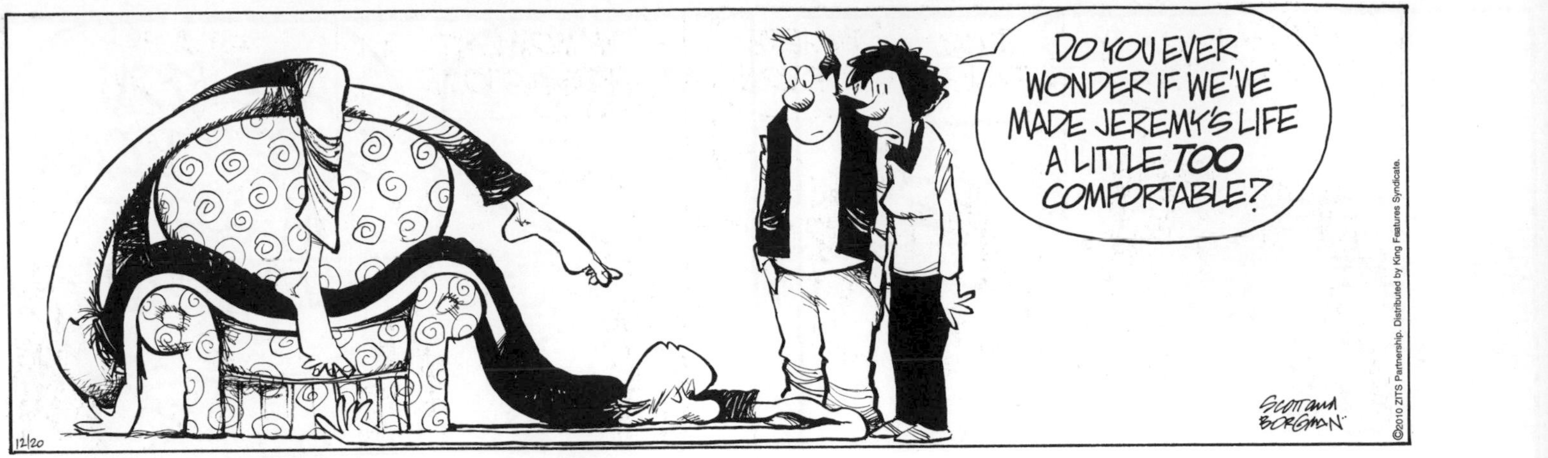
DO YOU EVER WONDER IF WE'VE MADE JEREMY'S LIFE A LITTLE **TOO** COMFORTABLE?
©2010 ZITS Partnership. Distributed by King Features Syndicate.

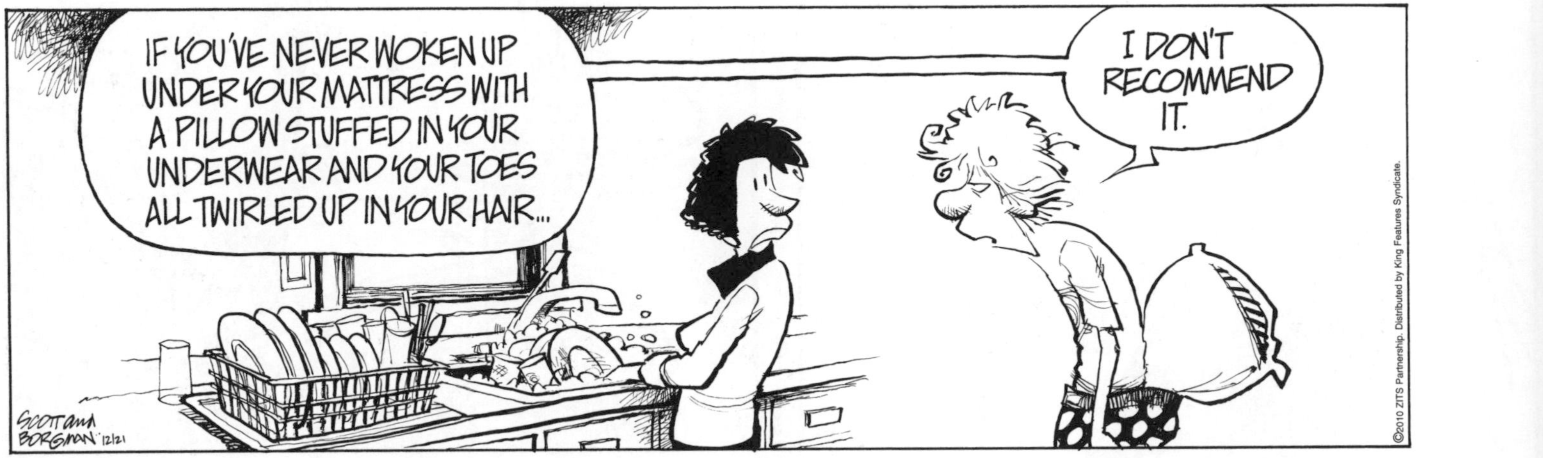
IF YOU'VE NEVER WOKEN UP UNDER YOUR MATTRESS WITH A PILLOW STUFFED IN YOUR UNDERWEAR AND YOUR TOES ALL TWIRLED UP IN YOUR HAIR...
I DON'T RECOMMEND IT.
©2010 ZITS Partnership. Distributed by King Features Syndicate.

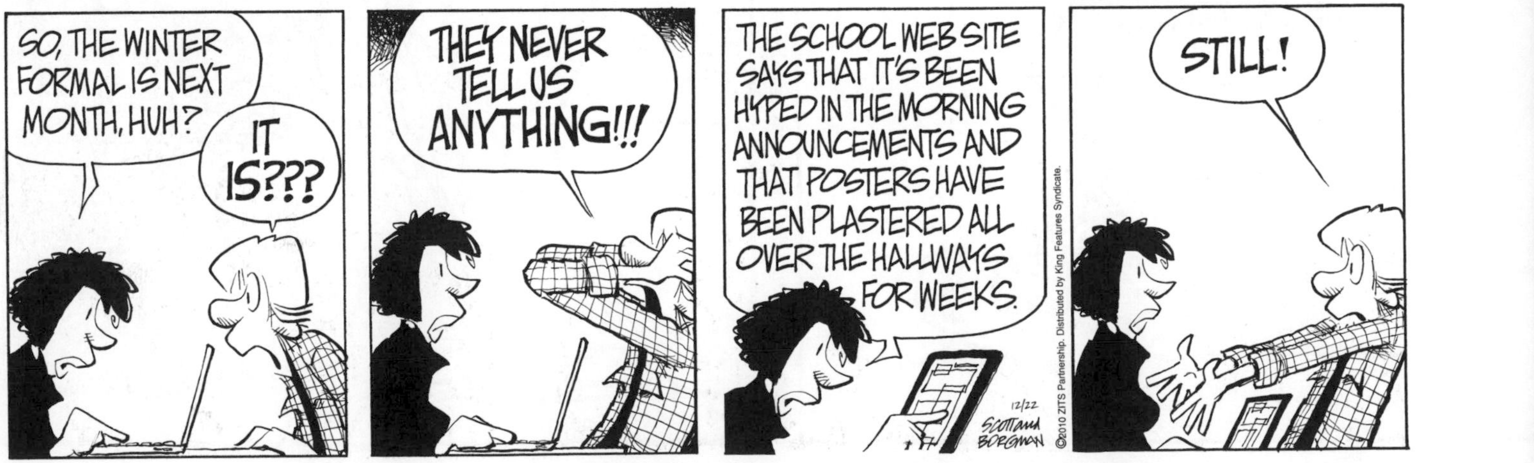
SO, THE WINTER FORMAL IS NEXT MONTH, HUH?
IT IS???
THEY NEVER TELL US ANYTHING!!!
THE SCHOOL WEB SITE SAYS THAT IT'S BEEN HYPED IN THE MORNING ANNOUNCEMENTS AND THAT POSTERS HAVE BEEN PLASTERED ALL OVER THE HALLWAYS FOR WEEKS.
STILL!
©2010 ZITS Partnership. Distributed by King Features Syndicate.

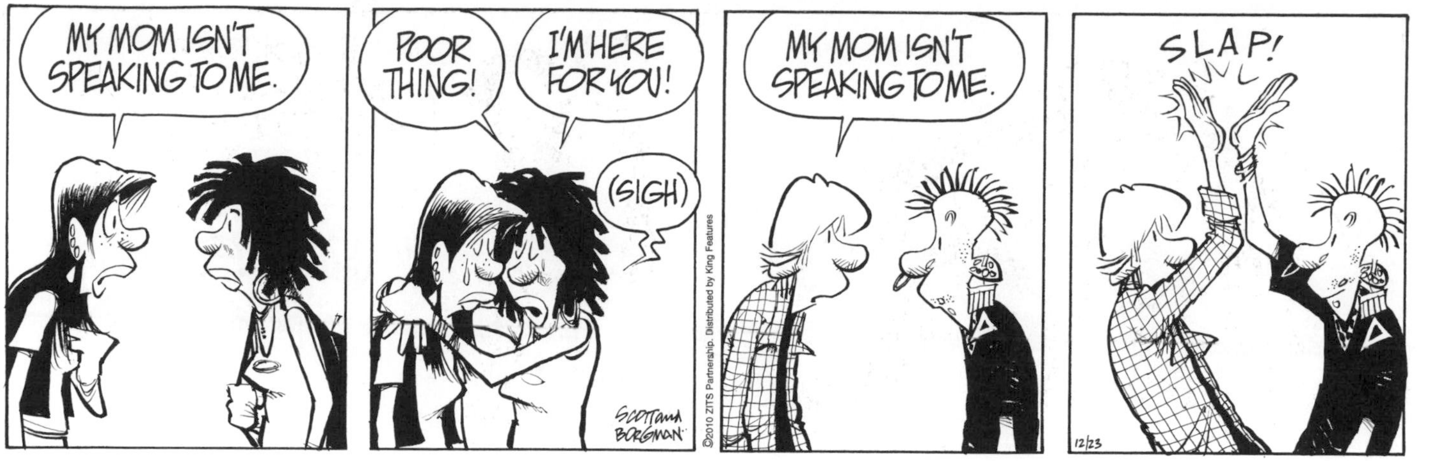
MY MOM ISN'T SPEAKING TO ME.
POOR THING!
I'M HERE FOR YOU!
(SIGH)
MY MOM ISN'T SPEAKING TO ME.
SLAP!
SCOTT AND BORGMAN
©2010 ZITS Partnership. Distributed by King Features
12/23

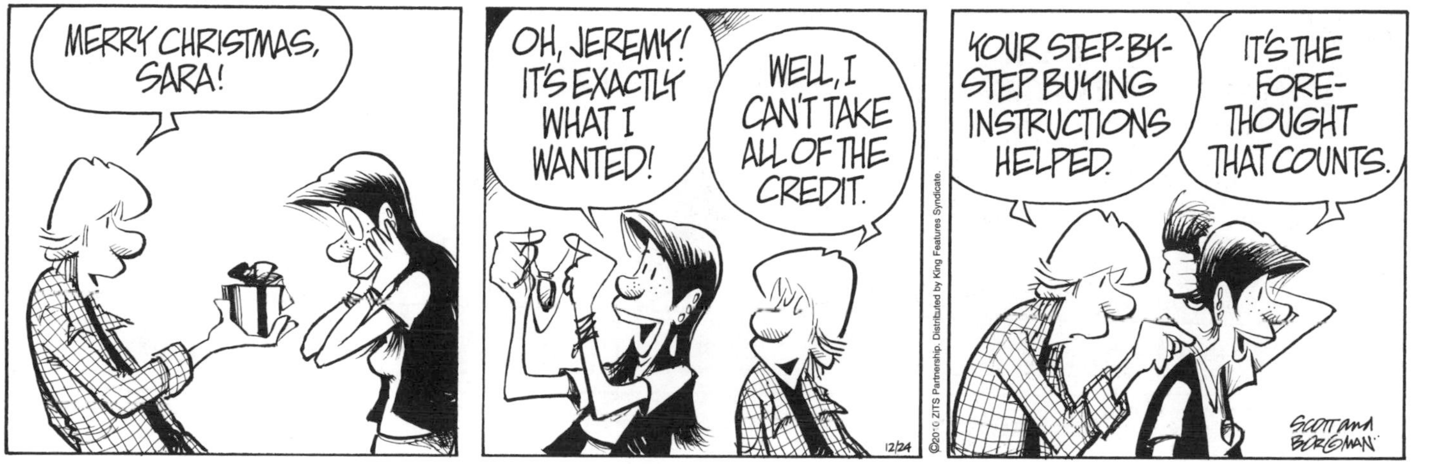
MERRY CHRISTMAS, SARA!
OH, JEREMY! IT'S EXACTLY WHAT I WANTED!
WELL, I CAN'T TAKE ALL OF THE CREDIT.
12/24
©2010 ZITS Partnership. Distributed by King Features Syndicate.
YOUR STEP-BY-STEP BUYING INSTRUCTIONS HELPED.
IT'S THE FORE-THOUGHT THAT COUNTS.
SCOTT AND BORGMAN

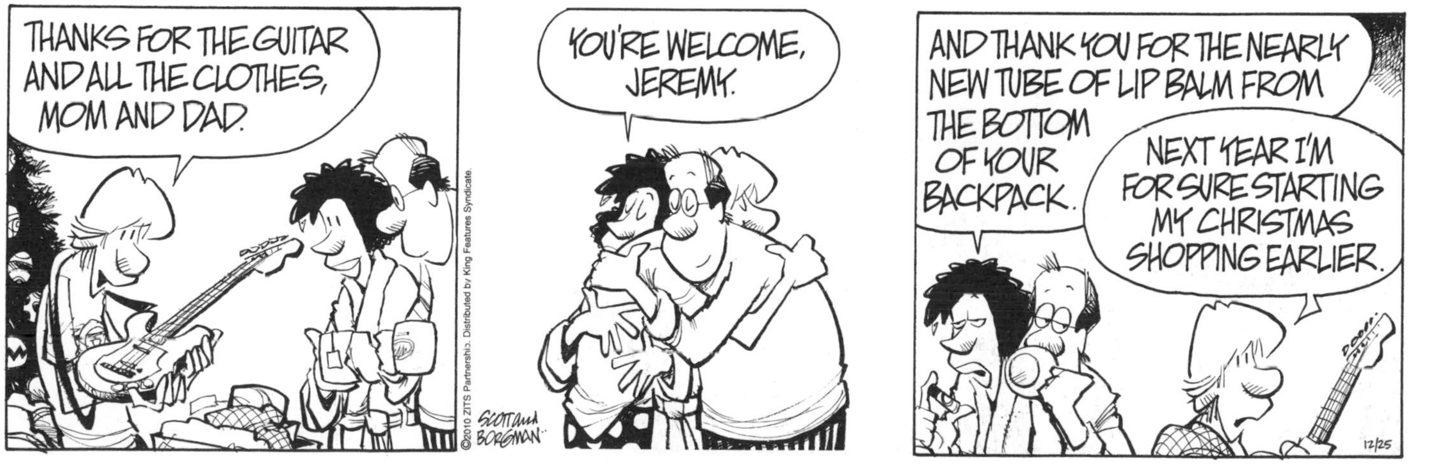
THANKS FOR THE GUITAR AND ALL THE CLOTHES, MOM AND DAD.
©2010 ZITS Partnership. Distributed by King Features Syndicate.
YOU'RE WELCOME, JEREMY.
SCOTT AND BORGMAN
AND THANK YOU FOR THE NEARLY NEW TUBE OF LIP BALM FROM THE BOTTOM OF YOUR BACKPACK.
NEXT YEAR I'M FOR SURE STARTING MY CHRISTMAS SHOPPING EARLIER.
12/25

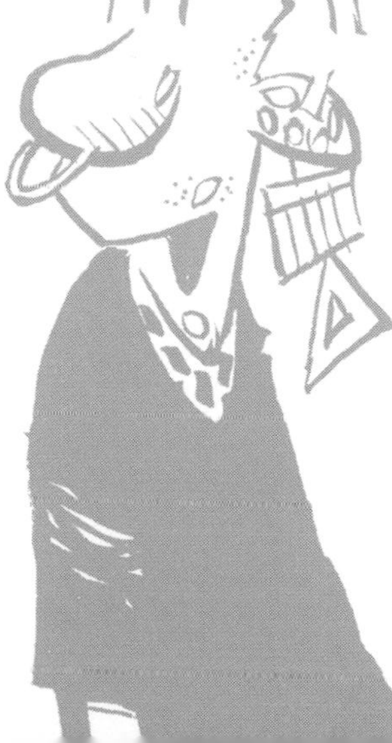

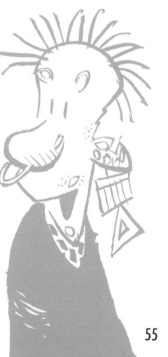

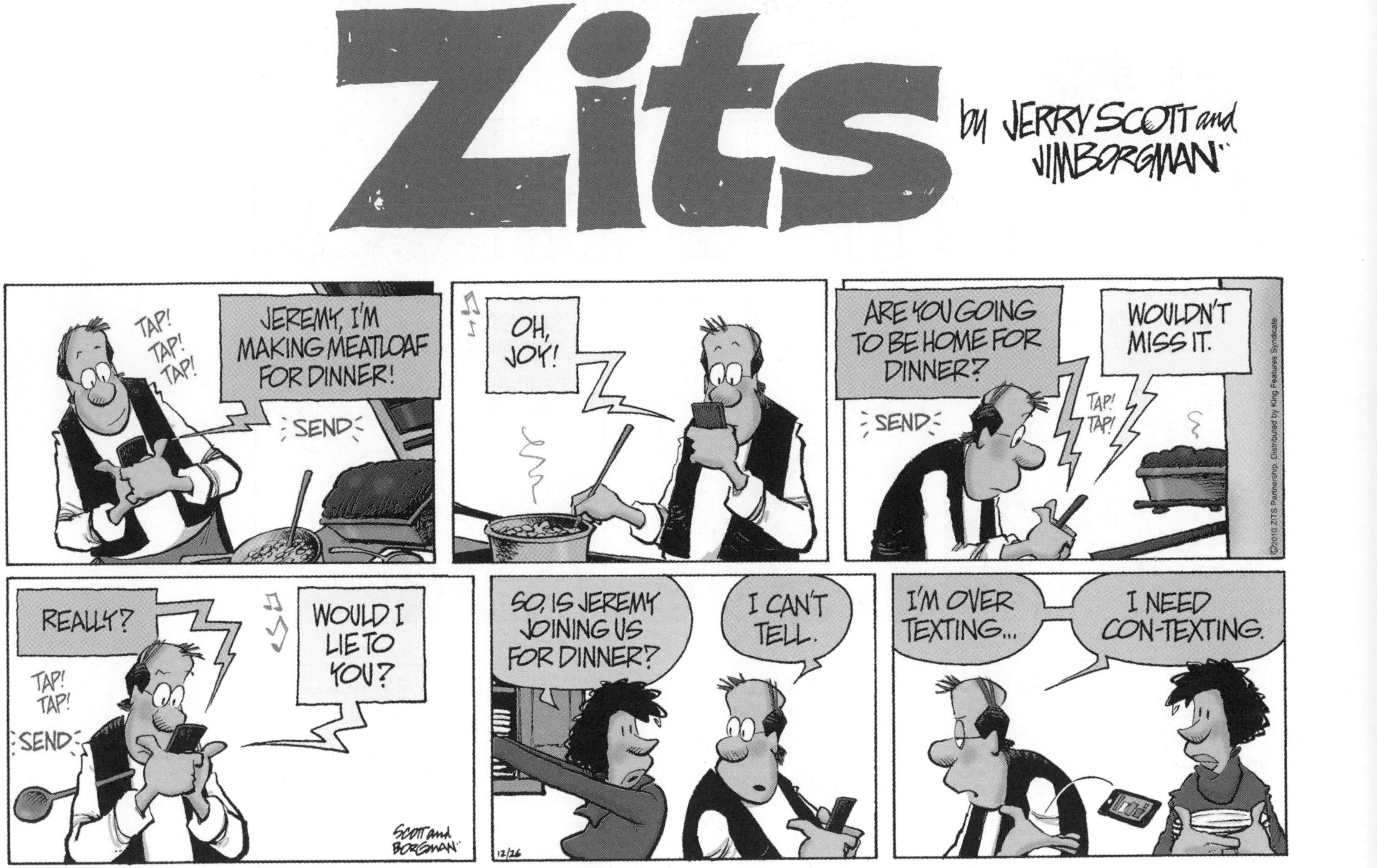
Zits
by JERRY SCOTT and JIM BORGMAN
TAP! TAP! TAP!
JEREMY, I'M MAKING MEATLOAF FOR DINNER!
SEND
OH, JOY!
ARE YOU GOING TO BE HOME FOR DINNER?
SEND
WOULDN'T MISS IT.
TAP! TAP!
©2010 ZITS Partnership. Distributed by King Features Syndicate.
REALLY?
TAP! TAP!
SEND
WOULD I LIE TO YOU?
SCOTT and BORGMAN
SO, IS JEREMY JOINING US FOR DINNER?
I CAN'T TELL.
12/26
I'M OVER TEXTING...
I NEED CON-TEXTING.

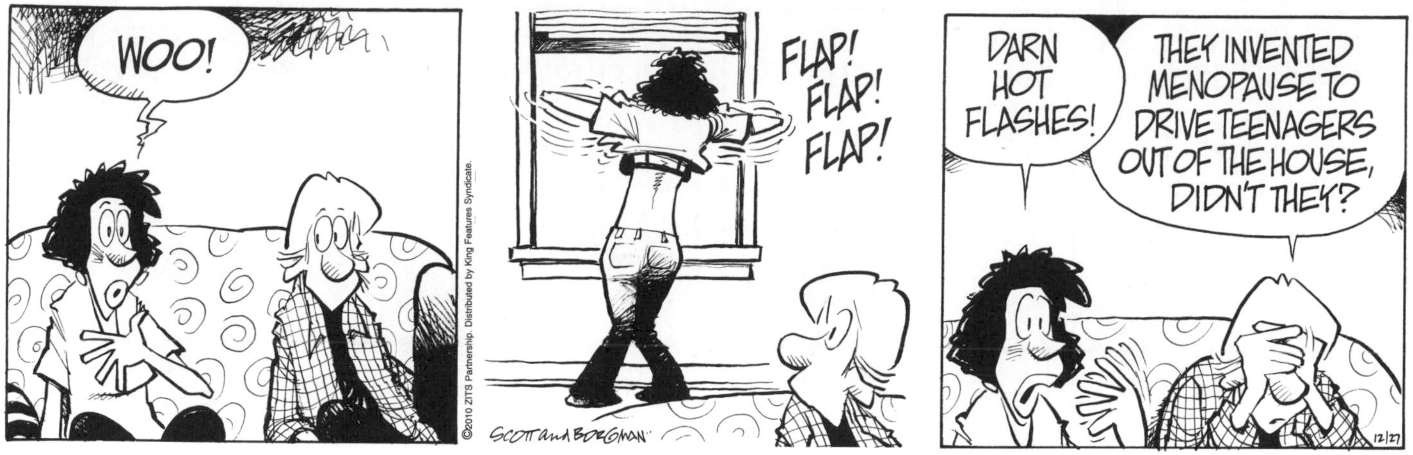
WOO!
FLAP! FLAP! FLAP!
©2010 ZITS Partnership. Distributed by King Features Syndicate.
SCOTT and BORGMAN
DARN HOT FLASHES!
THEY INVENTED MENOPAUSE TO DRIVE TEENAGERS OUT OF THE HOUSE, DIDN'T THEY?
12/27

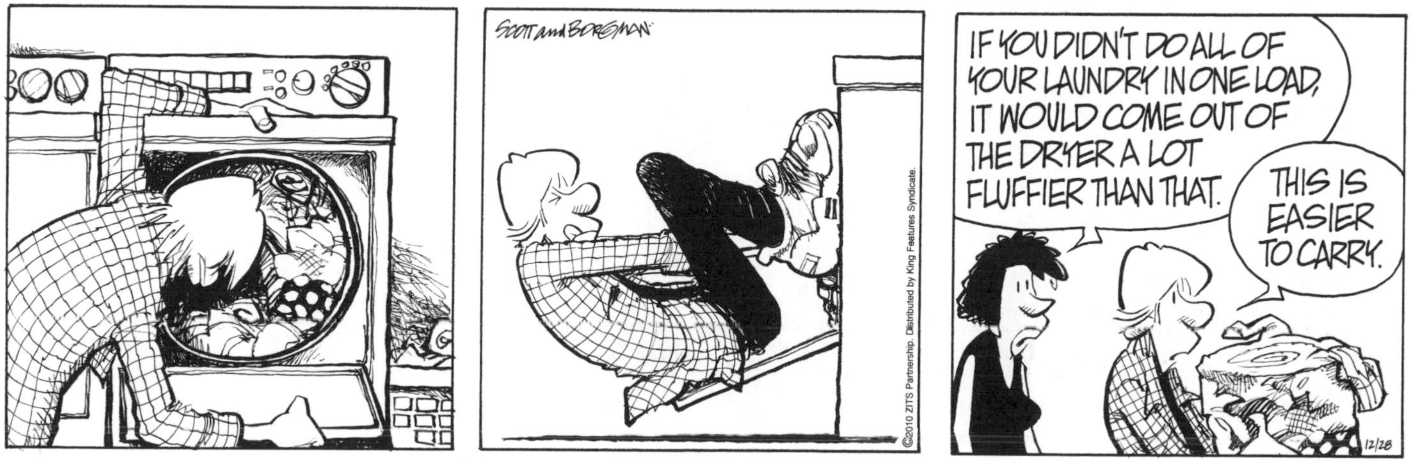
SCOTT and BORGMAN
©2010 ZITS Partnership. Distributed by King Features Syndicate.
IF YOU DIDN'T DO ALL OF YOUR LAUNDRY IN ONE LOAD, IT WOULD COME OUT OF THE DRYER A LOT FLUFFIER THAN THAT.
THIS IS EASIER TO CARRY.
12/28

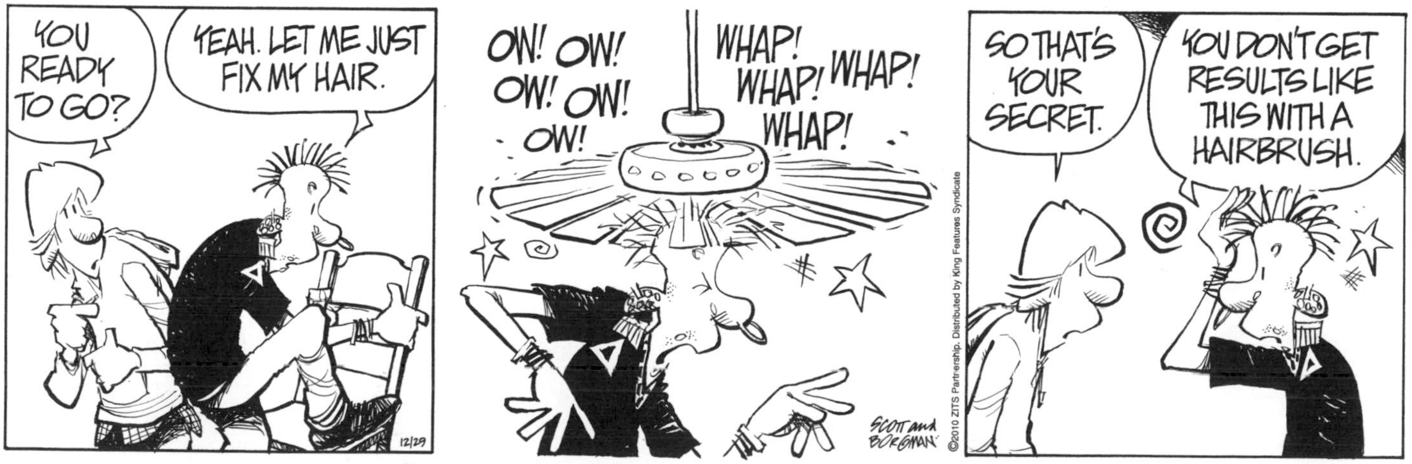
YOU READY TO GO?
YEAH. LET ME JUST FIX MY HAIR.
12/29
OW! OW! OW! OW! OW!
WHAP! WHAP! WHAP! WHAP!
SCOTT and BORGMAN
©2010 ZITS Partnership. Distributed by King Features Syndicate
SO THAT'S YOUR SECRET.
YOU DON'T GET RESULTS LIKE THIS WITH A HAIRBRUSH.

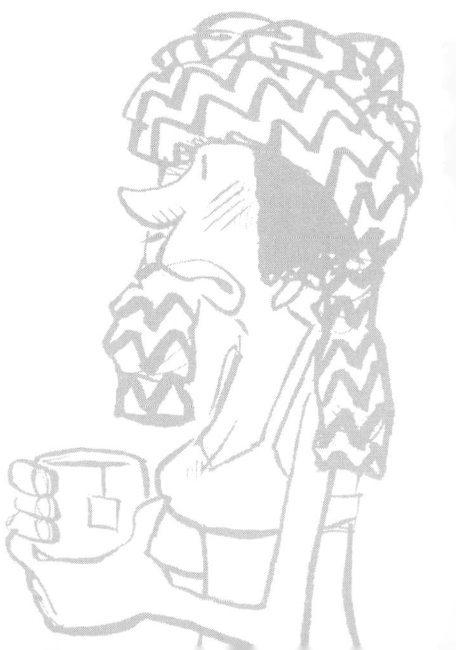

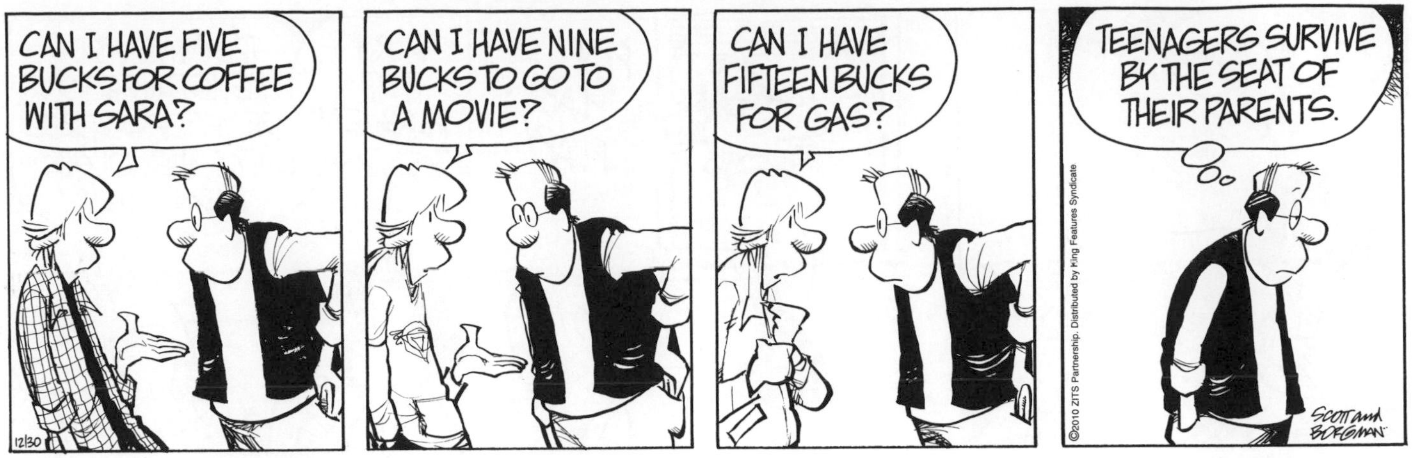
CAN I HAVE FIVE BUCKS FOR COFFEE WITH SARA?
CAN I HAVE NINE BUCKS TO GO TO A MOVIE?
CAN I HAVE FIFTEEN BUCKS FOR GAS?
TEENAGERS SURVIVE BY THE SEAT OF THEIR PARENTS.
12/30
©2010 ZITS Partnership. Distributed by King Features Syndicate
SCOTT and BORGMAN

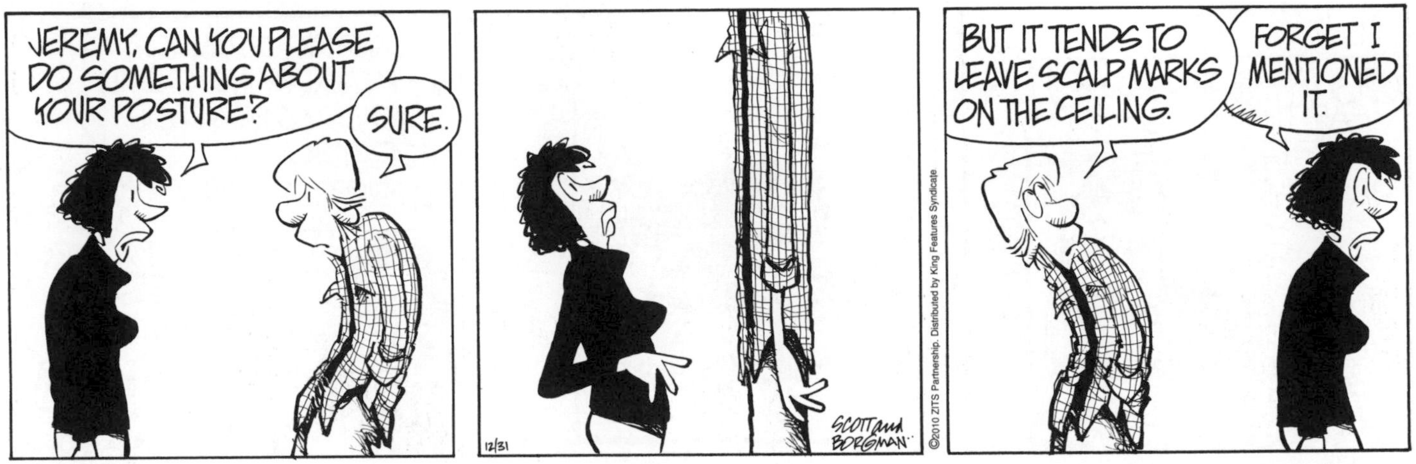
JEREMY, CAN YOU PLEASE DO SOMETHING ABOUT YOUR POSTURE?
SURE.
12/31
SCOTT and BORGMAN
©2010 ZITS Partnership. Distributed by King Features Syndicate
BUT IT TENDS TO LEAVE SCALP MARKS ON THE CEILING.
FORGET I MENTIONED IT.

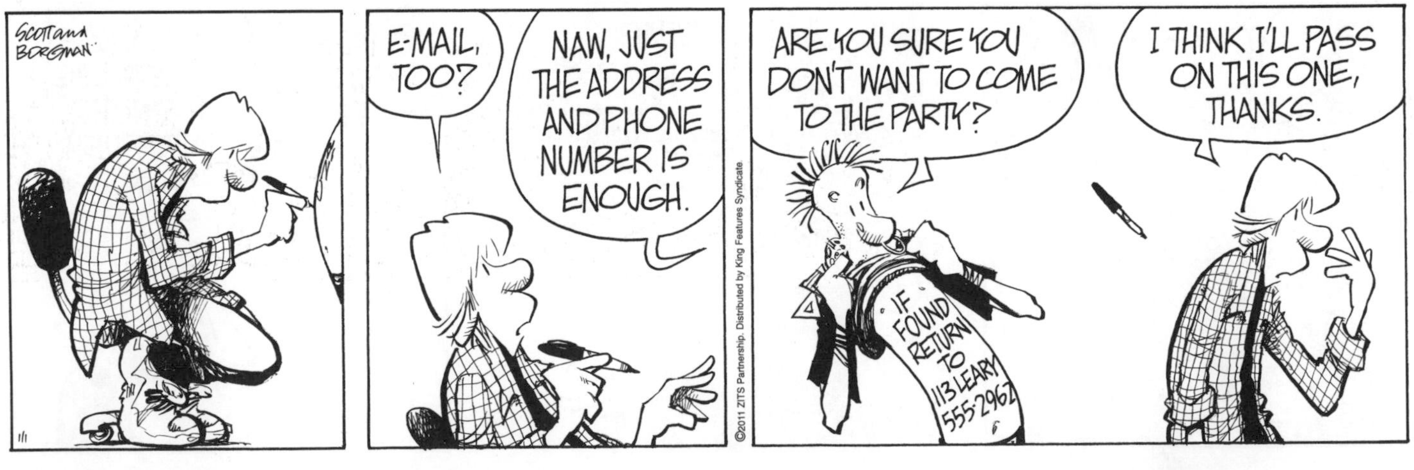
SCOTT and BORGMAN
1/1
E-MAIL, TOO?
NAW, JUST THE ADDRESS AND PHONE NUMBER IS ENOUGH.
©2011 ZITS Partnership. Distributed by King Features Syndicate
ARE YOU SURE YOU DON'T WANT TO COME TO THE PARTY?
IF FOUND RETURN TO 113 LEARY 555-2962
I THINK I'LL PASS ON THIS ONE, THANKS.

Zits

by JERRY SCOTT and JIMBORGMAN

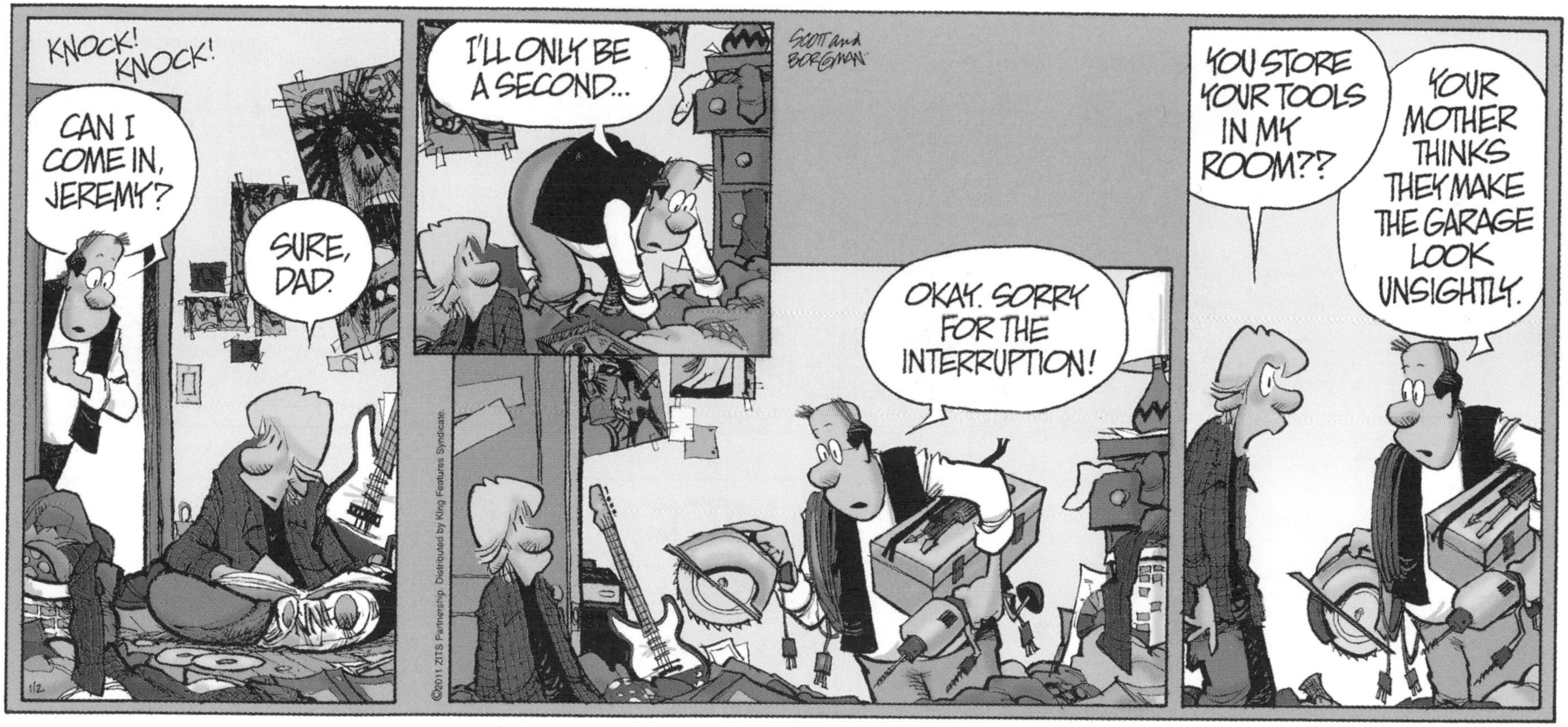

KNOCK! KNOCK!
CAN I COME IN, JEREMY?
SURE, DAD.
I'LL ONLY BE A SECOND...
SCOTT and BORGMAN
©2011 ZITS Partnership. Distributed by King Features Syndicate.
OKAY. SORRY FOR THE INTERRUPTION!
YOU STORE YOUR TOOLS IN MY ROOM??
YOUR MOTHER THINKS THEY MAKE THE GARAGE LOOK UNSIGHTLY.

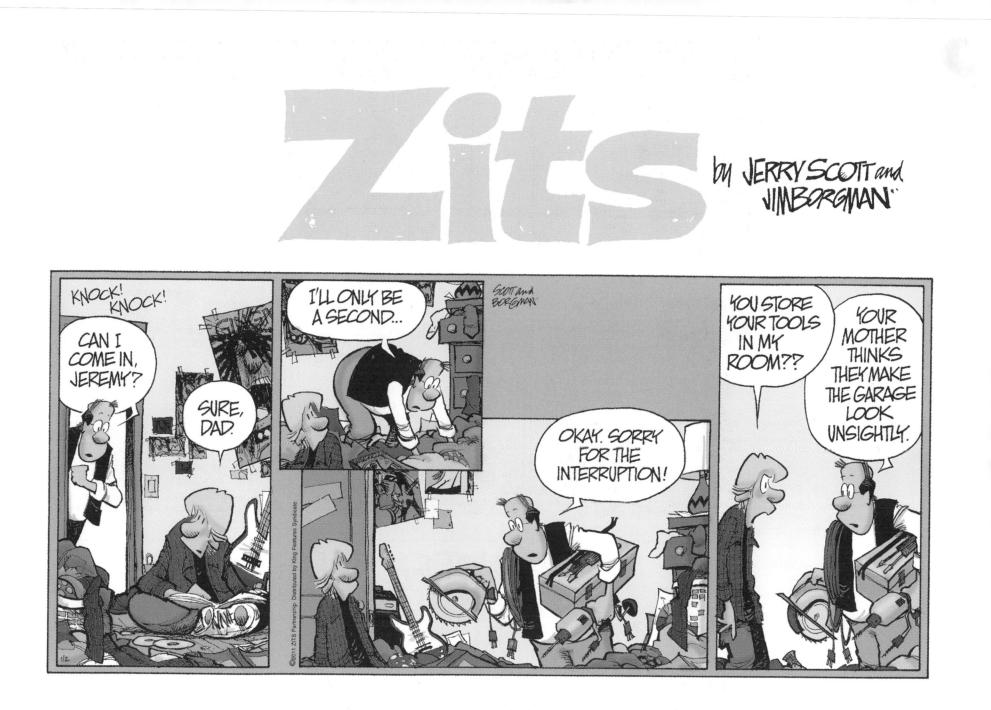

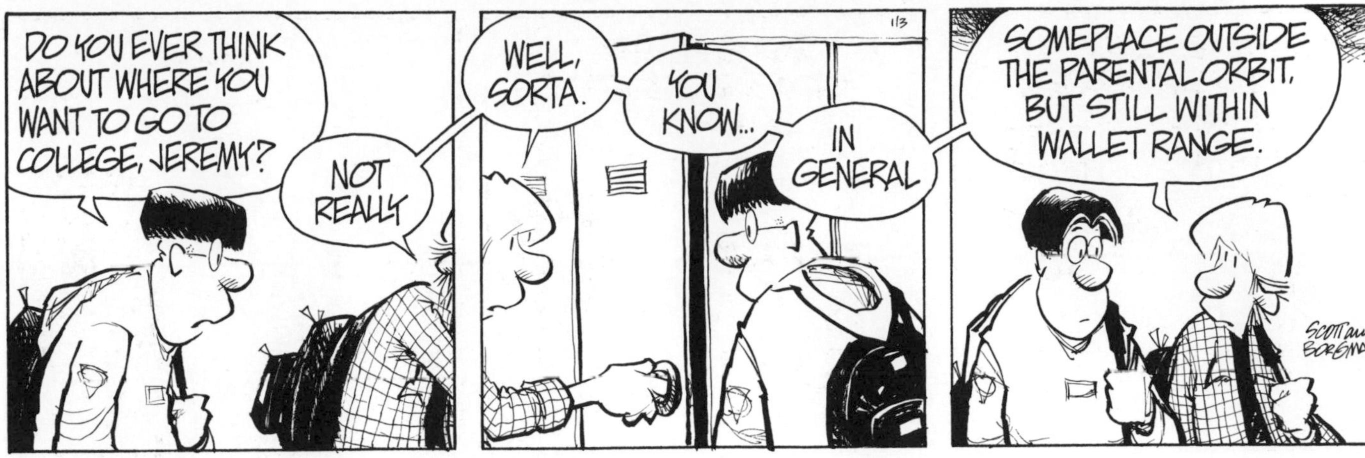
DO YOU EVER THINK ABOUT WHERE YOU WANT TO GO TO COLLEGE, JEREMY?
NOT REALLY
WELL, SORTA.
YOU KNOW...
IN GENERAL
SOMEPLACE OUTSIDE THE PARENTAL ORBIT, BUT STILL WITHIN WALLET RANGE.
1/3
SCOTT and BORGMAN
©2010 ZITS Partnership. Distributed by King Features Syndicate.

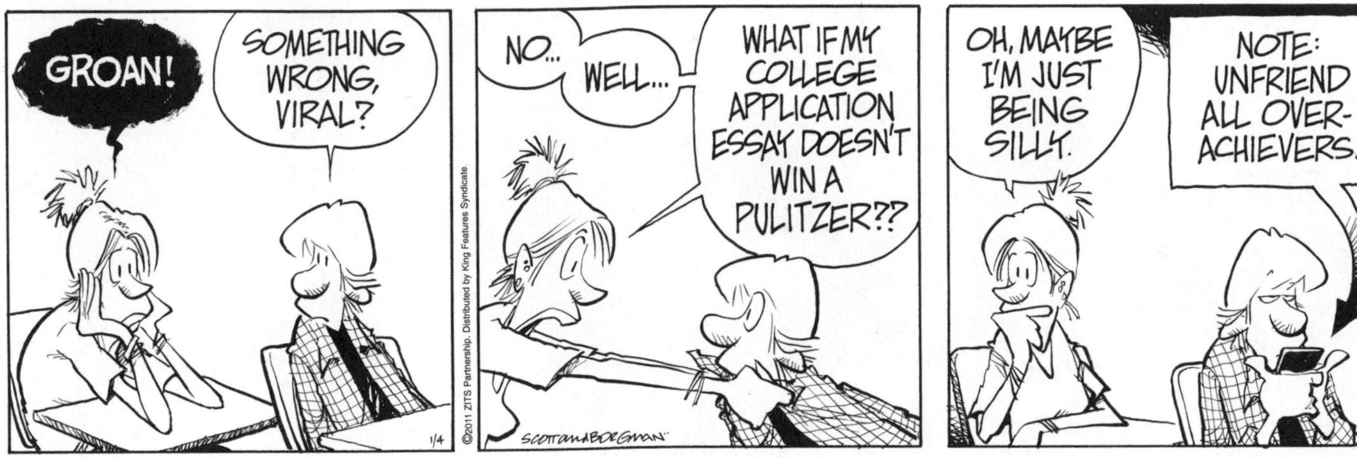
GROAN!
SOMETHING WRONG, VIRAL?
1/4
©2011 ZITS Partnership. Distributed by King Features Syndicate
NO...
WELL...
WHAT IF MY COLLEGE APPLICATION ESSAY DOESN'T WIN A PULITZER??
SCOTT and BORGMAN
OH, MAYBE I'M JUST BEING SILLY.
NOTE: UNFRIEND ALL OVER-ACHIEVERS.

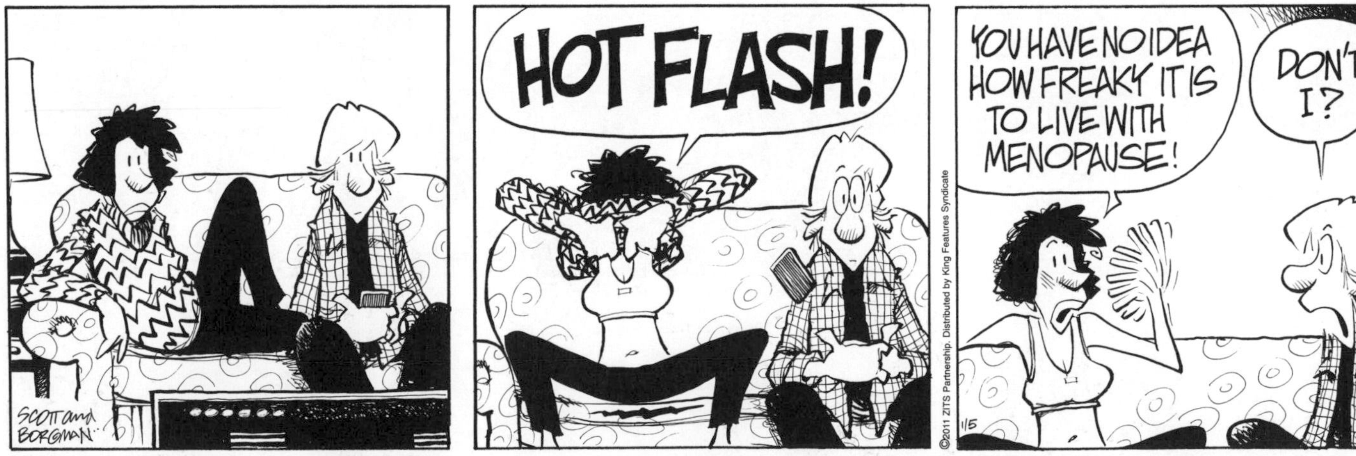
SCOTT and BORGMAN
HOT FLASH!
©2011 ZITS Partnership. Distributed by King Features Syndicate
1/5
YOU HAVE NO IDEA HOW FREAKY IT IS TO LIVE WITH MENOPAUSE!
DON'T I?

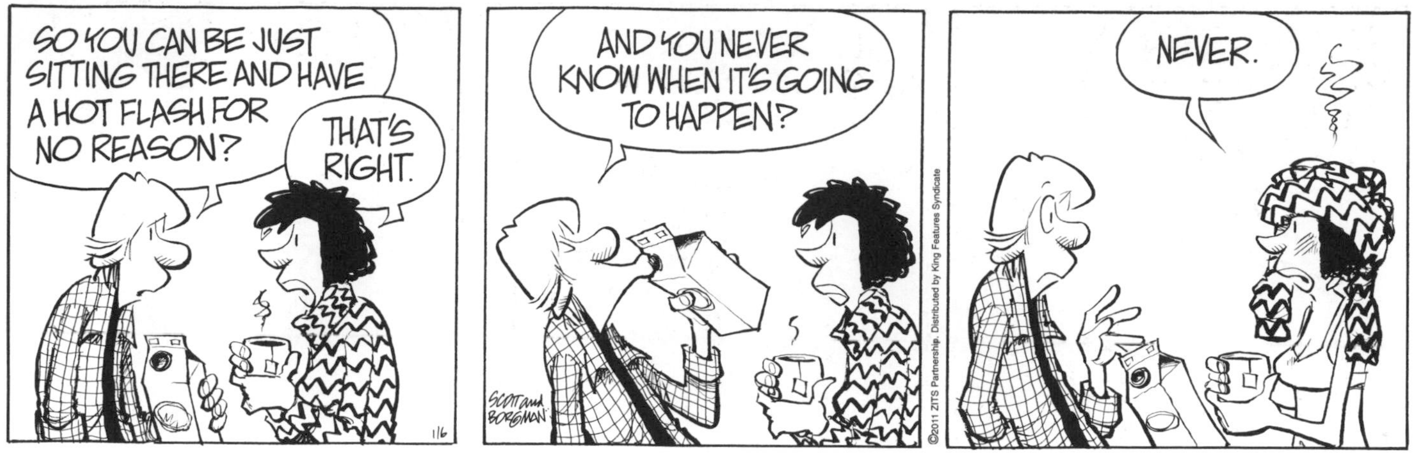
SO YOU CAN BE JUST SITTING THERE AND HAVE A HOT FLASH FOR NO REASON?
THAT'S RIGHT.
AND YOU NEVER KNOW WHEN IT'S GOING TO HAPPEN?
NEVER.
©2011 ZITS Partnership. Distributed by King Features Syndicate

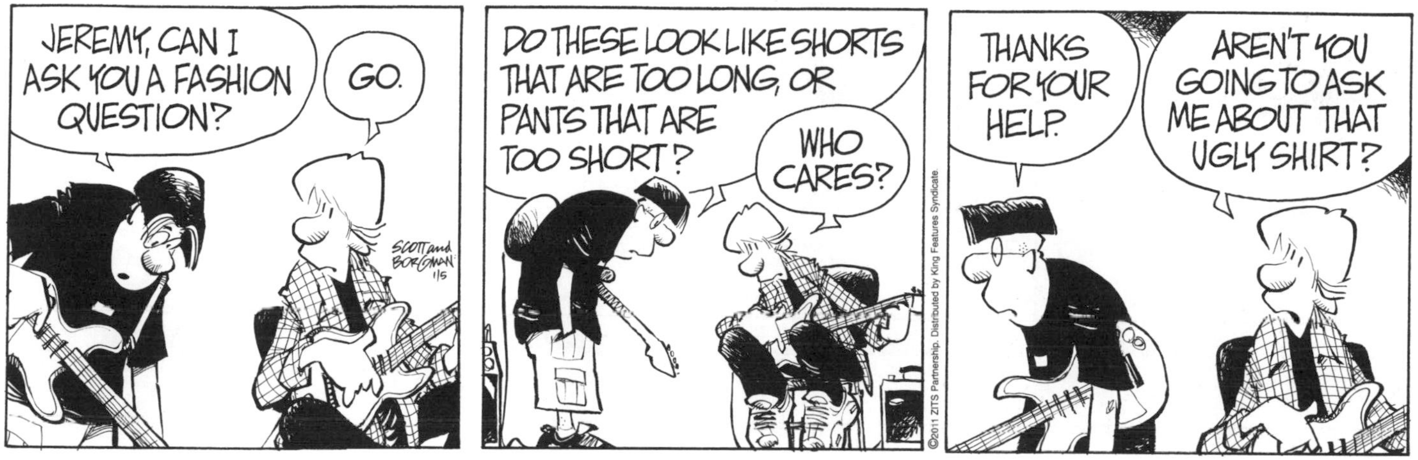
JEREMY, CAN I ASK YOU A FASHION QUESTION?
GO.
DO THESE LOOK LIKE SHORTS THAT ARE TOO LONG, OR PANTS THAT ARE TOO SHORT?
WHO CARES?
THANKS FOR YOUR HELP.
AREN'T YOU GOING TO ASK ME ABOUT THAT UGLY SHIRT?
©2011 ZITS Partnership. Distributed by King Features Syndicate

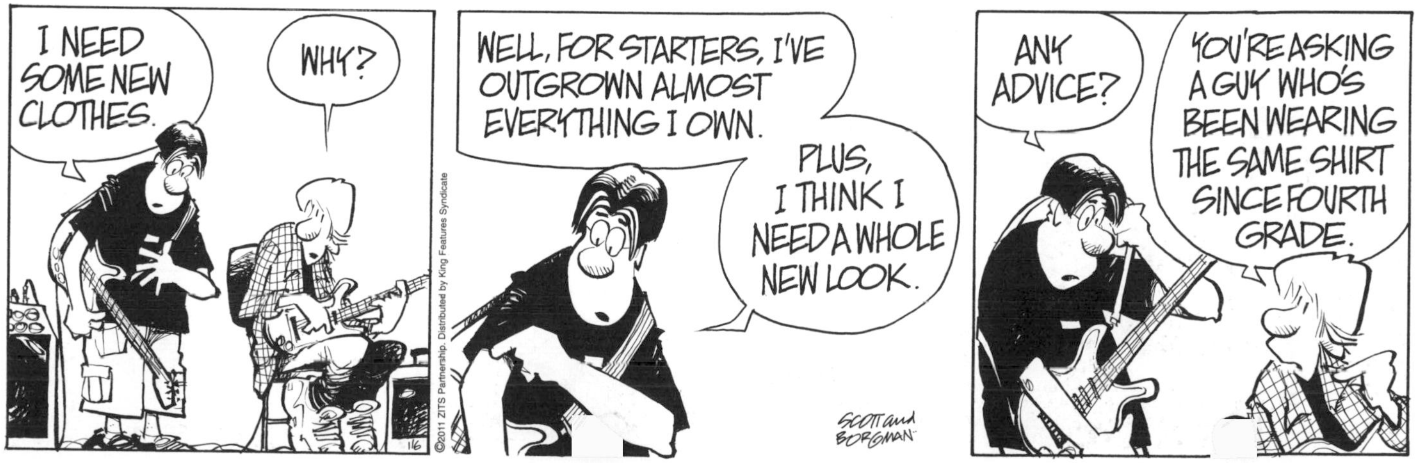
I NEED SOME NEW CLOTHES.
WHY?
WELL, FOR STARTERS, I'VE OUTGROWN ALMOST EVERYTHING I OWN.
PLUS, I THINK I NEED A WHOLE NEW LOOK.
ANY ADVICE?
YOU'RE ASKING A GUY WHO'S BEEN WEARING THE SAME SHIRT SINCE FOURTH GRADE.
©2011 ZITS Partnership. Distributed by King Features Syndicate

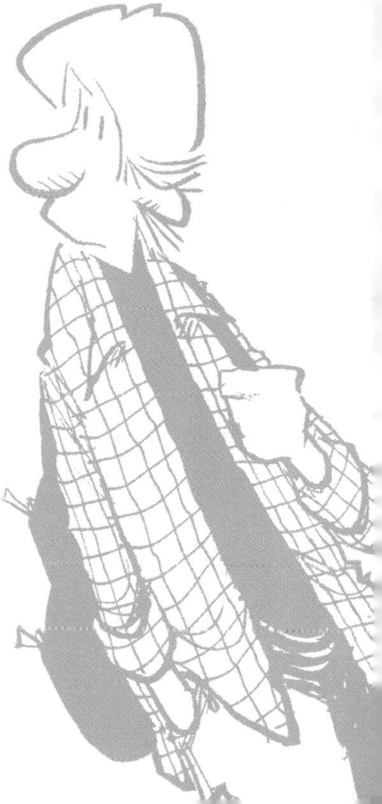

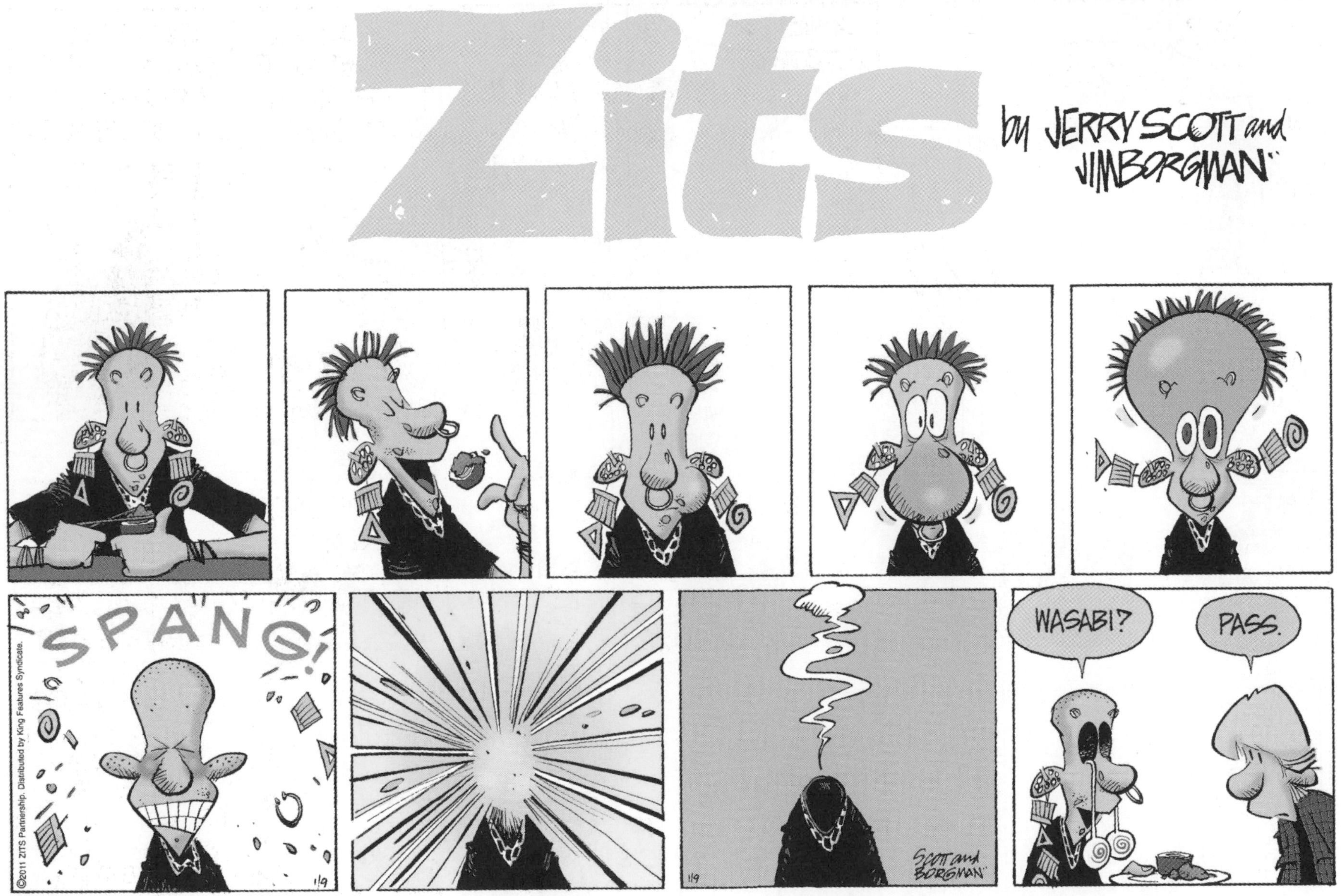
Zits
by JERRY SCOTT and JIM BORGMAN
©2011 ZITS Partnership. Distributed by King Features Syndicate.
SPANG!
SCOTT and BORGMAN
WASABI?
PASS.

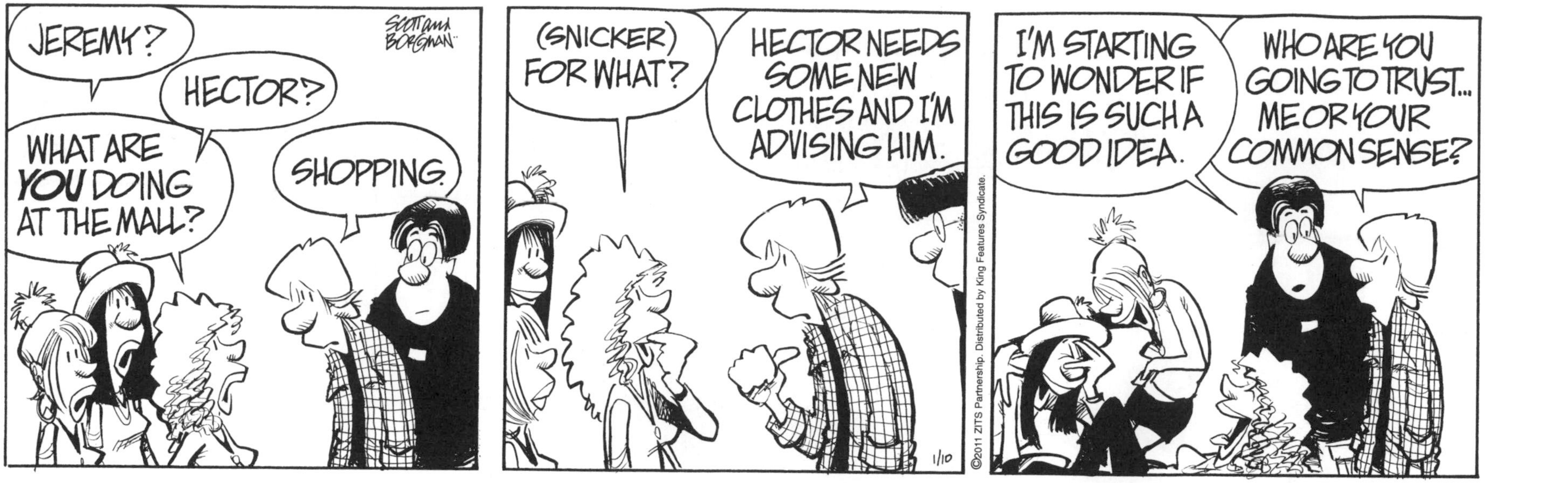
SCOTT AND BORGMAN
JEREMY?
HECTOR?
WHAT ARE **YOU** DOING AT THE MALL?
SHOPPING.
(SNICKER) FOR WHAT?
HECTOR NEEDS SOME NEW CLOTHES AND I'M ADVISING HIM.
1/10
©2011 ZITS Partnership. Distributed by King Features Syndicate.
I'M STARTING TO WONDER IF THIS IS SUCH A GOOD IDEA.
WHO ARE YOU GOING TO TRUST... ME OR YOUR COMMON SENSE?

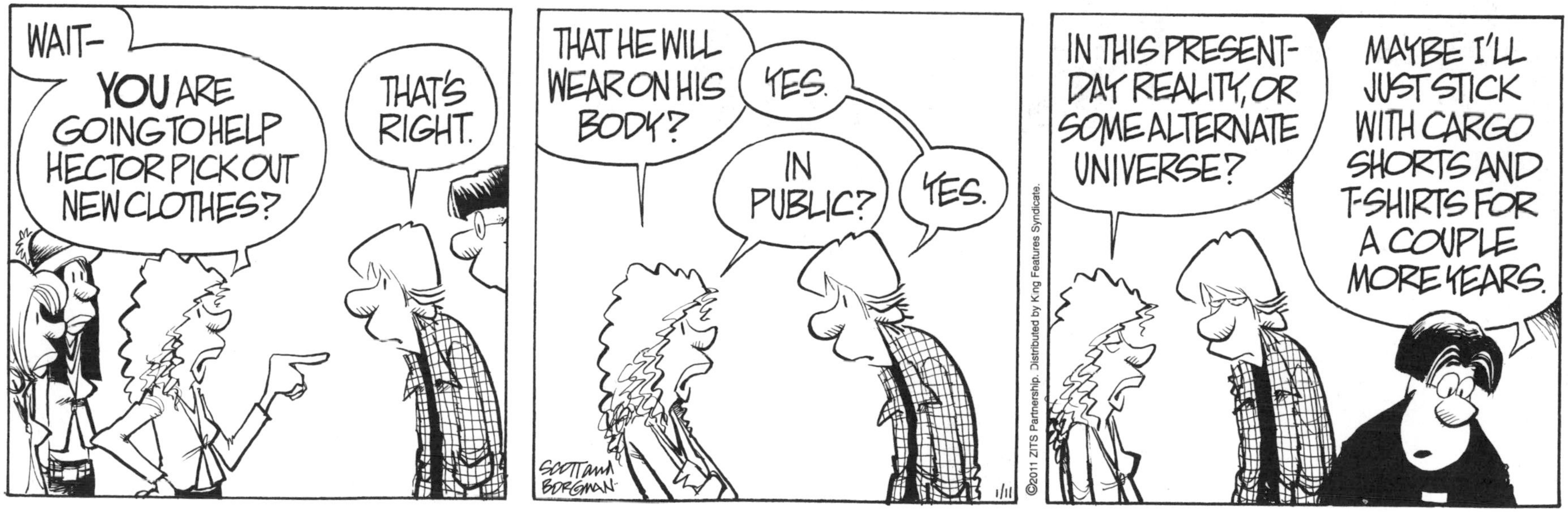
WAIT-
YOU ARE GOING TO HELP HECTOR PICK OUT NEW CLOTHES?
THAT'S RIGHT.
THAT HE WILL WEAR ON HIS BODY?
YES.
IN PUBLIC?
YES.
SCOTT AND BORGMAN
1/11
©2011 ZITS Partnership. Distributed by King Features Syndicate.
IN THIS PRESENT-DAY REALITY, OR SOME ALTERNATE UNIVERSE?
MAYBE I'LL JUST STICK WITH CARGO SHORTS AND T-SHIRTS FOR A COUPLE MORE YEARS.

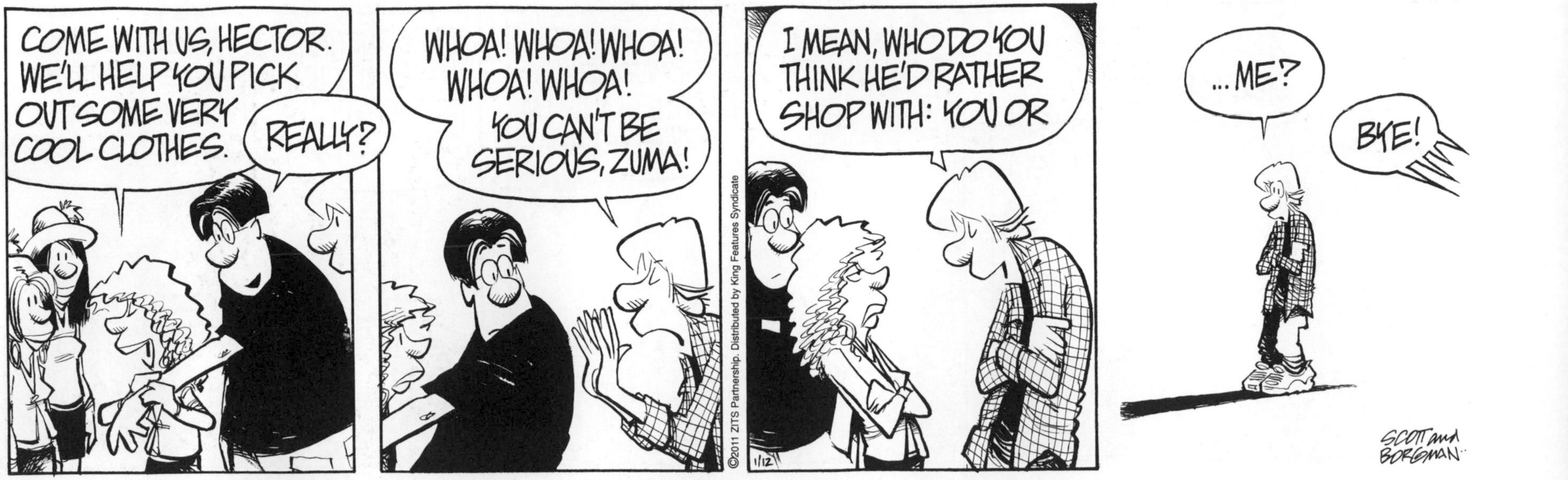
COME WITH US, HECTOR. WE'LL HELP YOU PICK OUT SOME VERY COOL CLOTHES.
REALLY?
WHOA! WHOA! WHOA! WHOA! WHOA!
YOU CAN'T BE SERIOUS, ZUMA!
©2011 ZITS Partnership. Distributed by King Features Syndicate
1/12
I MEAN, WHO DO YOU THINK HE'D RATHER SHOP WITH: YOU OR
...ME?
BYE!
SCOTT and BORGMAN

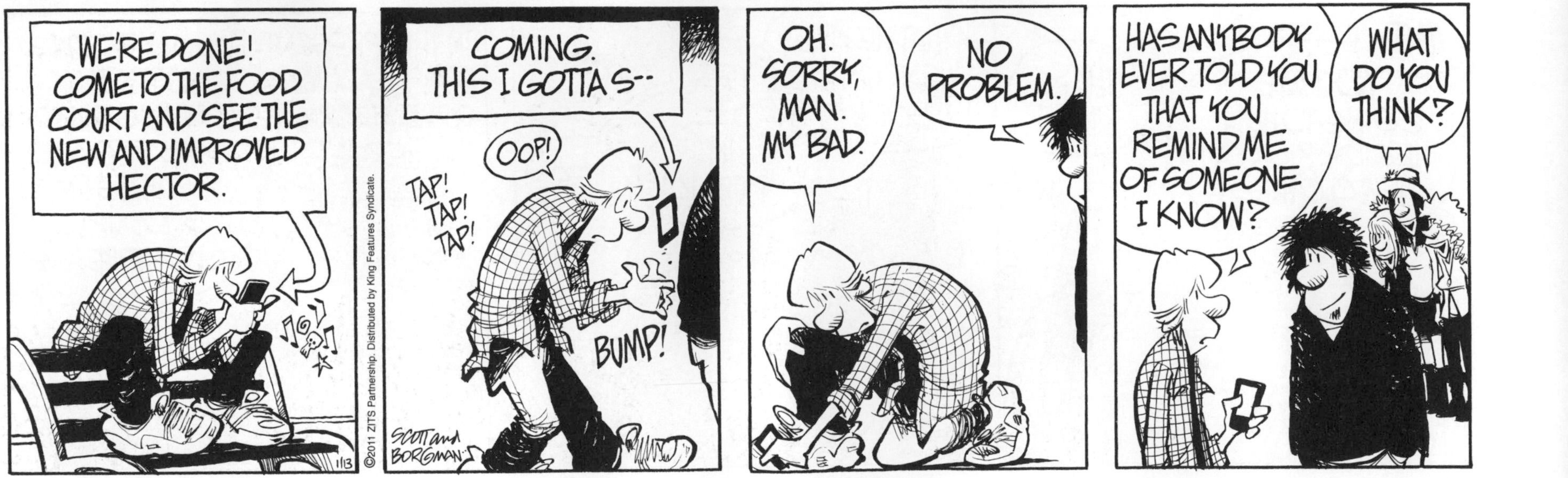
WE'RE DONE! COME TO THE FOOD COURT AND SEE THE NEW AND IMPROVED HECTOR.
1/13
©2011 ZITS Partnership. Distributed by King Features Syndicate.
COMING. THIS I GOTTA S--
OOP!
TAP! TAP! TAP!
BUMP!
SCOTT and BORGMAN
OH. SORRY, MAN. MY BAD.
NO PROBLEM.
HAS ANYBODY EVER TOLD YOU THAT YOU REMIND ME OF SOMEONE I KNOW?
WHAT DO YOU THINK?

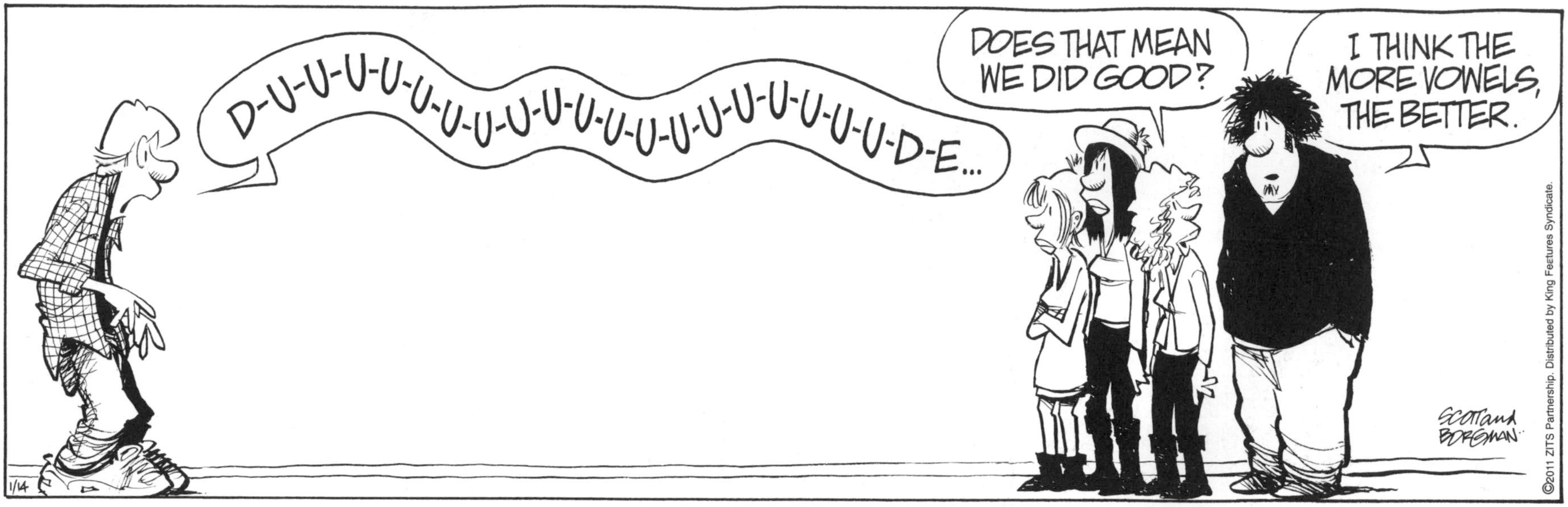
D-U-U-U-U-U-U-U-U-U-U-U-U-U-U-U-U-U-U-U-D-E...
DOES THAT MEAN WE DID GOOD?
I THINK THE MORE VOWELS, THE BETTER.
SCOTT and BORGMAN
©2011 ZITS Partnership. Distributed by King Features Syndicate.

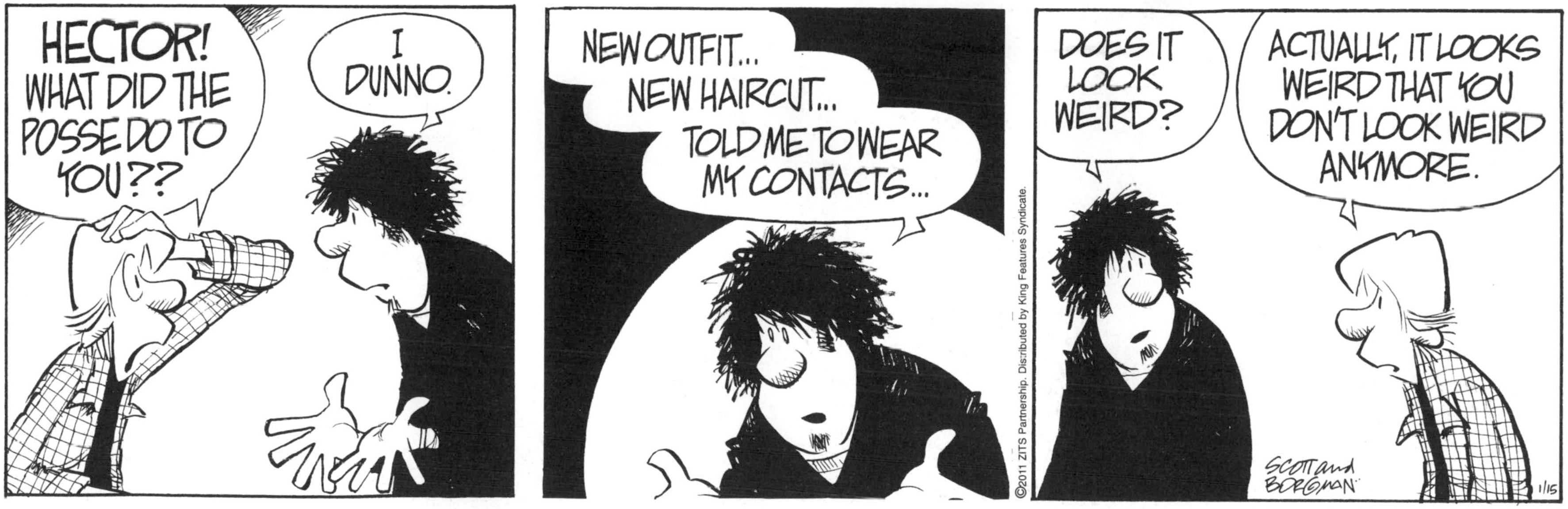
HECTOR! WHAT DID THE POSSE DO TO YOU??
I DUNNO.
NEW OUTFIT...
NEW HAIRCUT...
TOLD ME TO WEAR MY CONTACTS...
©2011 ZITS Partnership. Distributed by King Features Syndicate.
DOES IT LOOK WEIRD?
ACTUALLY, IT LOOKS WEIRD THAT YOU DON'T LOOK WEIRD ANYMORE.
SCOTT and BORGMAN

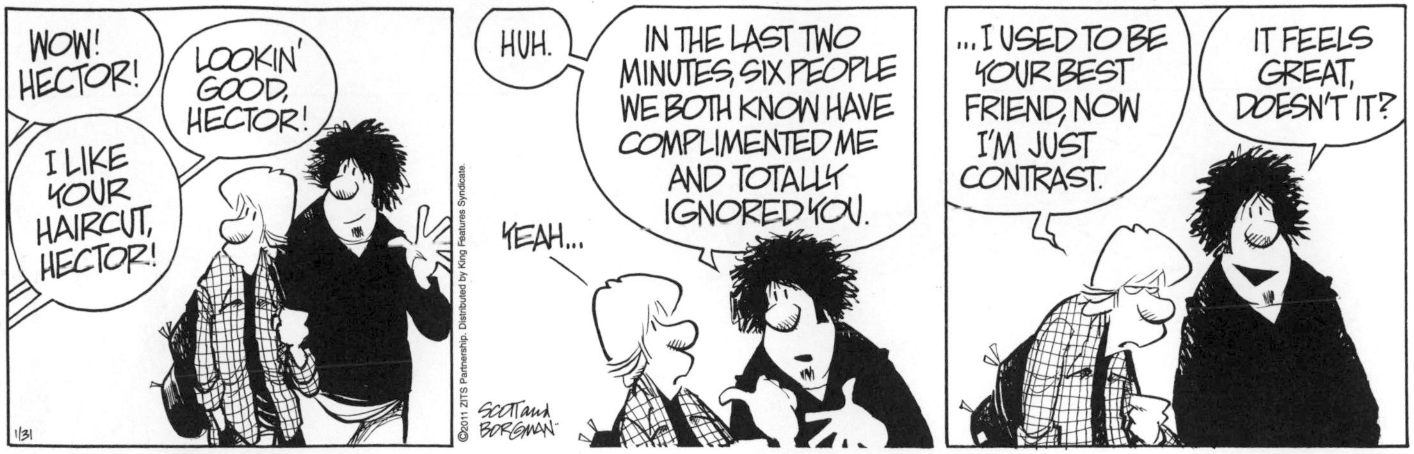
WOW! HECTOR!
LOOKIN' GOOD, HECTOR!
I LIKE YOUR HAIRCUT, HECTOR!
1/31
©2011 ZITS Partnership. Distributed by King Features Syndicate.
HUH.
IN THE LAST TWO MINUTES, SIX PEOPLE WE BOTH KNOW HAVE COMPLIMENTED ME AND TOTALLY IGNORED YOU.
YEAH...
SCOTT and BORGMAN
...I USED TO BE YOUR BEST FRIEND, NOW I'M JUST CONTRAST.
IT FEELS GREAT, DOESN'T IT?

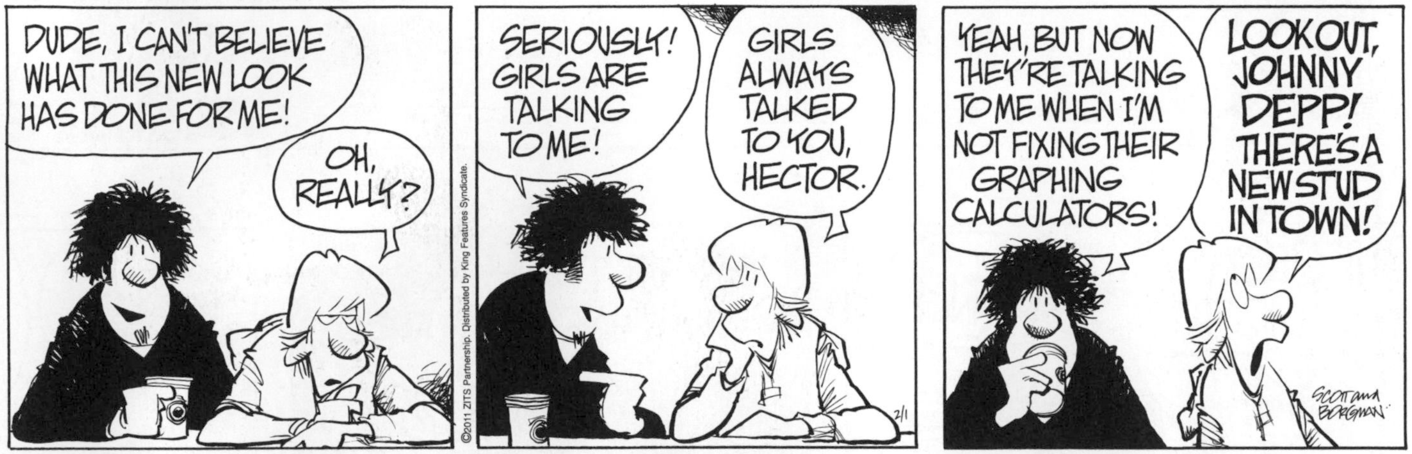
DUDE, I CAN'T BELIEVE WHAT THIS NEW LOOK HAS DONE FOR ME!
OH, REALLY?
©2011 ZITS Partnership. Distributed by King Features Syndicate.
SERIOUSLY! GIRLS ARE TALKING TO ME!
GIRLS ALWAYS TALKED TO YOU, HECTOR.
2/1
YEAH, BUT NOW THEY'RE TALKING TO ME WHEN I'M NOT FIXING THEIR GRAPHING CALCULATORS!
LOOK OUT, JOHNNY DEPP! THERE'S A NEW STUD IN TOWN!
SCOTT and BORGMAN

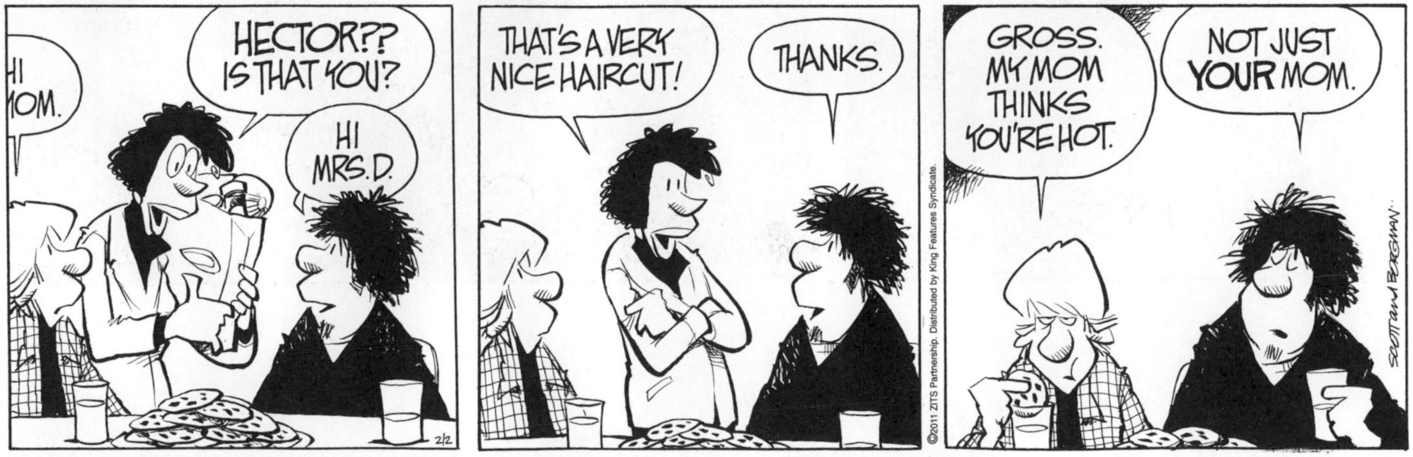
HI MOM.
HECTOR?? IS THAT YOU?
HI MRS. D.
2/2
THAT'S A VERY NICE HAIRCUT!
THANKS.
©2011 ZITS Partnership. Distributed by King Features Syndicate.
GROSS. MY MOM THINKS YOU'RE HOT.
NOT JUST YOUR MOM.
SCOTT and BORGMAN

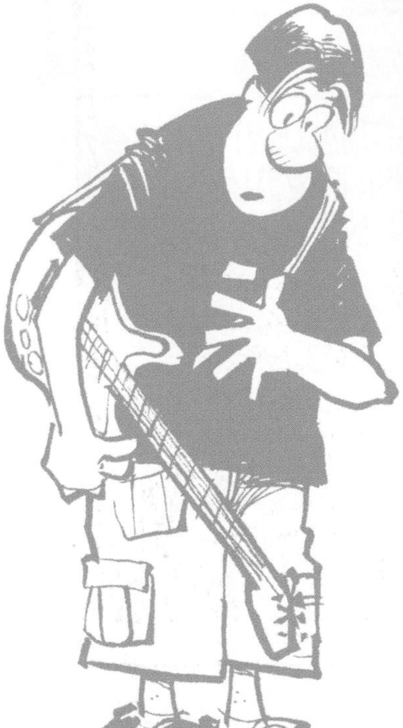

Zits

by JERRY SCOTT and JIM BORGMAN

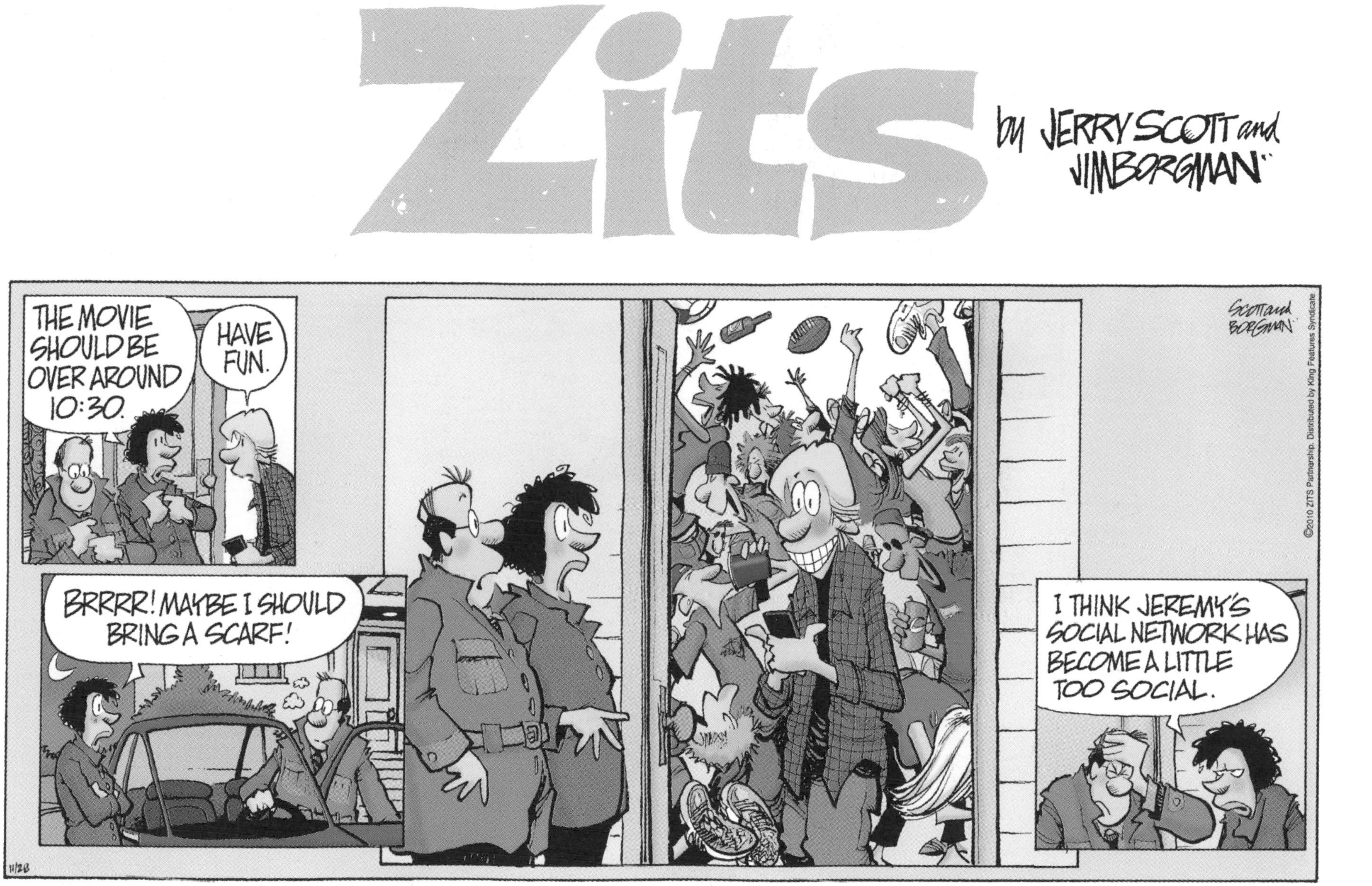
THE MOVIE SHOULD BE OVER AROUND 10:30.
HAVE FUN.
BRRRR! MAYBE I SHOULD BRING A SCARF!
I THINK JEREMY'S SOCIAL NETWORK HAS BECOME A LITTLE TOO SOCIAL.
SCOTT and BORGMAN
©2010 ZITS Partnership. Distributed by King Features Syndicate
11/28

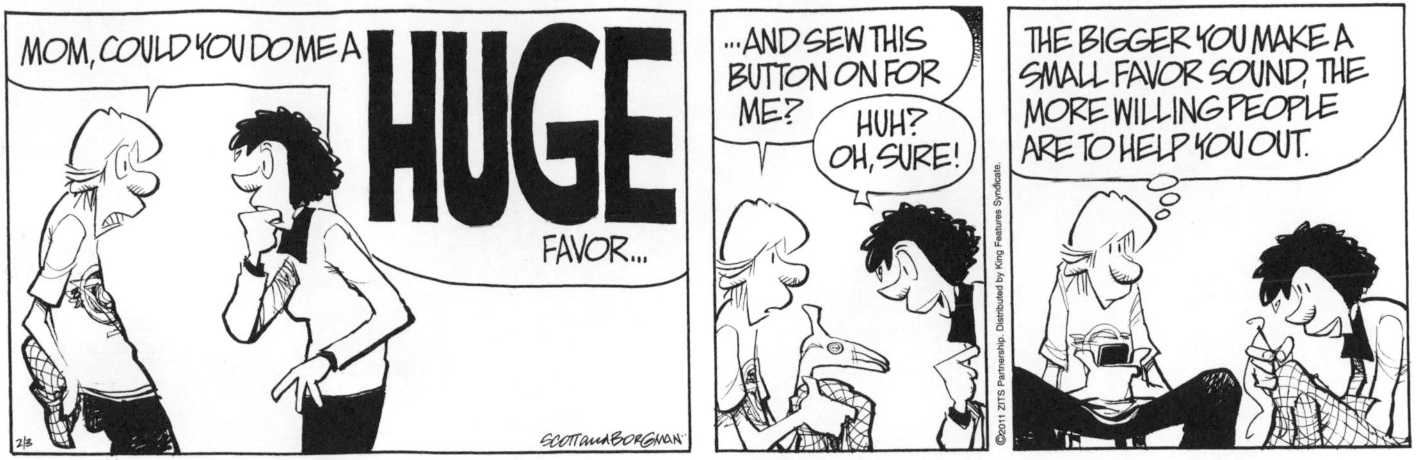
MOM, COULD YOU DO ME A HUGE FAVOR...
2/3
SCOTT and BORGMAN
...AND SEW THIS BUTTON ON FOR ME?
HUH? OH, SURE!
©2011 ZITS Partnership. Distributed by King Features Syndicate.
THE BIGGER YOU MAKE A SMALL FAVOR SOUND, THE MORE WILLING PEOPLE ARE TO HELP YOU OUT.

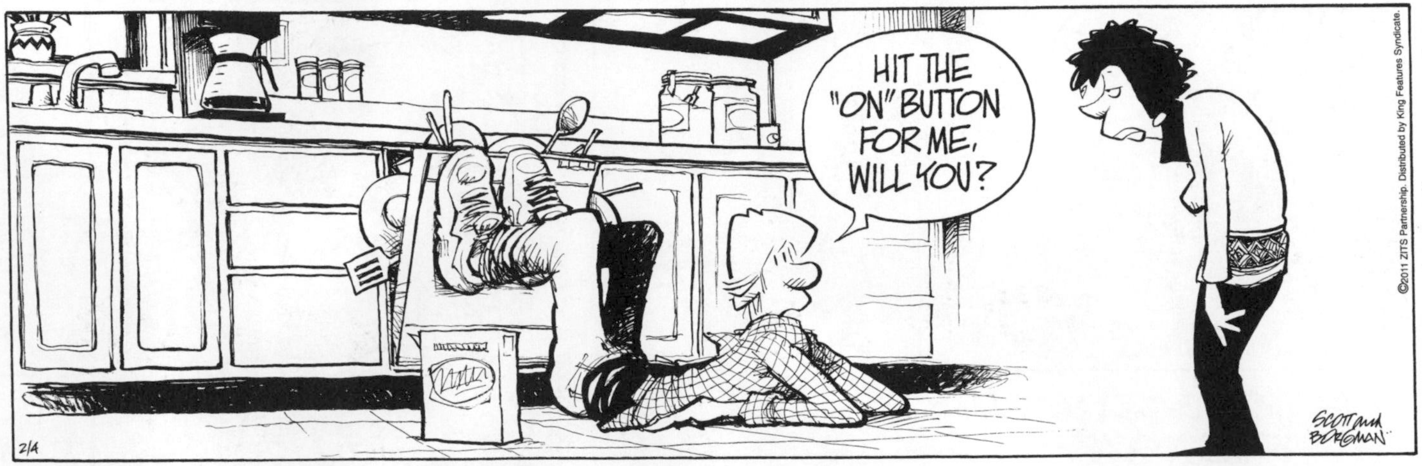
HIT THE "ON" BUTTON FOR ME, WILL YOU?
2/4
SCOTT and BORGMAN
©2011 ZITS Partnership. Distributed by King Features Syndicate.

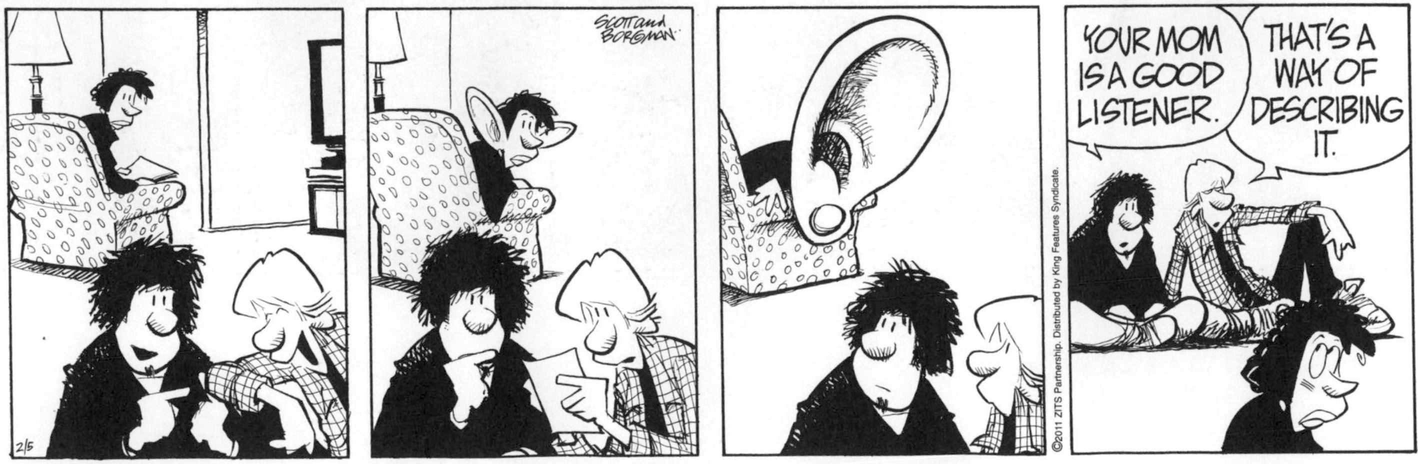
2/5
SCOTT and BORGMAN
©2011 ZITS Partnership. Distributed by King Features Syndicate.
YOUR MOM IS A GOOD LISTENER.
THAT'S A WAY OF DESCRIBING IT.

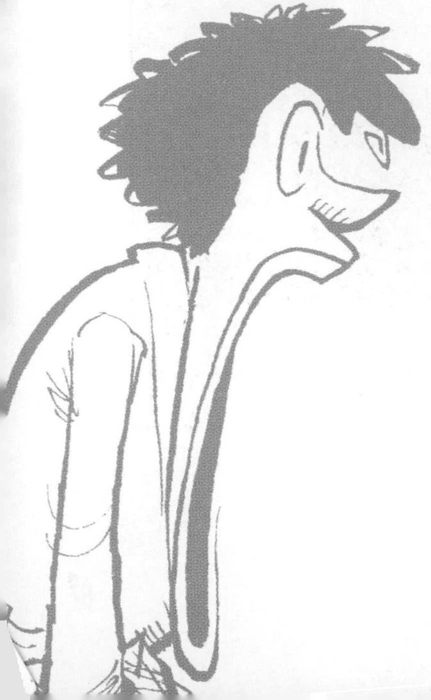

Zits

by JERRY SCOTT and JIM BORGMAN

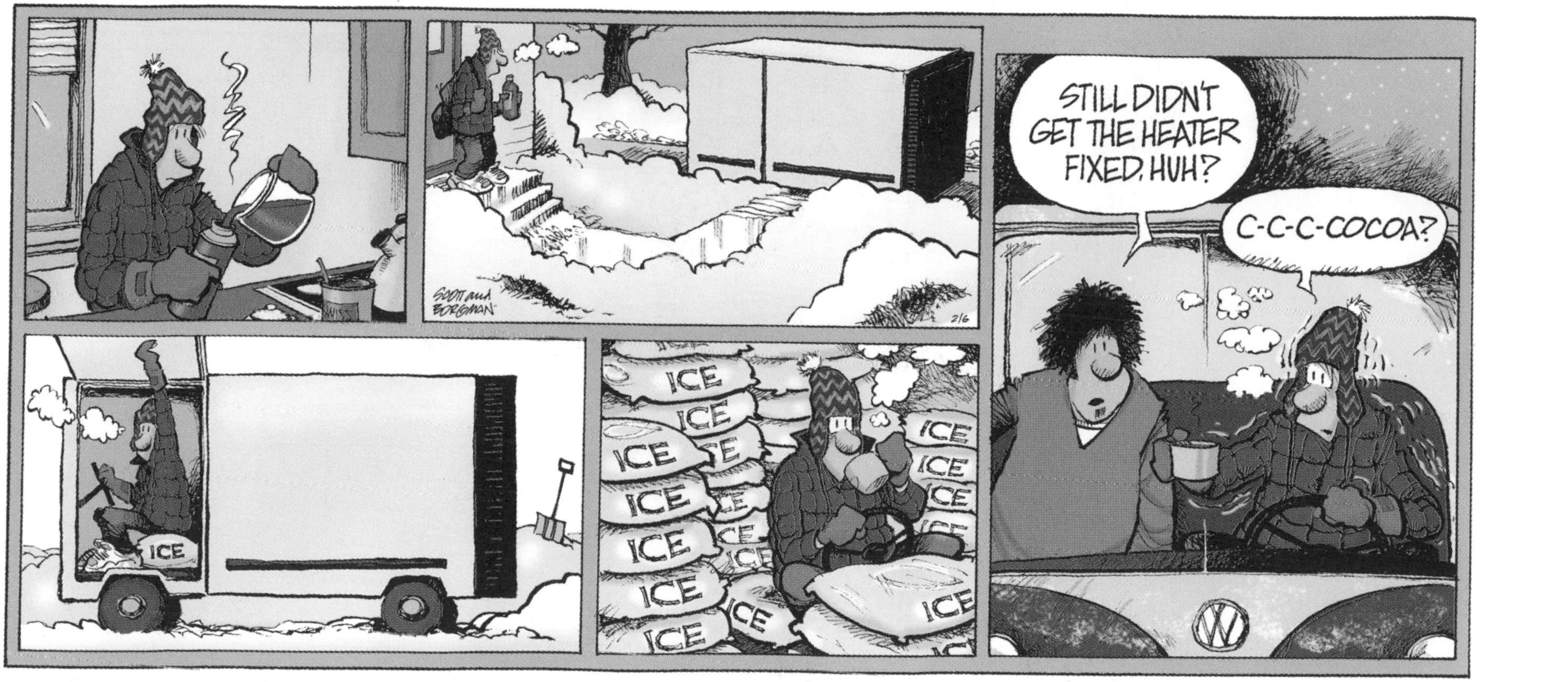
SCOTT and BORGMAN
2/16
ICE
STILL DIDN'T GET THE HEATER FIXED, HUH?
C-C-C-COCOA?

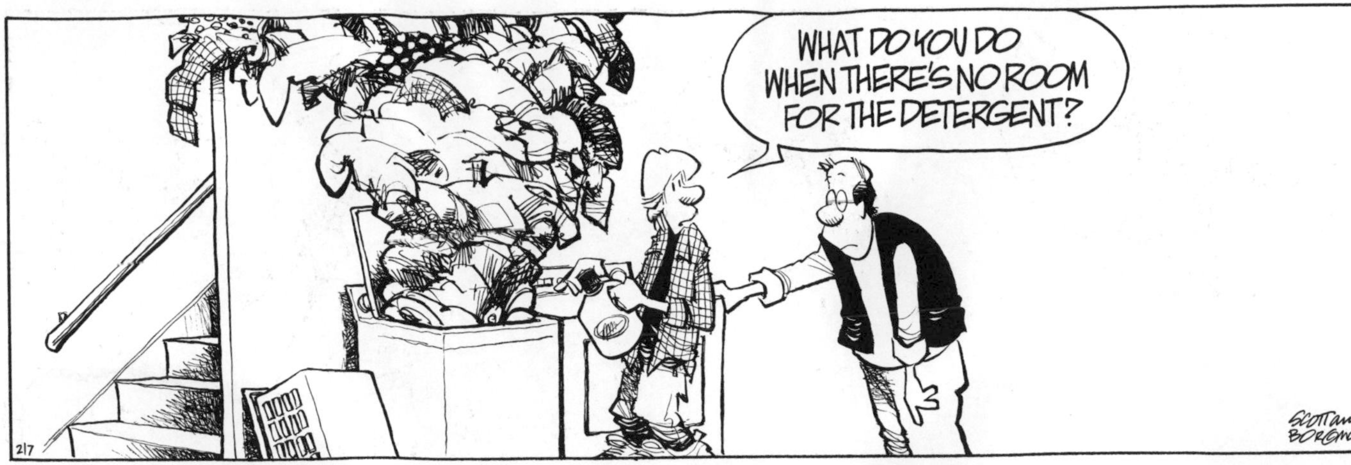
WHAT DO YOU DO WHEN THERE'S NO ROOM FOR THE DETERGENT?
2/7
SCOTT and BORGMAN
©2011 ZITS Partnership. Distributed by King Features Syndicate.

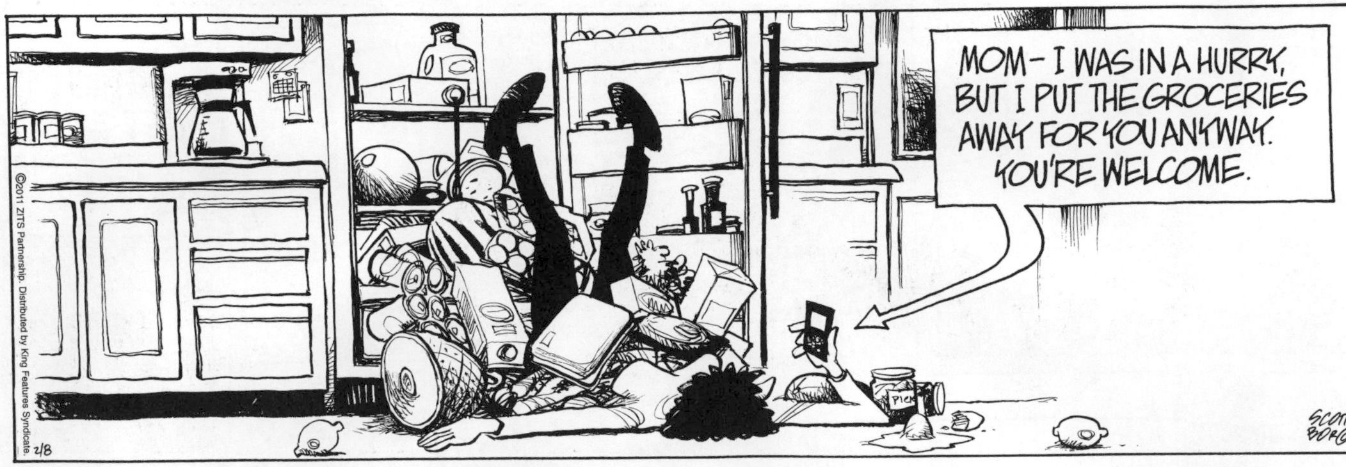
MOM - I WAS IN A HURRY, BUT I PUT THE GROCERIES AWAY FOR YOU ANYWAY. YOU'RE WELCOME.
2/8
SCOTT and BORGMAN
©2011 ZITS Partnership. Distributed by King Features Syndicate.

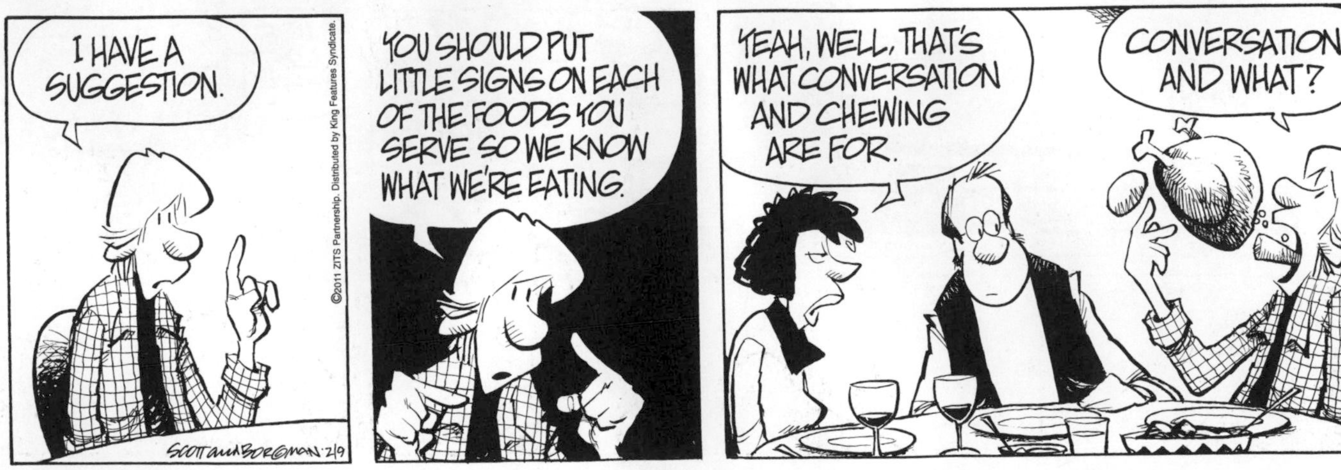
I HAVE A SUGGESTION.
YOU SHOULD PUT LITTLE SIGNS ON EACH OF THE FOODS YOU SERVE SO WE KNOW WHAT WE'RE EATING.
YEAH, WELL, THAT'S WHAT CONVERSATION AND CHEWING ARE FOR.
CONVERSATION AND WHAT?
SCOTT and BORGMAN 2/9
©2011 ZITS Partnership. Distributed by King Features Syndicate.

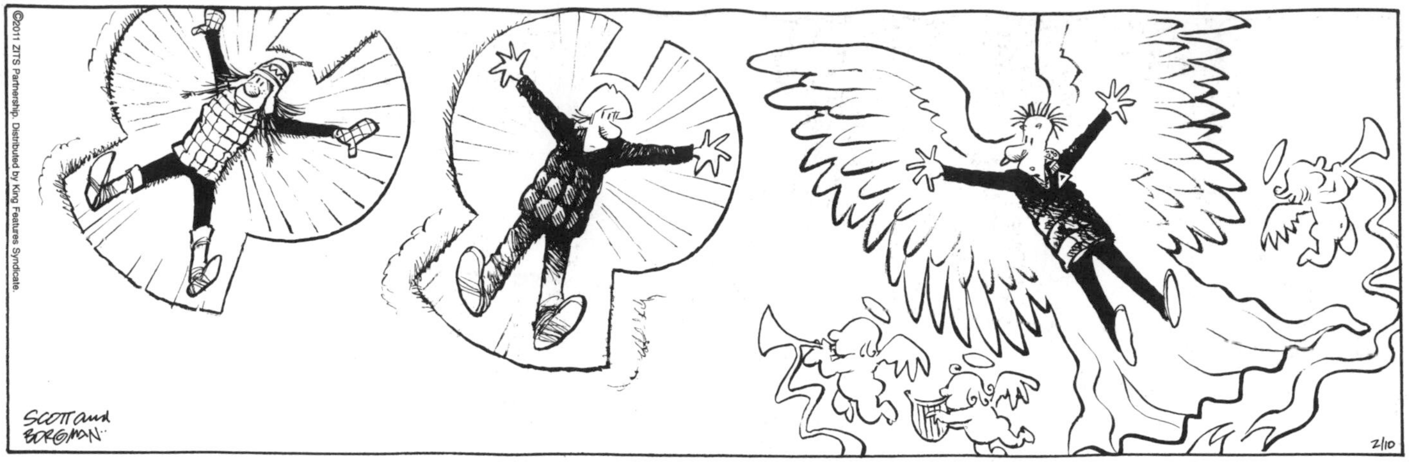
©2011 ZITS Partnership. Distributed by King Features Syndicate.
SCOTT and BORGMAN
2/10

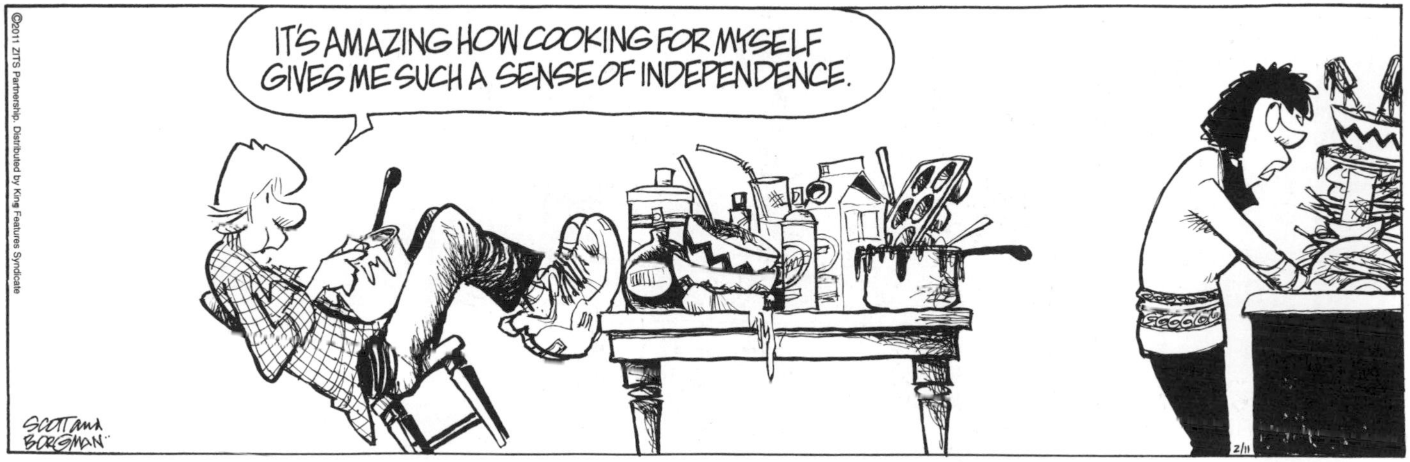
©2011 ZITS Partnership. Distributed by King Features Syndicate
IT'S AMAZING HOW COOKING FOR MYSELF GIVES ME SUCH A SENSE OF INDEPENDENCE.
SCOTT and BORGMAN
2/11

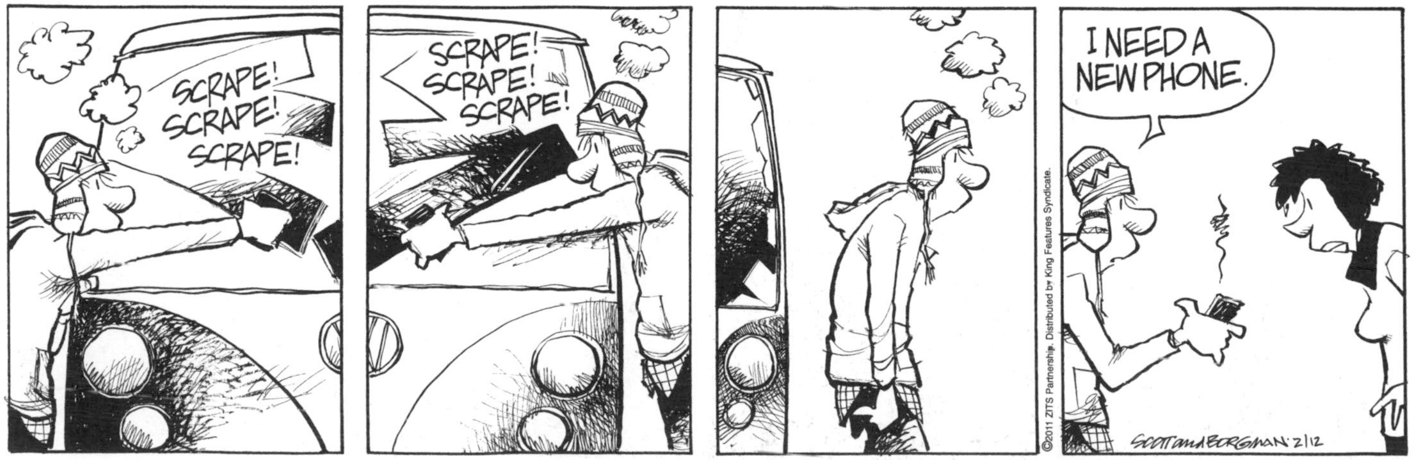
SCRAPE! SCRAPE! SCRAPE!
SCRAPE! SCRAPE! SCRAPE!
I NEED A NEW PHONE.
©2011 ZITS Partnership. Distributed by King Features Syndicate.
SCOTT and BORGMAN 2/12

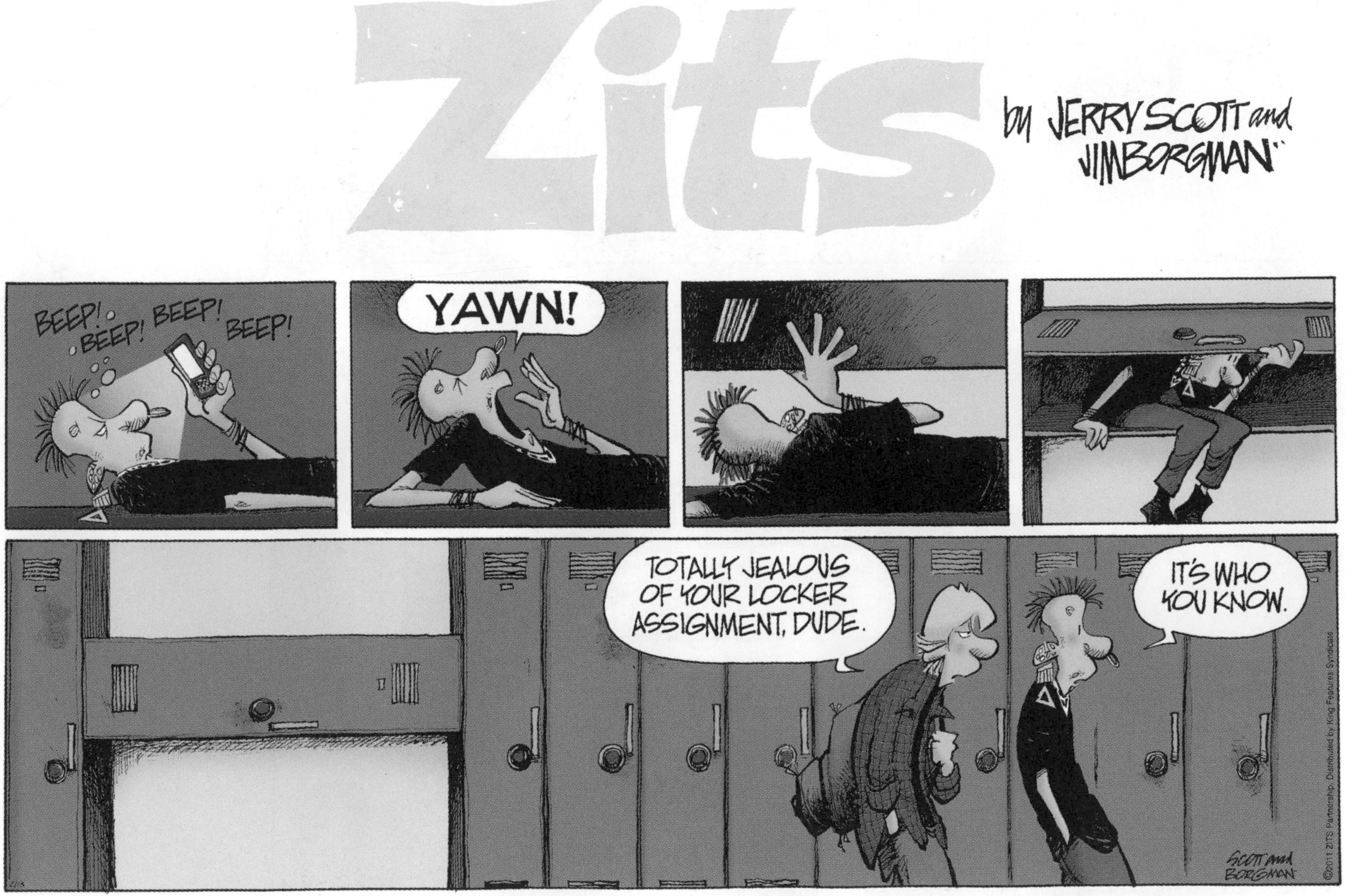
Zits
by JERRY SCOTT and JIM BORGMAN
BEEP! BEEP! BEEP! BEEP!
YAWN!
TOTALLY JEALOUS OF YOUR LOCKER ASSIGNMENT, DUDE.
IT'S WHO YOU KNOW.
SCOTT and BORGMAN
©2011 ZITS Partnership. Distributed by King Features Syndicate

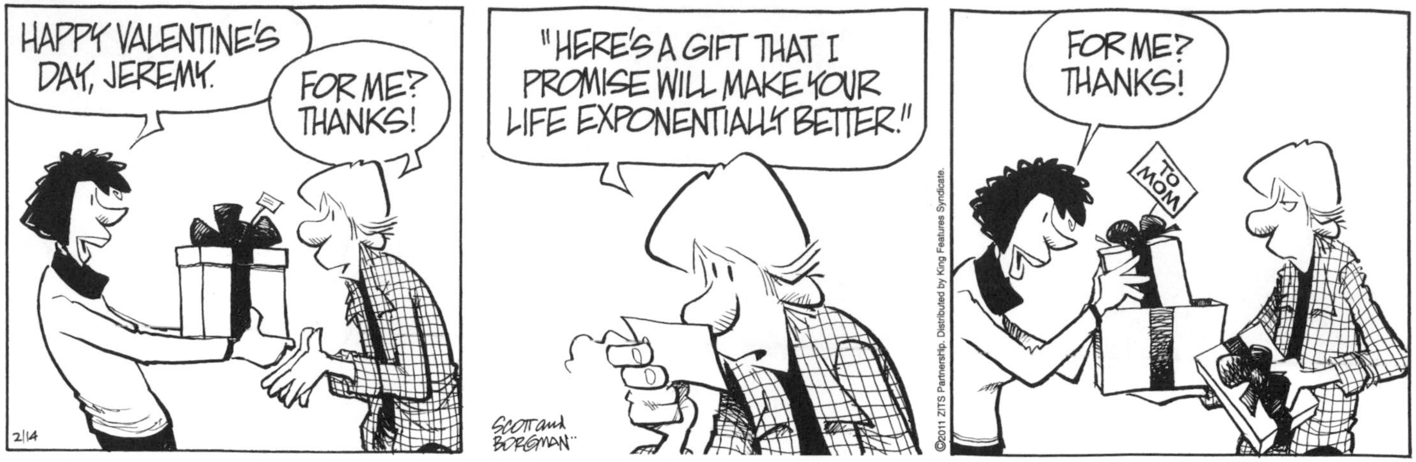
HAPPY VALENTINE'S DAY, JEREMY.
FOR ME? THANKS!
"HERE'S A GIFT THAT I PROMISE WILL MAKE YOUR LIFE EXPONENTIALLY BETTER."
FOR ME? THANKS!
TO MOM
2/14
SCOTT and BORGMAN
©2011 ZITS Partnership. Distributed by King Features Syndicate.

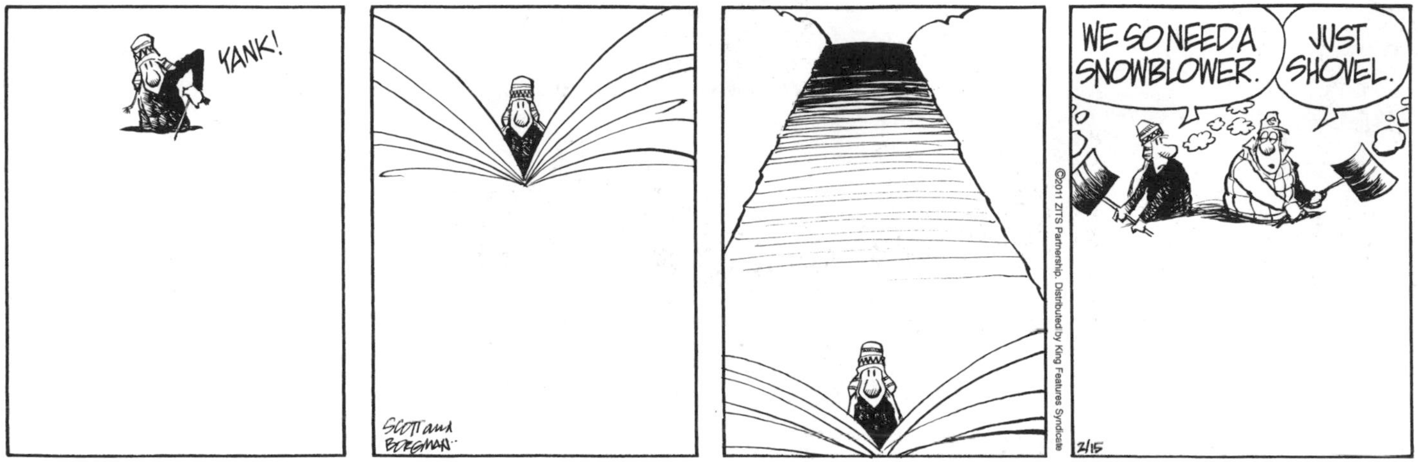
YANK!
SCOTT and BORGMAN
WE SO NEED A SNOWBLOWER.
JUST SHOVEL.
2/15
©2011 ZITS Partnership. Distributed by King Features Syndicate

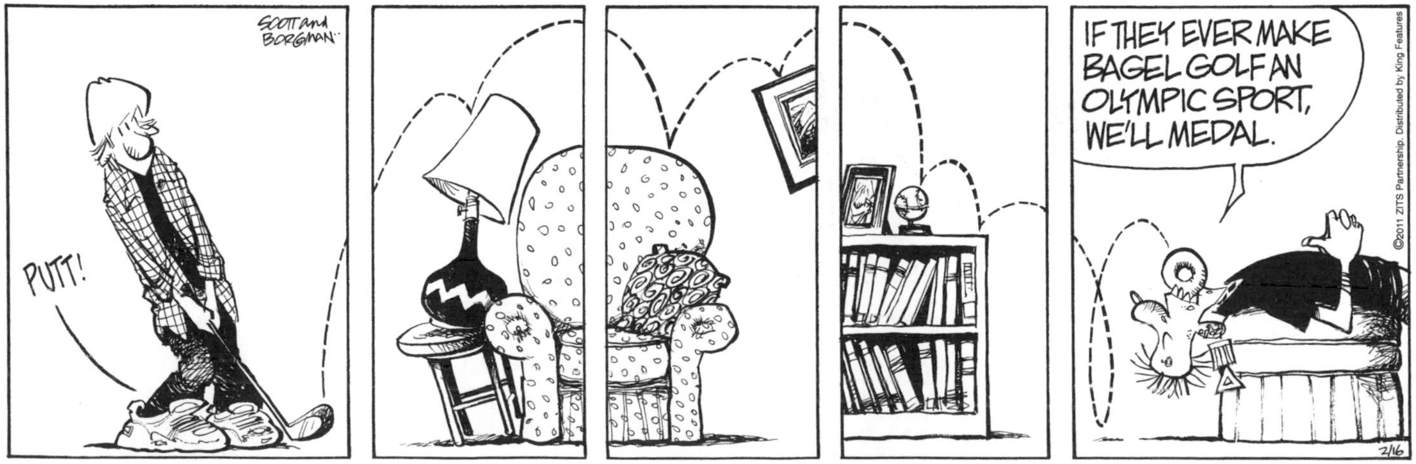
SCOTT and BORGMAN
PUTT!
IF THEY EVER MAKE BAGEL GOLF AN OLYMPIC SPORT, WE'LL MEDAL.
2/16
©2011 ZITS Partnership. Distributed by King Features

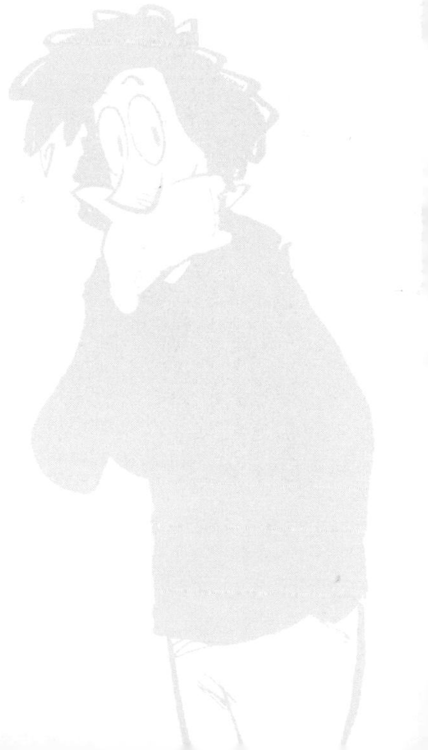

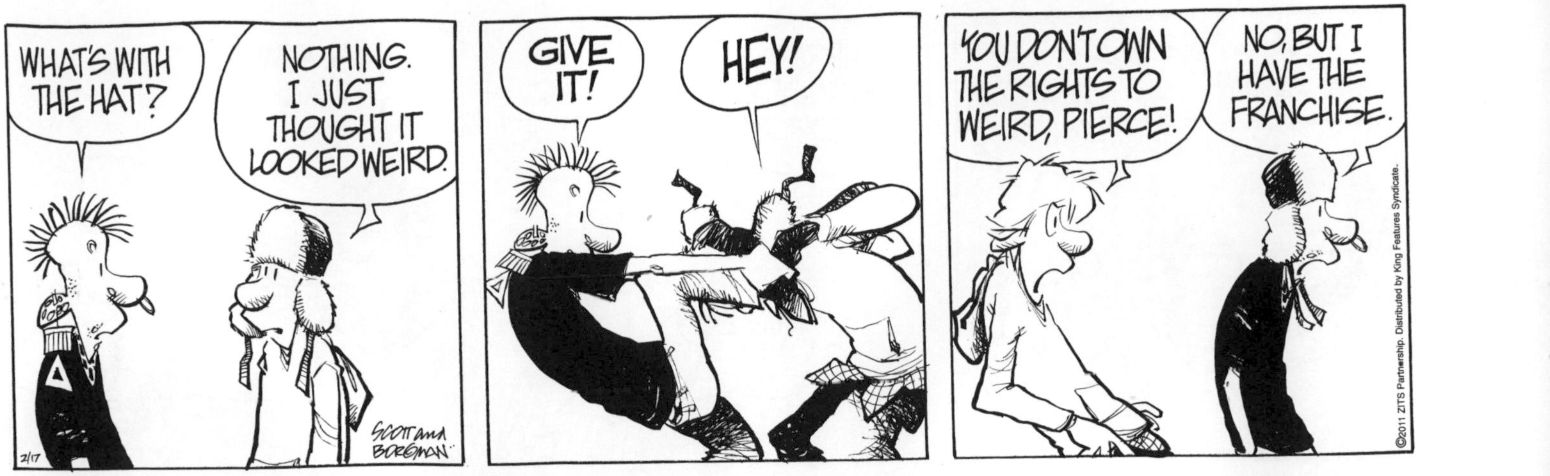
WHAT'S WITH THE HAT?
NOTHING. I JUST THOUGHT IT LOOKED WEIRD.
SCOTT and BORGMAN
2/17
GIVE IT!
HEY!
YOU DON'T OWN THE RIGHTS TO WEIRD, PIERCE!
NO, BUT I HAVE THE FRANCHISE.
©2011 ZITS Partnership. Distributed by King Features Syndicate.

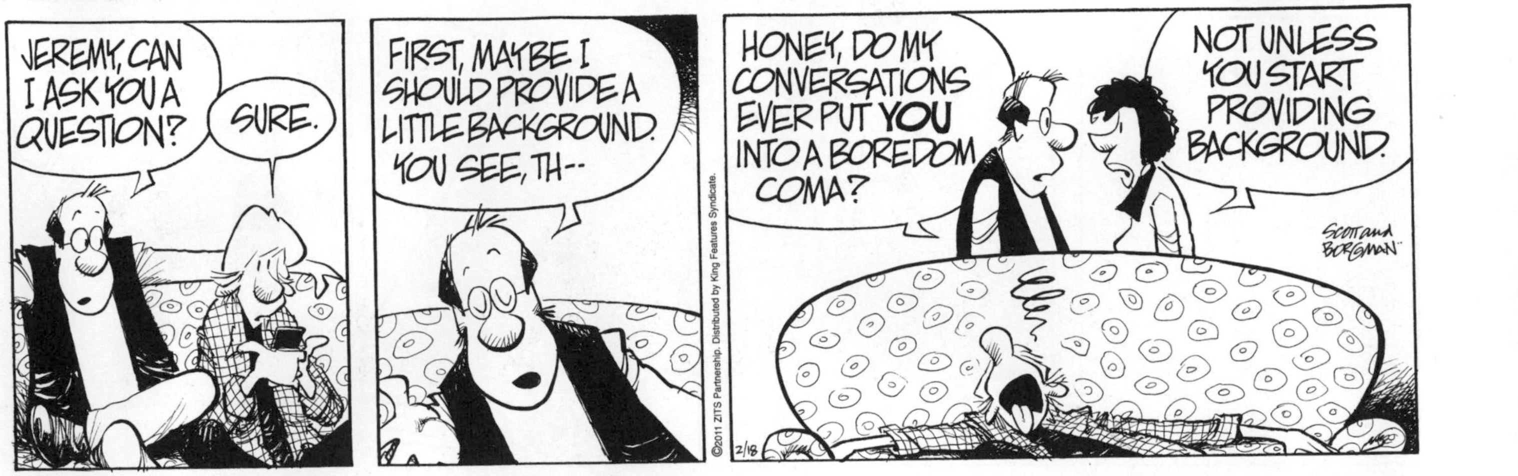
JEREMY, CAN I ASK YOU A QUESTION?
SURE.
FIRST, MAYBE I SHOULD PROVIDE A LITTLE BACKGROUND. YOU SEE, TH--
©2011 ZITS Partnership. Distributed by King Features Syndicate.
HONEY, DO MY CONVERSATIONS EVER PUT **YOU** INTO A BOREDOM COMA?
NOT UNLESS YOU START PROVIDING BACKGROUND.
SCOTT and BORGMAN
2/18

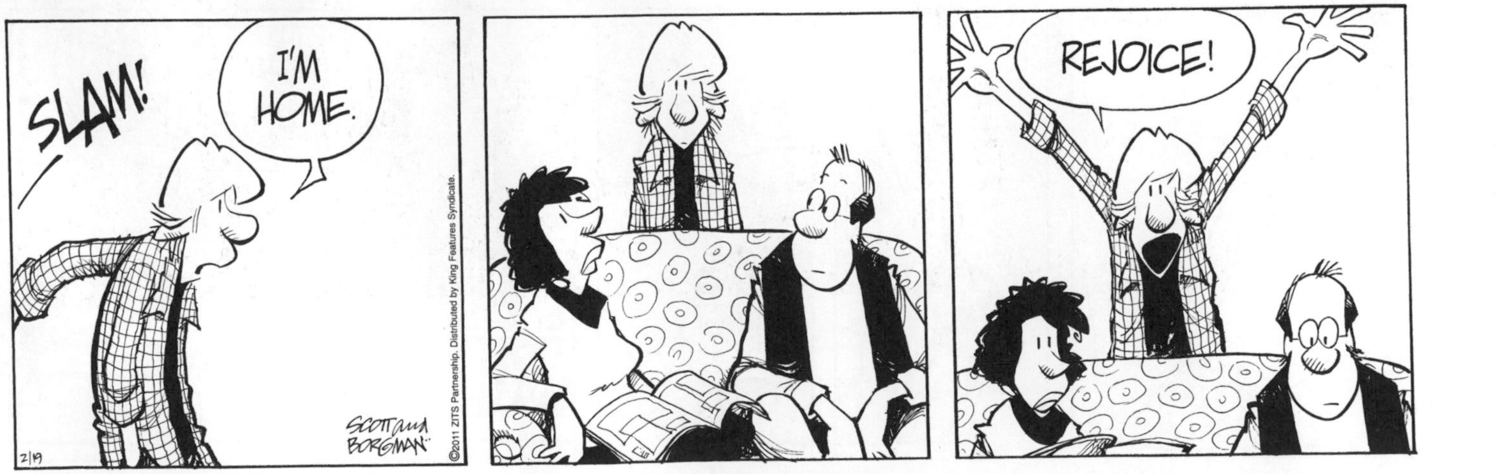
SLAM!
I'M HOME.
SCOTT and BORGMAN
2/19
©2011 ZITS Partnership. Distributed by King Features Syndicate.
REJOICE!

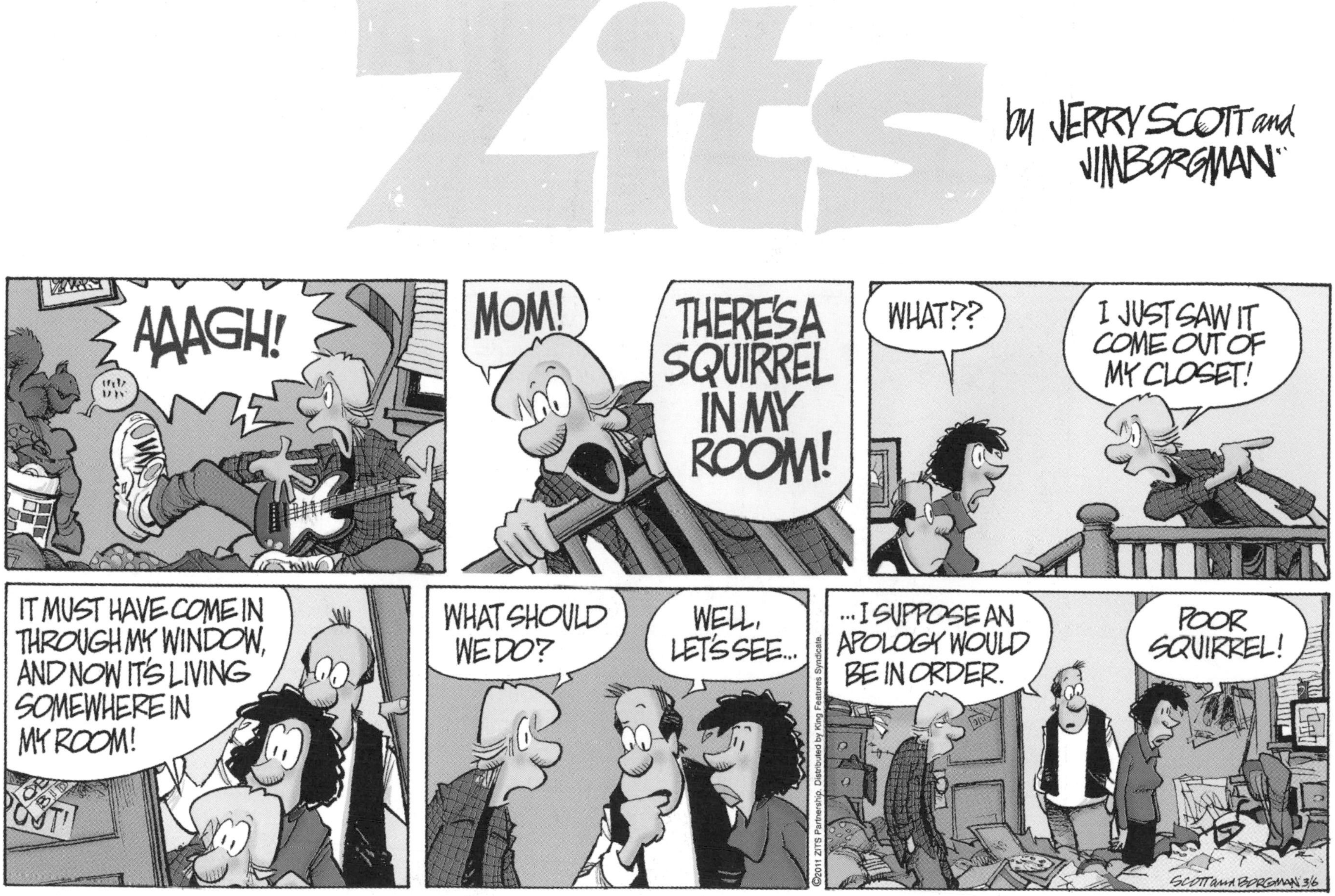
Zits
by JERRY SCOTT and JIM BORGMAN
AAAGH!
MOM!
THERE'S A SQUIRREL IN MY ROOM!
WHAT??
I JUST SAW IT COME OUT OF MY CLOSET!
IT MUST HAVE COME IN THROUGH MY WINDOW, AND NOW IT'S LIVING SOMEWHERE IN MY ROOM!
WHAT SHOULD WE DO?
WELL, LET'S SEE...
©2011 ZITS Partnership. Distributed by King Features Syndicate.
...I SUPPOSE AN APOLOGY WOULD BE IN ORDER.
POOR SQUIRREL!
SCOTT and BORGMAN 3/6

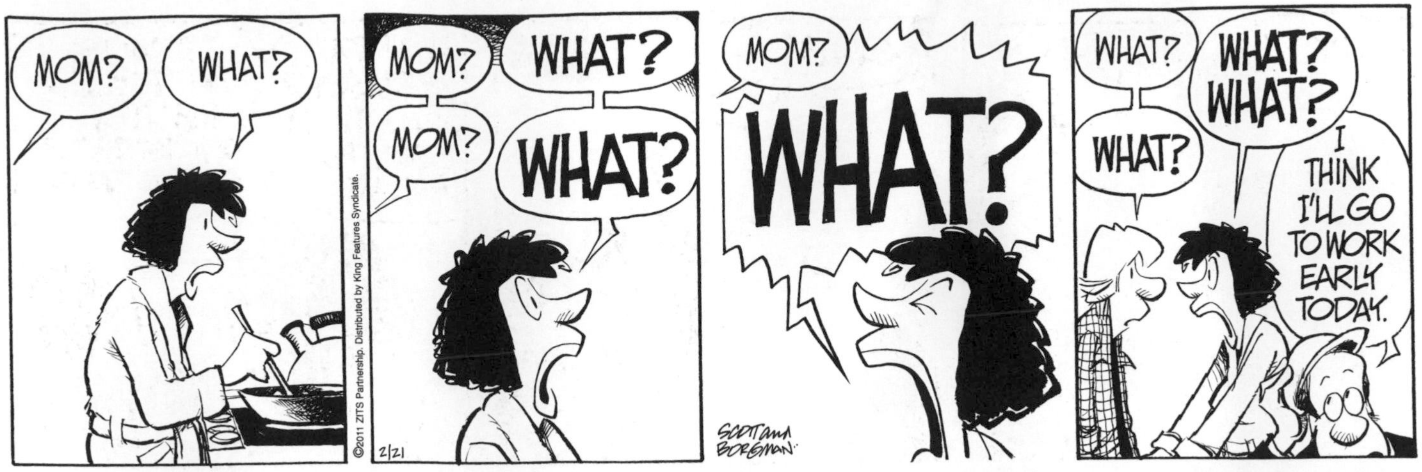
MOM?
WHAT?
MOM?
WHAT?
MOM?
WHAT?
©2011 ZITS Partnership. Distributed by King Features Syndicate.
2/21
MOM?
WHAT?
SCOTT AND BORGMAN
WHAT?
WHAT?
WHAT? WHAT?
I THINK I'LL GO TO WORK EARLY TODAY.

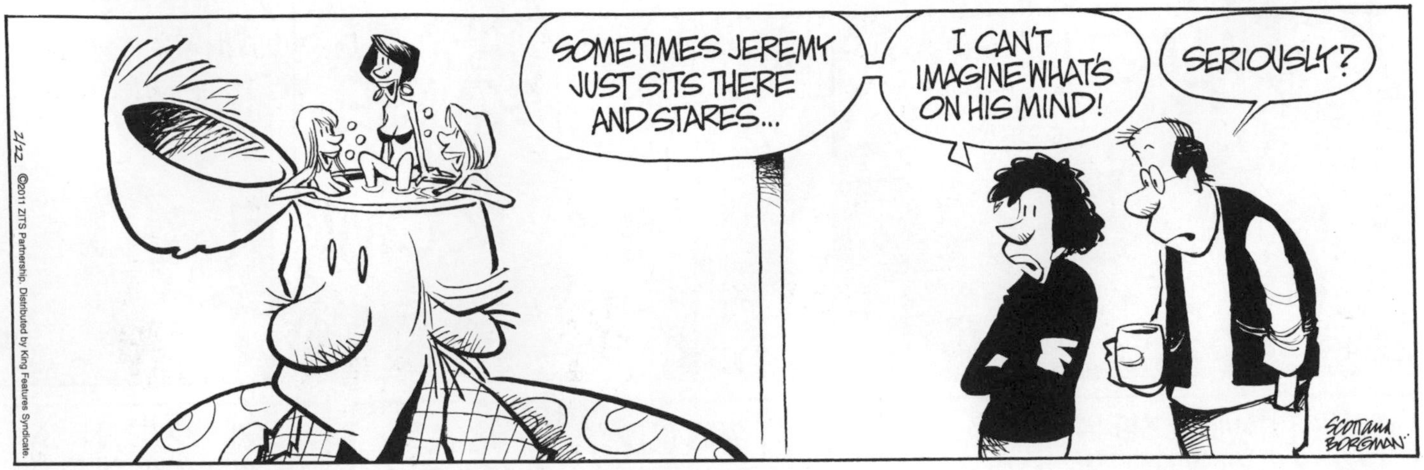
2/22
©2011 ZITS Partnership. Distributed by King Features Syndicate.
SOMETIMES JEREMY JUST SITS THERE AND STARES...
I CAN'T IMAGINE WHAT'S ON HIS MIND!
SERIOUSLY?
SCOTT AND BORGMAN

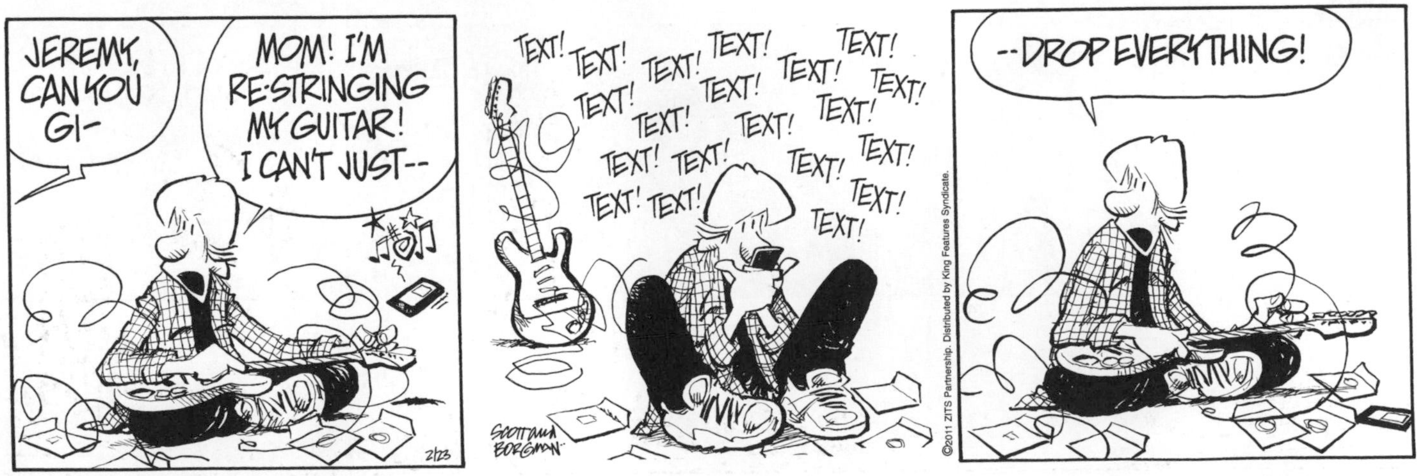
JEREMY, CAN YOU GI-
MOM! I'M RE-STRINGING MY GUITAR! I CAN'T JUST--
2/23
TEXT! TEXT!
SCOTT AND BORGMAN
©2011 ZITS Partnership. Distributed by King Features Syndicate.
--DROP EVERYTHING!

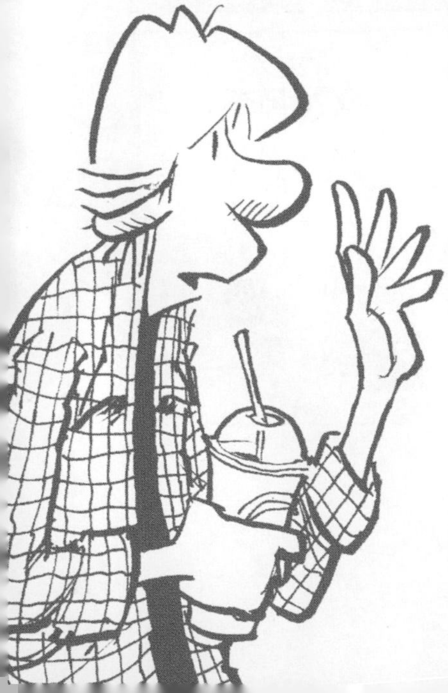

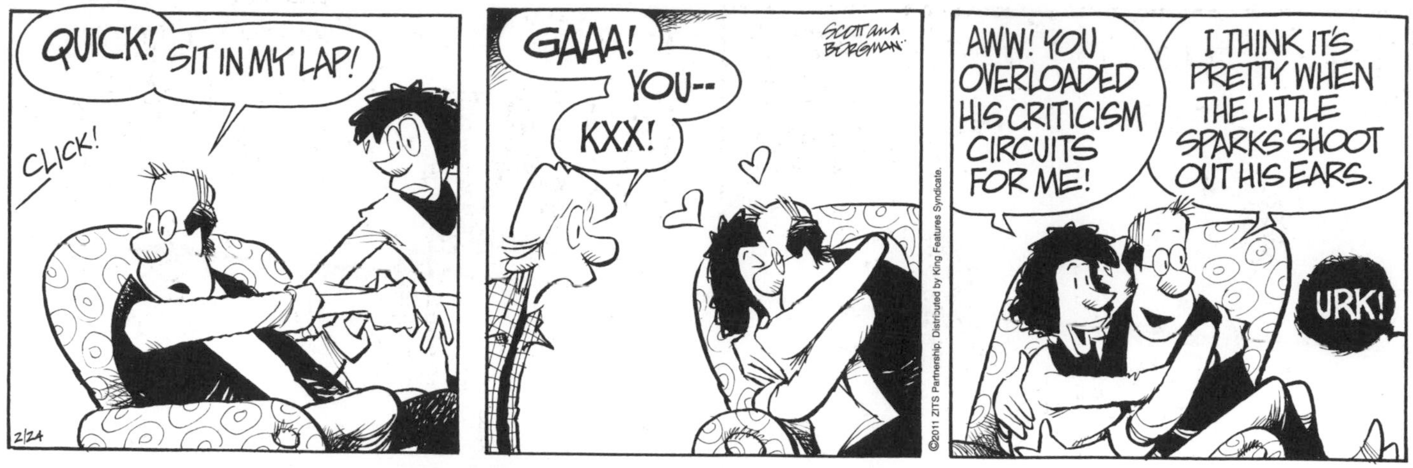
QUICK! SIT IN MY LAP!
CLICK!
2/24
SCOTT and BORGMAN
GAAA! YOU-- KXX!
©2011 ZITS Partnership. Distributed by King Features Syndicate.
AWW! YOU OVERLOADED HIS CRITICISM CIRCUITS FOR ME!
I THINK IT'S PRETTY WHEN THE LITTLE SPARKS SHOOT OUT HIS EARS.
URK!

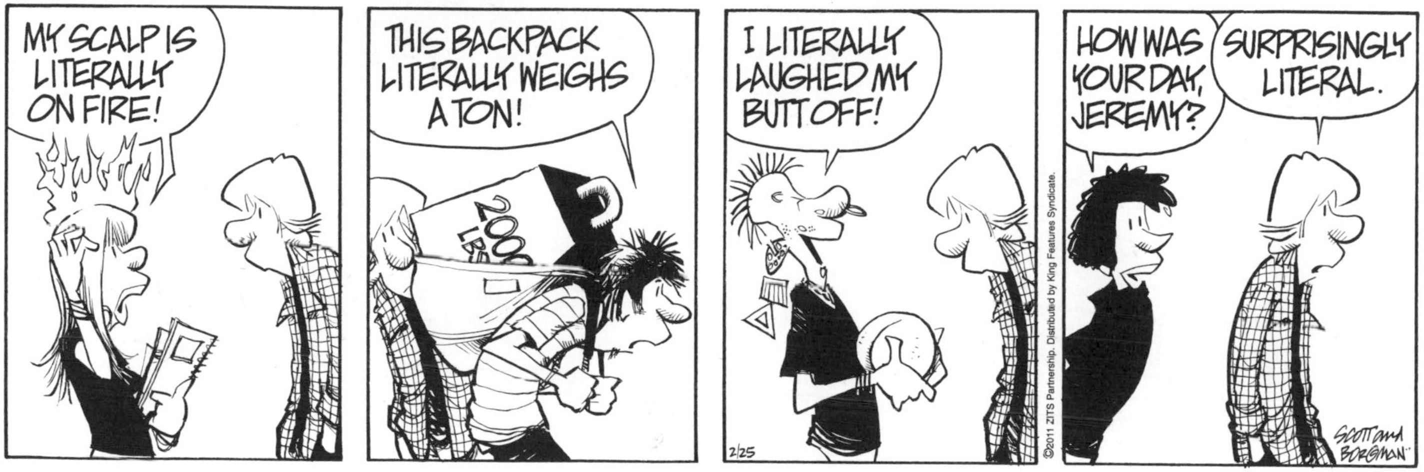
MY SCALP IS LITERALLY ON FIRE!
THIS BACKPACK LITERALLY WEIGHS A TON!
2000 LBS
I LITERALLY LAUGHED MY BUTT OFF!
2/25
©2011 ZITS Partnership. Distributed by King Features Syndicate.
HOW WAS YOUR DAY, JEREMY?
SURPRISINGLY LITERAL.
SCOTT and BORGMAN

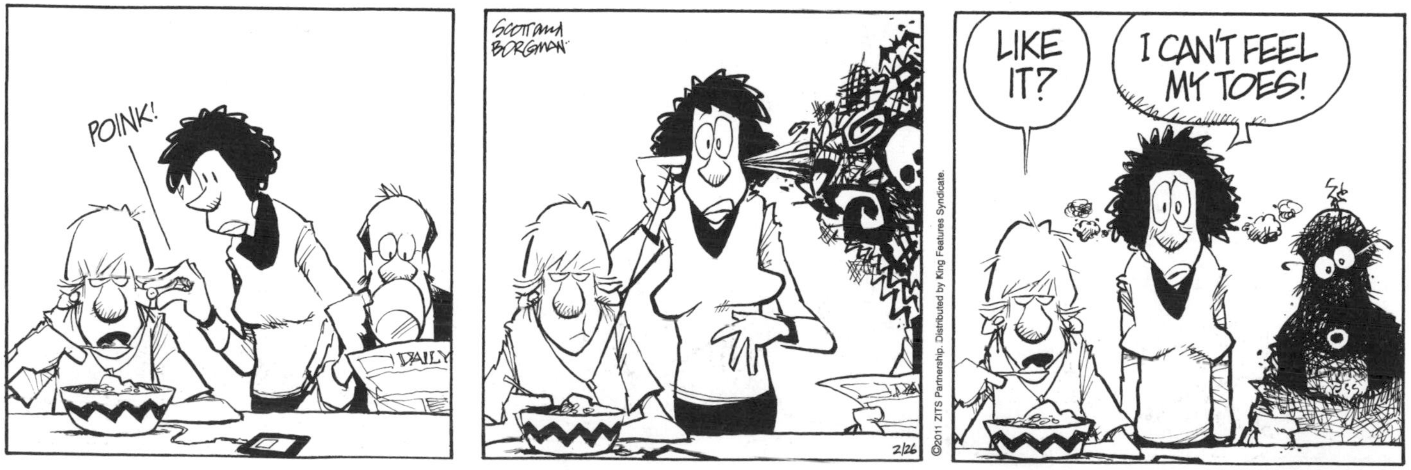
POINK!
DAILY
SCOTT and BORGMAN
2/26
©2011 ZITS Partnership. Distributed by King Features Syndicate.
LIKE IT?
I CAN'T FEEL MY TOES!

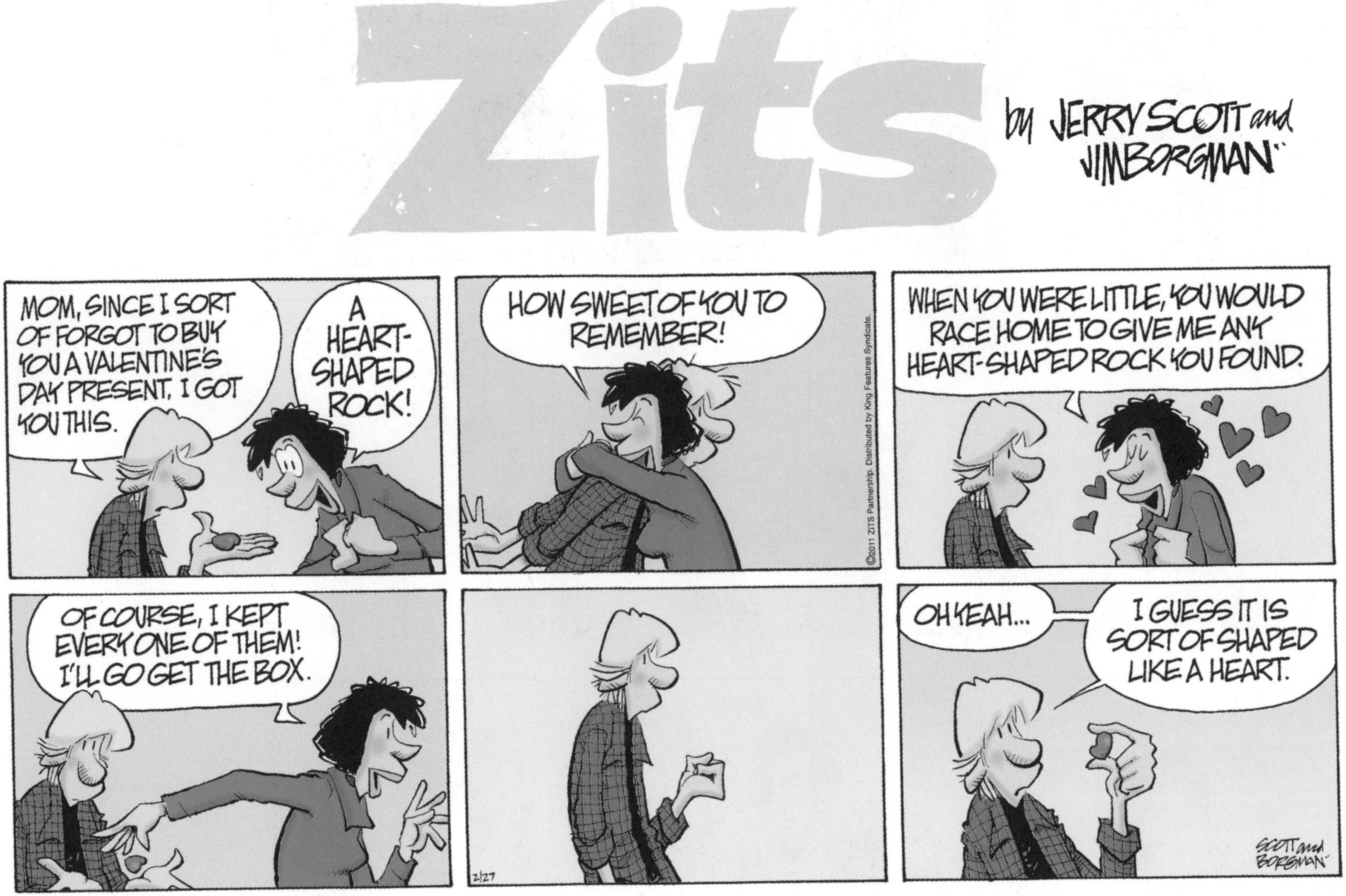
Zits
by JERRY SCOTT and JIM BORGMAN
MOM, SINCE I SORT OF FORGOT TO BUY YOU A VALENTINE'S DAY PRESENT, I GOT YOU THIS.
A HEART-SHAPED ROCK!
HOW SWEET OF YOU TO REMEMBER!
©2011 ZITS Partnership. Distributed by King Features Syndicate.
WHEN YOU WERE LITTLE, YOU WOULD RACE HOME TO GIVE ME ANY HEART-SHAPED ROCK YOU FOUND.
OF COURSE, I KEPT EVERY ONE OF THEM! I'LL GO GET THE BOX.
2/27
OH YEAH...
I GUESS IT IS SORT OF SHAPED LIKE A HEART.
SCOTT and BORGMAN

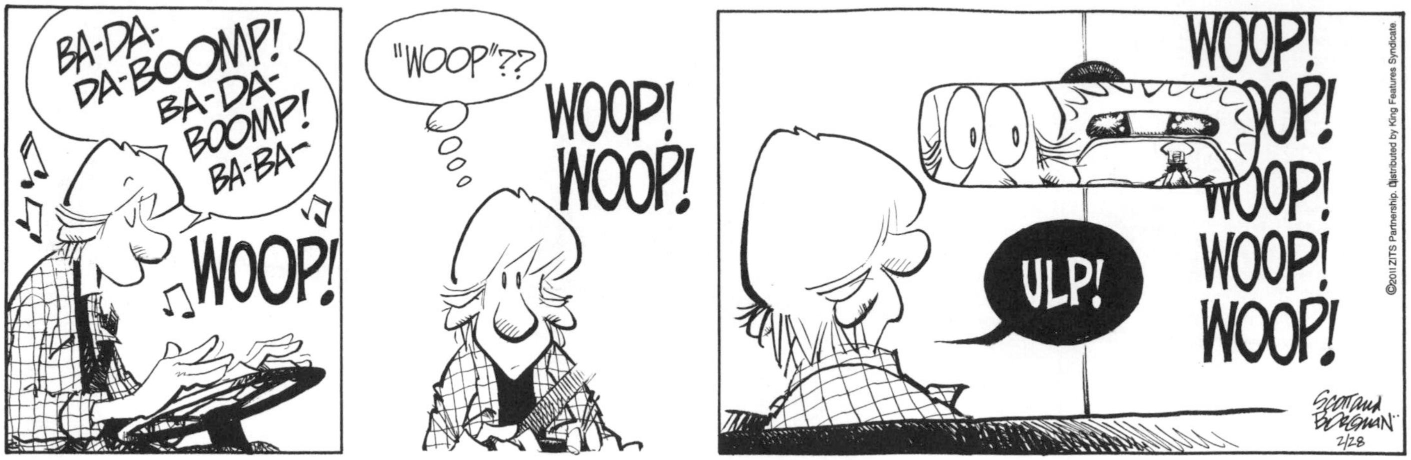
BA-DA-DA-BOOMP! BA-DA-BOOMP! BA-BA-
WOOP!
"WOOP"??
WOOP! WOOP!
WOOP! WOOP! WOOP! WOOP! WOOP!
ULP!
©2011 ZITS Partnership. Distributed by King Features Syndicate.
SCOTT and BORGMAN
2/28

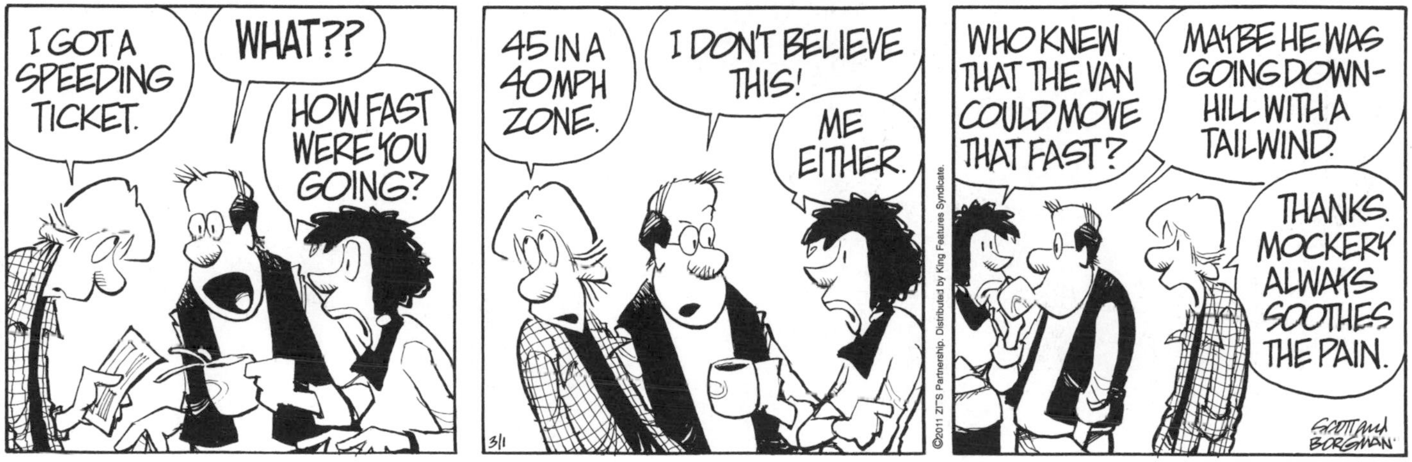
I GOT A SPEEDING TICKET.
WHAT??
HOW FAST WERE YOU GOING?
45 IN A 40 MPH ZONE.
I DON'T BELIEVE THIS!
ME EITHER.
3/1
©2011 ZITS Partnership. Distributed by King Features Syndicate.
WHO KNEW THAT THE VAN COULD MOVE THAT FAST?
MAYBE HE WAS GOING DOWN-HILL WITH A TAILWIND.
THANKS. MOCKERY ALWAYS SOOTHES THE PAIN.
SCOTT and BORGMAN

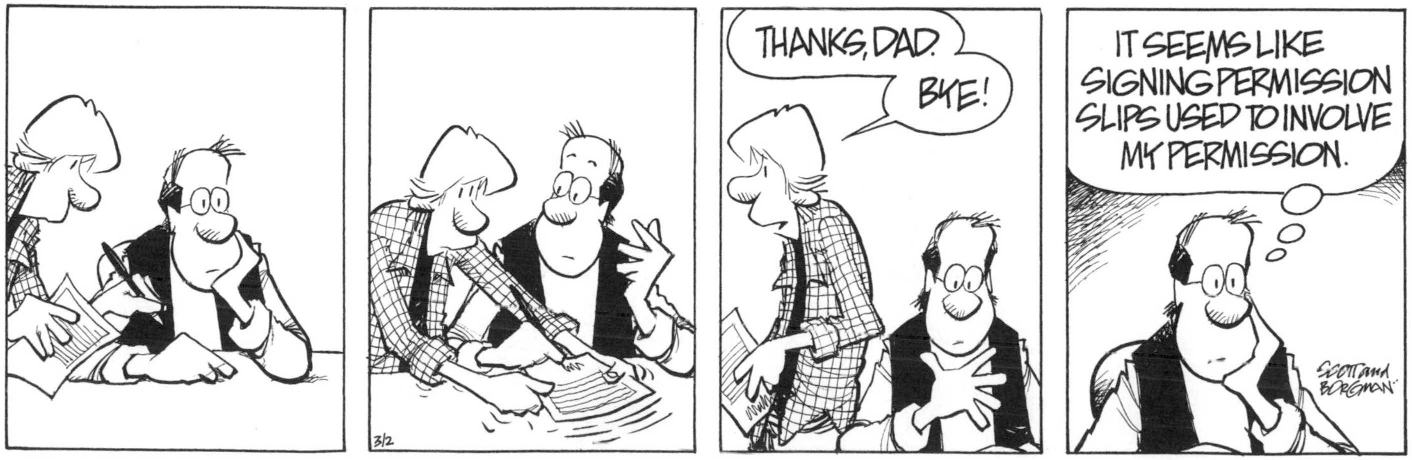
3/2
THANKS, DAD.
BYE!
IT SEEMS LIKE SIGNING PERMISSION SLIPS USED TO INVOLVE MY PERMISSION.
SCOTT and BORGMAN

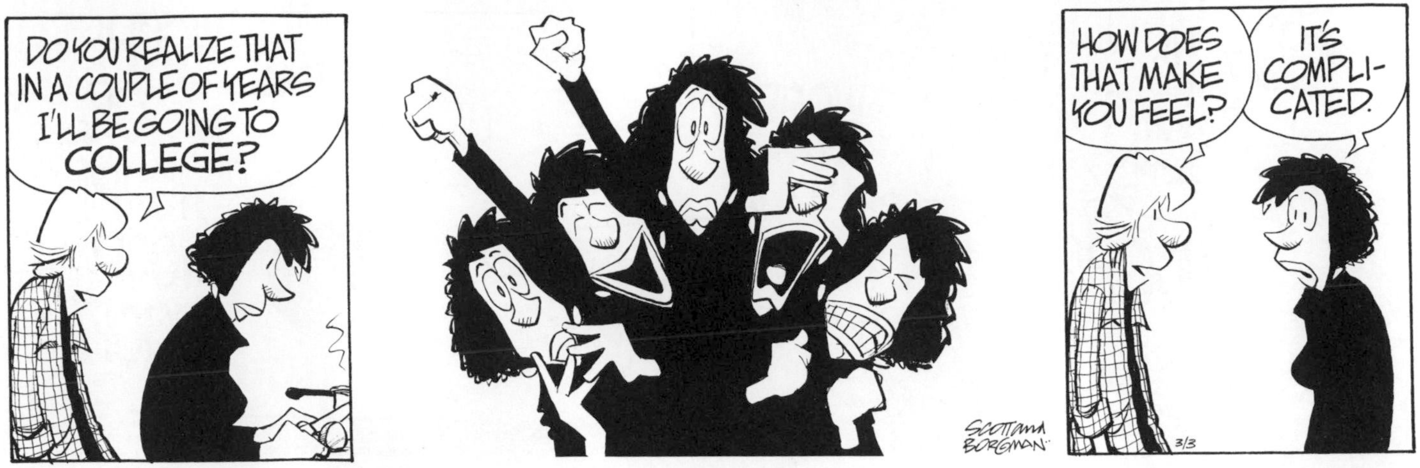
DO YOU REALIZE THAT IN A COUPLE OF YEARS I'LL BE GOING TO COLLEGE?
HOW DOES THAT MAKE YOU FEEL?
IT'S COMPLI-CATED.
SCOTT and BORGMAN
3/3

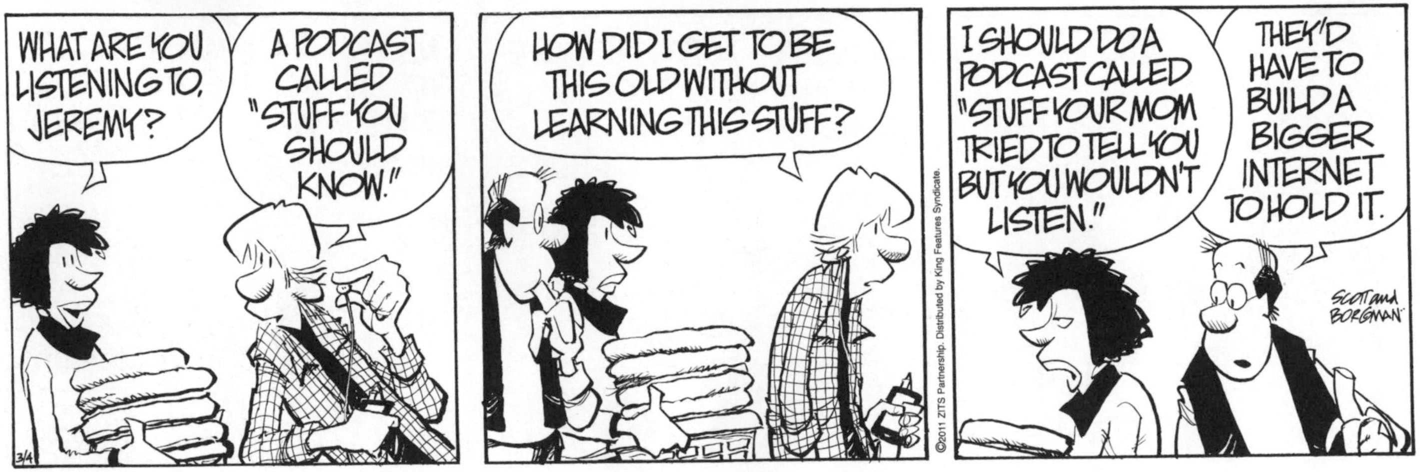
WHAT ARE YOU LISTENING TO, JEREMY?
A PODCAST CALLED "STUFF YOU SHOULD KNOW."
3/4
HOW DID I GET TO BE THIS OLD WITHOUT LEARNING THIS STUFF?
©2011 ZITS Partnership. Distributed by King Features Syndicate.
I SHOULD DO A PODCAST CALLED "STUFF YOUR MOM TRIED TO TELL YOU BUT YOU WOULDN'T LISTEN."
THEY'D HAVE TO BUILD A BIGGER INTERNET TO HOLD IT.
SCOTT and BORGMAN

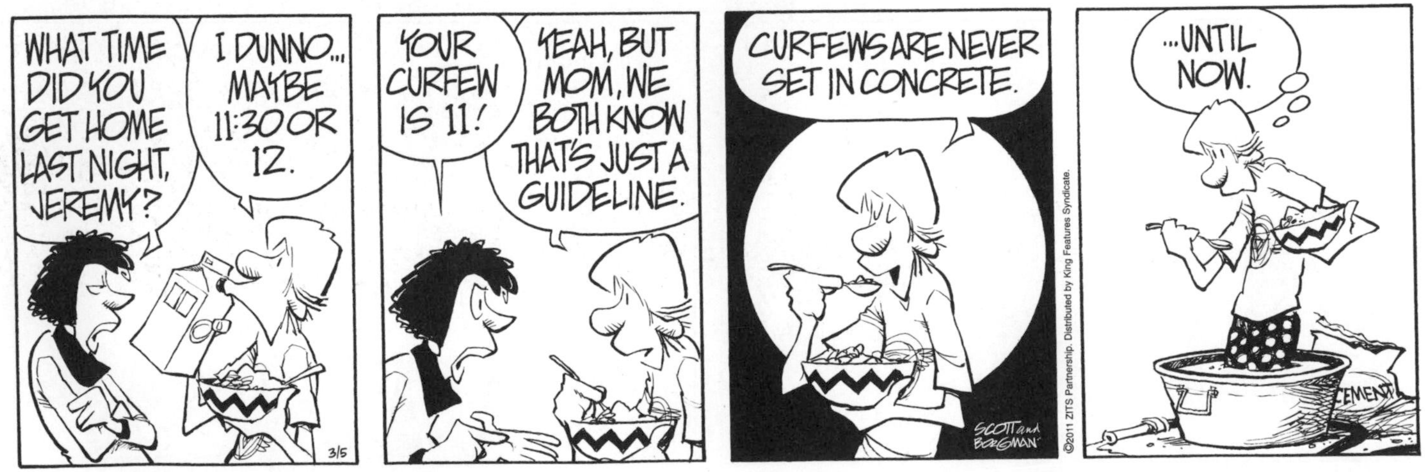
WHAT TIME DID YOU GET HOME LAST NIGHT, JEREMY?
I DUNNO... MAYBE 11:30 OR 12.
3/5
YOUR CURFEW IS 11!
YEAH, BUT MOM, WE BOTH KNOW THAT'S JUST A GUIDELINE.
CURFEWS ARE NEVER SET IN CONCRETE.
SCOTT and BORGMAN
©2011 ZITS Partnership. Distributed by King Features Syndicate.
...UNTIL NOW.
CEMENT

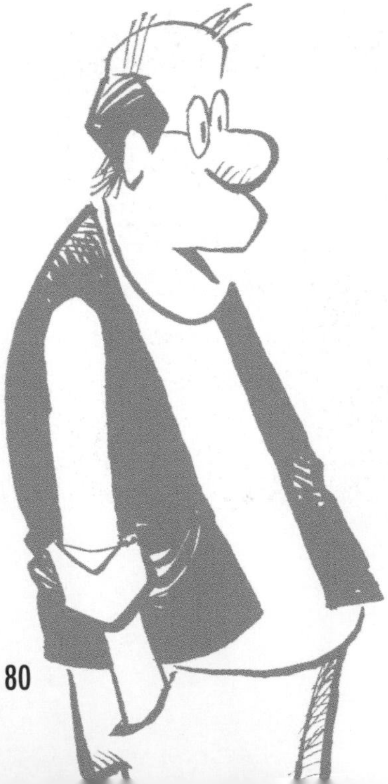

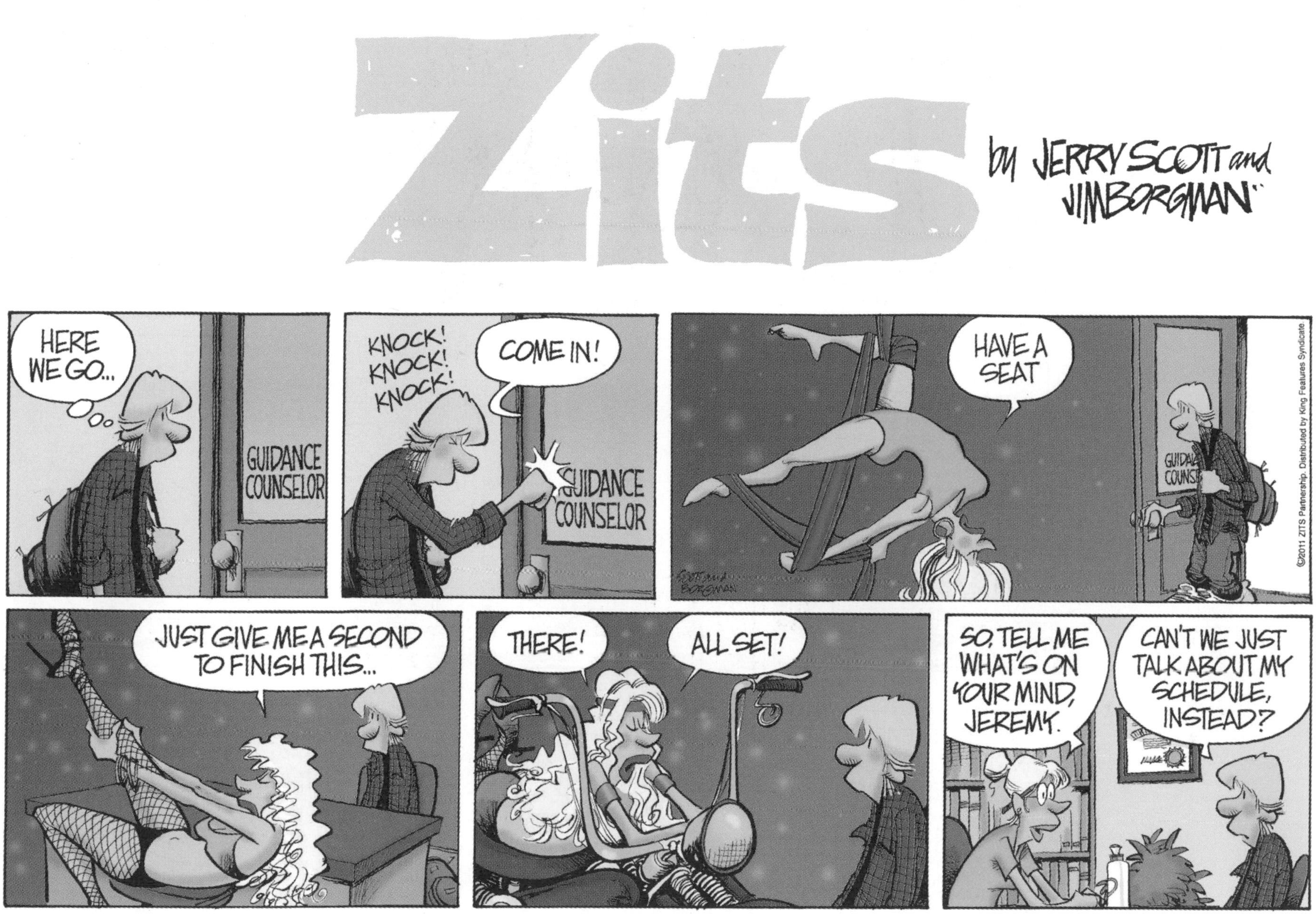
Zits
by JERRY SCOTT and JIM BORGMAN
HERE WE GO...
GUIDANCE COUNSELOR
KNOCK! KNOCK! KNOCK!
COME IN!
GUIDANCE COUNSELOR
HAVE A SEAT
©2011 ZITS Partnership. Distributed by King Features Syndicate.
JUST GIVE ME A SECOND TO FINISH THIS...
THERE!
ALL SET!
SO, TELL ME WHAT'S ON YOUR MIND, JEREMY.
CAN'T WE JUST TALK ABOUT MY SCHEDULE, INSTEAD?

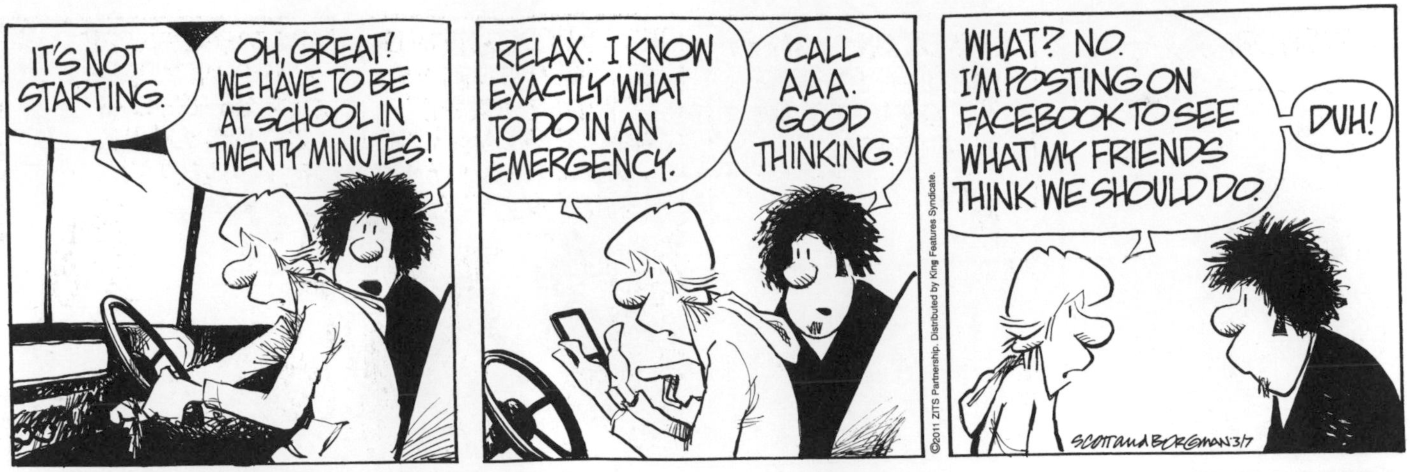
IT'S NOT STARTING.
OH, GREAT! WE HAVE TO BE AT SCHOOL IN TWENTY MINUTES!
RELAX. I KNOW EXACTLY WHAT TO DO IN AN EMERGENCY.
CALL AAA. GOOD THINKING.
WHAT? NO. I'M POSTING ON FACEBOOK TO SEE WHAT MY FRIENDS THINK WE SHOULD DO.
DUH!
SCOTT and BORGMAN 3/7
©2011 ZITS Partnership. Distributed by King Features Syndicate.

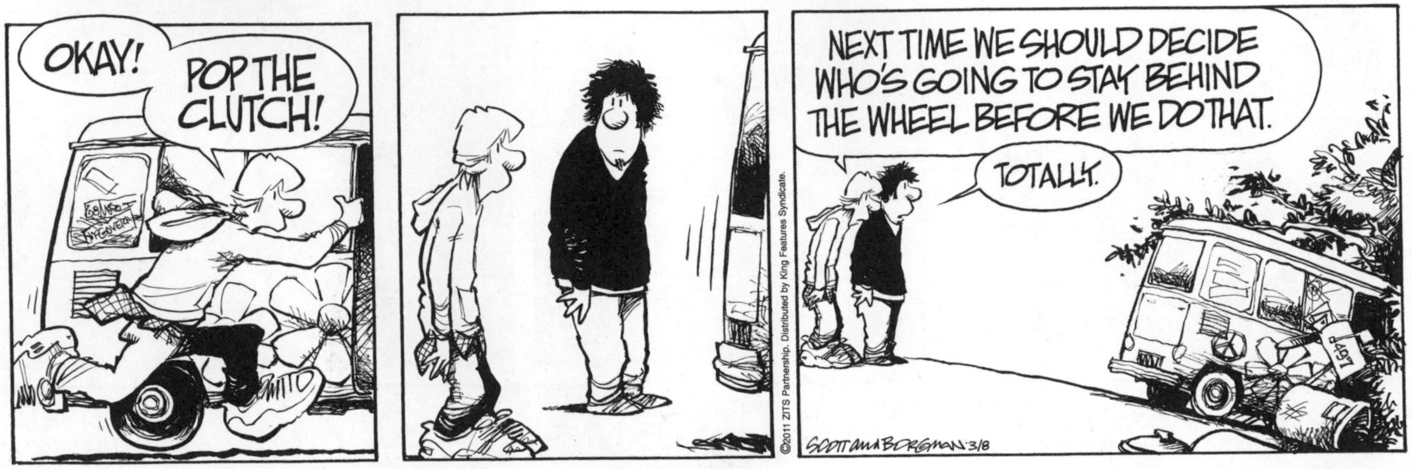
OKAY!
POP THE CLUTCH!
NEXT TIME WE SHOULD DECIDE WHO'S GOING TO STAY BEHIND THE WHEEL BEFORE WE DO THAT.
TOTALLY.
SCOTT and BORGMAN 3/8
©2011 ZITS Partnership. Distributed by King Features Syndicate.

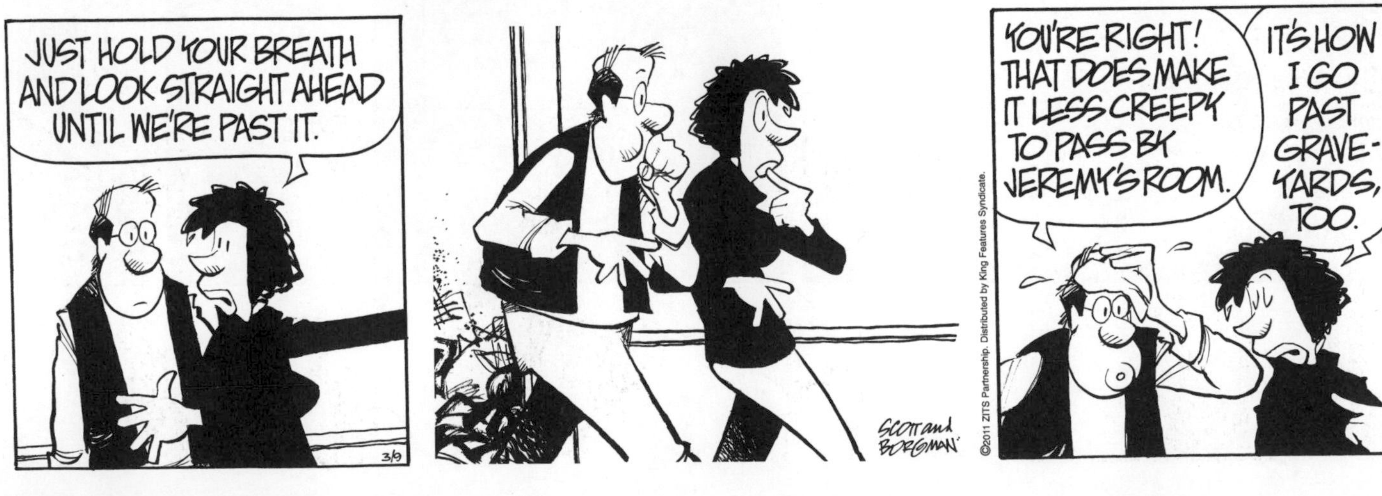
JUST HOLD YOUR BREATH AND LOOK STRAIGHT AHEAD UNTIL WE'RE PAST IT.
3/9
SCOTT and BORGMAN
YOU'RE RIGHT! THAT DOES MAKE IT LESS CREEPY TO PASS BY JEREMY'S ROOM.
IT'S HOW I GO PAST GRAVE-YARDS, TOO.
©2011 ZITS Partnership. Distributed by King Features Syndicate.

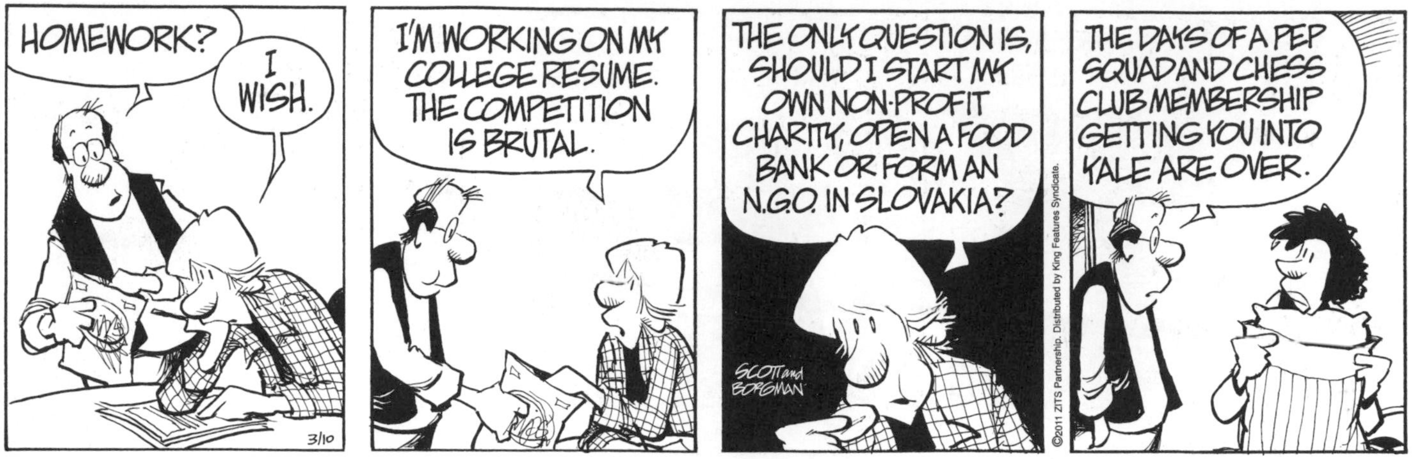
HOMEWORK?
I WISH.
I'M WORKING ON MY COLLEGE RESUME. THE COMPETITION IS BRUTAL.
THE ONLY QUESTION IS, SHOULD I START MY OWN NON-PROFIT CHARITY, OPEN A FOOD BANK OR FORM AN N.G.O. IN SLOVAKIA?
SCOTT and BORGMAN
©2011 ZITS Partnership. Distributed by King Features Syndicate.
THE DAYS OF A PEP SQUAD AND CHESS CLUB MEMBERSHIP GETTING YOU INTO YALE ARE OVER.
3/10

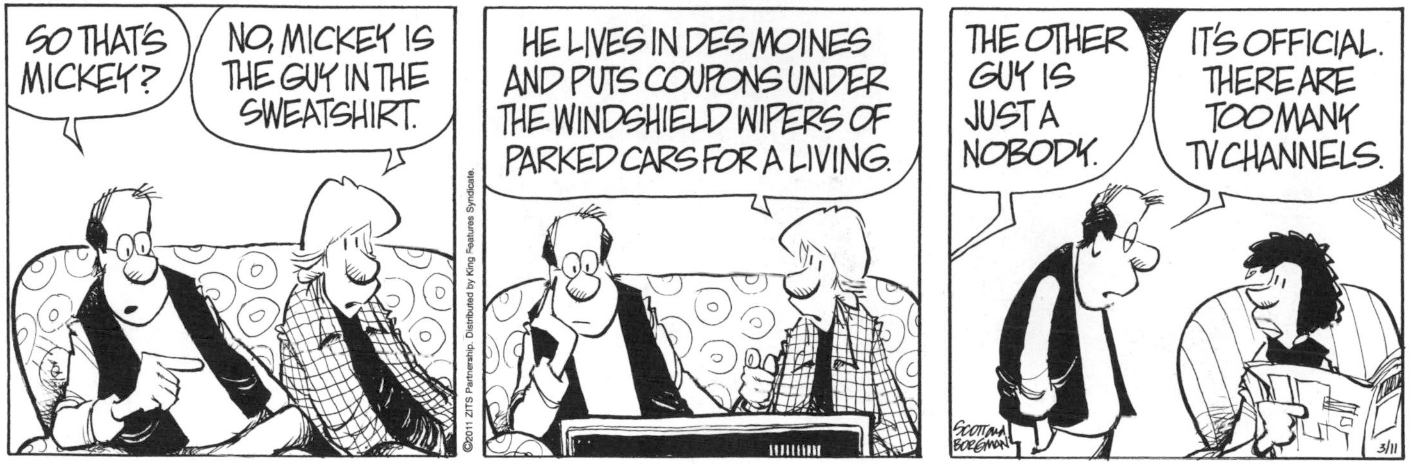
SO THAT'S MICKEY?
NO, MICKEY IS THE GUY IN THE SWEATSHIRT.
©2011 ZITS Partnership. Distributed by King Features Syndicate.
HE LIVES IN DES MOINES AND PUTS COUPONS UNDER THE WINDSHIELD WIPERS OF PARKED CARS FOR A LIVING.
THE OTHER GUY IS JUST A NOBODY.
IT'S OFFICIAL. THERE ARE TOO MANY TV CHANNELS.
SCOTT and BORGMAN
3/11

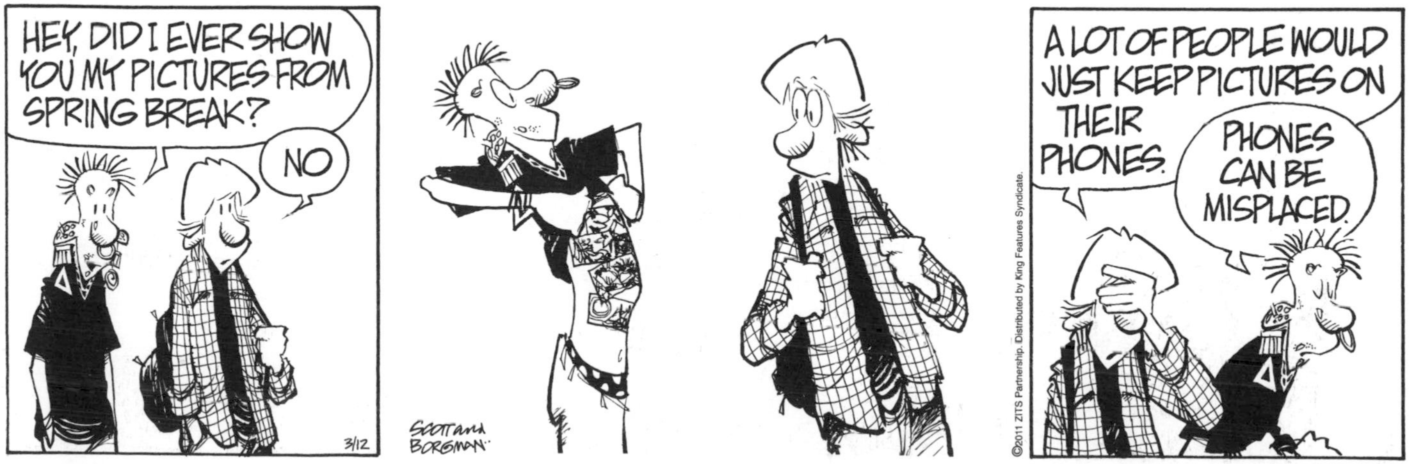
HEY, DID I EVER SHOW YOU MY PICTURES FROM SPRING BREAK?
NO
3/12
SCOTT and BORGMAN
©2011 ZITS Partnership. Distributed by King Features Syndicate.
A LOT OF PEOPLE WOULD JUST KEEP PICTURES ON THEIR PHONES.
PHONES CAN BE MISPLACED.

Zits

by JERRY SCOTT and JIM BORGMAN

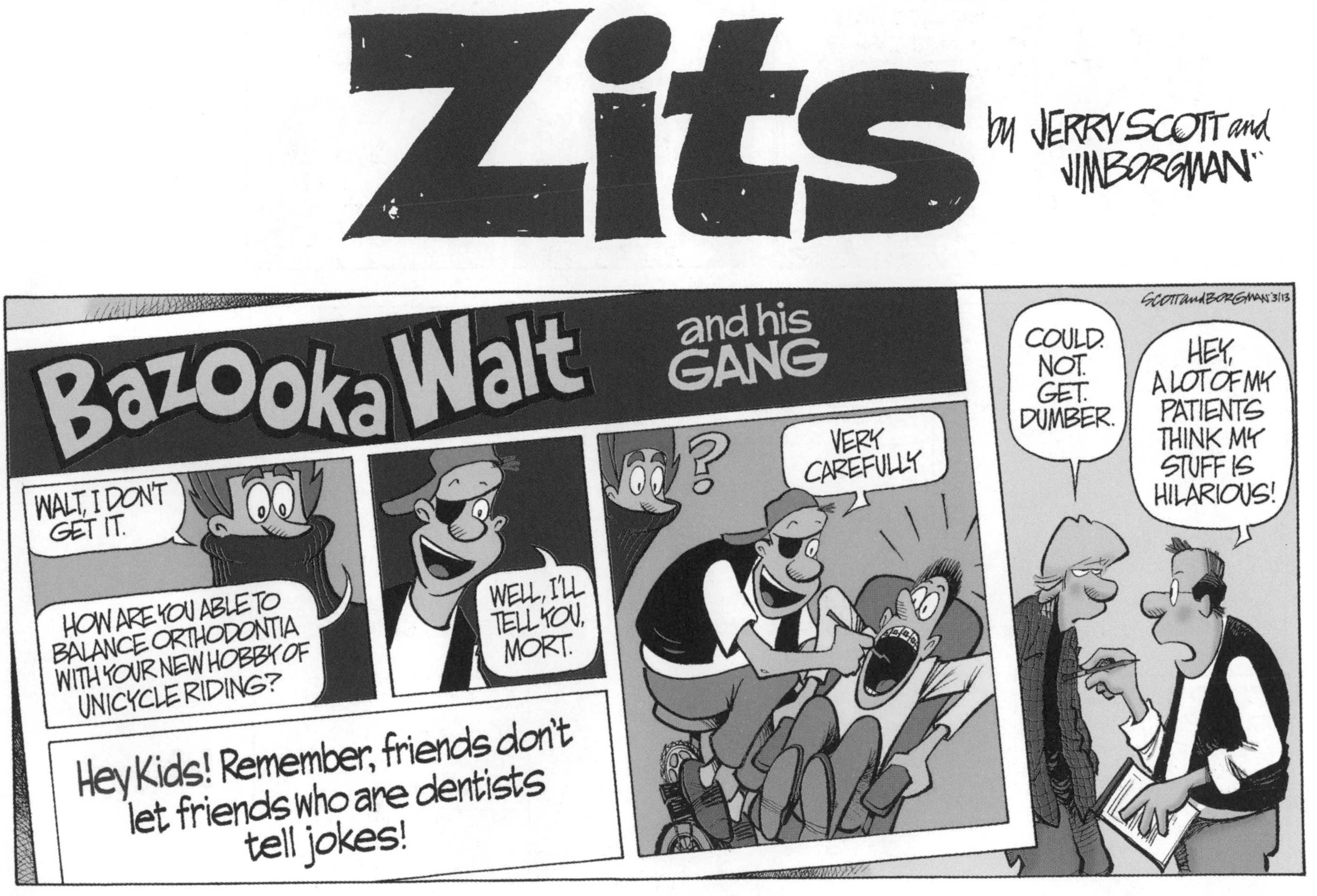

SCOTT and BORGMAN 3/13
Bazooka Walt and his GANG
WALT, I DON'T GET IT.
HOW ARE YOU ABLE TO BALANCE ORTHODONTIA WITH YOUR NEW HOBBY OF UNICYCLE RIDING?
WELL, I'LL TELL YOU, MORT.
VERY CAREFULLY
?
Hey Kids! Remember, friends don't let friends who are dentists tell jokes!
COULD. NOT. GET. DUMBER.
HEY, A LOT OF MY PATIENTS THINK MY STUFF IS HILARIOUS!

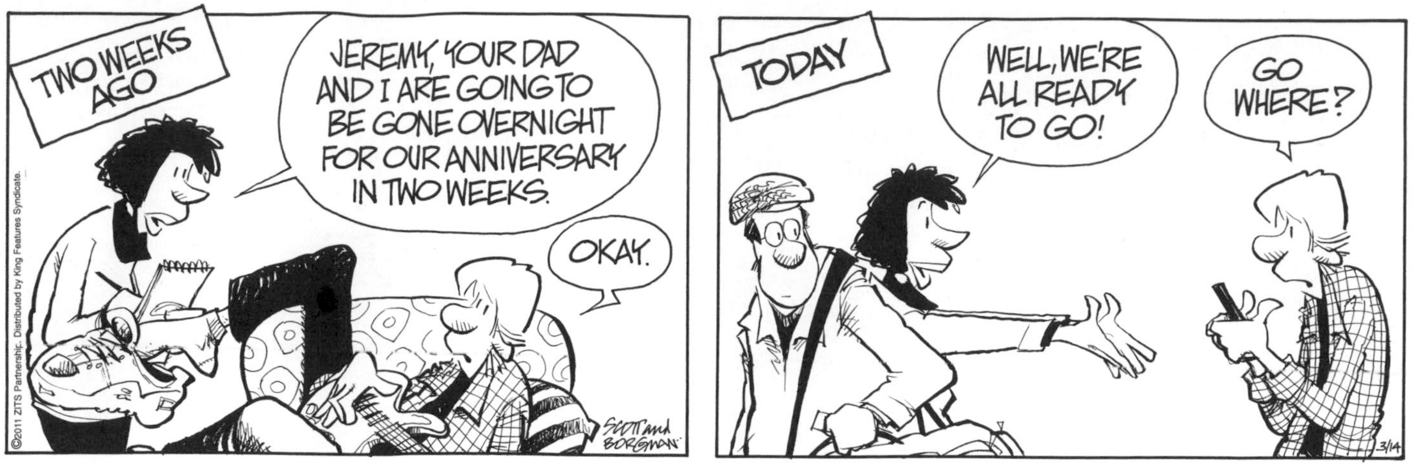
TWO WEEKS AGO
JEREMY, YOUR DAD AND I ARE GOING TO BE GONE OVERNIGHT FOR OUR ANNIVERSARY IN TWO WEEKS.
OKAY.
©2011 ZITS Partnership. Distributed by King Features Syndicate.
SCOTT and BORGMAN
TODAY
WELL, WE'RE ALL READY TO GO!
GO WHERE?
3/14

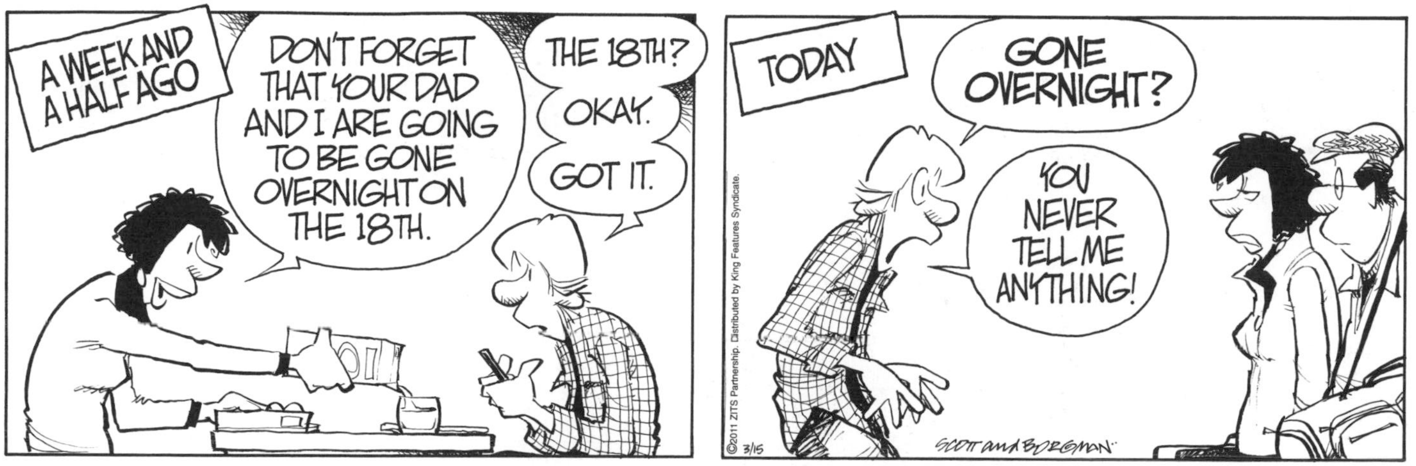
A WEEK AND A HALF AGO
DON'T FORGET THAT YOUR DAD AND I ARE GOING TO BE GONE OVERNIGHT ON THE 18TH.
THE 18TH?
OKAY.
GOT IT.
TODAY
GONE OVERNIGHT?
YOU NEVER TELL ME ANYTHING!
©2011 ZITS Partnership. Distributed by King Features Syndicate.
3/15
SCOTT and BORGMAN

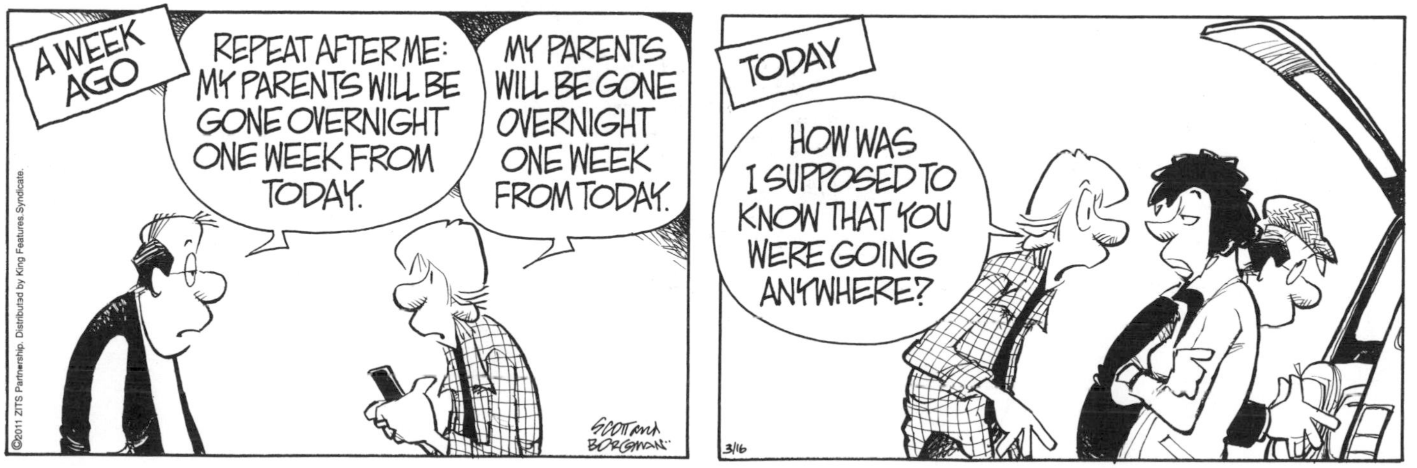
A WEEK AGO
REPEAT AFTER ME: MY PARENTS WILL BE GONE OVERNIGHT ONE WEEK FROM TODAY.
MY PARENTS WILL BE GONE OVERNIGHT ONE WEEK FROM TODAY.
©2011 ZITS Partnership. Distributed by King Features Syndicate.
SCOTT and BORGMAN
3/16
TODAY
HOW WAS I SUPPOSED TO KNOW THAT YOU WERE GOING ANYWHERE?

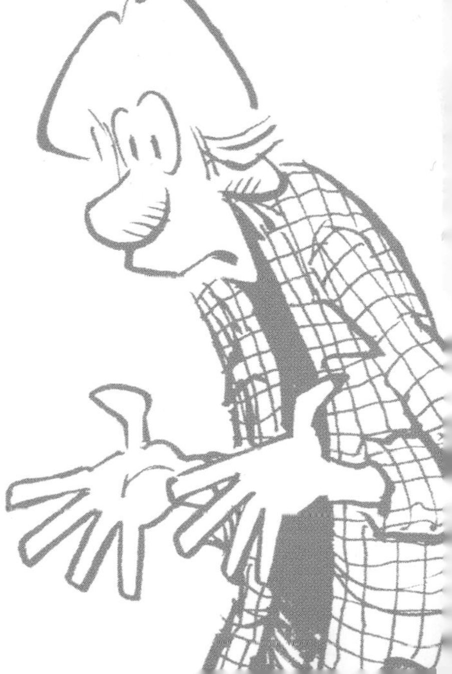

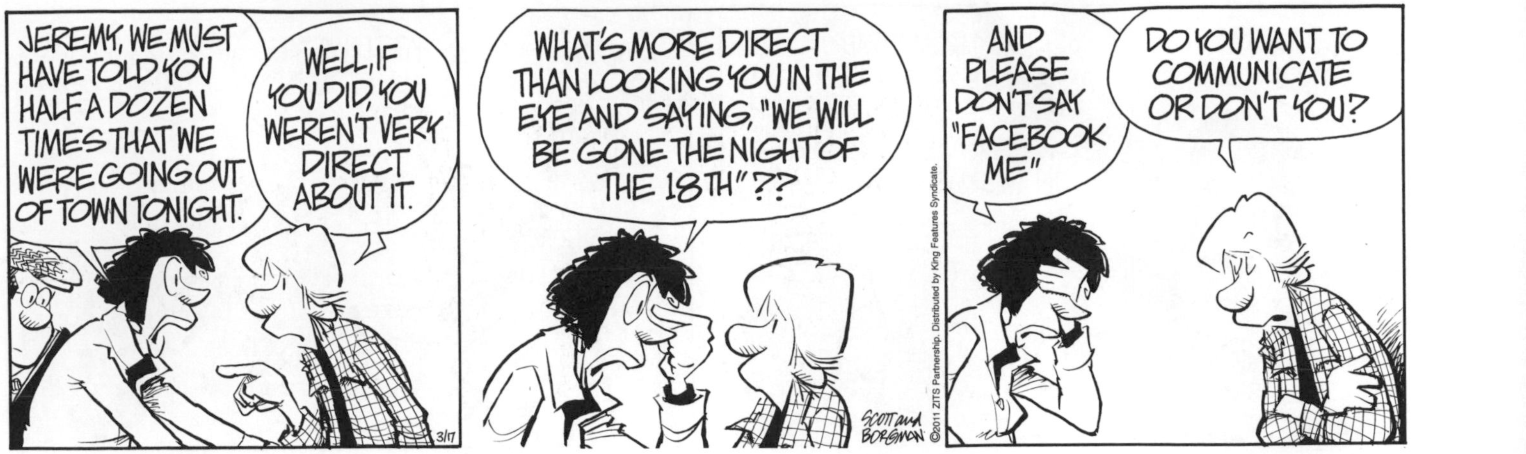
JEREMY, WE MUST HAVE TOLD YOU HALF A DOZEN TIMES THAT WE WERE GOING OUT OF TOWN TONIGHT.
WELL, IF YOU DID, YOU WEREN'T VERY DIRECT ABOUT IT.
3/17
WHAT'S MORE DIRECT THAN LOOKING YOU IN THE EYE AND SAYING, "WE WILL BE GONE THE NIGHT OF THE 18TH"??
SCOTT and BORGMAN
©2011 ZITS Partnership. Distributed by King Features Syndicate.
AND PLEASE DON'T SAY "FACEBOOK ME"
DO YOU WANT TO COMMUNICATE OR DON'T YOU?

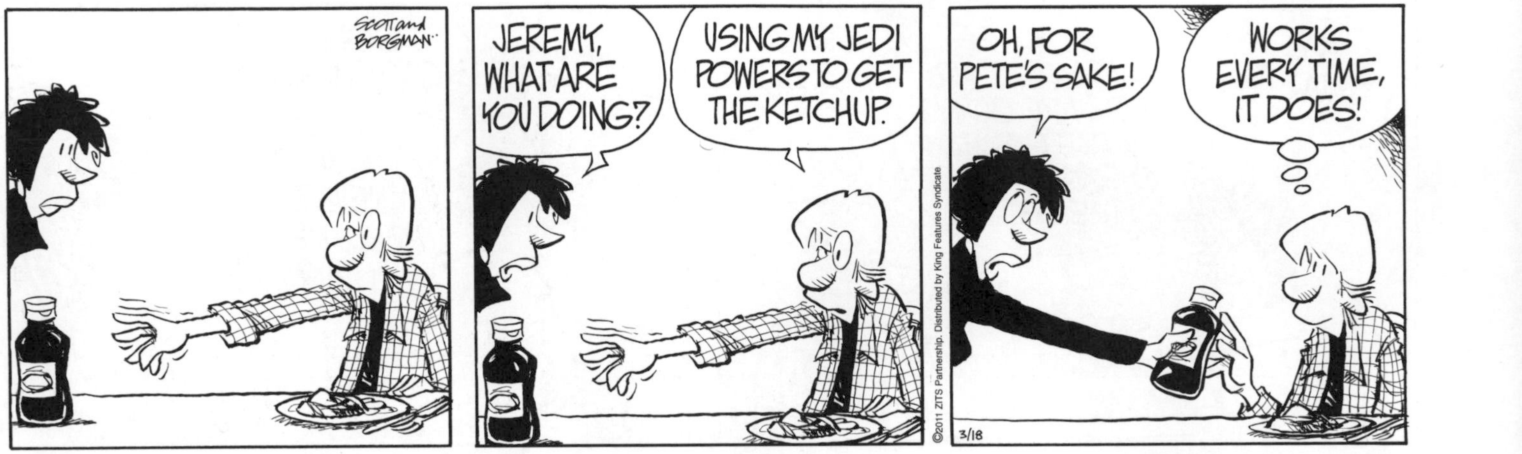
SCOTT and BORGMAN
JEREMY, WHAT ARE YOU DOING?
USING MY JEDI POWERS TO GET THE KETCHUP.
©2011 ZITS Partnership. Distributed by King Features Syndicate
OH, FOR PETE'S SAKE!
WORKS EVERY TIME, IT DOES!
3/18

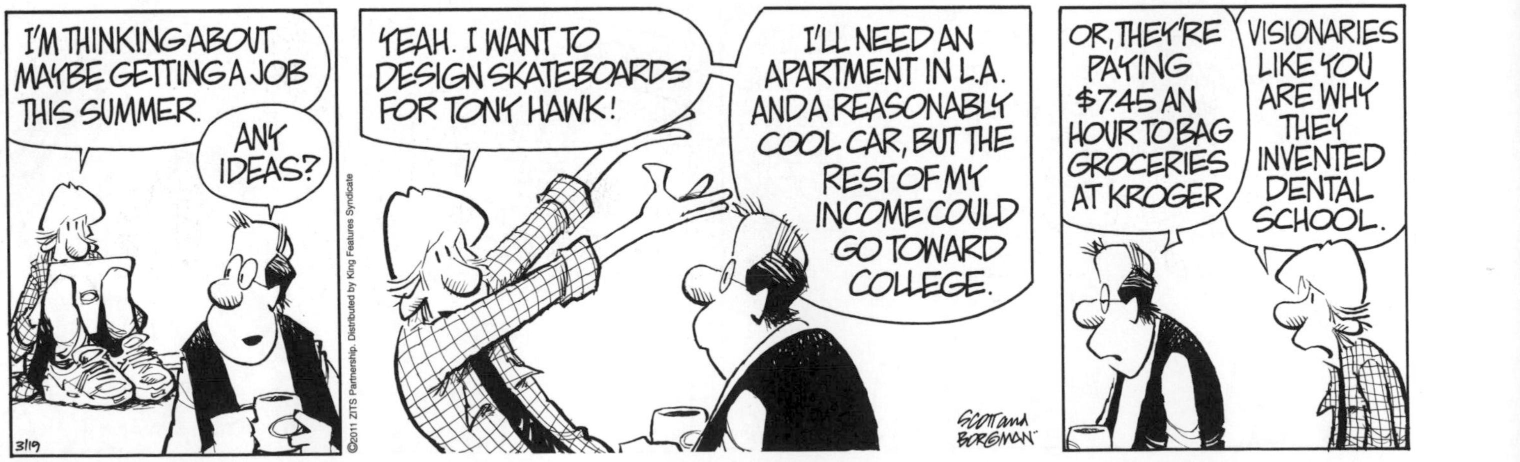
I'M THINKING ABOUT MAYBE GETTING A JOB THIS SUMMER.
ANY IDEAS?
3/19
©2011 ZITS Partnership. Distributed by King Features Syndicate
YEAH. I WANT TO DESIGN SKATEBOARDS FOR TONY HAWK!
I'LL NEED AN APARTMENT IN L.A. AND A REASONABLY COOL CAR, BUT THE REST OF MY INCOME COULD GO TOWARD COLLEGE.
SCOTT and BORGMAN
OR, THEY'RE PAYING $7.45 AN HOUR TO BAG GROCERIES AT KROGER
VISIONARIES LIKE YOU ARE WHY THEY INVENTED DENTAL SCHOOL.

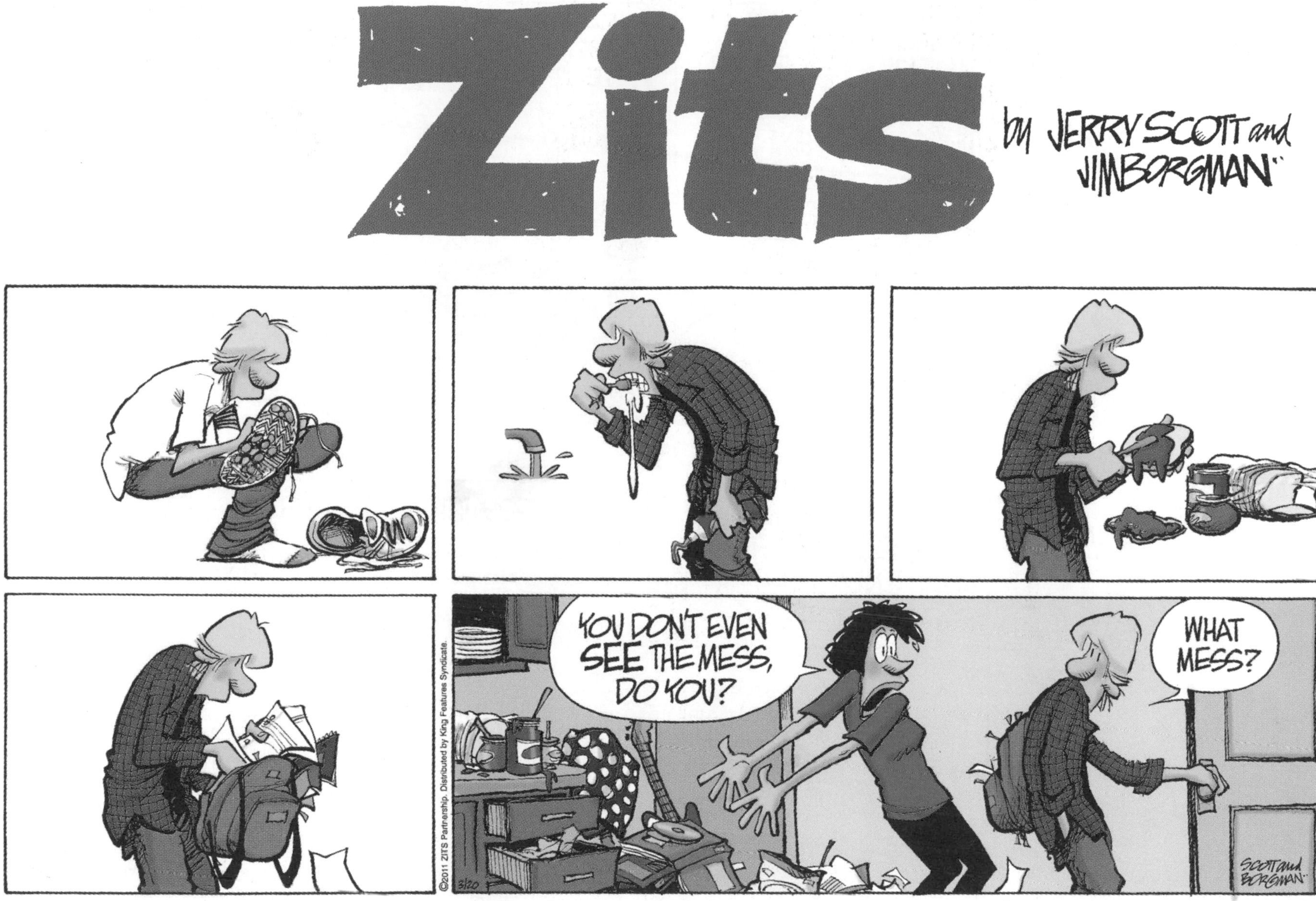
Zits
by JERRY SCOTT and JIM BORGMAN
©2011 ZITS Partnership. Distributed by King Features Syndicate.
YOU DON'T EVEN SEE THE MESS, DO YOU?
WHAT MESS?
SCOTT and BORGMAN

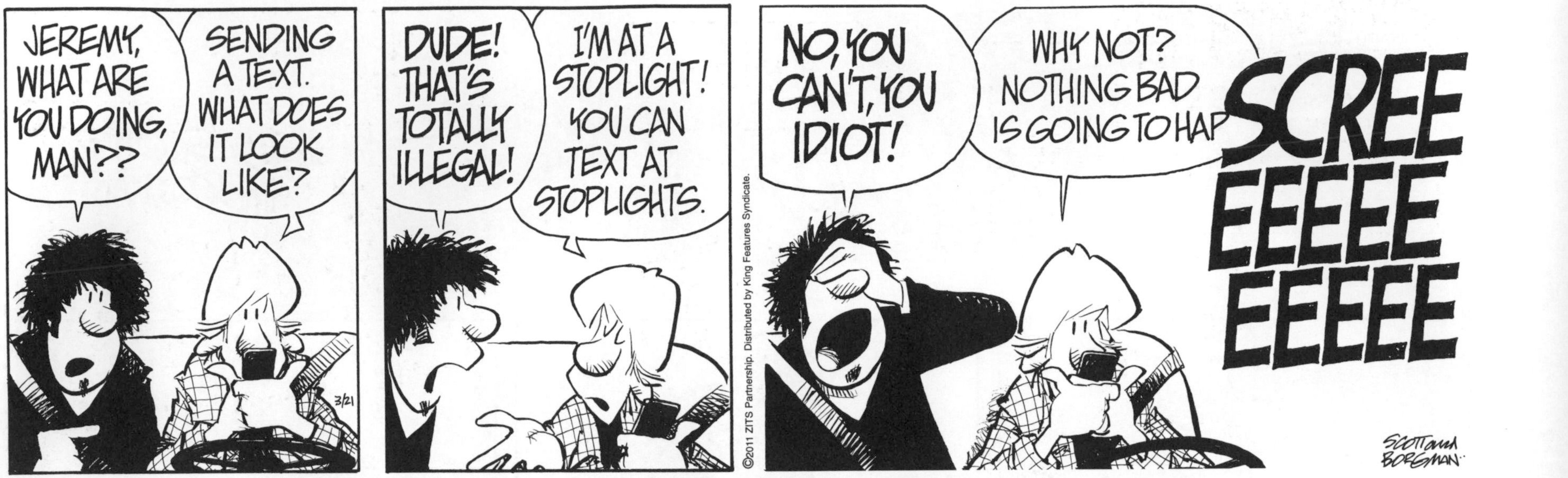
JEREMY, WHAT ARE YOU DOING, MAN??
SENDING A TEXT. WHAT DOES IT LOOK LIKE?
3/21
DUDE! THAT'S TOTALLY ILLEGAL!
I'M AT A STOPLIGHT! YOU CAN TEXT AT STOPLIGHTS.
NO, YOU CAN'T, YOU IDIOT!
WHY NOT? NOTHING BAD IS GOING TO HAP
SCREEEEEEEEEEEE
SCOTT and BORGMAN

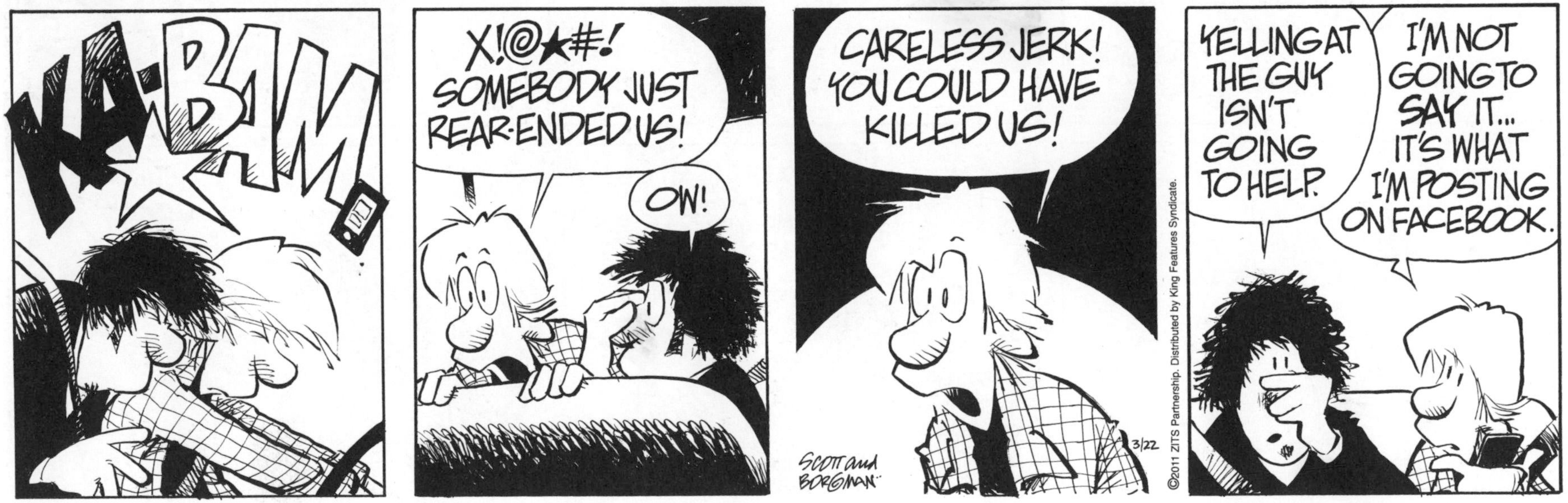
KA-BAM
X!@★#! SOMEBODY JUST REAR-ENDED US!
OW!
CARELESS JERK! YOU COULD HAVE KILLED US!
SCOTT and BORGMAN
3/22
YELLING AT THE GUY ISN'T GOING TO HELP.
I'M NOT GOING TO SAY IT... IT'S WHAT I'M POSTING ON FACEBOOK.

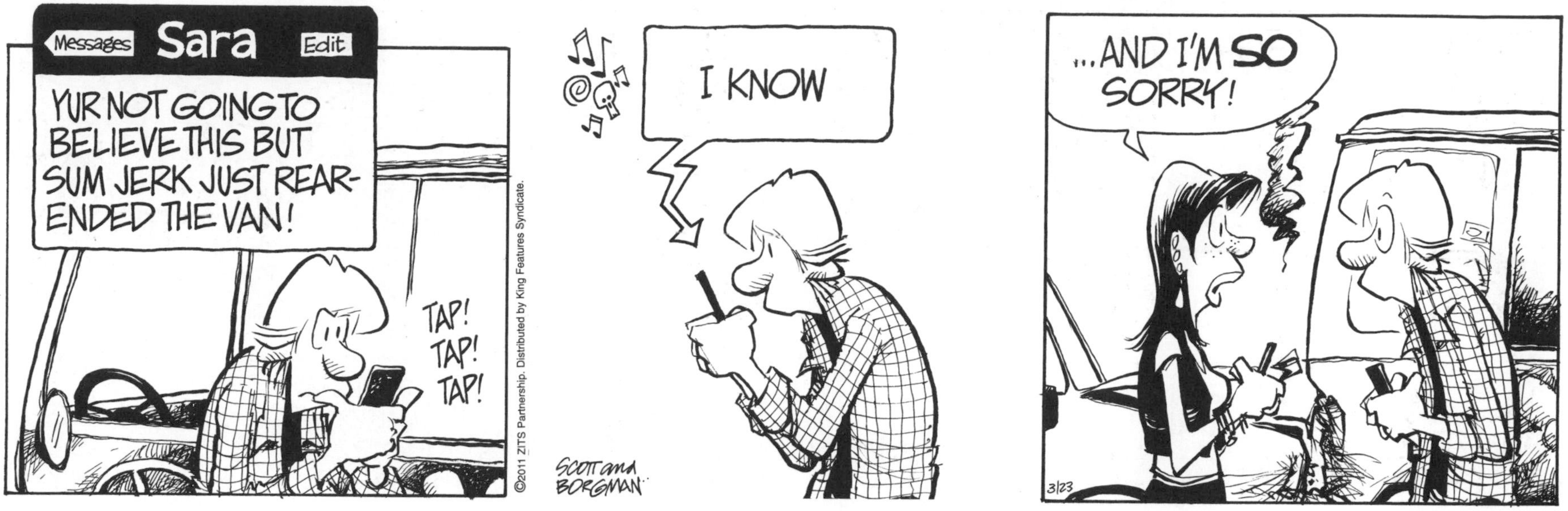
Messages
Sara
Edit
YUR NOT GOING TO BELIEVE THIS BUT SUM JERK JUST REAR-ENDED THE VAN!
TAP! TAP! TAP!
©2011 ZITS Partnership. Distributed by King Features Syndicate.
SCOTT and BORGMAN
I KNOW
...AND I'M SO SORRY!
3/23

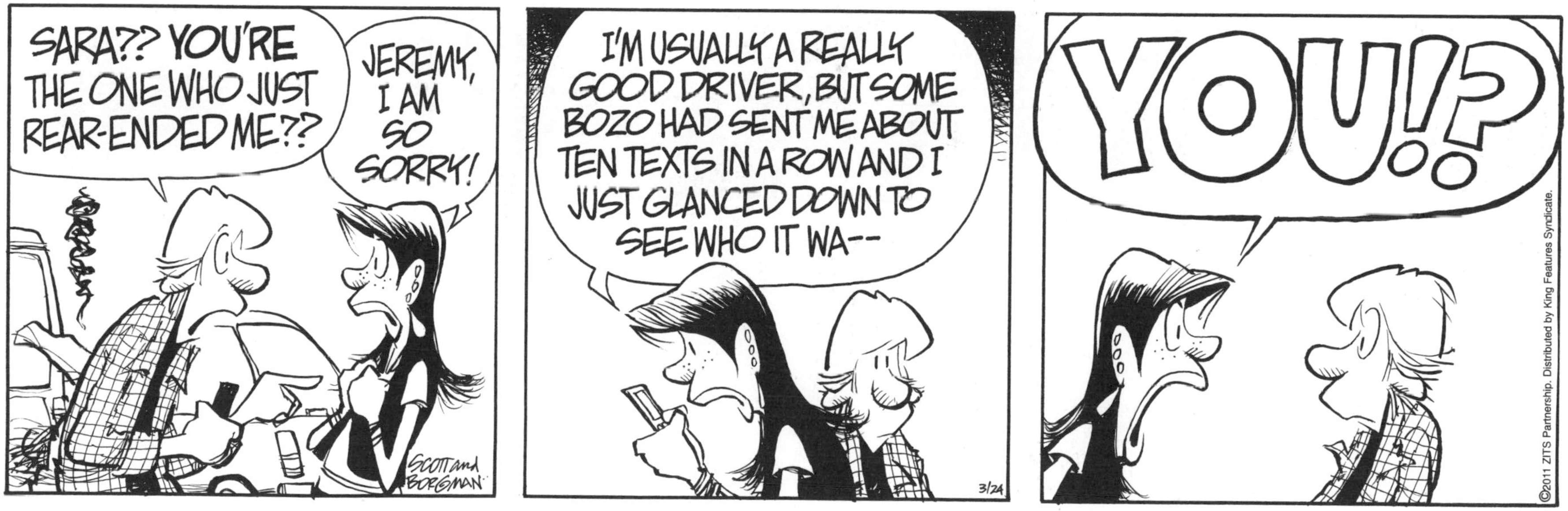
SARA?? YOU'RE THE ONE WHO JUST REAR-ENDED ME??
JEREMY, I AM SO SORRY!
SCOTT and BORGMAN
I'M USUALLY A REALLY GOOD DRIVER, BUT SOME BOZO HAD SENT ME ABOUT TEN TEXTS IN A ROW AND I JUST GLANCED DOWN TO SEE WHO IT WA--
3/24
YOU!?
©2011 ZITS Partnership. Distributed by King Features Syndicate.

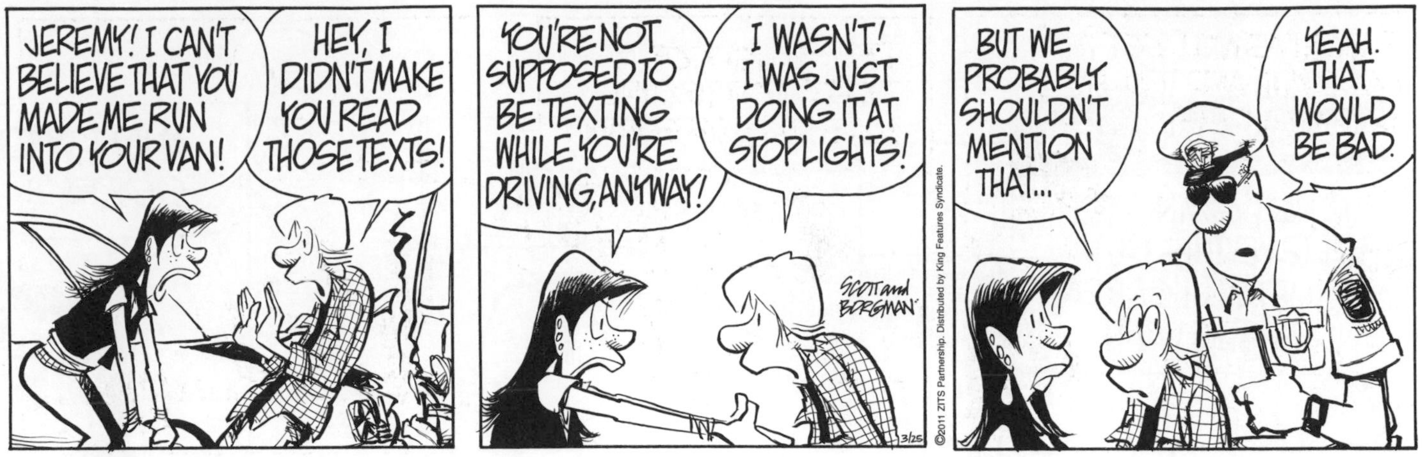
JEREMY! I CAN'T BELIEVE THAT YOU MADE ME RUN INTO YOUR VAN!
HEY, I DIDN'T MAKE YOU READ THOSE TEXTS!
YOU'RE NOT SUPPOSED TO BE TEXTING WHILE YOU'RE DRIVING, ANYWAY!
I WASN'T! I WAS JUST DOING IT AT STOPLIGHTS!
SCOTT and BORGMAN
3/25
©2011 ZITS Partnership. Distributed by King Features Syndicate.
BUT WE PROBABLY SHOULDN'T MENTION THAT...
YEAH. THAT WOULD BE BAD.

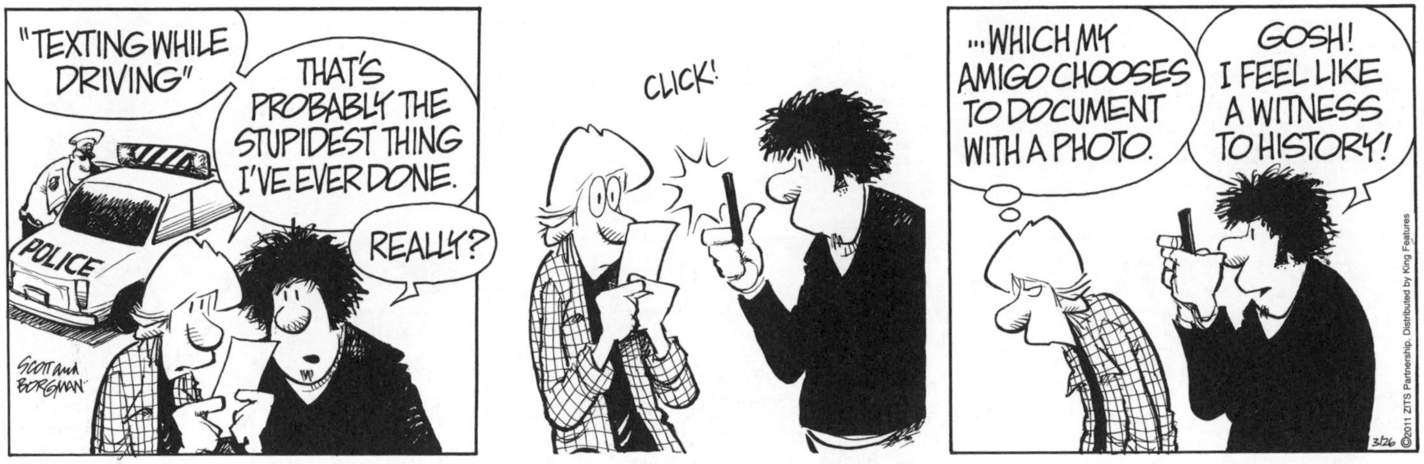
"TEXTING WHILE DRIVING"
THAT'S PROBABLY THE STUPIDEST THING I'VE EVER DONE.
REALLY?
POLICE
SCOTT and BORGMAN
CLICK!
...WHICH MY AMIGO CHOOSES TO DOCUMENT WITH A PHOTO.
GOSH! I FEEL LIKE A WITNESS TO HISTORY!
3/26
©2011 ZITS Partnership. Distributed by King Features

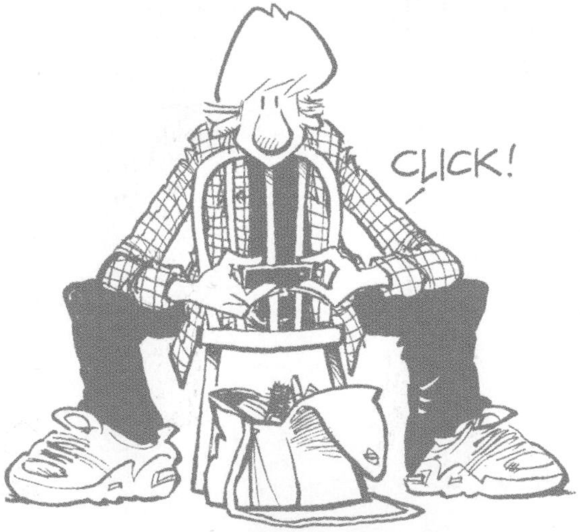
CLICK!

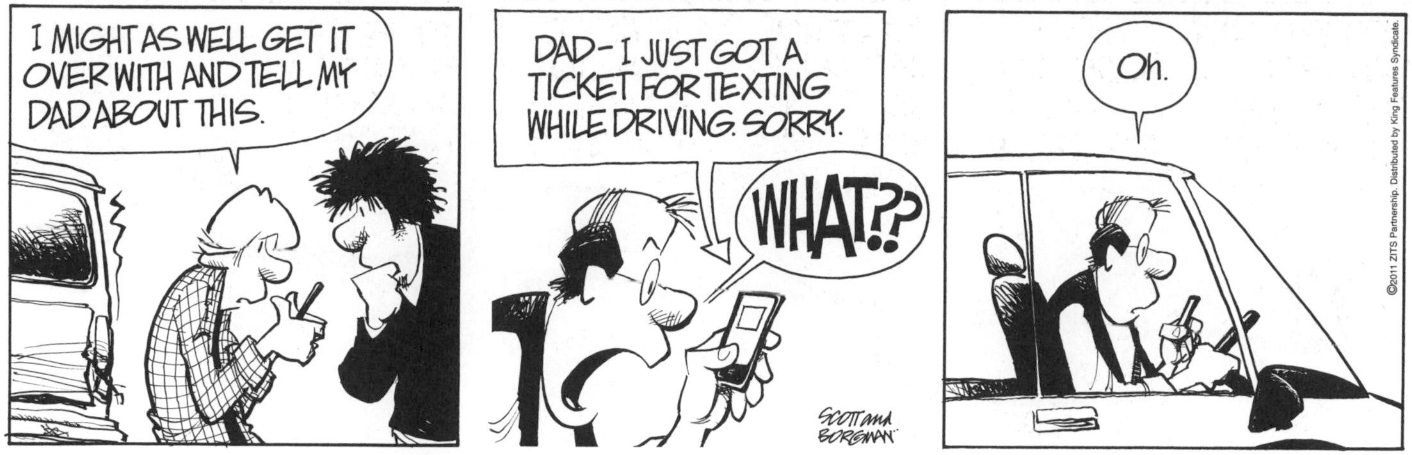
I MIGHT AS WELL GET IT OVER WITH AND TELL MY DAD ABOUT THIS.
DAD- I JUST GOT A TICKET FOR TEXTING WHILE DRIVING. SORRY.
WHAT??
Oh.
SCOTT and BORGMAN
©2011 ZITS Partnership. Distributed by King Features Syndicate.

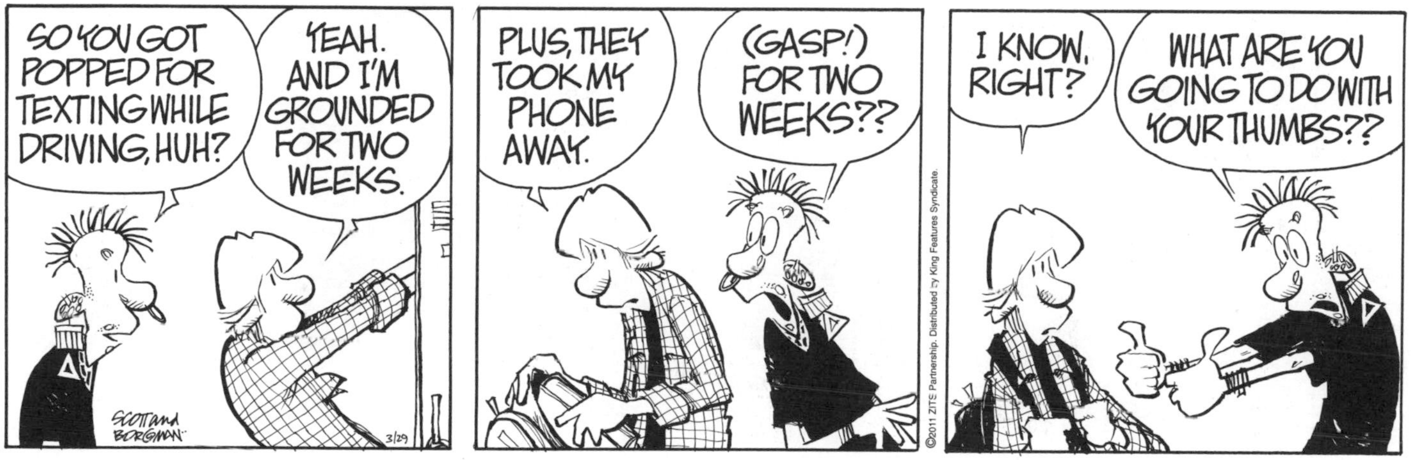
SO YOU GOT POPPED FOR TEXTING WHILE DRIVING, HUH?
YEAH. AND I'M GROUNDED FOR TWO WEEKS.
SCOTT and BORGMAN
3/29
PLUS, THEY TOOK MY PHONE AWAY.
(GASP!) FOR TWO WEEKS??
©2011 ZITS Partnership. Distributed by King Features Syndicate.
I KNOW, RIGHT?
WHAT ARE YOU GOING TO DO WITH YOUR THUMBS??

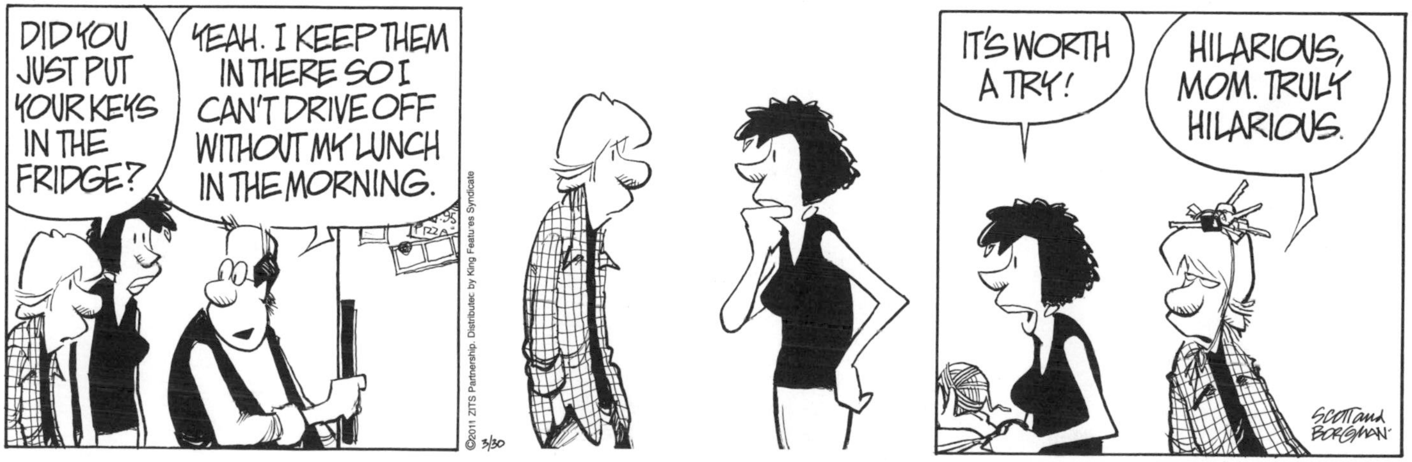
DID YOU JUST PUT YOUR KEYS IN THE FRIDGE?
YEAH. I KEEP THEM IN THERE SO I CAN'T DRIVE OFF WITHOUT MY LUNCH IN THE MORNING.
©2011 ZITS Partnership. Distributed by King Features Syndicate
3/30
IT'S WORTH A TRY!
HILARIOUS, MOM. TRULY HILARIOUS.
SCOTT and BORGMAN

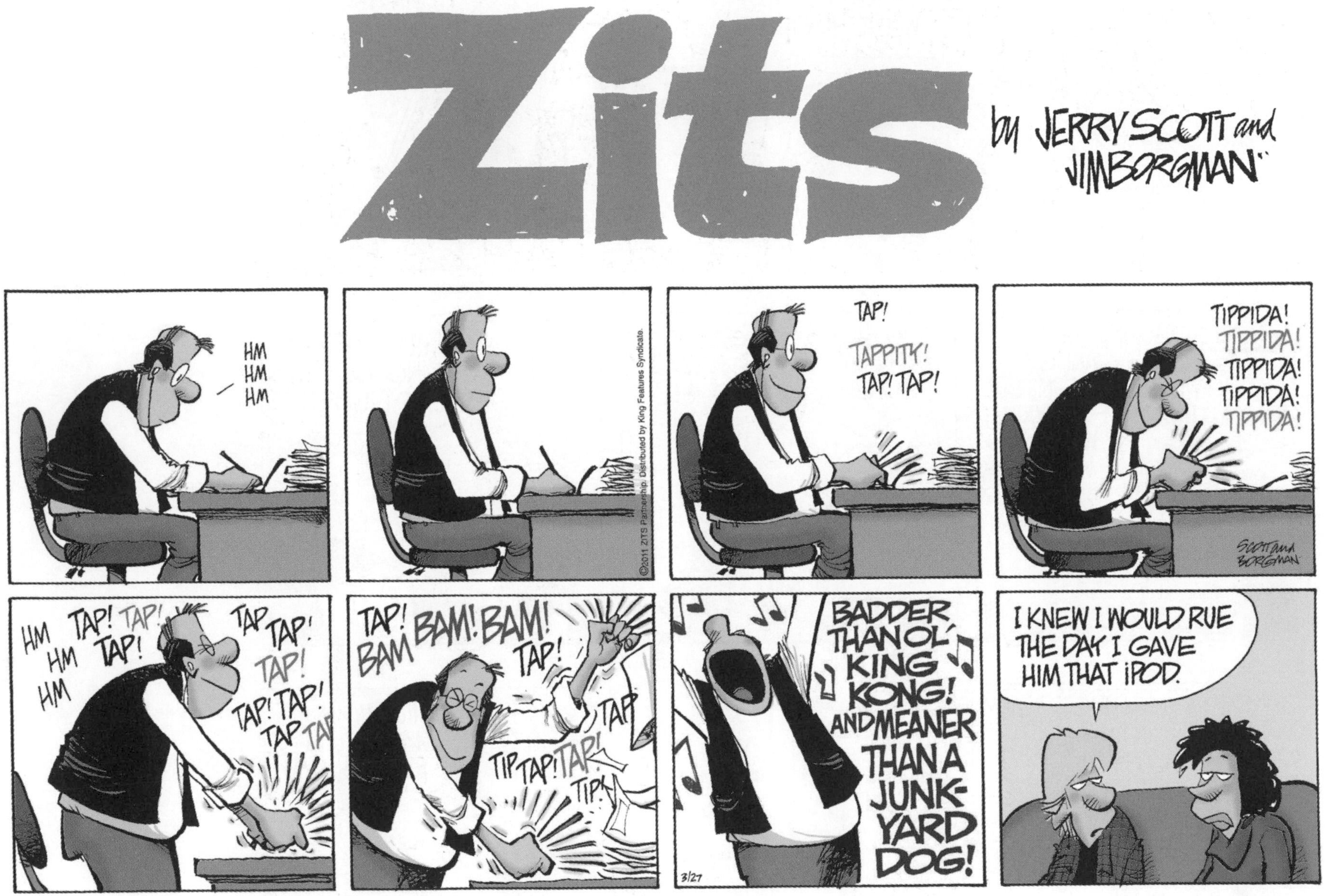
Zits
by JERRY SCOTT and JIM BORGMAN
HM HM HM
©2011 ZITS Partnership. Distributed by King Features Syndicate.
TAP!
TAPPITY!
TAP! TAP!
TIPPIDA!
TIPPIDA!
TIPPIDA!
TIPPIDA!
TIPPIDA!
SCOTT and BORGMAN
HM HM HM
TAP! TAP! TAP!
TAP TAP! TAP!
TAP! TAP! TAP
TAP! BAM BAM! BAM! TAP!
TAP
TIP TAP! TAP!
TIP!
3/27
BADDER THAN OL' KING KONG! AND MEANER THAN A JUNK-YARD DOG!
I KNEW I WOULD RUE THE DAY I GAVE HIM THAT iPOD.

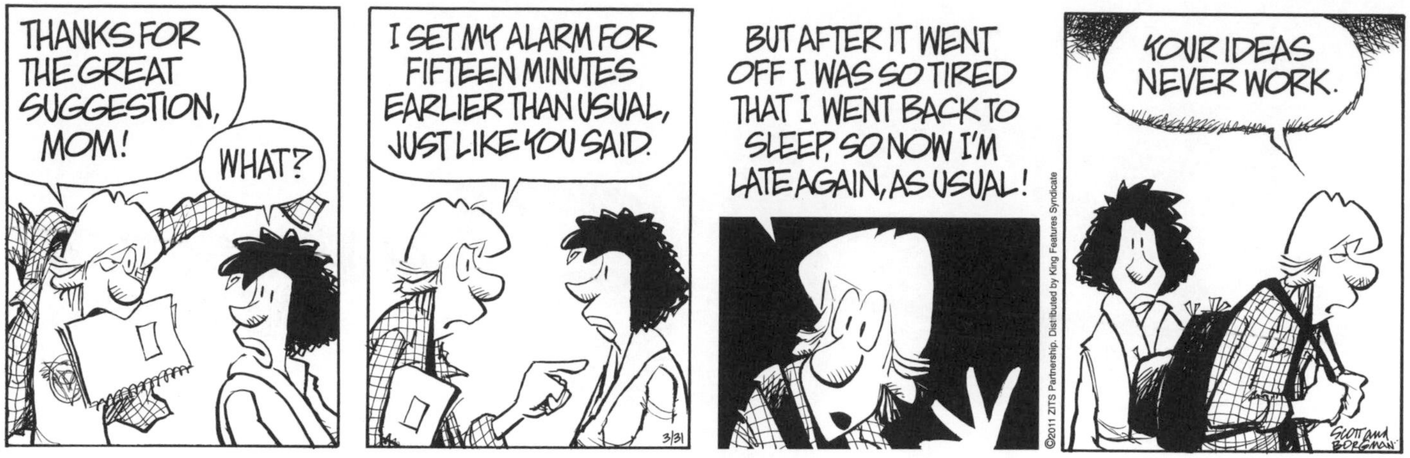
THANKS FOR THE GREAT SUGGESTION, MOM!
WHAT?
I SET MY ALARM FOR FIFTEEN MINUTES EARLIER THAN USUAL, JUST LIKE YOU SAID.
3/31
BUT AFTER IT WENT OFF I WAS SO TIRED THAT I WENT BACK TO SLEEP, SO NOW I'M LATE AGAIN, AS USUAL!
©2011 ZITS Partnership. Distributed by King Features Syndicate
YOUR IDEAS NEVER WORK.
SCOTT AND BORGMAN

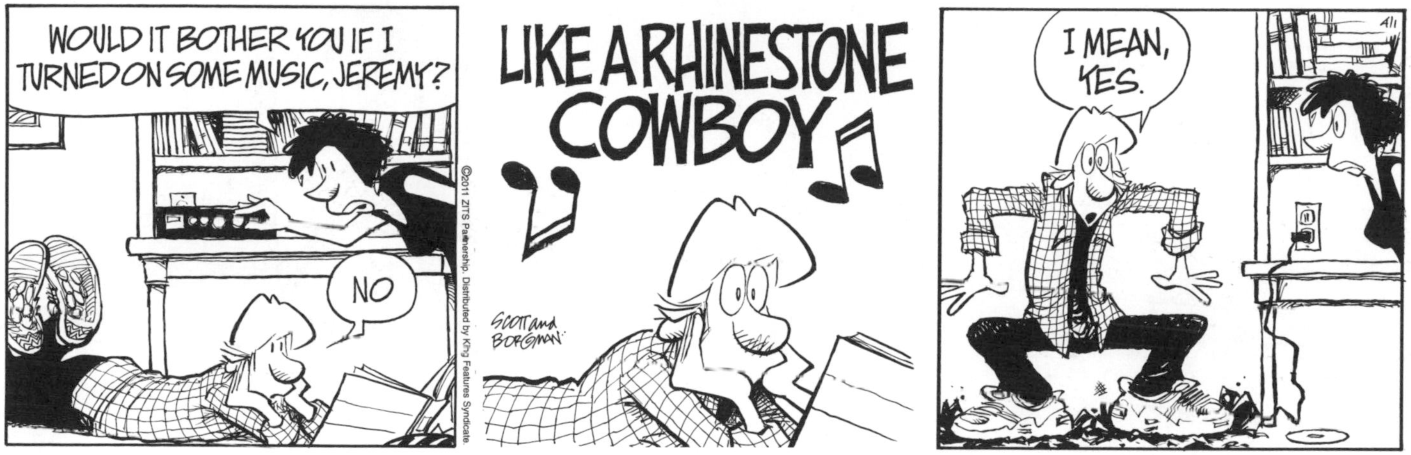
WOULD IT BOTHER YOU IF I TURNED ON SOME MUSIC, JEREMY?
NO
©2011 ZITS Partnership. Distributed by King Features Syndicate.
LIKE A RHINESTONE COWBOY
SCOTT AND BORGMAN
4/1
I MEAN, YES.

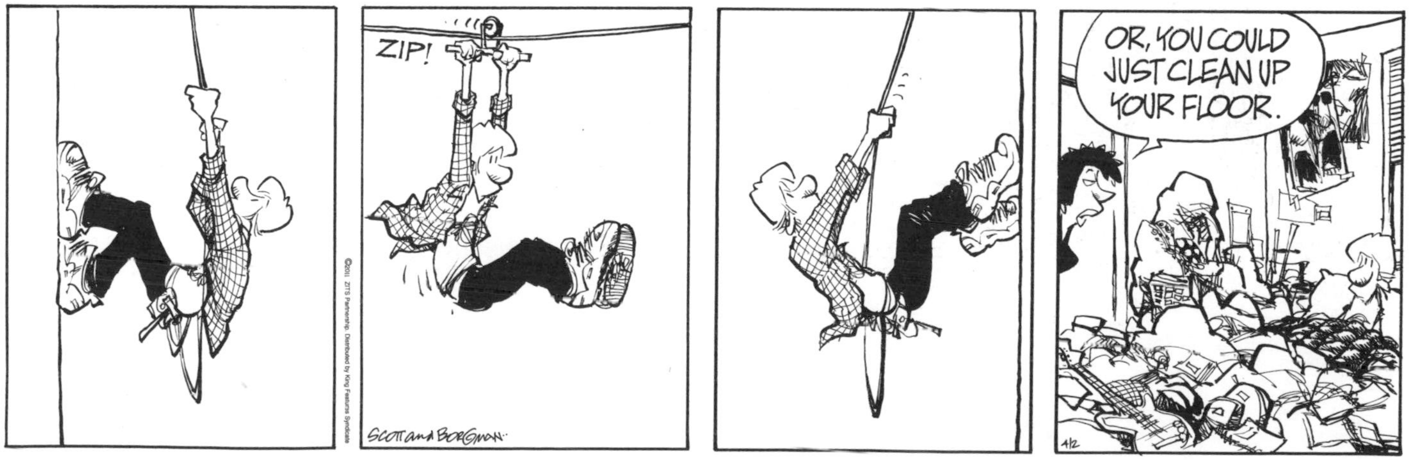
ZIP!
SCOTT AND BORGMAN
OR, YOU COULD JUST CLEAN UP YOUR FLOOR.
4/2

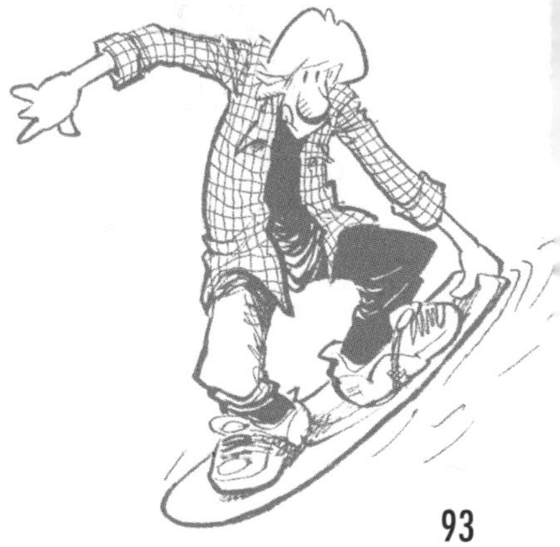

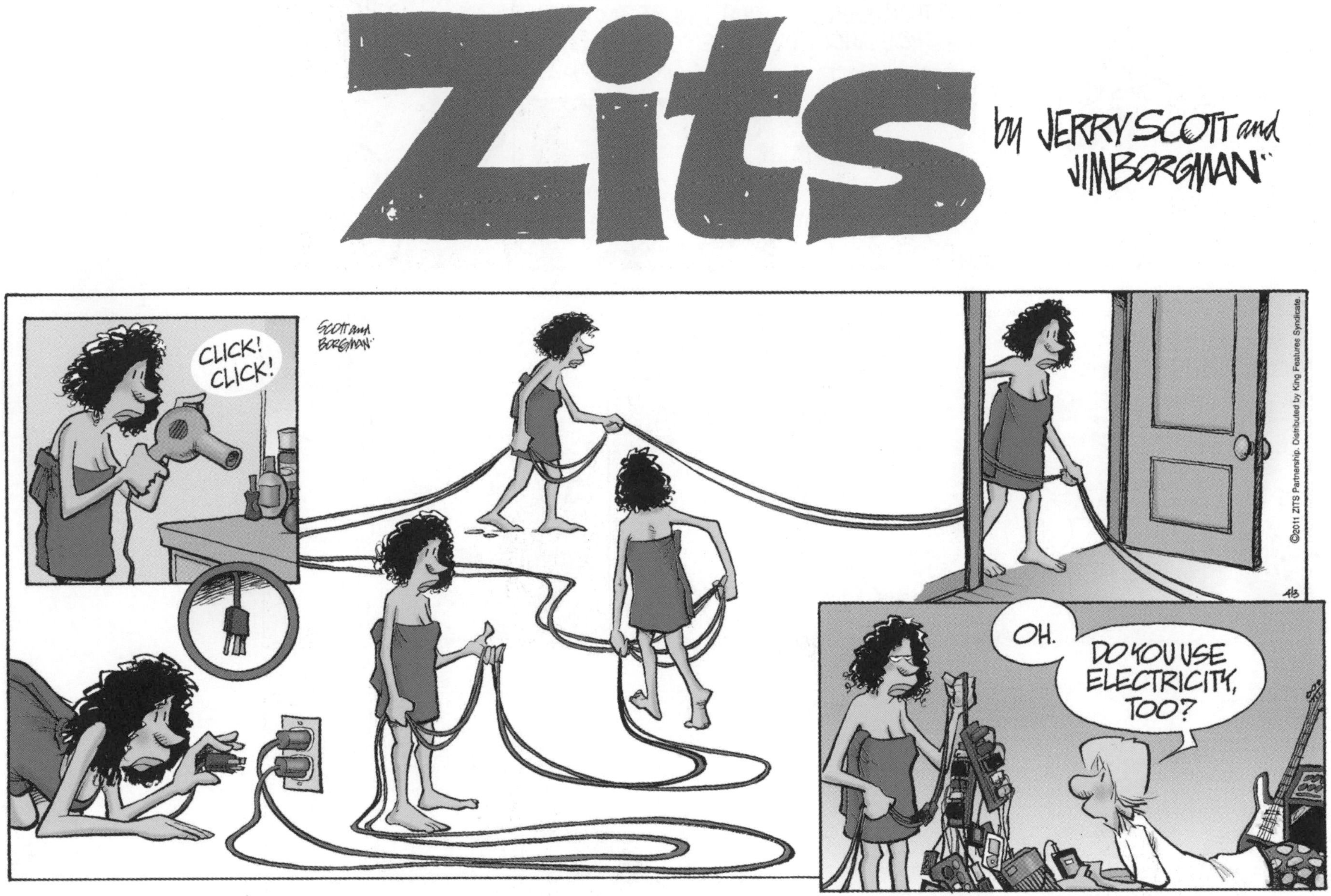
Zits
by JERRY SCOTT and JIM BORGMAN
SCOTT and BORGMAN
CLICK! CLICK!
©2011 ZITS Partnership. Distributed by King Features Syndicate.
OH.
DO YOU USE ELECTRICITY, TOO?

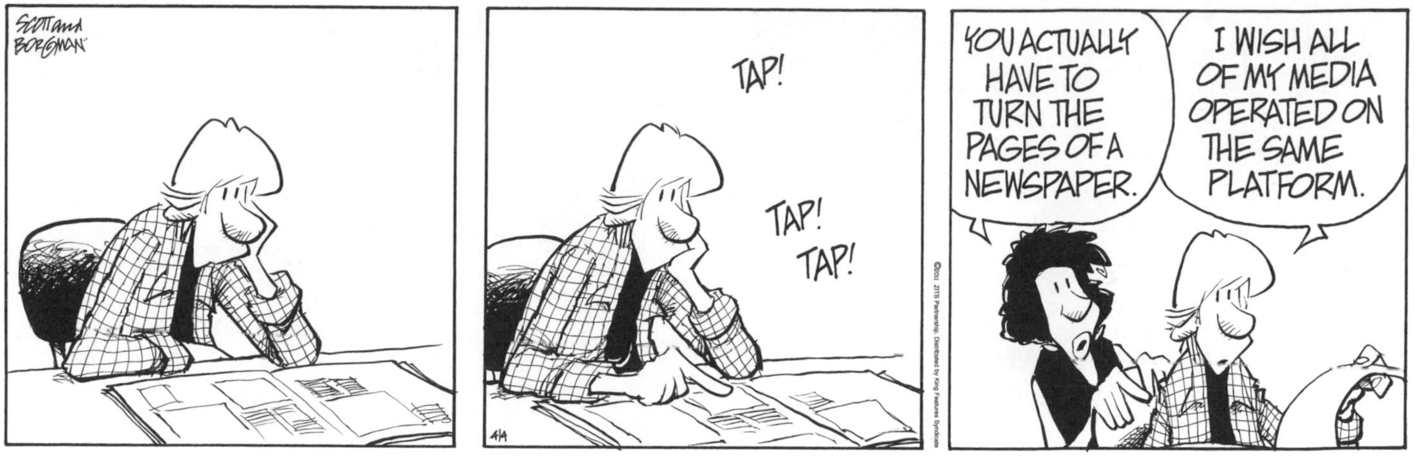
SCOTT and BORGMAN
TAP!
TAP!
TAP!
4/4
©2011 ZITS Partnership. Distributed by King Features Syndicate
YOU ACTUALLY HAVE TO TURN THE PAGES OF A NEWSPAPER.
I WISH ALL OF MY MEDIA OPERATED ON THE SAME PLATFORM.

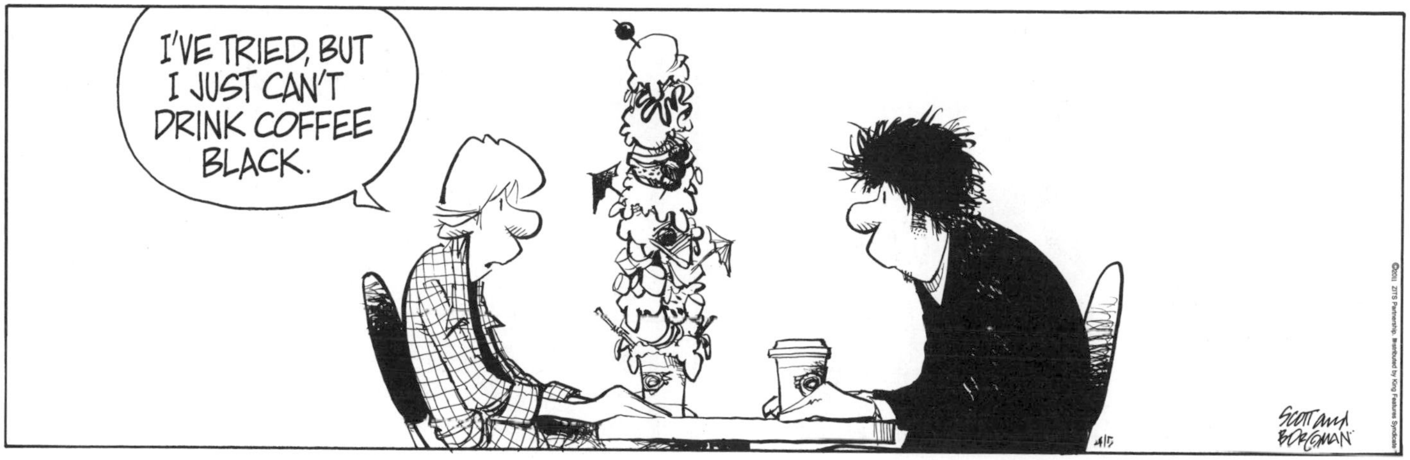
I'VE TRIED, BUT I JUST CAN'T DRINK COFFEE BLACK.
4/5
SCOTT and BORGMAN
©2011 ZITS Partnership. Distributed by King Features Syndicate

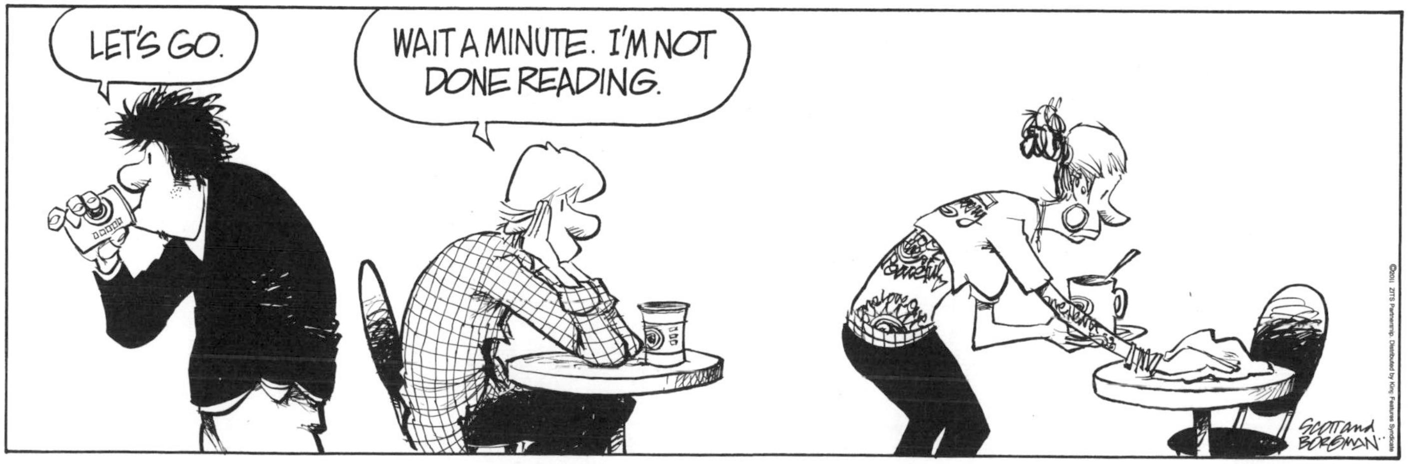
LET'S GO.
WAIT A MINUTE. I'M NOT DONE READING.
SCOTT and BORGMAN
©2011 ZITS Partnership. Distributed by King Features Syndicate

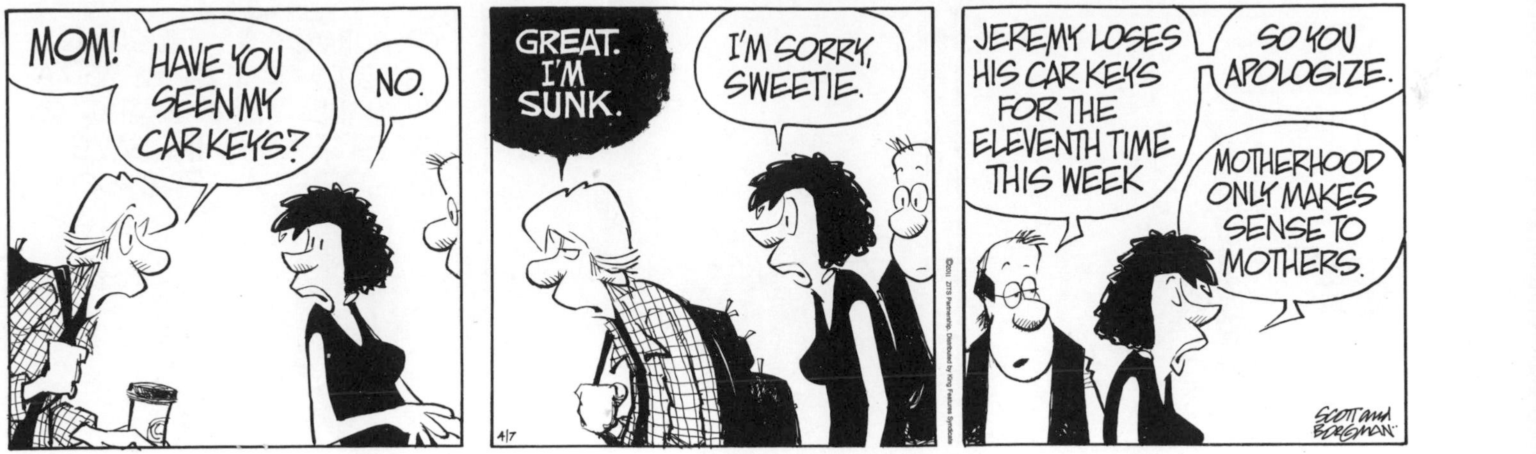
MOM!
HAVE YOU SEEN MY CAR KEYS?
NO.
GREAT. I'M SUNK.
I'M SORRY, SWEETIE.
JEREMY LOSES HIS CAR KEYS FOR THE ELEVENTH TIME THIS WEEK
SO YOU APOLOGIZE.
MOTHERHOOD ONLY MAKES SENSE TO MOTHERS.
4/7
©2011 ZITS Partnership. Distributed by King Features Syndicate
SCOTT and BORGMAN

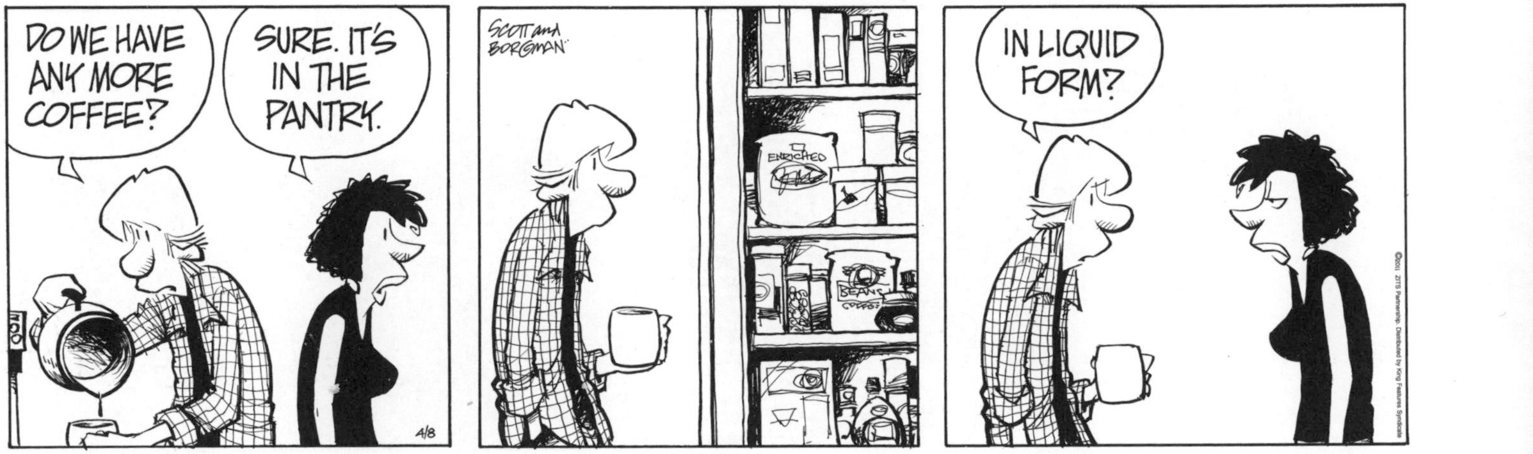
DO WE HAVE ANY MORE COFFEE?
SURE. IT'S IN THE PANTRY.
4/8
SCOTT and BORGMAN
ENRICHED
BEANS
COFFEE
IN LIQUID FORM?
©2011 ZITS Partnership. Distributed by King Features Syndicate

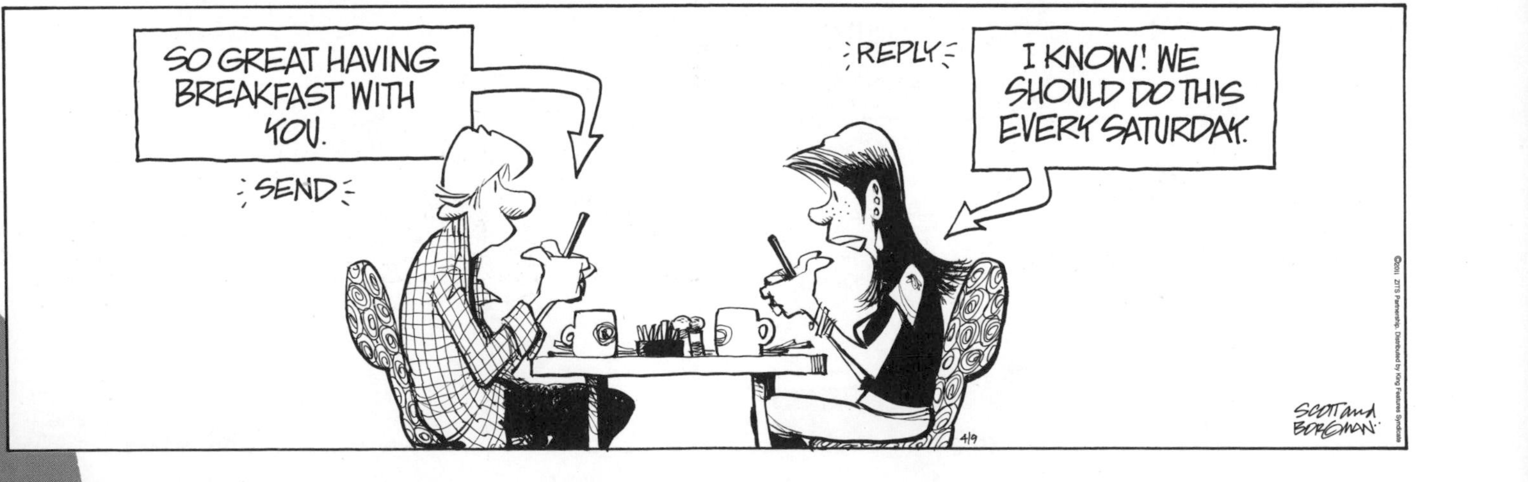
SO GREAT HAVING BREAKFAST WITH YOU.
SEND
REPLY
I KNOW! WE SHOULD DO THIS EVERY SATURDAY.
©2011 ZITS Partnership. Distributed by King Features Syndicate
4/9
SCOTT and BORGMAN

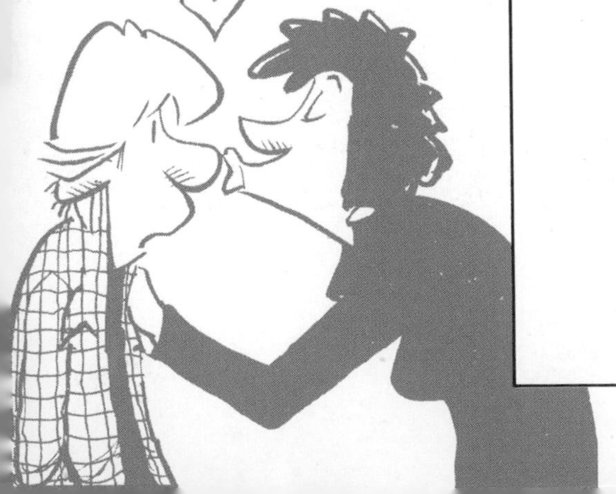

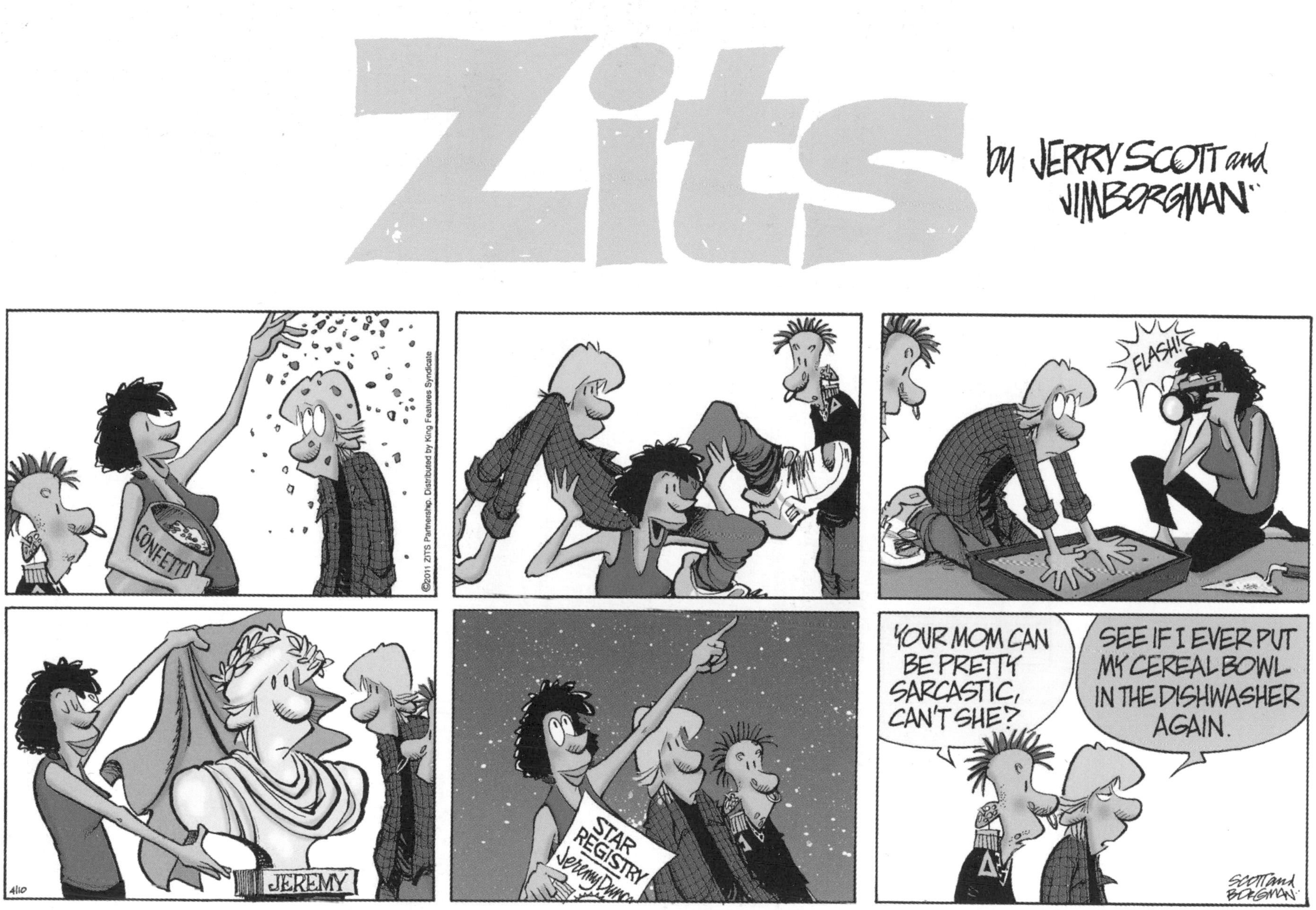
Zits
by JERRY SCOTT and JIM BORGMAN
CONFETTI
©2011 ZITS Partnership. Distributed by King Features Syndicate
FLASH!
4/10
JEREMY
STAR REGISTRY
Jeremy Dunc
YOUR MOM CAN BE PRETTY SARCASTIC, CAN'T SHE?
SEE IF I EVER PUT MY CEREAL BOWL IN THE DISHWASHER AGAIN.
SCOTT and BORGMAN

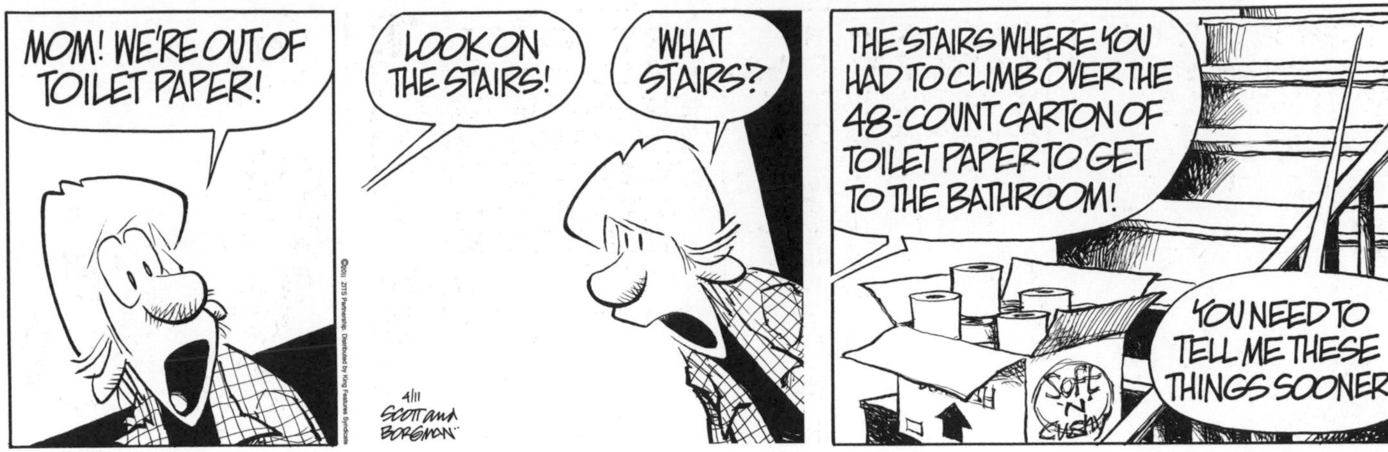
MOM! WE'RE OUT OF TOILET PAPER!
LOOK ON THE STAIRS!
WHAT STAIRS?
THE STAIRS WHERE YOU HAD TO CLIMB OVER THE 48-COUNT CARTON OF TOILET PAPER TO GET TO THE BATHROOM!
YOU NEED TO TELL ME THESE THINGS SOONER!
4/11
SCOTT and BORGMAN

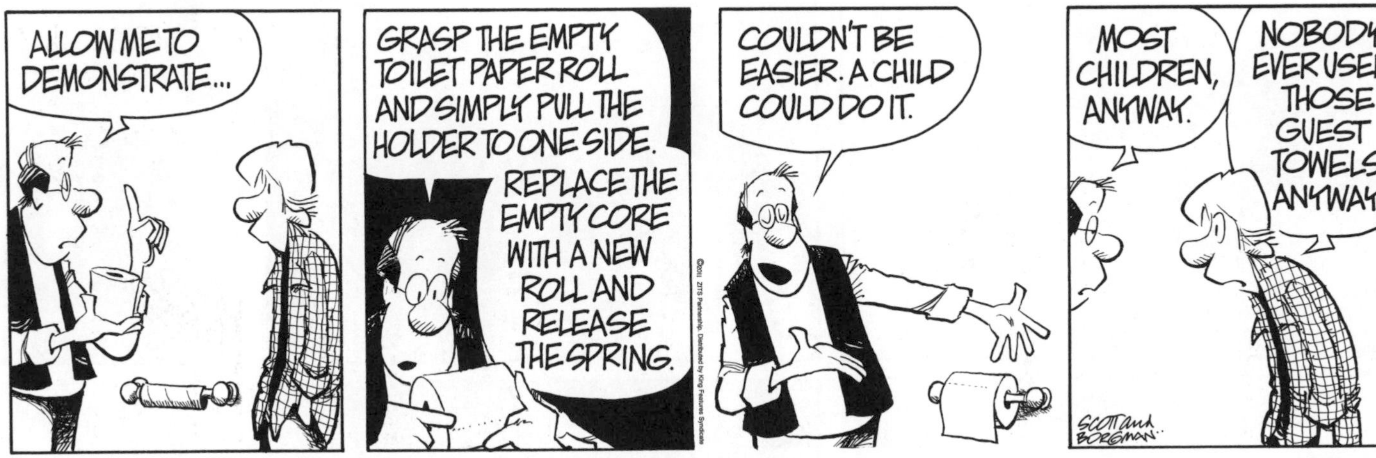
ALLOW ME TO DEMONSTRATE...
GRASP THE EMPTY TOILET PAPER ROLL AND SIMPLY PULL THE HOLDER TO ONE SIDE.
REPLACE THE EMPTY CORE WITH A NEW ROLL AND RELEASE THE SPRING.
COULDN'T BE EASIER. A CHILD COULD DO IT.
MOST CHILDREN, ANYWAY.
NOBODY EVER USED THOSE GUEST TOWELS, ANYWAY!
SCOTT and BORGMAN
4/12

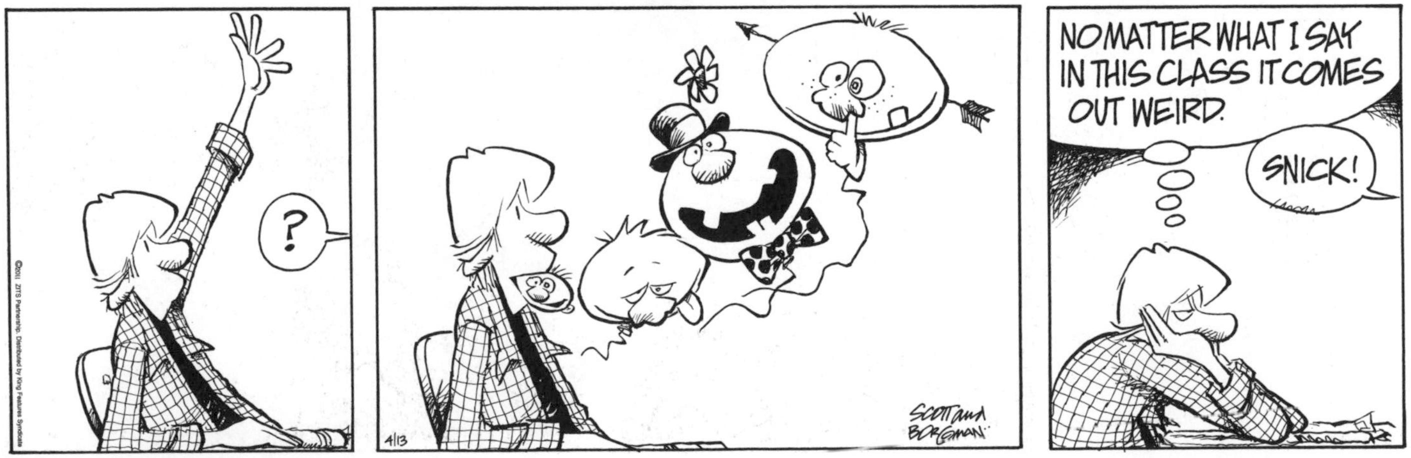
?
4/13
SCOTT and BORGMAN
NO MATTER WHAT I SAY IN THIS CLASS IT COMES OUT WEIRD.
SNICK!

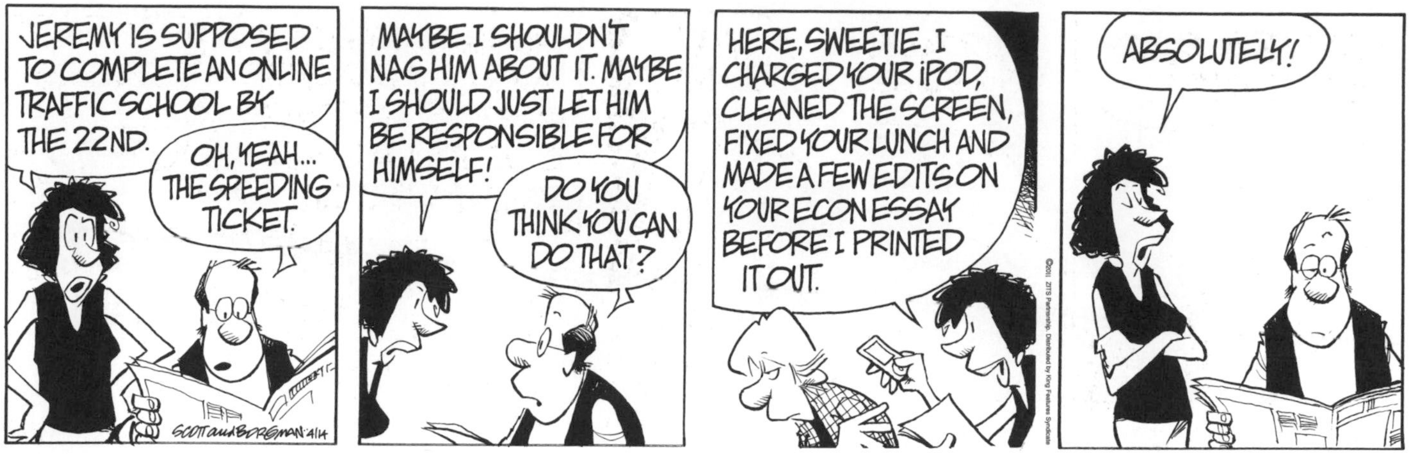
JEREMY IS SUPPOSED TO COMPLETE AN ONLINE TRAFFIC SCHOOL BY THE 22ND.
OH, YEAH... THE SPEEDING TICKET.
MAYBE I SHOULDN'T NAG HIM ABOUT IT. MAYBE I SHOULD JUST LET HIM BE RESPONSIBLE FOR HIMSELF!
DO YOU THINK YOU CAN DO THAT?
HERE, SWEETIE. I CHARGED YOUR iPOD, CLEANED THE SCREEN, FIXED YOUR LUNCH AND MADE A FEW EDITS ON YOUR ECON ESSAY BEFORE I PRINTED IT OUT.
ABSOLUTELY!
SCOTT and BORGMAN 4/14

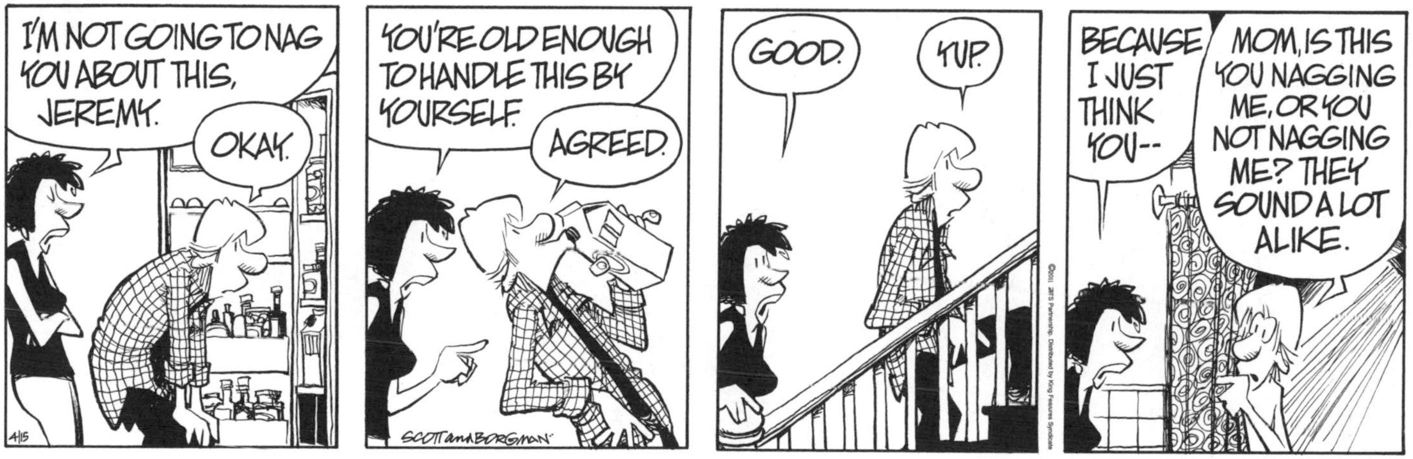
I'M NOT GOING TO NAG YOU ABOUT THIS, JEREMY.
OKAY.
YOU'RE OLD ENOUGH TO HANDLE THIS BY YOURSELF.
AGREED.
GOOD.
YUP.
BECAUSE I JUST THINK YOU--
MOM, IS THIS YOU NAGGING ME, OR YOU NOT NAGGING ME? THEY SOUND A LOT ALIKE.
4/15
SCOTT and BORGMAN

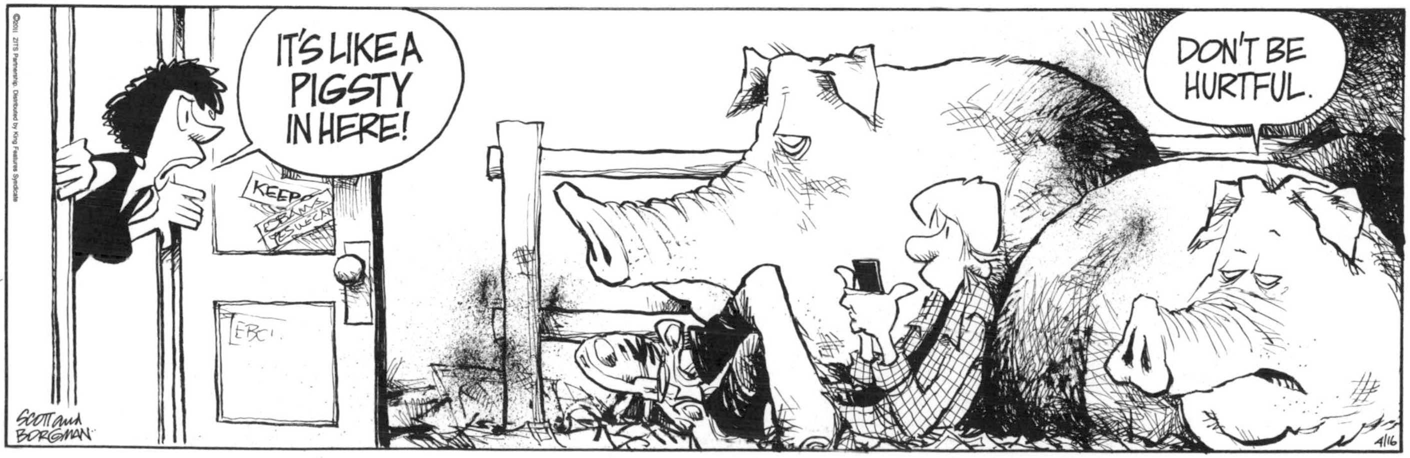
IT'S LIKE A PIGSTY IN HERE!
DON'T BE HURTFUL.
KEEP
SCOTT and BORGMAN
4/16

Zits

by JERRY SCOTT and JIM BORGMAN

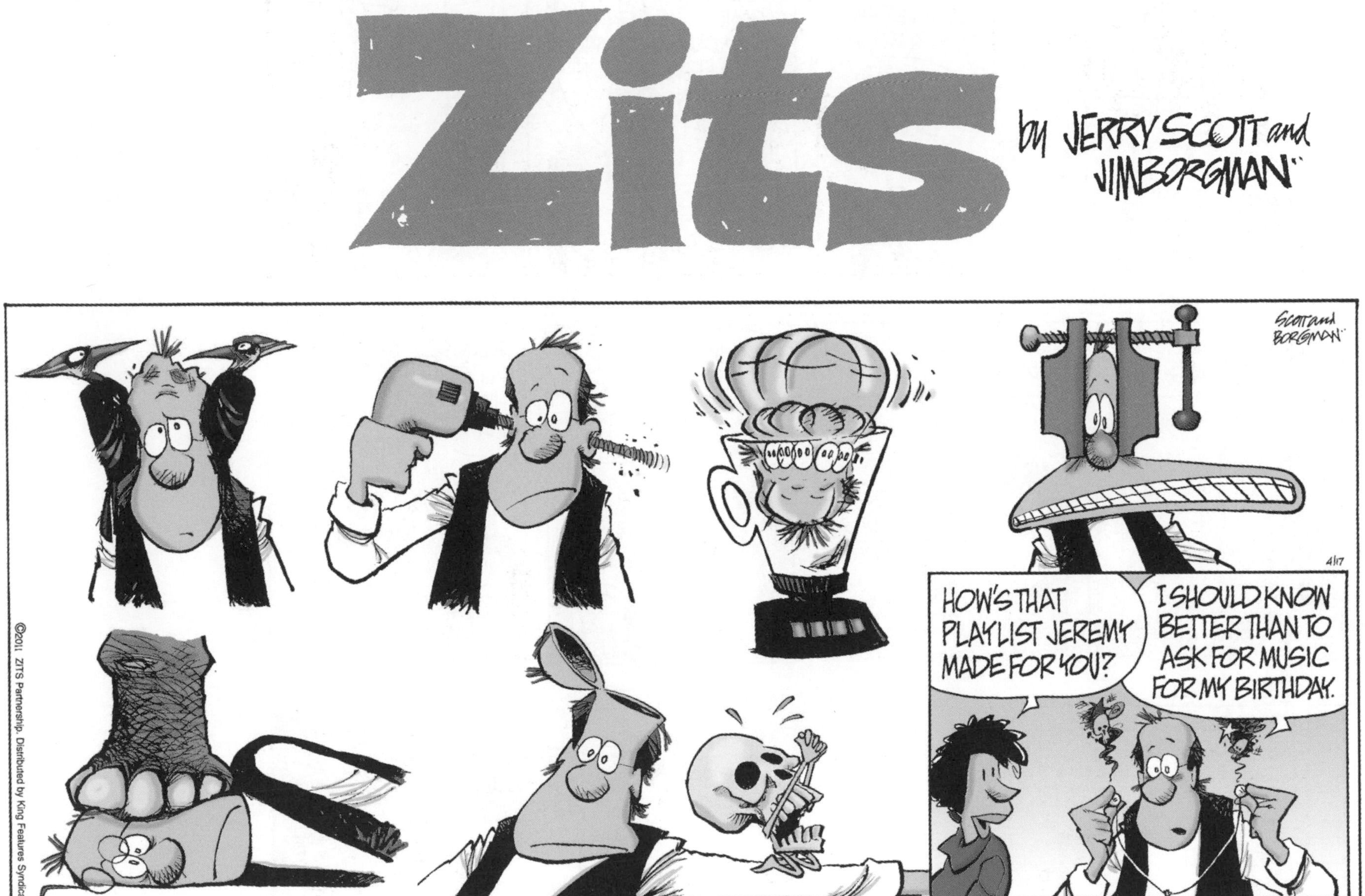
SCOTT and BORGMAN
4/17
HOW'S THAT PLAYLIST JEREMY MADE FOR YOU?
I SHOULD KNOW BETTER THAN TO ASK FOR MUSIC FOR MY BIRTHDAY.
©2011 ZITS Partnership. Distributed by King Features Syndicate

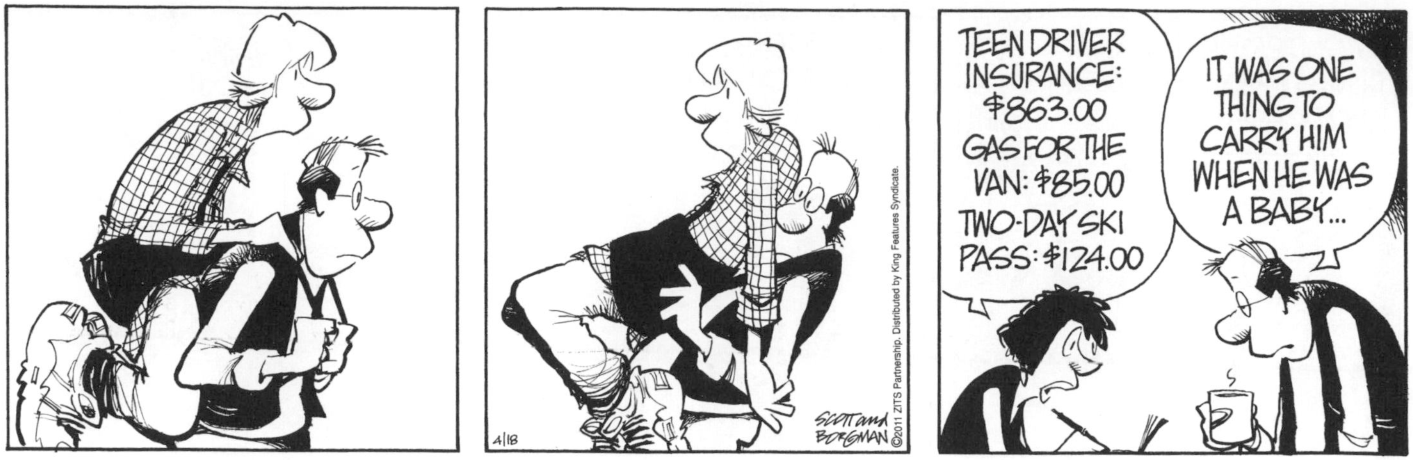
4/18
SCOTT and BORGMAN
©2011 ZITS Partnership. Distributed by King Features Syndicate.
TEEN DRIVER INSURANCE: $863.00 GAS FOR THE VAN: $85.00 TWO-DAY SKI PASS: $124.00
IT WAS ONE THING TO CARRY HIM WHEN HE WAS A BABY...

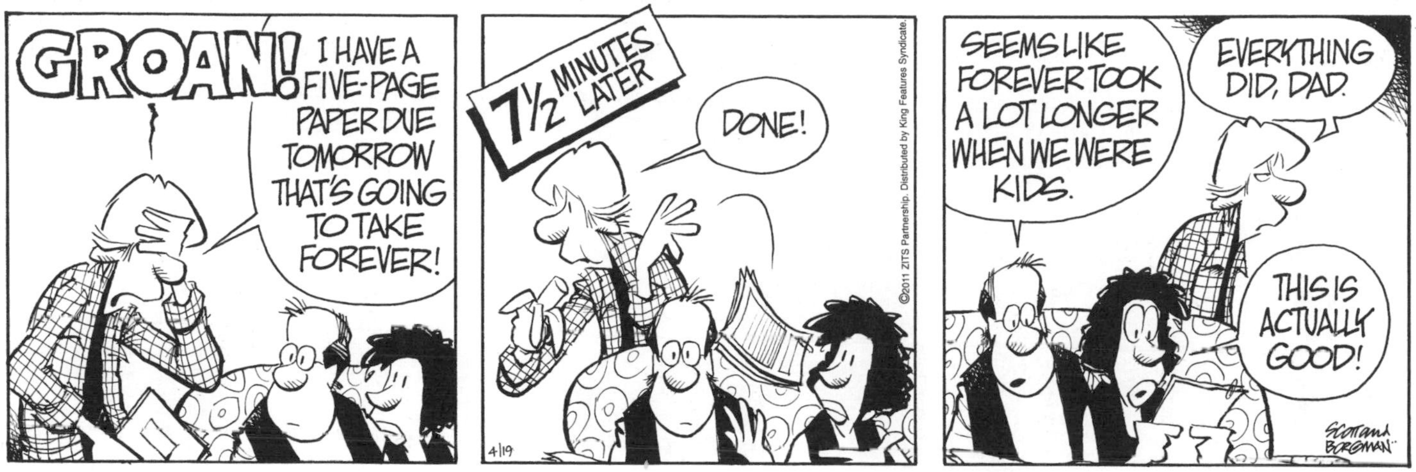
GROAN!
I HAVE A FIVE-PAGE PAPER DUE TOMORROW THAT'S GOING TO TAKE FOREVER!
7½ MINUTES LATER
DONE!
4/19
©2011 ZITS Partnership. Distributed by King Features Syndicate.
SEEMS LIKE FOREVER TOOK A LOT LONGER WHEN WE WERE KIDS.
EVERYTHING DID, DAD.
THIS IS ACTUALLY GOOD!
SCOTT and BORGMAN

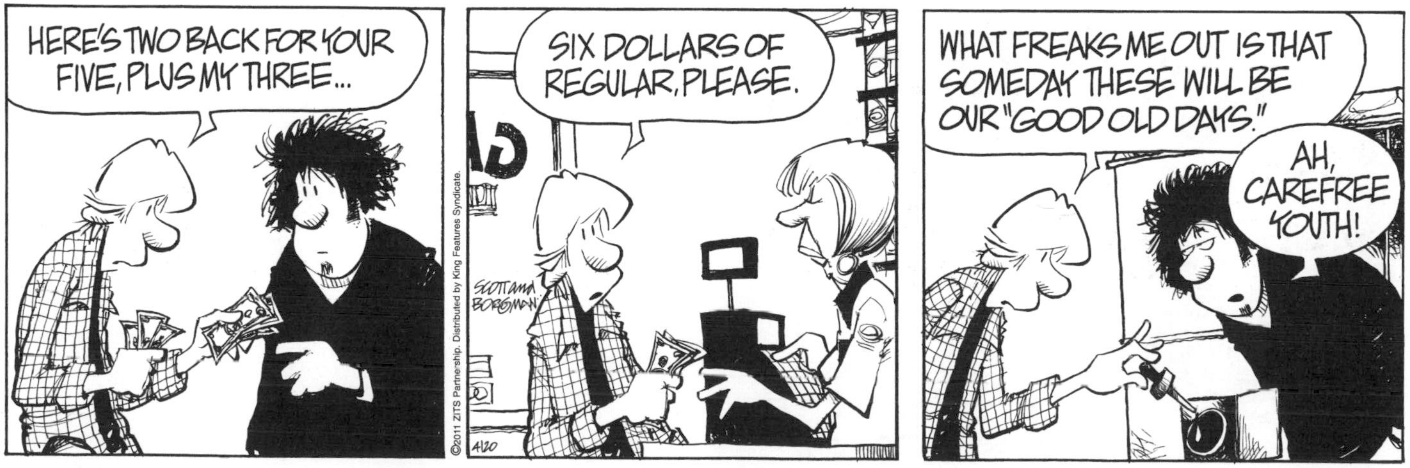
HERE'S TWO BACK FOR YOUR FIVE, PLUS MY THREE...
©2011 ZITS Partnership. Distributed by King Features Syndicate.
4/20
SIX DOLLARS OF REGULAR, PLEASE.
SCOTT and BORGMAN
WHAT FREAKS ME OUT IS THAT SOMEDAY THESE WILL BE OUR "GOOD OLD DAYS."
AH, CAREFREE YOUTH!

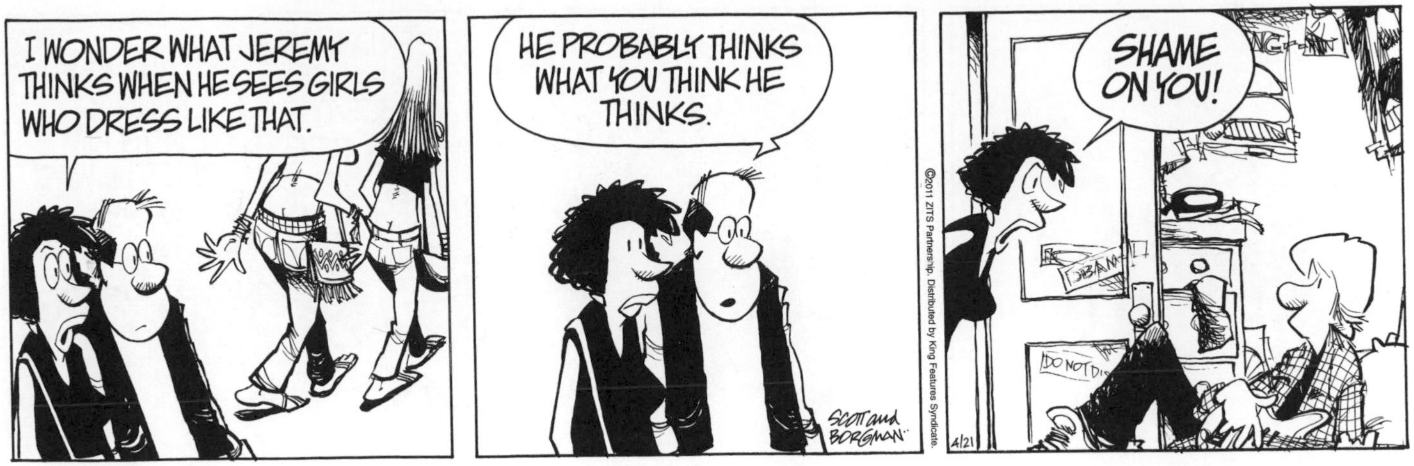
I WONDER WHAT JEREMY THINKS WHEN HE SEES GIRLS WHO DRESS LIKE THAT.
HE PROBABLY THINKS WHAT YOU THINK HE THINKS.
SHAME ON YOU!
©2011 ZITS Partnership. Distributed by King Features Syndicate.
SCOTT and BORGMAN
4/21

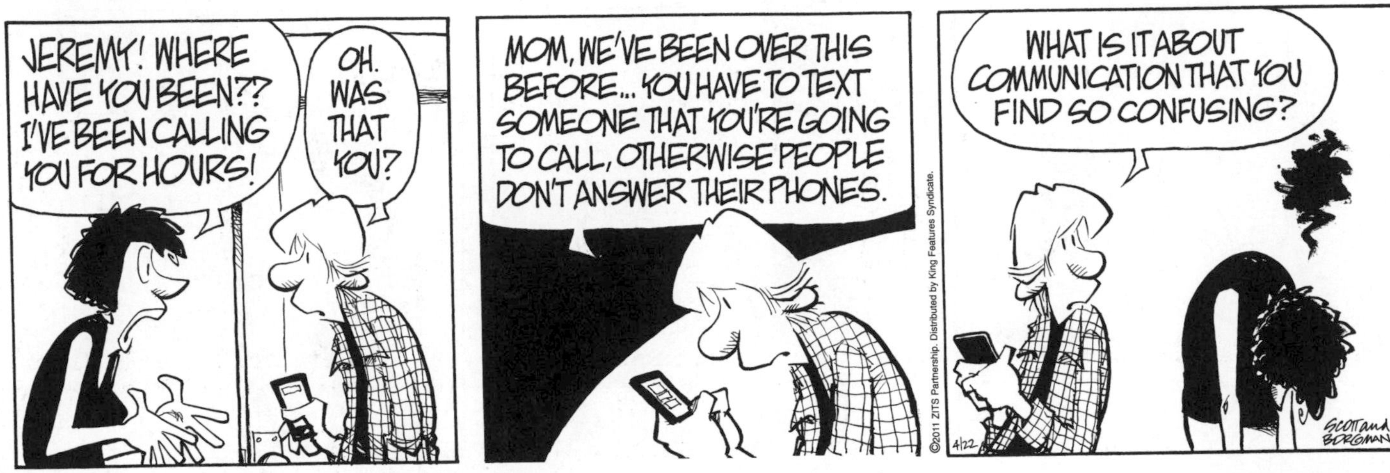
JEREMY! WHERE HAVE YOU BEEN?? I'VE BEEN CALLING YOU FOR HOURS!
OH. WAS THAT YOU?
MOM, WE'VE BEEN OVER THIS BEFORE... YOU HAVE TO TEXT SOMEONE THAT YOU'RE GOING TO CALL, OTHERWISE PEOPLE DON'T ANSWER THEIR PHONES.
WHAT IS IT ABOUT COMMUNICATION THAT YOU FIND SO CONFUSING?
©2011 ZITS Partnership. Distributed by King Features Syndicate.
4/22
SCOTT and BORGMAN

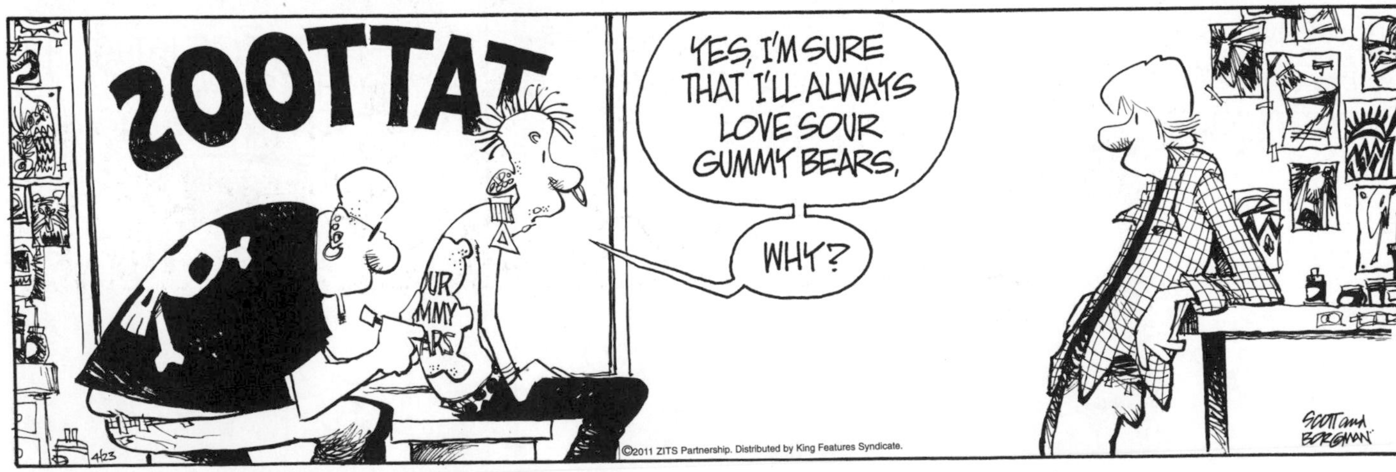
YES, I'M SURE THAT I'LL ALWAYS LOVE SOUR GUMMY BEARS.
WHY?
4/23
©2011 ZITS Partnership. Distributed by King Features Syndicate.
SCOTT and BORGMAN

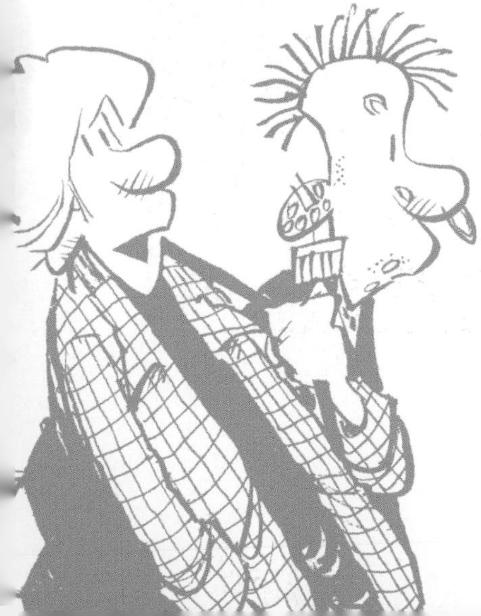

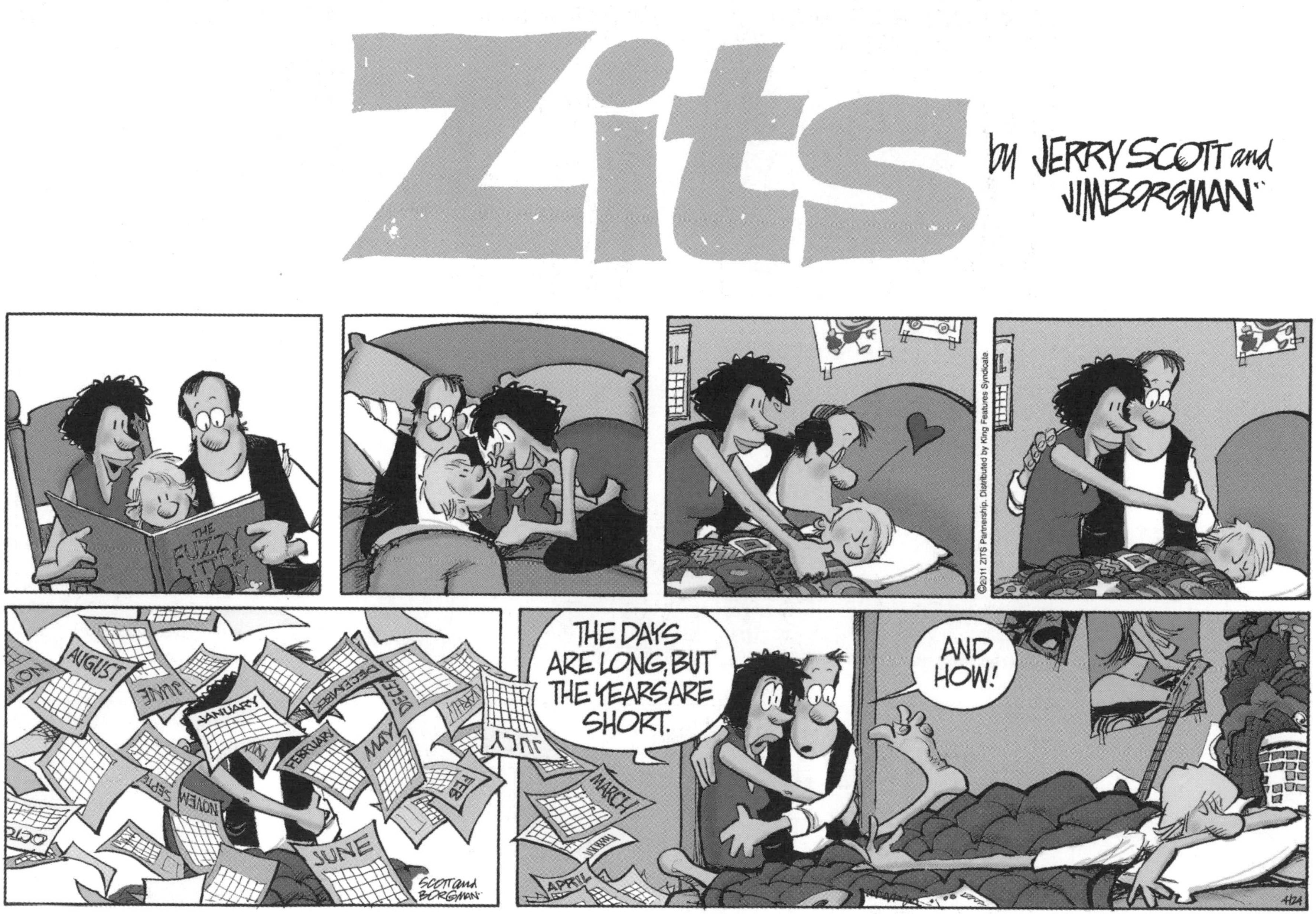
Zits
by JERRY SCOTT and JIM BORGMAN
THE FUZZY LITTLE
©2011 ZITS Partnership. Distributed by King Features Syndicate.
AUGUST
JUNE
JANUARY
FEBRUARY
MAY
JULY
FEB
MARCH
APRIL
SCOTT and BORGMAN
THE DAYS ARE LONG, BUT THE YEARS ARE SHORT.
AND HOW!
4/24

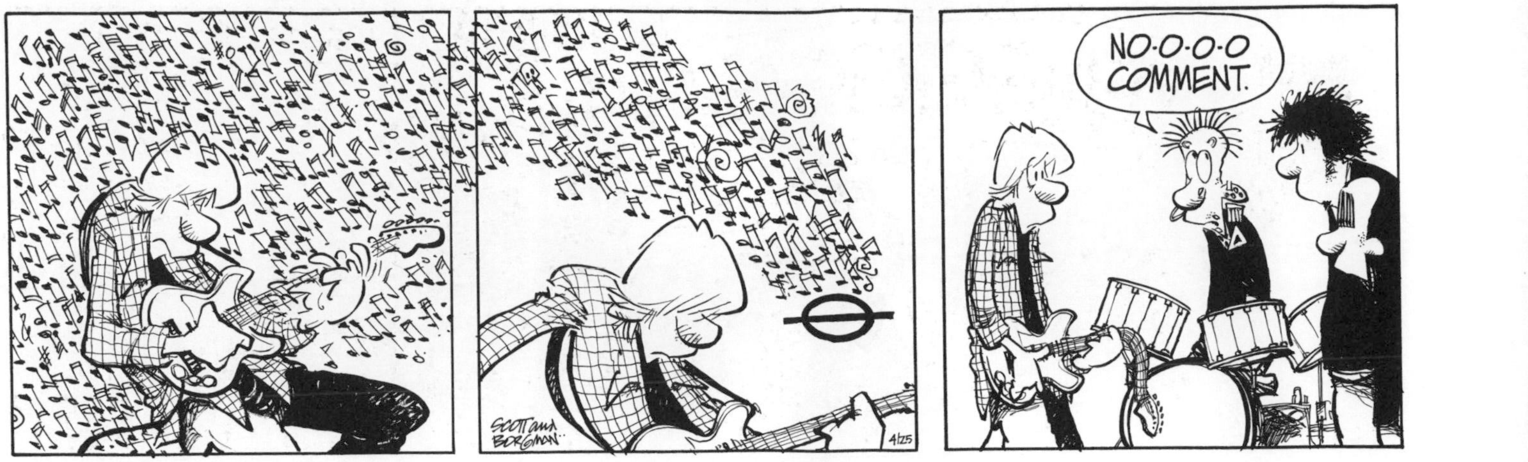
NO-O-O-O COMMENT.

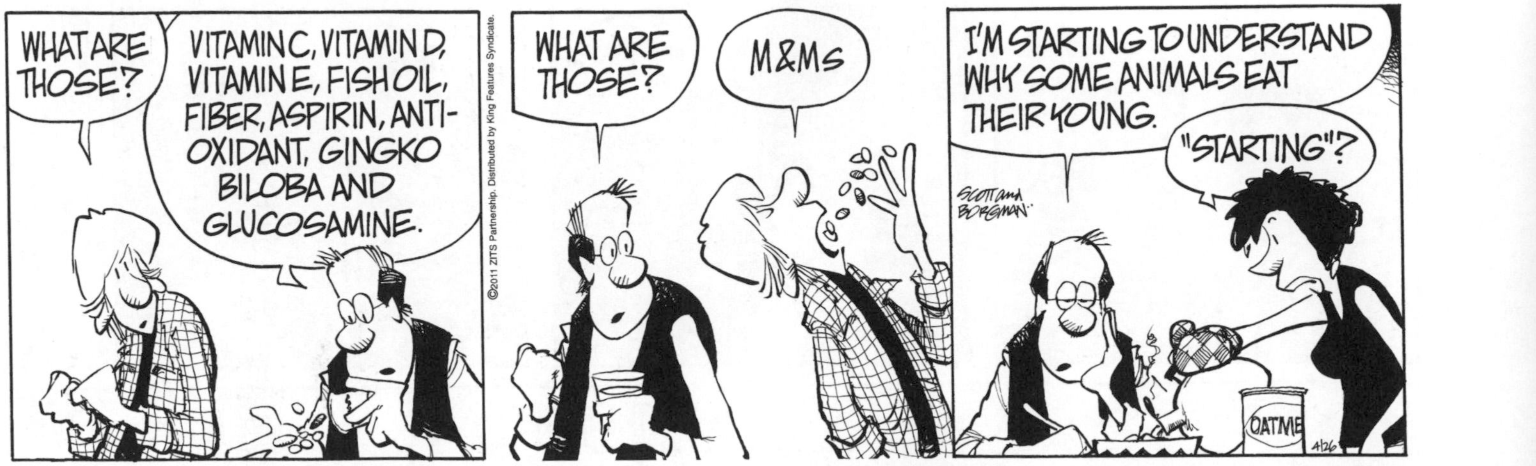
WHAT ARE THOSE?
VITAMIN C, VITAMIN D, VITAMIN E, FISH OIL, FIBER, ASPIRIN, ANTI-OXIDANT, GINGKO BILOBA AND GLUCOSAMINE.
©2011 ZITS Partnership. Distributed by King Features Syndicate.
WHAT ARE THOSE?
M&Ms
I'M STARTING TO UNDERSTAND WHY SOME ANIMALS EAT THEIR YOUNG.
"STARTING"?

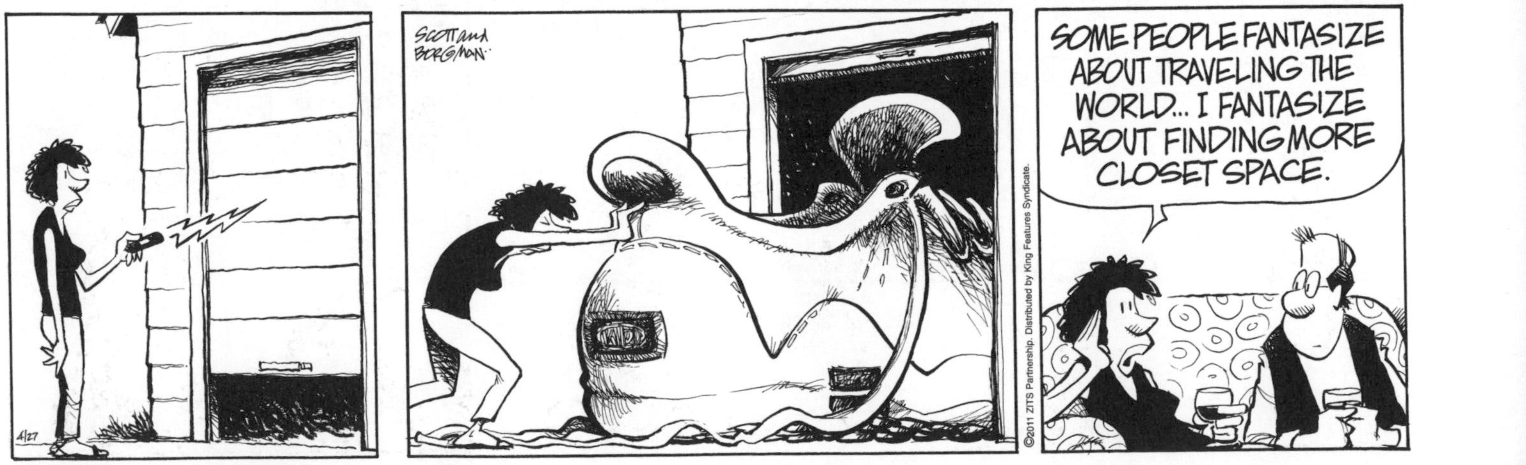
©2011 ZITS Partnership. Distributed by King Features Syndicate.
SOME PEOPLE FANTASIZE ABOUT TRAVELING THE WORLD... I FANTASIZE ABOUT FINDING MORE CLOSET SPACE.

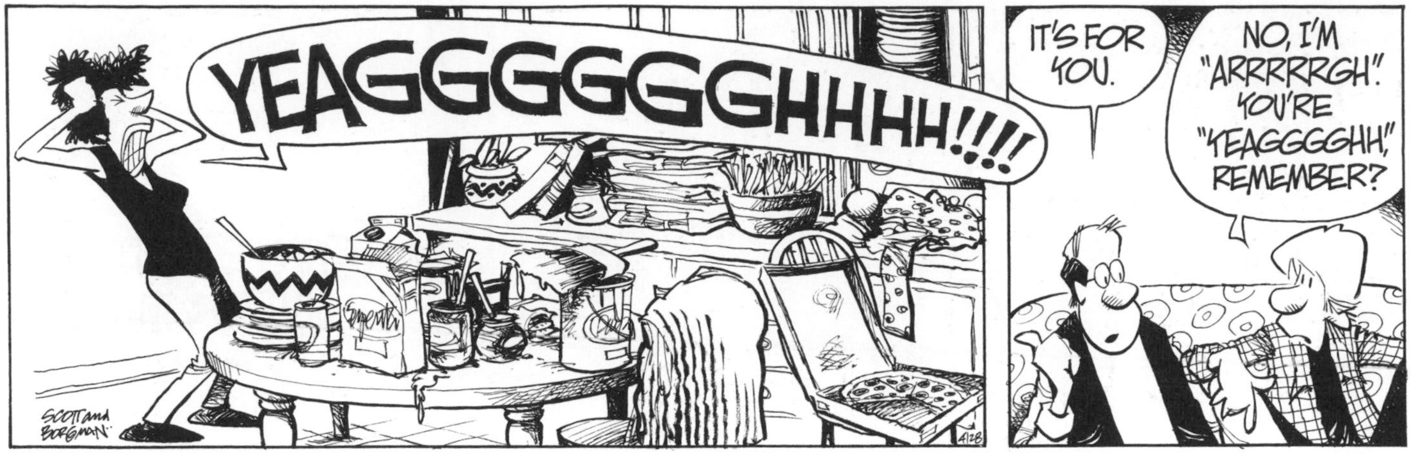
YEAGGGGGGHHHH!!!!
SCOTT and BORGMAN
4/28
IT'S FOR YOU.
NO, I'M "ARRRRRGH". YOU'RE "YEAGGGGHH," REMEMBER?

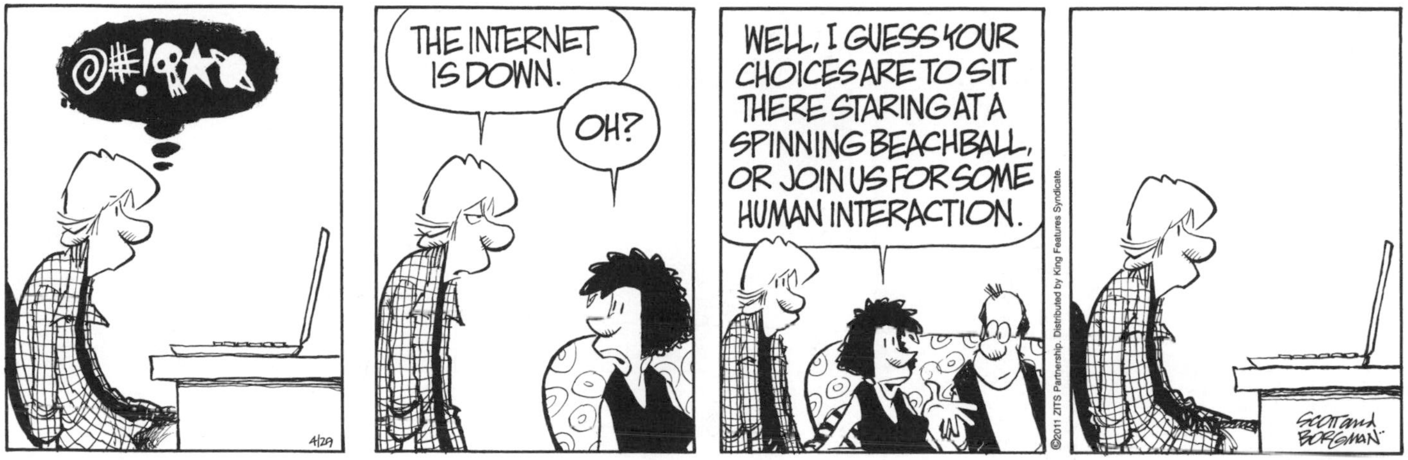
@#!
4/29
THE INTERNET IS DOWN.
OH?
WELL, I GUESS YOUR CHOICES ARE TO SIT THERE STARING AT A SPINNING BEACHBALL, OR JOIN US FOR SOME HUMAN INTERACTION.
©2011 ZITS Partnership. Distributed by King Features Syndicate.
SCOTT and BORGMAN

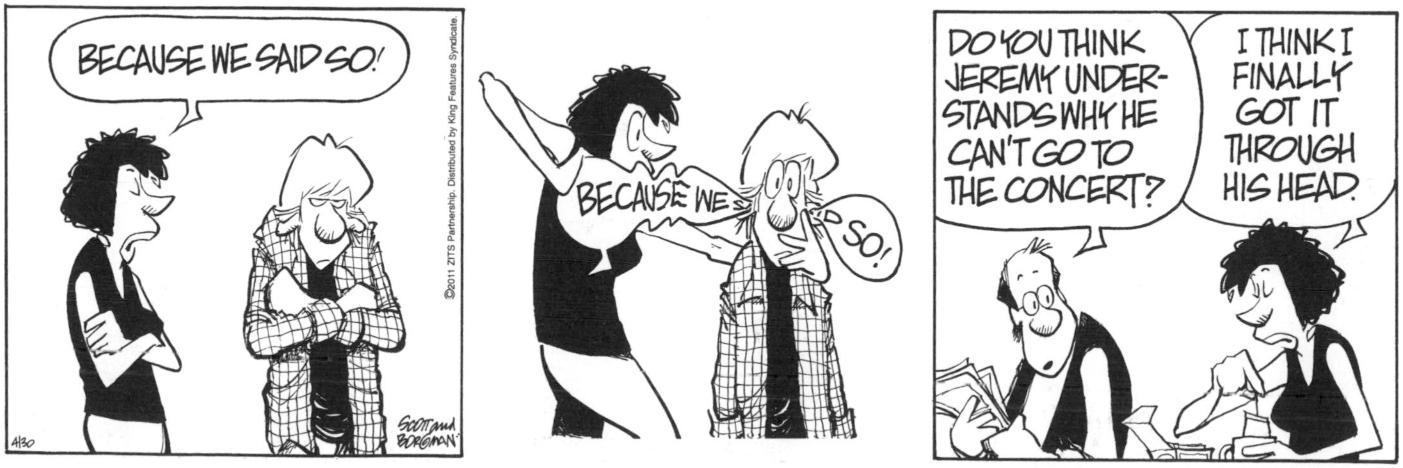
BECAUSE WE SAID SO!
©2011 ZITS Partnership. Distributed by King Features Syndicate.
4/30
SCOTT and BORGMAN
BECAUSE WE
SO!
DO YOU THINK JEREMY UNDERSTANDS WHY HE CAN'T GO TO THE CONCERT?
I THINK I FINALLY GOT IT THROUGH HIS HEAD.

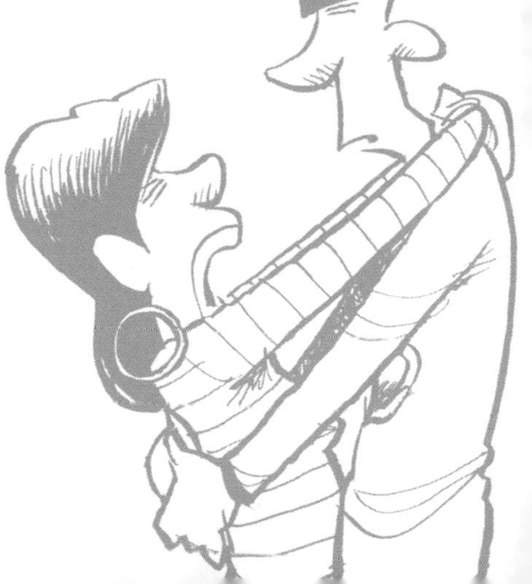

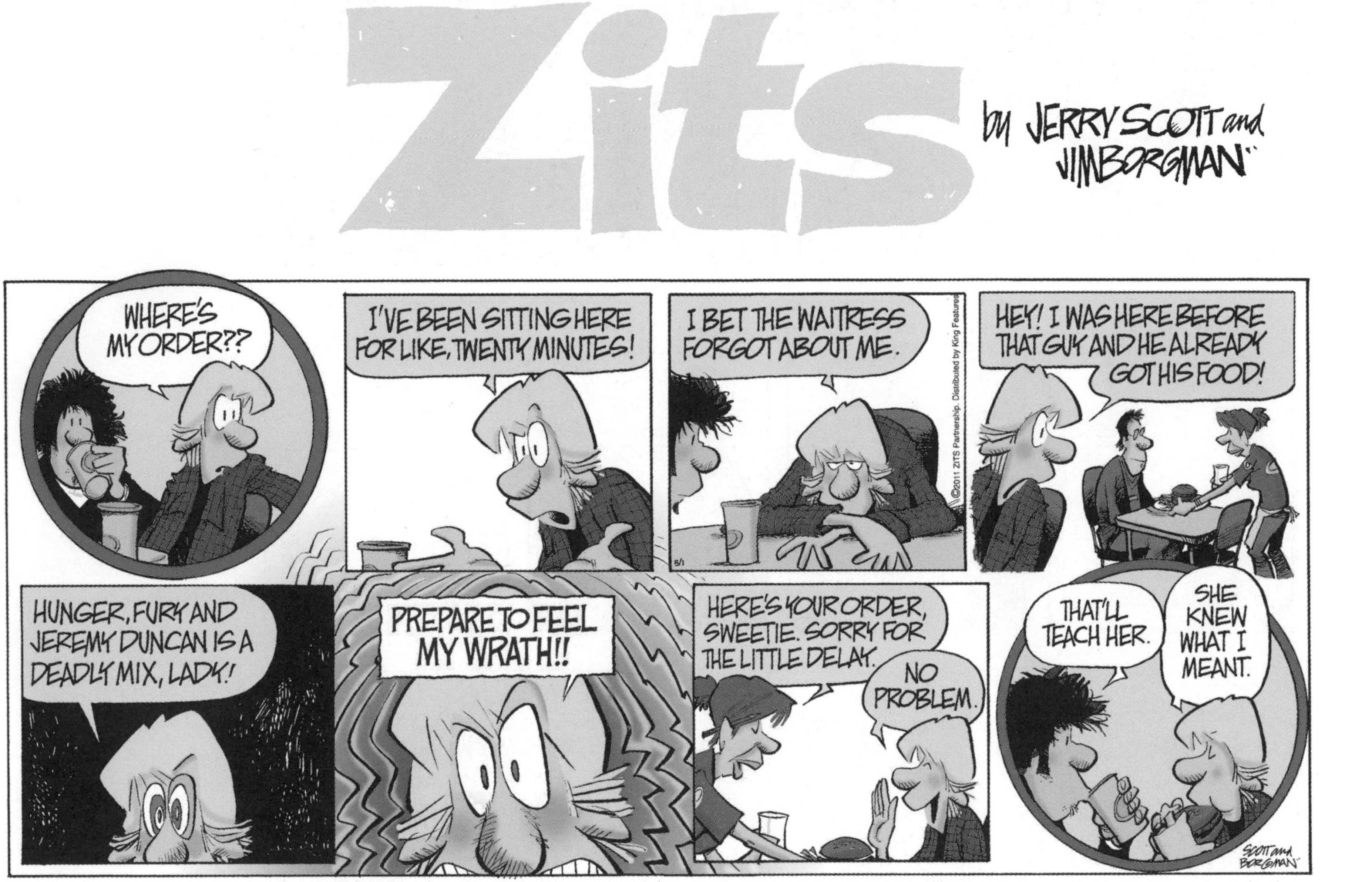
Zits
by JERRY SCOTT and JIM BORGMAN
WHERE'S MY ORDER??
I'VE BEEN SITTING HERE FOR LIKE, TWENTY MINUTES!
I BET THE WAITRESS FORGOT ABOUT ME.
©2011 ZITS Partnership. Distributed by King Features
HEY! I WAS HERE BEFORE THAT GUY AND HE ALREADY GOT HIS FOOD!
HUNGER, FURY AND JEREMY DUNCAN IS A DEADLY MIX, LADY!
PREPARE TO FEEL MY WRATH!!
HERE'S YOUR ORDER, SWEETIE. SORRY FOR THE LITTLE DELAY.
NO PROBLEM.
THAT'LL TEACH HER.
SHE KNEW WHAT I MEANT.
SCOTT and BORGMAN

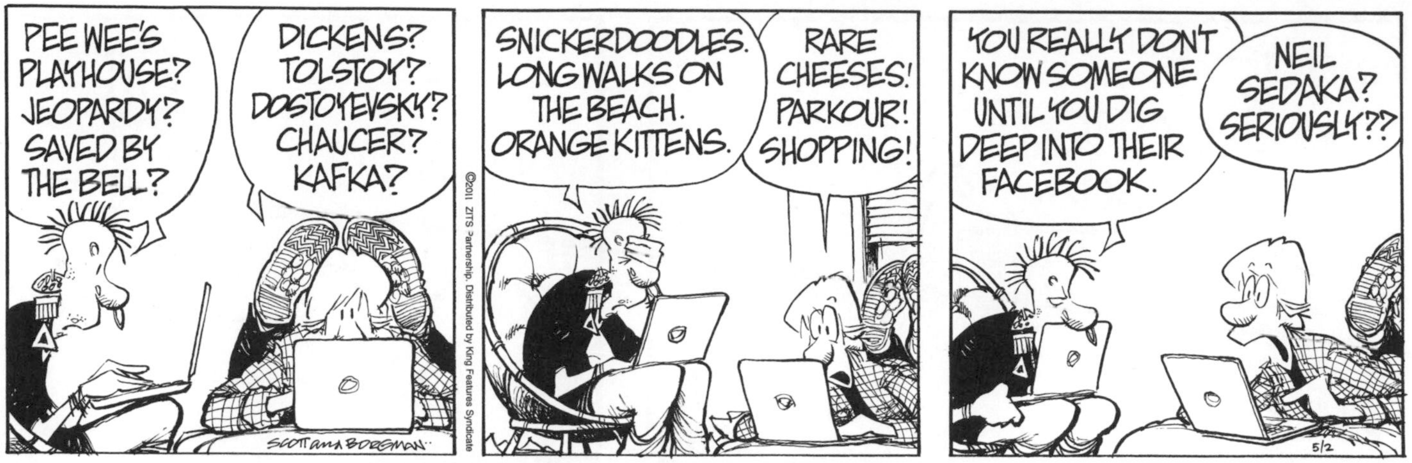
PEE WEE'S PLAYHOUSE? JEOPARDY? SAVED BY THE BELL?
DICKENS? TOLSTOY? DOSTOYEVSKY? CHAUCER? KAFKA?
SNICKERDOODLES. LONG WALKS ON THE BEACH. ORANGE KITTENS.
RARE CHEESES! PARKOUR! SHOPPING!
YOU REALLY DON'T KNOW SOMEONE UNTIL YOU DIG DEEP INTO THEIR FACEBOOK.
NEIL SEDAKA? SERIOUSLY??
©2011 ZITS Partnership. Distributed by King Features Syndicate
SCOTT and BORGMAN
5/2

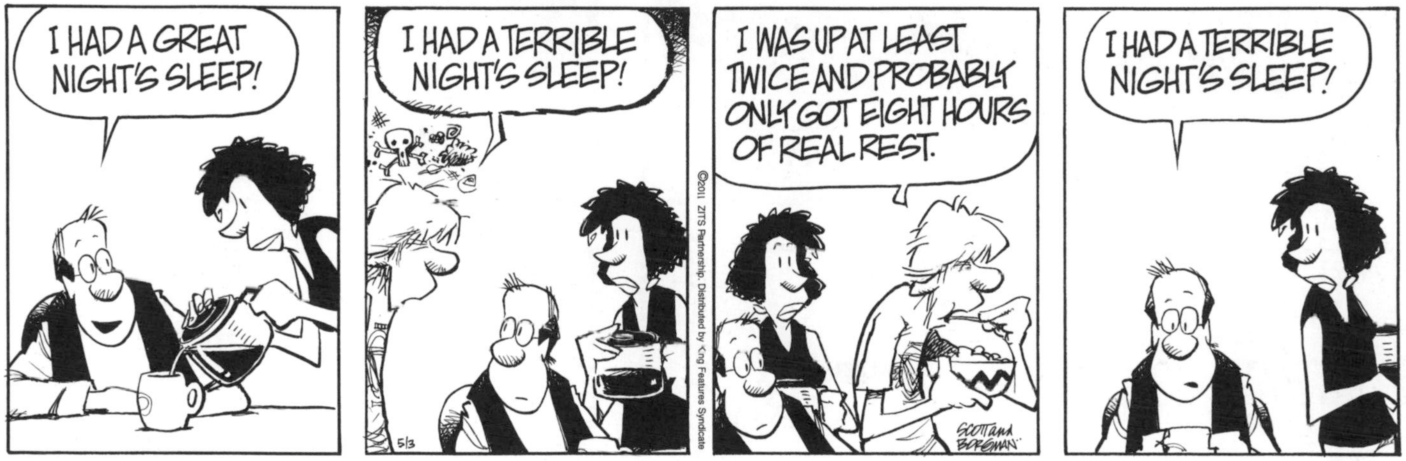
I HAD A GREAT NIGHT'S SLEEP!
I HAD A TERRIBLE NIGHT'S SLEEP!
I WAS UP AT LEAST TWICE AND PROBABLY ONLY GOT EIGHT HOURS OF REAL REST.
I HAD A TERRIBLE NIGHT'S SLEEP!
©2011 ZITS Partnership. Distributed by King Features Syndicate
5/3
SCOTT and BORGMAN

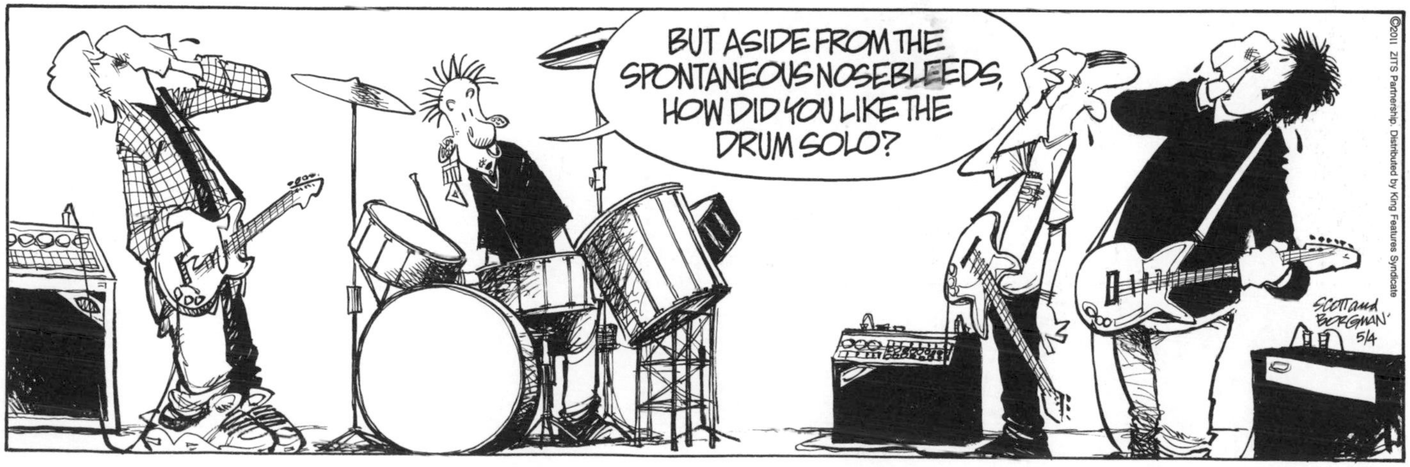
BUT ASIDE FROM THE SPONTANEOUS NOSEBLEEDS, HOW DID YOU LIKE THE DRUM SOLO?
©2011 ZITS Partnership. Distributed by King Features Syndicate
SCOTT and BORGMAN
5/4

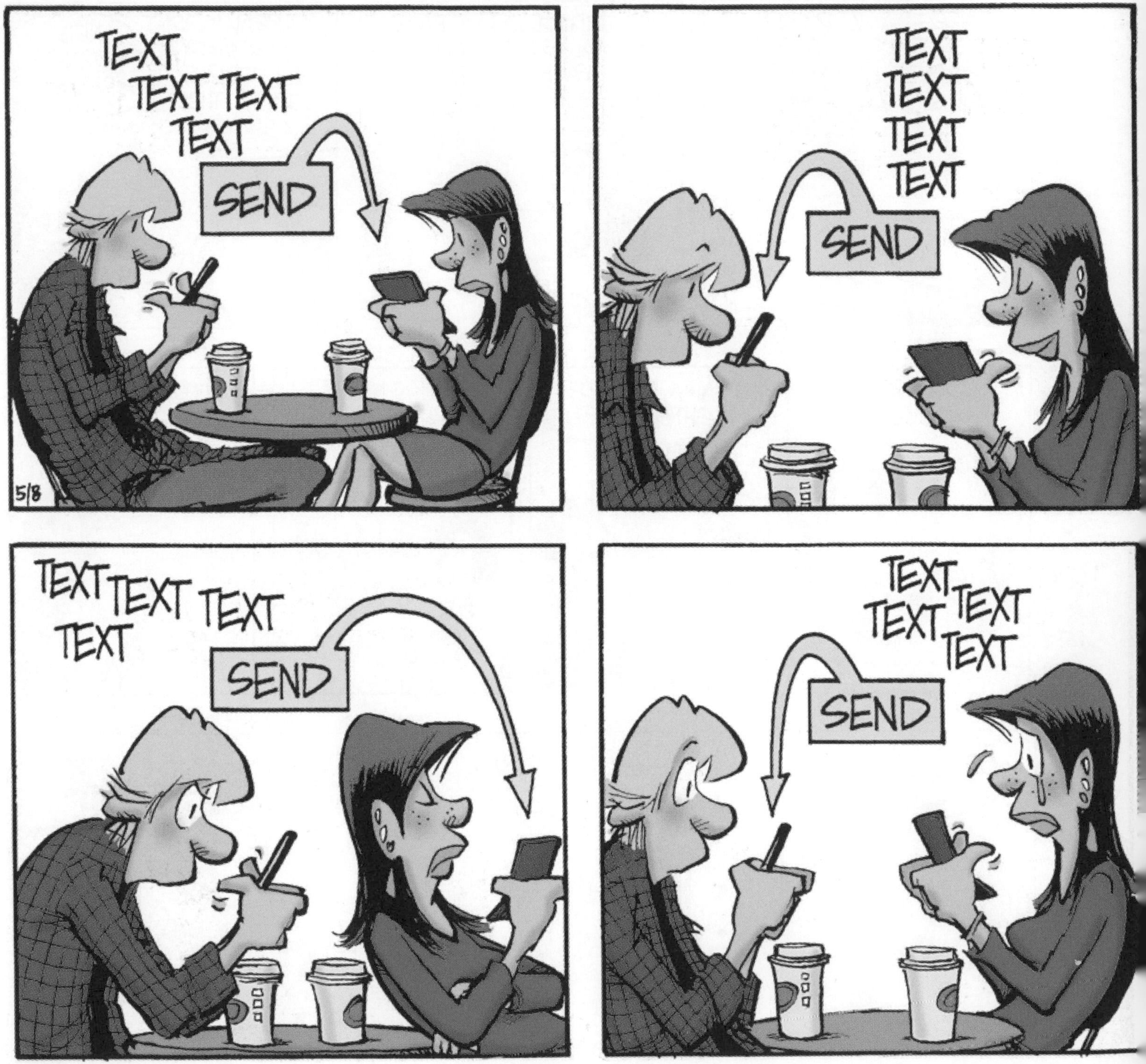
TEXT
TEXT TEXT
TEXT
SEND
5/8
TEXT
TEXT
TEXT
TEXT
SEND
TEXT TEXT TEXT
TEXT
SEND
TEXT
TEXT TEXT
TEXT
SEND

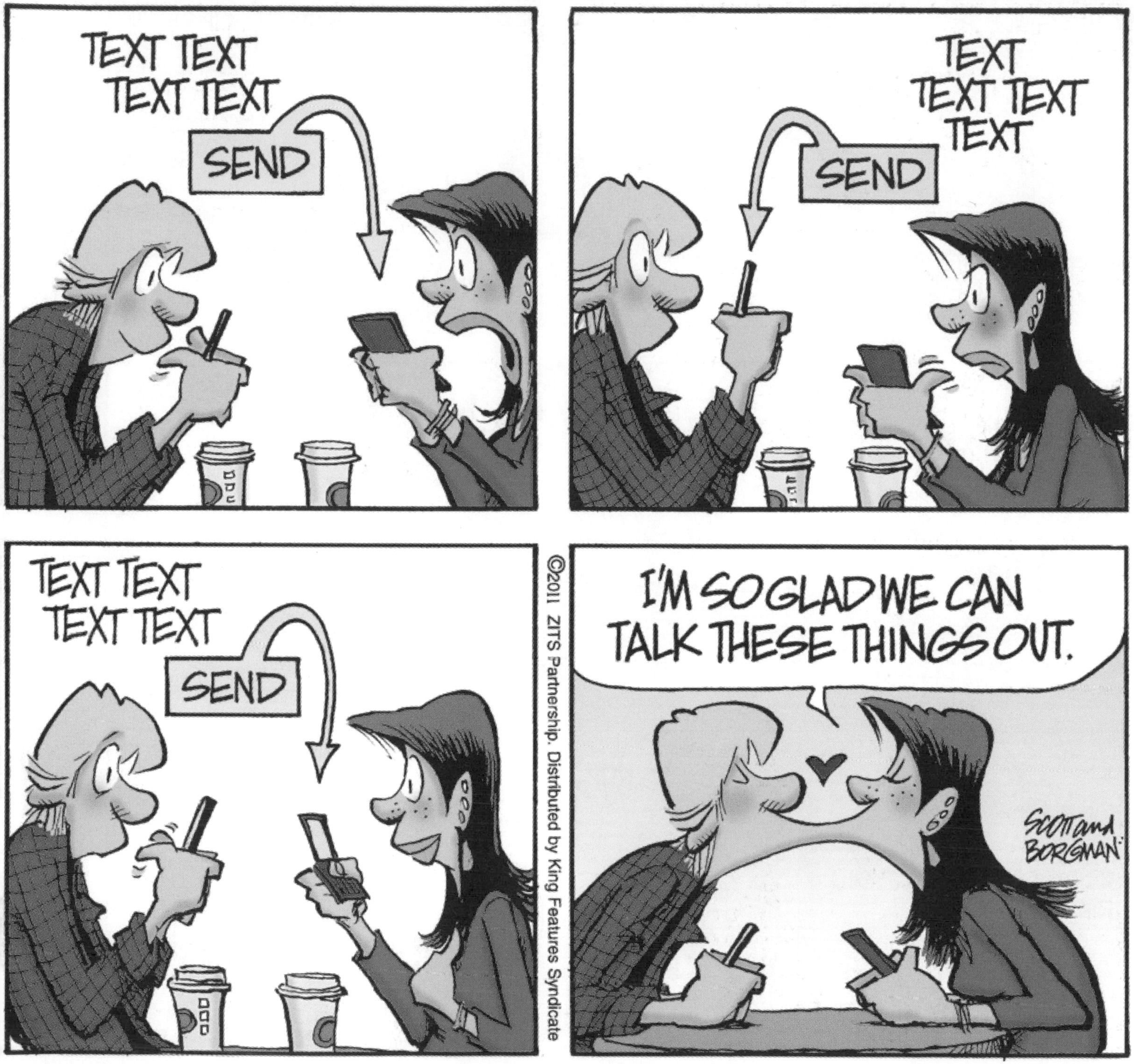

TEXT TEXT
TEXT TEXT
SEND
TEXT
TEXT TEXT
TEXT
SEND
TEXT TEXT
TEXT TEXT
SEND
I'M SO GLAD WE CAN TALK THESE THINGS OUT.
SCOTT and BORGMAN

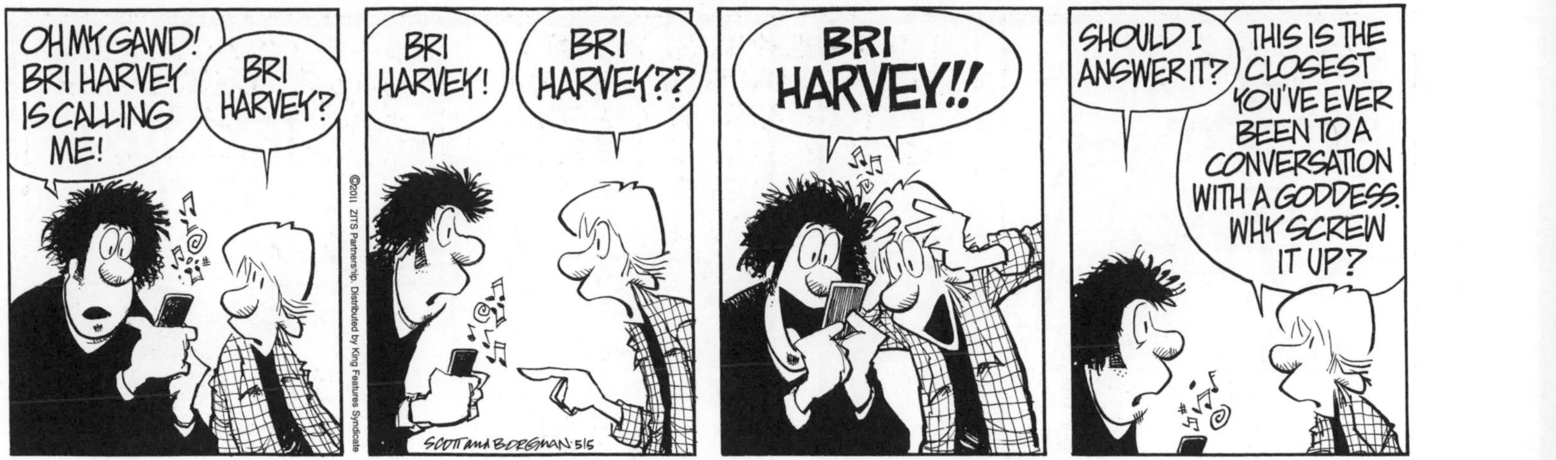
OH MY GAWD! BRI HARVEY IS CALLING ME!
BRI HARVEY?
©2011 ZITS Partnership. Distributed by King Features Syndicate
BRI HARVEY!
BRI HARVEY??
SCOTT AND BORGMAN 5/5
BRI HARVEY!!
SHOULD I ANSWER IT?
THIS IS THE CLOSEST YOU'VE EVER BEEN TO A CONVERSATION WITH A GODDESS. WHY SCREW IT UP?

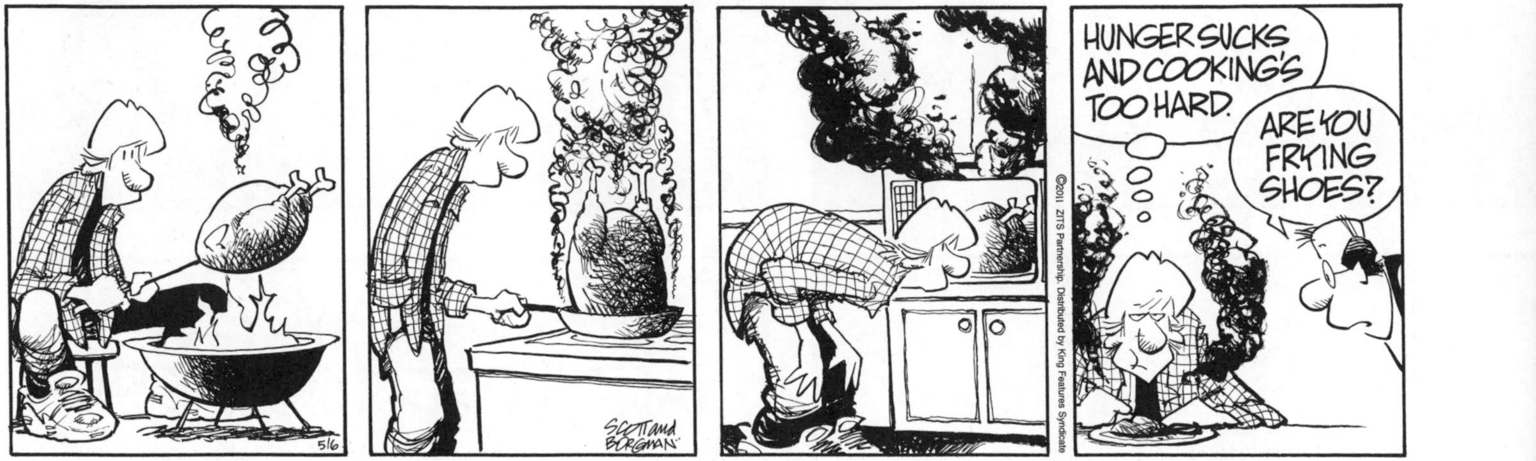
5/6
SCOTT AND BORGMAN
©2011 ZITS Partnership. Distributed by King Features Syndicate
HUNGER SUCKS AND COOKING'S TOO HARD.
ARE YOU FRYING SHOES?

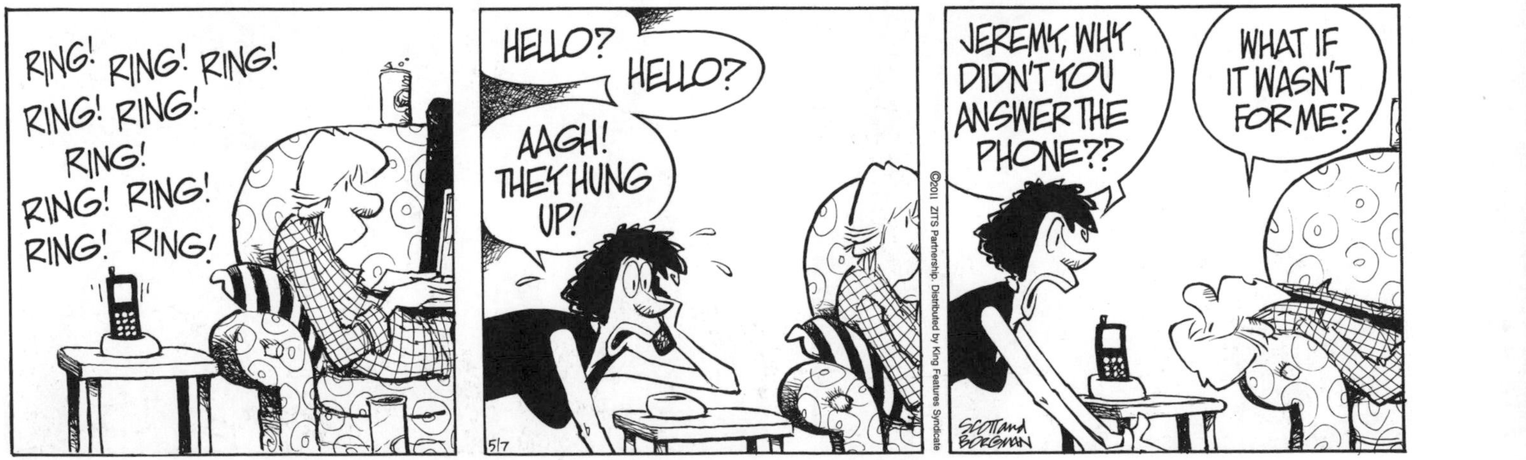
RING! RING! RING!
RING! RING!
RING!
RING! RING!
RING! RING!
HELLO?
HELLO?
AAGH! THEY HUNG UP!
5/7
©2011 ZITS Partnership. Distributed by King Features Syndicate
JEREMY, WHY DIDN'T YOU ANSWER THE PHONE??
WHAT IF IT WASN'T FOR ME?
SCOTT AND BORGMAN

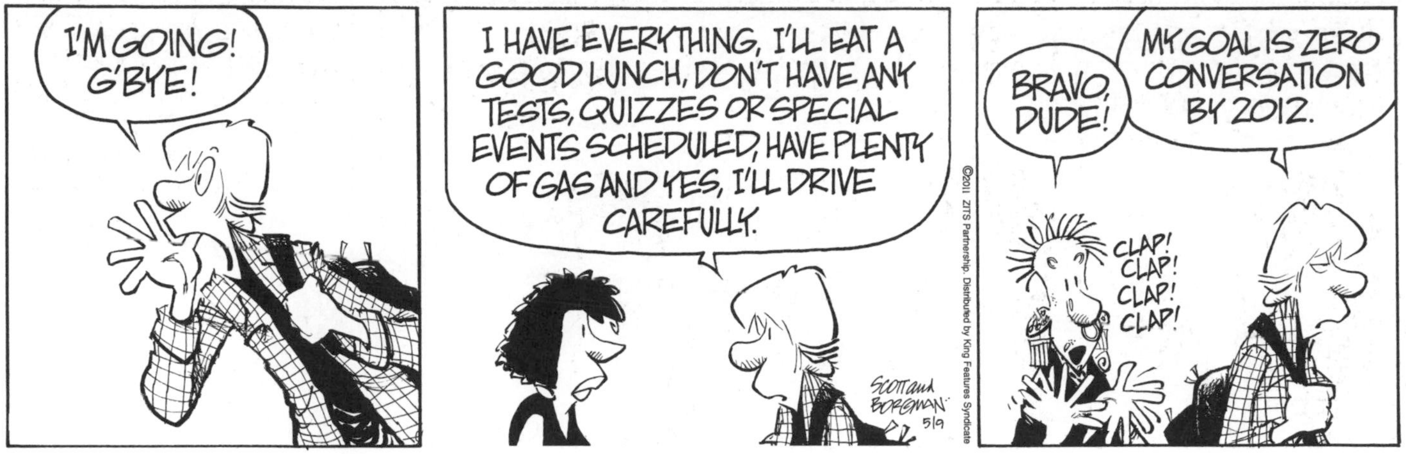
I'M GOING! G'BYE!
I HAVE EVERYTHING, I'LL EAT A GOOD LUNCH, DON'T HAVE ANY TESTS, QUIZZES OR SPECIAL EVENTS SCHEDULED, HAVE PLENTY OF GAS AND YES, I'LL DRIVE CAREFULLY.
SCOTT and BORGMAN 5/9
BRAVO, DUDE!
MY GOAL IS ZERO CONVERSATION BY 2012.
CLAP! CLAP! CLAP! CLAP!
©2011 ZITS Partnership. Distributed by King Features Syndicate

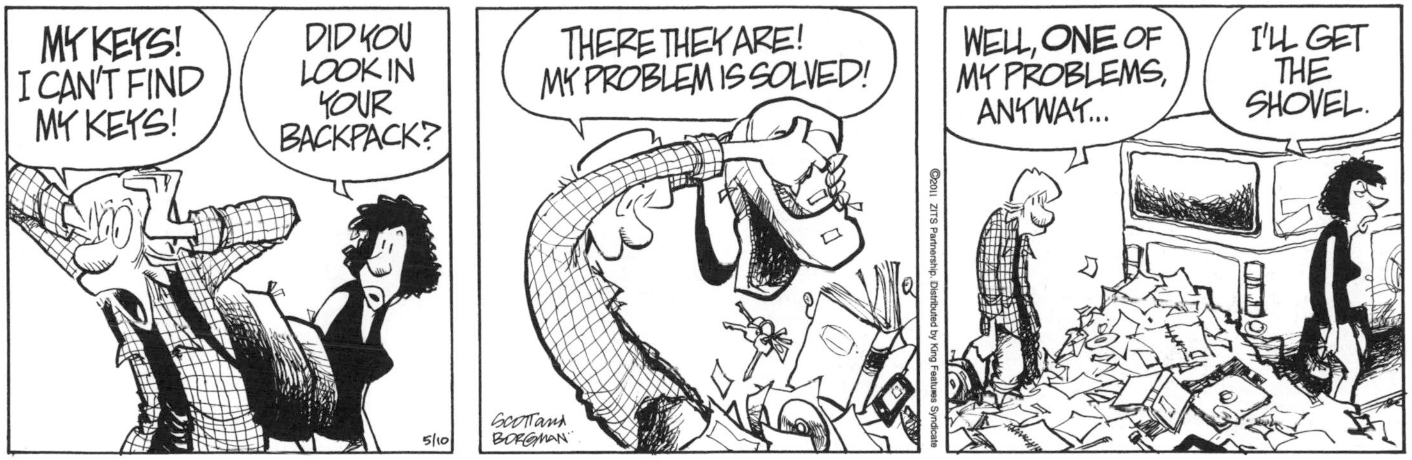
MY KEYS! I CAN'T FIND MY KEYS!
DID YOU LOOK IN YOUR BACKPACK?
5/10
THERE THEY ARE! MY PROBLEM IS SOLVED!
SCOTT and BORGMAN
WELL, ONE OF MY PROBLEMS, ANYWAY...
I'LL GET THE SHOVEL.
©2011 ZITS Partnership. Distributed by King Features Syndicate

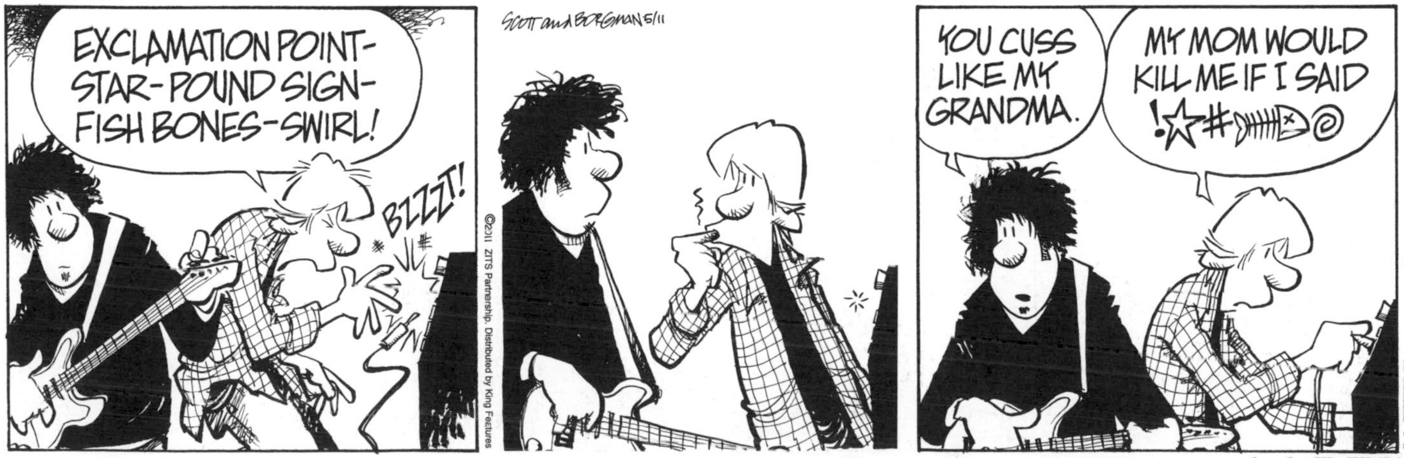
EXCLAMATION POINT-STAR-POUND SIGN-FISH BONES-SWIRL!
BZZZT!
©2011 ZITS Partnership. Distributed by King Features
SCOTT and BORGMAN 5/11
YOU CUSS LIKE MY GRANDMA.
MY MOM WOULD KILL ME IF I SAID !☆#

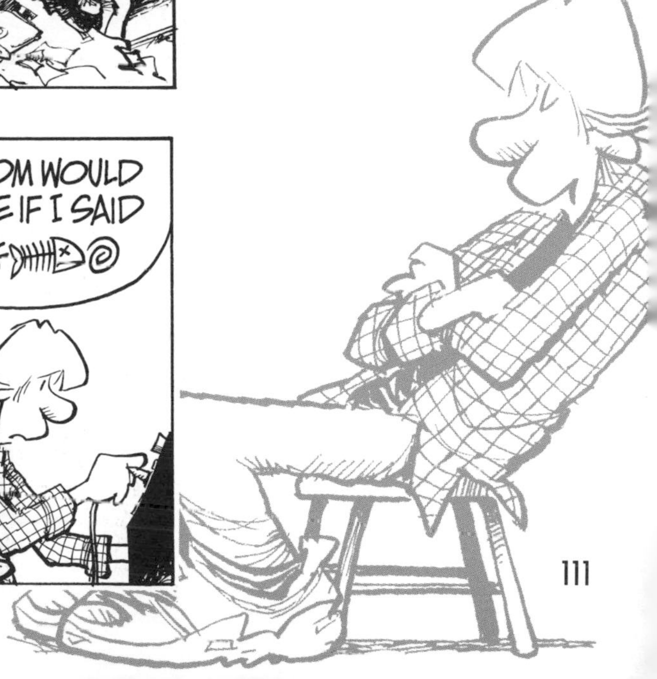

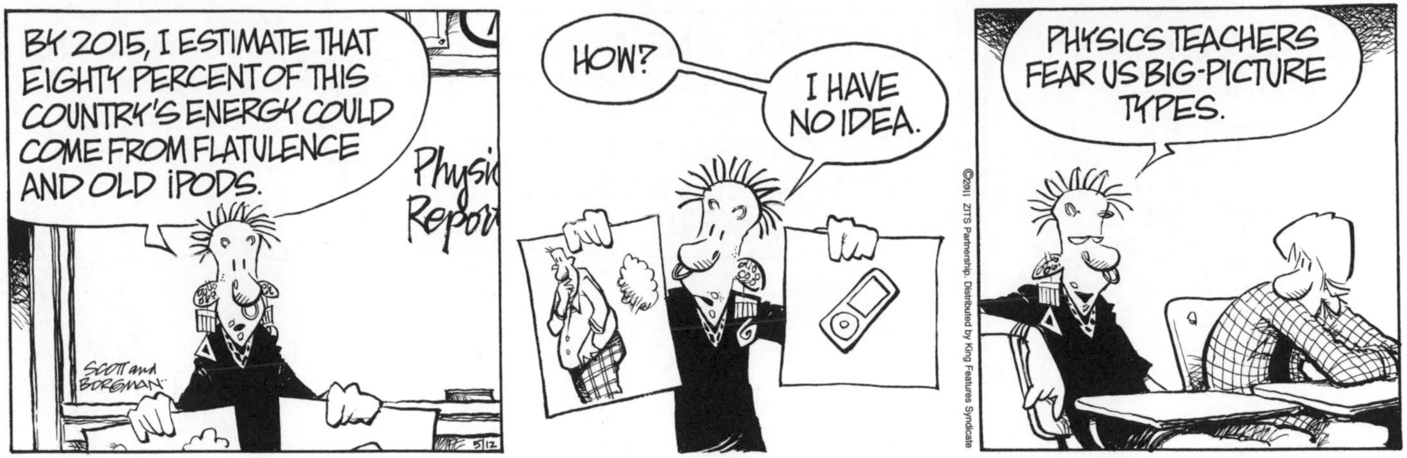
BY 2015, I ESTIMATE THAT EIGHTY PERCENT OF THIS COUNTRY'S ENERGY COULD COME FROM FLATULENCE AND OLD iPODS.
Physic
Repor
SCOTT and BORGMAN
5/12
HOW?
I HAVE NO IDEA.
©2011 ZITS Partnership. Distributed by King Features Syndicate
PHYSICS TEACHERS FEAR US BIG-PICTURE TYPES.

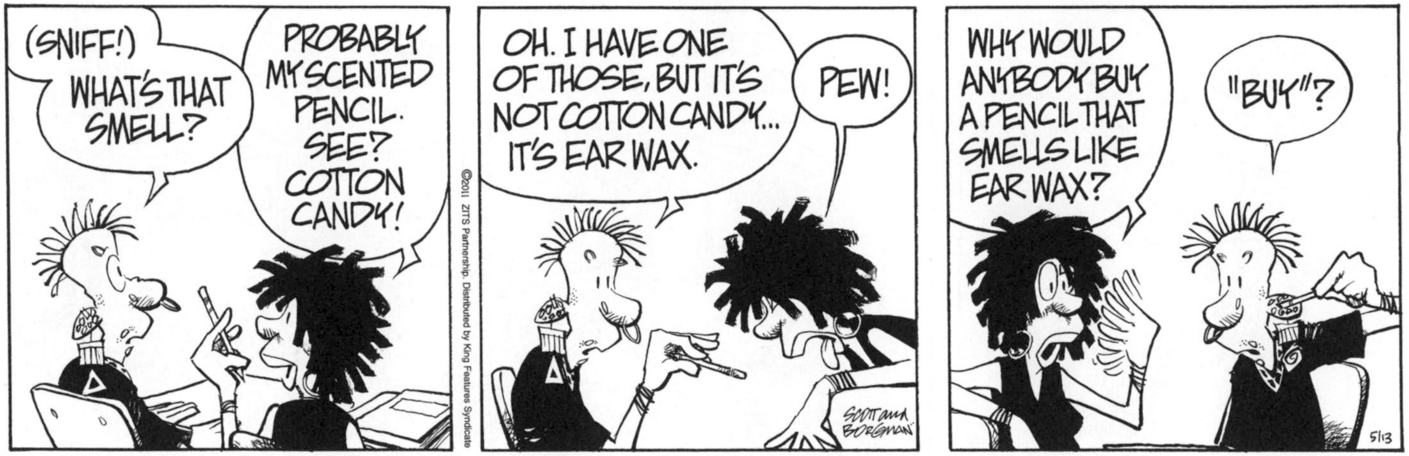
(SNIFF!)
WHAT'S THAT SMELL?
PROBABLY MY SCENTED PENCIL. SEE? COTTON CANDY!
©2011 ZITS Partnership. Distributed by King Features Syndicate
OH. I HAVE ONE OF THOSE, BUT IT'S NOT COTTON CANDY... IT'S EAR WAX.
PEW!
SCOTT and BORGMAN
WHY WOULD ANYBODY BUY A PENCIL THAT SMELLS LIKE EAR WAX?
"BUY"?
5/13

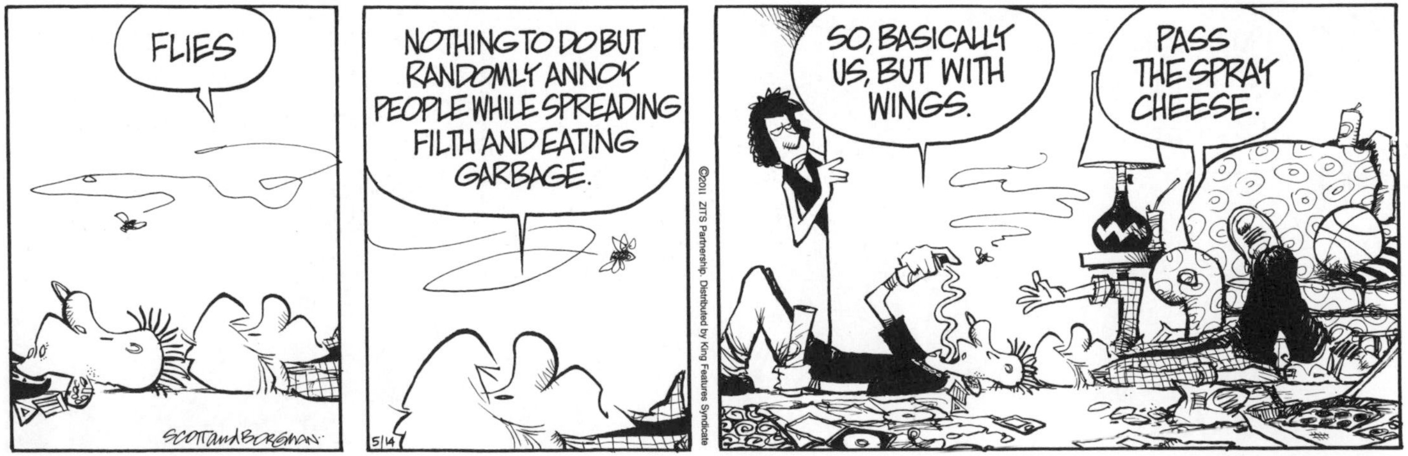
FLIES
SCOTT and BORGMAN
NOTHING TO DO BUT RANDOMLY ANNOY PEOPLE WHILE SPREADING FILTH AND EATING GARBAGE.
5/14
©2011 ZITS Partnership. Distributed by King Features Syndicate
SO, BASICALLY US, BUT WITH WINGS.
PASS THE SPRAY CHEESE.

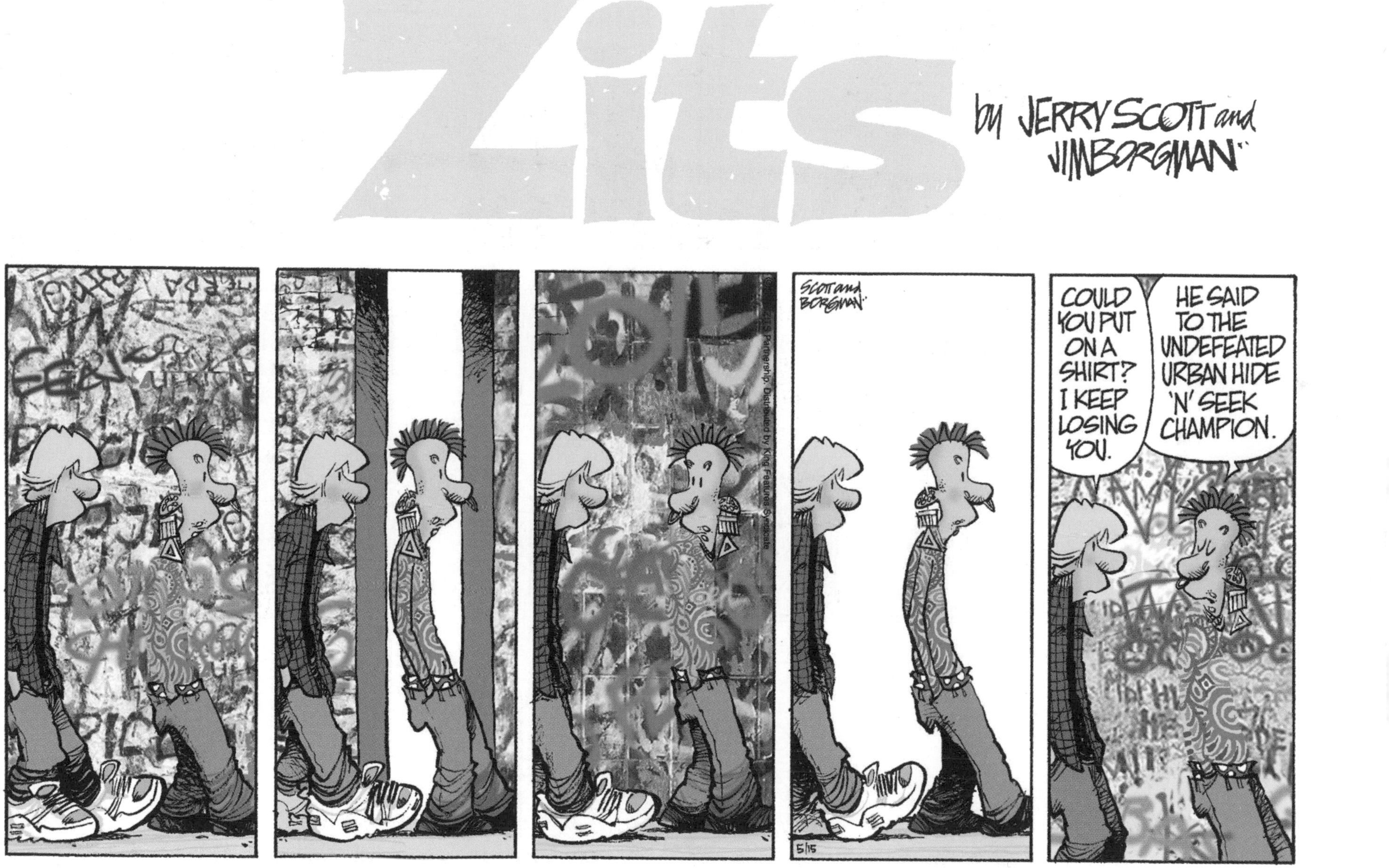
Zits
by JERRY SCOTT and JIM BORGMAN
ZITS Partnership. Distributed by King Features Syndicate
SCOTT and BORGMAN
5/15
COULD YOU PUT ON A SHIRT? I KEEP LOSING YOU.
HE SAID TO THE UNDEFEATED URBAN HIDE 'N' SEEK CHAMPION.

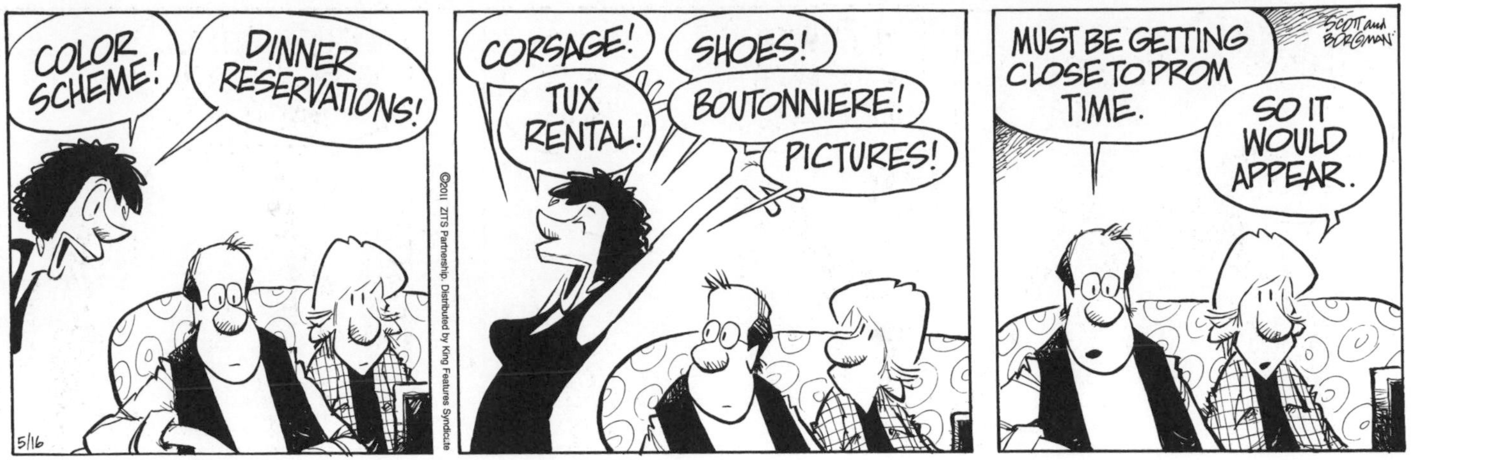
COLOR SCHEME!
DINNER RESERVATIONS!
5/16
©2011 ZITS Partnership. Distributed by King Features Syndicate
CORSAGE!
TUX RENTAL!
SHOES!
BOUTONNIERE!
PICTURES!
MUST BE GETTING CLOSE TO PROM TIME.
SO IT WOULD APPEAR.
SCOTT and BORGMAN

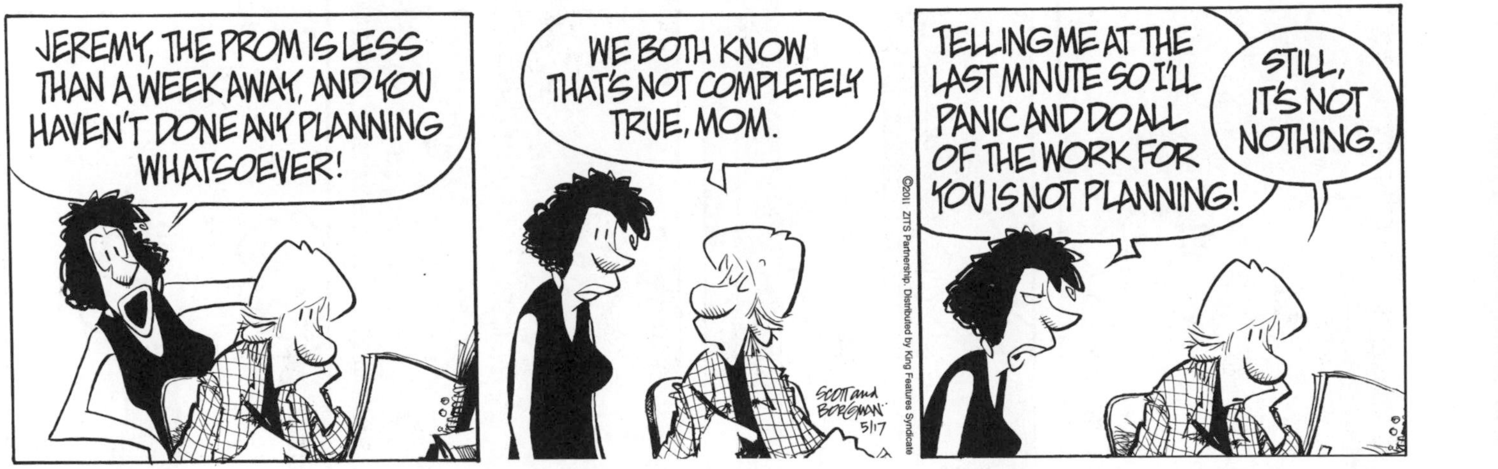
JEREMY, THE PROM IS LESS THAN A WEEK AWAY, AND YOU HAVEN'T DONE ANY PLANNING WHATSOEVER!
WE BOTH KNOW THAT'S NOT COMPLETELY TRUE, MOM.
SCOTT and BORGMAN
5/17
©2011 ZITS Partnership. Distributed by King Features Syndicate
TELLING ME AT THE LAST MINUTE SO I'LL PANIC AND DO ALL OF THE WORK FOR YOU IS NOT PLANNING!
STILL, IT'S NOT NOTHING.

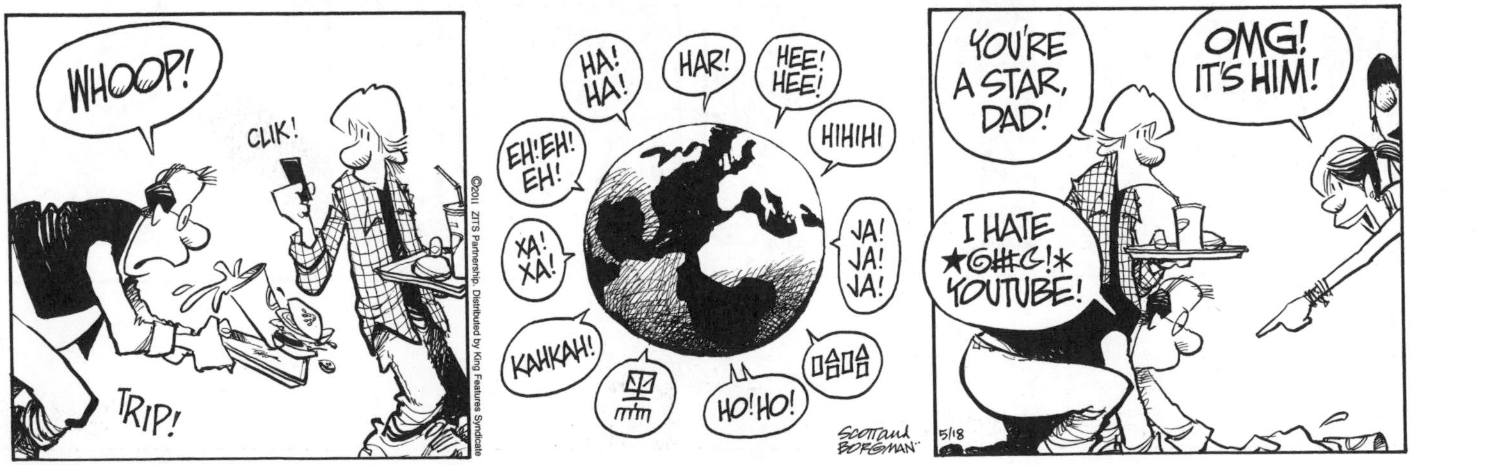
WHOOP!
CLIK!
TRIP!
©2011 ZITS Partnership. Distributed by King Features Syndicate
HA! HA!
HAR!
HEE! HEE!
EH! EH! EH!
HIHIHI
XA! XA!
JA! JA! JA!
KAHKAH!
HO! HO!
SCOTT and BORGMAN
YOU'RE A STAR, DAD!
OMG! IT'S HIM!
I HATE ★@#G!* YOUTUBE!
5/18

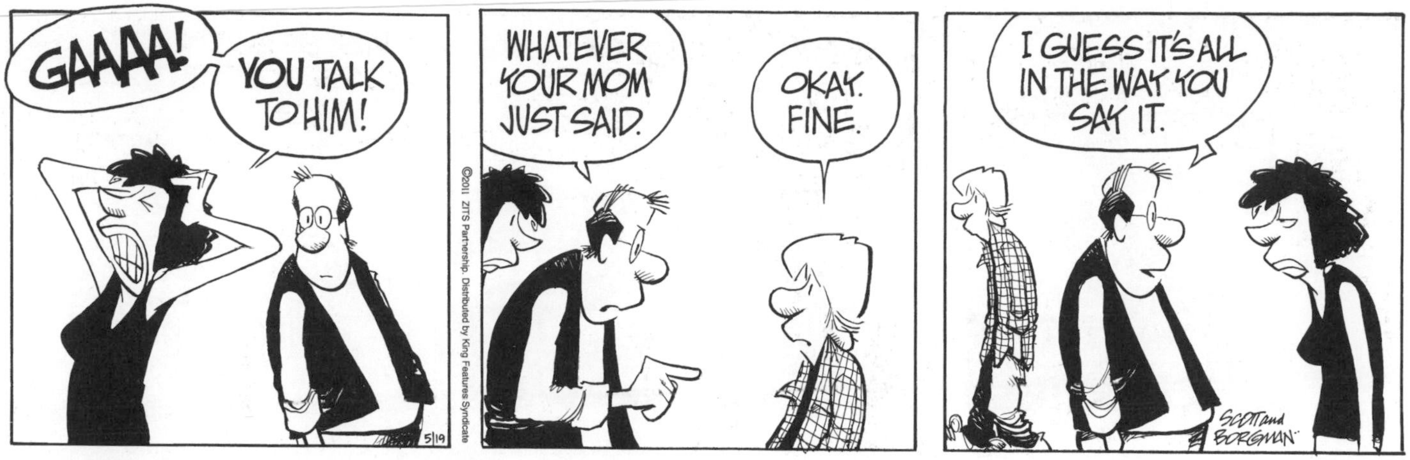
GAAAA!
YOU TALK TO HIM!
WHATEVER YOUR MOM JUST SAID.
OKAY. FINE.
I GUESS IT'S ALL IN THE WAY YOU SAY IT.
5/19
©2011 ZITS Partnership. Distributed by King Features Syndicate
SCOTT and BORGMAN

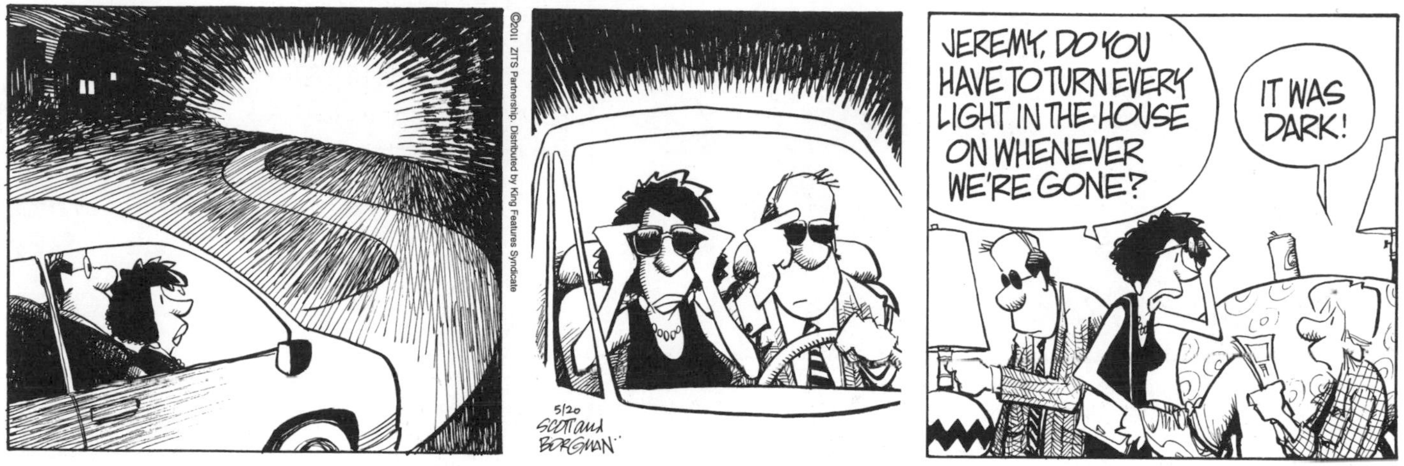
JEREMY, DO YOU HAVE TO TURN EVERY LIGHT IN THE HOUSE ON WHENEVER WE'RE GONE?
IT WAS DARK!
5/20
©2011 ZITS Partnership. Distributed by King Features Syndicate
SCOTT and BORGMAN

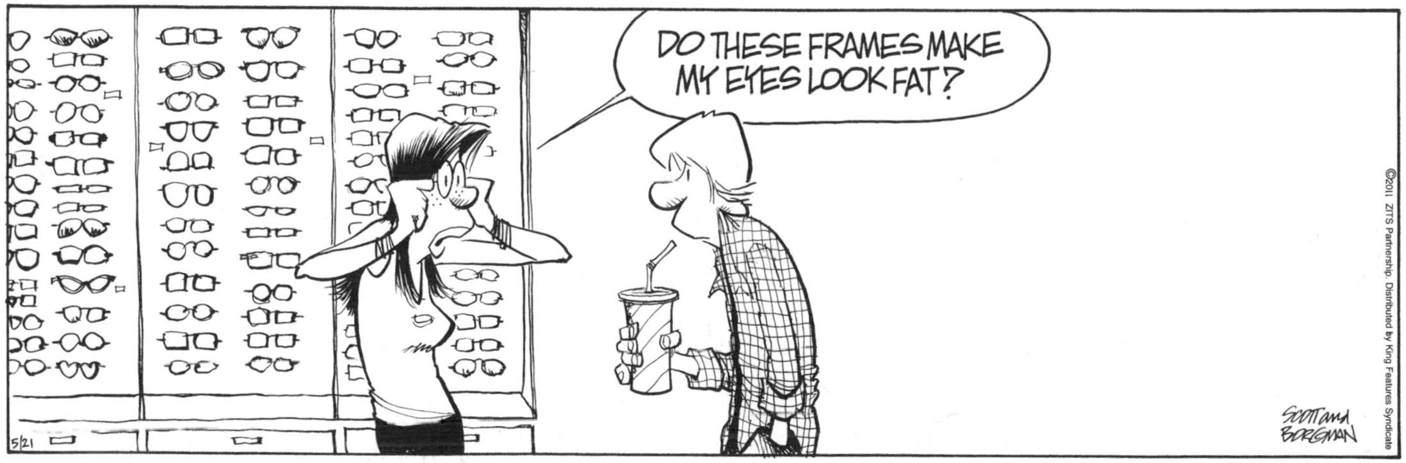
DO THESE FRAMES MAKE MY EYES LOOK FAT?
5/21
©2011 ZITS Partnership. Distributed by King Features Syndicate
SCOTT and BORGMAN

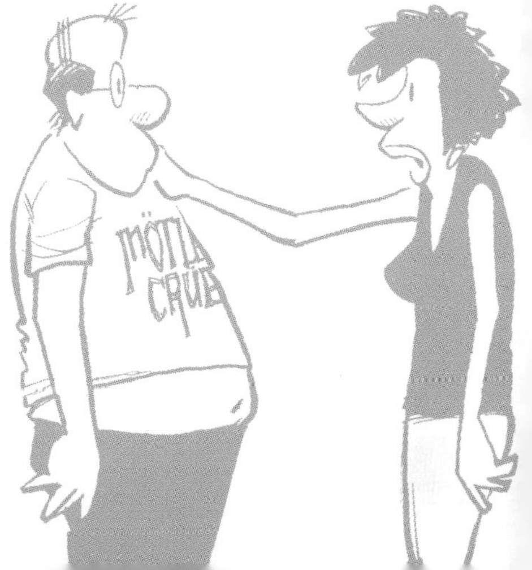

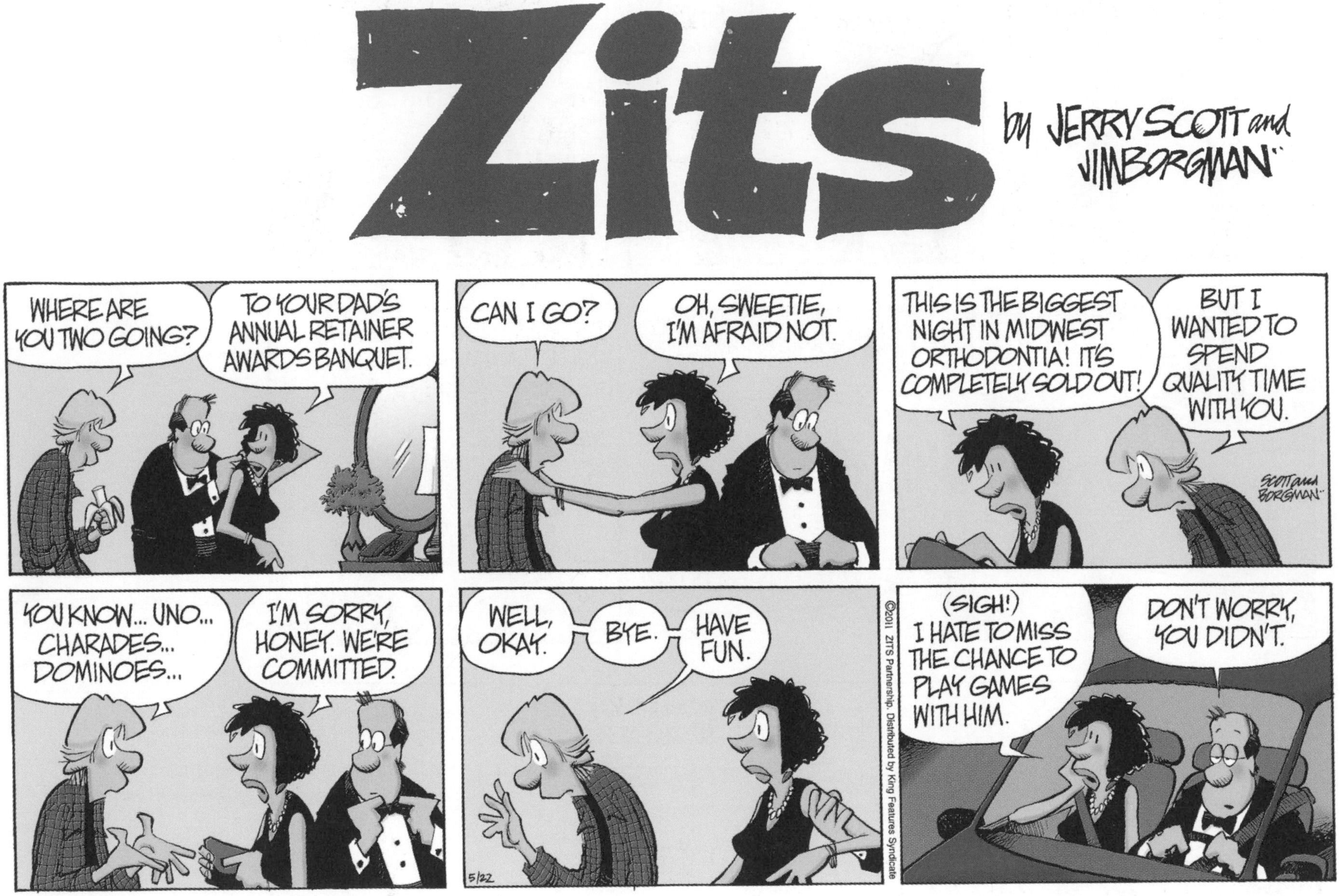
Zits
by JERRY SCOTT and JIM BORGMAN
WHERE ARE YOU TWO GOING?
TO YOUR DAD'S ANNUAL RETAINER AWARDS BANQUET.
CAN I GO?
OH, SWEETIE, I'M AFRAID NOT.
THIS IS THE BIGGEST NIGHT IN MIDWEST ORTHODONTIA! IT'S COMPLETELY SOLD OUT!
BUT I WANTED TO SPEND QUALITY TIME WITH YOU.
SCOTT and BORGMAN
YOU KNOW... UNO... CHARADES... DOMINOES...
I'M SORRY, HONEY. WE'RE COMMITTED.
WELL, OKAY.
BYE.
HAVE FUN.
5/22
©2011 ZITS Partnership. Distributed by King Features Syndicate
(SIGH!) I HATE TO MISS THE CHANCE TO PLAY GAMES WITH HIM.
DON'T WORRY, YOU DIDN'T.

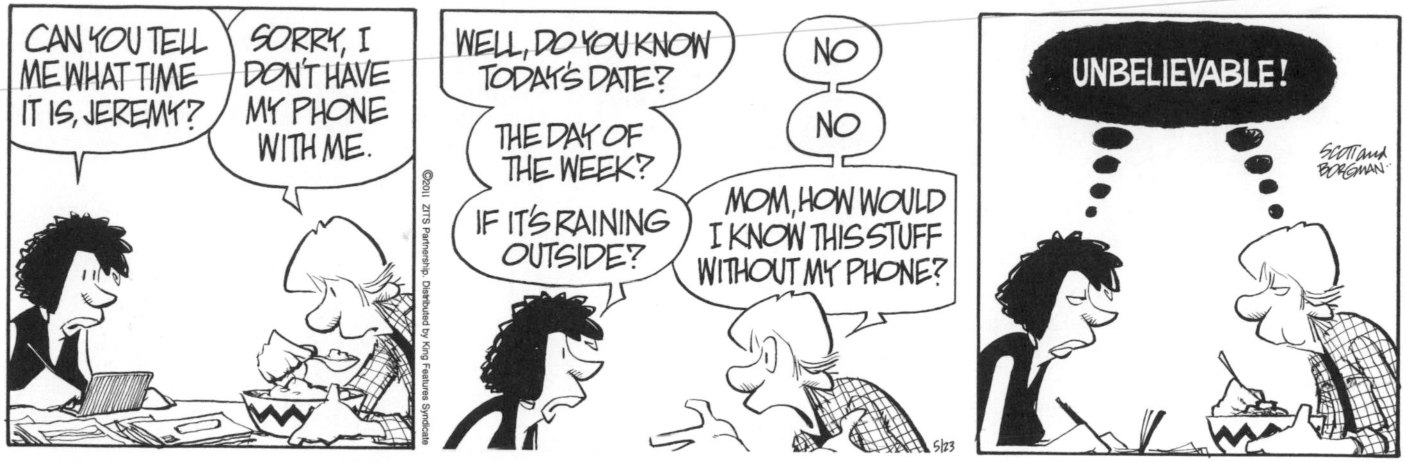
CAN YOU TELL ME WHAT TIME IT IS, JEREMY?
SORRY, I DON'T HAVE MY PHONE WITH ME.
WELL, DO YOU KNOW TODAY'S DATE?
NO
THE DAY OF THE WEEK?
NO
IF IT'S RAINING OUTSIDE?
MOM, HOW WOULD I KNOW THIS STUFF WITHOUT MY PHONE?
UNBELIEVABLE!
©2011 ZITS Partnership. Distributed by King Features Syndicate
5/23
SCOTT and BORGMAN

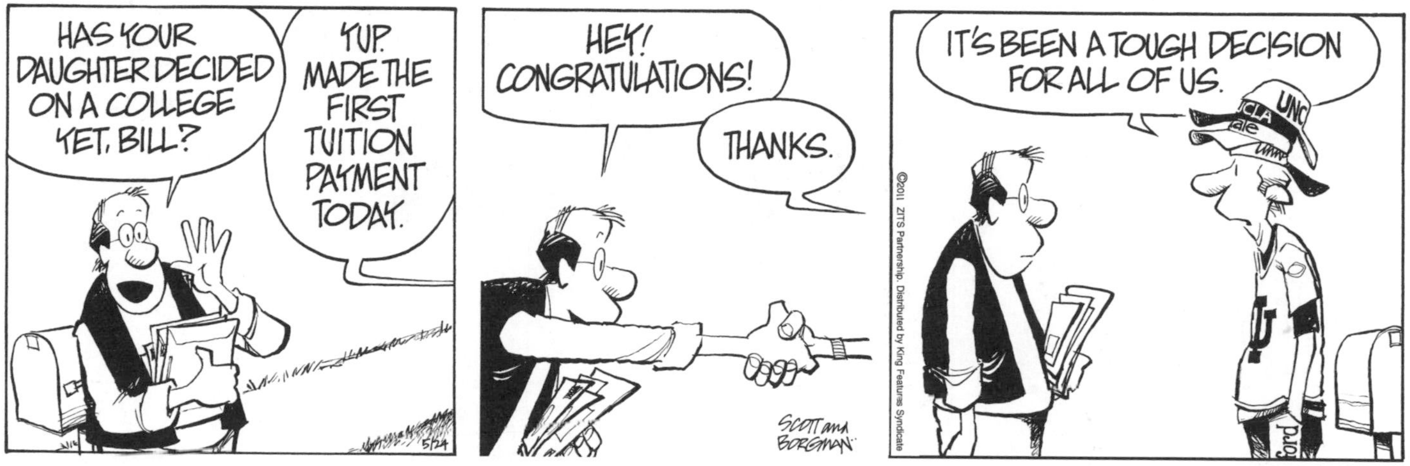
HAS YOUR DAUGHTER DECIDED ON A COLLEGE YET, BILL?
YUP. MADE THE FIRST TUITION PAYMENT TODAY.
5/24
HEY! CONGRATULATIONS!
THANKS.
SCOTT and BORGMAN
©2011 ZITS Partnership. Distributed by King Features Syndicate
IT'S BEEN A TOUGH DECISION FOR ALL OF US.

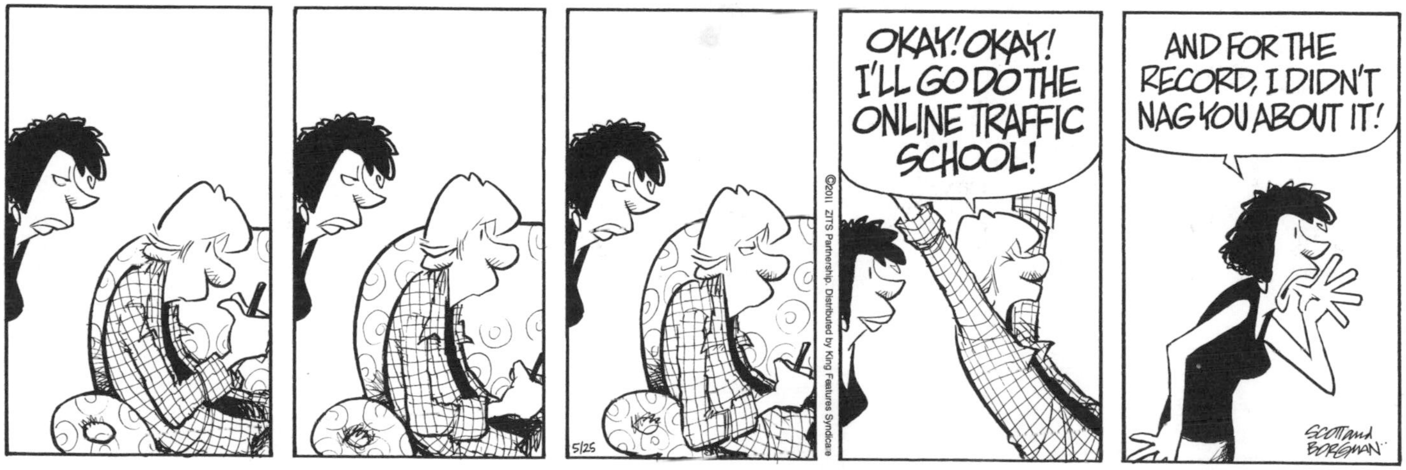
5/25
©2011 ZITS Partnership. Distributed by King Features Syndicate
OKAY! OKAY! I'LL GO DO THE ONLINE TRAFFIC SCHOOL!
AND FOR THE RECORD, I DIDN'T NAG YOU ABOUT IT!
SCOTT and BORGMAN

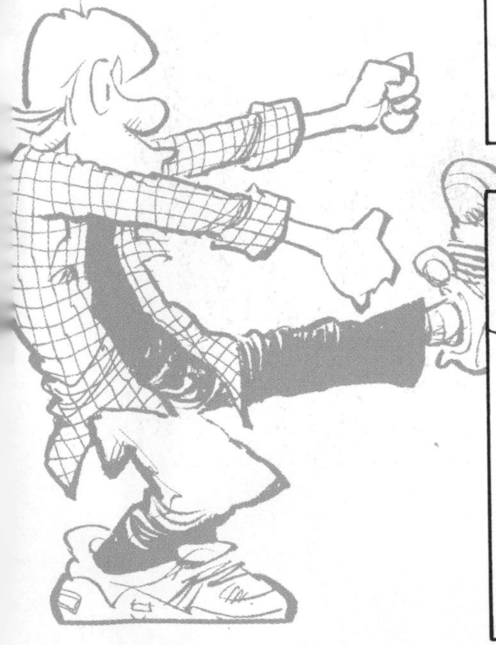

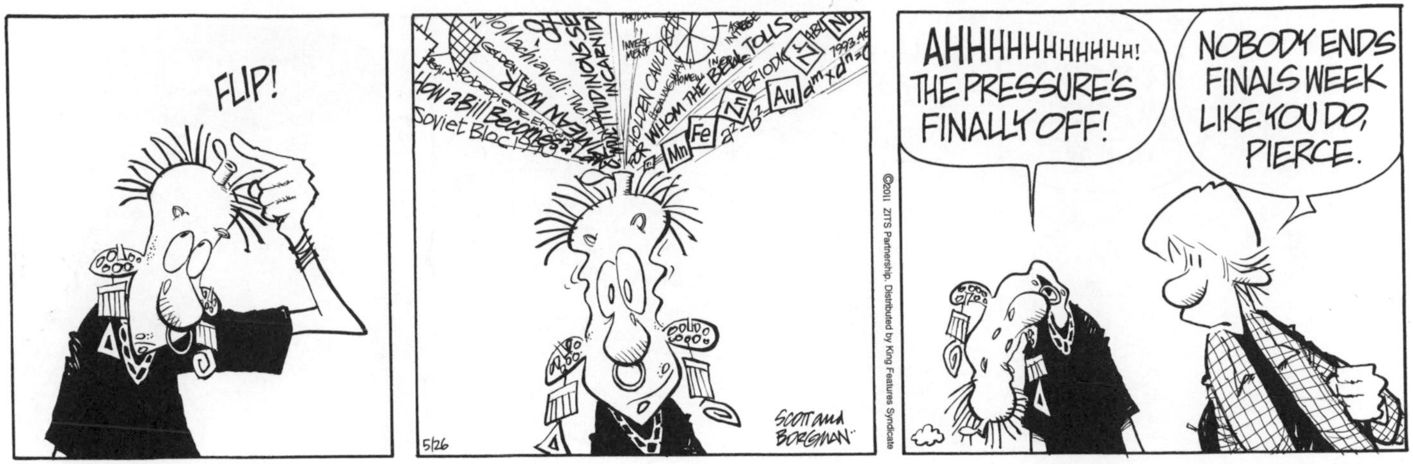

FLIP!
5/26
SCOTT and BORGMAN
©2011 ZITS Partnership. Distributed by King Features Syndicate
AHHHHHHHHHH! THE PRESSURE'S FINALLY OFF!
NOBODY ENDS FINALS WEEK LIKE YOU DO, PIERCE.

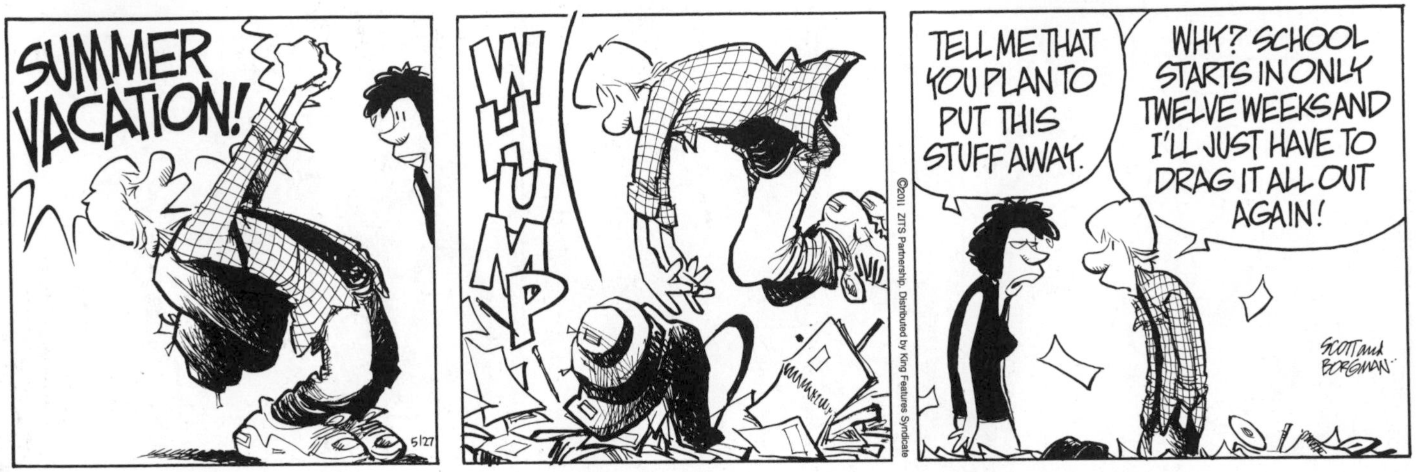

SUMMER VACATION!
5/27
WHUMP
©2011 ZITS Partnership. Distributed by King Features Syndicate
TELL ME THAT YOU PLAN TO PUT THIS STUFF AWAY.
WHY? SCHOOL STARTS IN ONLY TWELVE WEEKS AND I'LL JUST HAVE TO DRAG IT ALL OUT AGAIN!
SCOTT and BORGMAN

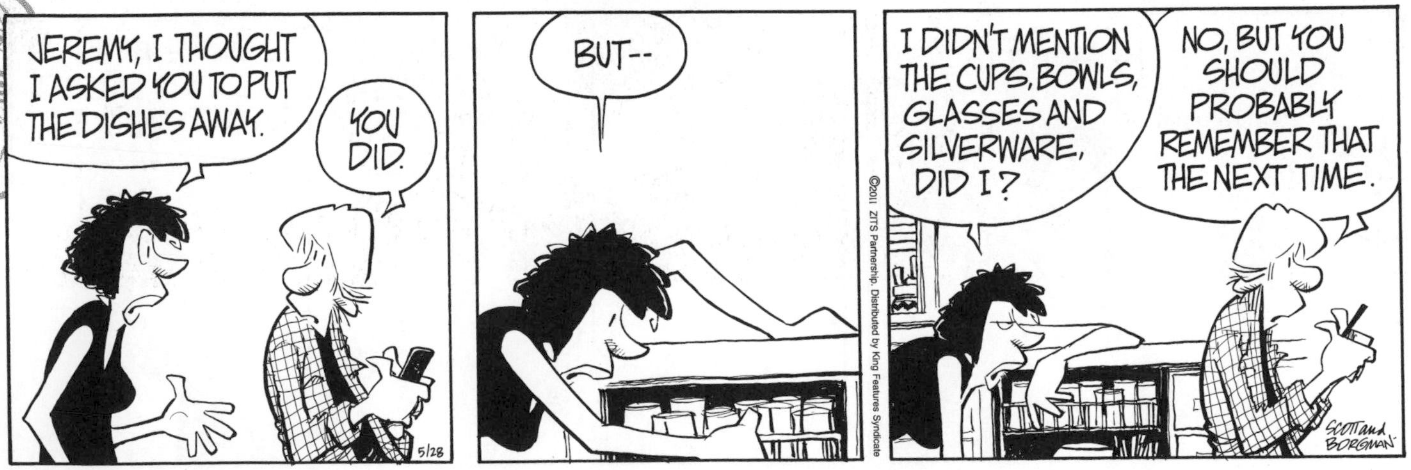

JEREMY, I THOUGHT I ASKED YOU TO PUT THE DISHES AWAY.
YOU DID.
5/28
BUT--
©2011 ZITS Partnership. Distributed by King Features Syndicate
I DIDN'T MENTION THE CUPS, BOWLS, GLASSES AND SILVERWARE, DID I?
NO, BUT YOU SHOULD PROBABLY REMEMBER THAT THE NEXT TIME.
SCOTT and BORGMAN

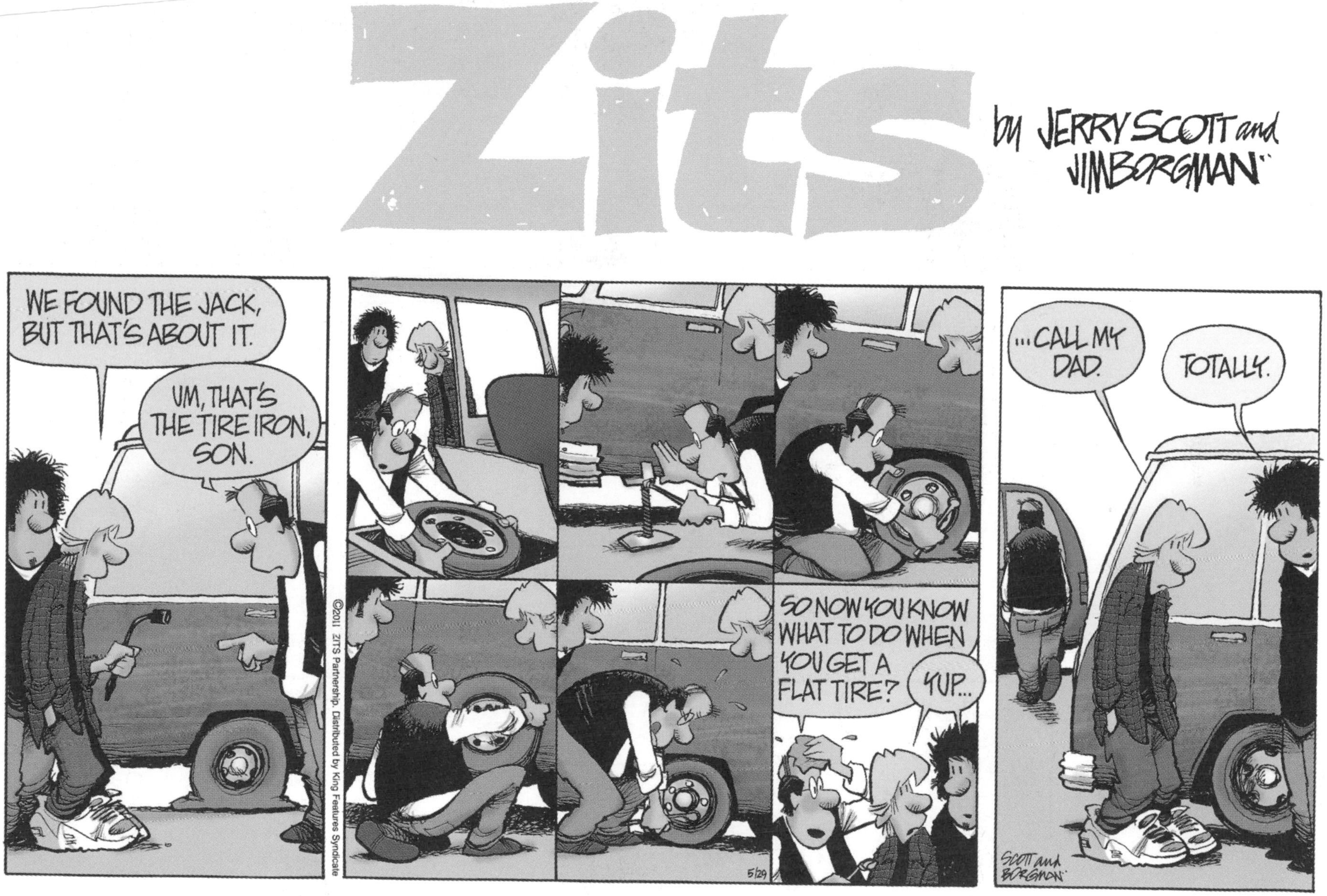
Zits
by JERRY SCOTT and JIM BORGMAN
WE FOUND THE JACK, BUT THAT'S ABOUT IT.
UM, THAT'S THE TIRE IRON, SON.
©2011 ZITS Partnership. Distributed by King Features Syndicate
5/29
SO NOW YOU KNOW WHAT TO DO WHEN YOU GET A FLAT TIRE?
YUP...
...CALL MY DAD.
TOTALLY.
SCOTT and BORGMAN

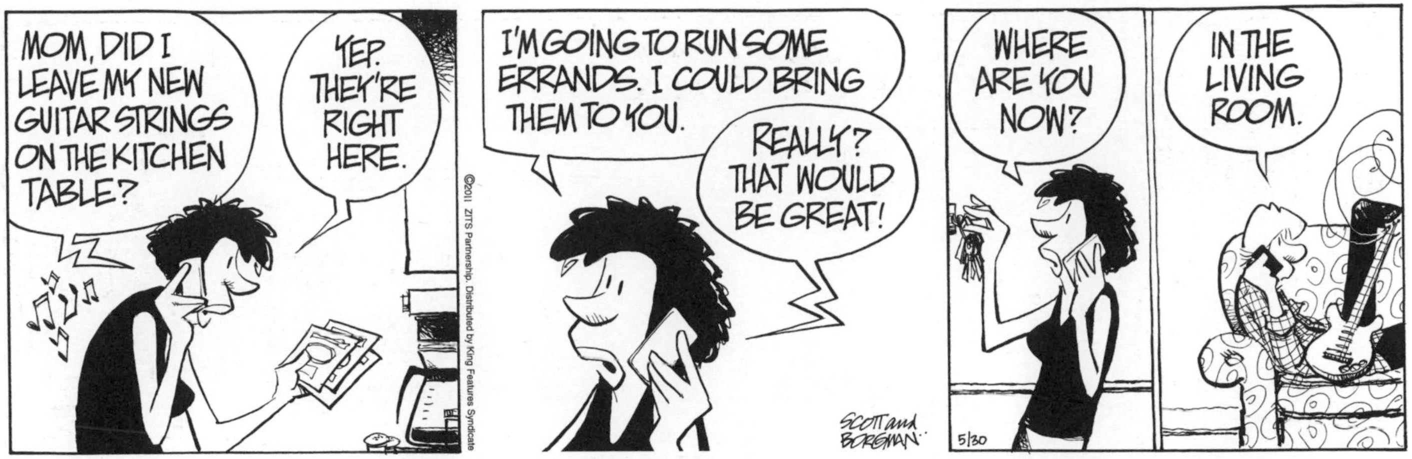

MOM, DID I LEAVE MY NEW GUITAR STRINGS ON THE KITCHEN TABLE?
YEP. THEY'RE RIGHT HERE.
©2011 ZITS Partnership. Distributed by King Features Syndicate
I'M GOING TO RUN SOME ERRANDS. I COULD BRING THEM TO YOU.
REALLY? THAT WOULD BE GREAT!
SCOTT and BORGMAN
WHERE ARE YOU NOW?
IN THE LIVING ROOM.
5/30

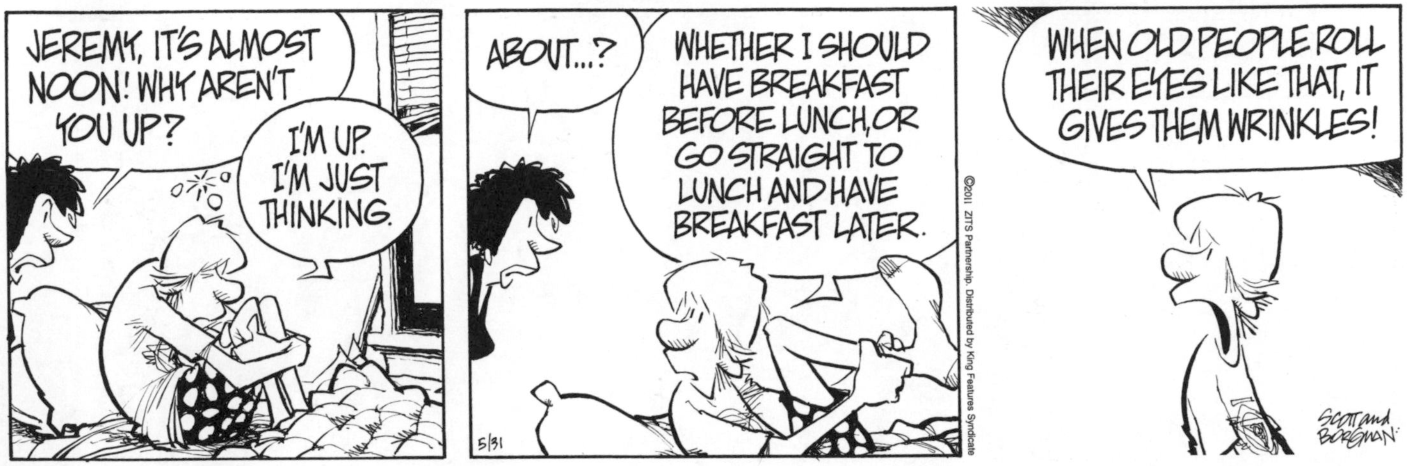

JEREMY, IT'S ALMOST NOON! WHY AREN'T YOU UP?
I'M UP. I'M JUST THINKING.
5/31
ABOUT...?
WHETHER I SHOULD HAVE BREAKFAST BEFORE LUNCH, OR GO STRAIGHT TO LUNCH AND HAVE BREAKFAST LATER.
©2011 ZITS Partnership. Distributed by King Features Syndicate
WHEN OLD PEOPLE ROLL THEIR EYES LIKE THAT, IT GIVES THEM WRINKLES!
SCOTT and BORGMAN

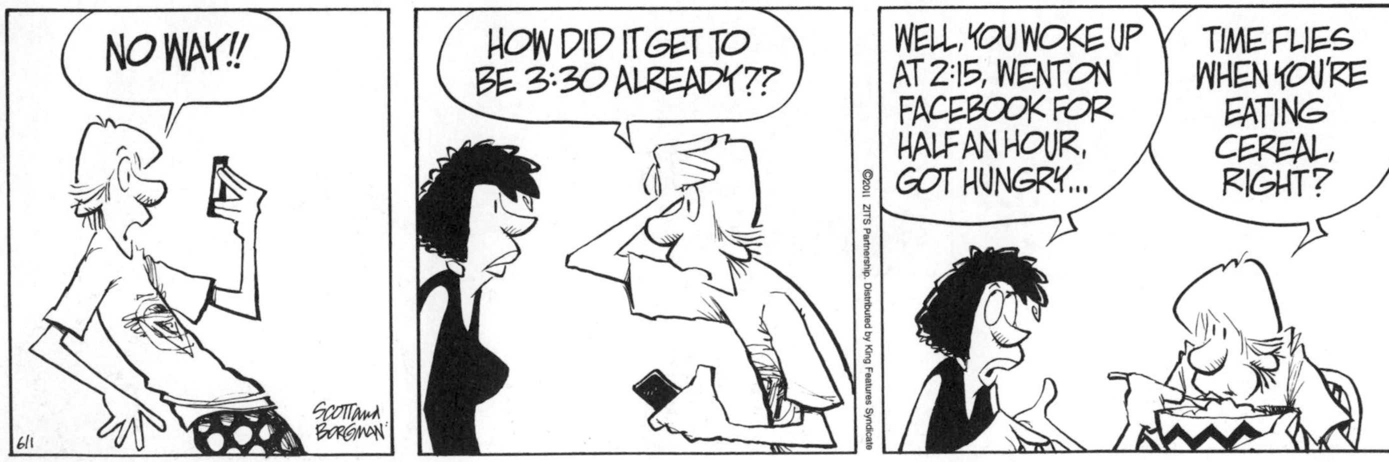

NO WAY!!
SCOTT and BORGMAN
6/1
HOW DID IT GET TO BE 3:30 ALREADY??
©2011 ZITS Partnership. Distributed by King Features Syndicate
WELL, YOU WOKE UP AT 2:15, WENT ON FACEBOOK FOR HALF AN HOUR, GOT HUNGRY...
TIME FLIES WHEN YOU'RE EATING CEREAL, RIGHT?

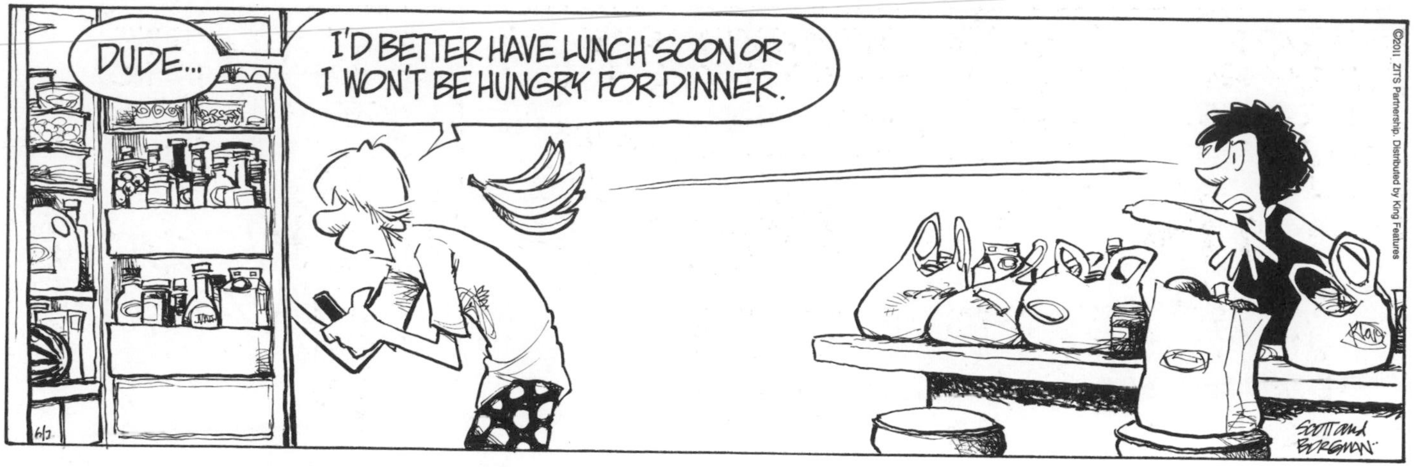
DUDE...
I'D BETTER HAVE LUNCH SOON OR I WON'T BE HUNGRY FOR DINNER.
©2011 ZITS Partnership. Distributed by King Features
SCOTT and BORGMAN

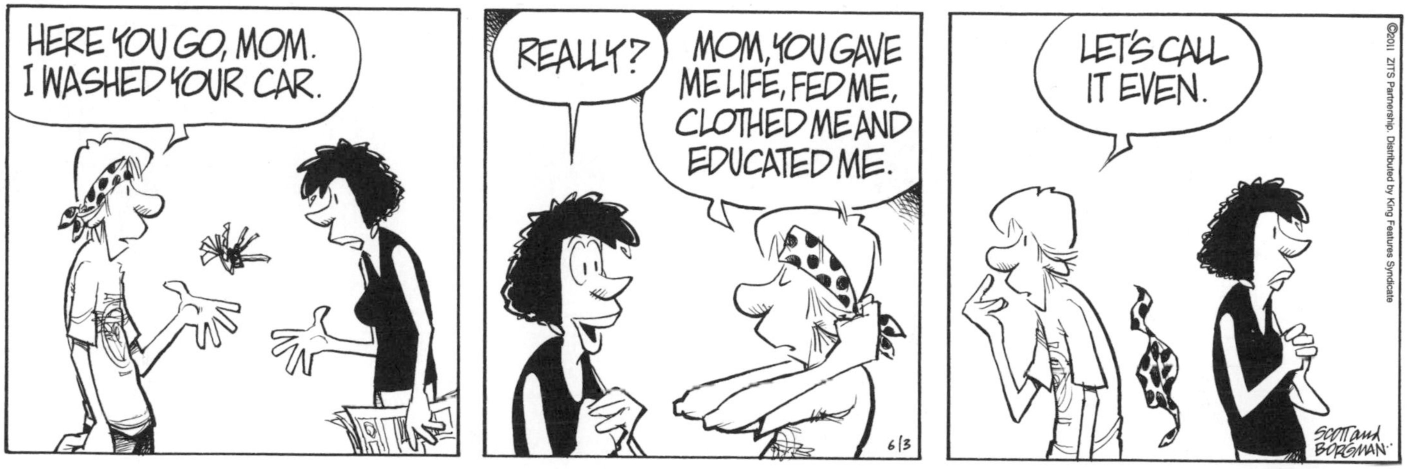
HERE YOU GO, MOM. I WASHED YOUR CAR.
REALLY?
MOM, YOU GAVE ME LIFE, FED ME, CLOTHED ME AND EDUCATED ME.
LET'S CALL IT EVEN.
©2011 ZITS Partnership. Distributed by King Features Syndicate
SCOTT and BORGMAN

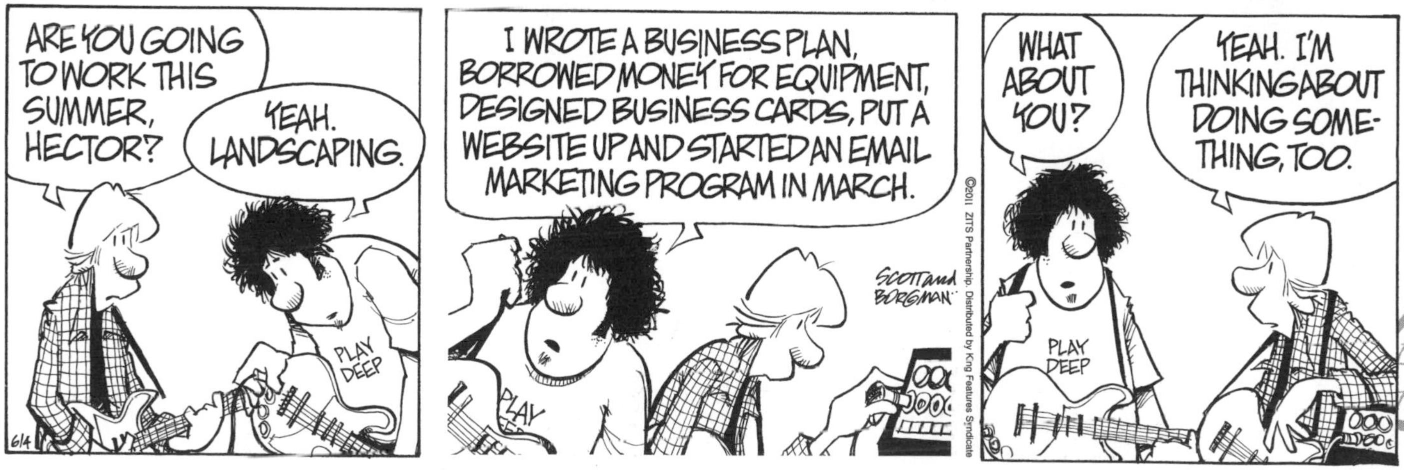
ARE YOU GOING TO WORK THIS SUMMER, HECTOR?
YEAH. LANDSCAPING.
PLAY DEEP
I WROTE A BUSINESS PLAN, BORROWED MONEY FOR EQUIPMENT, DESIGNED BUSINESS CARDS, PUT A WEBSITE UP AND STARTED AN EMAIL MARKETING PROGRAM IN MARCH.
SCOTT and BORGMAN
©2011 ZITS Partnership. Distributed by King Features Syndicate
WHAT ABOUT YOU?
YEAH. I'M THINKING ABOUT DOING SOME-THING, TOO.
PLAY DEEP

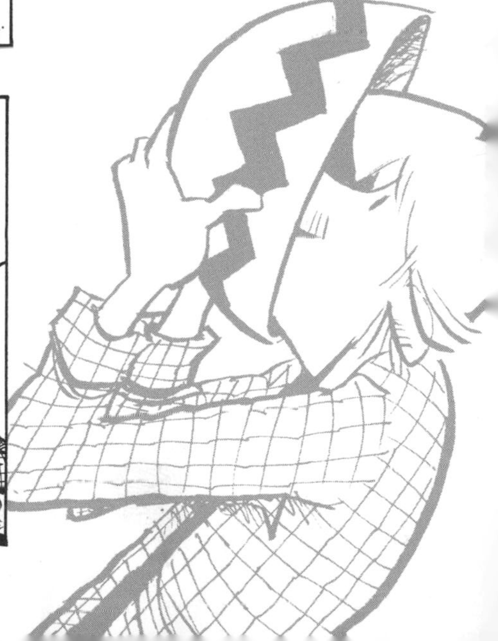

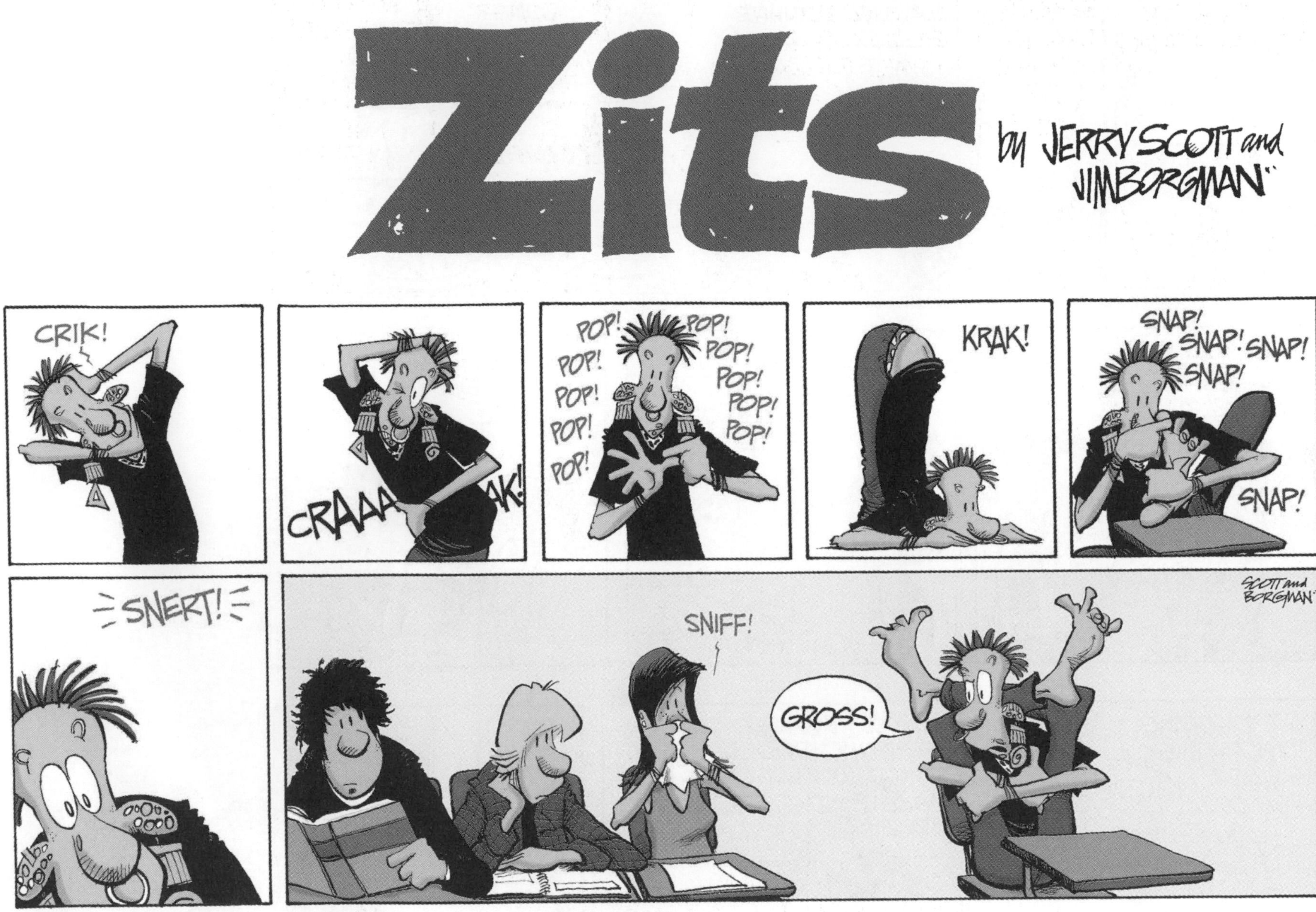
Zits
by JERRY SCOTT and JIM BORGMAN
CRIK!
CRAAA AK!
POP! POP! POP! POP! POP! POP! POP! POP! POP! POP! POP!
KRAK!
SNAP! SNAP! SNAP! SNAP! SNAP!
SNERT!
SCOTT and BORGMAN
SNIFF!
GROSS!

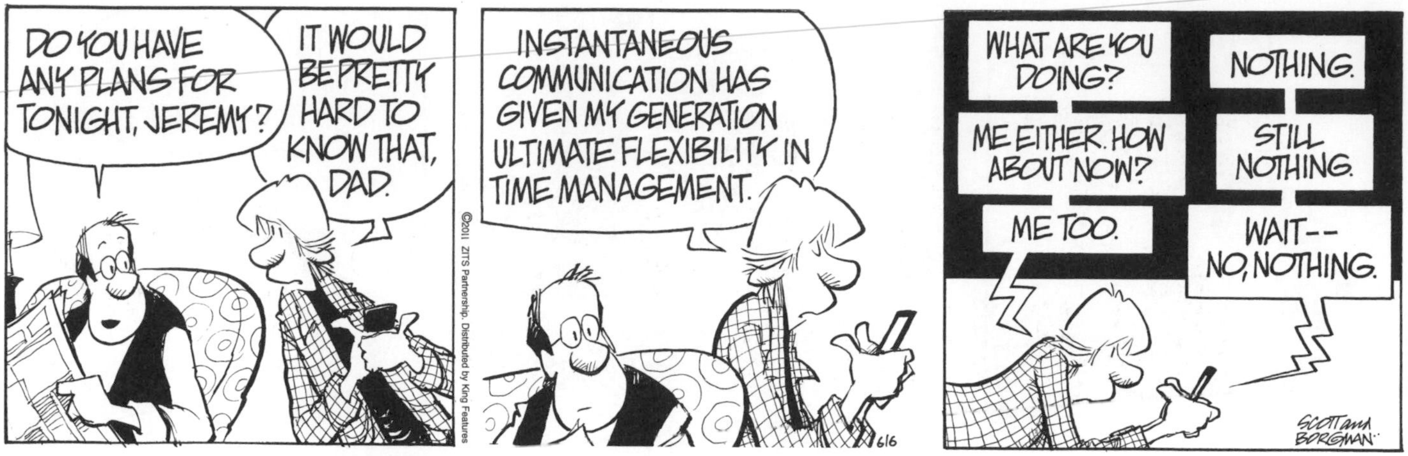
DO YOU HAVE ANY PLANS FOR TONIGHT, JEREMY?
IT WOULD BE PRETTY HARD TO KNOW THAT, DAD.
INSTANTANEOUS COMMUNICATION HAS GIVEN MY GENERATION ULTIMATE FLEXIBILITY IN TIME MANAGEMENT.
WHAT ARE YOU DOING?
NOTHING.
ME EITHER. HOW ABOUT NOW?
STILL NOTHING.
ME TOO.
WAIT-- NO, NOTHING.
©2011 ZITS Partnership. Distributed by King Features

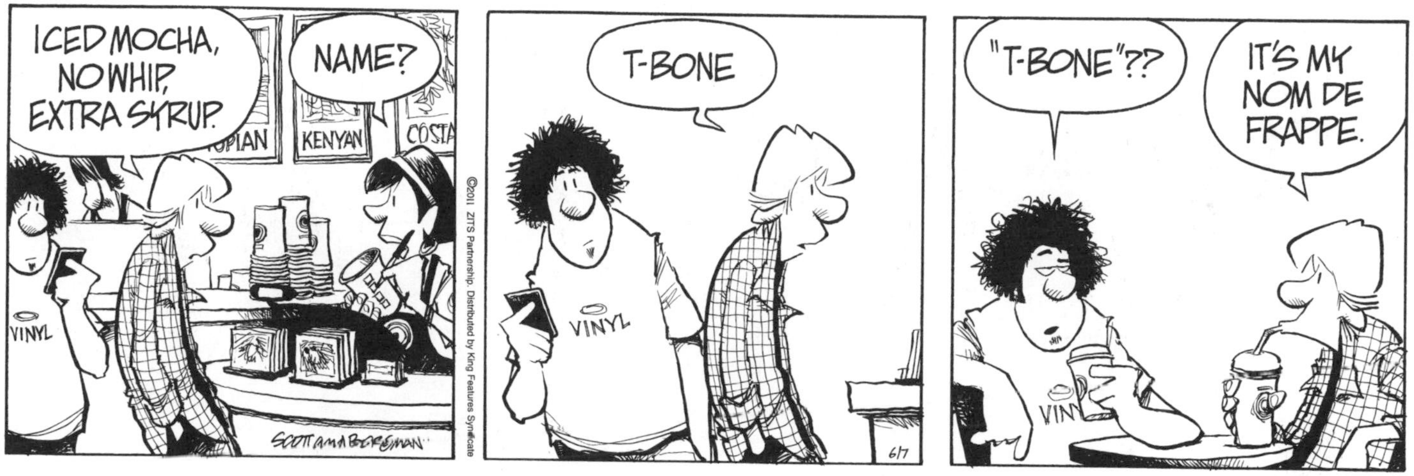
ICED MOCHA, NO WHIP, EXTRA SYRUP.
NAME?
KENYAN
T-BONE
"T-BONE"??
IT'S MY NOM DE FRAPPE.
VINYL
©2011 ZITS Partnership. Distributed by King Features Syndicate

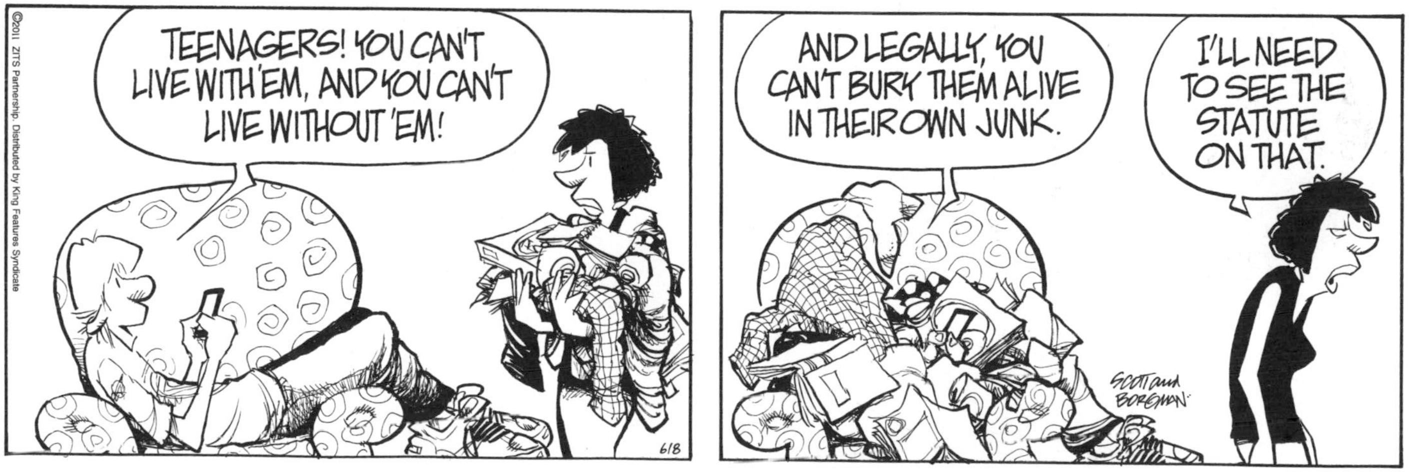
TEENAGERS! YOU CAN'T LIVE WITH 'EM, AND YOU CAN'T LIVE WITHOUT 'EM!
AND LEGALLY, YOU CAN'T BURY THEM ALIVE IN THEIR OWN JUNK.
I'LL NEED TO SEE THE STATUTE ON THAT.
©2011 ZITS Partnership. Distributed by King Features Syndicate

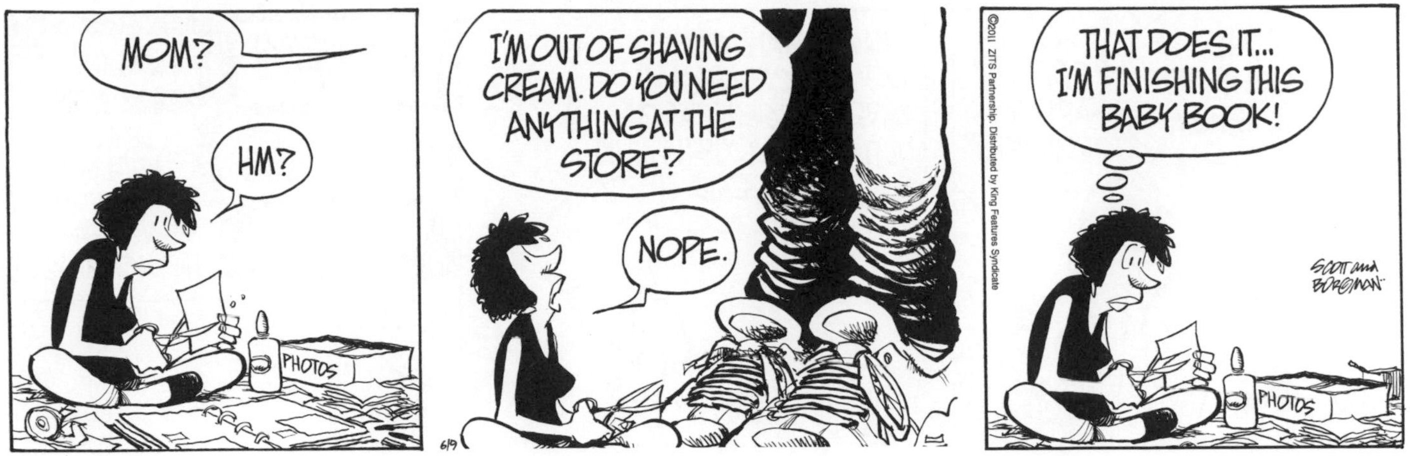
MOM?
HM?
I'M OUT OF SHAVING CREAM. DO YOU NEED ANYTHING AT THE STORE?
NOPE.
6/9
THAT DOES IT... I'M FINISHING THIS BABY BOOK!
PHOTOS
©2011 ZITS Partnership. Distributed by King Features Syndicate
SCOTT and BORGMAN

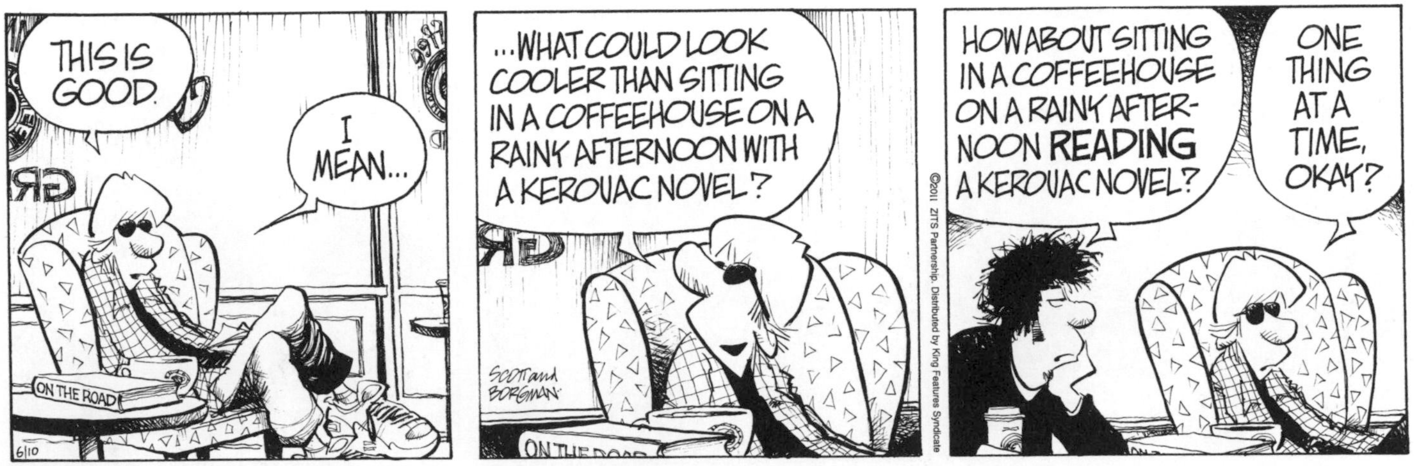
THIS IS GOOD.
I MEAN...
ON THE ROAD
6/10
...WHAT COULD LOOK COOLER THAN SITTING IN A COFFEEHOUSE ON A RAINY AFTERNOON WITH A KEROUAC NOVEL?
SCOTT and BORGMAN
©2011 ZITS Partnership. Distributed by King Features Syndicate
HOW ABOUT SITTING IN A COFFEEHOUSE ON A RAINY AFTERNOON **READING** A KEROUAC NOVEL?
ONE THING AT A TIME, OKAY?

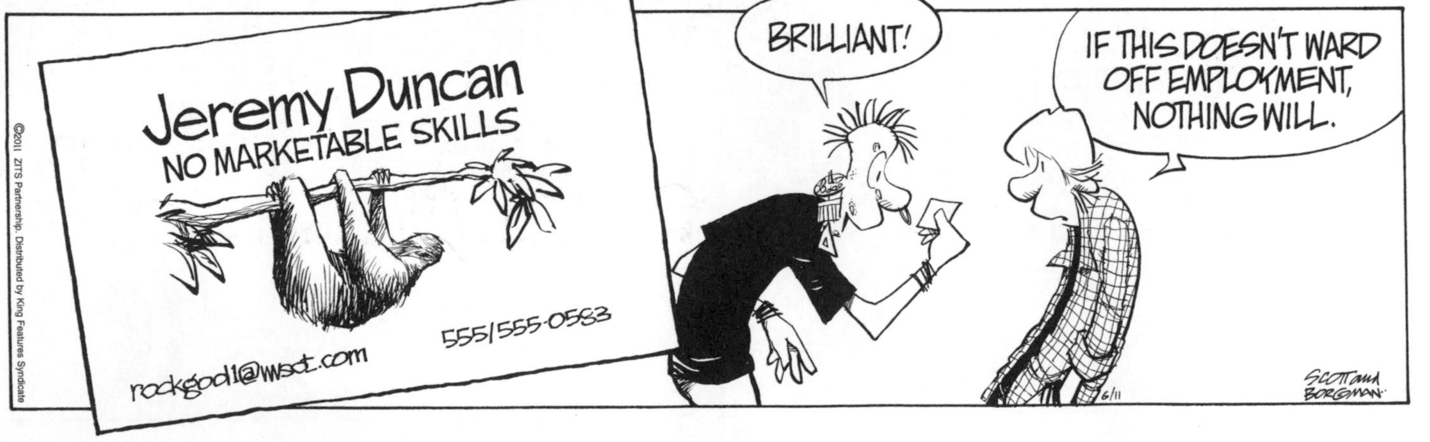
©2011 ZITS Partnership. Distributed by King Features Syndicate
Jeremy Duncan
NO MARKETABLE SKILLS
555/555-0583
rockgod1@wsct.com
BRILLIANT!
IF THIS DOESN'T WARD OFF EMPLOYMENT, NOTHING WILL.
SCOTT and BORGMAN
6/11

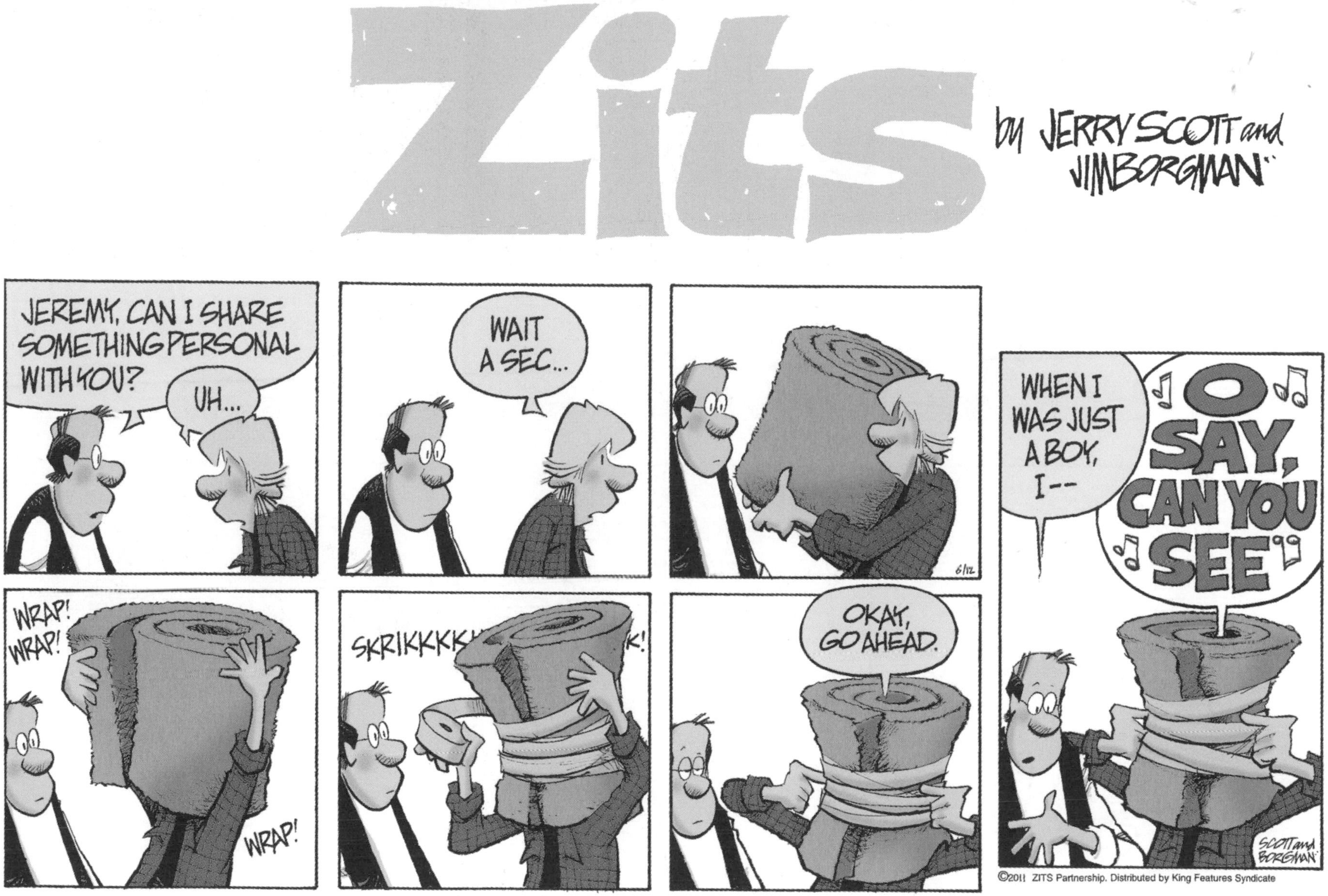
Zits
by JERRY SCOTT and JIM BORGMAN
JEREMY, CAN I SHARE SOMETHING PERSONAL WITH YOU?
UH...
WAIT A SEC...
WRAP! WRAP!
WRAP!
SKRIKKKK
K!
OKAY, GO AHEAD.
WHEN I WAS JUST A BOY, I--
O SAY, CAN YOU SEE
SCOTT and BORGMAN

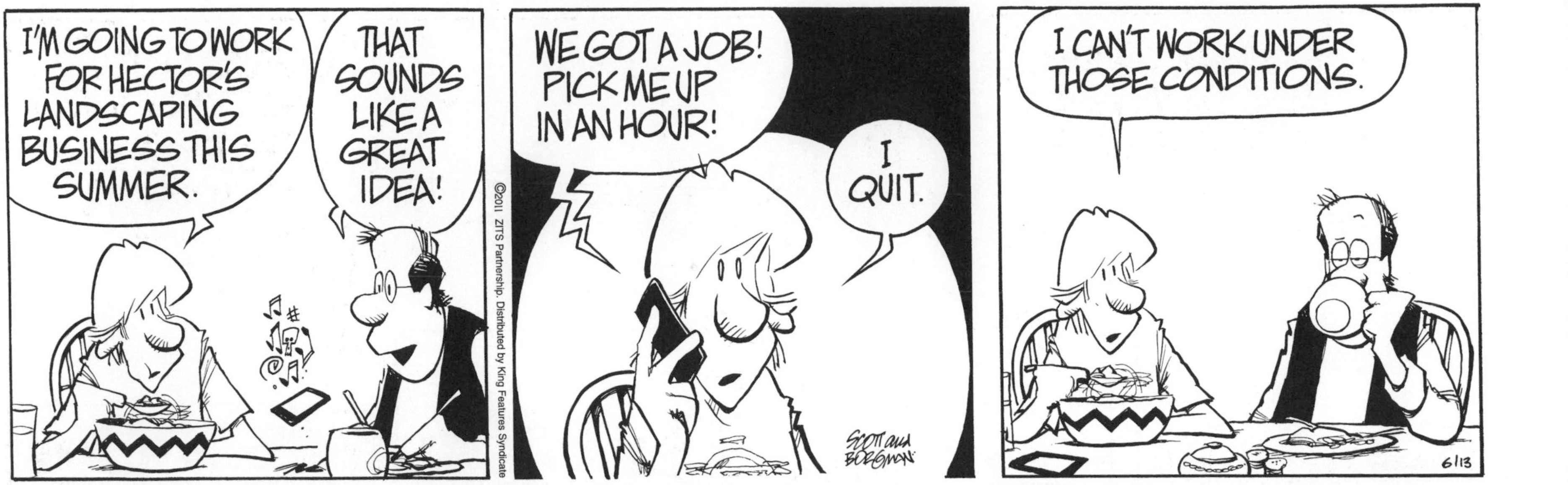
I'M GOING TO WORK FOR HECTOR'S LANDSCAPING BUSINESS THIS SUMMER.
THAT SOUNDS LIKE A GREAT IDEA!
©2011 ZITS Partnership. Distributed by King Features Syndicate
WE GOT A JOB! PICK ME UP IN AN HOUR!
I QUIT.
SCOTT and BORGMAN
I CAN'T WORK UNDER THOSE CONDITIONS.
6/13

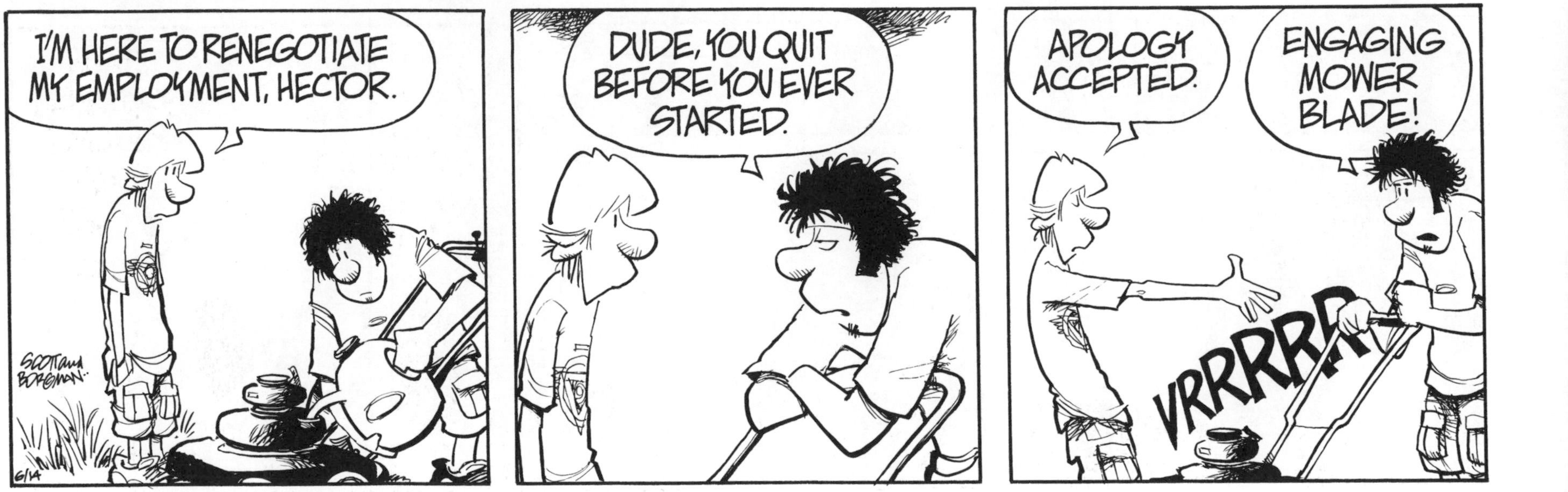
I'M HERE TO RENEGOTIATE MY EMPLOYMENT, HECTOR.
SCOTT and BORGMAN
6/14
DUDE, YOU QUIT BEFORE YOU EVER STARTED.
APOLOGY ACCEPTED.
ENGAGING MOWER BLADE!
VRRRRR

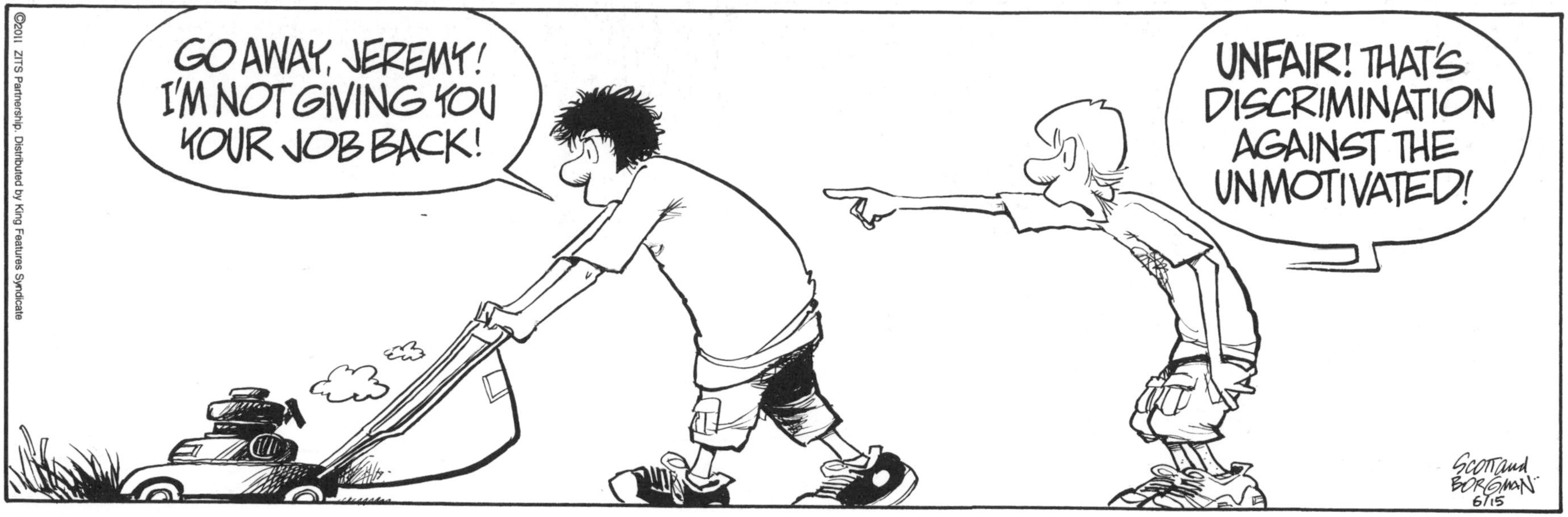
GO AWAY, JEREMY! I'M NOT GIVING YOU YOUR JOB BACK!
UNFAIR! THAT'S DISCRIMINATION AGAINST THE UNMOTIVATED!
SCOTT and BORGMAN 6/15

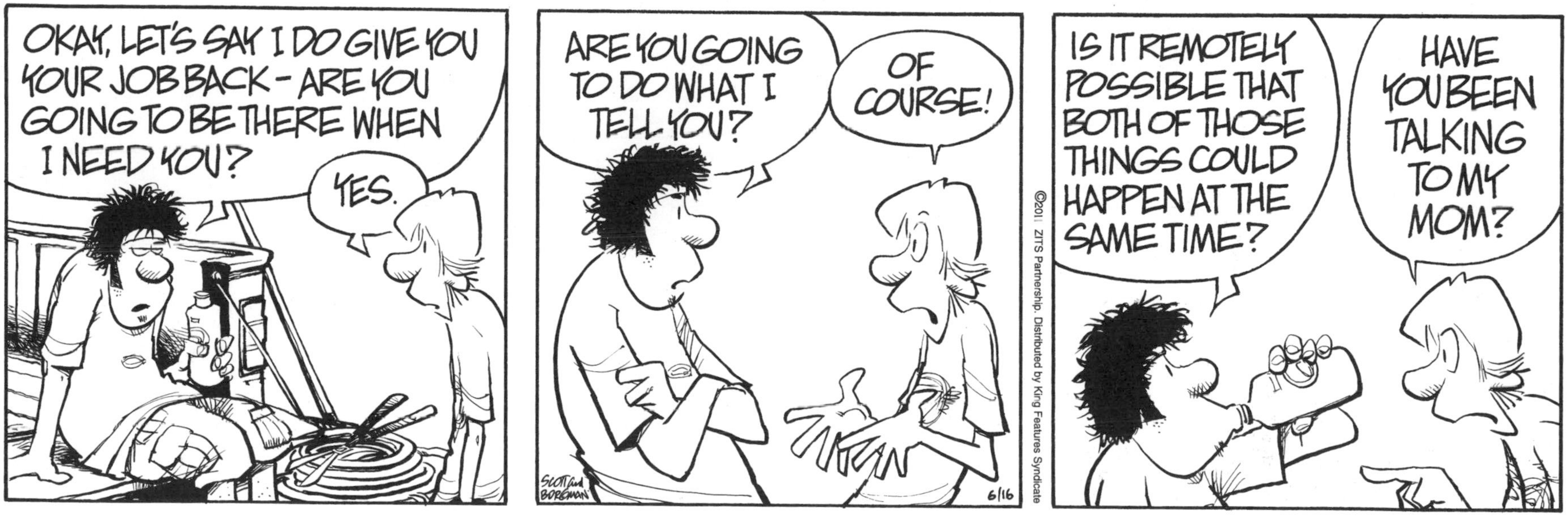
OKAY, LET'S SAY I DO GIVE YOU YOUR JOB BACK - ARE YOU GOING TO BE THERE WHEN I NEED YOU?
YES.
ARE YOU GOING TO DO WHAT I TELL YOU?
OF COURSE!
SCOTT and BORGMAN
6/16
IS IT REMOTELY POSSIBLE THAT BOTH OF THOSE THINGS COULD HAPPEN AT THE SAME TIME?
HAVE YOU BEEN TALKING TO MY MOM?

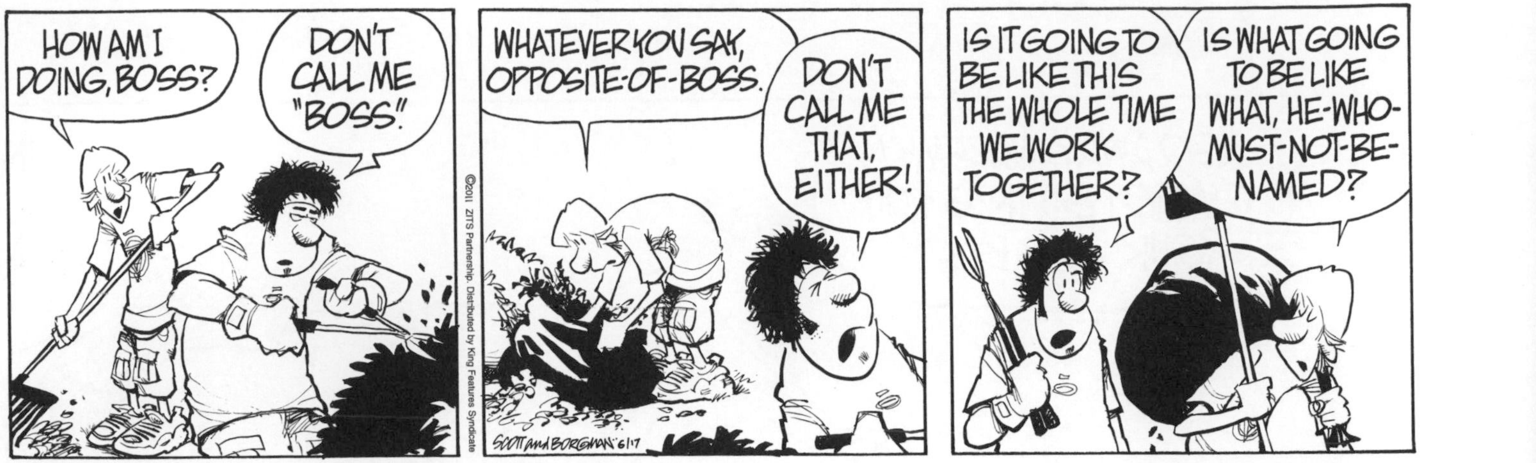
HOW AM I DOING, BOSS?
DON'T CALL ME "BOSS."
©2011 ZITS Partnership. Distributed by King Features Syndicate
WHATEVER YOU SAY, OPPOSITE-OF-BOSS.
DON'T CALL ME THAT, EITHER!
SCOTT AND BORGMAN 6/17
IS IT GOING TO BE LIKE THIS THE WHOLE TIME WE WORK TOGETHER?
IS WHAT GOING TO BE LIKE WHAT, HE-WHO-MUST-NOT-BE-NAMED?

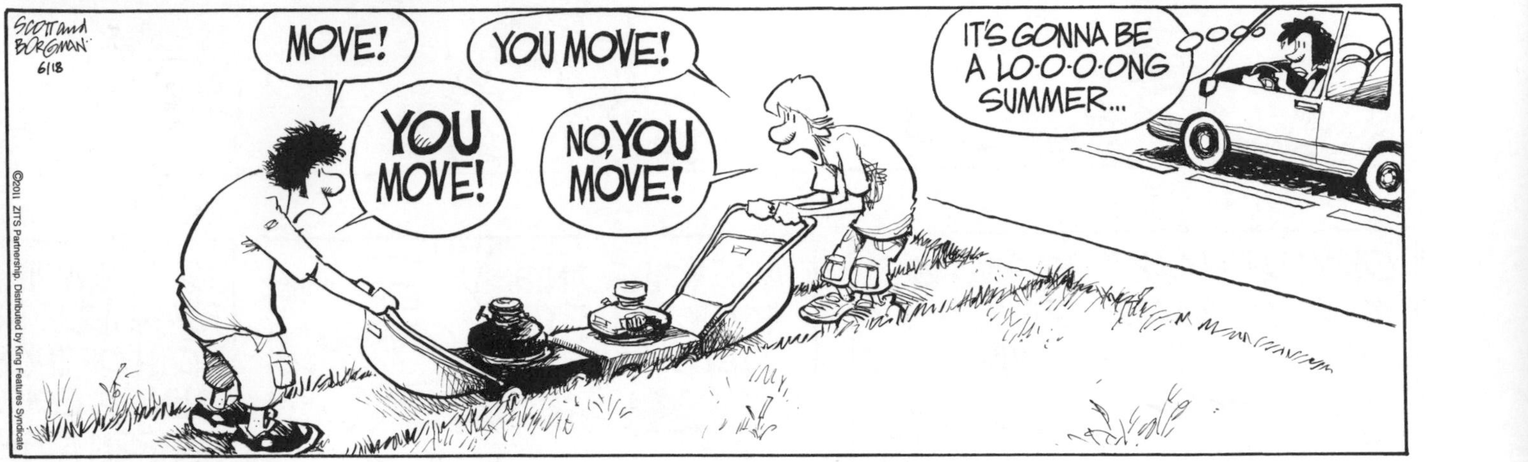
SCOTT AND BORGMAN 6/18
©2011 ZITS Partnership. Distributed by King Features Syndicate
MOVE!
YOU MOVE!
YOU MOVE!
NO, YOU MOVE!
IT'S GONNA BE A LO-O-O-ONG SUMMER...

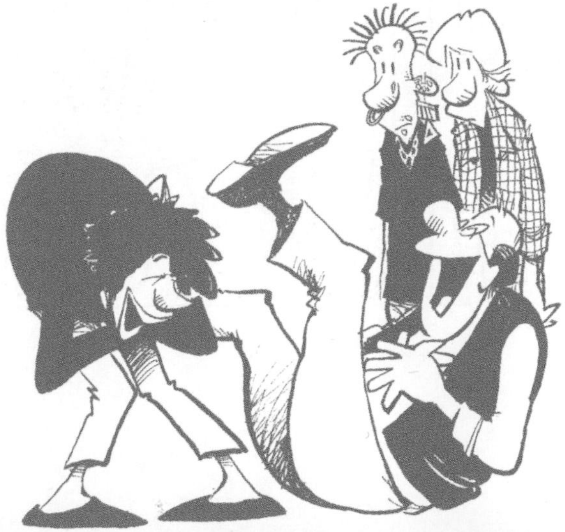

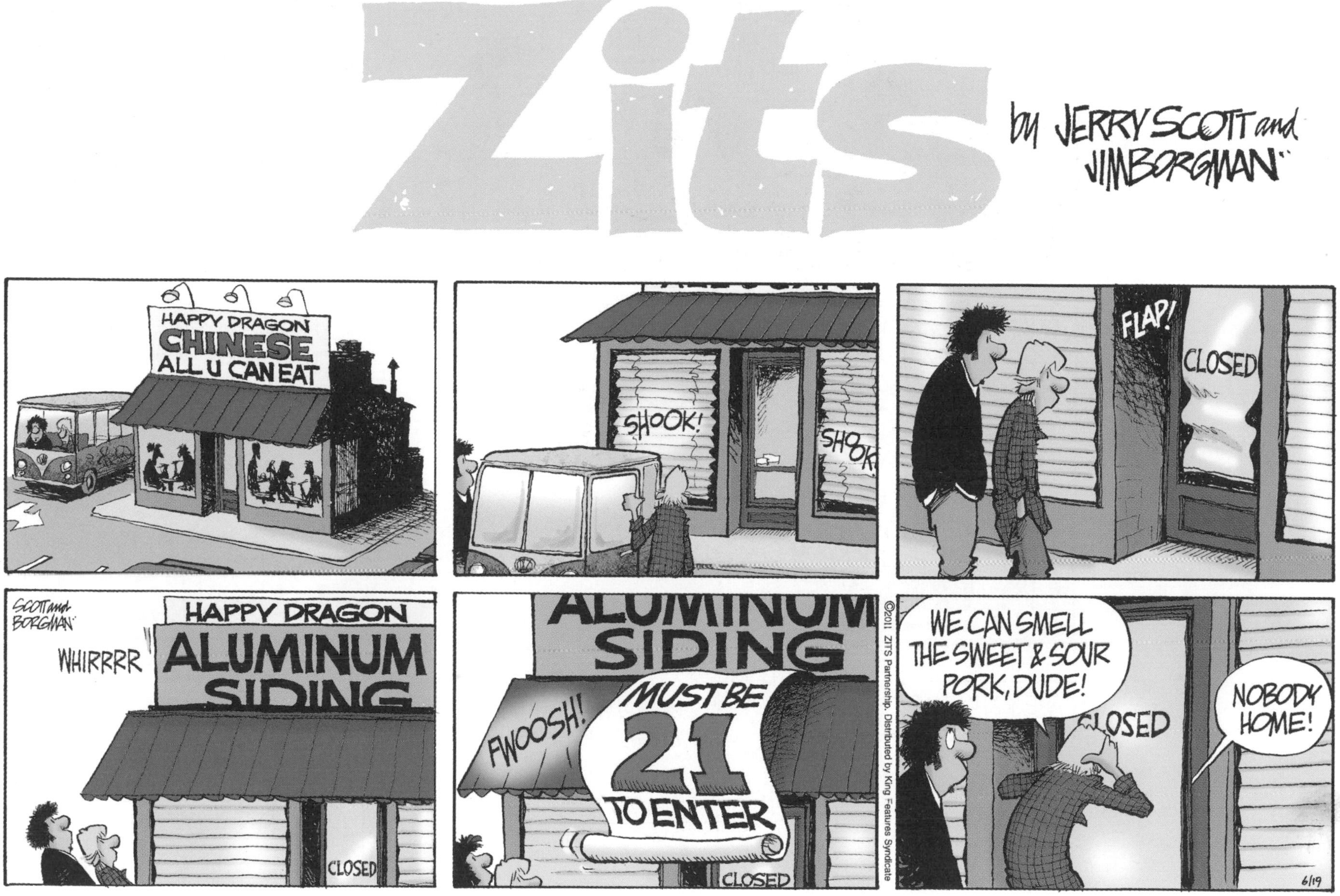
Zits
by JERRY SCOTT and JIM BORGMAN
HAPPY DRAGON
CHINESE
ALL U CAN EAT
SHOOK!
SHOOK!
FLAP!
CLOSED
SCOTT and BORGMAN
HAPPY DRAGON
WHIRRRR
ALUMINUM
SIDING
CLOSED
ALUMINUM
SIDING
FWOOSH!
MUST BE
21
TO ENTER
CLOSED
©2011 ZITS Partnership. Distributed by King Features Syndicate
WE CAN SMELL THE SWEET & SOUR PORK, DUDE!
CLOSED
NOBODY HOME!
6/19

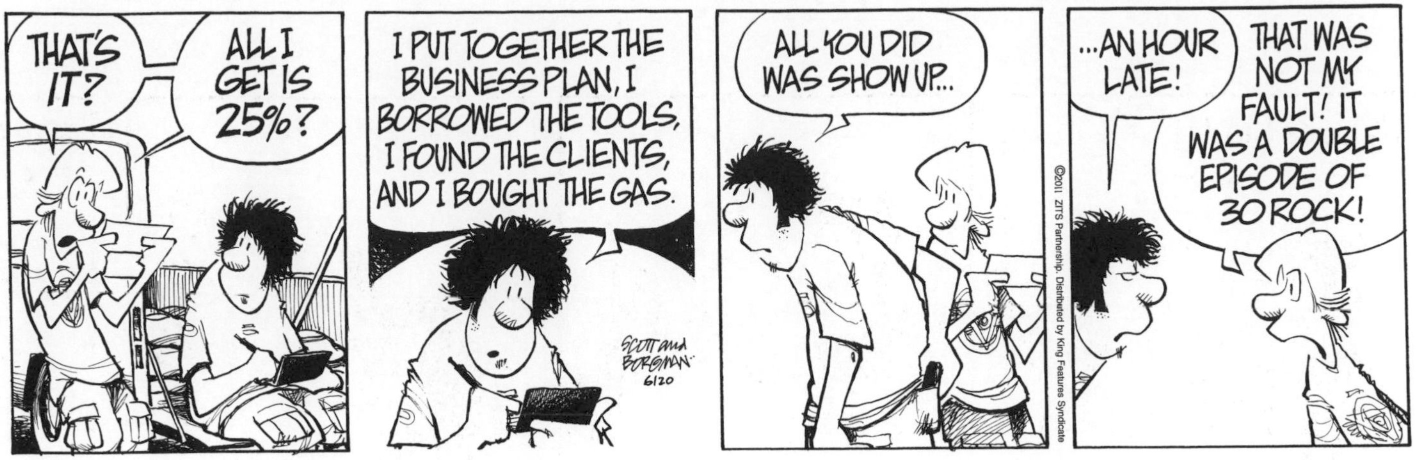
THAT'S IT?
ALL I GET IS 25%?
I PUT TOGETHER THE BUSINESS PLAN, I BORROWED THE TOOLS, I FOUND THE CLIENTS, AND I BOUGHT THE GAS.
SCOTT and BORGMAN 6/20
ALL YOU DID WAS SHOW UP...
...AN HOUR LATE!
THAT WAS NOT MY FAULT! IT WAS A DOUBLE EPISODE OF 30 ROCK!
©2011 ZITS Partnership. Distributed by King Features Syndicate

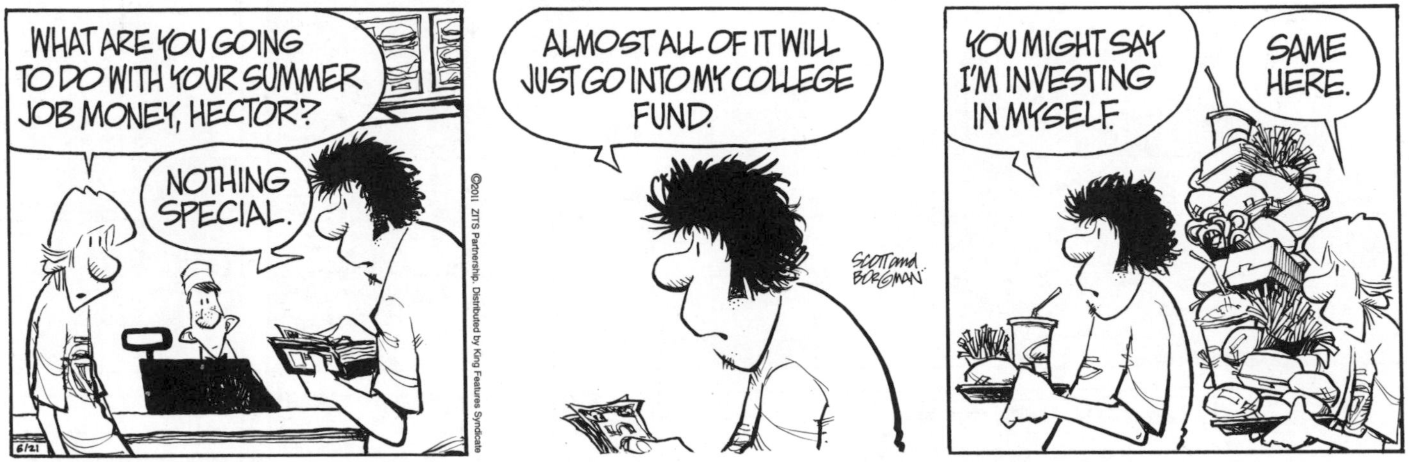
WHAT ARE YOU GOING TO DO WITH YOUR SUMMER JOB MONEY, HECTOR?
NOTHING SPECIAL.
6/21
©2011 ZITS Partnership. Distributed by King Features Syndicate
ALMOST ALL OF IT WILL JUST GO INTO MY COLLEGE FUND.
SCOTT and BORGMAN
YOU MIGHT SAY I'M INVESTING IN MYSELF.
SAME HERE.

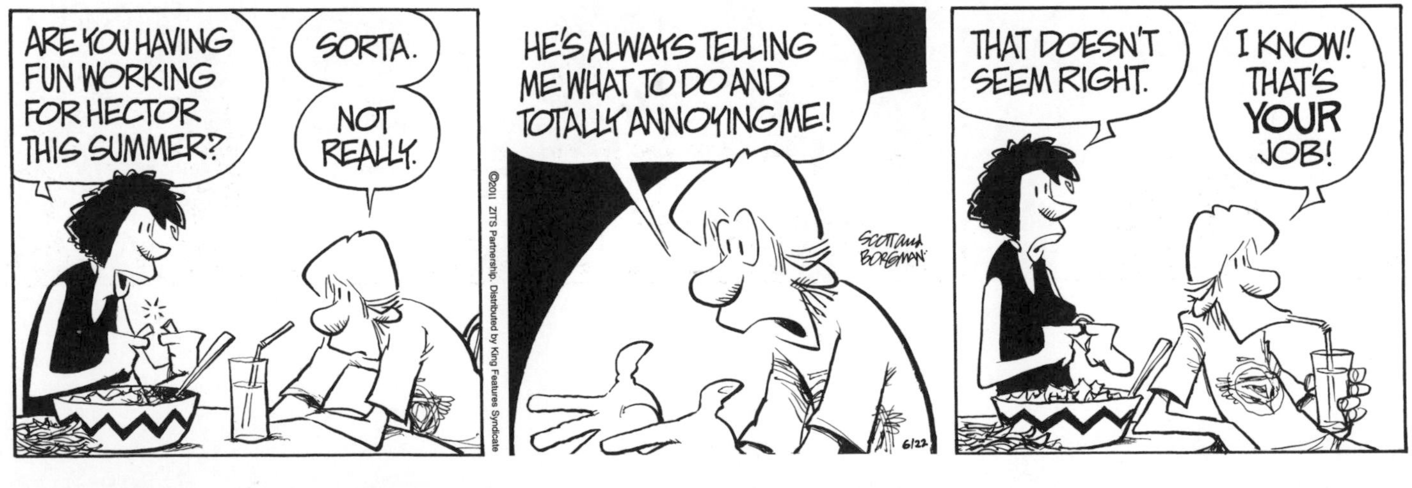
ARE YOU HAVING FUN WORKING FOR HECTOR THIS SUMMER?
SORTA.
NOT REALLY.
©2011 ZITS Partnership. Distributed by King Features Syndicate
HE'S ALWAYS TELLING ME WHAT TO DO AND TOTALLY ANNOYING ME!
SCOTT and BORGMAN 6/22
THAT DOESN'T SEEM RIGHT.
I KNOW! THAT'S YOUR JOB!

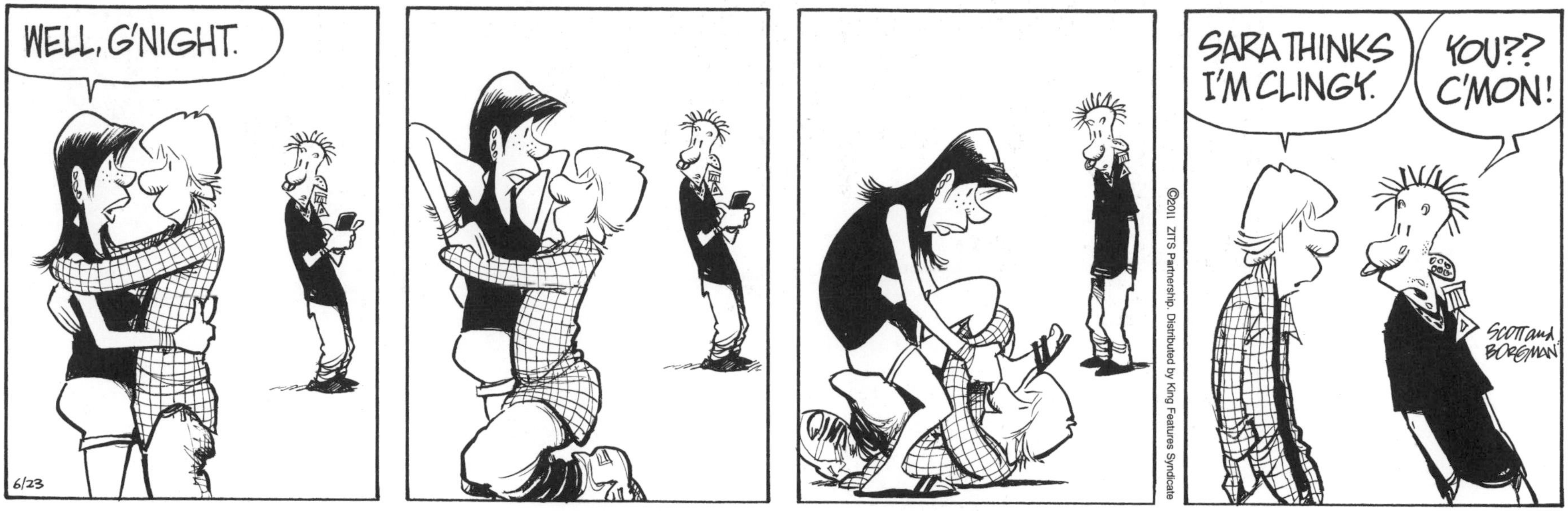
WELL, G'NIGHT.
SARA THINKS I'M CLINGY.
YOU?? C'MON!
SCOTT and BORGMAN
6/23
©2011 ZITS Partnership. Distributed by King Features Syndicate

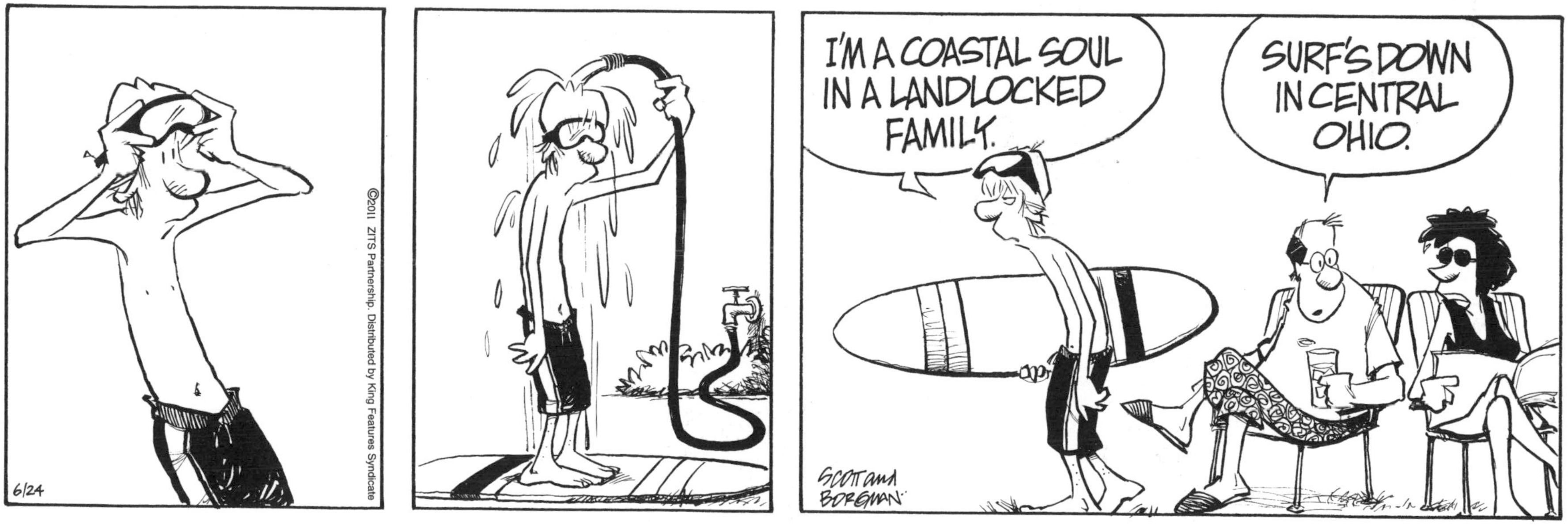
6/24
©2011 ZITS Partnership. Distributed by King Features Syndicate
I'M A COASTAL SOUL IN A LANDLOCKED FAMILY.
SURF'S DOWN IN CENTRAL OHIO.
SCOTT and BORGMAN

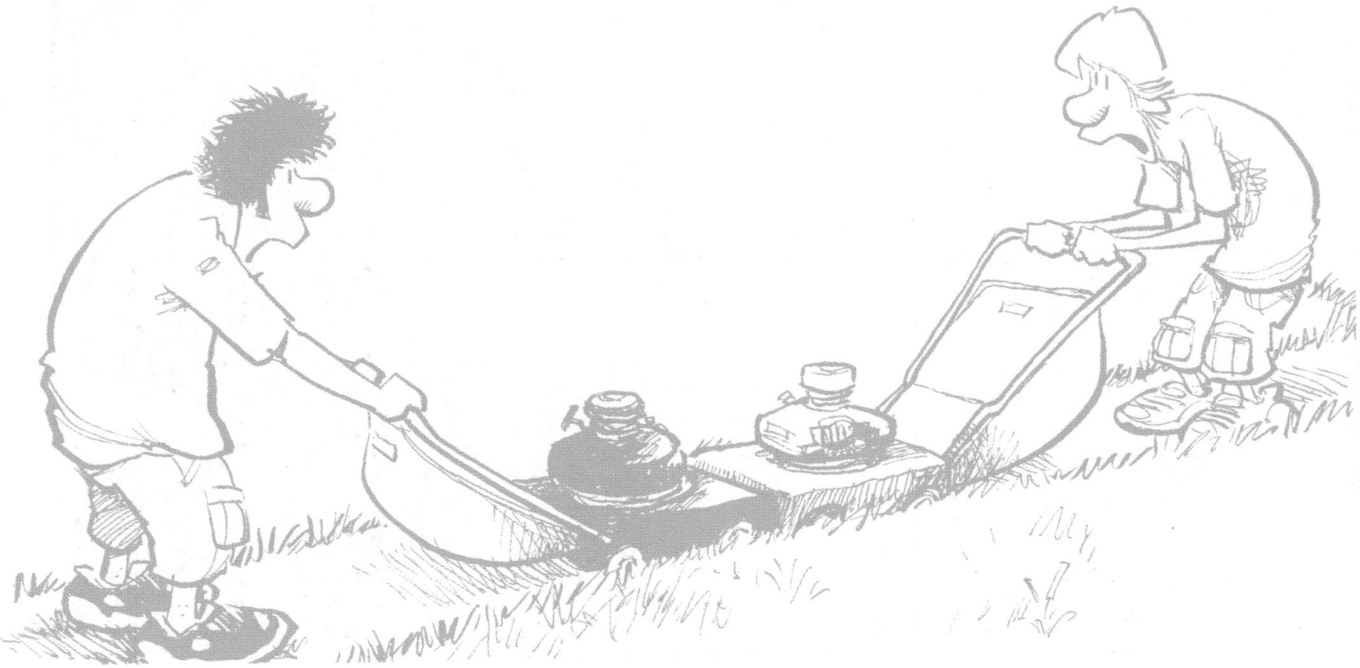

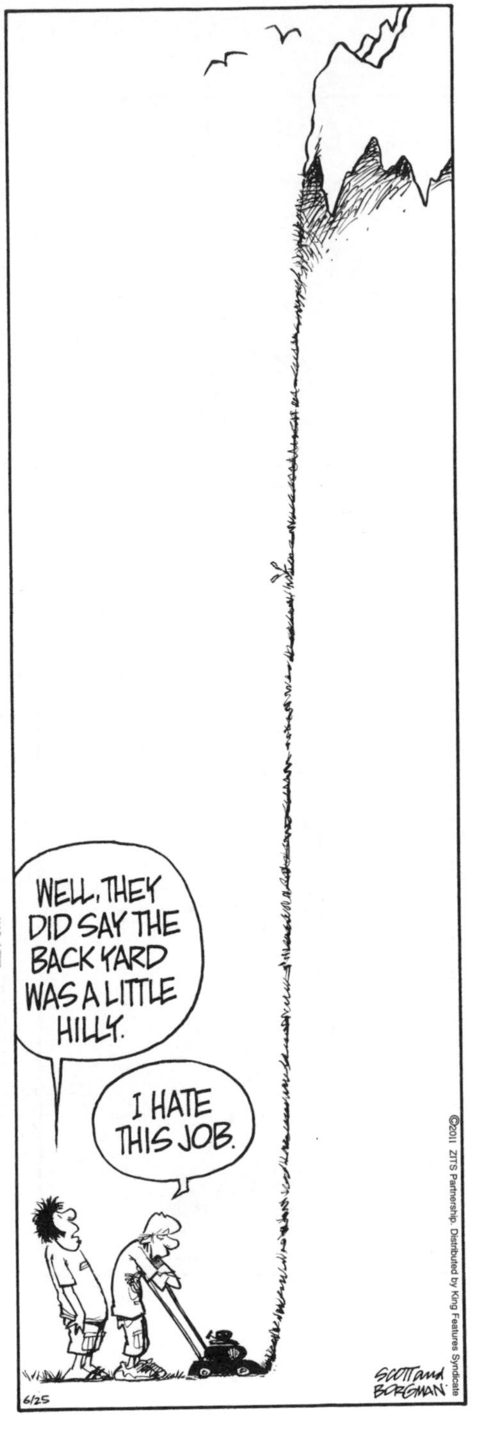
WELL, THEY DID SAY THE BACK YARD WAS A LITTLE HILLY.
I HATE THIS JOB.
©2011 ZITS Partnership. Distributed by King Features Syndicate
SCOTT and BORGMAN
6/25

Zits

by JERRY SCOTT and JIM BORGMAN

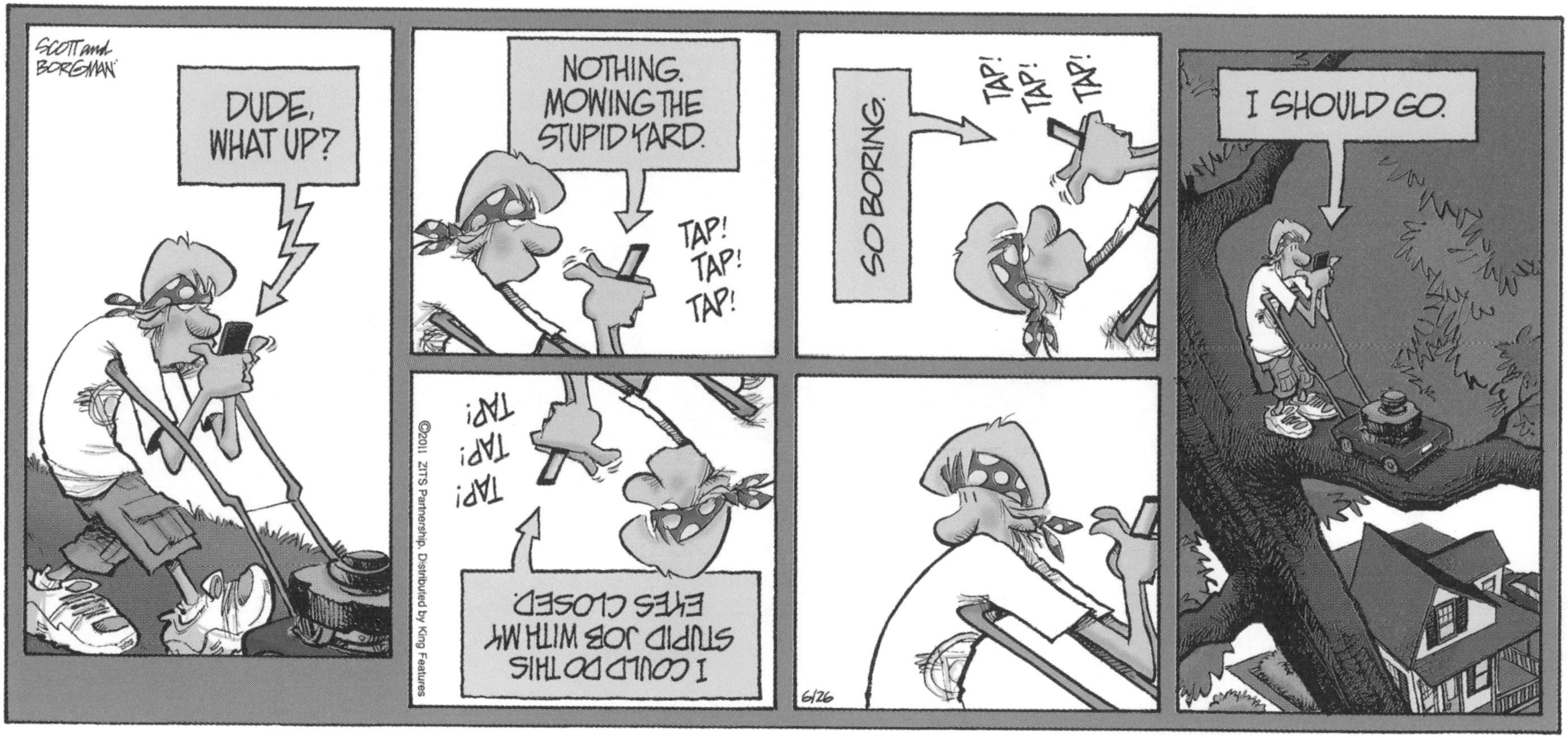
SCOTT and BORGMAN
DUDE, WHAT UP?
NOTHING. MOWING THE STUPID YARD.
TAP! TAP! TAP!
SO BORING.
TAP! TAP! TAP!
I COULD DO THIS STUPID JOB WITH MY EYES CLOSED.
TAP! TAP! TAP!
©2011 ZITS Partnership. Distributed by King Features
6/26
I SHOULD GO.

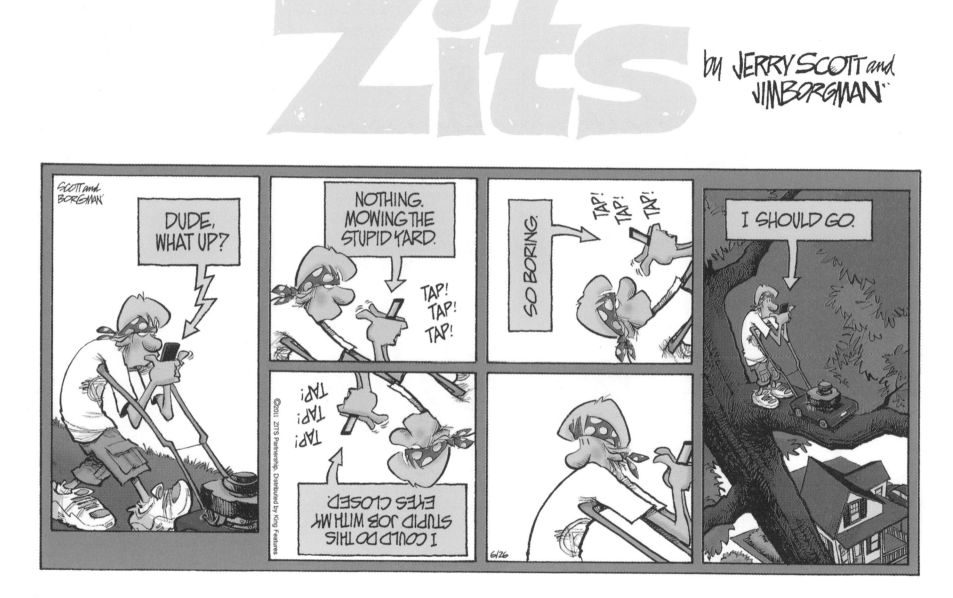

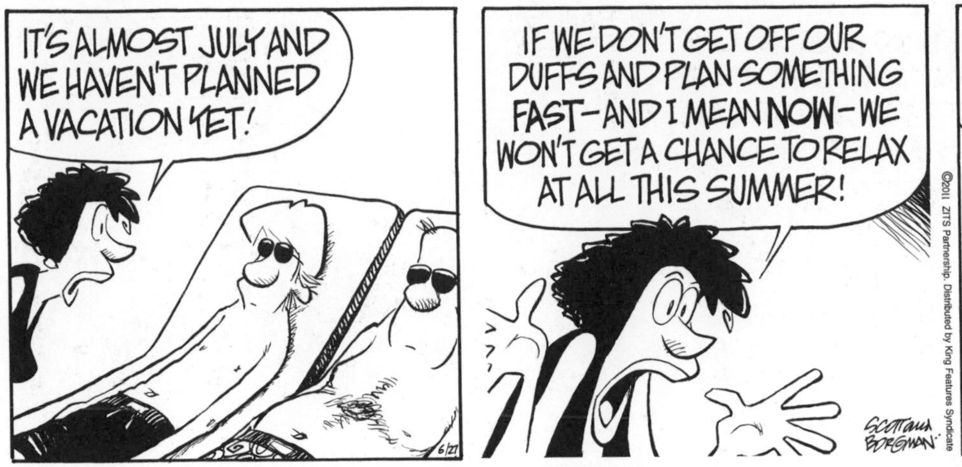
IT'S ALMOST JULY AND WE HAVEN'T PLANNED A VACATION YET!
IF WE DON'T GET OFF OUR DUFFS AND PLAN SOMETHING FAST—AND I MEAN NOW—WE WON'T GET A CHANCE TO RELAX AT ALL THIS SUMMER!
I'LL START A SPREAD-SHEET!
CAN SHE HEAR HERSELF?
6/27
SCOTT and BORGMAN
©2011 ZITS Partnership. Distributed by King Features Syndicate

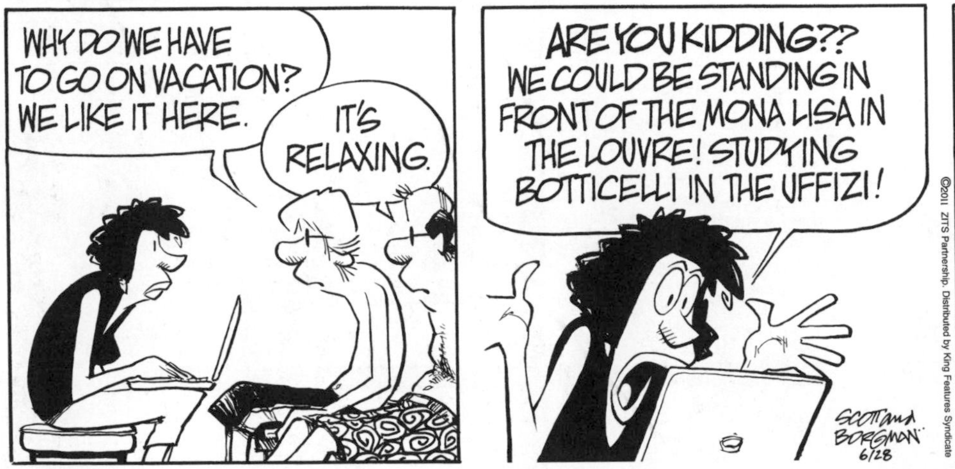
WHY DO WE HAVE TO GO ON VACATION? WE LIKE IT HERE.
IT'S RELAXING.
ARE YOU KIDDING?? WE COULD BE STANDING IN FRONT OF THE MONA LISA IN THE LOUVRE! STUDYING BOTTICELLI IN THE UFFIZI!
SHE'S RIGHT. A DANK, SWEATY MUSEUM IS THE PLACE TO BE.
SEND ME A POSTCARD.
SCOTT and BORGMAN
6/28
©2011 ZITS Partnership. Distributed by King Features Syndicate

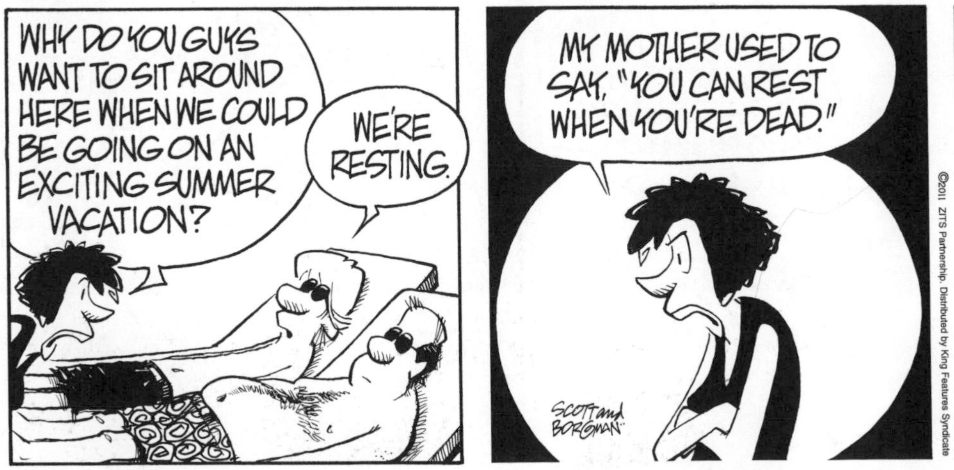
WHY DO YOU GUYS WANT TO SIT AROUND HERE WHEN WE COULD BE GOING ON AN EXCITING SUMMER VACATION?
WE'RE RESTING.
MY MOTHER USED TO SAY, "YOU CAN REST WHEN YOU'RE DEAD."
SCOTT and BORGMAN
JUST CURIOUS—HOW DID GRANDPA DIE?
BUNGEE JUMPING WITH THE DOLPHINS, WHY?
6/29
©2011 ZITS Partnership. Distributed by King Features Syndicate

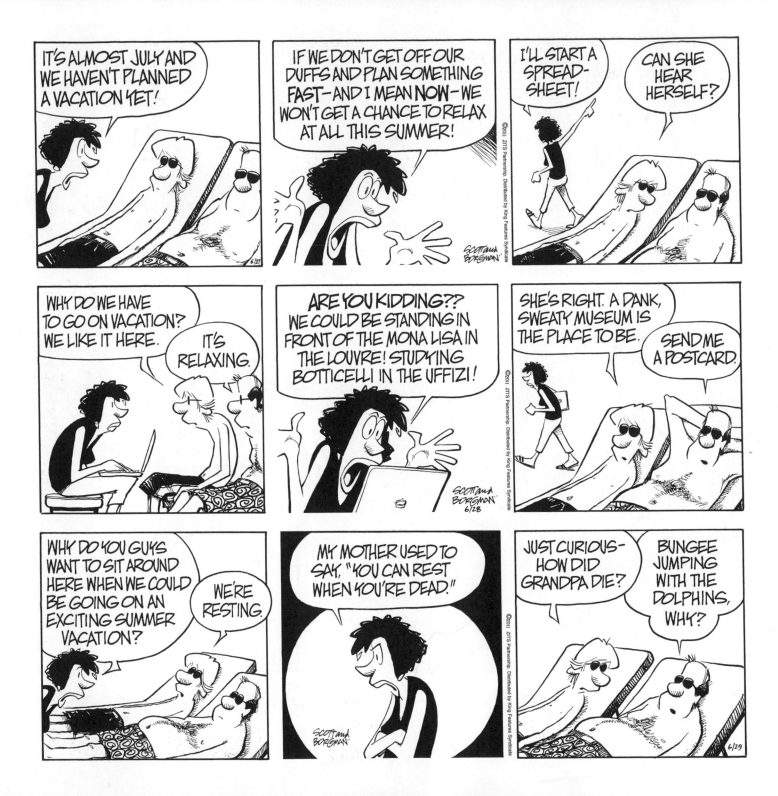

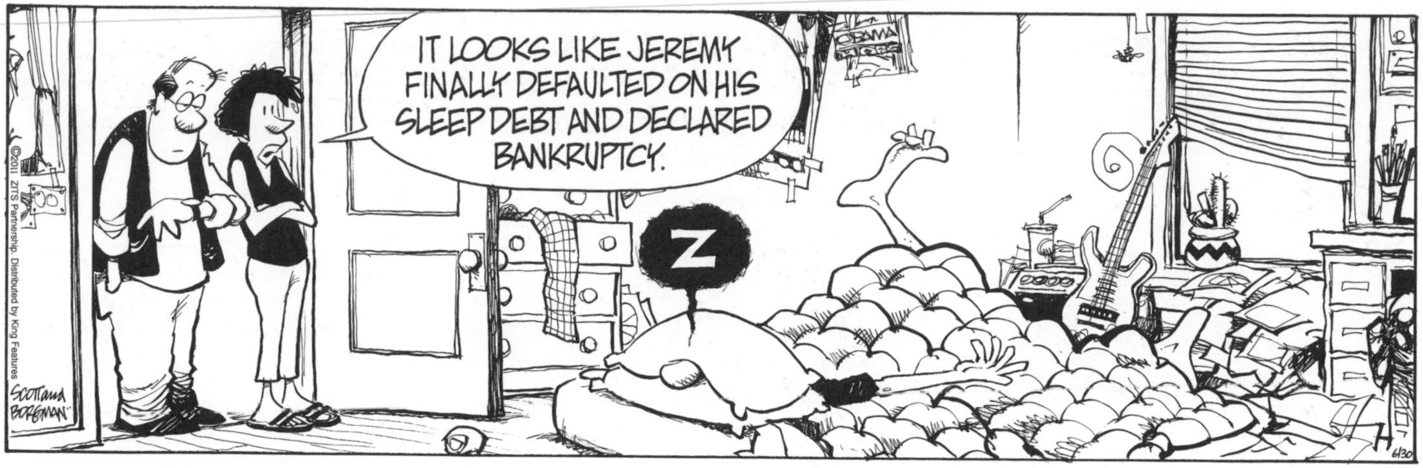
IT LOOKS LIKE JEREMY FINALLY DEFAULTED ON HIS SLEEP DEBT AND DECLARED BANKRUPTCY.
Z
©2011 ZITS Partnership. Distributed by King Features

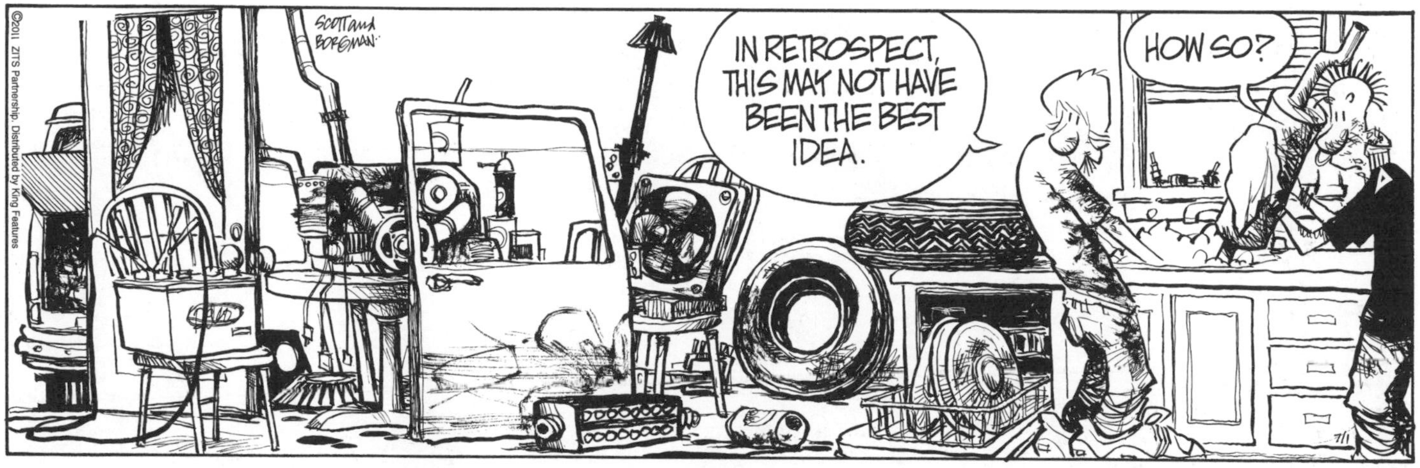
IN RETROSPECT, THIS MAY NOT HAVE BEEN THE BEST IDEA.
HOW SO?
©2011 ZITS Partnership. Distributed by King Features

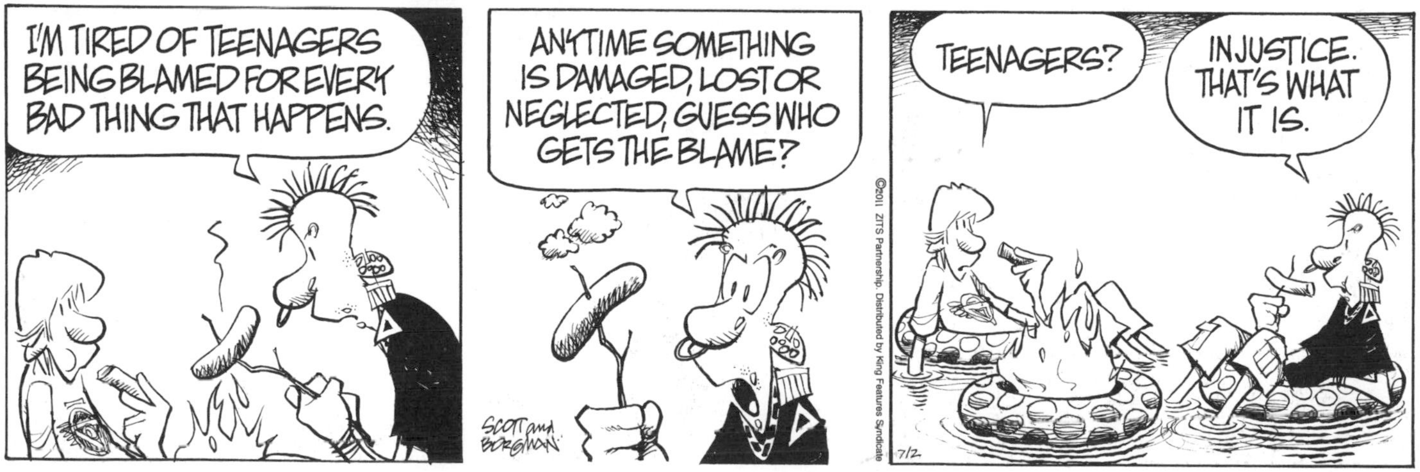
I'M TIRED OF TEENAGERS BEING BLAMED FOR EVERY BAD THING THAT HAPPENS.
ANYTIME SOMETHING IS DAMAGED, LOST OR NEGLECTED, GUESS WHO GETS THE BLAME?
TEENAGERS?
INJUSTICE. THAT'S WHAT IT IS.
©2011 ZITS Partnership. Distributed by King Features Syndicate

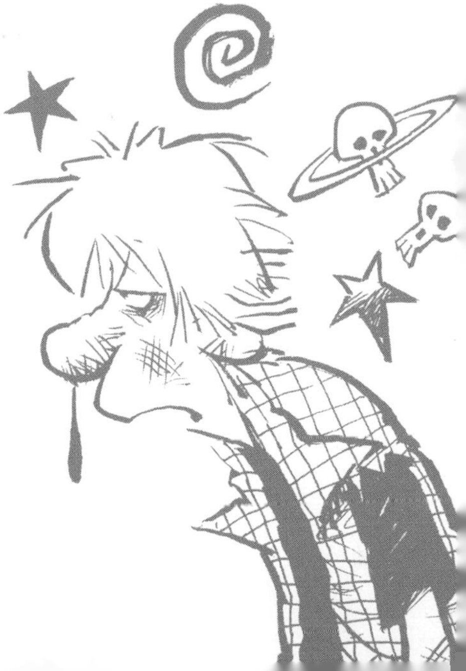

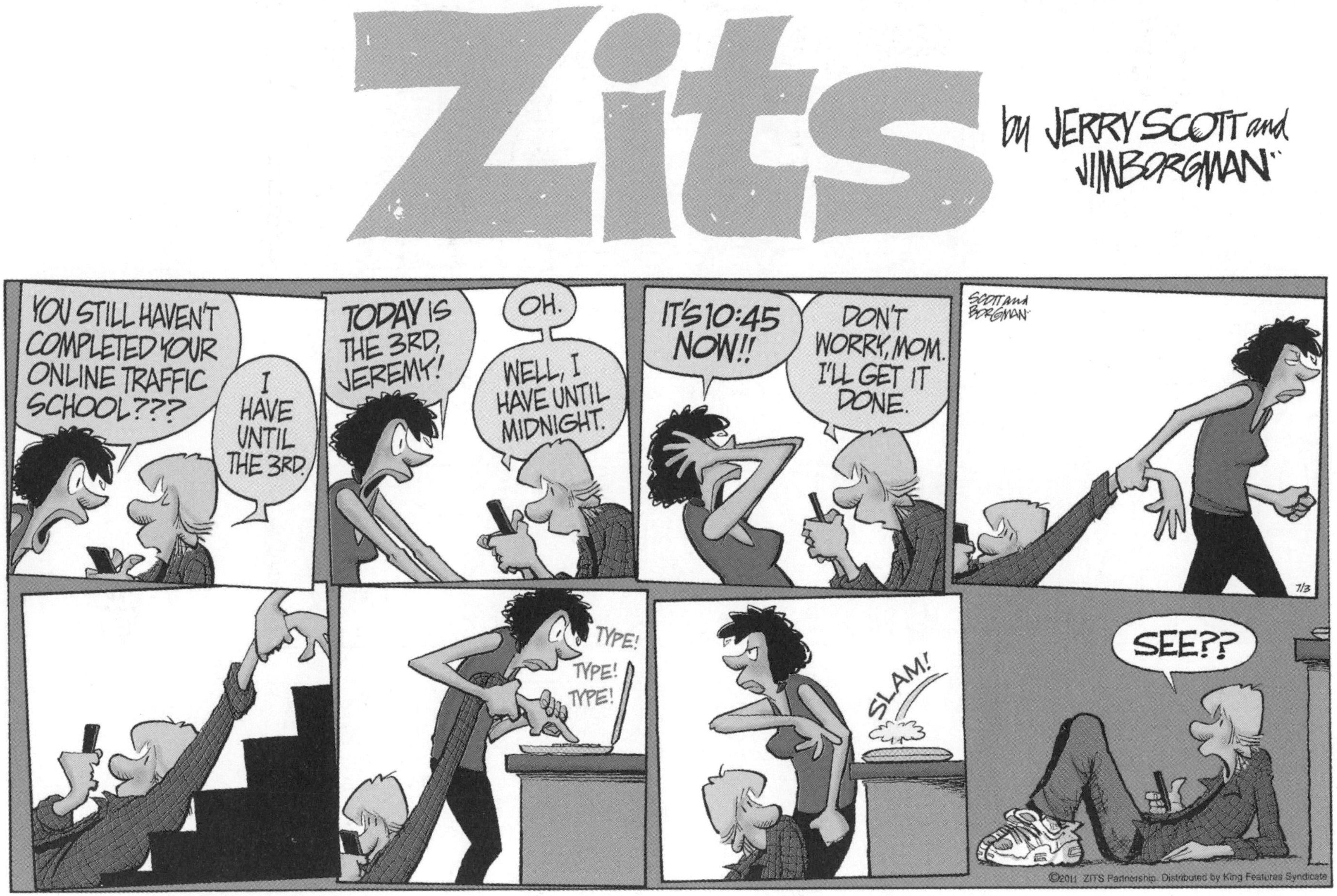
Zits
by JERRY SCOTT and JIM BORGMAN
YOU STILL HAVEN'T COMPLETED YOUR ONLINE TRAFFIC SCHOOL???
I HAVE UNTIL THE 3RD.
TODAY IS THE 3RD, JEREMY!
OH.
WELL, I HAVE UNTIL MIDNIGHT.
IT'S 10:45 NOW!!
DON'T WORRY, MOM. I'LL GET IT DONE.
SCOTT and BORGMAN
7/3
TYPE!
TYPE!
TYPE!
SLAM!
SEE??
©2011 ZITS Partnership. Distributed by King Features Syndicate

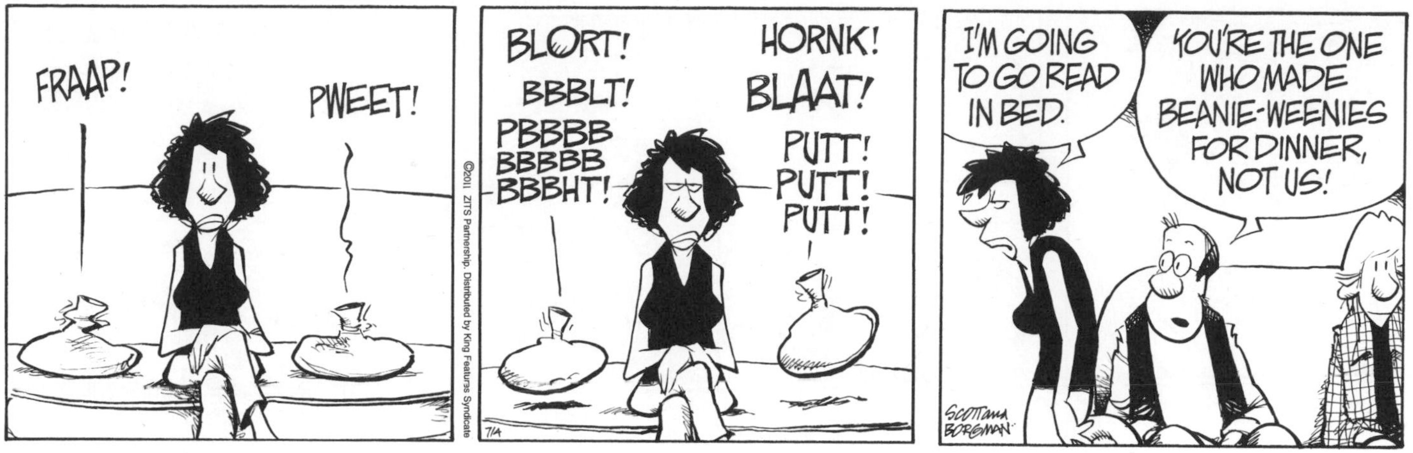
FRAAP!
PWEET!
BLORT!
BBBLT!
PBBBB BBBBB BBBHT!
HORNK!
BLAAT!
PUTT! PUTT! PUTT!
I'M GOING TO GO READ IN BED.
YOU'RE THE ONE WHO MADE BEANIE-WEENIES FOR DINNER, NOT US!
©2011 ZITS Partnership. Distributed by King Features Syndicate
7/4
SCOTT and BORGMAN

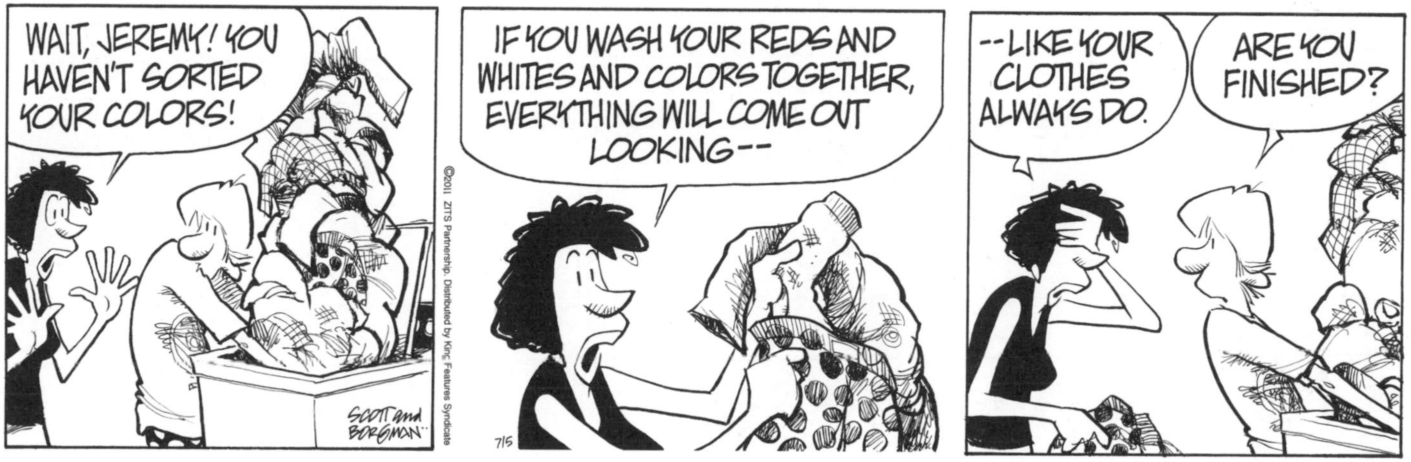
WAIT, JEREMY! YOU HAVEN'T SORTED YOUR COLORS!
IF YOU WASH YOUR REDS AND WHITES AND COLORS TOGETHER, EVERYTHING WILL COME OUT LOOKING--
--LIKE YOUR CLOTHES ALWAYS DO.
ARE YOU FINISHED?
©2011 ZITS Partnership. Distributed by King Features Syndicate
7/15
SCOTT and BORGMAN

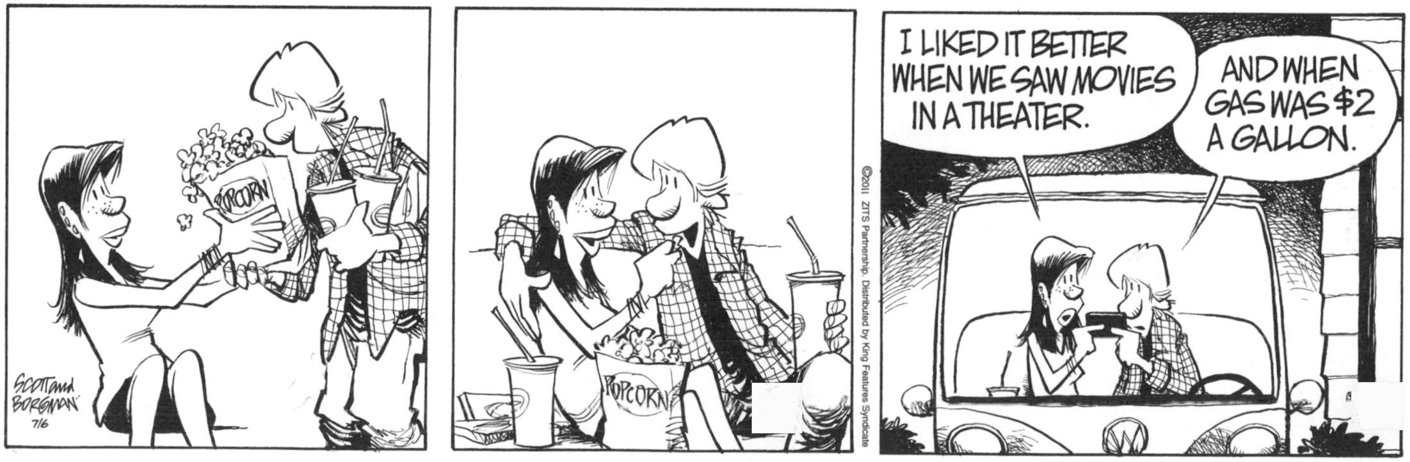
POPCORN
POPCORN
I LIKED IT BETTER WHEN WE SAW MOVIES IN A THEATER.
AND WHEN GAS WAS $2 A GALLON.
©2011 ZITS Partnership. Distributed by King Features Syndicate
SCOTT and BORGMAN
7/6

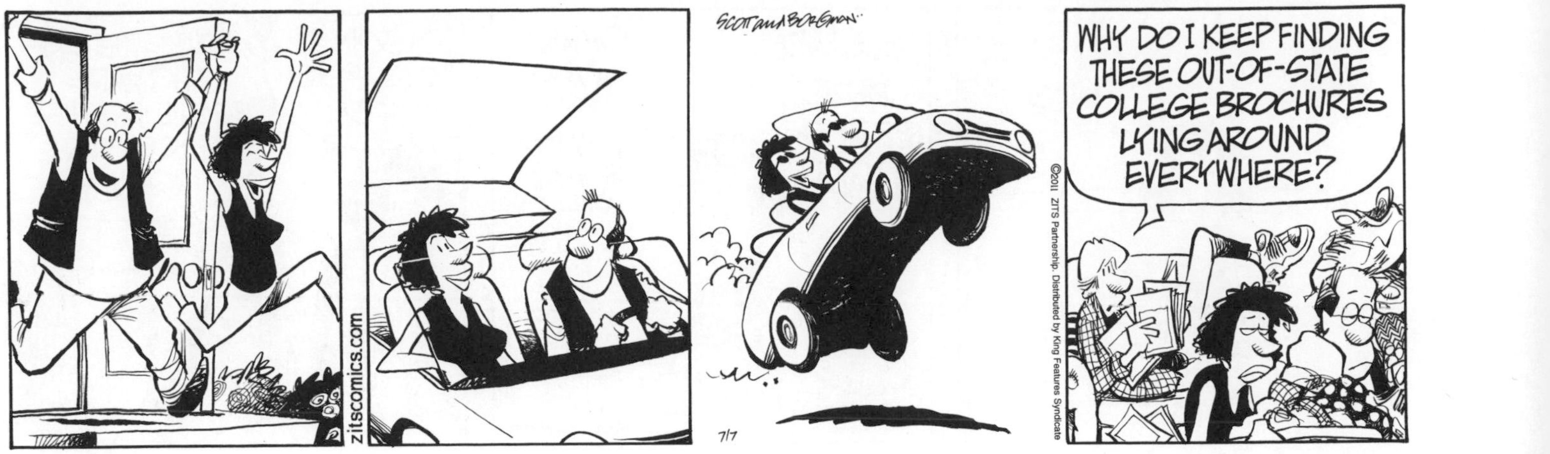
zitscomics.com
SCOTT and BORGMAN
7/7
©2011 ZITS Partnership. Distributed by King Features Syndicate
WHY DO I KEEP FINDING THESE OUT-OF-STATE COLLEGE BROCHURES LYING AROUND EVERYWHERE?

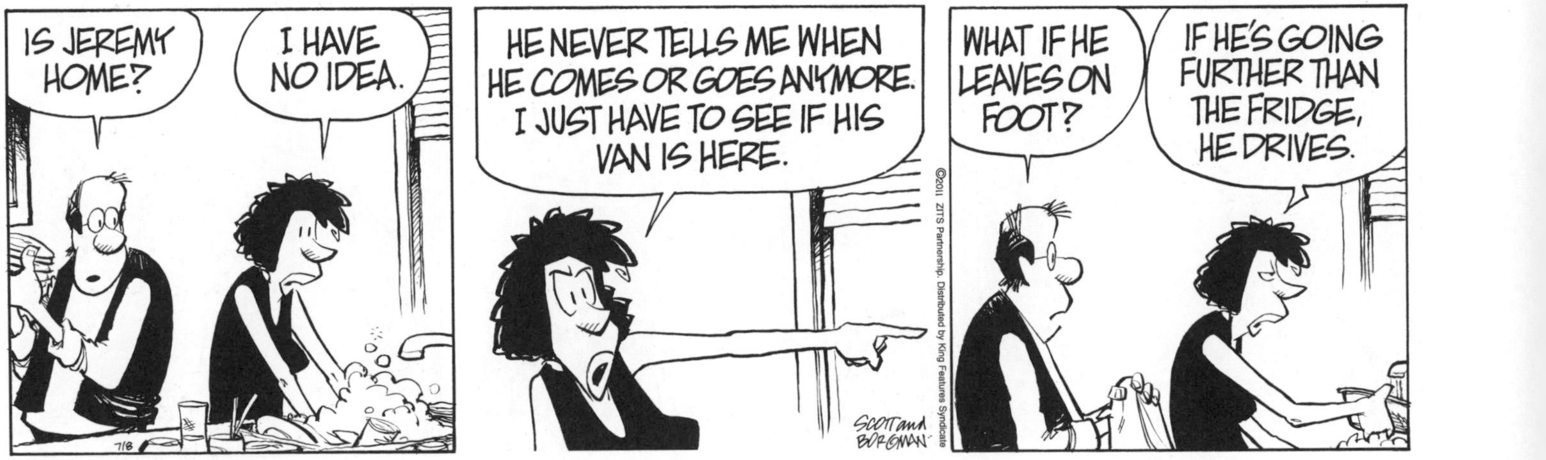
IS JEREMY HOME?
I HAVE NO IDEA.
7/8
HE NEVER TELLS ME WHEN HE COMES OR GOES ANYMORE. I JUST HAVE TO SEE IF HIS VAN IS HERE.
SCOTT and BORGMAN
©2011 ZITS Partnership. Distributed by King Features Syndicate
WHAT IF HE LEAVES ON FOOT?
IF HE'S GOING FURTHER THAN THE FRIDGE, HE DRIVES.

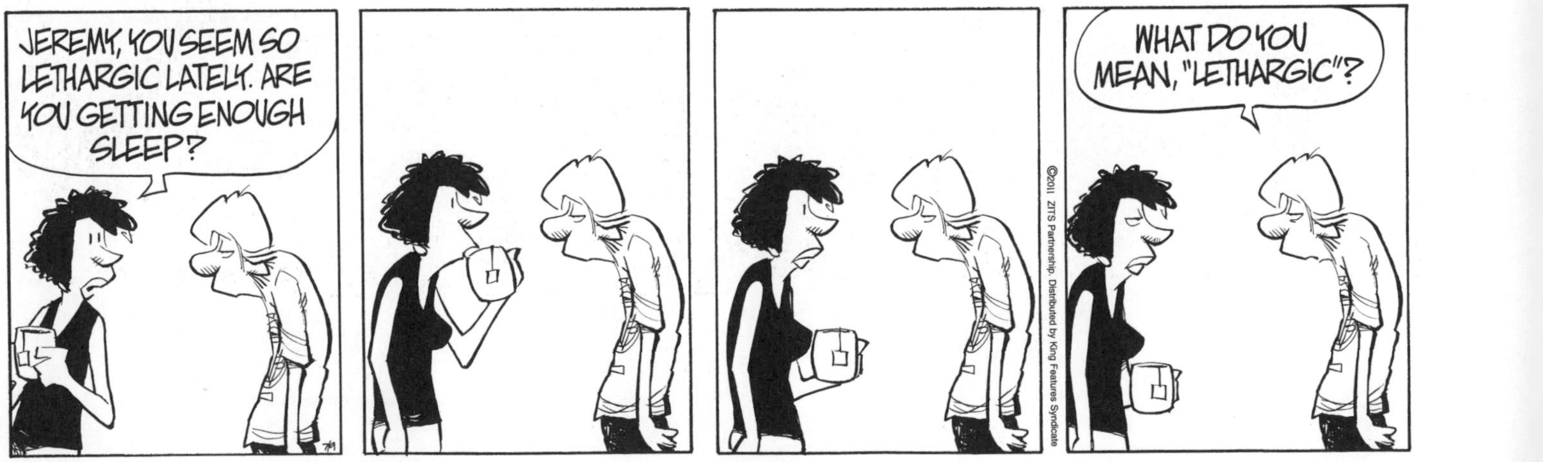
JEREMY, YOU SEEM SO LETHARGIC LATELY. ARE YOU GETTING ENOUGH SLEEP?
7/9
©2011 ZITS Partnership. Distributed by King Features Syndicate
WHAT DO YOU MEAN, "LETHARGIC"?

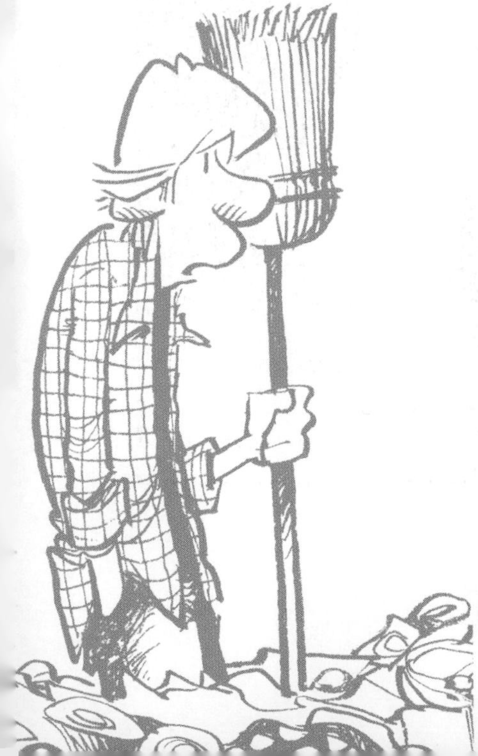

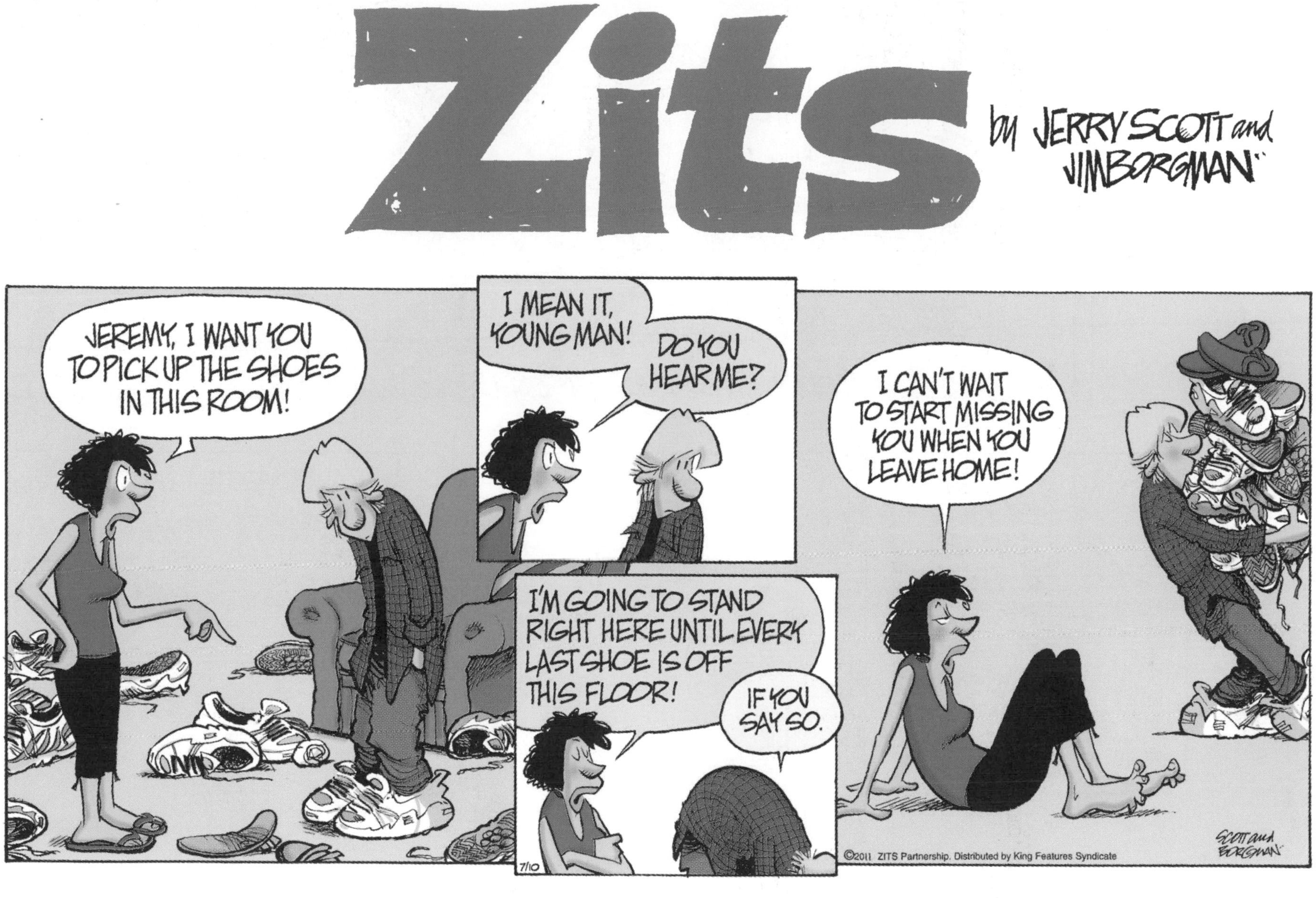
Zits
by JERRY SCOTT and JIM BORGMAN
JEREMY, I WANT YOU TO PICK UP THE SHOES IN THIS ROOM!
I MEAN IT, YOUNG MAN!
DO YOU HEAR ME?
I'M GOING TO STAND RIGHT HERE UNTIL EVERY LAST SHOE IS OFF THIS FLOOR!
IF YOU SAY SO.
I CAN'T WAIT TO START MISSING YOU WHEN YOU LEAVE HOME!
7/10
©2011 ZITS Partnership. Distributed by King Features Syndicate
SCOTT and BORGMAN

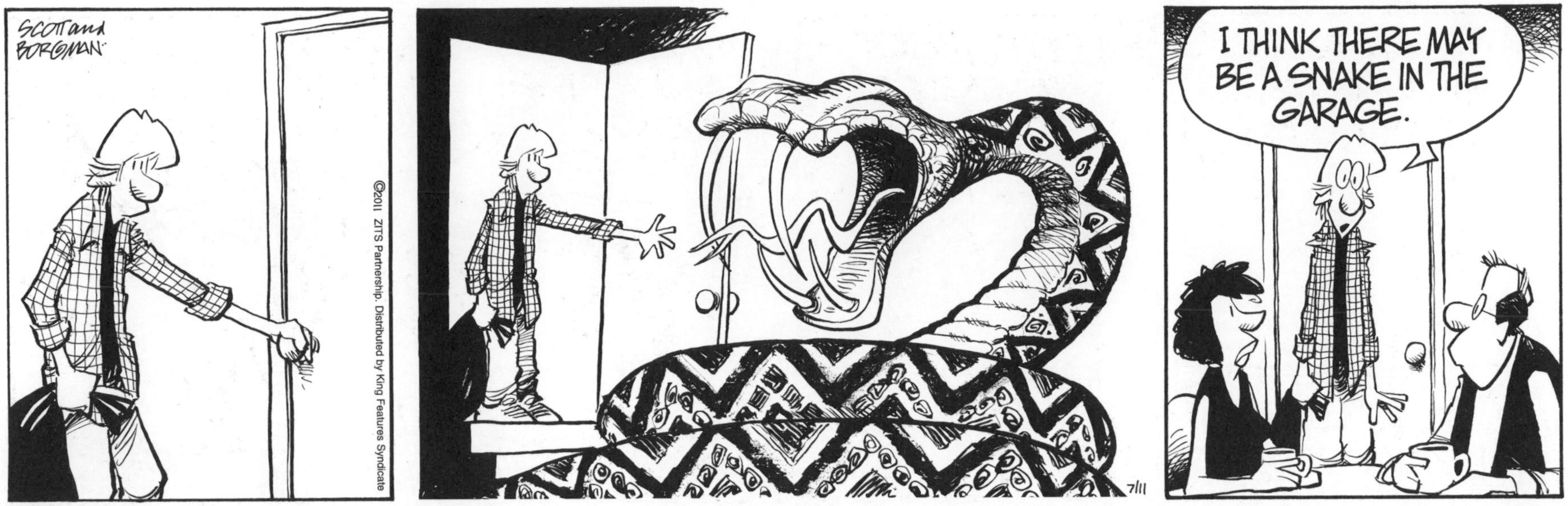
SCOTT and BORGMAN
©2011 ZITS Partnership. Distributed by King Features Syndicate
7/11
I THINK THERE MAY BE A SNAKE IN THE GARAGE.

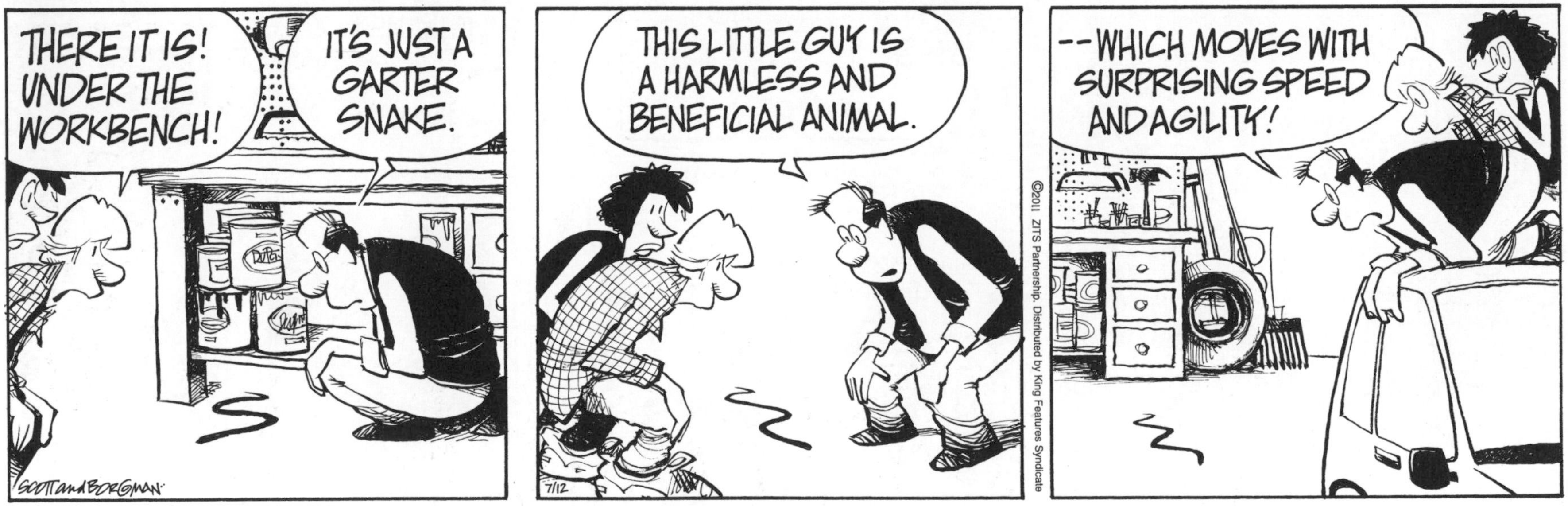
THERE IT IS! UNDER THE WORKBENCH!
IT'S JUST A GARTER SNAKE.
SCOTT and BORGMAN
THIS LITTLE GUY IS A HARMLESS AND BENEFICIAL ANIMAL.
7/12
©2011 ZITS Partnership. Distributed by King Features Syndicate
--WHICH MOVES WITH SURPRISING SPEED AND AGILITY!

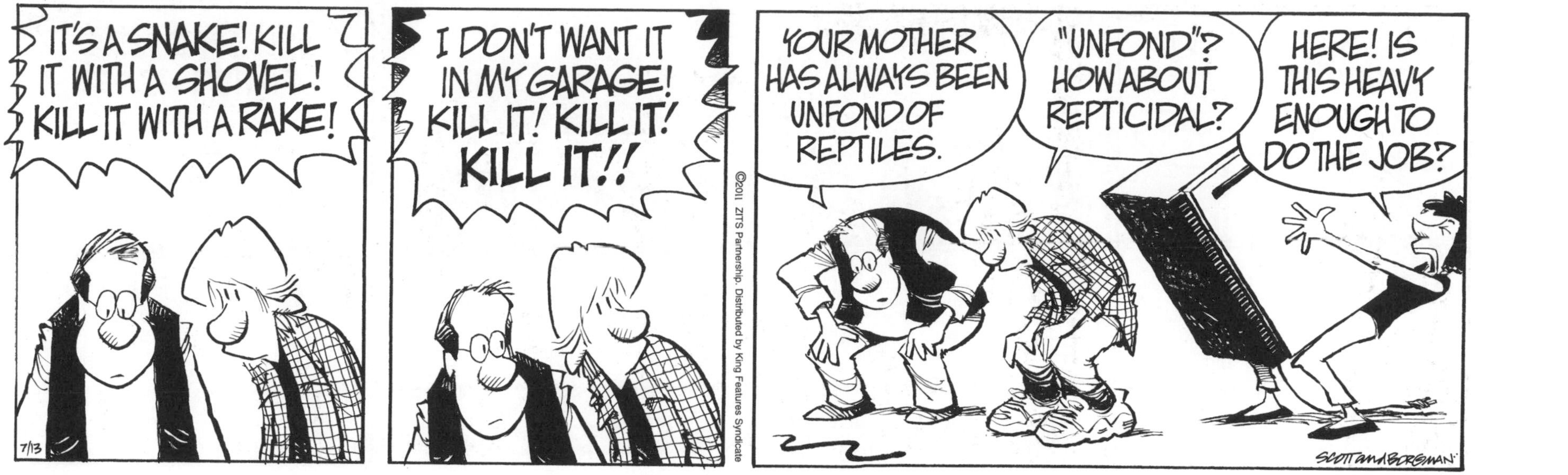
IT'S A SNAKE! KILL IT WITH A SHOVEL! KILL IT WITH A RAKE!
7/13
I DON'T WANT IT IN MY GARAGE! KILL IT! KILL IT! KILL IT!!
©2011 ZITS Partnership. Distributed by King Features Syndicate
YOUR MOTHER HAS ALWAYS BEEN UNFOND OF REPTILES.
"UNFOND"? HOW ABOUT REPTICIDAL?
HERE! IS THIS HEAVY ENOUGH TO DO THE JOB?
SCOTT AND BORGMAN

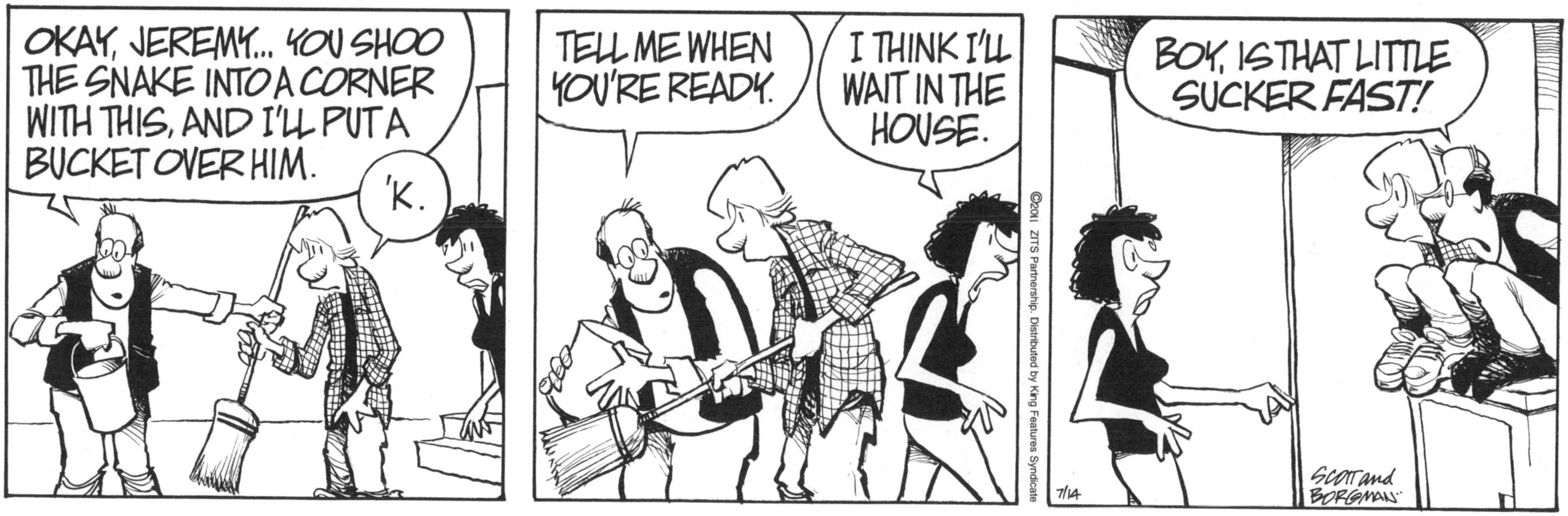
OKAY, JEREMY... YOU SHOO THE SNAKE INTO A CORNER WITH THIS, AND I'LL PUT A BUCKET OVER HIM.
'K.
TELL ME WHEN YOU'RE READY.
I THINK I'LL WAIT IN THE HOUSE.
©2011 ZITS Partnership. Distributed by King Features Syndicate
BOY, IS THAT LITTLE SUCKER FAST!
7/14
SCOTT and BORGMAN

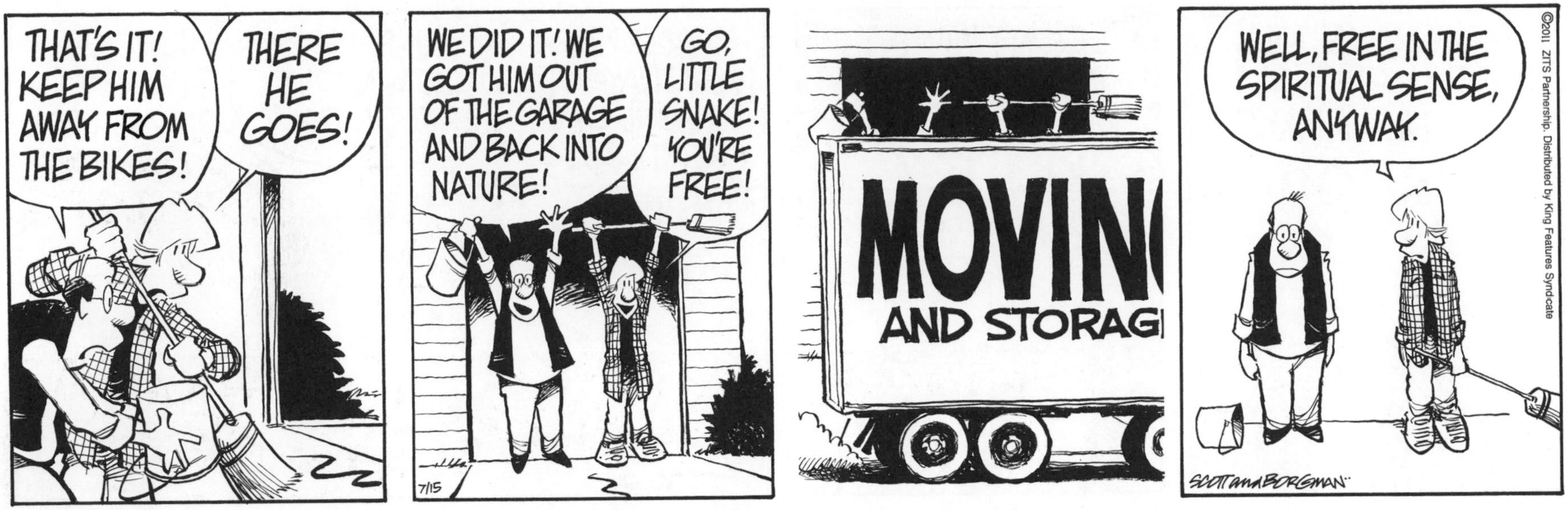
THAT'S IT! KEEP HIM AWAY FROM THE BIKES!
THERE HE GOES!
WE DID IT! WE GOT HIM OUT OF THE GARAGE AND BACK INTO NATURE!
GO, LITTLE SNAKE! YOU'RE FREE!
7/15
MOVING
AND STORAG
WELL, FREE IN THE SPIRITUAL SENSE, ANYWAY.
SCOTT AND BORGMAN
©2011 ZITS Partnership. Distributed by King Features Syndicate

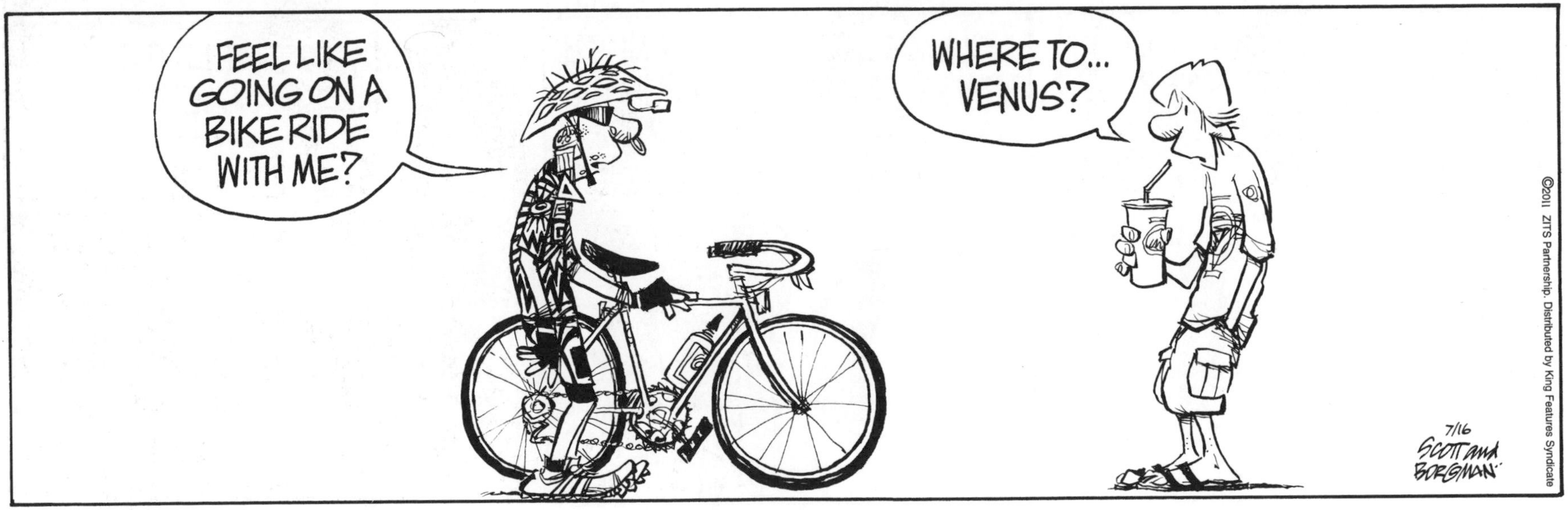
FEEL LIKE GOING ON A BIKE RIDE WITH ME?
WHERE TO... VENUS?
7/16
SCOTT AND BORGMAN
©2011 ZITS Partnership. Distributed by King Features Syndicate

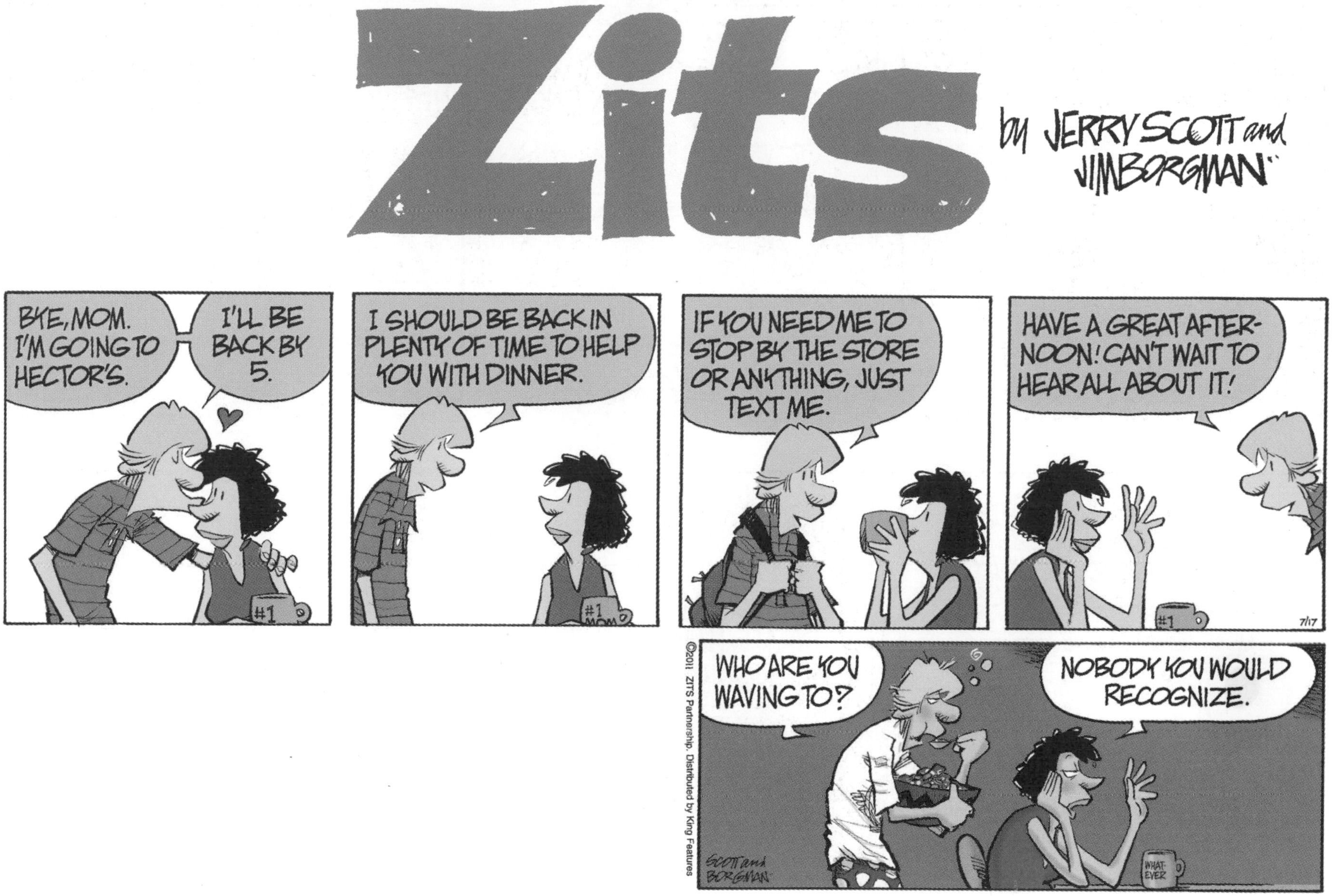
Zits
by JERRY SCOTT and JIM BORGMAN
BYE, MOM. I'M GOING TO HECTOR'S.
I'LL BE BACK BY 5.
#1
I SHOULD BE BACK IN PLENTY OF TIME TO HELP YOU WITH DINNER.
#1 MOM
IF YOU NEED ME TO STOP BY THE STORE OR ANYTHING, JUST TEXT ME.
HAVE A GREAT AFTER-NOON! CAN'T WAIT TO HEAR ALL ABOUT IT!
#1
7/17
WHO ARE YOU WAVING TO?
NOBODY YOU WOULD RECOGNIZE.
WHAT-EVER
SCOTT and BORGMAN
©2011 ZITS Partnership. Distributed by King Features

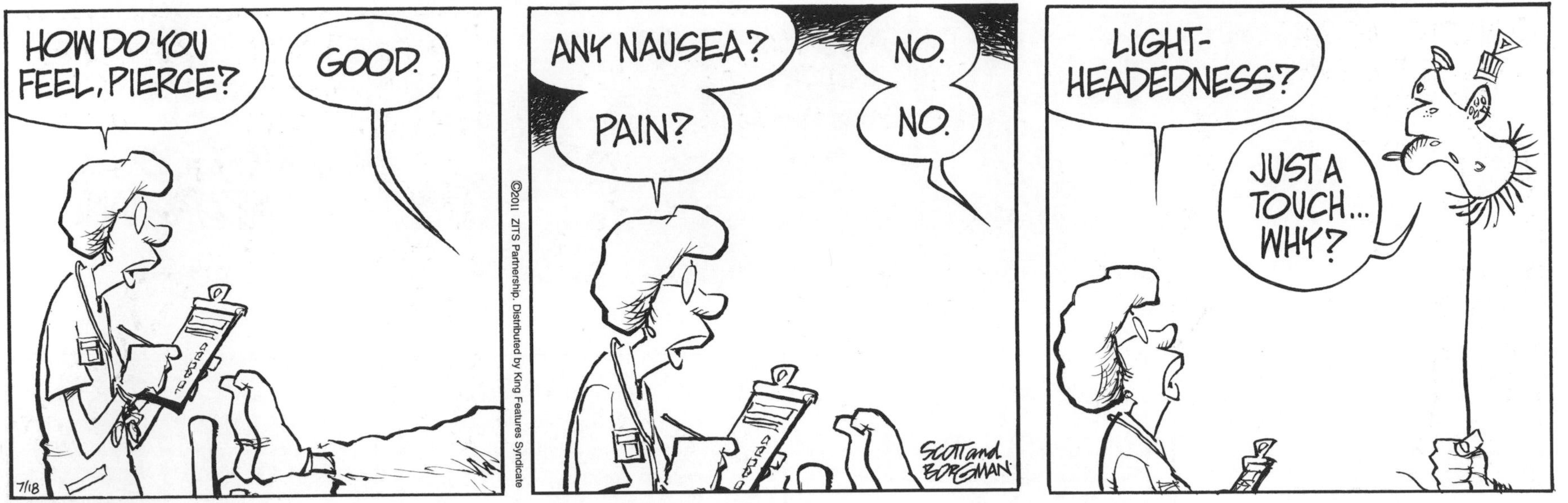
HOW DO YOU FEEL, PIERCE?
GOOD.
ANY NAUSEA?
NO.
PAIN?
NO.
LIGHT-HEADEDNESS?
JUST A TOUCH... WHY?
©2011 ZITS Partnership. Distributed by King Features Syndicate
SCOTT and BORGMAN
7/18

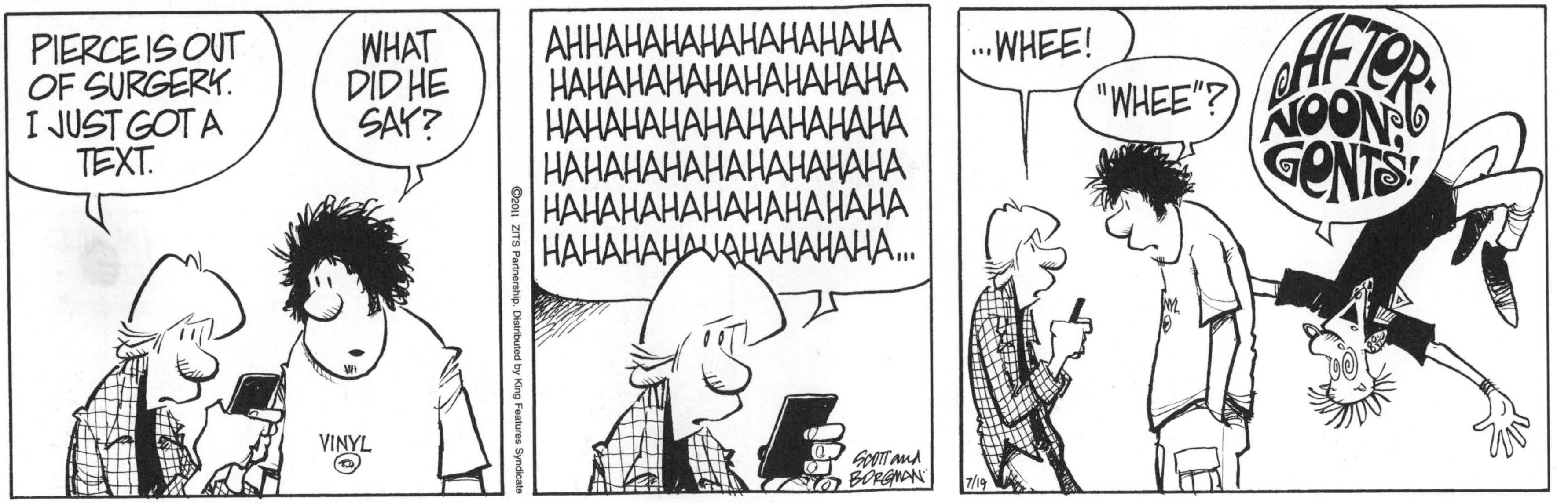
PIERCE IS OUT OF SURGERY. I JUST GOT A TEXT.
WHAT DID HE SAY?
VINYL
AHHAHAHAHAHAHAHAHAHA HAHAHAHAHAHAHAHAHAHA HAHAHAHAHAHAHAHAHAHA HAHAHAHAHAHAHAHAHAHA HAHAHAHAHAHAHAHAHAHA HAHAHAHAHAHAHAHAHAHA...
...WHEE!
"WHEE"?
AFTERNOON, GENTS!
©2011 ZITS Partnership. Distributed by King Features Syndicate
SCOTT and BORGMAN
7/19

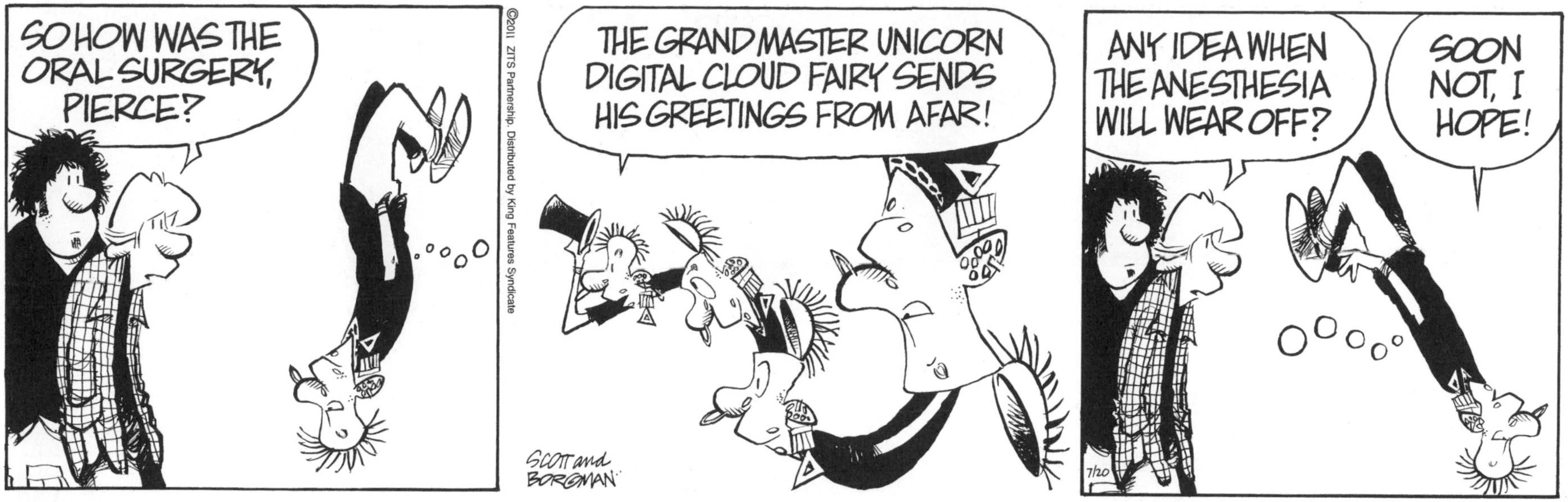
SO HOW WAS THE ORAL SURGERY, PIERCE?
©2011 ZITS Partnership. Distributed by King Features Syndicate
THE GRAND MASTER UNICORN DIGITAL CLOUD FAIRY SENDS HIS GREETINGS FROM AFAR!
SCOTT and BORGMAN
ANY IDEA WHEN THE ANESTHESIA WILL WEAR OFF?
SOON NOT, I HOPE!
7/20

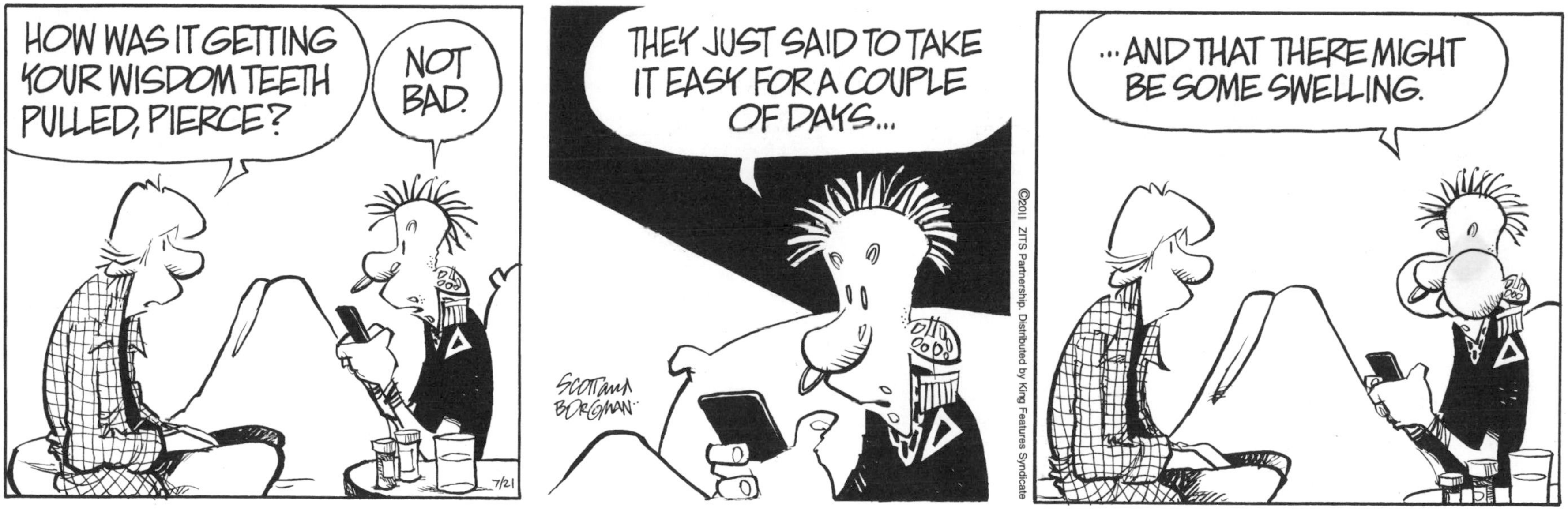
HOW WAS IT GETTING YOUR WISDOM TEETH PULLED, PIERCE?
NOT BAD.
7/21
THEY JUST SAID TO TAKE IT EASY FOR A COUPLE OF DAYS...
SCOTT and BORGMAN
©2011 ZITS Partnership. Distributed by King Features Syndicate
...AND THAT THERE MIGHT BE SOME SWELLING.

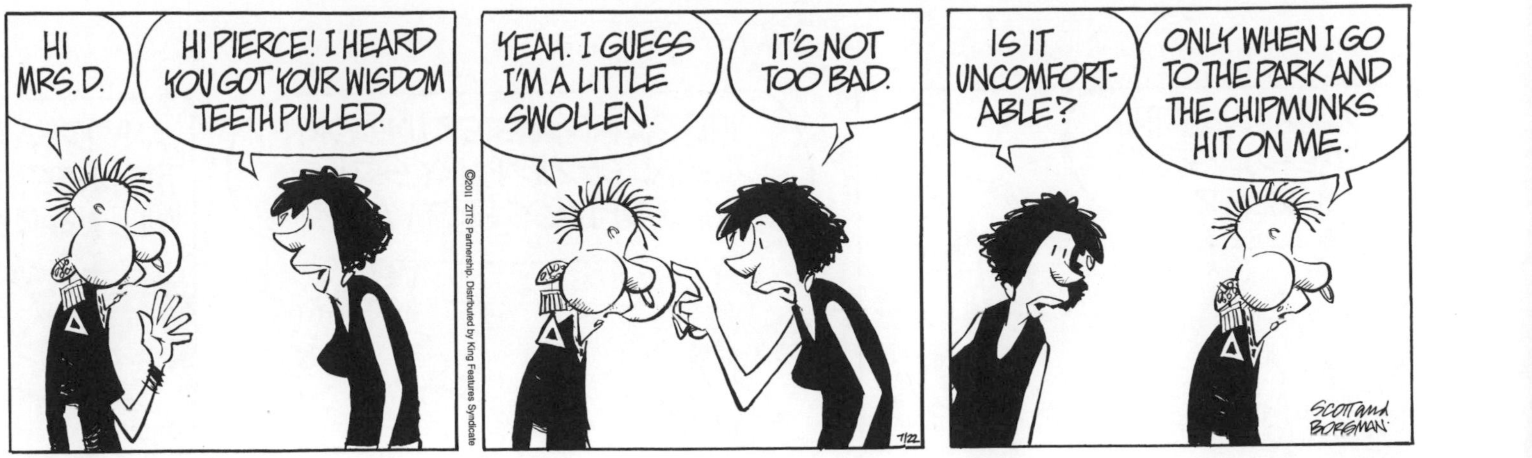
HI MRS. D.
HI PIERCE! I HEARD YOU GOT YOUR WISDOM TEETH PULLED.
YEAH. I GUESS I'M A LITTLE SWOLLEN.
IT'S NOT TOO BAD.
IS IT UNCOMFORT-ABLE?
ONLY WHEN I GO TO THE PARK AND THE CHIPMUNKS HIT ON ME.
©2011 ZITS Partnership. Distributed by King Features Syndicate
7/22
SCOTT and BORGMAN

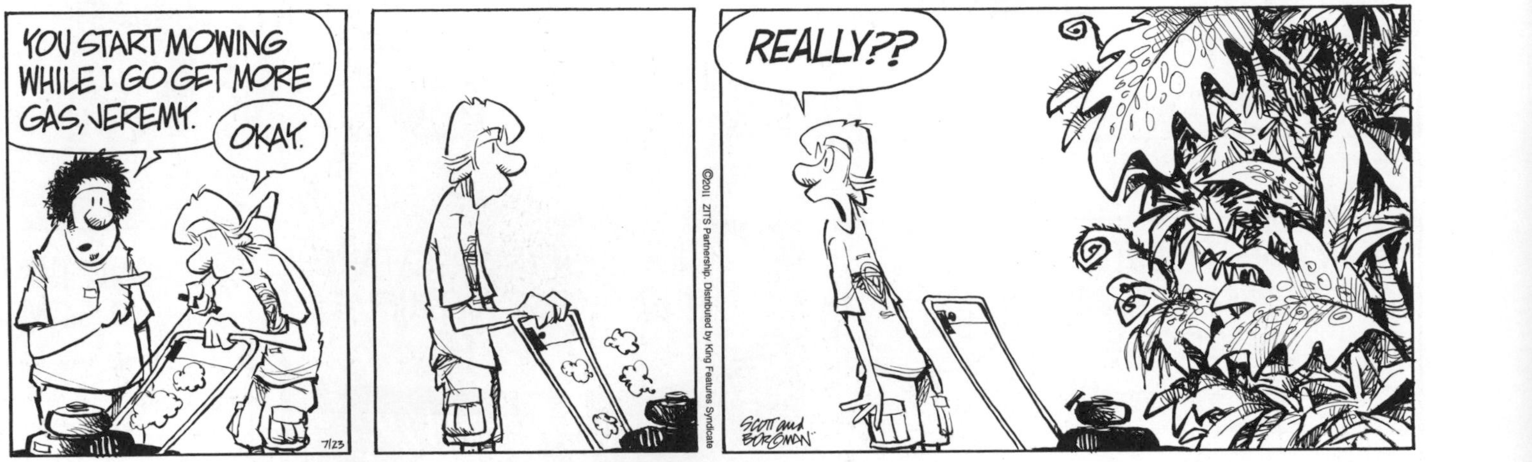
YOU START MOWING WHILE I GO GET MORE GAS, JEREMY.
OKAY.
7/23
©2011 ZITS Partnership. Distributed by King Features Syndicate
REALLY??
SCOTT and BORGMAN

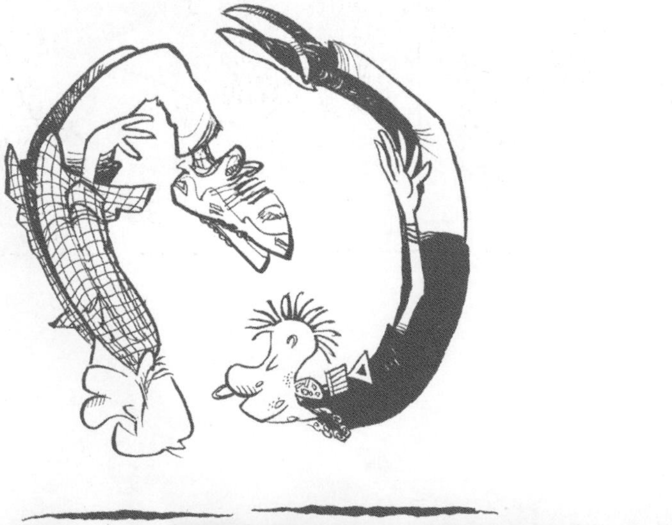

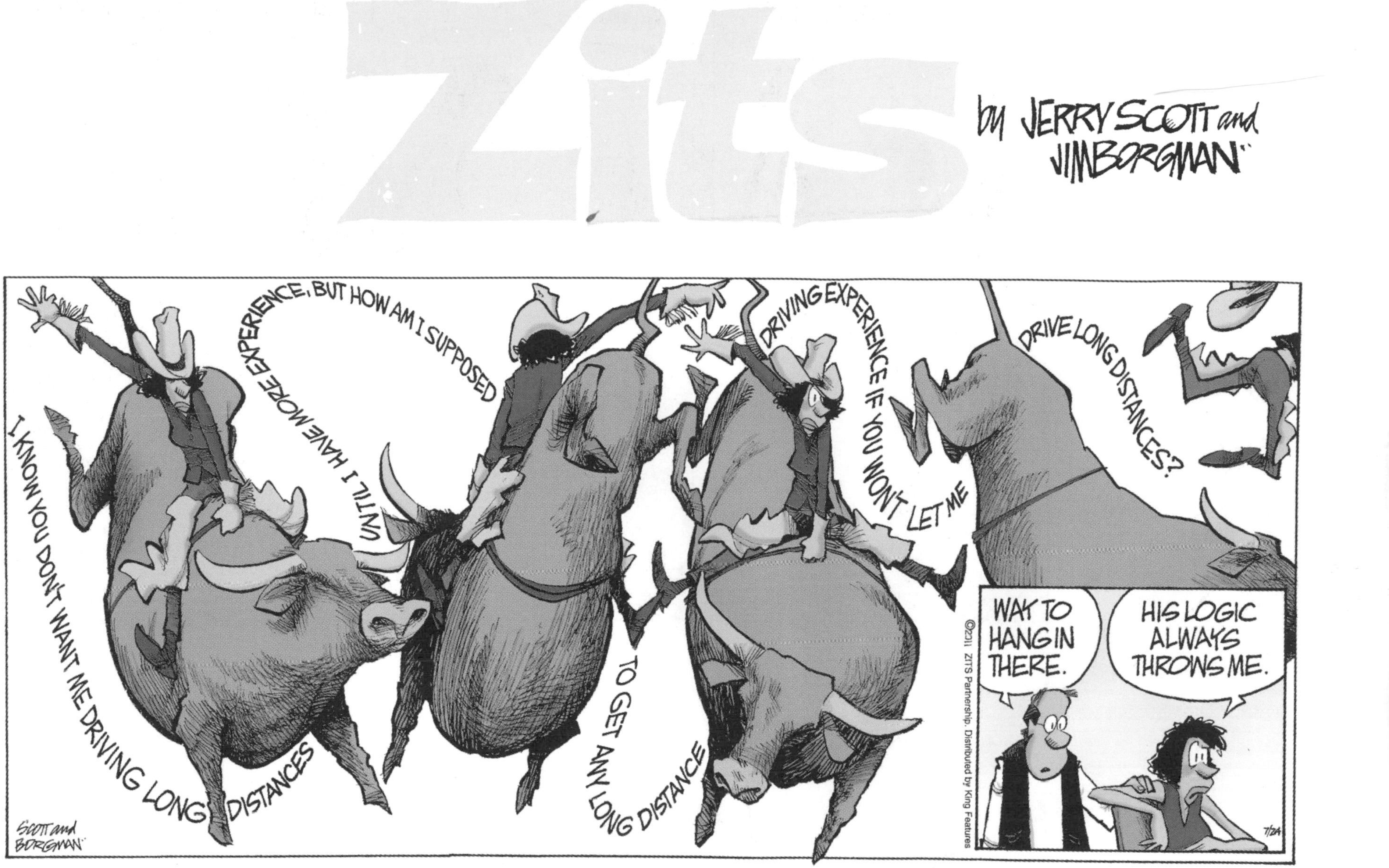
Zits
by JERRY SCOTT and JIM BORGMAN
I KNOW YOU DON'T WANT ME DRIVING LONG DISTANCES
UNTIL I HAVE MORE EXPERIENCE, BUT HOW AM I SUPPOSED
TO GET ANY LONG DISTANCE
DRIVING EXPERIENCE IF YOU WON'T LET ME
DRIVE LONG DISTANCES?
WAY TO HANG IN THERE.
HIS LOGIC ALWAYS THROWS ME.
SCOTT and BORGMAN
©2011 ZITS Partnership. Distributed by King Features

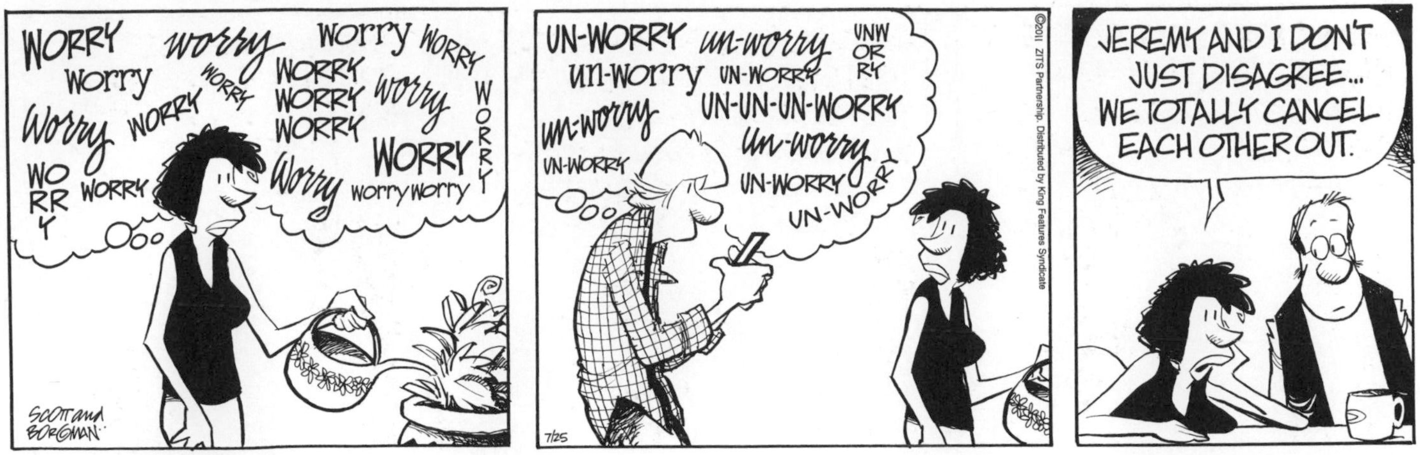
WORRY worry worry WORRY
worry WORRY
Worry WORRY WORRY WORRY WORRY worry
WORRY
WO RR Y WORRY Worry WORRY worry worry
WORRY
SCOTT and BORGMAN
UN-WORRY un-worry UNW OR RY
un-worry UN-WORRY
UN-UN-UN-WORRY
un-worry
UN-WORRY Un-worry
UN-WORRY
UN-WORRY
©2011 ZITS Partnership. Distributed by King Features Syndicate
7/25
JEREMY AND I DON'T JUST DISAGREE... WE TOTALLY CANCEL EACH OTHER OUT.

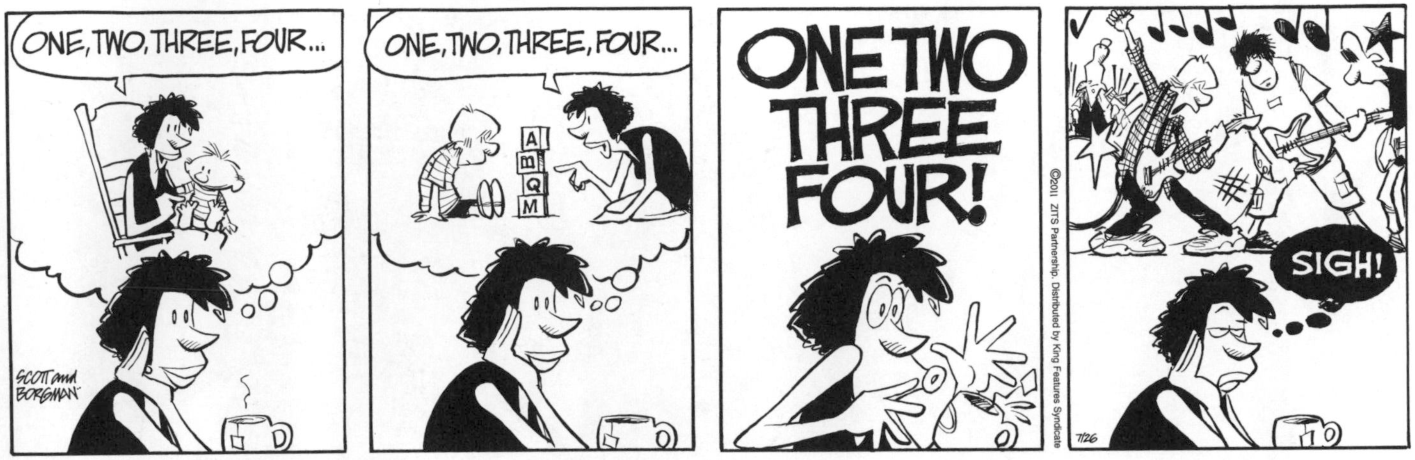
ONE, TWO, THREE, FOUR...
SCOTT and BORGMAN
ONE, TWO, THREE, FOUR...
ONE TWO THREE FOUR!
©2011 ZITS Partnership. Distributed by King Features Syndicate
SIGH!
7/26

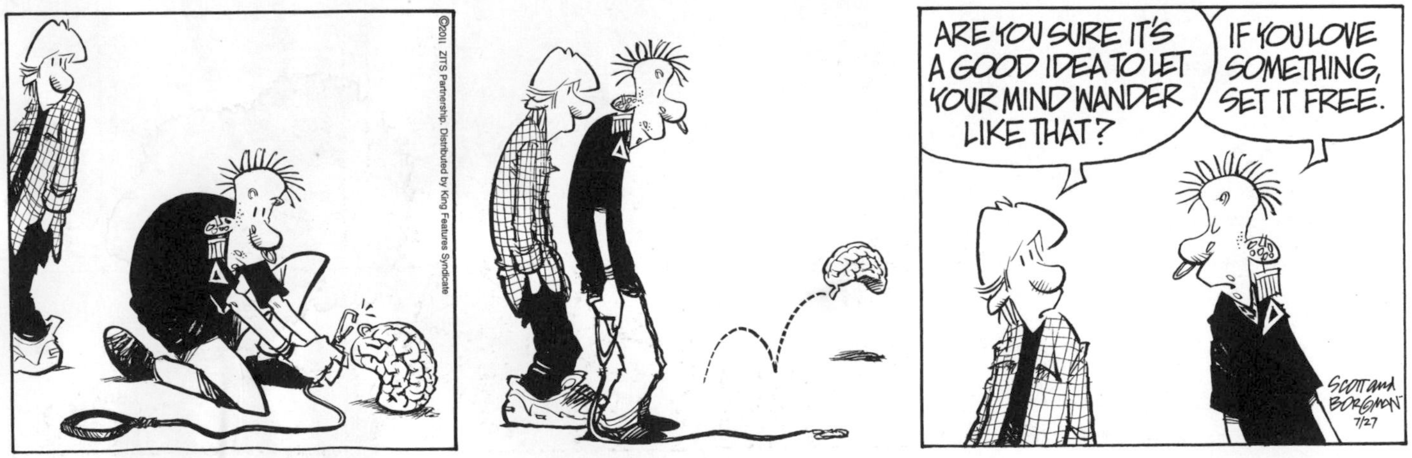
©2011 ZITS Partnership. Distributed by King Features Syndicate
ARE YOU SURE IT'S A GOOD IDEA TO LET YOUR MIND WANDER LIKE THAT?
IF YOU LOVE SOMETHING, SET IT FREE.
SCOTT and BORGMAN
7/27

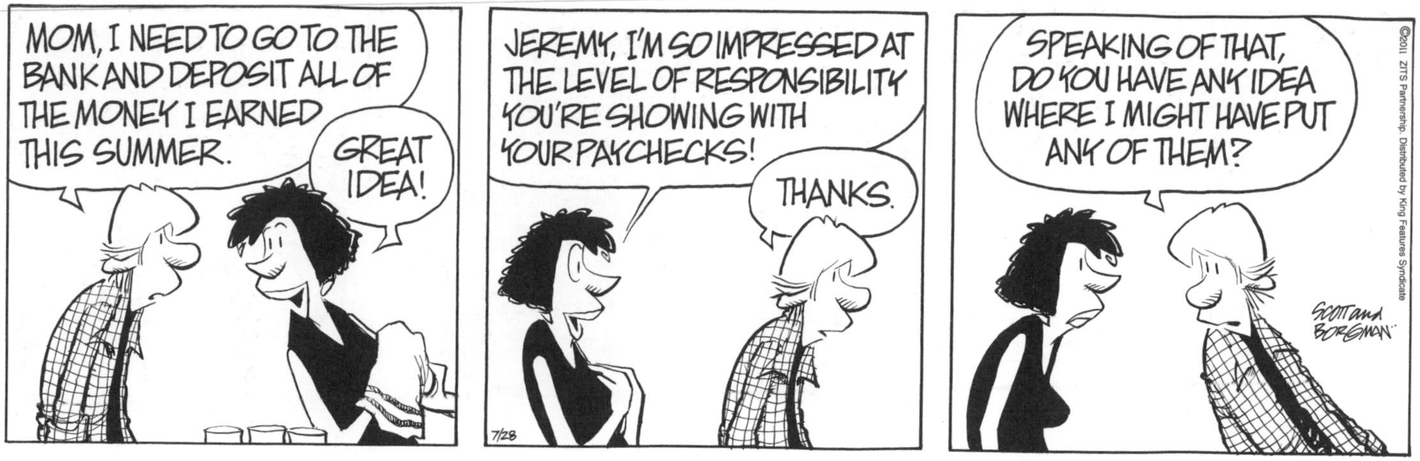
MOM, I NEED TO GO TO THE BANK AND DEPOSIT ALL OF THE MONEY I EARNED THIS SUMMER.
GREAT IDEA!
7/28
JEREMY, I'M SO IMPRESSED AT THE LEVEL OF RESPONSIBILITY YOU'RE SHOWING WITH YOUR PAYCHECKS!
THANKS.
SPEAKING OF THAT, DO YOU HAVE ANY IDEA WHERE I MIGHT HAVE PUT ANY OF THEM?
SCOTT and BORGMAN
©2011 ZITS Partnership. Distributed by King Features Syndicate

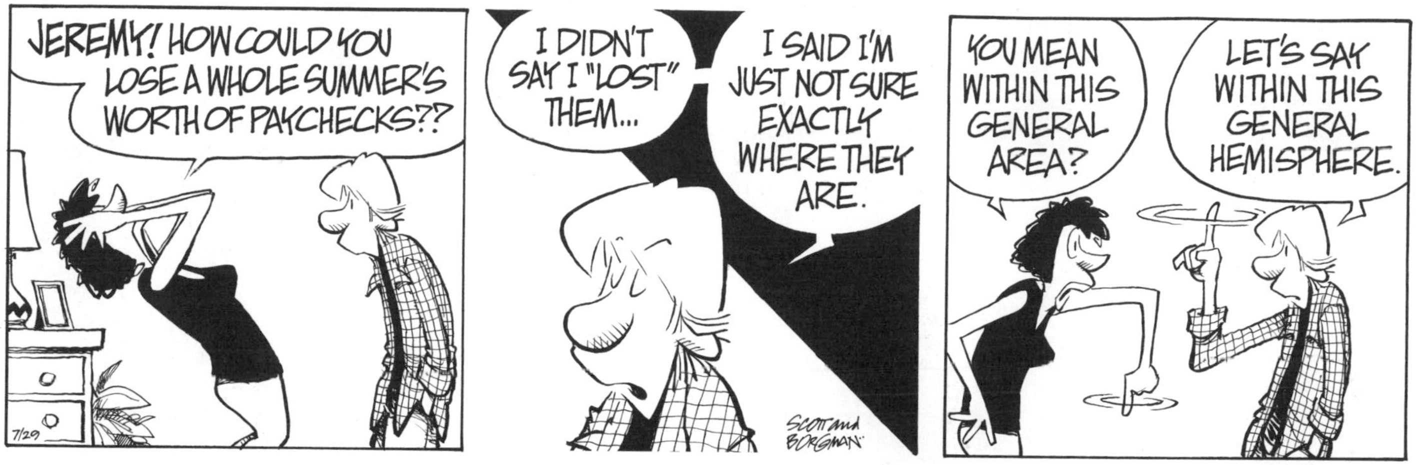
JEREMY! HOW COULD YOU LOSE A WHOLE SUMMER'S WORTH OF PAYCHECKS??
7/29
I DIDN'T SAY I "LOST" THEM...
I SAID I'M JUST NOT SURE EXACTLY WHERE THEY ARE.
SCOTT and BORGMAN
YOU MEAN WITHIN THIS GENERAL AREA?
LET'S SAY WITHIN THIS GENERAL HEMISPHERE.

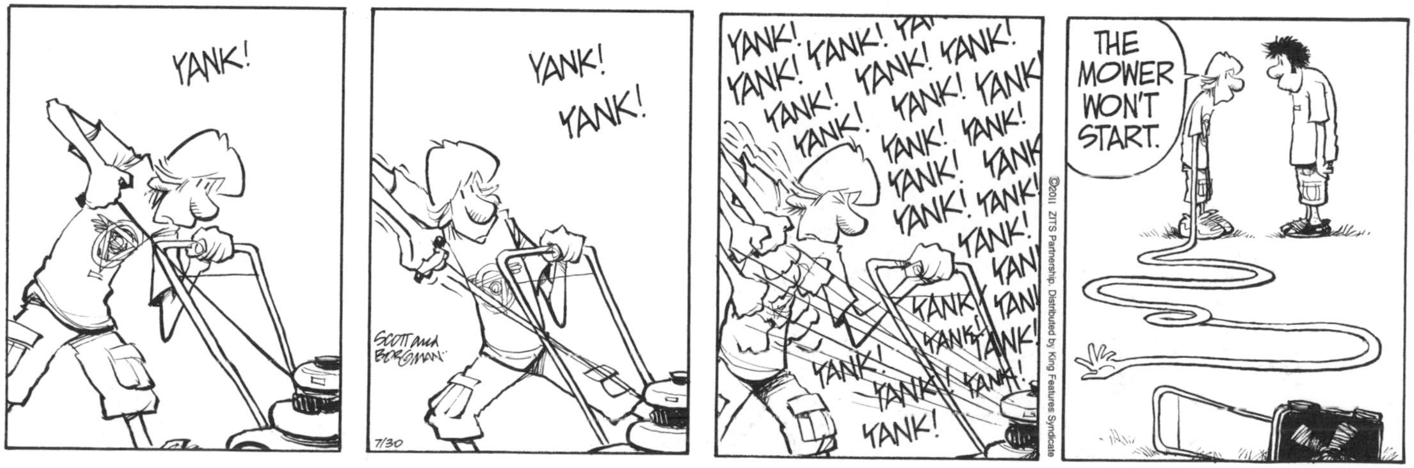
YANK!
YANK! YANK!
SCOTT and BORGMAN
7/30
YANK! YANK!
©2011 ZITS Partnership. Distributed by King Features Syndicate
THE MOWER WON'T START.

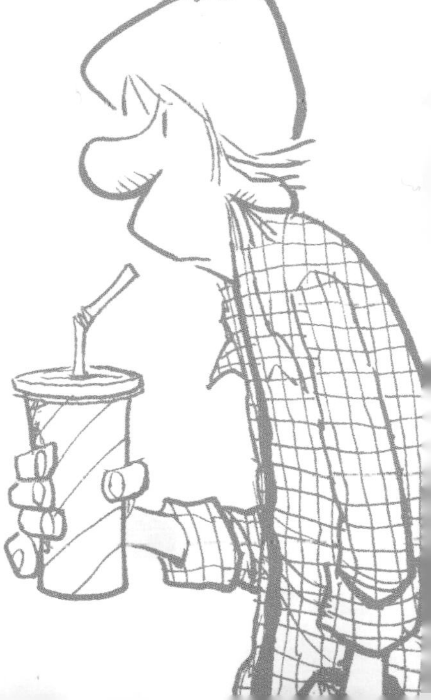

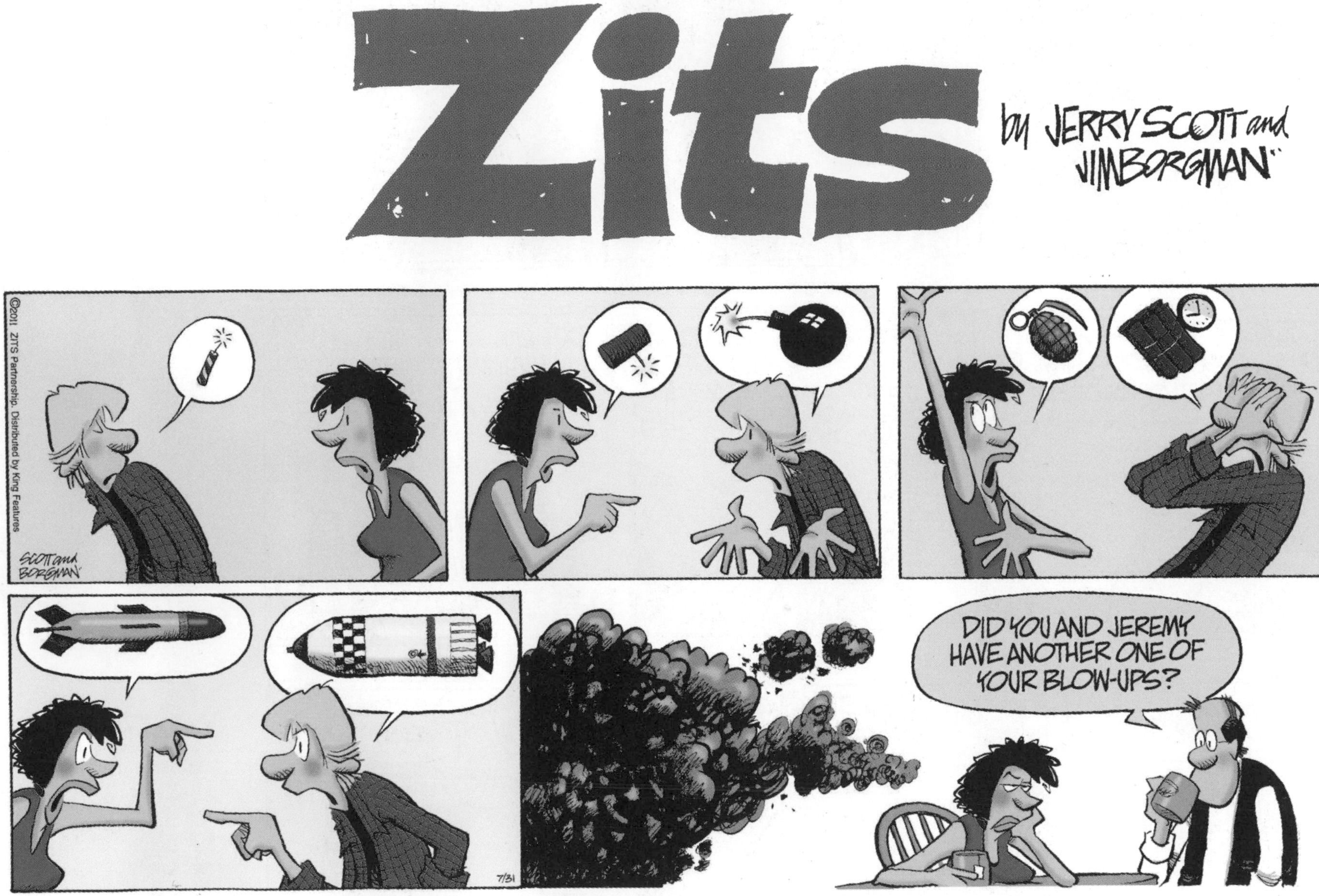
Zits
by JERRY SCOTT and JIM BORGMAN
©2011 ZITS Partnership. Distributed by King Features
SCOTT and BORGMAN
7/31
DID YOU AND JEREMY HAVE ANOTHER ONE OF YOUR BLOW-UPS?

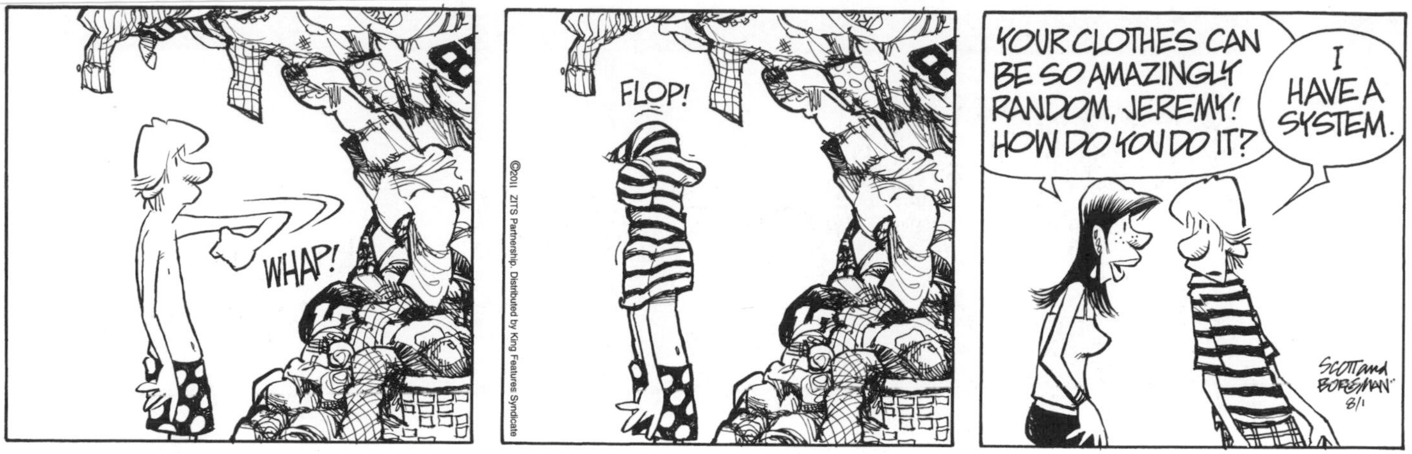
WHAP!
FLOP!
©2011 ZITS Partnership. Distributed by King Features Syndicate
YOUR CLOTHES CAN BE SO AMAZINGLY RANDOM, JEREMY! HOW DO YOU DO IT?
I HAVE A SYSTEM.
SCOTT and BORGMAN 8/1

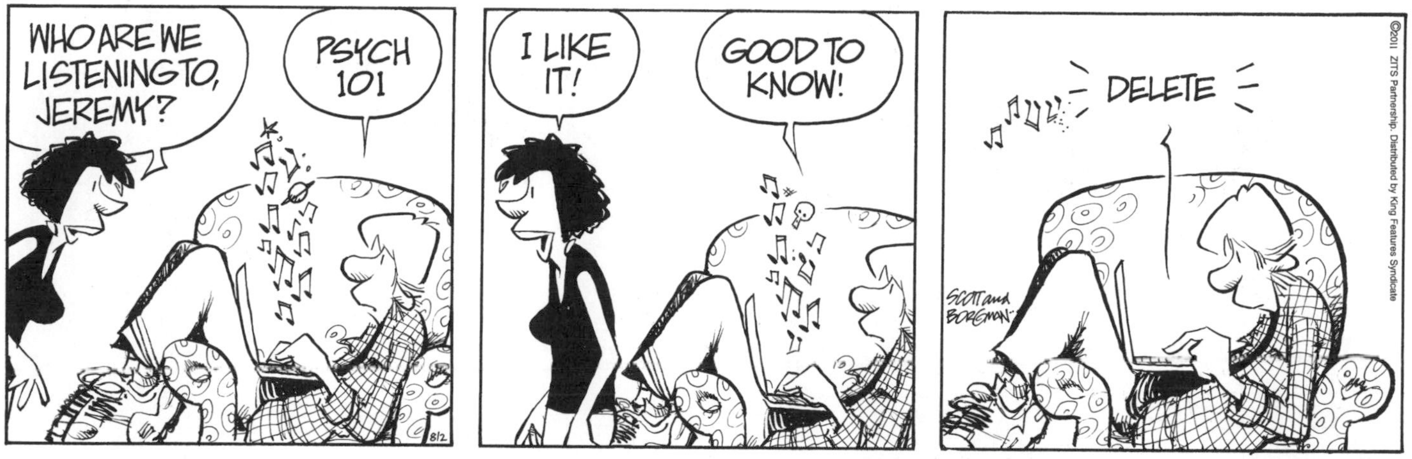
WHO ARE WE LISTENING TO, JEREMY?
PSYCH 101
8/2
I LIKE IT!
GOOD TO KNOW!
DELETE
SCOTT and BORGMAN
©2011 ZITS Partnership. Distributed by King Features Syndicate

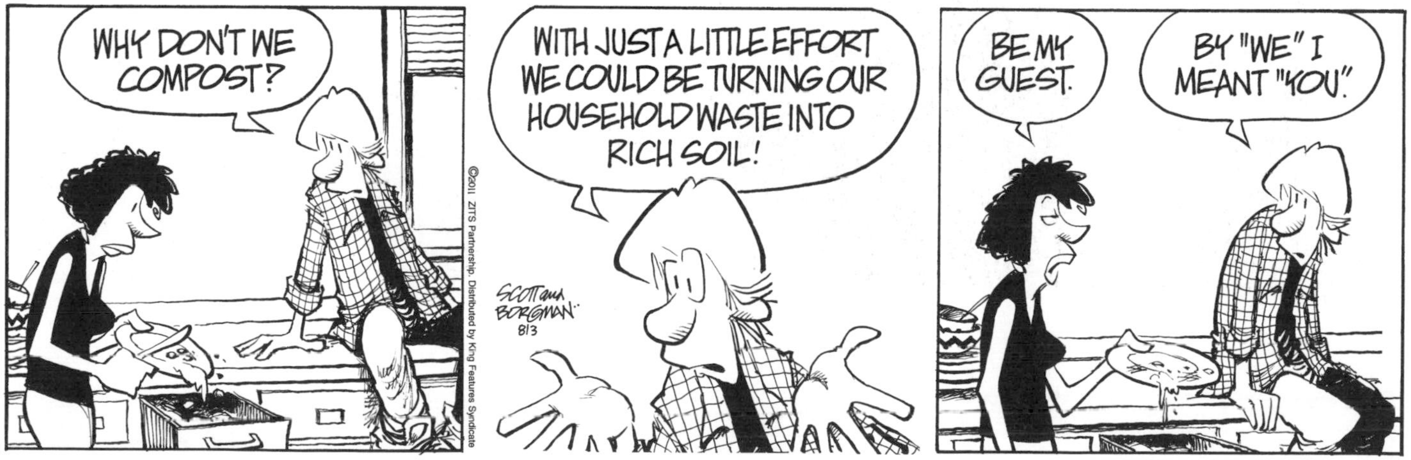
WHY DON'T WE COMPOST?
©2011 ZITS Partnership. Distributed by King Features Syndicate
WITH JUST A LITTLE EFFORT WE COULD BE TURNING OUR HOUSEHOLD WASTE INTO RICH SOIL!
SCOTT and BORGMAN 8/3
BE MY GUEST.
BY "WE" I MEANT "YOU".

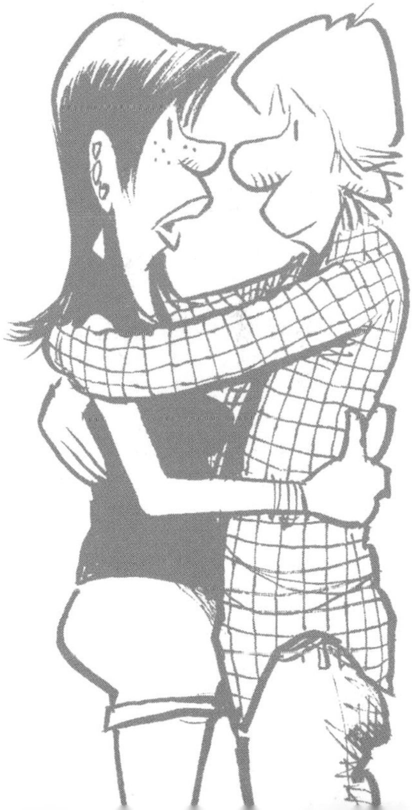

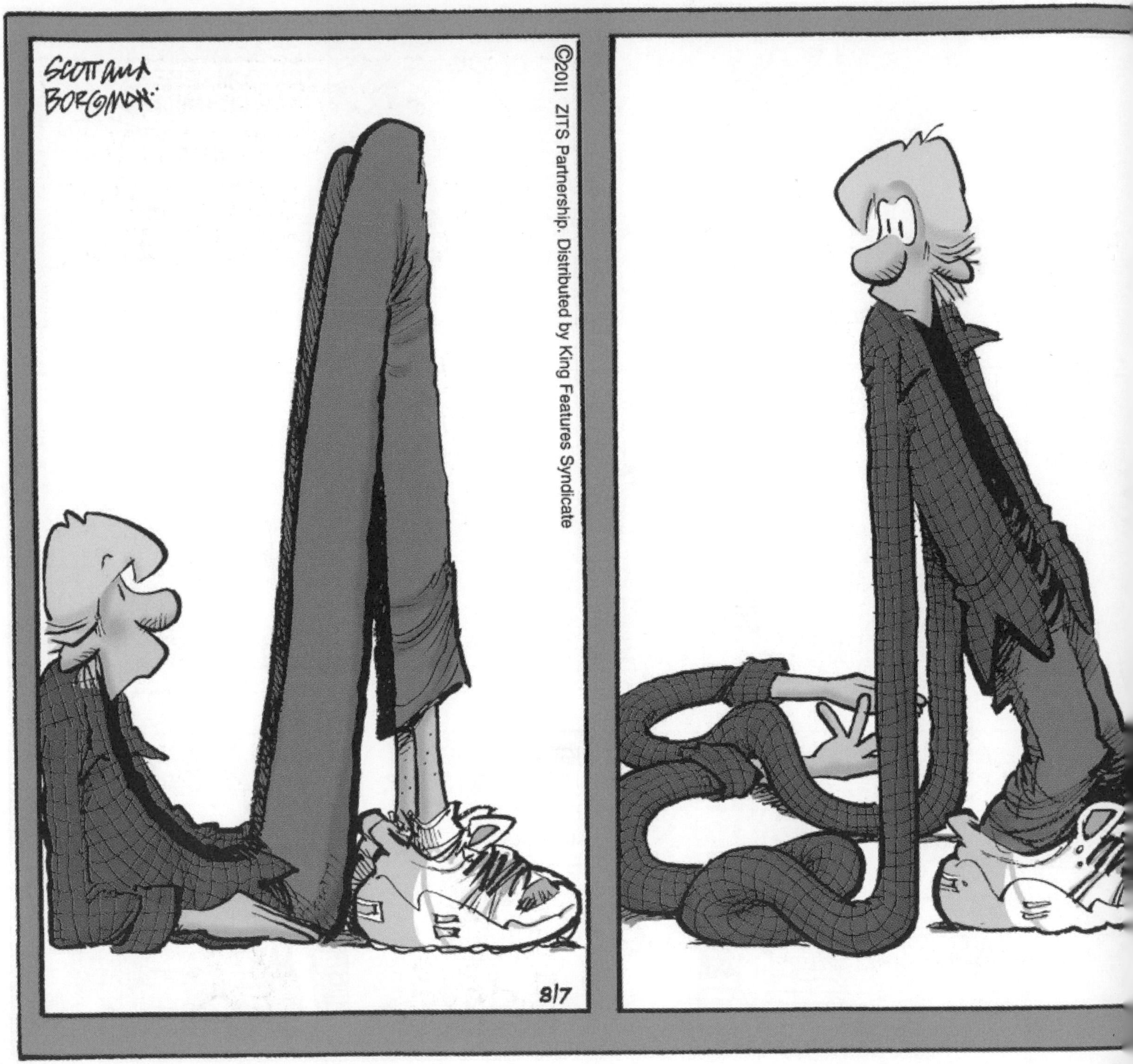
SCOTT AND BORGMAN
©2011 ZITS Partnership. Distributed by King Features Syndicate
8/7

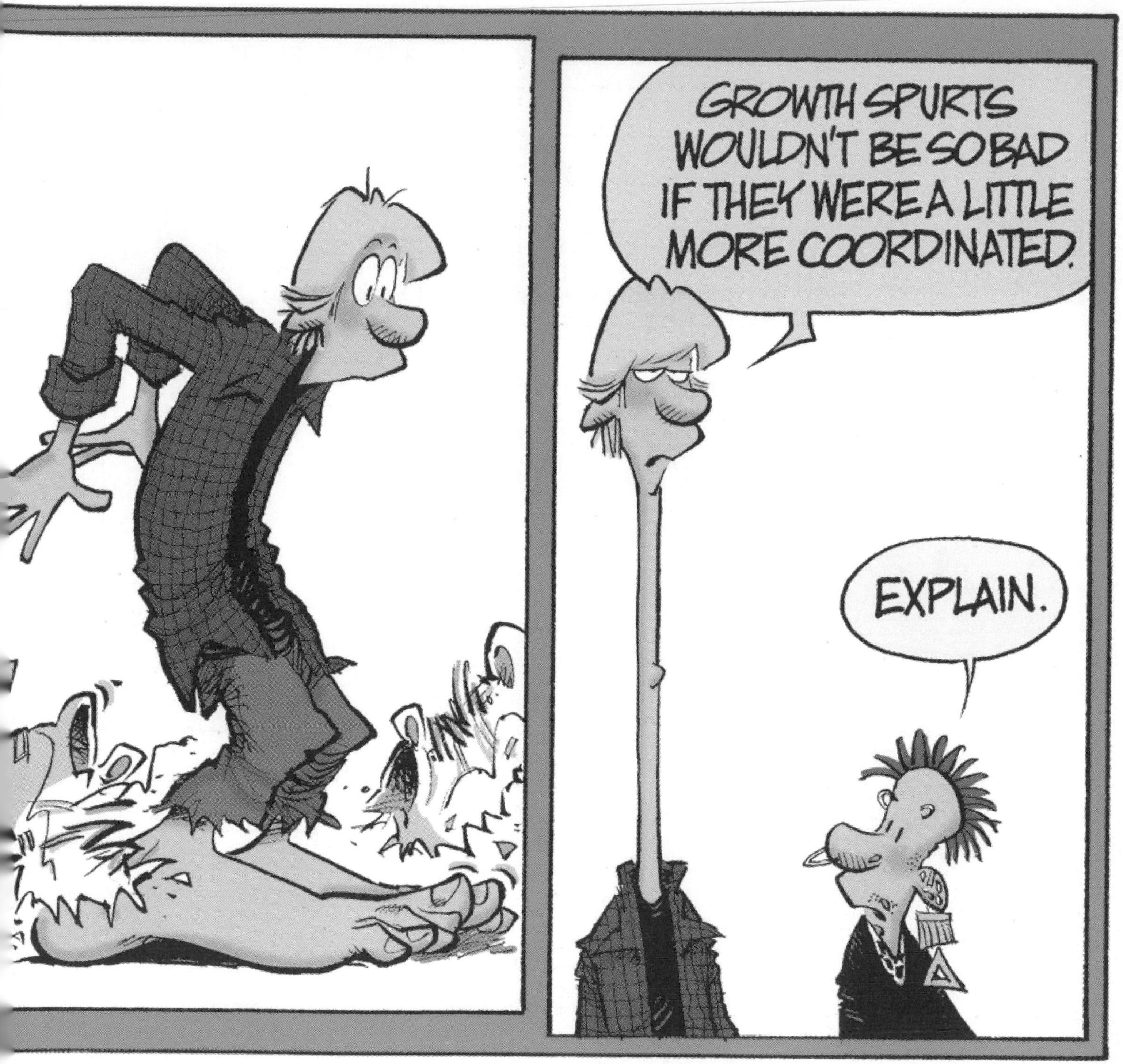
GROWTH SPURTS WOULDN'T BE SO BAD IF THEY WERE A LITTLE MORE COORDINATED.
EXPLAIN.

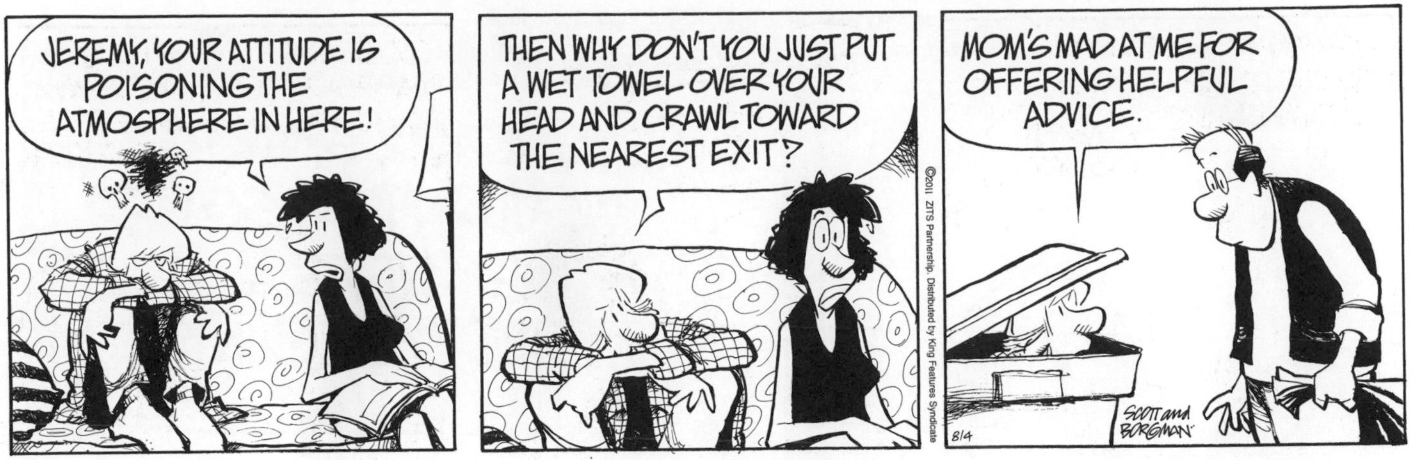
JEREMY, YOUR ATTITUDE IS POISONING THE ATMOSPHERE IN HERE!
THEN WHY DON'T YOU JUST PUT A WET TOWEL OVER YOUR HEAD AND CRAWL TOWARD THE NEAREST EXIT?
©2011 ZITS Partnership. Distributed by King Features Syndicate
MOM'S MAD AT ME FOR OFFERING HELPFUL ADVICE.
8/4
SCOTT and BORGMAN

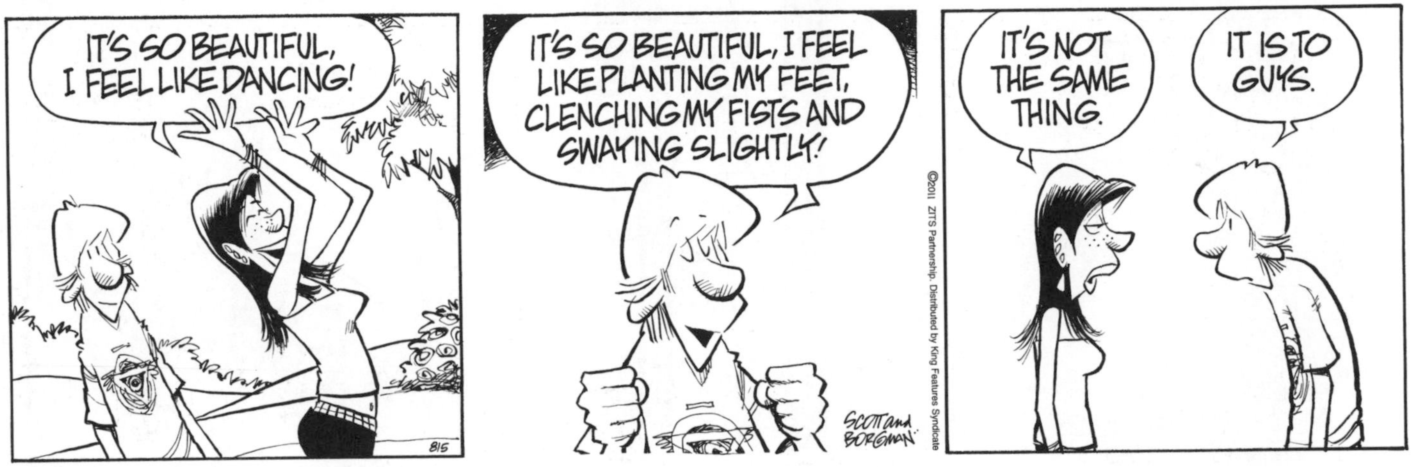
IT'S SO BEAUTIFUL, I FEEL LIKE DANCING!
8/5
IT'S SO BEAUTIFUL, I FEEL LIKE PLANTING MY FEET, CLENCHING MY FISTS AND SWAYING SLIGHTLY!
SCOTT and BORGMAN
©2011 ZITS Partnership. Distributed by King Features Syndicate
IT'S NOT THE SAME THING.
IT IS TO GUYS.

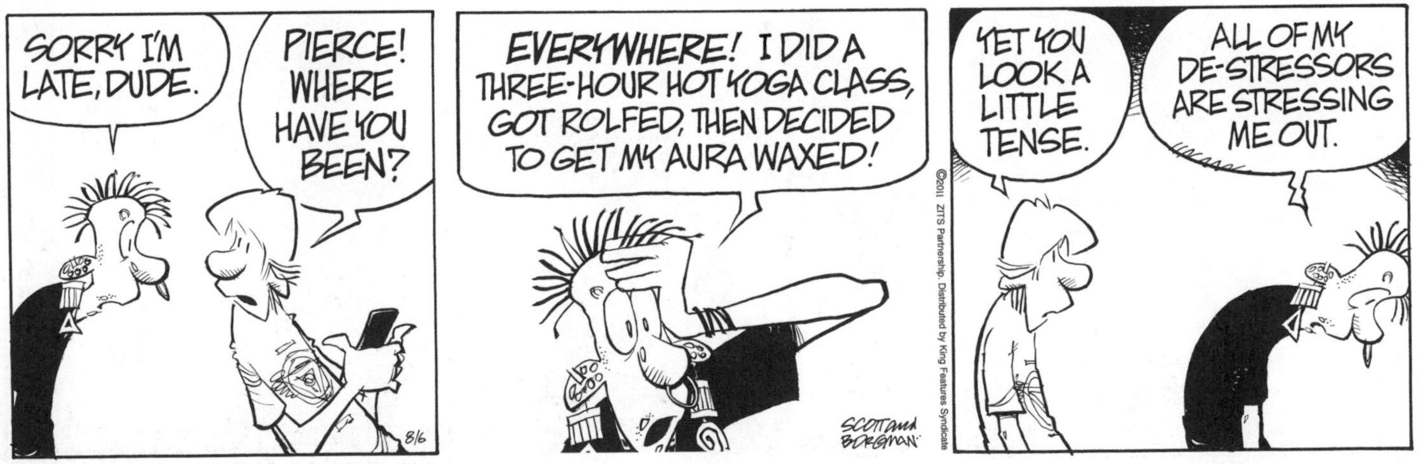
SORRY I'M LATE, DUDE.
PIERCE! WHERE HAVE YOU BEEN?
8/6
EVERYWHERE! I DID A THREE-HOUR HOT YOGA CLASS, GOT ROLFED, THEN DECIDED TO GET MY AURA WAXED!
SCOTT and BORGMAN
©2011 ZITS Partnership. Distributed by King Features Syndicate
YET YOU LOOK A LITTLE TENSE.
ALL OF MY DE-STRESSORS ARE STRESSING ME OUT.

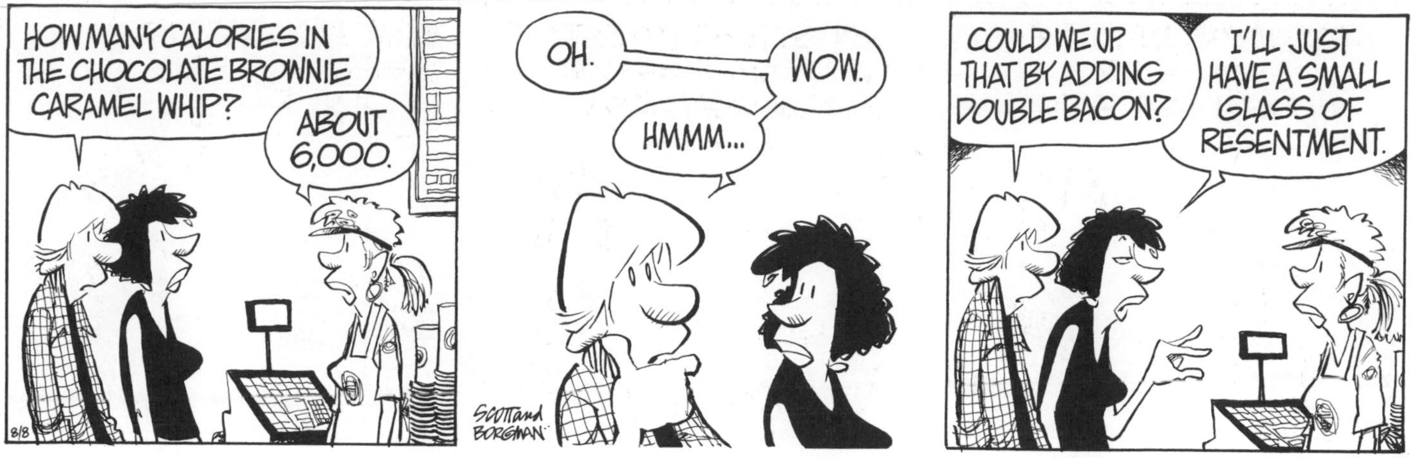
HOW MANY CALORIES IN THE CHOCOLATE BROWNIE CARAMEL WHIP?
ABOUT 6,000.
OH.
WOW.
HMMM...
COULD WE UP THAT BY ADDING DOUBLE BACON?
I'LL JUST HAVE A SMALL GLASS OF RESENTMENT.
8/8
SCOTT and BORGMAN

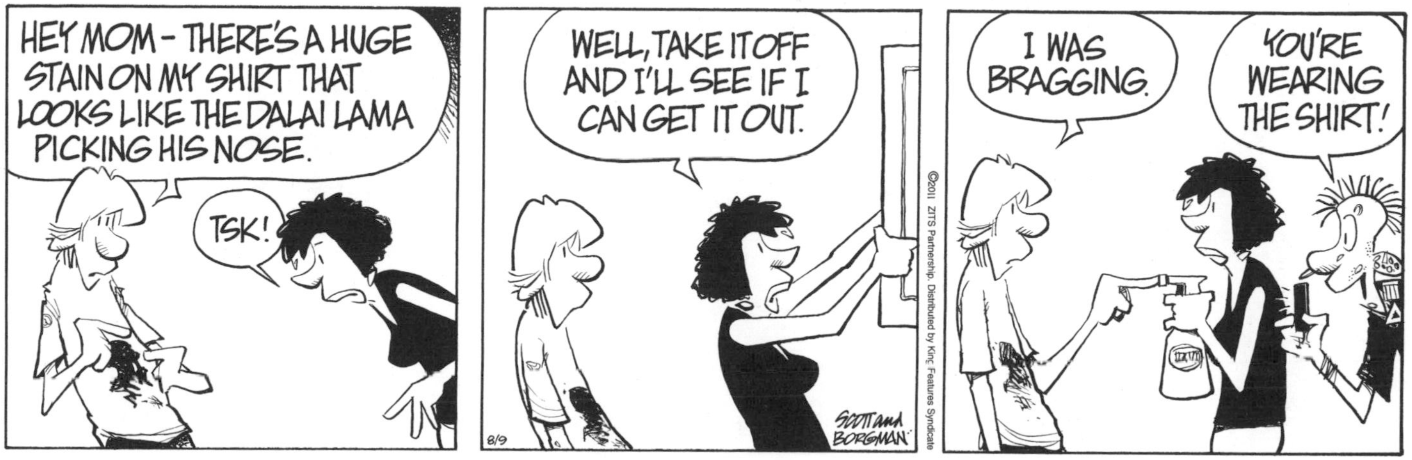
HEY MOM - THERE'S A HUGE STAIN ON MY SHIRT THAT LOOKS LIKE THE DALAI LAMA PICKING HIS NOSE.
TSK!
WELL, TAKE IT OFF AND I'LL SEE IF I CAN GET IT OUT.
I WAS BRAGGING.
YOU'RE WEARING THE SHIRT!
8/9
SCOTT and BORGMAN
©2011 ZITS Partnership. Distributed by King Features Syndicate

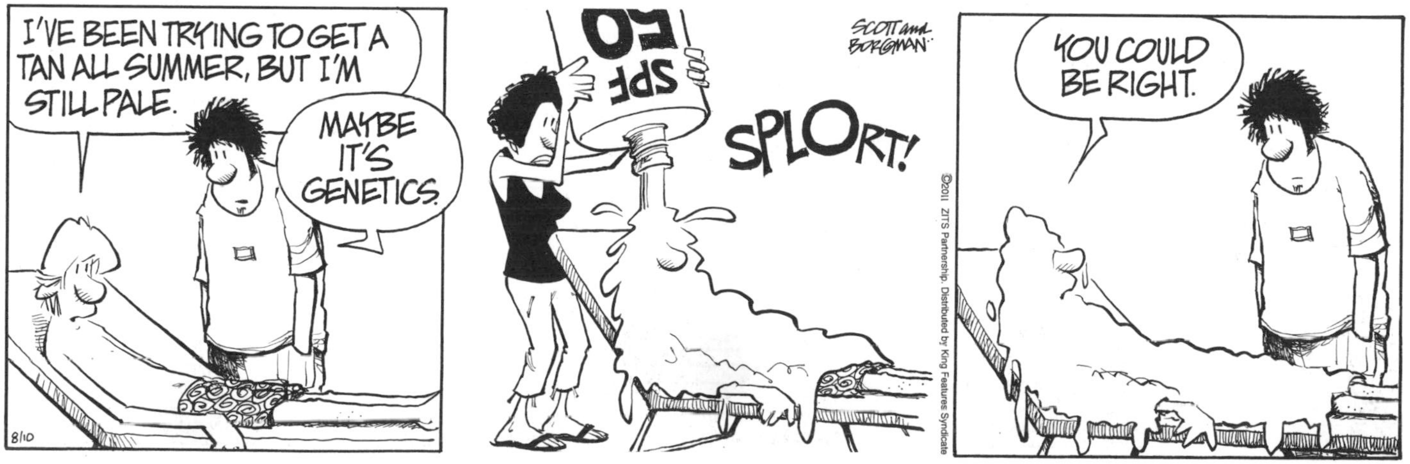
I'VE BEEN TRYING TO GET A TAN ALL SUMMER, BUT I'M STILL PALE.
MAYBE IT'S GENETICS.
SPF 50
SPLORT!
YOU COULD BE RIGHT.
8/10
SCOTT and BORGMAN
©2011 ZITS Partnership. Distributed by King Features Syndicate

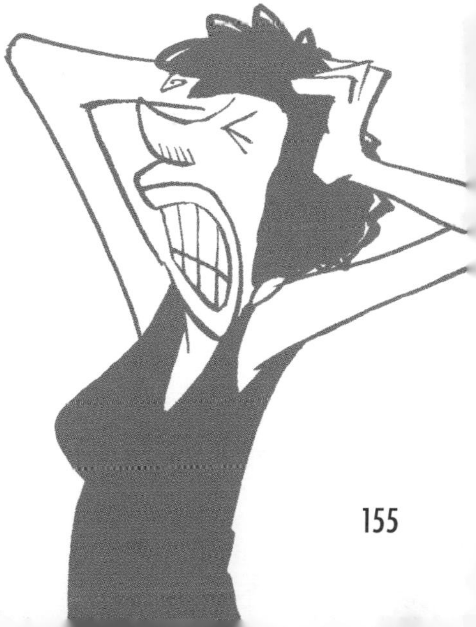

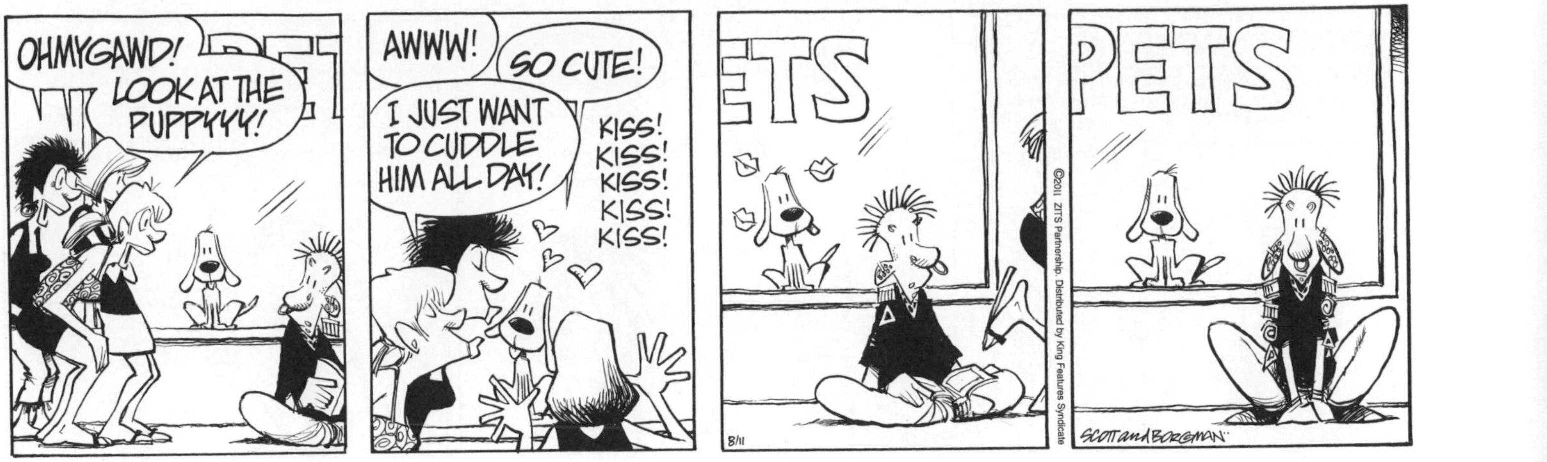
OHMYGAWD!
LOOK AT THE PUPPYYY!
AWWW!
SO CUTE!
I JUST WANT TO CUDDLE HIM ALL DAY!
KISS! KISS! KISS! KISS! KISS!
PETS
8/11
PETS
©2011 ZITS Partnership. Distributed by King Features Syndicate
SCOTT and BORGMAN

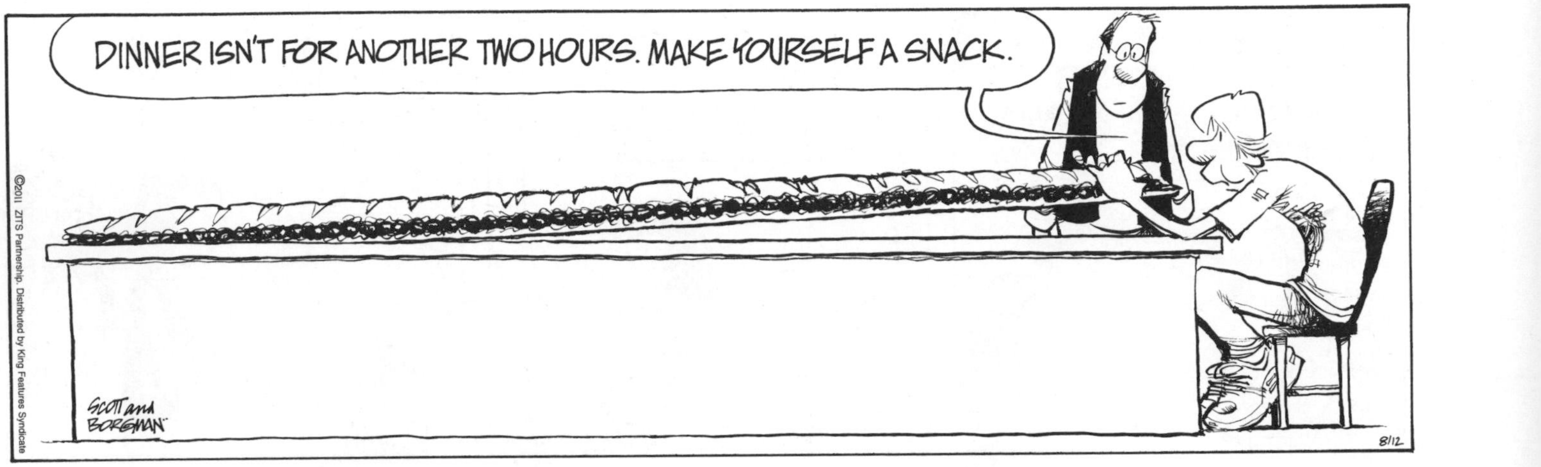
DINNER ISN'T FOR ANOTHER TWO HOURS. MAKE YOURSELF A SNACK.
©2011 ZITS Partnership. Distributed by King Features Syndicate
SCOTT and BORGMAN
8/12

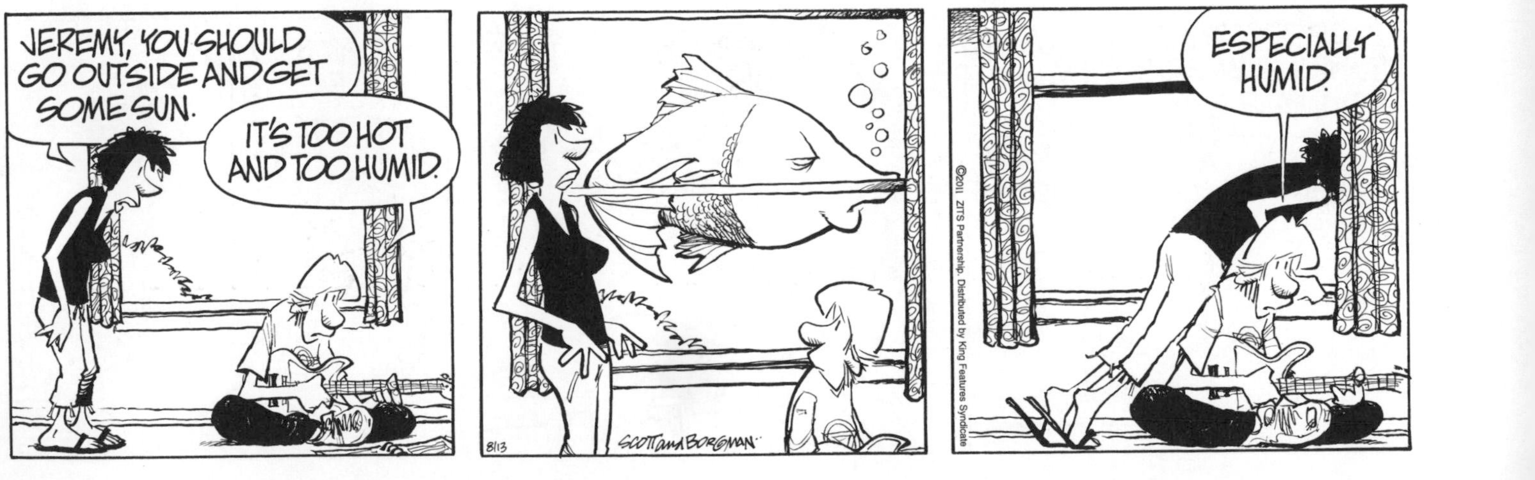
JEREMY, YOU SHOULD GO OUTSIDE AND GET SOME SUN.
IT'S TOO HOT AND TOO HUMID.
8/13
SCOTT and BORGMAN
ESPECIALLY HUMID.
©2011 ZITS Partnership. Distributed by King Features Syndicate

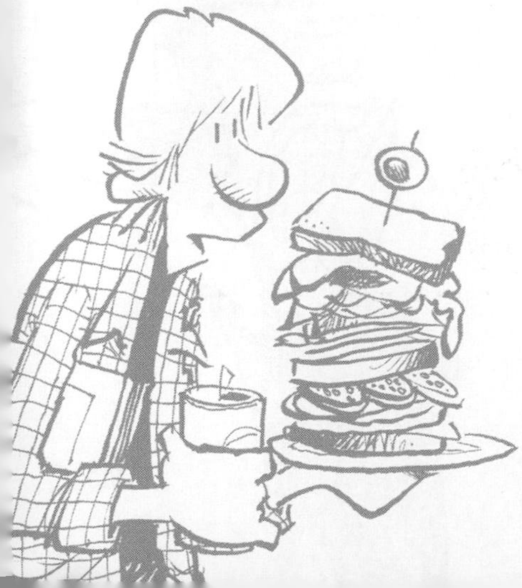

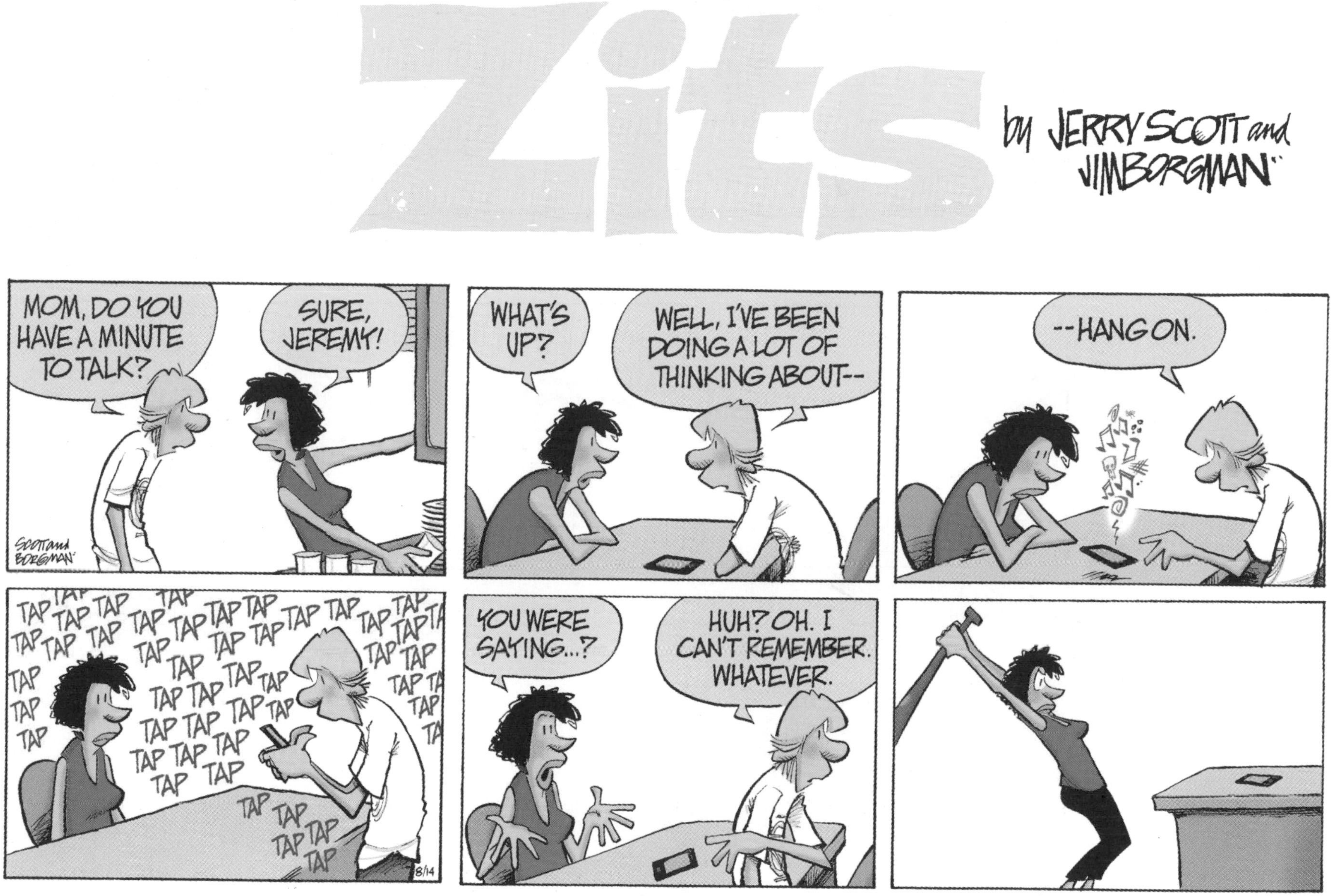
Zits
by JERRY SCOTT and JIM BORGMAN
MOM, DO YOU HAVE A MINUTE TO TALK?
SURE, JEREMY!
SCOTT and BORGMAN
WHAT'S UP?
WELL, I'VE BEEN DOING A LOT OF THINKING ABOUT--
--HANG ON.
TAP TAP TAP TAP TAP TAP TAP TAP TAP TAP TAP TAP TAP TAP TAP TAP TAP TAP TAP TAP TAP TAP TAP TAP TAP TAP TAP TAP TAP TAP TAP TAP TAP TAP TAP TAP TAP TAP TAP TAP
8/14
YOU WERE SAYING...?
HUH? OH. I CAN'T REMEMBER. WHATEVER.

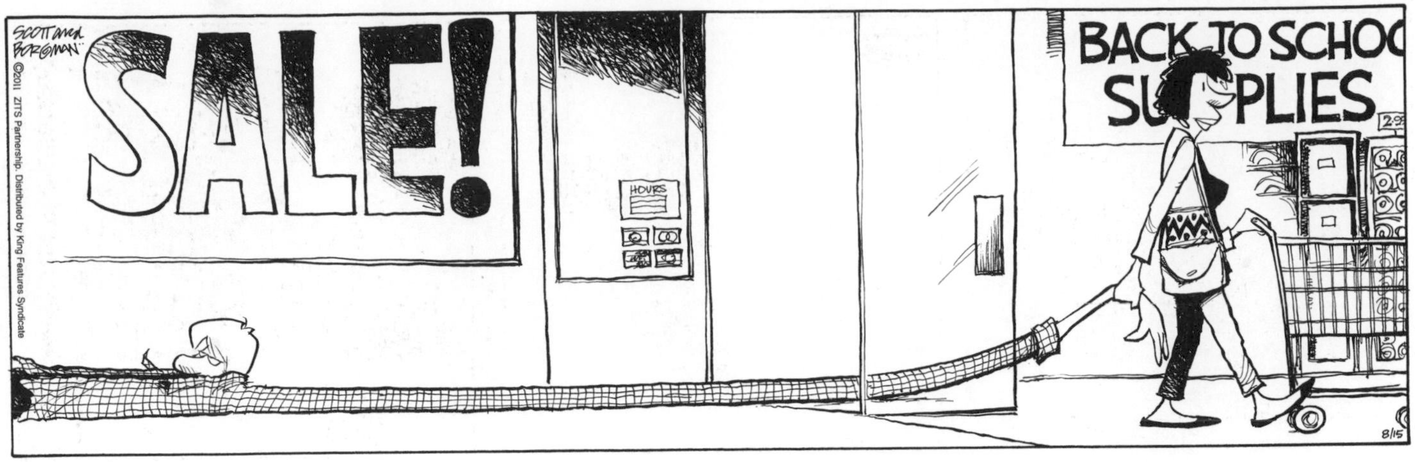
SCOTT and BORGMAN
©2011 ZITS Partnership. Distributed by King Features Syndicate
SALE!
HOURS
BACK TO SCHO
SU PLIES
8/15

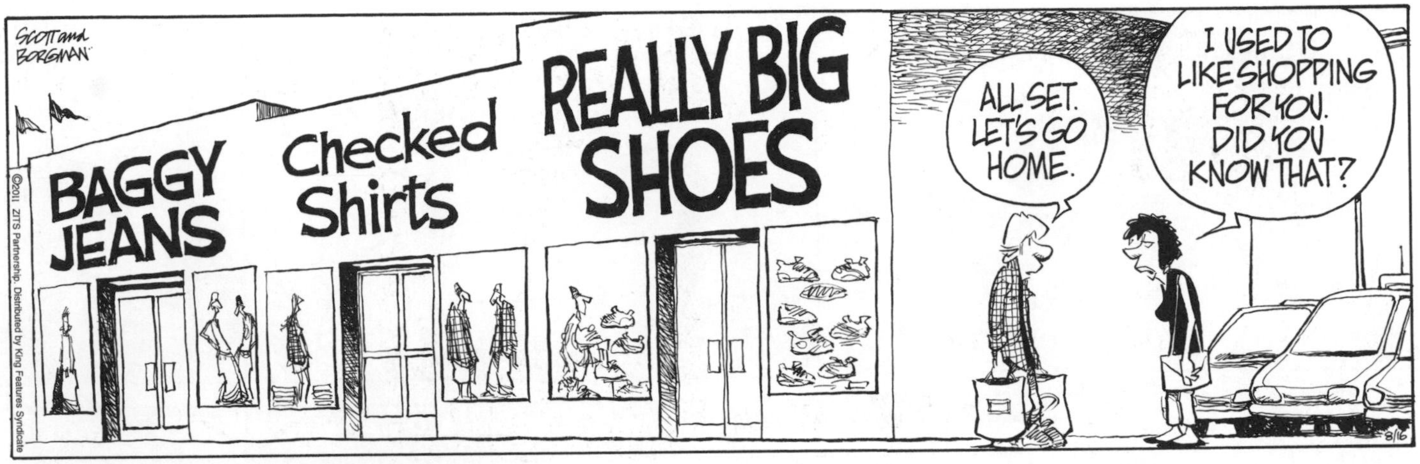
SCOTT and BORGMAN
©2011 ZITS Partnership. Distributed by King Features Syndicate
BAGGY JEANS
Checked Shirts
REALLY BIG SHOES
ALL SET. LET'S GO HOME.
I USED TO LIKE SHOPPING FOR YOU. DID YOU KNOW THAT?
8/16

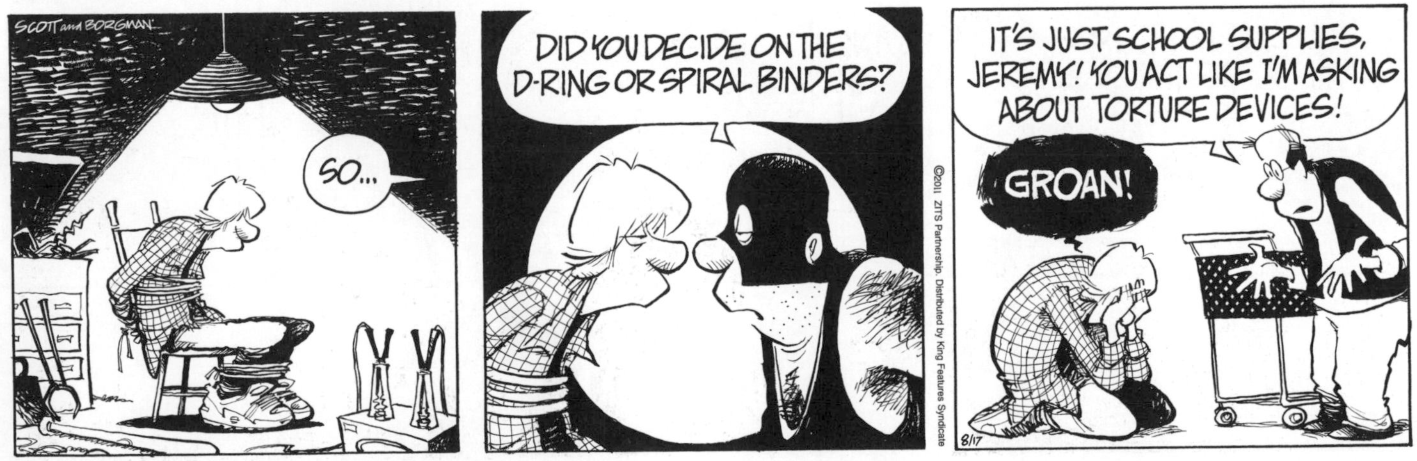
SCOTT and BORGMAN
SO...
DID YOU DECIDE ON THE D-RING OR SPIRAL BINDERS?
©2011 ZITS Partnership. Distributed by King Features Syndicate
IT'S JUST SCHOOL SUPPLIES, JEREMY! YOU ACT LIKE I'M ASKING ABOUT TORTURE DEVICES!
GROAN!
8/17

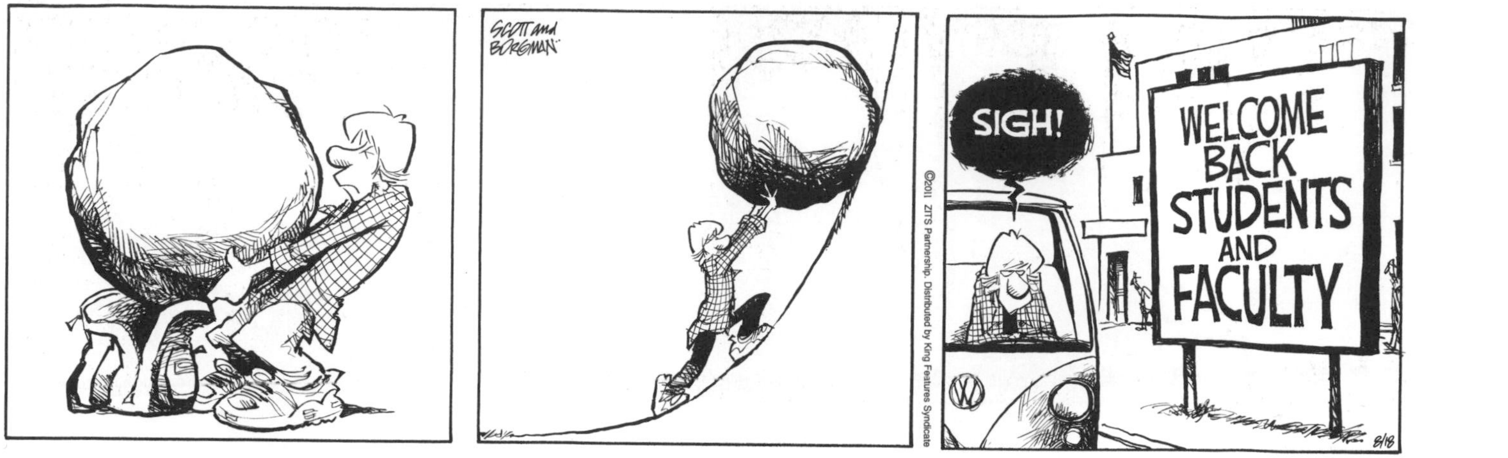
SCOTT and BORGMAN
SIGH!
WELCOME BACK STUDENTS AND FACULTY
©2011 ZITS Partnership. Distributed by King Features Syndicate
8/18

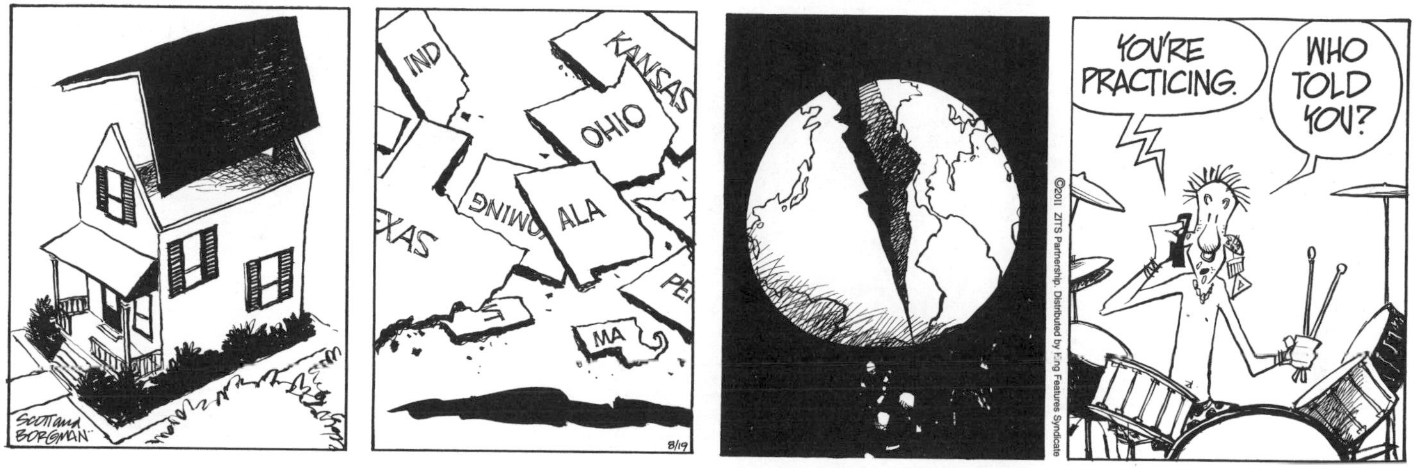
SCOTT and BORGMAN
IND
KANSAS
OHIO
EXAS
OMING
ALA
MA
8/19
YOU'RE PRACTICING.
WHO TOLD YOU?
©2011 ZITS Partnership. Distributed by King Features Syndicate

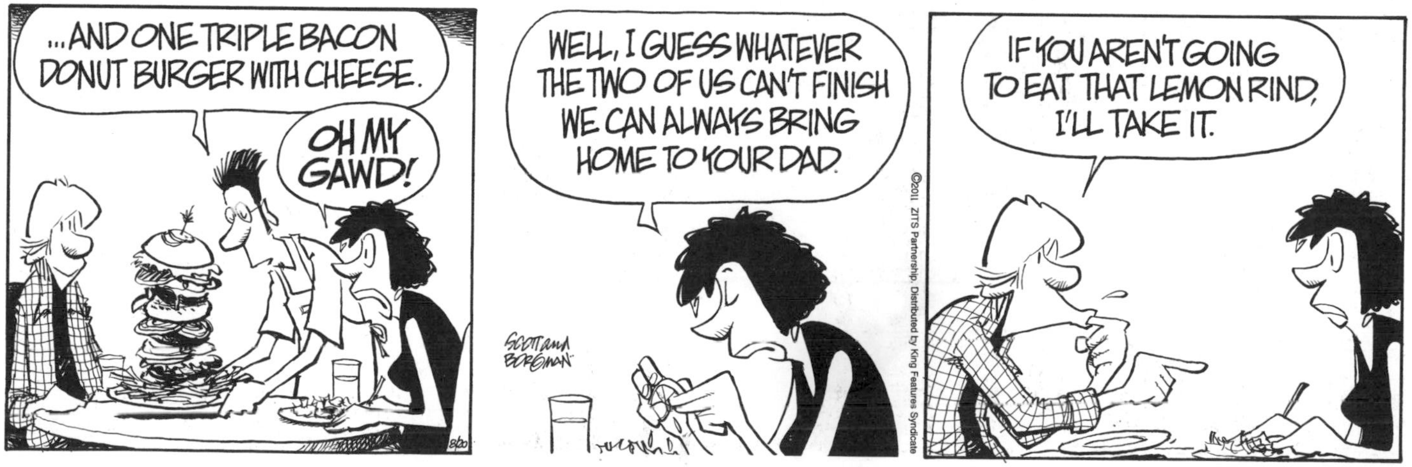
...AND ONE TRIPLE BACON DONUT BURGER WITH CHEESE.
OH MY GAWD!
8/20
WELL, I GUESS WHATEVER THE TWO OF US CAN'T FINISH WE CAN ALWAYS BRING HOME TO YOUR DAD.
SCOTT and BORGMAN
©2011 ZITS Partnership. Distributed by King Features Syndicate
IF YOU AREN'T GOING TO EAT THAT LEMON RIND, I'LL TAKE IT.

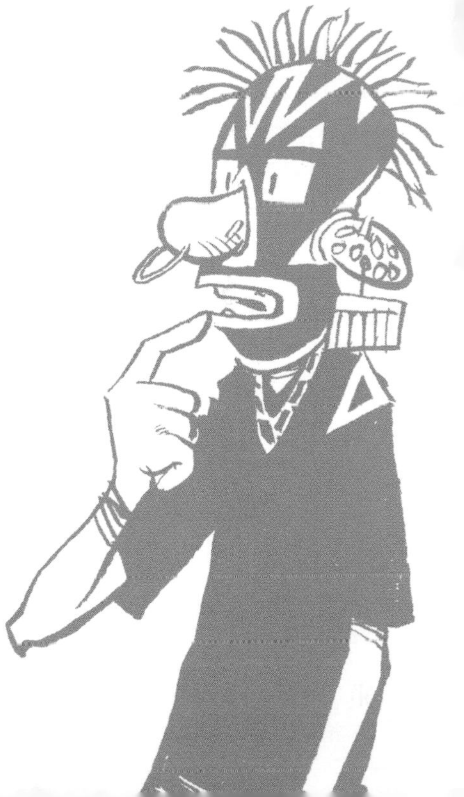

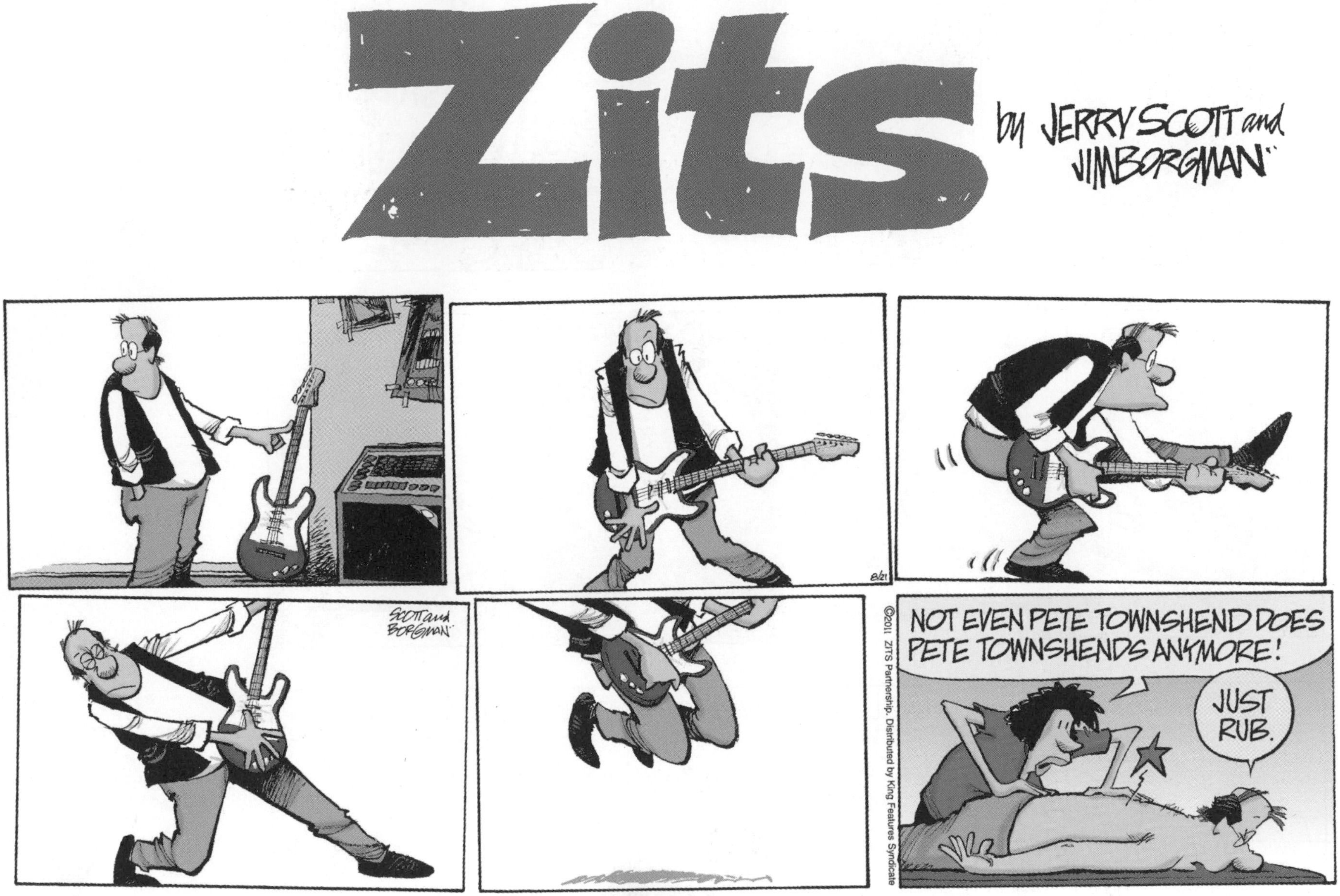
Zits
by JERRY SCOTT and JIM BORGMAN
SCOTT and BORGMAN
8/21
©2011 ZITS Partnership. Distributed by King Features Syndicate
NOT EVEN PETE TOWNSHEND DOES PETE TOWNSHENDS ANYMORE!
JUST RUB.

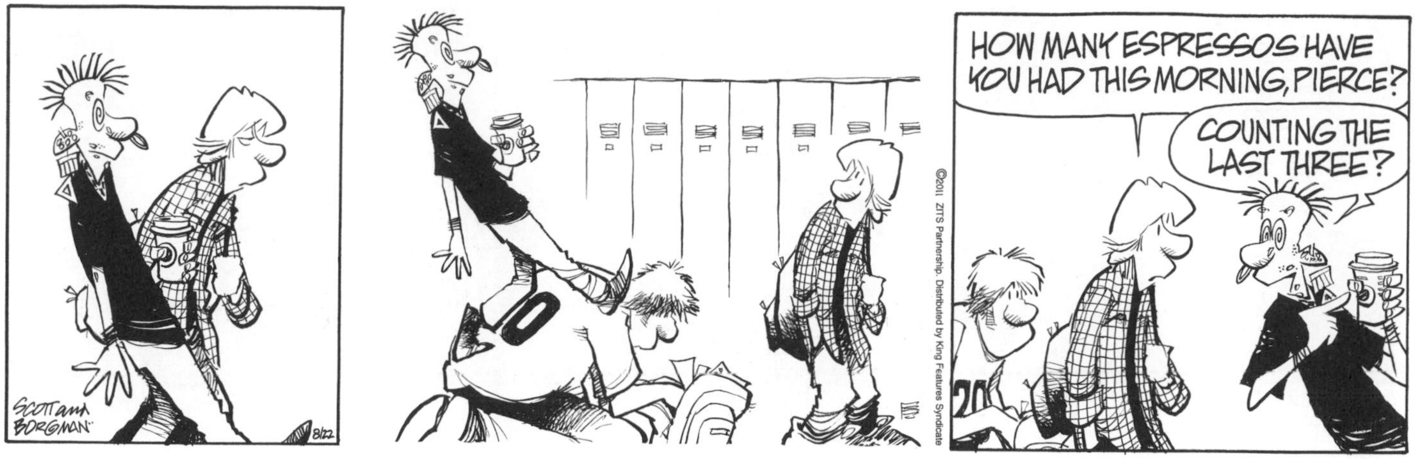
SCOTT and BORGMAN 8/22
©2011 ZITS Partnership. Distributed by King Features Syndicate
HOW MANY ESPRESSOS HAVE YOU HAD THIS MORNING, PIERCE?
COUNTING THE LAST THREE?

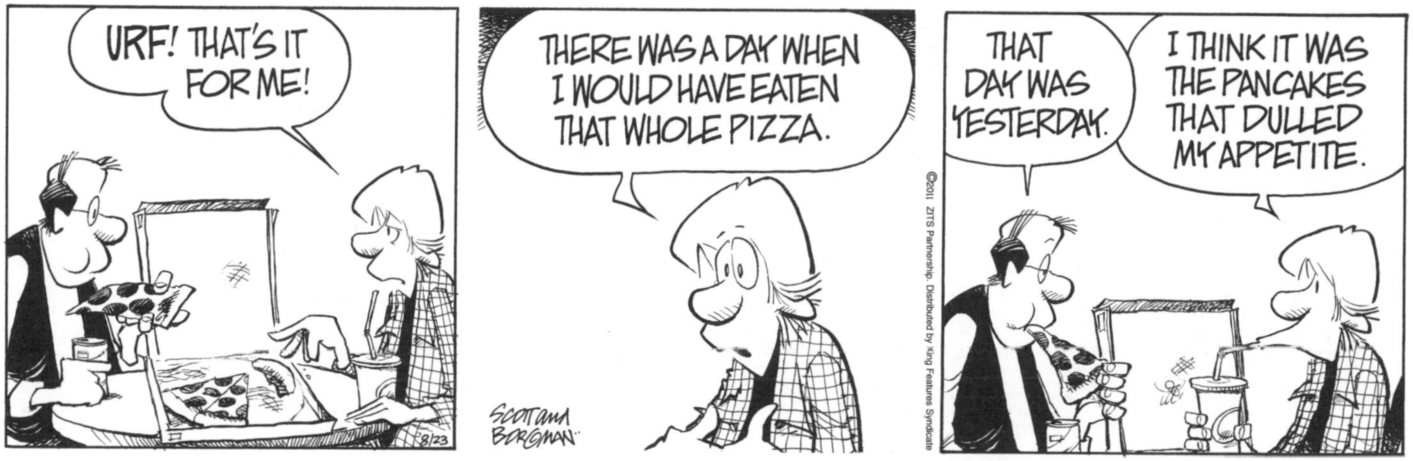
URF! THAT'S IT FOR ME!
8/23
SCOTT and BORGMAN
THERE WAS A DAY WHEN I WOULD HAVE EATEN THAT WHOLE PIZZA.
©2011 ZITS Partnership. Distributed by King Features Syndicate
THAT DAY WAS YESTERDAY.
I THINK IT WAS THE PANCAKES THAT DULLED MY APPETITE.

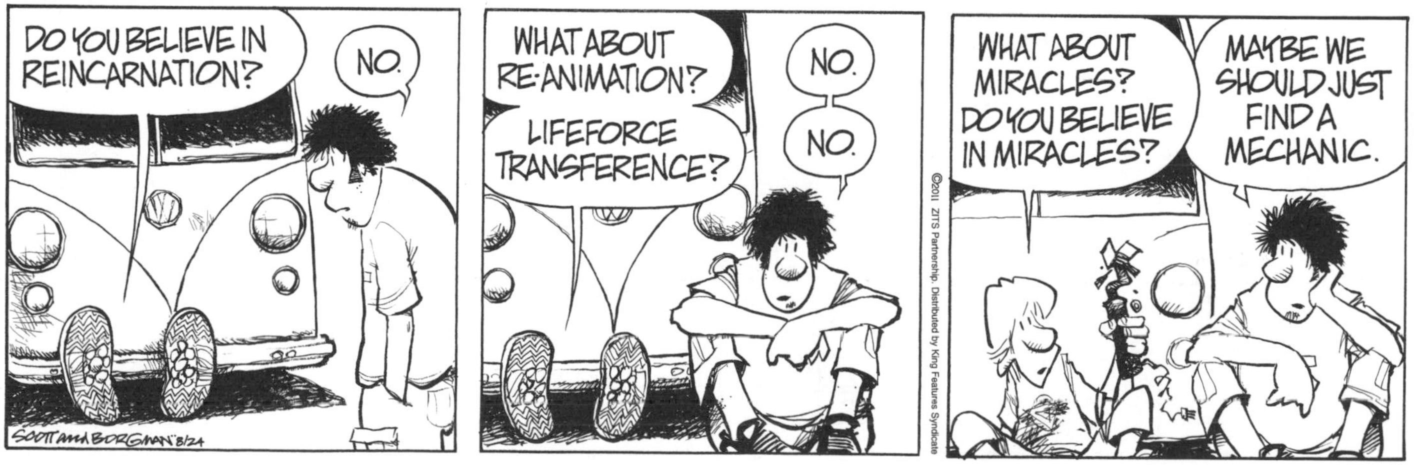
DO YOU BELIEVE IN REINCARNATION?
NO.
SCOTT and BORGMAN 8/24
WHAT ABOUT RE-ANIMATION?
NO.
LIFEFORCE TRANSFERENCE?
NO.
©2011 ZITS Partnership. Distributed by King Features Syndicate
WHAT ABOUT MIRACLES? DO YOU BELIEVE IN MIRACLES?
MAYBE WE SHOULD JUST FIND A MECHANIC.

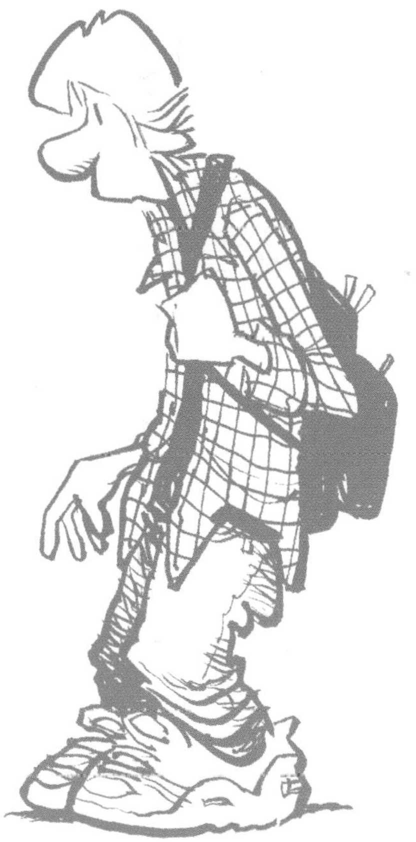

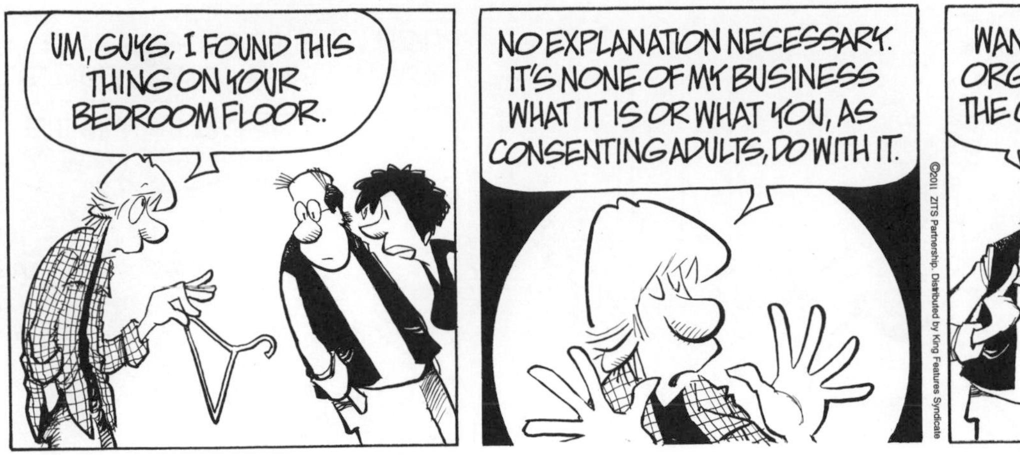
UM, GUYS, I FOUND THIS THING ON YOUR BEDROOM FLOOR.
NO EXPLANATION NECESSARY. IT'S NONE OF MY BUSINESS WHAT IT IS OR WHAT YOU, AS CONSENTING ADULTS, DO WITH IT.
©2011 ZITS Partnership. Distributed by King Features Syndicate
WANT TO GO ORGANIZE THE CLOSET?
NOT IN FRONT OF THE MINOR!

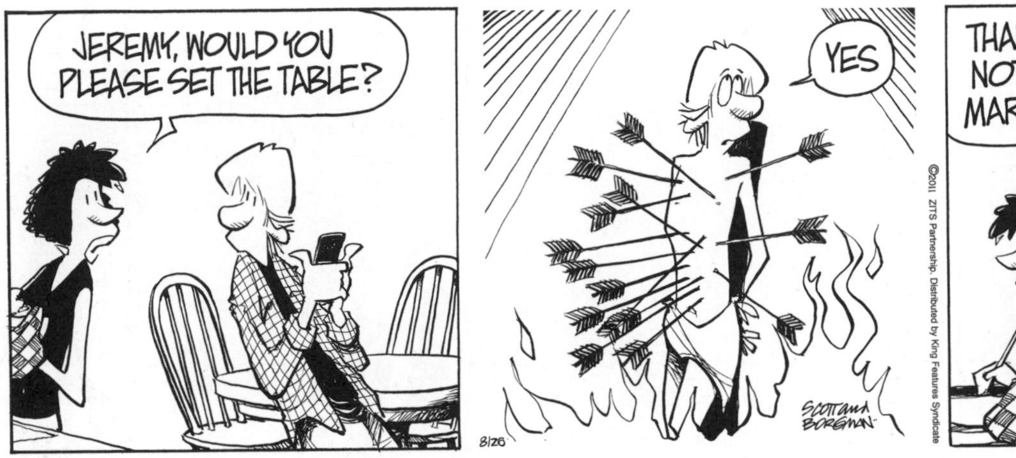
JEREMY, WOULD YOU PLEASE SET THE TABLE?
YES
8/26
SCOTT and BORGMAN
©2011 ZITS Partnership. Distributed by King Features Syndicate
THANK YOU FOR NOT BEING A MARTYR ABOUT IT.
WHO, ME?

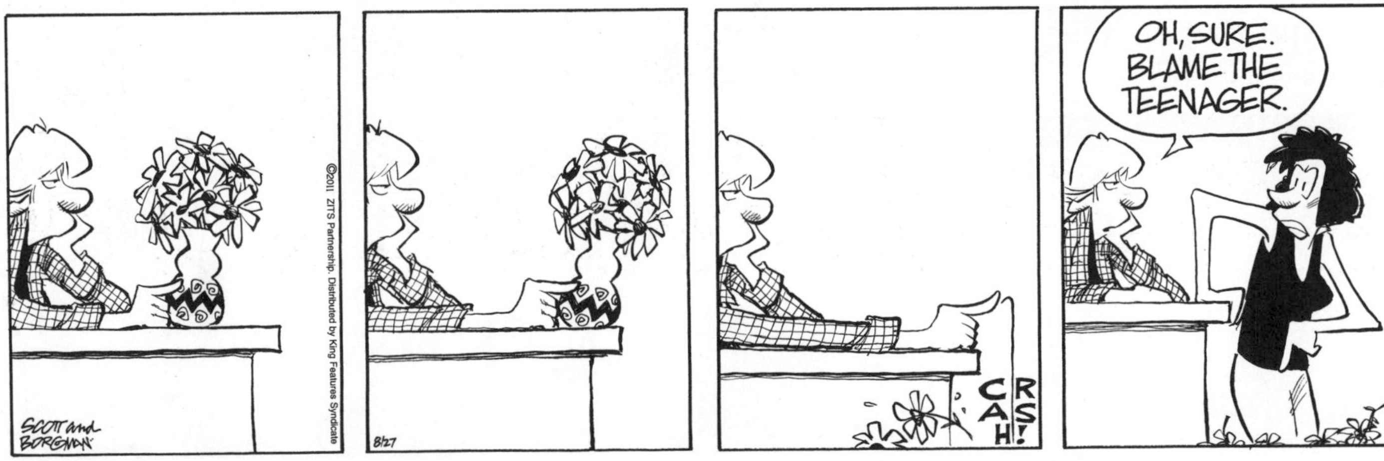
SCOTT and BORGMAN
©2011 ZITS Partnership. Distributed by King Features Syndicate
8/27
CRASH!
OH, SURE. BLAME THE TEENAGER.

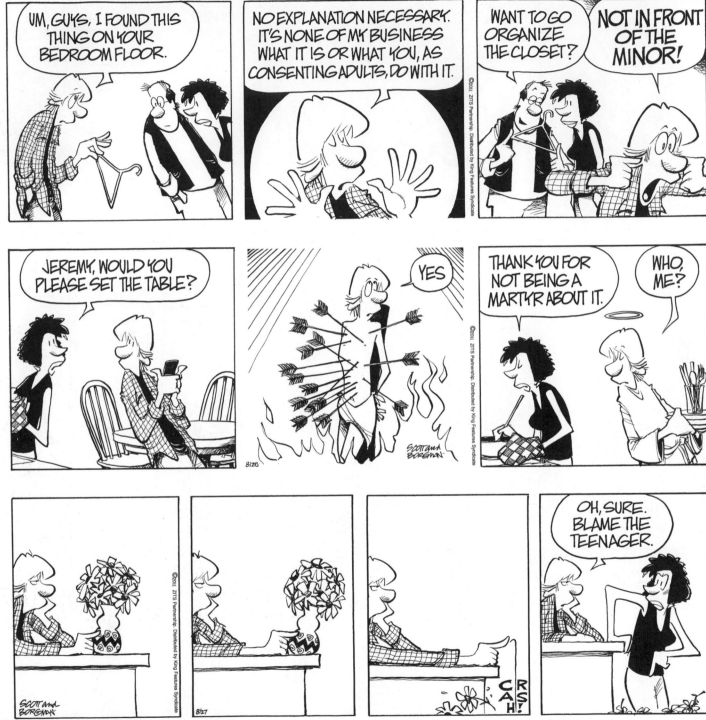

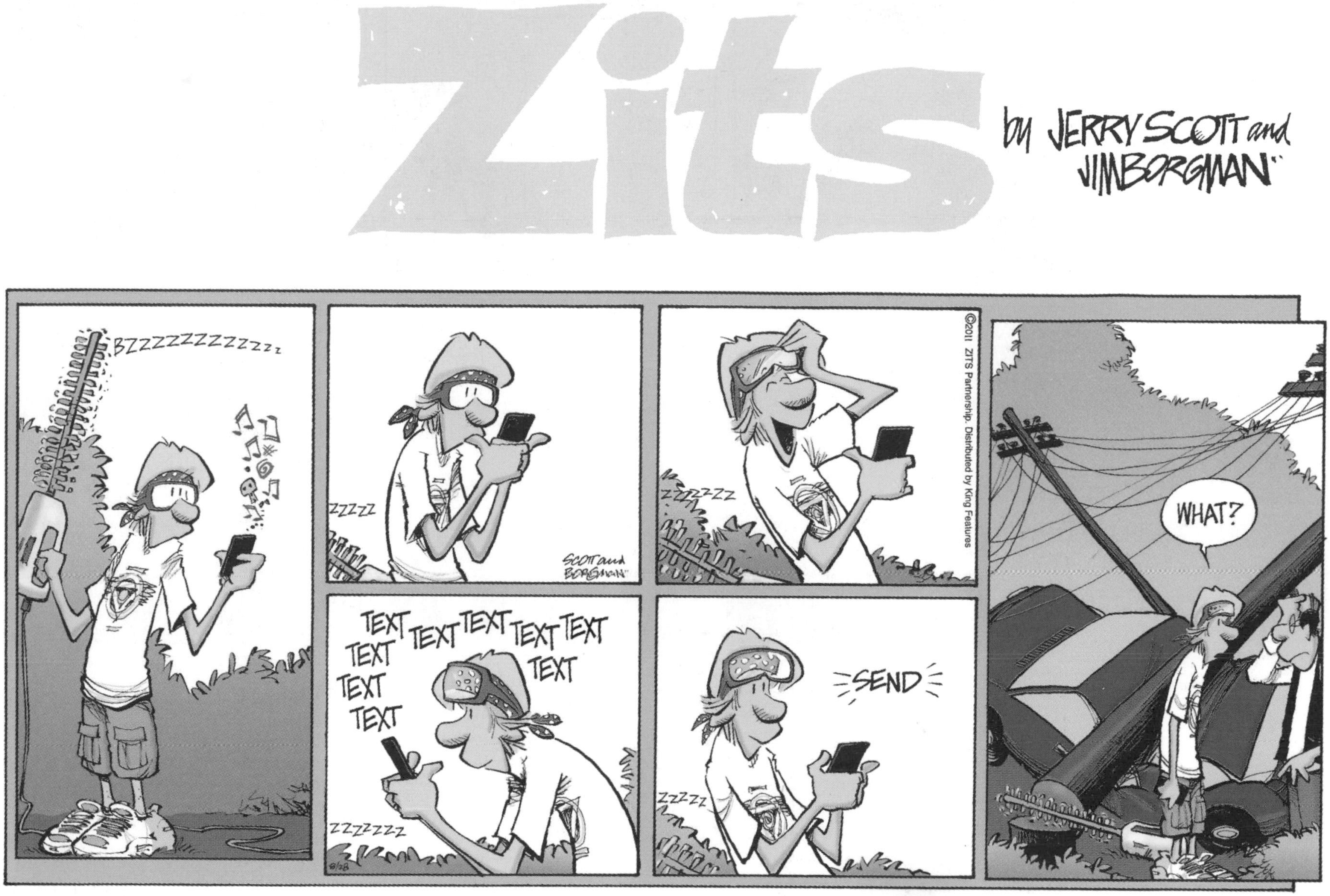
Zits
by JERRY SCOTT and JIM BORGMAN
BZZZZZZZZZZzzz
ZZZZZ
SCOTT and BORGMAN
ZZZZZZZ
©2011 ZITS Partnership. Distributed by King Features
TEXT TEXT TEXT TEXT TEXT TEXT TEXT TEXT TEXT TEXT
ZZZZZZZ
SEND
ZZZZZ
WHAT?

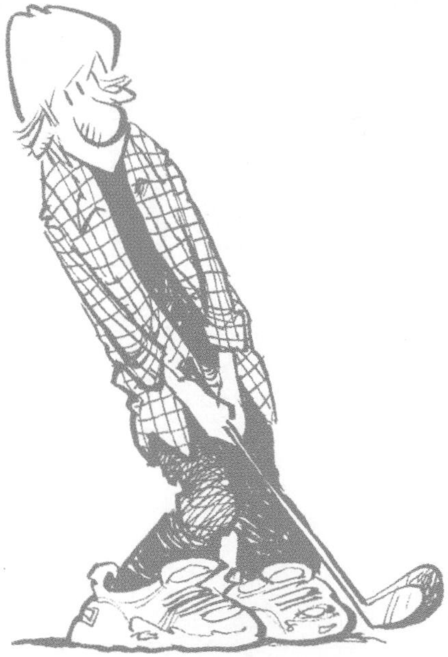

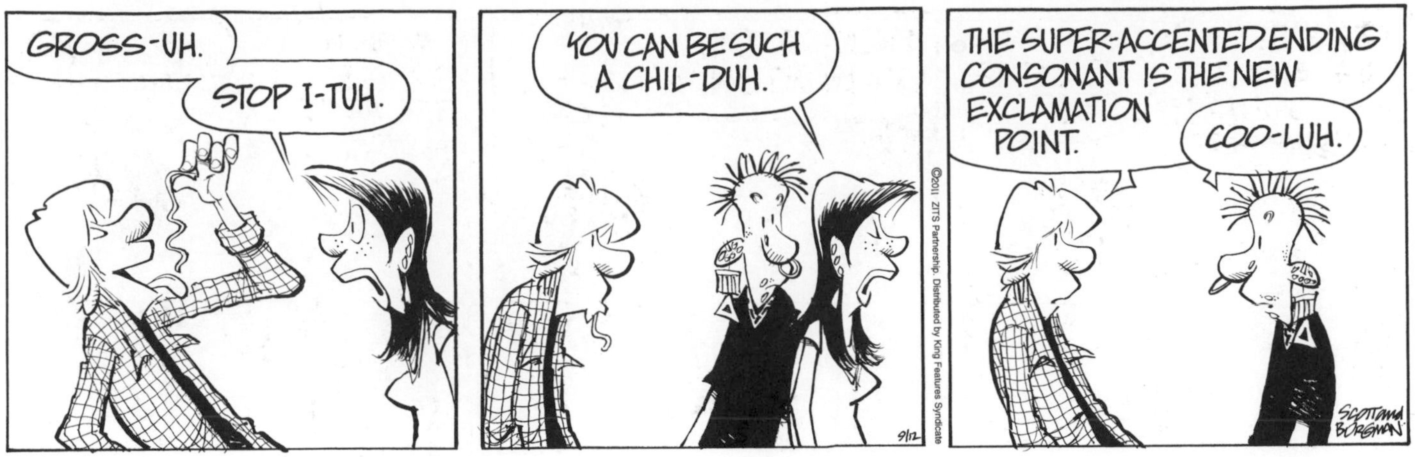

GROSS-UH.
STOP I-TUH.
YOU CAN BE SUCH A CHIL-DUH.
©2011 ZITS Partnership. Distributed by King Features Syndicate
9/12
THE SUPER-ACCENTED ENDING CONSONANT IS THE NEW EXCLAMATION POINT.
COO-LUH.
SCOTT and BORGMAN

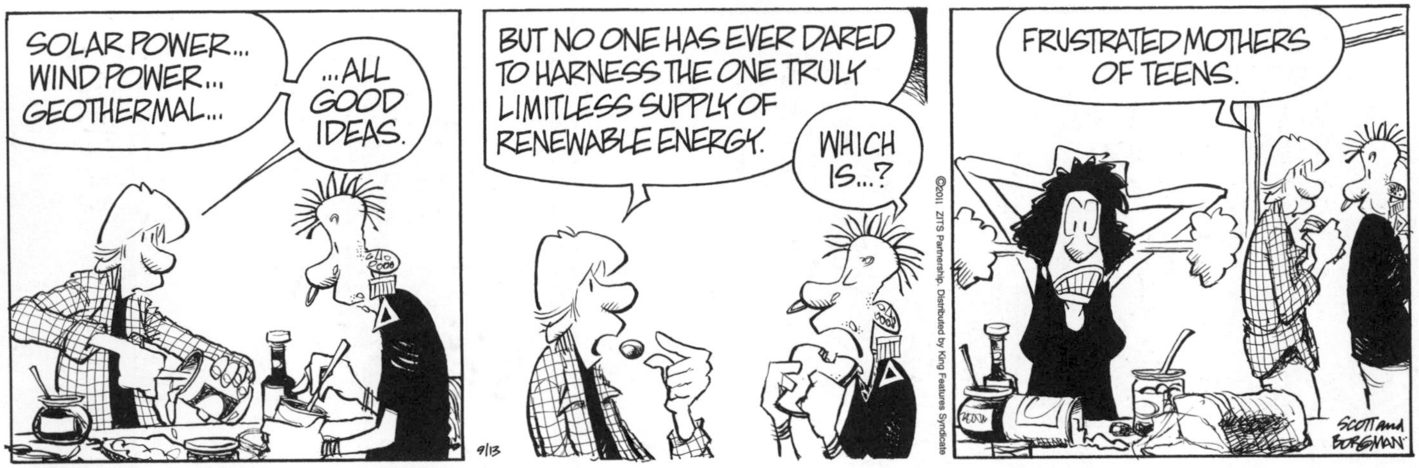

SOLAR POWER... WIND POWER... GEOTHERMAL...
...ALL GOOD IDEAS.
9/13
BUT NO ONE HAS EVER DARED TO HARNESS THE ONE TRULY LIMITLESS SUPPLY OF RENEWABLE ENERGY.
WHICH IS...?
©2011 ZITS Partnership. Distributed by King Features Syndicate
FRUSTRATED MOTHERS OF TEENS.
SCOTT and BORGMAN

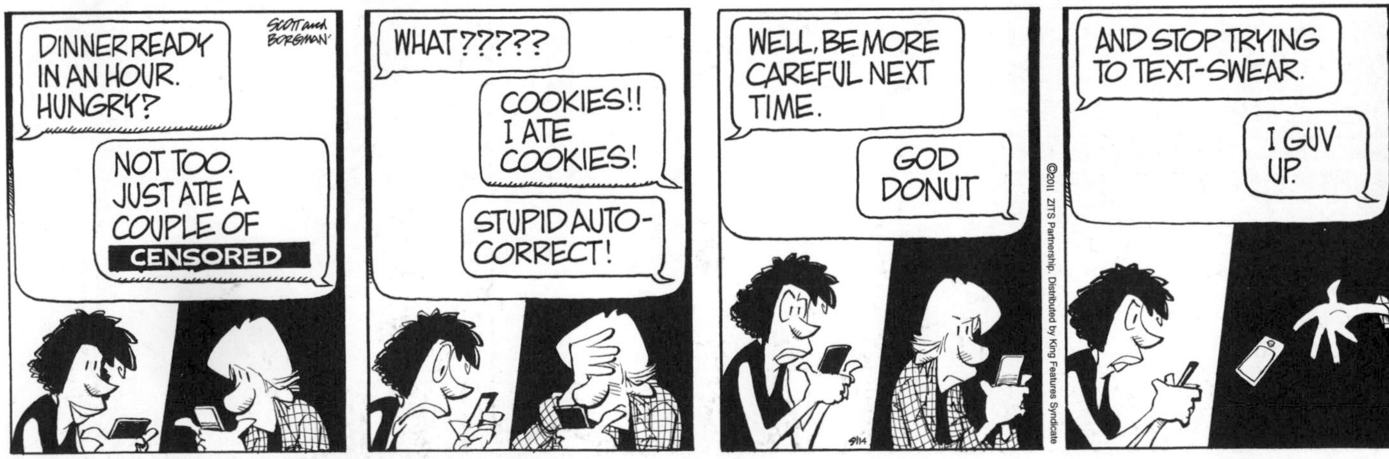

SCOTT and BORGMAN
DINNER READY IN AN HOUR. HUNGRY?
NOT TOO. JUST ATE A COUPLE OF CENSORED
WHAT?????
COOKIES!! I ATE COOKIES!
STUPID AUTO-CORRECT!
WELL, BE MORE CAREFUL NEXT TIME.
GOD DONUT
9/14
©2011 ZITS Partnership. Distributed by King Features Syndicate
AND STOP TRYING TO TEXT-SWEAR.
I GUV UP.

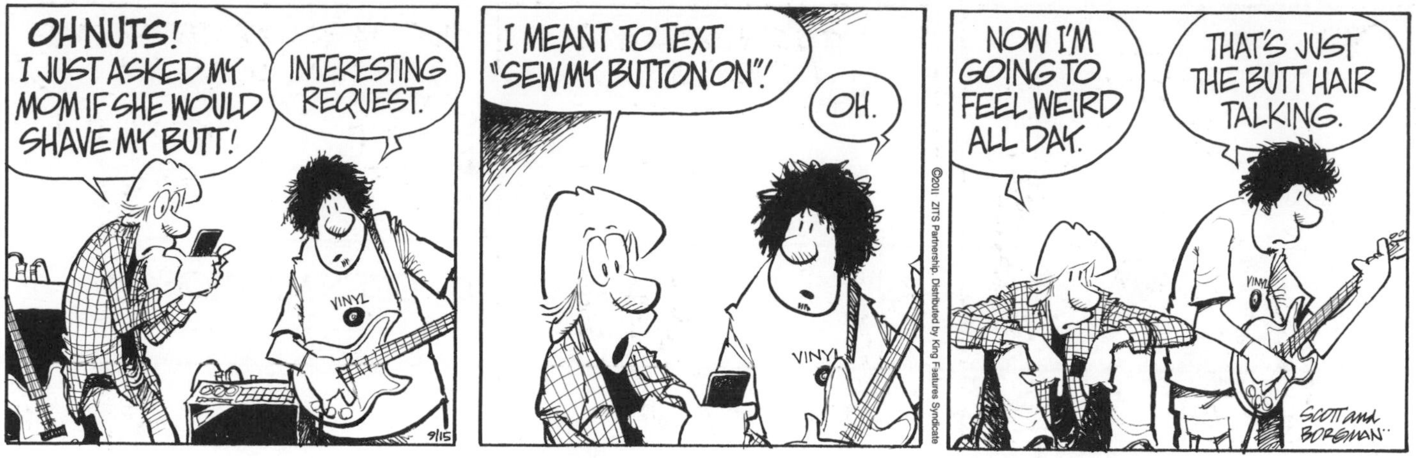
OH NUTS! I JUST ASKED MY MOM IF SHE WOULD SHAVE MY BUTT!
INTERESTING REQUEST.
VINYL
9/15
I MEANT TO TEXT "SEW MY BUTTON ON"!
OH.
VINYL
©2011 ZITS Partnership. Distributed by King Features Syndicate
NOW I'M GOING TO FEEL WEIRD ALL DAY.
THAT'S JUST THE BUTT HAIR TALKING.
VINYL
SCOTT and BORGMAN

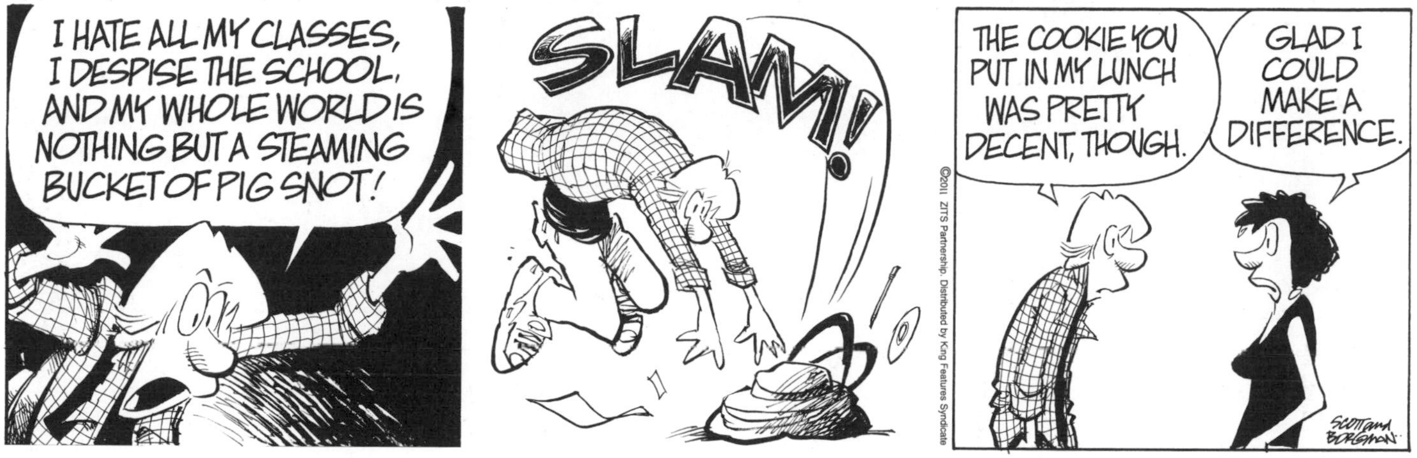
I HATE ALL MY CLASSES, I DESPISE THE SCHOOL, AND MY WHOLE WORLD IS NOTHING BUT A STEAMING BUCKET OF PIG SNOT!
SLAM!
©2011 ZITS Partnership. Distributed by King Features Syndicate
THE COOKIE YOU PUT IN MY LUNCH WAS PRETTY DECENT, THOUGH.
GLAD I COULD MAKE A DIFFERENCE.
SCOTT and BORGMAN

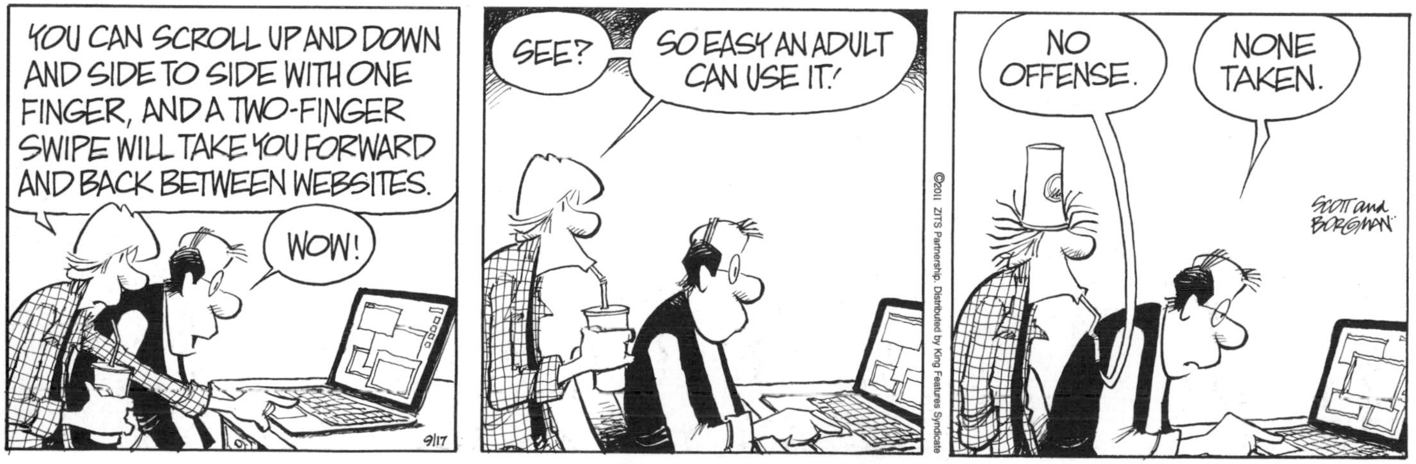
YOU CAN SCROLL UP AND DOWN AND SIDE TO SIDE WITH ONE FINGER, AND A TWO-FINGER SWIPE WILL TAKE YOU FORWARD AND BACK BETWEEN WEBSITES.
WOW!
9/17
SEE?
SO EASY AN ADULT CAN USE IT!
©2011 ZITS Partnership. Distributed by King Features Syndicate
NO OFFENSE.
NONE TAKEN.
SCOTT and BORGMAN

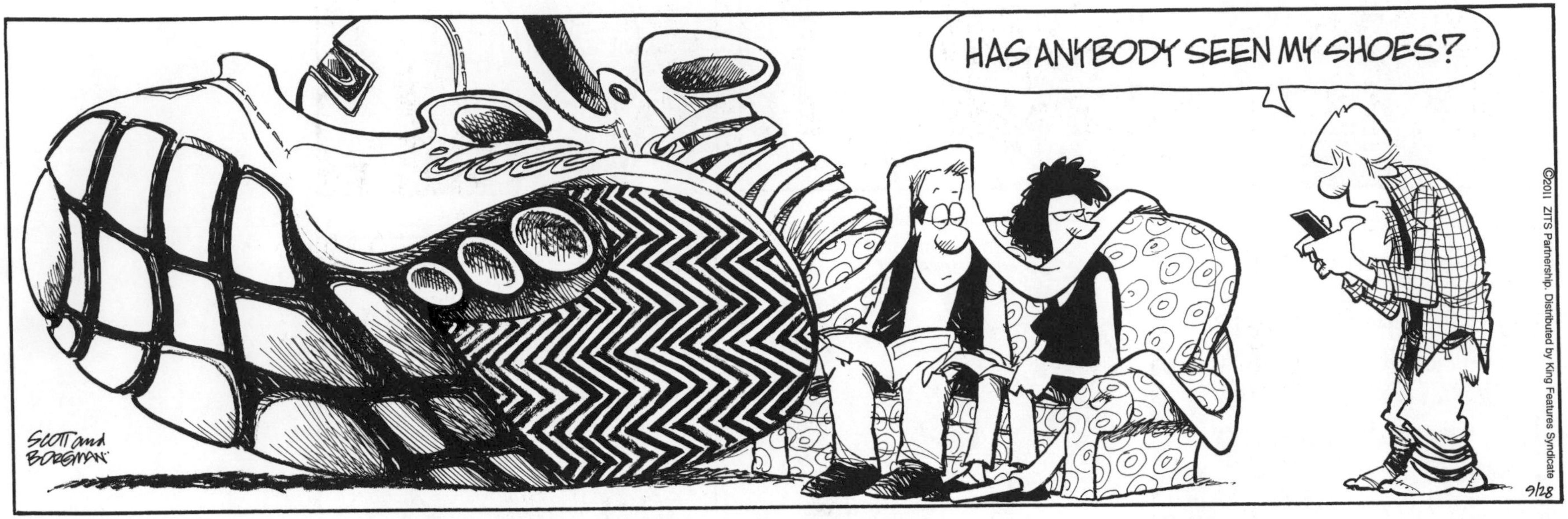
HAS ANYBODY SEEN MY SHOES?
SCOTT and BORGMAN
©2011 ZITS Partnership. Distributed by King Features Syndicate
9/28

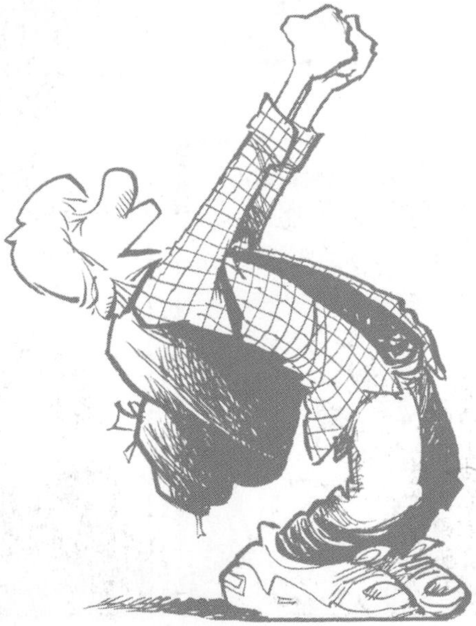

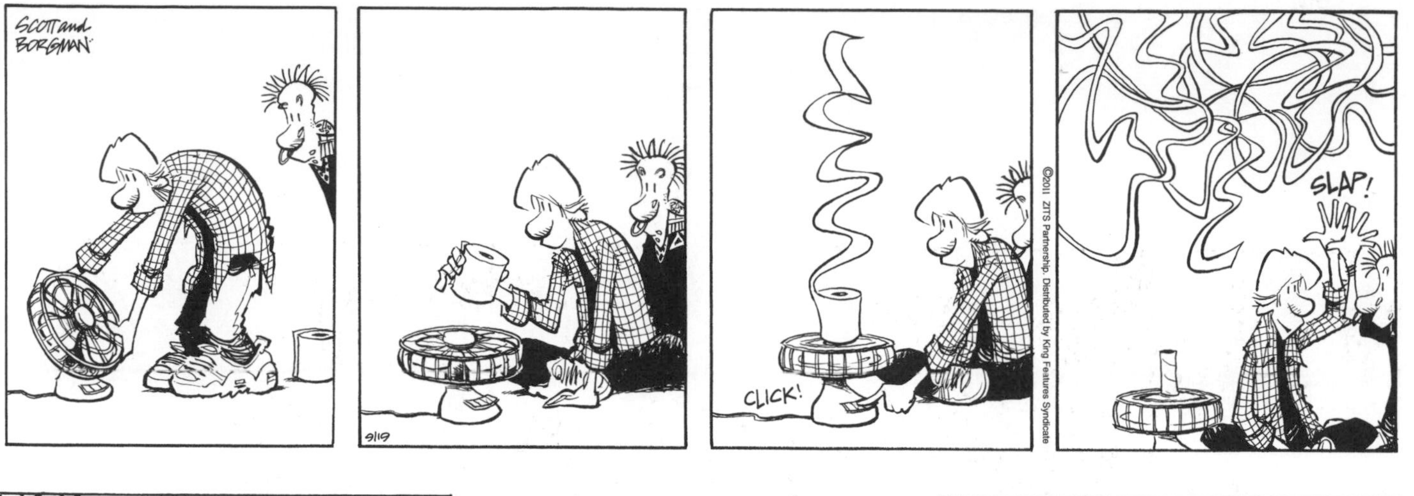
SCOTT and BORGMAN
9/19
CLICK!
©2011 ZITS Partnership. Distributed by King Features Syndicate
SLAP!

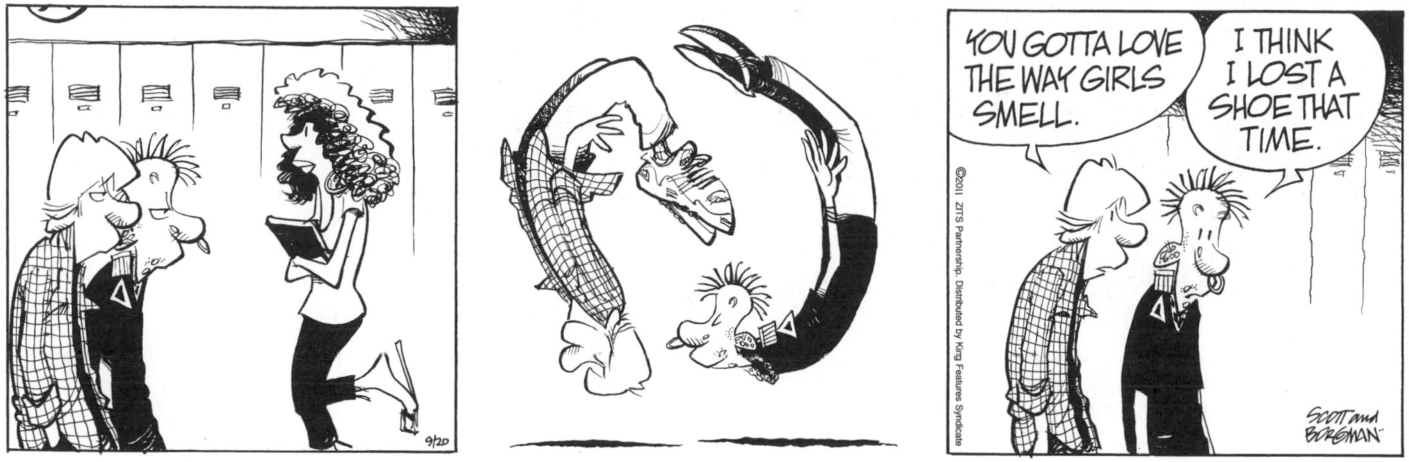
9/20
YOU GOTTA LOVE THE WAY GIRLS SMELL.
I THINK I LOST A SHOE THAT TIME.
©2011 ZITS Partnership. Distributed by King Features Syndicate
SCOTT and BORGMAN

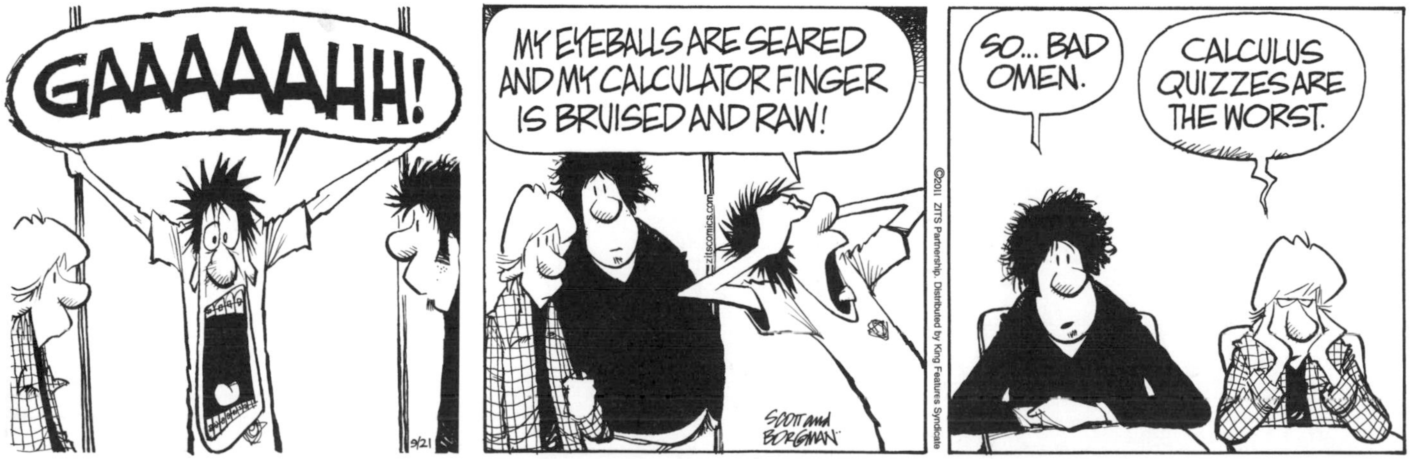
GAAAAAHH!
9/21
MY EYEBALLS ARE SEARED AND MY CALCULATOR FINGER IS BRUISED AND RAW!
zitscomics.com
SCOTT and BORGMAN
©2011 ZITS Partnership. Distributed by King Features Syndicate
SO... BAD OMEN.
CALCULUS QUIZZES ARE THE WORST.

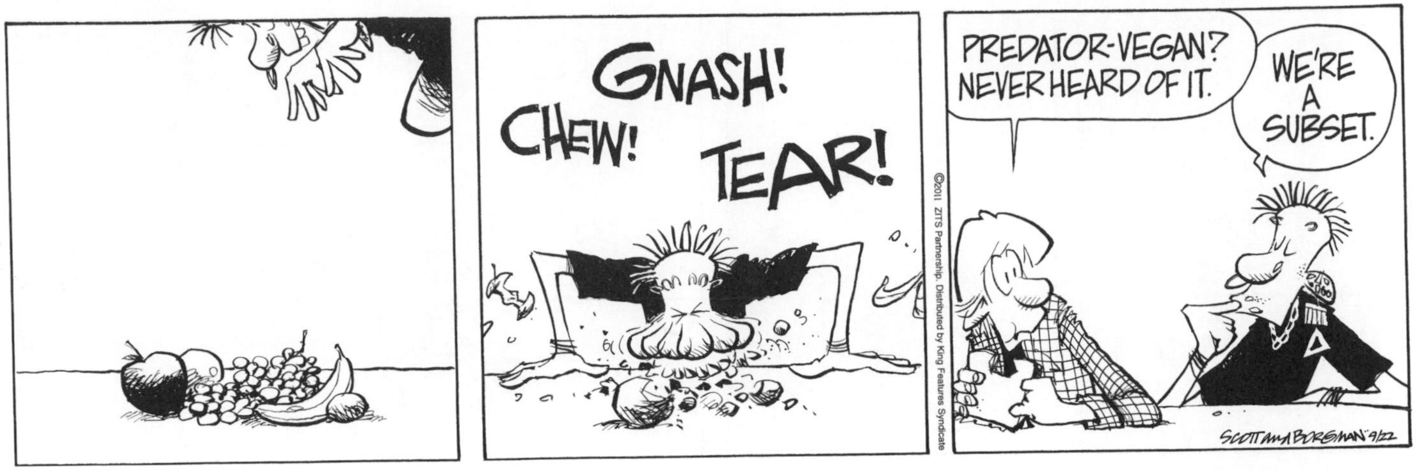
GNASH!
CHEW!
TEAR!
©2011 ZITS Partnership. Distributed by King Features Syndicate
PREDATOR-VEGAN? NEVER HEARD OF IT.
WE'RE A SUBSET.
SCOTT and BORGMAN 9/22

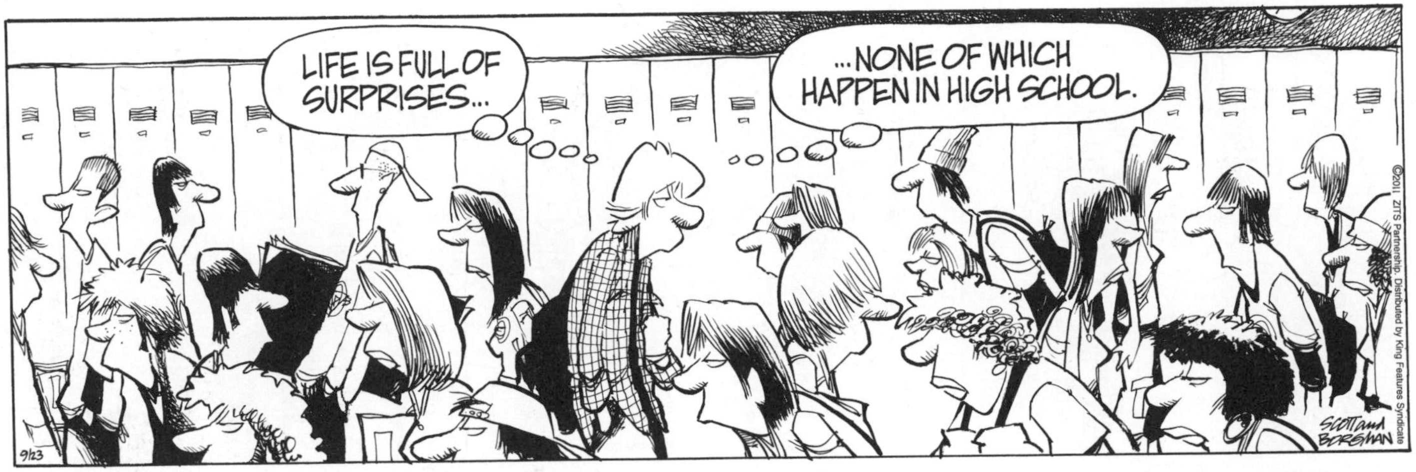
LIFE IS FULL OF SURPRISES...
...NONE OF WHICH HAPPEN IN HIGH SCHOOL.
©2011 ZITS Partnership. Distributed by King Features Syndicate
9/23
SCOTT and BORGMAN

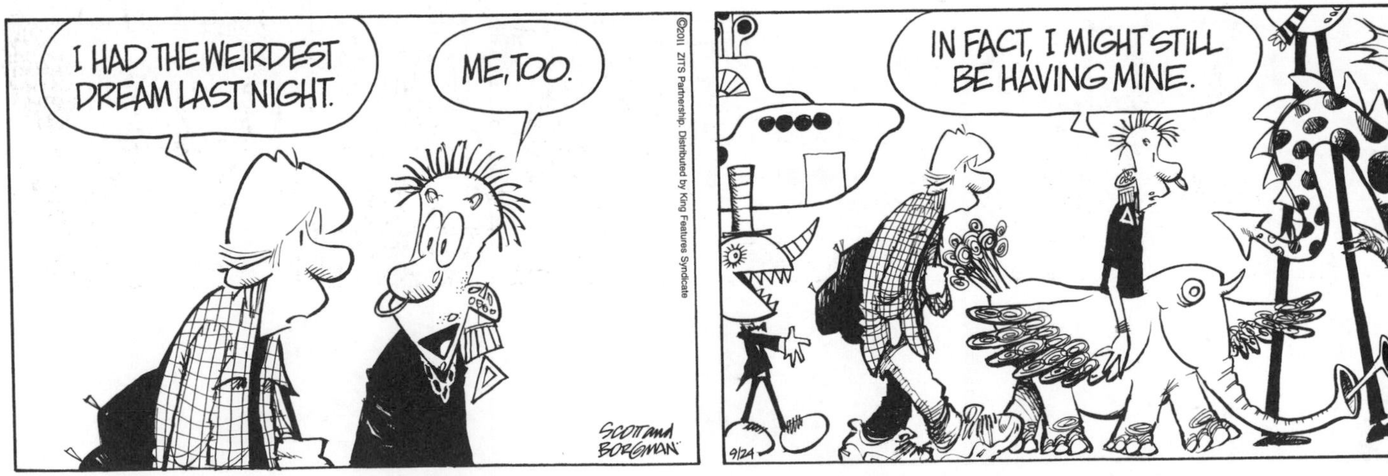
I HAD THE WEIRDEST DREAM LAST NIGHT.
ME, TOO.
©2011 ZITS Partnership. Distributed by King Features Syndicate
SCOTT and BORGMAN
IN FACT, I MIGHT STILL BE HAVING MINE.
9/24

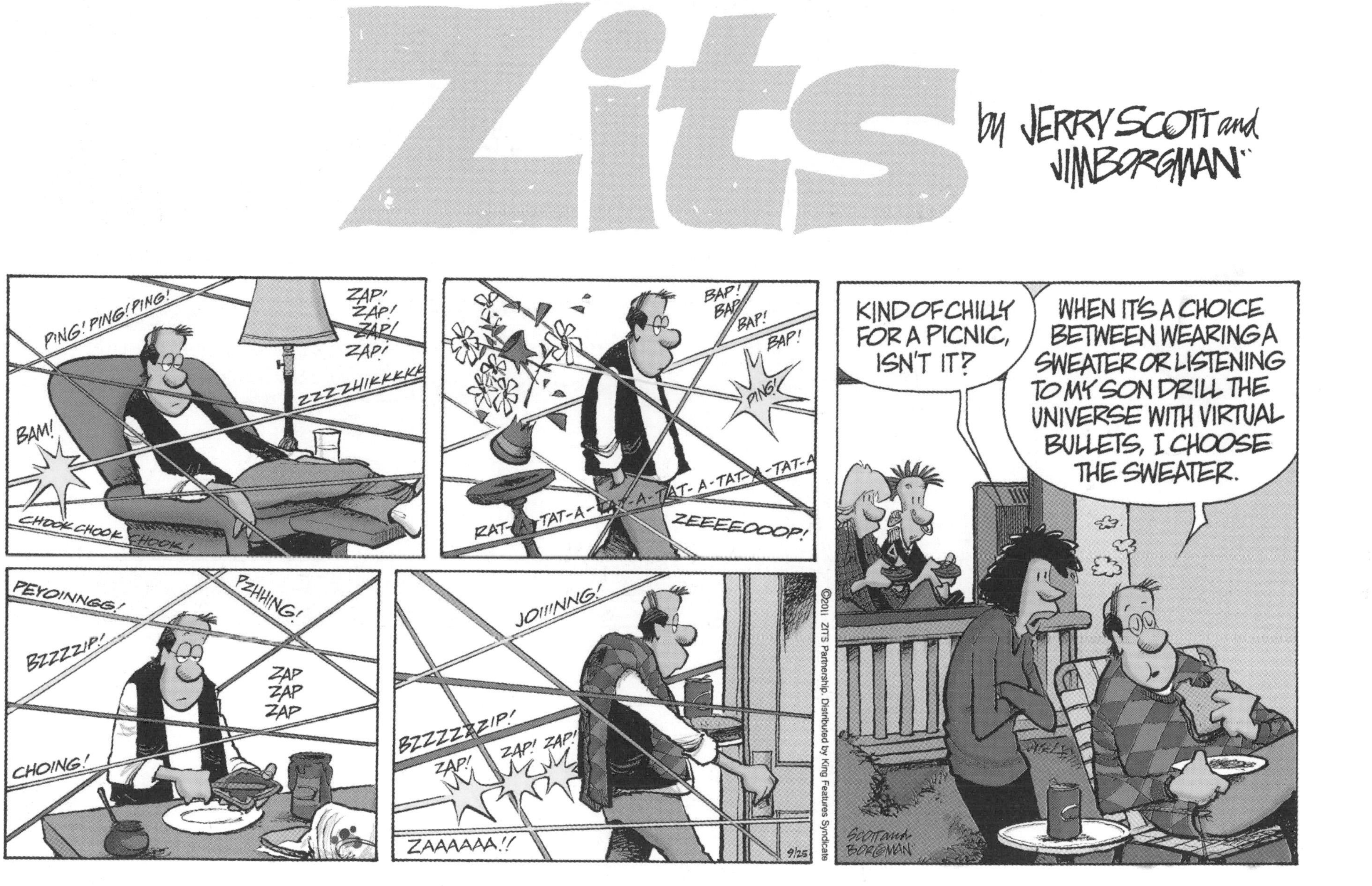
Zits
by JERRY SCOTT and JIM BORGMAN
PING! PING! PING!
ZAP! ZAP! ZAP! ZAP!
ZZZZHIKKKKK
BAM!
CHOOK CHOOK CHOOK!
BAP! BAP! BAP! BAP!
PING!
RAT-A-TAT-A-TAT-A-TAT-A-TAT-A-TAT-A
ZEEEEOOOP!
PEYOINNGG!
PZHHING!
BZZZZIP!
ZAP ZAP ZAP
CHOING!
JO!!!NNG!
BZZZZZZIP!
ZAP! ZAP! ZAP!
ZAAAAAA!!
9/25
©2011 ZITS Partnership. Distributed by King Features Syndicate
KIND OF CHILLY FOR A PICNIC, ISN'T IT?
WHEN IT'S A CHOICE BETWEEN WEARING A SWEATER OR LISTENING TO MY SON DRILL THE UNIVERSE WITH VIRTUAL BULLETS, I CHOOSE THE SWEATER.
SCOTT and BORGMAN

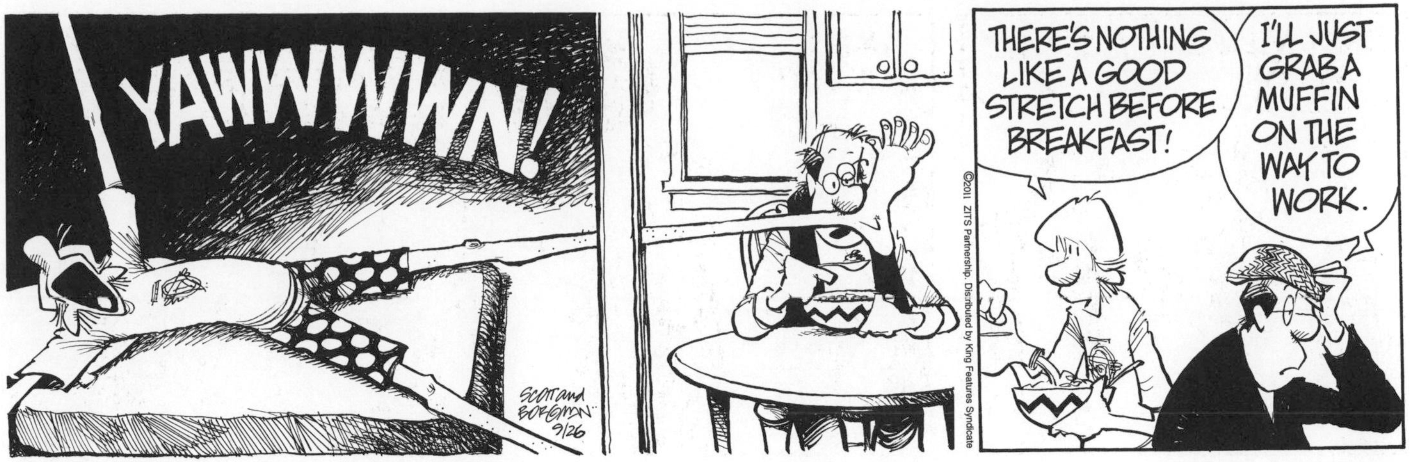
YAWWWWN!
SCOTT and BORGMAN 9/26
THERE'S NOTHING LIKE A GOOD STRETCH BEFORE BREAKFAST!
I'LL JUST GRAB A MUFFIN ON THE WAY TO WORK.
©2011 ZITS Partnership. Distributed by King Features Syndicate

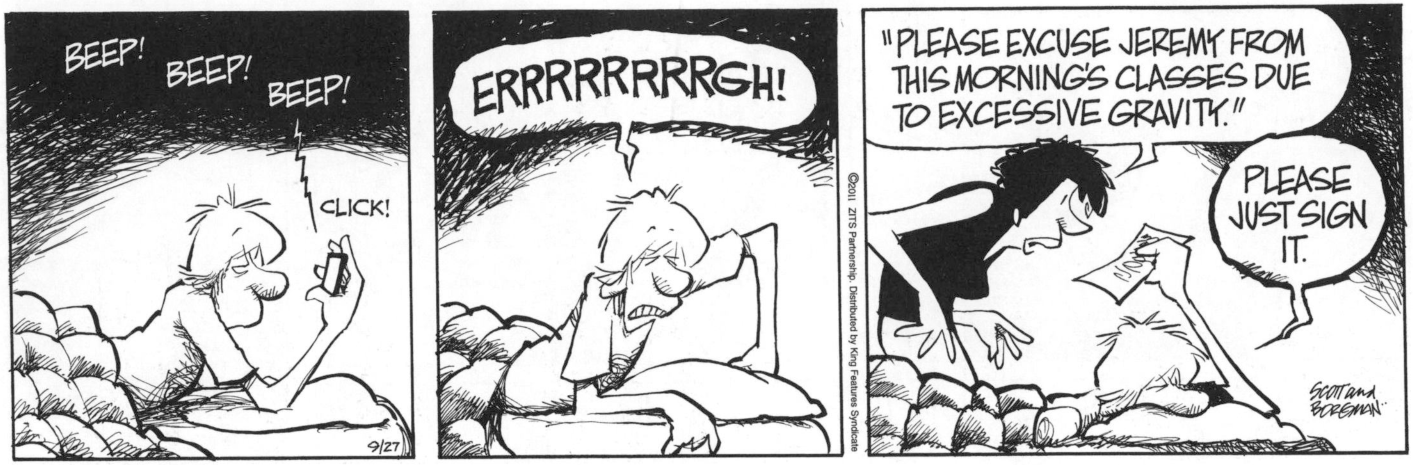
BEEP! BEEP! BEEP!
CLICK!
9/27
ERRRRRRRRGH!
©2011 ZITS Partnership. Distributed by King Features Syndicate
"PLEASE EXCUSE JEREMY FROM THIS MORNING'S CLASSES DUE TO EXCESSIVE GRAVITY."
PLEASE JUST SIGN IT.
SCOTT and BORGMAN

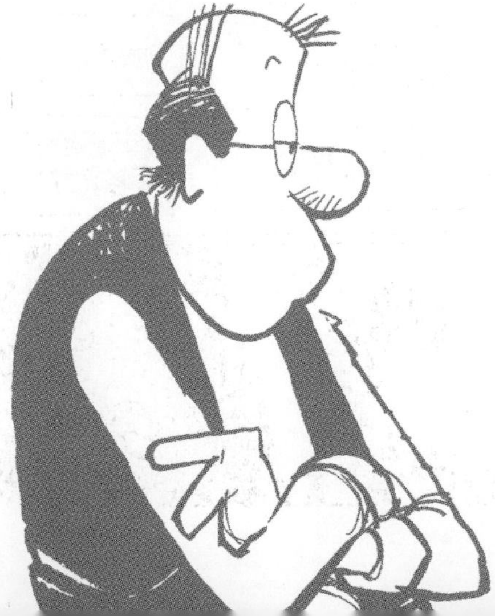

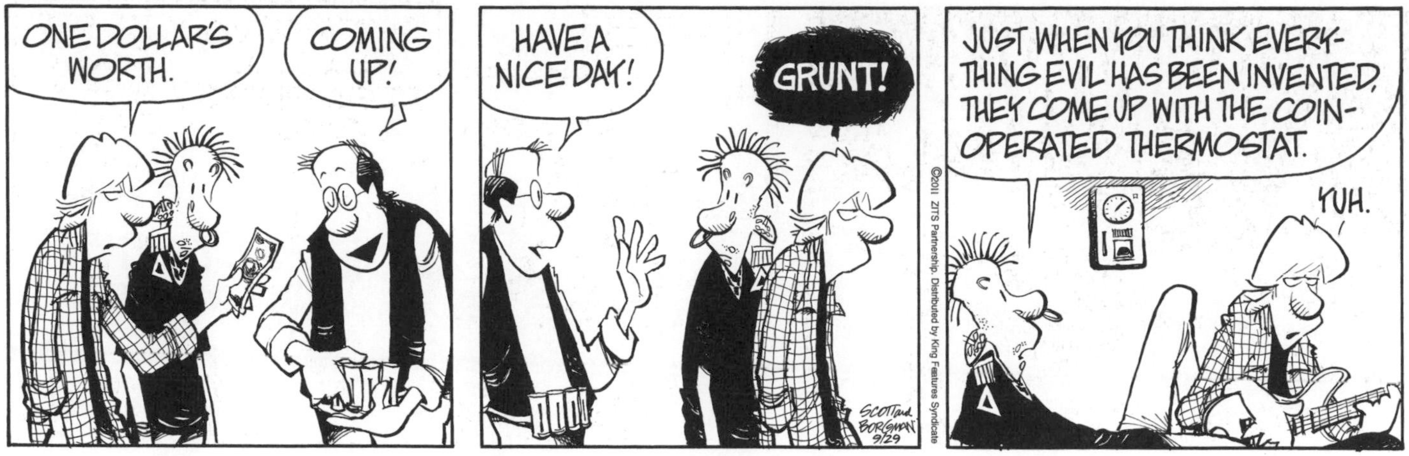
ONE DOLLAR'S WORTH.
COMING UP!
HAVE A NICE DAY!
GRUNT!
©2011 ZITS Partnership. Distributed by King Features Syndicate
SCOTT and BORGMAN 9/29
JUST WHEN YOU THINK EVERYTHING EVIL HAS BEEN INVENTED, THEY COME UP WITH THE COIN-OPERATED THERMOSTAT.
YUH.

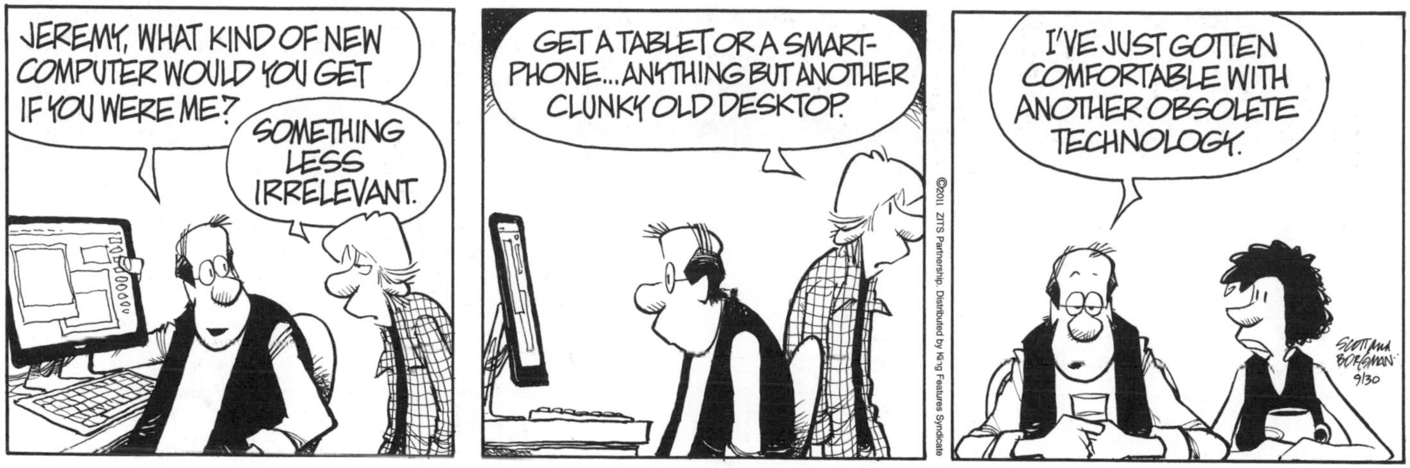
JEREMY, WHAT KIND OF NEW COMPUTER WOULD YOU GET IF YOU WERE ME?
SOMETHING LESS IRRELEVANT.
GET A TABLET OR A SMARTPHONE... ANYTHING BUT ANOTHER CLUNKY OLD DESKTOP.
©2011 ZITS Partnership. Distributed by King Features Syndicate
I'VE JUST GOTTEN COMFORTABLE WITH ANOTHER OBSOLETE TECHNOLOGY.
SCOTT and BORGMAN 9/30

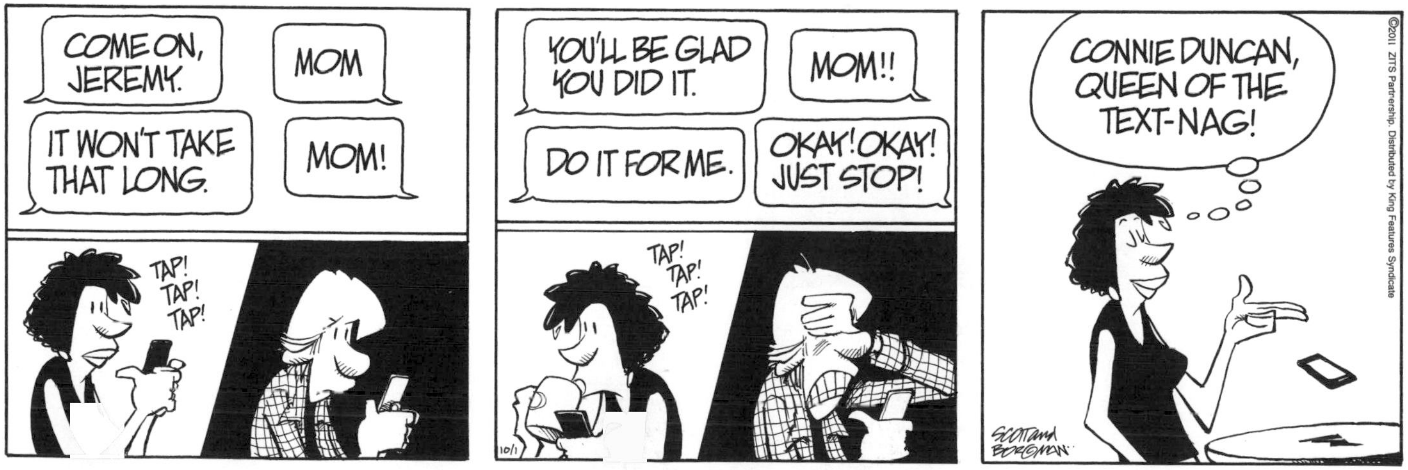
COME ON, JEREMY.
MOM
IT WON'T TAKE THAT LONG.
MOM!
TAP! TAP! TAP!
YOU'LL BE GLAD YOU DID IT.
MOM!!
DO IT FOR ME.
OKAY! OKAY! JUST STOP!
TAP! TAP! TAP!
10/1
CONNIE DUNCAN, QUEEN OF THE TEXT-NAG!
©2011 ZITS Partnership. Distributed by King Features Syndicate
SCOTT and BORGMAN

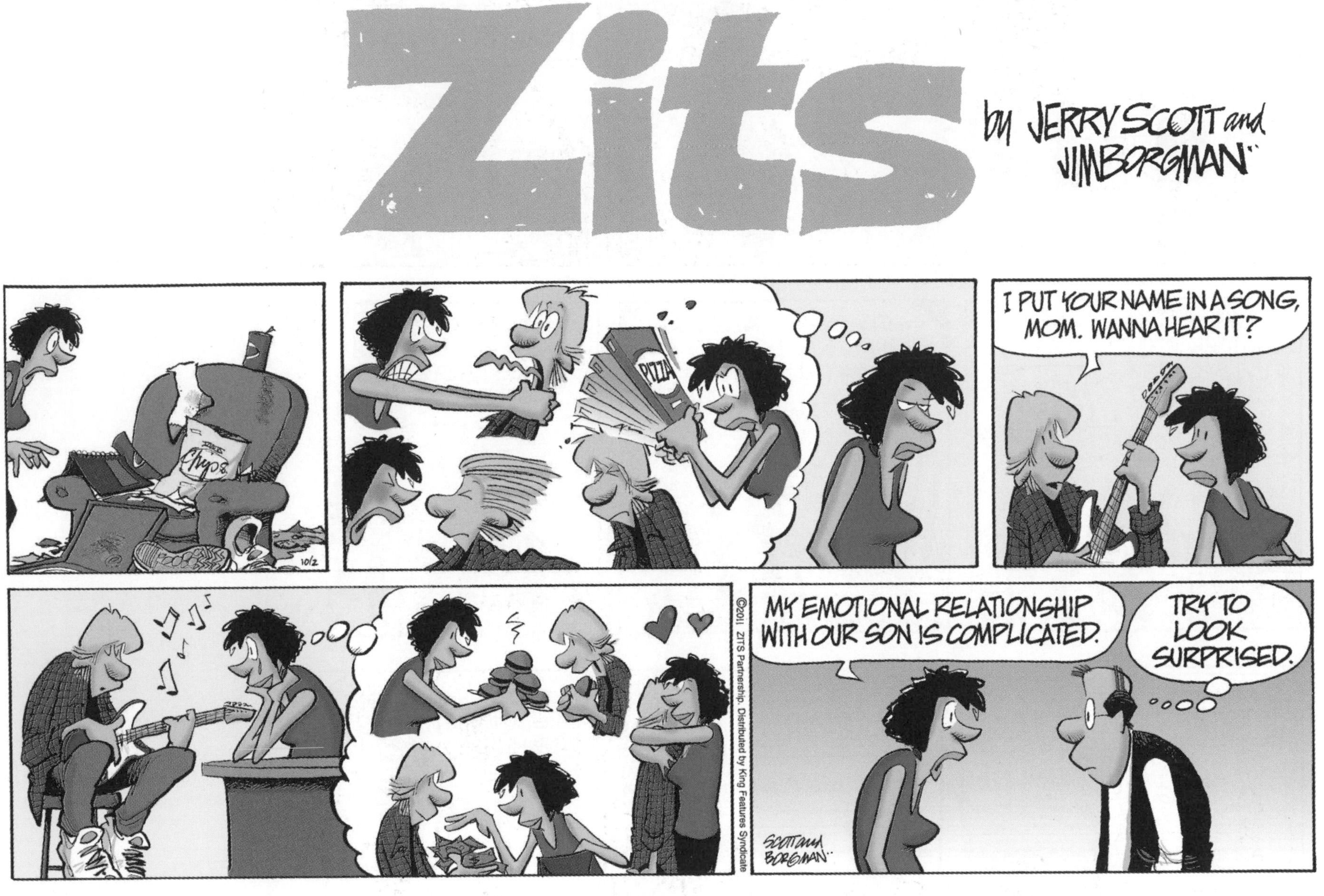

Zits
by JERRY SCOTT and JIM BORGMAN
10/2
PIZZA
I PUT YOUR NAME IN A SONG, MOM. WANNA HEAR IT?
©2011 ZITS Partnership. Distributed by King Features Syndicate
MY EMOTIONAL RELATIONSHIP WITH OUR SON IS COMPLICATED.
TRY TO LOOK SURPRISED.
SCOTT and BORGMAN

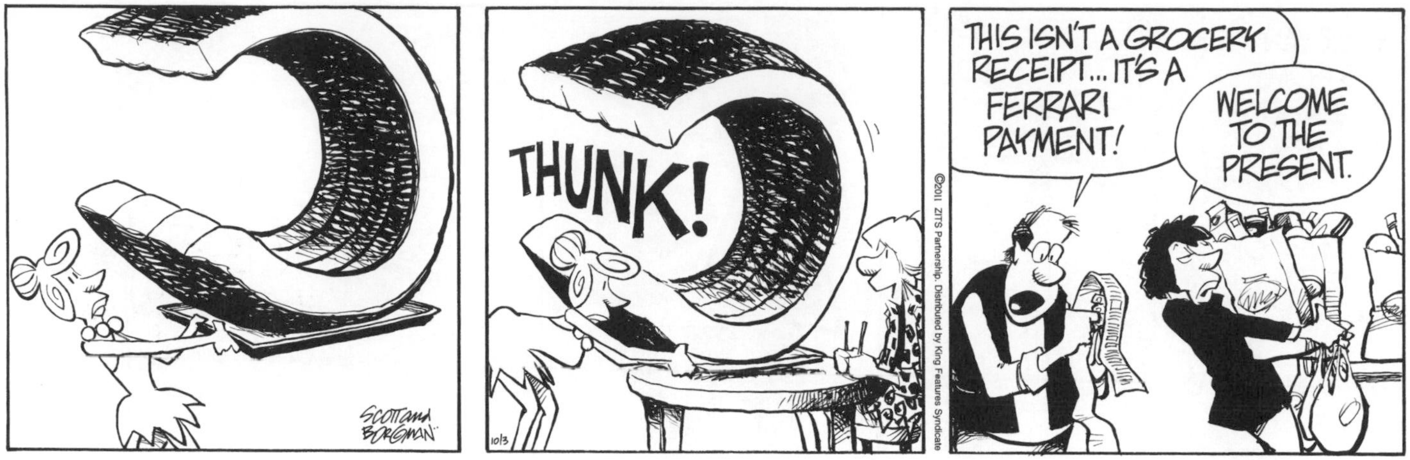
SCOTT and BORGMAN
10/3
THUNK!
©2011 ZITS Partnership. Distributed by King Features Syndicate
THIS ISN'T A GROCERY RECEIPT... IT'S A FERRARI PAYMENT!
WELCOME TO THE PRESENT.

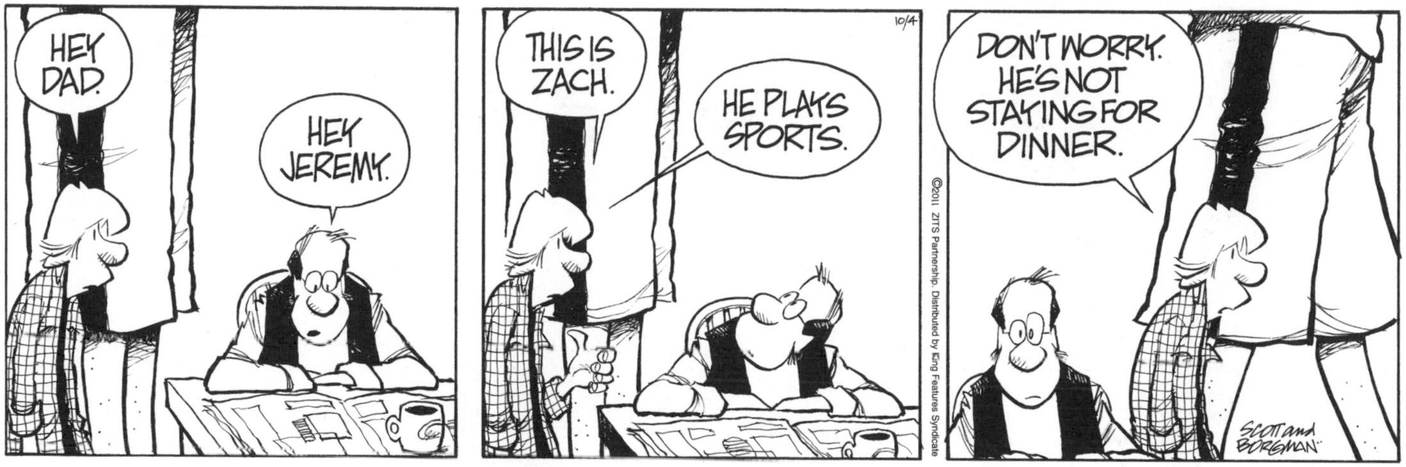
HEY DAD.
HEY JEREMY.
10/4
THIS IS ZACH.
HE PLAYS SPORTS.
©2011 ZITS Partnership. Distributed by King Features Syndicate
DON'T WORRY. HE'S NOT STAYING FOR DINNER.
SCOTT and BORGMAN

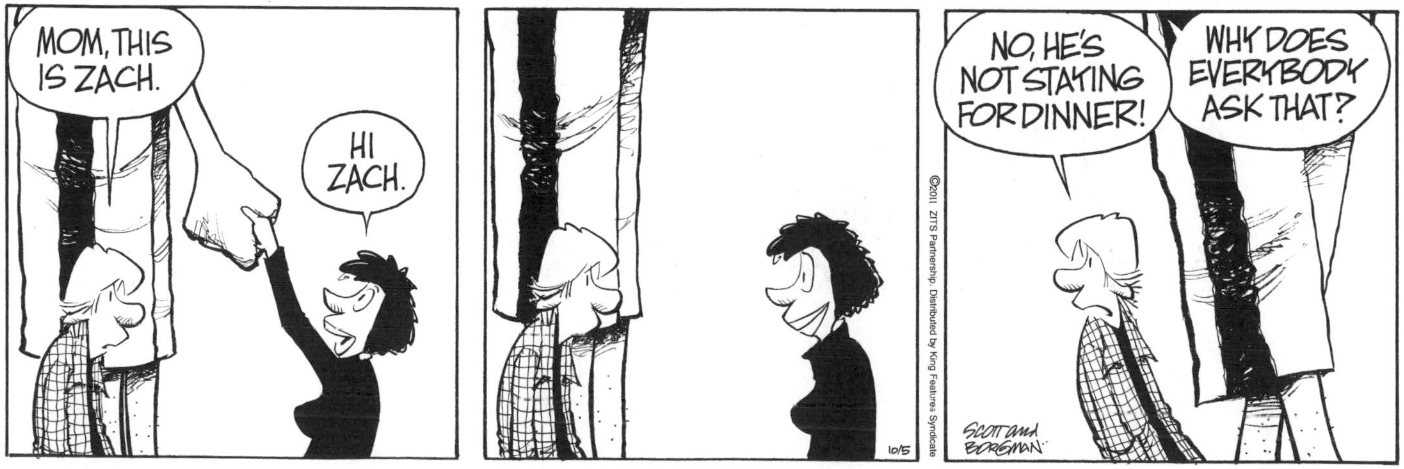
MOM, THIS IS ZACH.
HI ZACH.
10/5
©2011 ZITS Partnership. Distributed by King Features Syndicate
NO, HE'S NOT STAYING FOR DINNER!
WHY DOES EVERYBODY ASK THAT?
SCOTT and BORGMAN

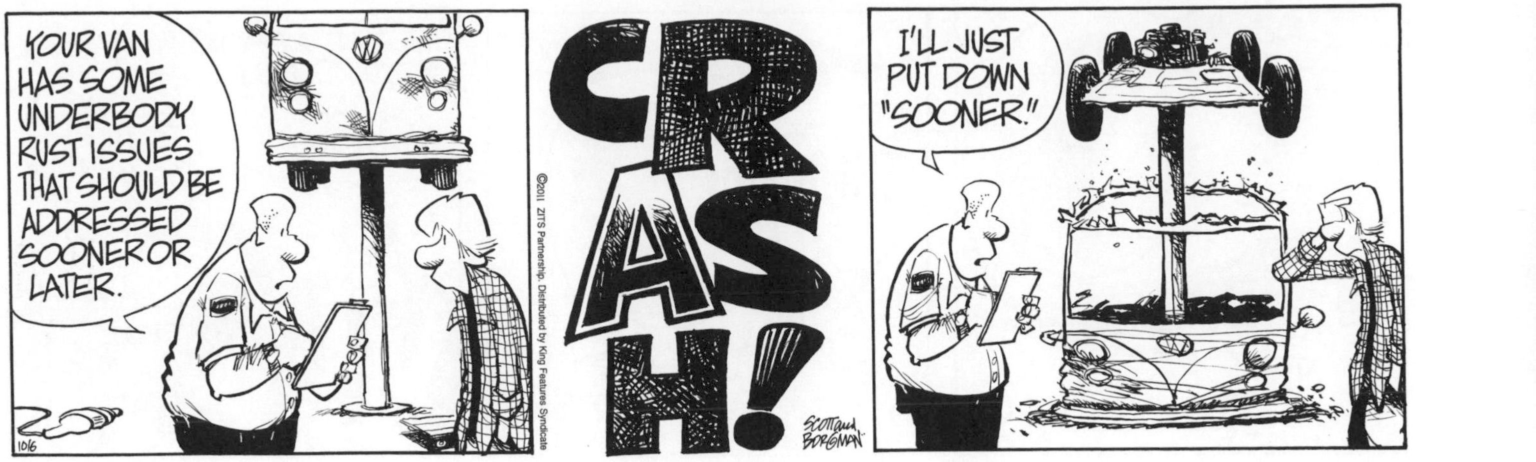
YOUR VAN HAS SOME UNDERBODY RUST ISSUES THAT SHOULD BE ADDRESSED SOONER OR LATER.
10/6
©2011 ZITS Partnership. Distributed by King Features Syndicate
CRASH!
SCOTT and BORGMAN
I'LL JUST PUT DOWN "SOONER."

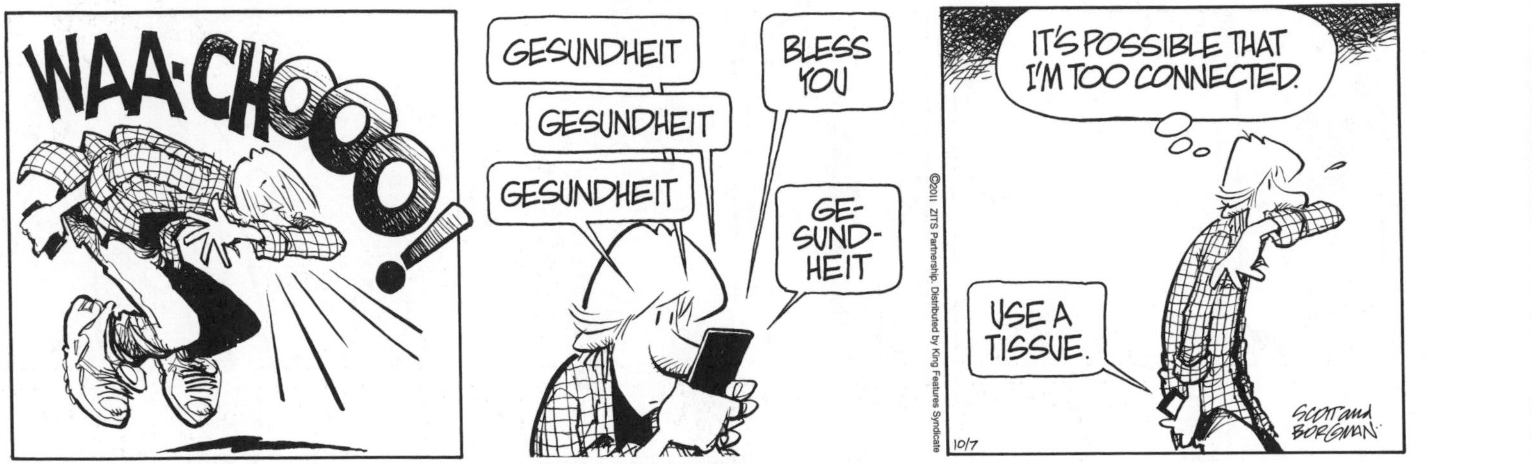
WAA-CHOOOO!
GESUNDHEIT
GESUNDHEIT
GESUNDHEIT
BLESS YOU
GE-SUND-HEIT
©2011 ZITS Partnership. Distributed by King Features Syndicate
IT'S POSSIBLE THAT I'M TOO CONNECTED.
USE A TISSUE.
10/7
SCOTT and BORGMAN

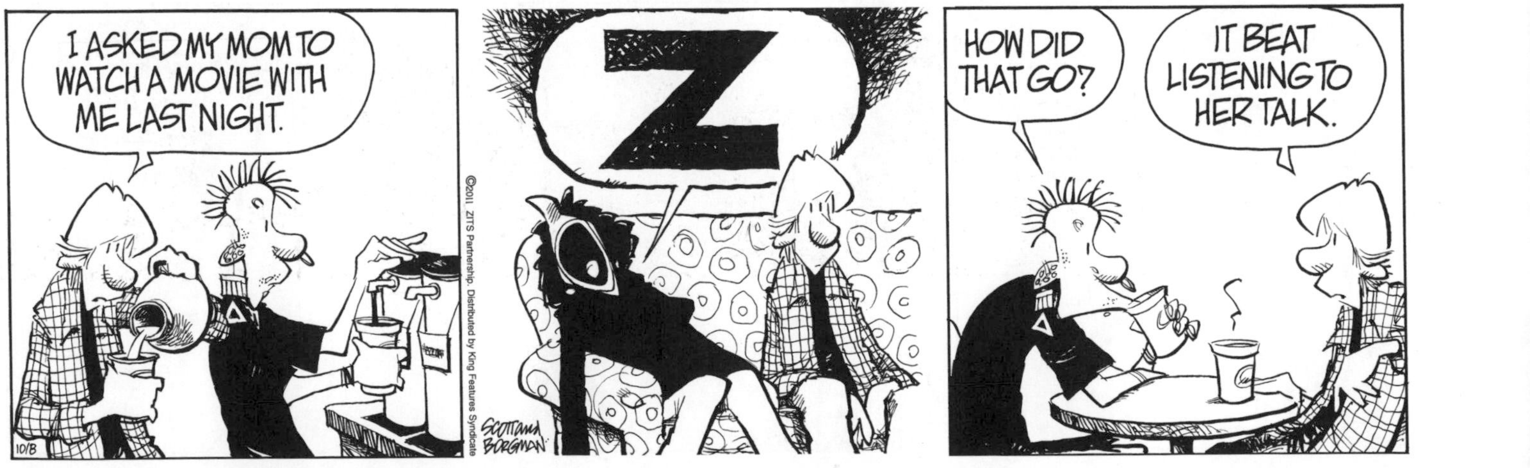
I ASKED MY MOM TO WATCH A MOVIE WITH ME LAST NIGHT.
10/8
©2011 ZITS Partnership. Distributed by King Features Syndicate
Z
SCOTT and BORGMAN
HOW DID THAT GO?
IT BEAT LISTENING TO HER TALK.

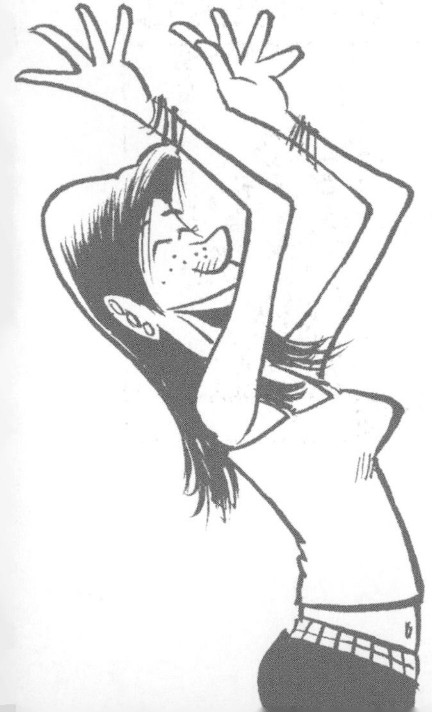

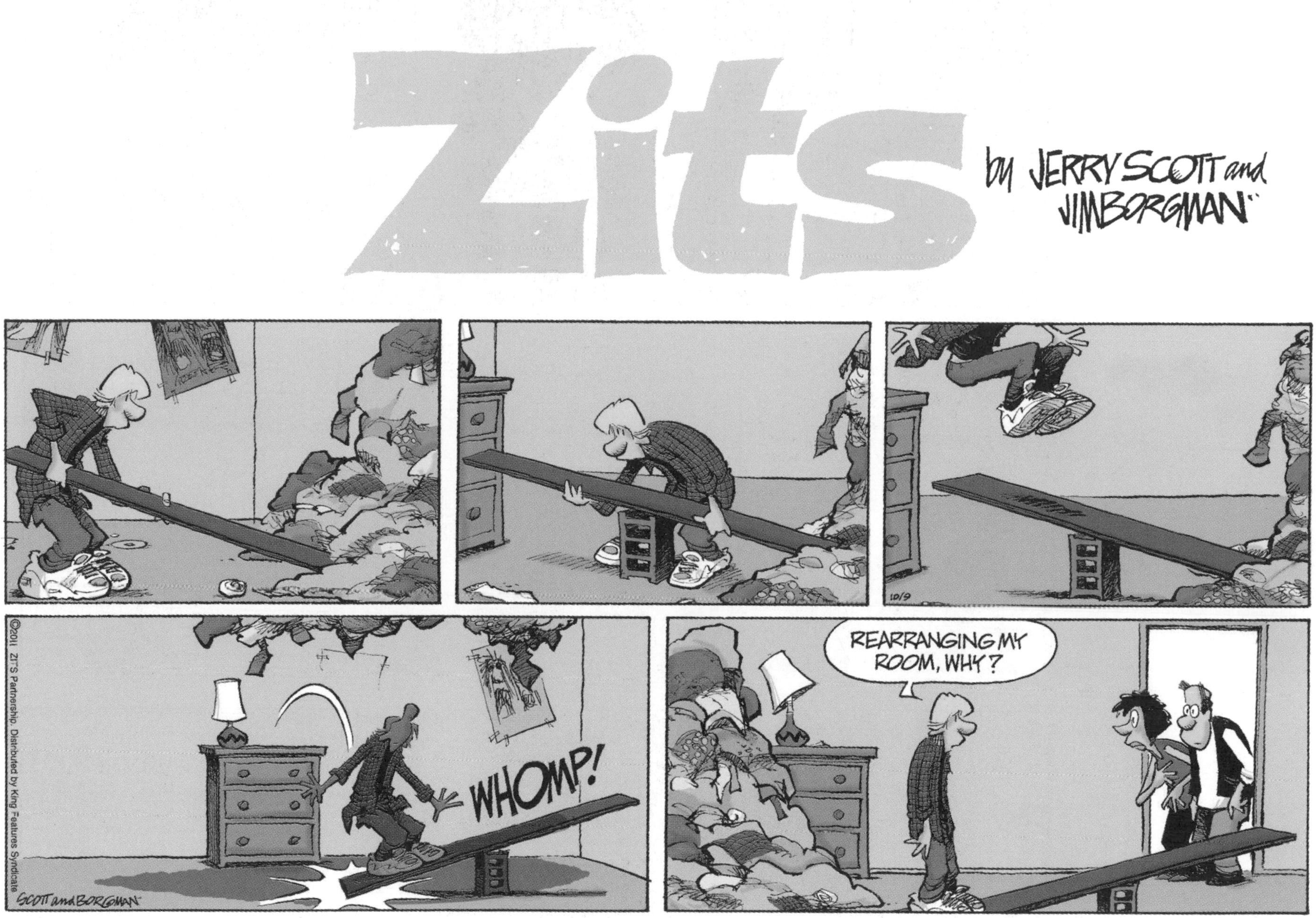
Zits
by JERRY SCOTT and JIM BORGMAN
10/9
©2011 ZITS Partnership. Distributed by King Features Syndicate
SCOTT and BORGMAN
WHOMP!
REARRANGING MY ROOM, WHY?

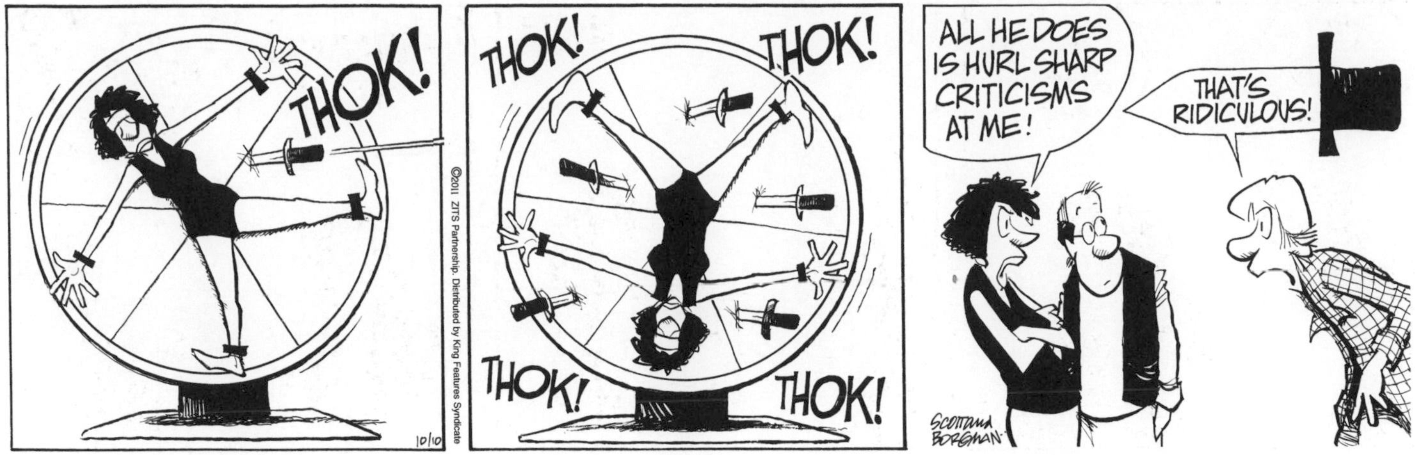
THOK!
THOK!
THOK!
THOK!
THOK!
ALL HE DOES IS HURL SHARP CRITICISMS AT ME!
THAT'S RIDICULOUS!
©2011 ZITS Partnership. Distributed by King Features Syndicate
10/10
SCOTT AND BORGMAN

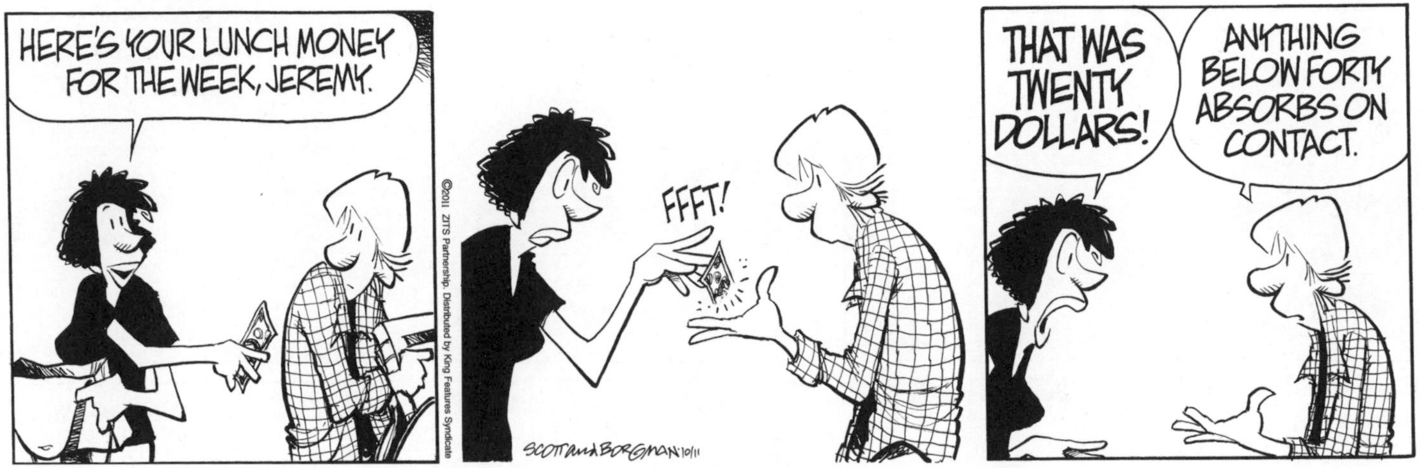
HERE'S YOUR LUNCH MONEY FOR THE WEEK, JEREMY.
FFFT!
THAT WAS TWENTY DOLLARS!
ANYTHING BELOW FORTY ABSORBS ON CONTACT.
©2011 ZITS Partnership. Distributed by King Features Syndicate
SCOTT AND BORGMAN 10/11

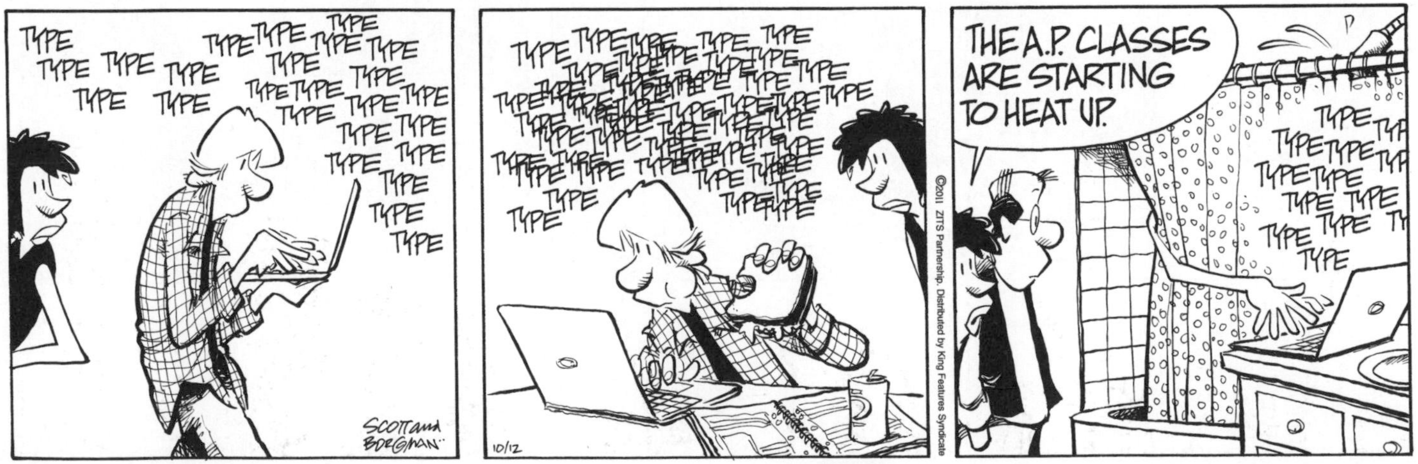
TYPE TYPE TYPE TYPE TYPE
THE A.P. CLASSES ARE STARTING TO HEAT UP.
©2011 ZITS Partnership. Distributed by King Features Syndicate
SCOTT AND BORGMAN
10/12

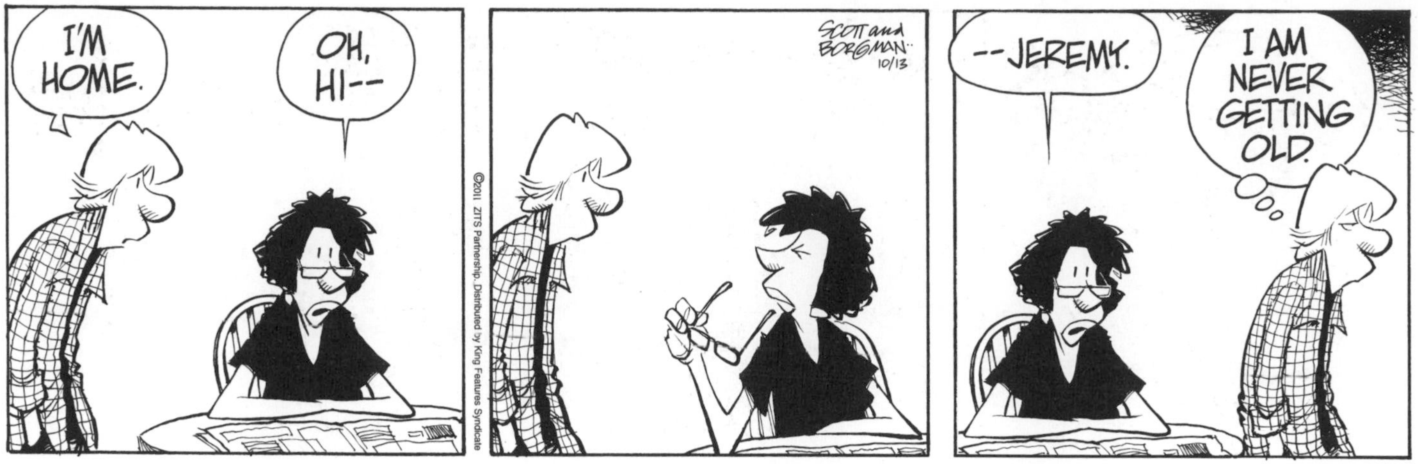
I'M HOME.
OH, HI--
SCOTT and BORGMAN 10/13
©2011 ZITS Partnership. Distributed by King Features Syndicate
--JEREMY.
I AM NEVER GETTING OLD.

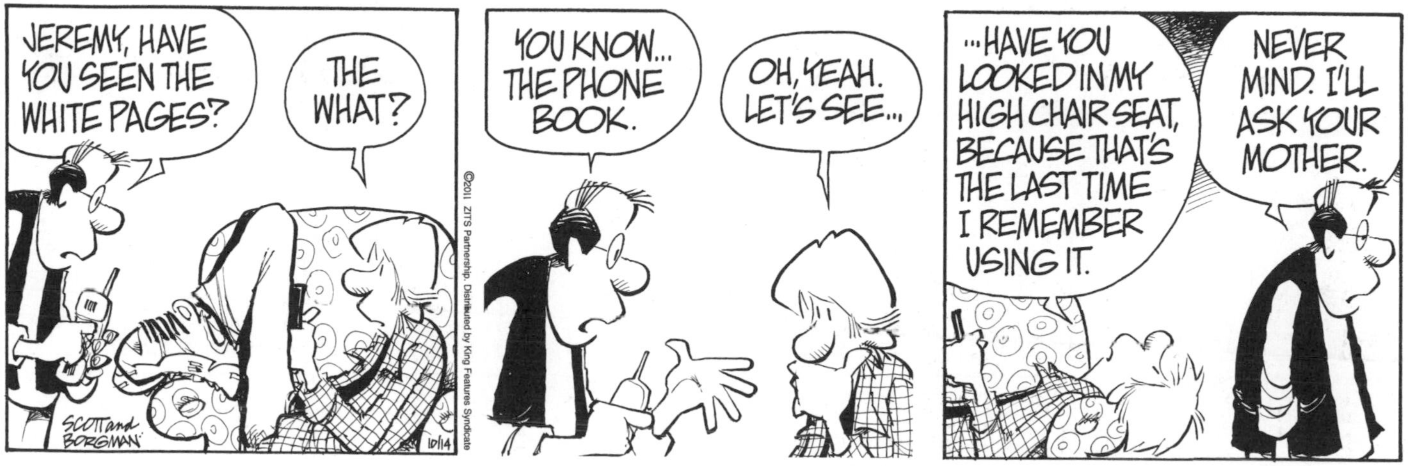
JEREMY, HAVE YOU SEEN THE WHITE PAGES?
THE WHAT?
SCOTT and BORGMAN 10/14
©2011 ZITS Partnership. Distributed by King Features Syndicate
YOU KNOW... THE PHONE BOOK.
OH, YEAH. LET'S SEE...
...HAVE YOU LOOKED IN MY HIGH CHAIR SEAT, BECAUSE THAT'S THE LAST TIME I REMEMBER USING IT.
NEVER MIND. I'LL ASK YOUR MOTHER.

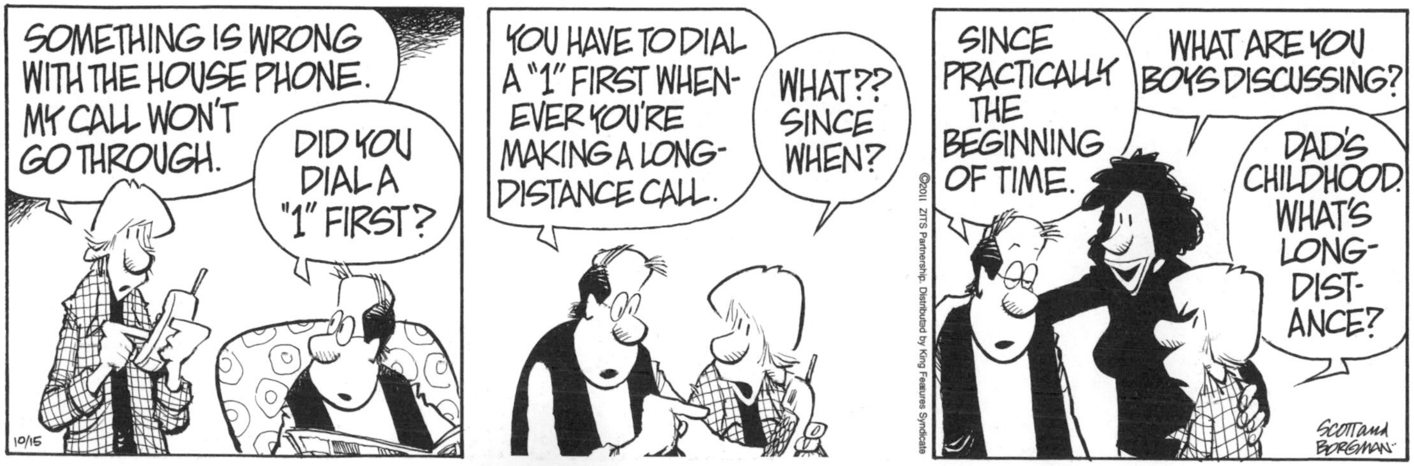
SOMETHING IS WRONG WITH THE HOUSE PHONE. MY CALL WON'T GO THROUGH.
DID YOU DIAL A "1" FIRST?
10/15
YOU HAVE TO DIAL A "1" FIRST WHENEVER YOU'RE MAKING A LONG-DISTANCE CALL.
WHAT?? SINCE WHEN?
©2011 ZITS Partnership. Distributed by King Features Syndicate
SINCE PRACTICALLY THE BEGINNING OF TIME.
WHAT ARE YOU BOYS DISCUSSING?
DAD'S CHILDHOOD. WHAT'S LONG-DISTANCE?
SCOTT and BORGMAN

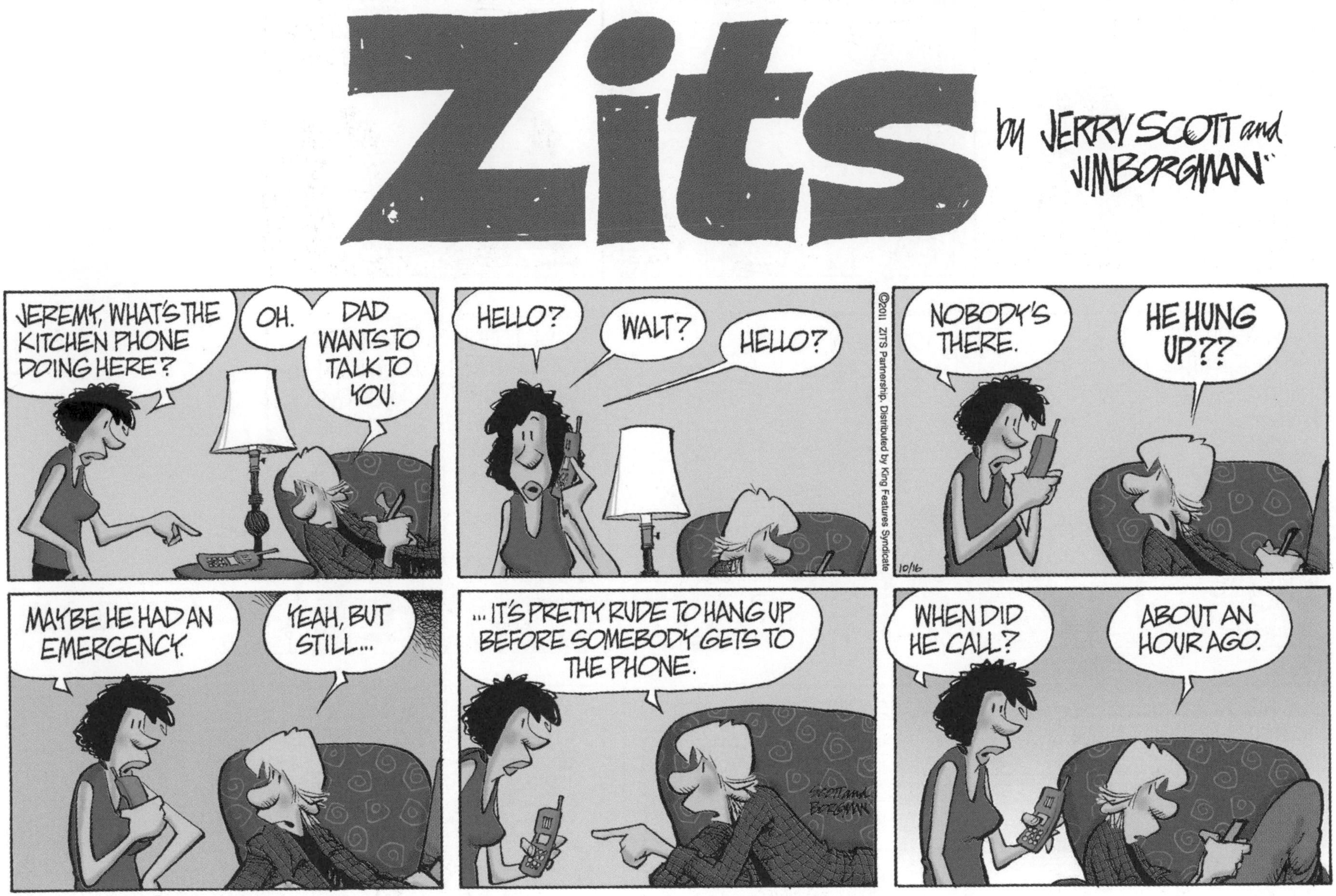
Zits
by JERRY SCOTT and JIM BORGMAN
JEREMY, WHAT'S THE KITCHEN PHONE DOING HERE?
OH.
DAD WANTS TO TALK TO YOU.
HELLO?
WALT?
HELLO?
©2011 ZITS Partnership. Distributed by King Features Syndicate
NOBODY'S THERE.
HE HUNG UP??
10/16
MAYBE HE HAD AN EMERGENCY.
YEAH, BUT STILL...
...IT'S PRETTY RUDE TO HANG UP BEFORE SOMEBODY GETS TO THE PHONE.
SCOTT and BORGMAN
WHEN DID HE CALL?
ABOUT AN HOUR AGO.

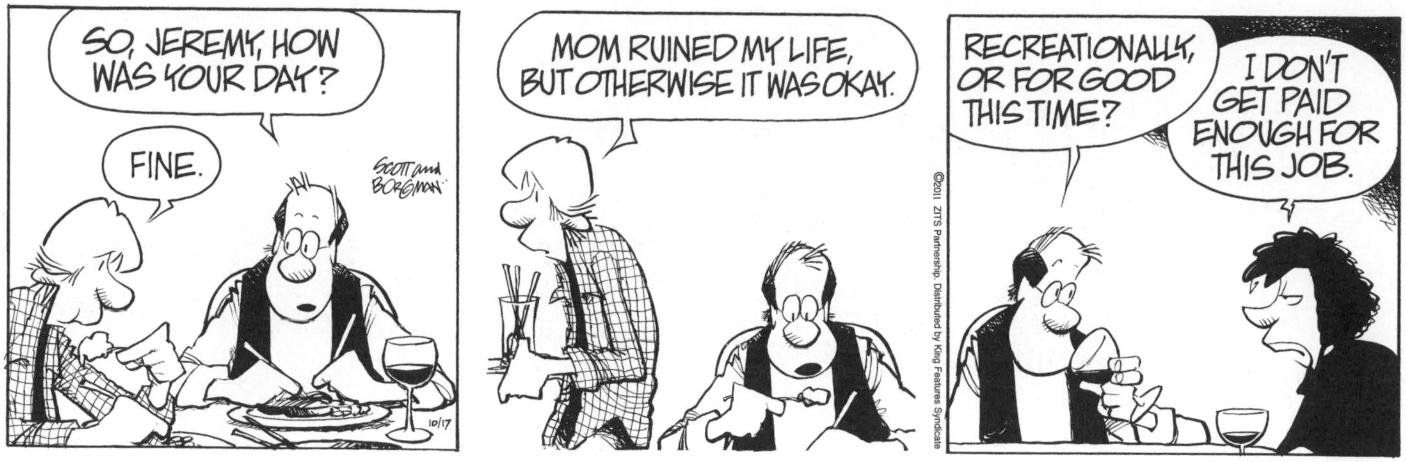
SO, JEREMY, HOW WAS YOUR DAY?
FINE.
SCOTT and BORGMAN
10/17
MOM RUINED MY LIFE, BUT OTHERWISE IT WAS OKAY.
©2011 ZITS Partnership. Distributed by King Features Syndicate
RECREATIONALLY, OR FOR GOOD THIS TIME?
I DON'T GET PAID ENOUGH FOR THIS JOB.

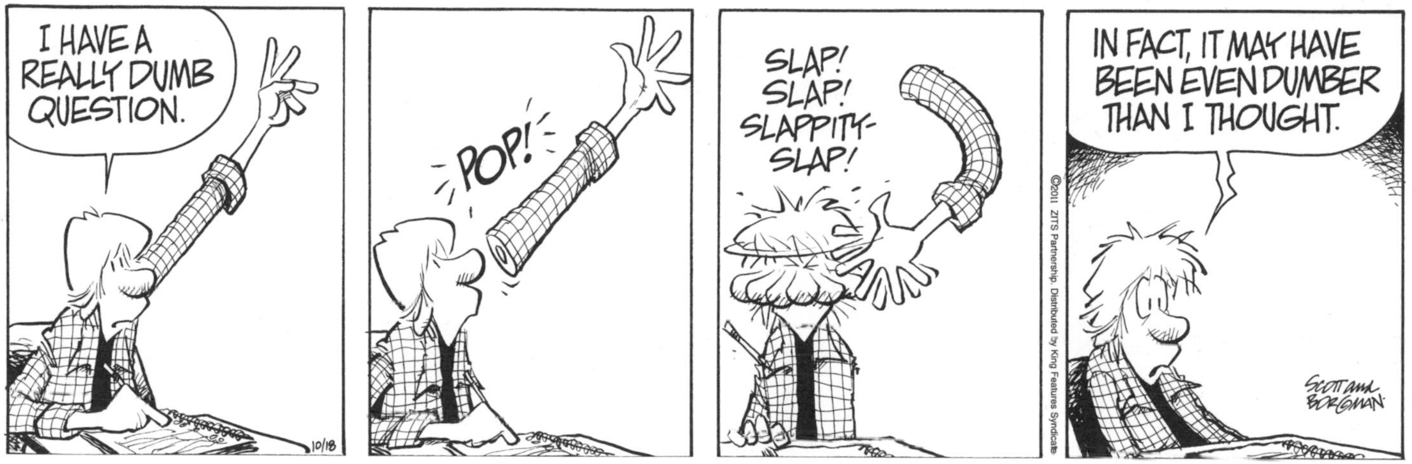
I HAVE A REALLY DUMB QUESTION.
10/18
POP!
SLAP! SLAP! SLAPPITY-SLAP!
©2011 ZITS Partnership. Distributed by King Features Syndicate
IN FACT, IT MAY HAVE BEEN EVEN DUMBER THAN I THOUGHT.
SCOTT and BORGMAN

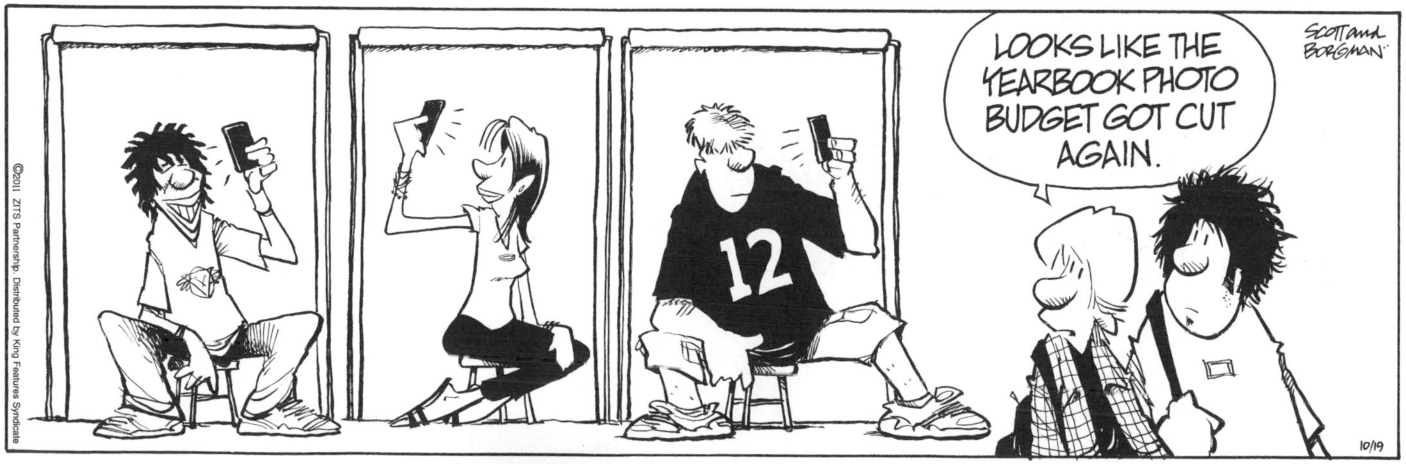
©2011 ZITS Partnership. Distributed by King Features Syndicate
12
LOOKS LIKE THE YEARBOOK PHOTO BUDGET GOT CUT AGAIN.
SCOTT and BORGMAN
10/19

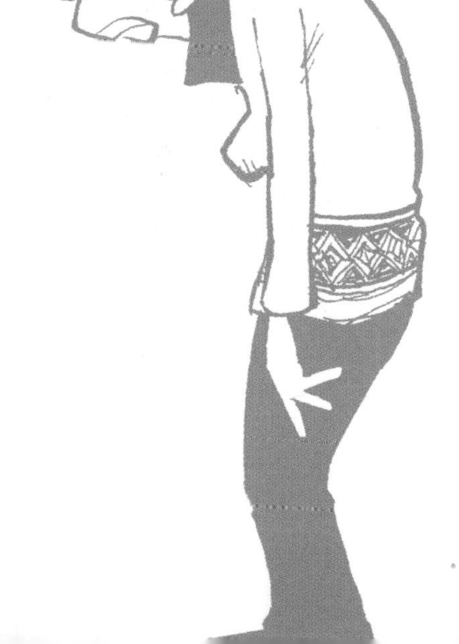

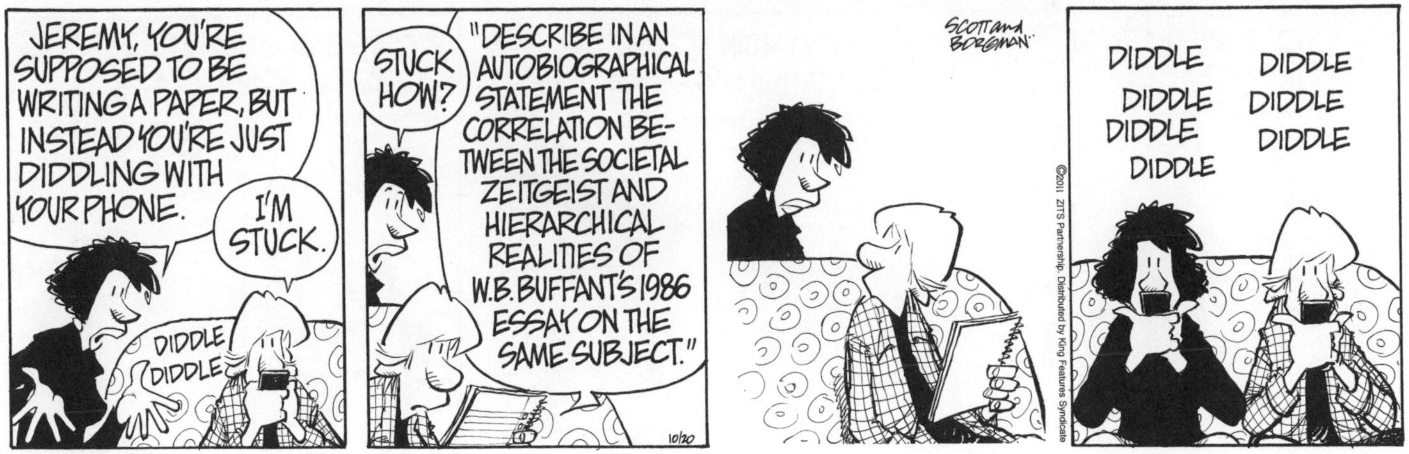
JEREMY, YOU'RE SUPPOSED TO BE WRITING A PAPER, BUT INSTEAD YOU'RE JUST DIDDLING WITH YOUR PHONE.
I'M STUCK.
DIDDLE DIDDLE
STUCK HOW?
"DESCRIBE IN AN AUTOBIOGRAPHICAL STATEMENT THE CORRELATION BETWEEN THE SOCIETAL ZEITGEIST AND HIERARCHICAL REALITIES OF W.B. BUFFANT'S 1986 ESSAY ON THE SAME SUBJECT."
10/20
SCOTT and BORGMAN
©2011 ZITS Partnership. Distributed by King Features Syndicate
DIDDLE DIDDLE DIDDLE DIDDLE DIDDLE DIDDLE DIDDLE

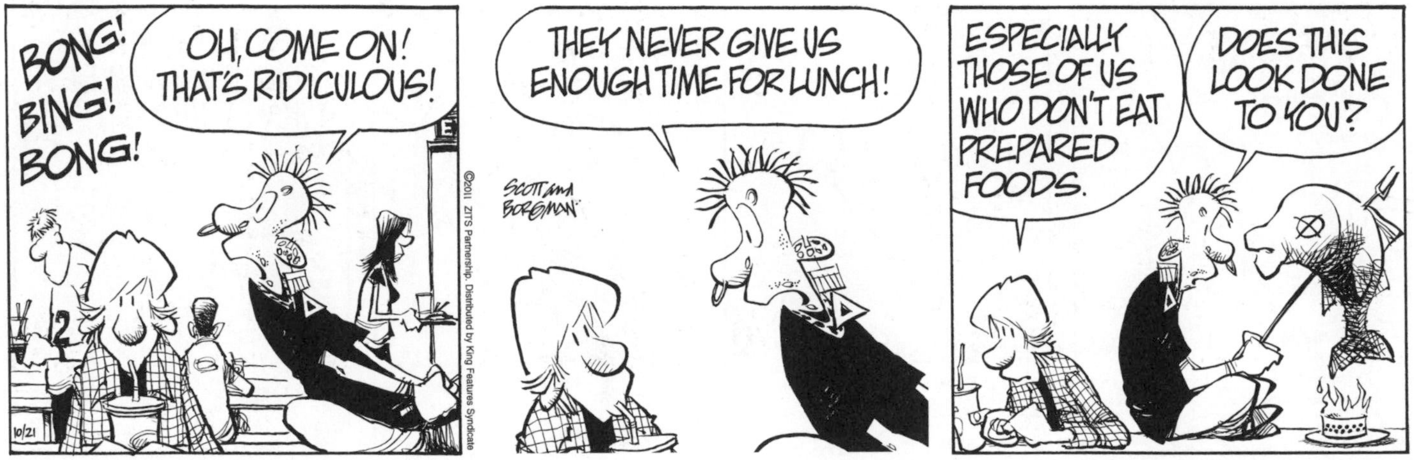
BONG! BING! BONG!
OH, COME ON! THAT'S RIDICULOUS!
10/21
©2011 ZITS Partnership. Distributed by King Features Syndicate
SCOTT and BORGMAN
THEY NEVER GIVE US ENOUGH TIME FOR LUNCH!
ESPECIALLY THOSE OF US WHO DON'T EAT PREPARED FOODS.
DOES THIS LOOK DONE TO YOU?

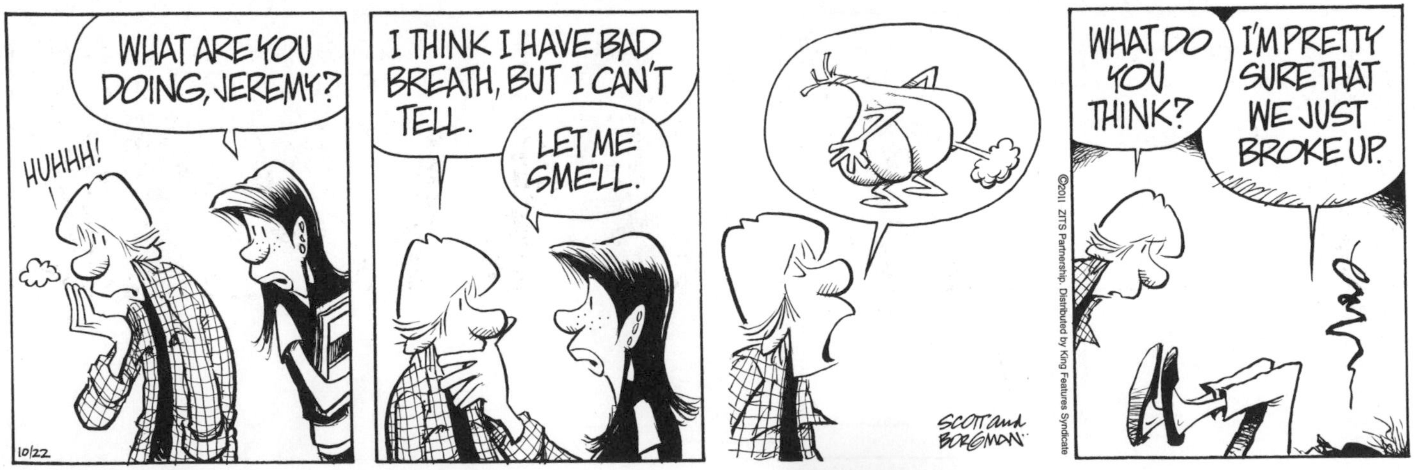
WHAT ARE YOU DOING, JEREMY?
HUHHH!
10/22
I THINK I HAVE BAD BREATH, BUT I CAN'T TELL.
LET ME SMELL.
SCOTT and BORGMAN
WHAT DO YOU THINK?
I'M PRETTY SURE THAT WE JUST BROKE UP.
©2011 ZITS Partnership. Distributed by King Features Syndicate

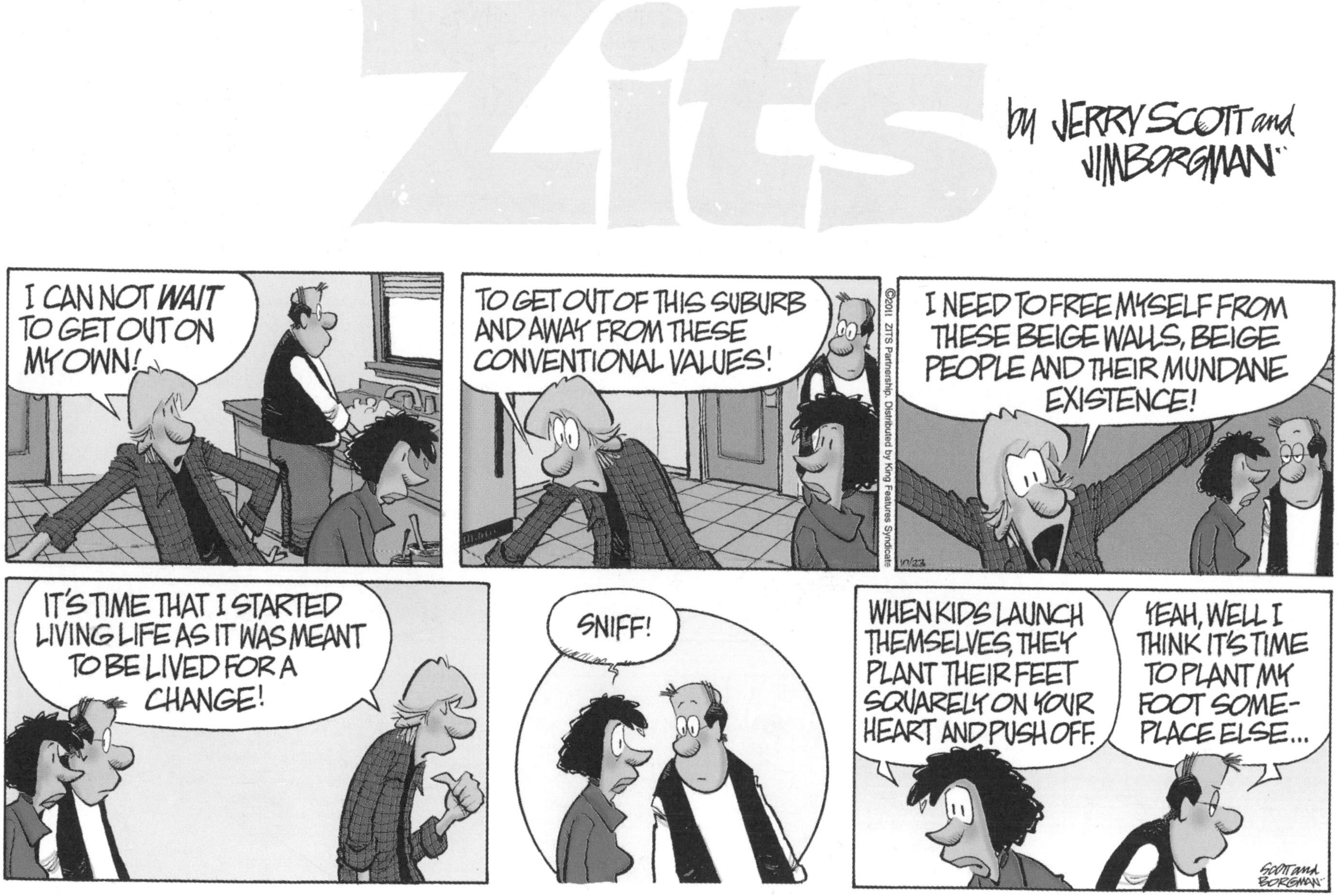
Zits
by JERRY SCOTT and JIM BORGMAN
I CAN NOT WAIT TO GET OUT ON MY OWN!
TO GET OUT OF THIS SUBURB AND AWAY FROM THESE CONVENTIONAL VALUES!
©2011 ZITS Partnership. Distributed by King Features Syndicate.
I NEED TO FREE MYSELF FROM THESE BEIGE WALLS, BEIGE PEOPLE AND THEIR MUNDANE EXISTENCE!
IT'S TIME THAT I STARTED LIVING LIFE AS IT WAS MEANT TO BE LIVED FOR A CHANGE!
SNIFF!
WHEN KIDS LAUNCH THEMSELVES, THEY PLANT THEIR FEET SQUARELY ON YOUR HEART AND PUSH OFF.
YEAH, WELL I THINK IT'S TIME TO PLANT MY FOOT SOMEPLACE ELSE...
SCOTT and BORGMAN

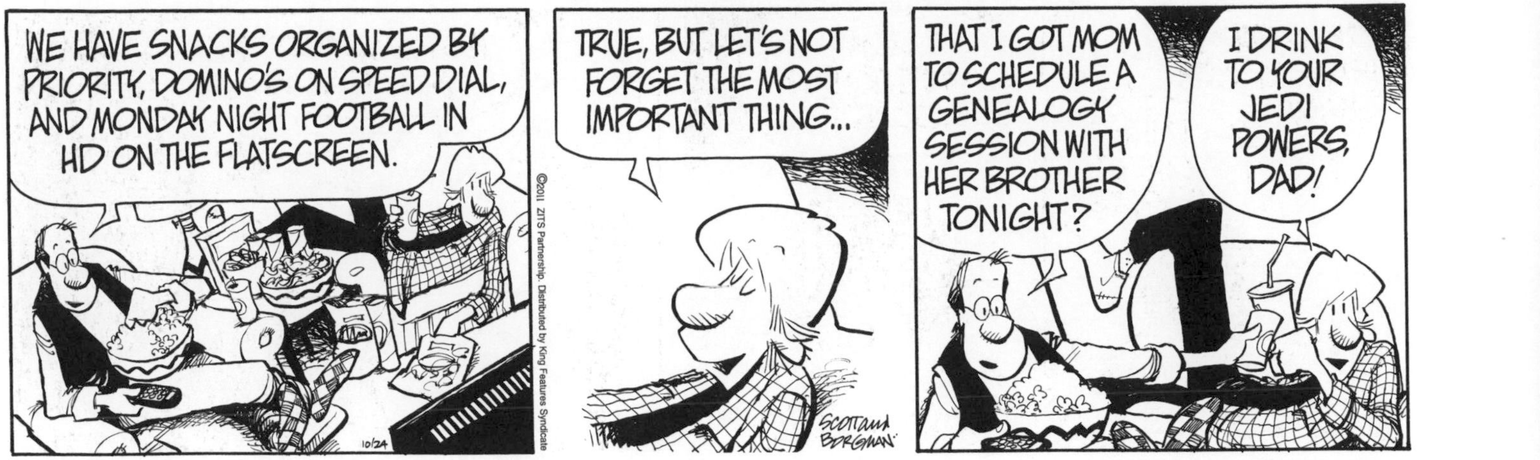
WE HAVE SNACKS ORGANIZED BY PRIORITY, DOMINO'S ON SPEED DIAL, AND MONDAY NIGHT FOOTBALL IN HD ON THE FLATSCREEN.
10/24
©2011 ZITS Partnership. Distributed by King Features Syndicate
TRUE, BUT LET'S NOT FORGET THE MOST IMPORTANT THING...
SCOTT and BORGMAN
THAT I GOT MOM TO SCHEDULE A GENEALOGY SESSION WITH HER BROTHER TONIGHT?
I DRINK TO YOUR JEDI POWERS, DAD!

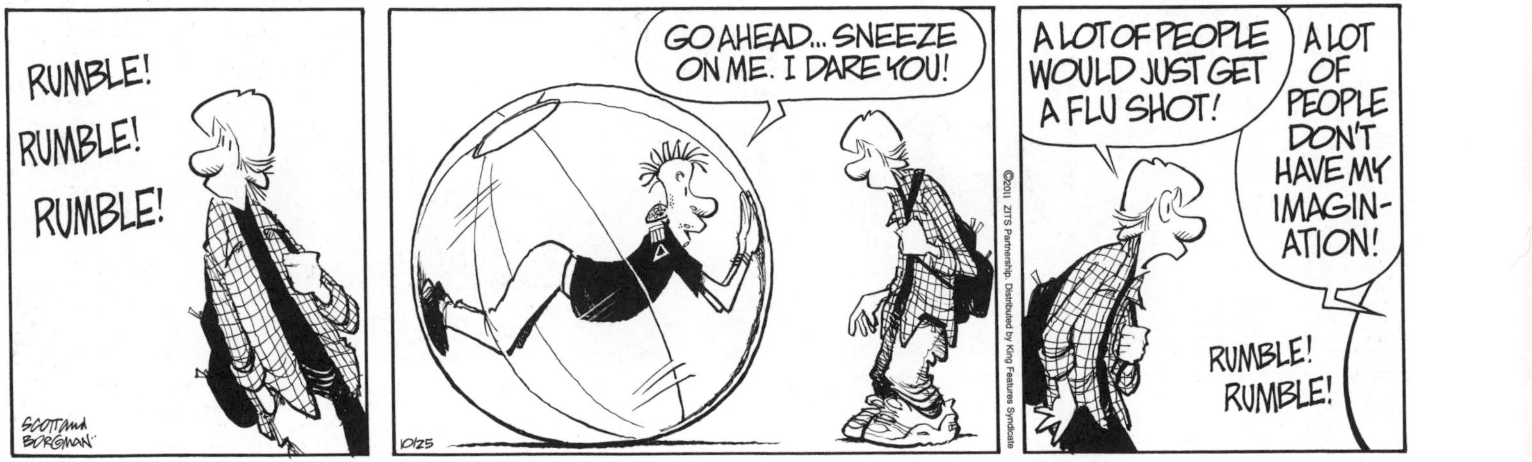
RUMBLE!
RUMBLE!
RUMBLE!
SCOTT and BORGMAN
GO AHEAD... SNEEZE ON ME. I DARE YOU!
10/25
©2011 ZITS Partnership. Distributed by King Features Syndicate
A LOT OF PEOPLE WOULD JUST GET A FLU SHOT!
A LOT OF PEOPLE DON'T HAVE MY IMAGINATION!
RUMBLE! RUMBLE!

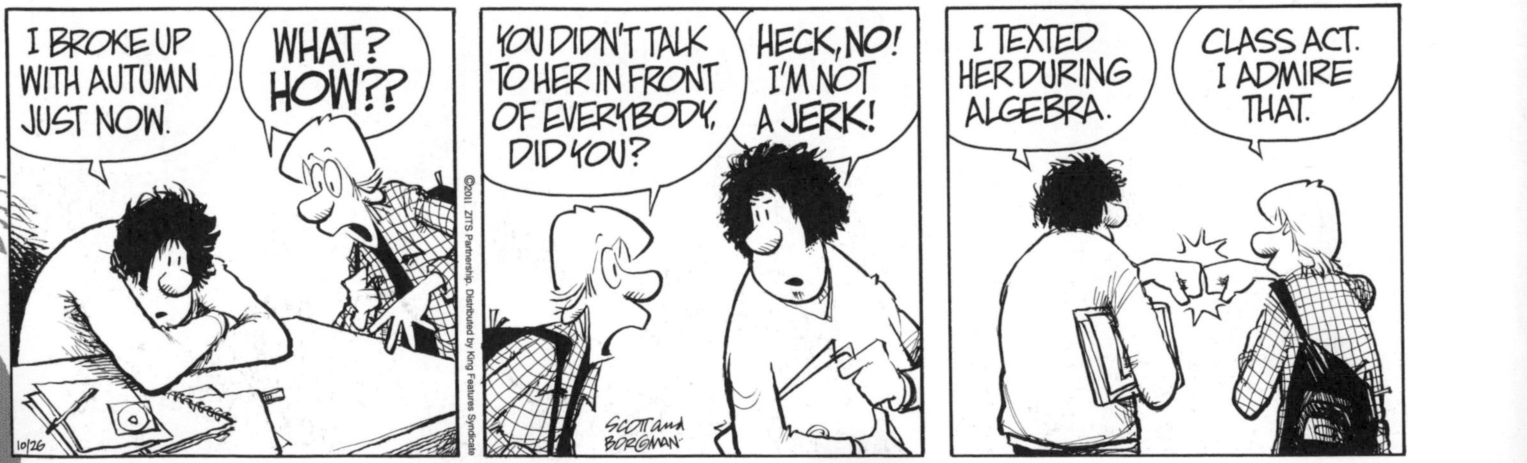
I BROKE UP WITH AUTUMN JUST NOW.
WHAT? HOW??
10/26
©2011 ZITS Partnership. Distributed by King Features Syndicate
YOU DIDN'T TALK TO HER IN FRONT OF EVERYBODY, DID YOU?
HECK, NO! I'M NOT A JERK!
SCOTT and BORGMAN
I TEXTED HER DURING ALGEBRA.
CLASS ACT. I ADMIRE THAT.

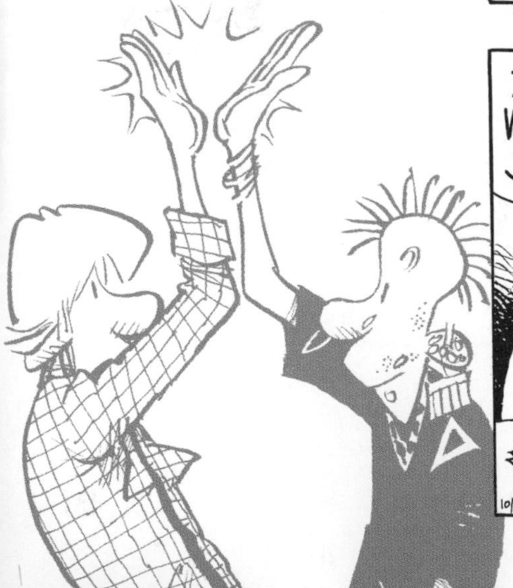

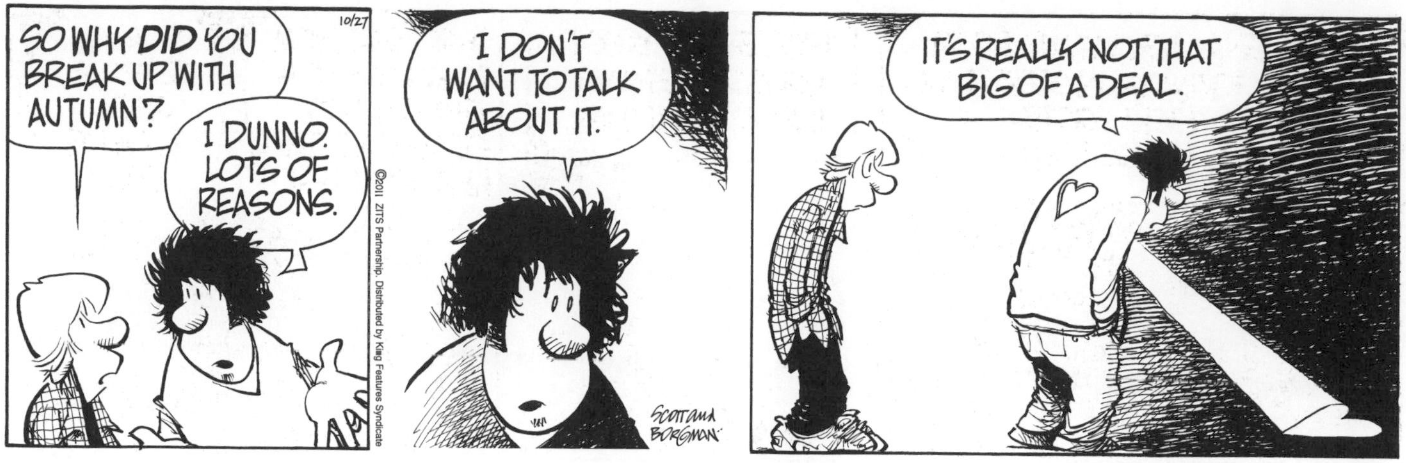

10/27
SO WHY **DID** YOU BREAK UP WITH AUTUMN?
I DUNNO. LOTS OF REASONS.
©2011 ZITS Partnership. Distributed by King Features Syndicate
I DON'T WANT TO TALK ABOUT IT.
SCOTT AND BORGMAN
IT'S REALLY NOT THAT BIG OF A DEAL.

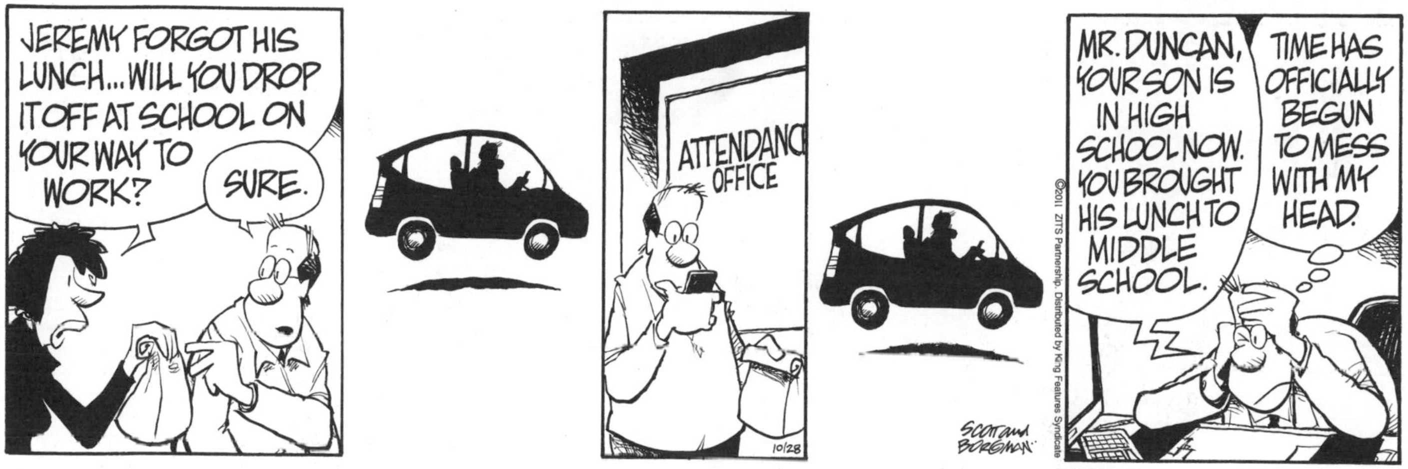

JEREMY FORGOT HIS LUNCH... WILL YOU DROP IT OFF AT SCHOOL ON YOUR WAY TO WORK?
SURE.
ATTENDANC
OFFICE
10/28
SCOTT AND BORGMAN
©2011 ZITS Partnership. Distributed by King Features Syndicate
MR. DUNCAN, YOUR SON IS IN HIGH SCHOOL NOW. YOU BROUGHT HIS LUNCH TO MIDDLE SCHOOL.
TIME HAS OFFICIALLY BEGUN TO MESS WITH MY HEAD.

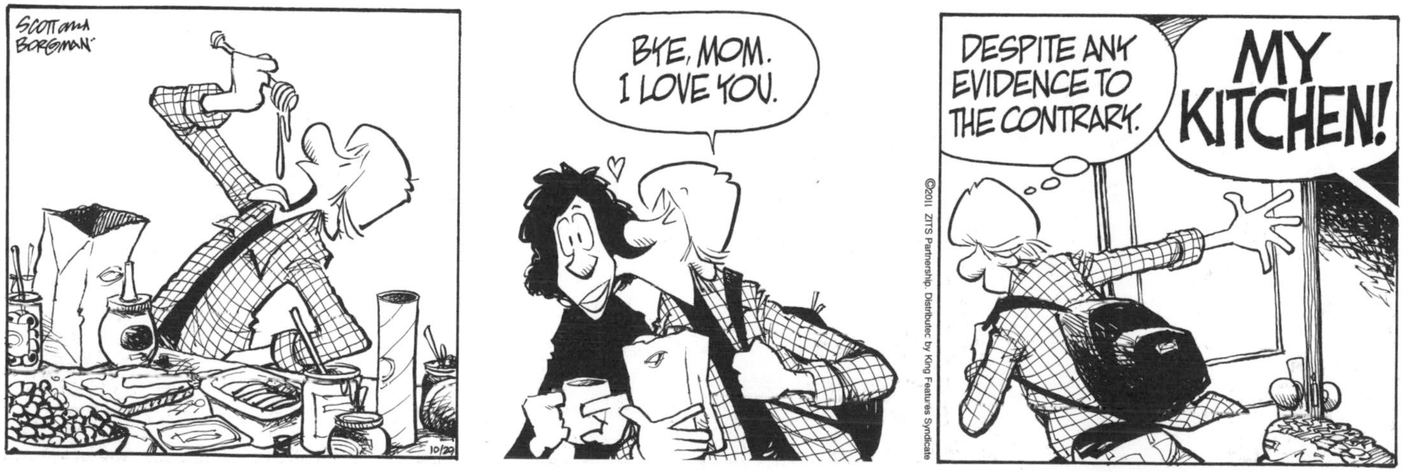

SCOTT AND BORGMAN
10/29
BYE, MOM. I LOVE YOU.
©2011 ZITS Partnership. Distributed by King Features Syndicate
DESPITE ANY EVIDENCE TO THE CONTRARY.
MY KITCHEN!

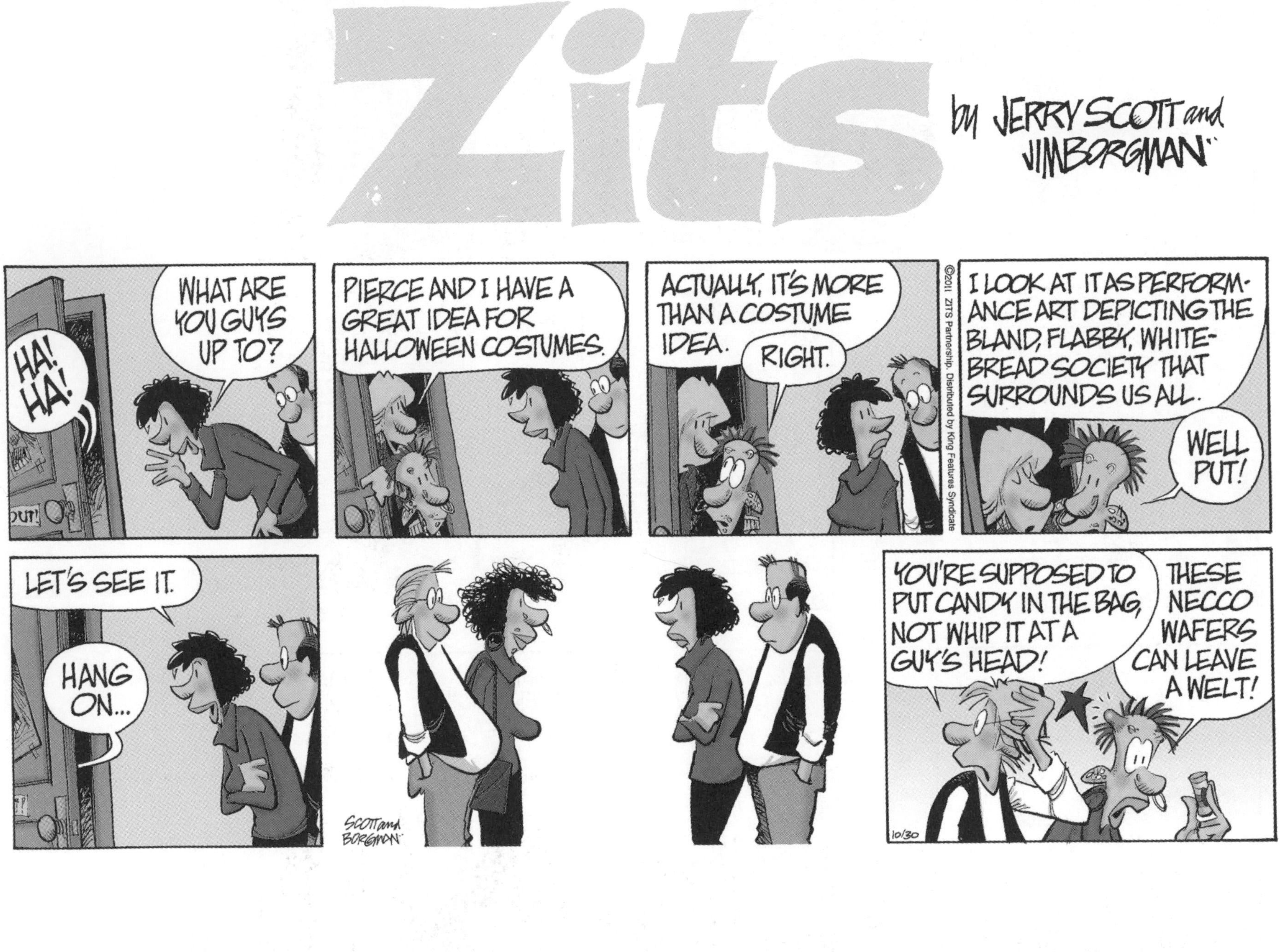
Zits
by JERRY SCOTT and JIM BORGMAN
HA! HA!
WHAT ARE YOU GUYS UP TO?
PIERCE AND I HAVE A GREAT IDEA FOR HALLOWEEN COSTUMES.
ACTUALLY, IT'S MORE THAN A COSTUME IDEA.
RIGHT.
©2011 ZITS Partnership. Distributed by King Features Syndicate
I LOOK AT IT AS PERFORMANCE ART DEPICTING THE BLAND, FLABBY, WHITE-BREAD SOCIETY THAT SURROUNDS US ALL.
WELL PUT!
LET'S SEE IT.
HANG ON...
SCOTT and BORGMAN
YOU'RE SUPPOSED TO PUT CANDY IN THE BAG, NOT WHIP IT AT A GUY'S HEAD!
THESE NECCO WAFERS CAN LEAVE A WELT!
10/30

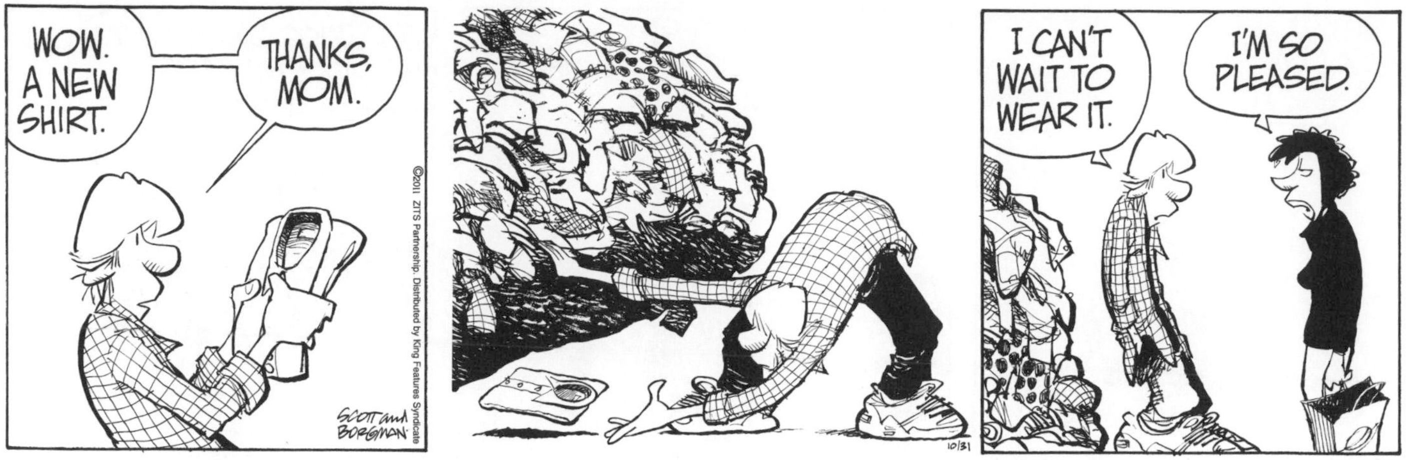
WOW. A NEW SHIRT.
THANKS, MOM.
©2011 ZITS Partnership. Distributed by King Features Syndicate
SCOTT AND BORGMAN
10/31
I CAN'T WAIT TO WEAR IT.
I'M SO PLEASED.

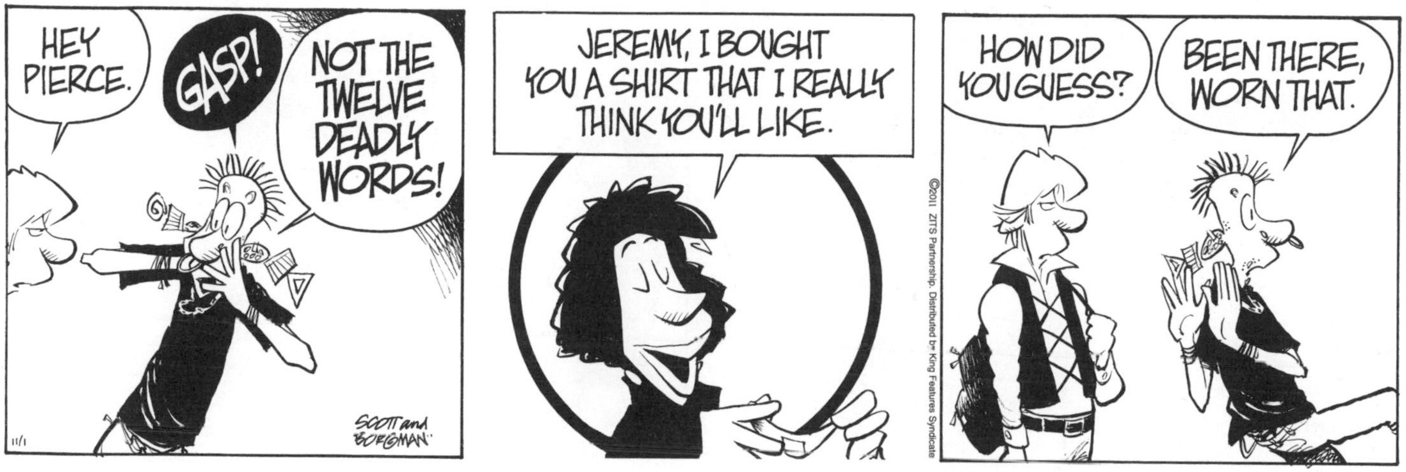
HEY PIERCE.
GASP!
NOT THE TWELVE DEADLY WORDS!
11/1
SCOTT AND BORGMAN
JEREMY, I BOUGHT YOU A SHIRT THAT I REALLY THINK YOU'LL LIKE.
©2011 ZITS Partnership. Distributed by King Features Syndicate
HOW DID YOU GUESS?
BEEN THERE, WORN THAT.

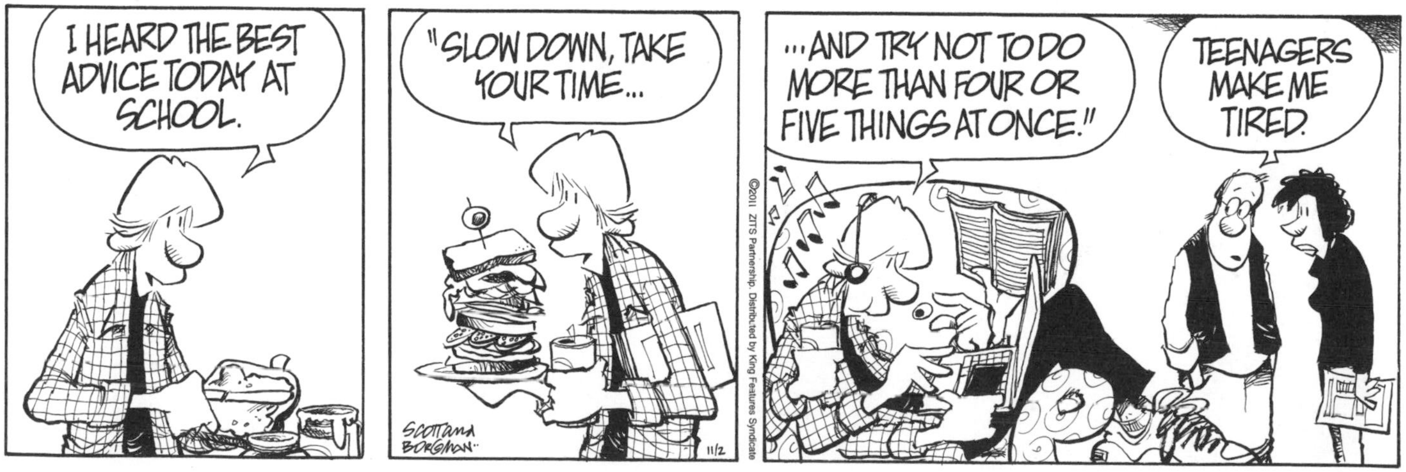
I HEARD THE BEST ADVICE TODAY AT SCHOOL.
"SLOW DOWN, TAKE YOUR TIME...
SCOTT AND BORGMAN
11/2
©2011 ZITS Partnership. Distributed by King Features Syndicate
...AND TRY NOT TO DO MORE THAN FOUR OR FIVE THINGS AT ONCE."
TEENAGERS MAKE ME TIRED.

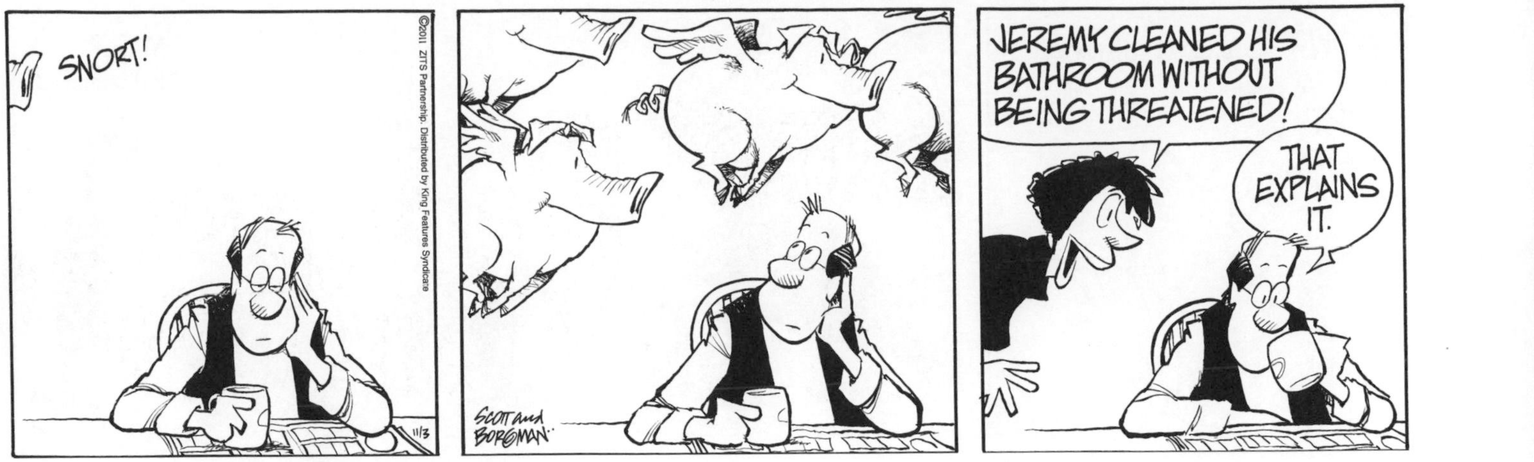
SNORT!
©2011 ZITS Partnership. Distributed by King Features Syndicate
11/3
SCOTT and BORGMAN
JEREMY CLEANED HIS BATHROOM WITHOUT BEING THREATENED!
THAT EXPLAINS IT.

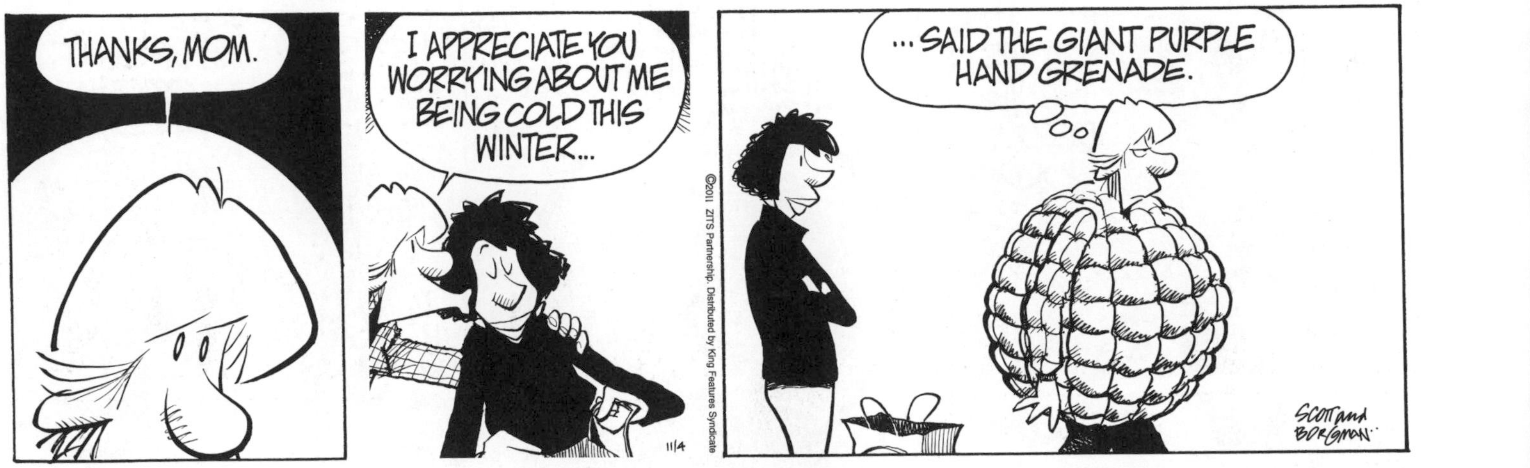
THANKS, MOM.
I APPRECIATE YOU WORRYING ABOUT ME BEING COLD THIS WINTER...
11/4
©2011 ZITS Partnership. Distributed by King Features Syndicate
... SAID THE GIANT PURPLE HAND GRENADE.
SCOTT and BORGMAN

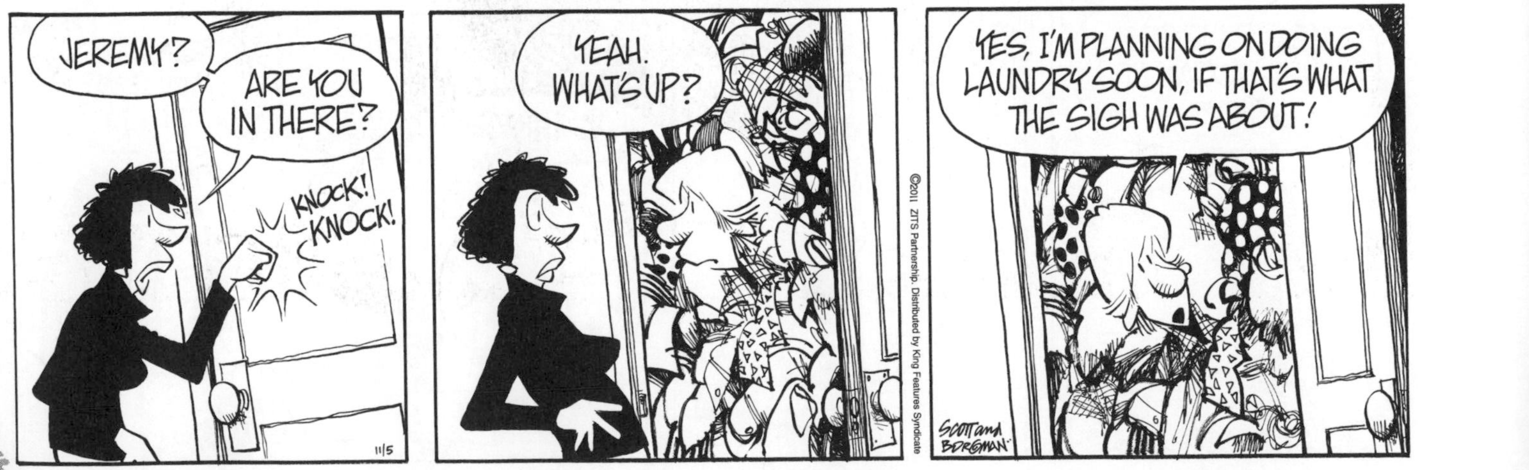
JEREMY?
ARE YOU IN THERE?
KNOCK! KNOCK!
11/5
YEAH. WHAT'S UP?
©2011 ZITS Partnership. Distributed by King Features Syndicate
YES, I'M PLANNING ON DOING LAUNDRY SOON, IF THAT'S WHAT THE SIGH WAS ABOUT!
SCOTT and BORGMAN

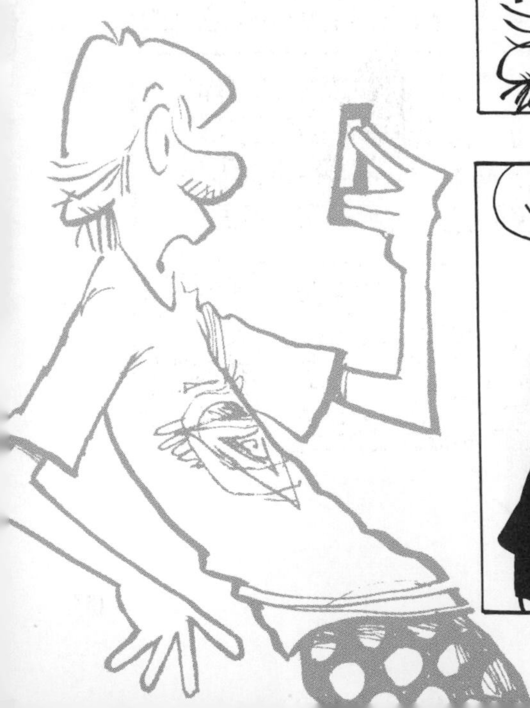

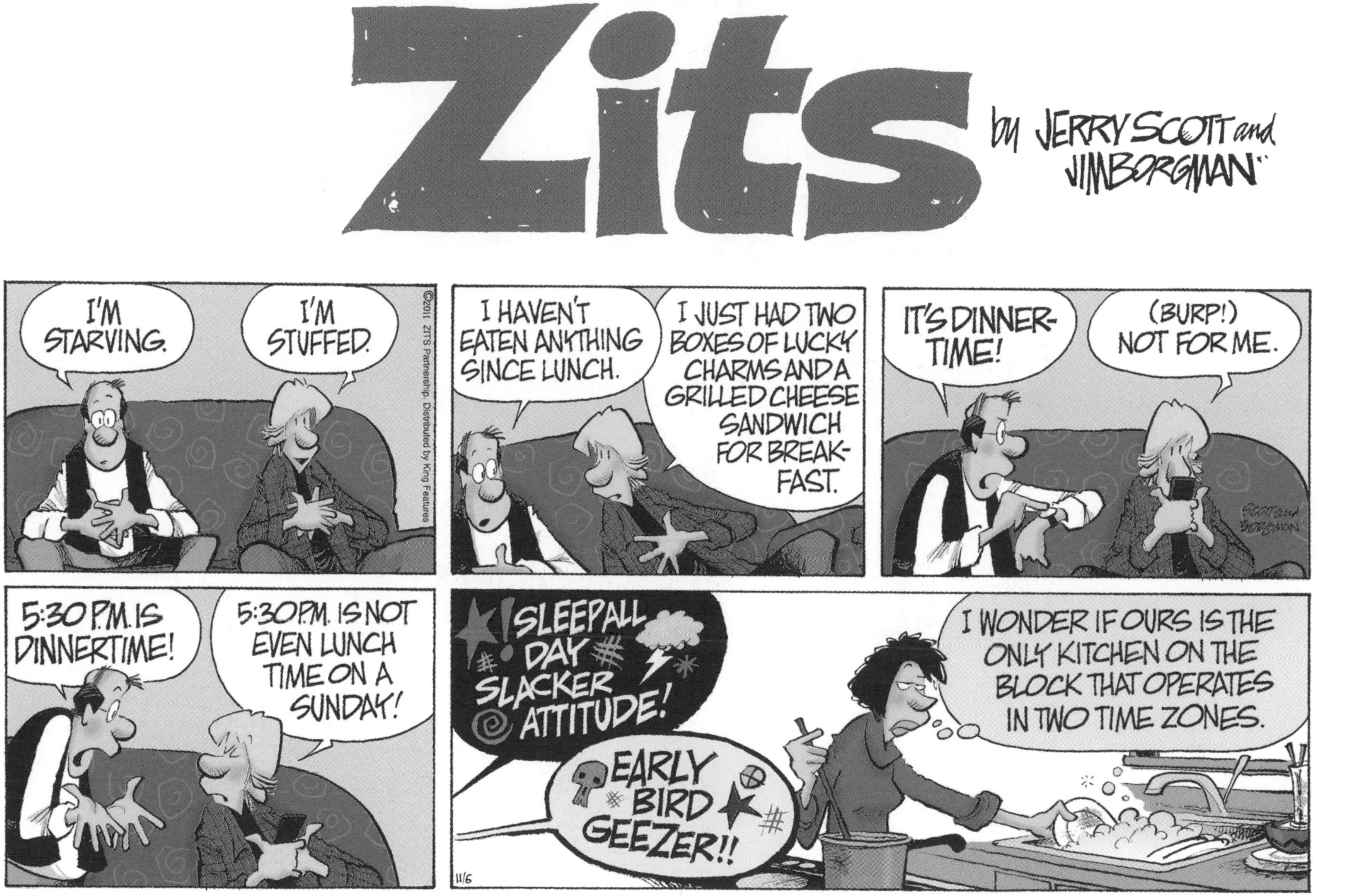
Zits
by JERRY SCOTT and JIM BORGMAN
I'M STARVING.
I'M STUFFED.
©2011 ZITS Partnership. Distributed by King Features
I HAVEN'T EATEN ANYTHING SINCE LUNCH.
I JUST HAD TWO BOXES OF LUCKY CHARMS AND A GRILLED CHEESE SANDWICH FOR BREAK-FAST.
IT'S DINNER-TIME!
(BURP!) NOT FOR ME.
SCOTT and BORGMAN
5:30 P.M. IS DINNERTIME!
5:30 P.M. IS NOT EVEN LUNCH TIME ON A SUNDAY!
SLEEP ALL DAY SLACKER ATTITUDE!
EARLY BIRD GEEZER!!
I WONDER IF OURS IS THE ONLY KITCHEN ON THE BLOCK THAT OPERATES IN TWO TIME ZONES.
11/6

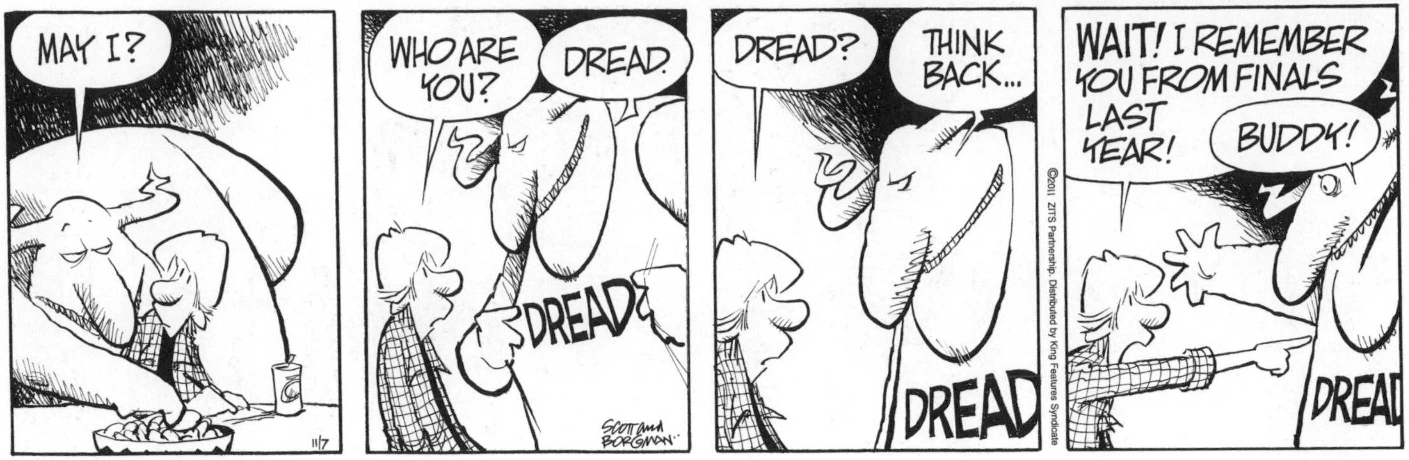
MAY I?
11/7
WHO ARE YOU?
DREAD.
DREAD
SCOTT and BORGMAN
DREAD?
THINK BACK...
DREAD
WAIT! I REMEMBER YOU FROM FINALS LAST YEAR!
BUDDY!
DREAD

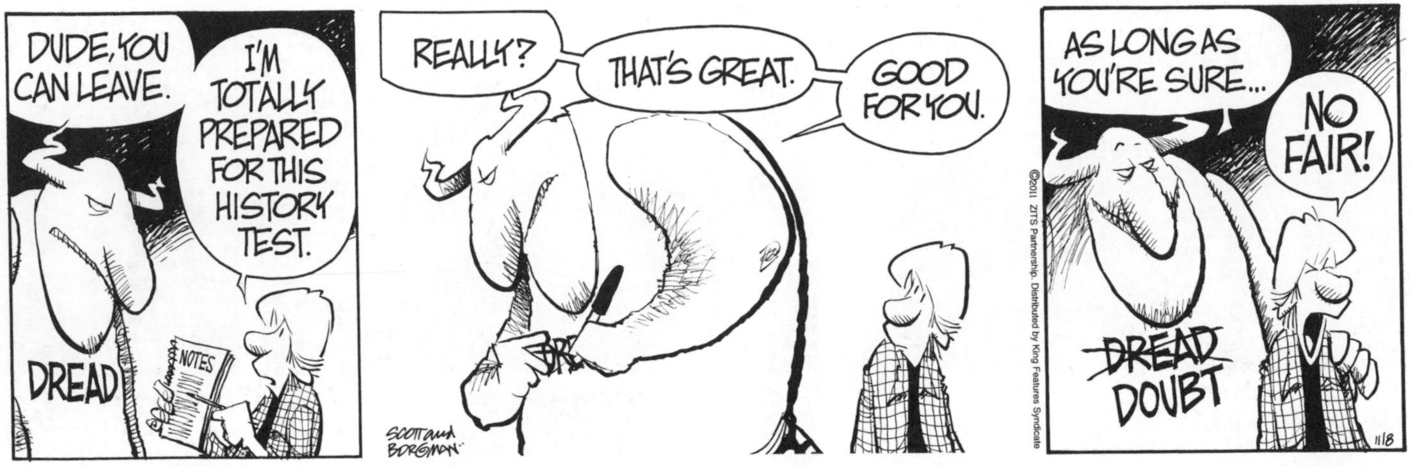
DUDE, YOU CAN LEAVE.
I'M TOTALLY PREPARED FOR THIS HISTORY TEST.
DREAD
NOTES
REALLY?
THAT'S GREAT.
GOOD FOR YOU.
SCOTT and BORGMAN
AS LONG AS YOU'RE SURE...
NO FAIR!
DREAD
DOUBT
11/8

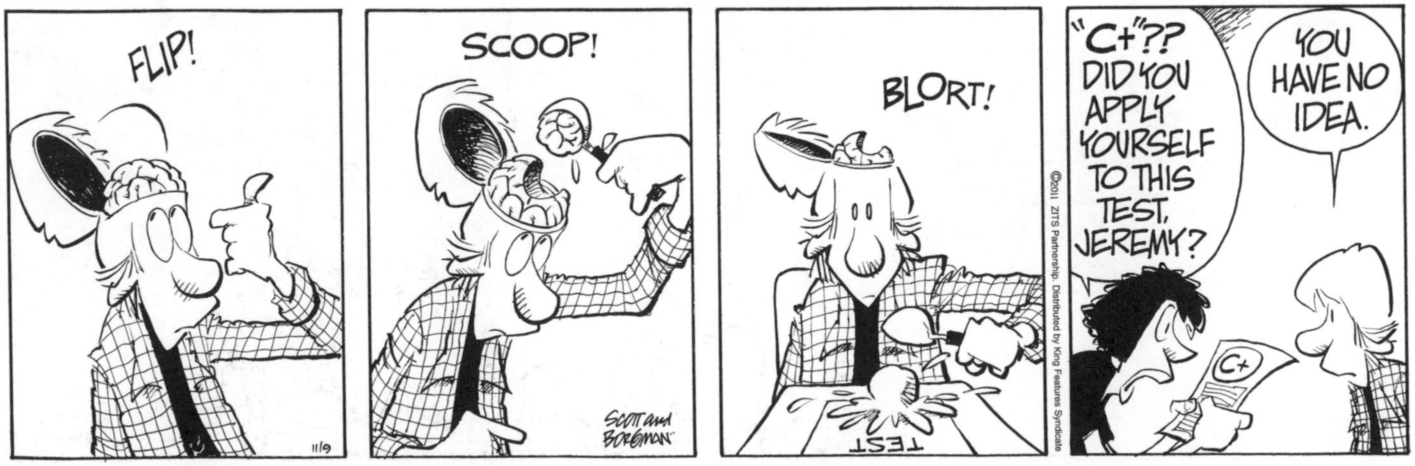
FLIP!
11/9
SCOOP!
SCOTT and BORGMAN
BLORT!
TEST
"C+"?? DID YOU APPLY YOURSELF TO THIS TEST, JEREMY?
YOU HAVE NO IDEA.
C+

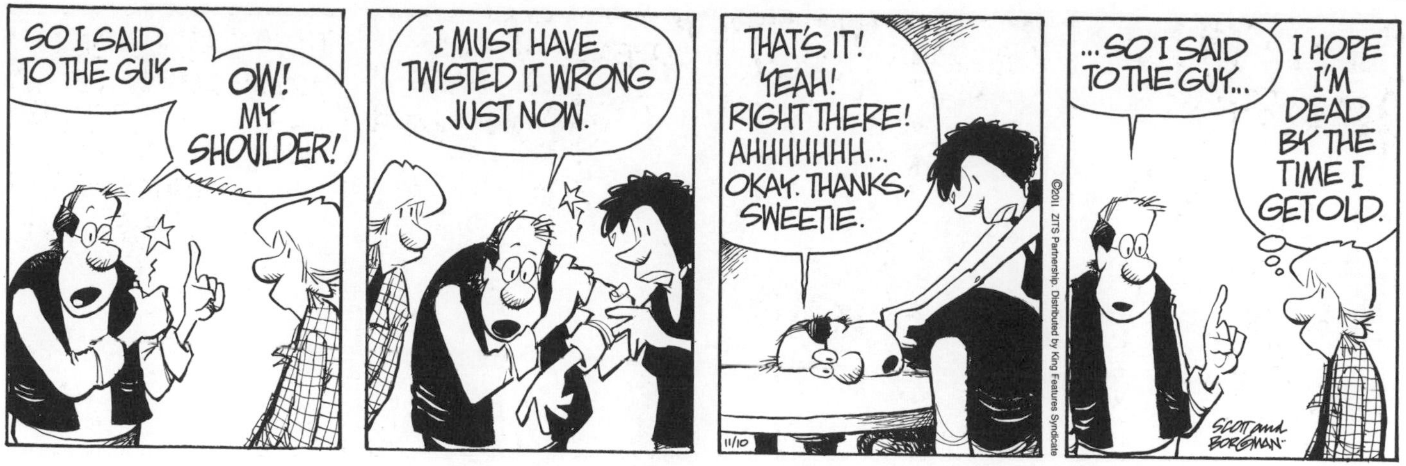

SO I SAID TO THE GUY–
OW! MY SHOULDER!
I MUST HAVE TWISTED IT WRONG JUST NOW.
THAT'S IT! YEAH! RIGHT THERE! AHHHHHHH... OKAY. THANKS, SWEETIE.
©2011 ZITS Partnership. Distributed by King Features Syndicate
11/10
...SO I SAID TO THE GUY...
I HOPE I'M DEAD BY THE TIME I GET OLD.
SCOTT and BORGMAN

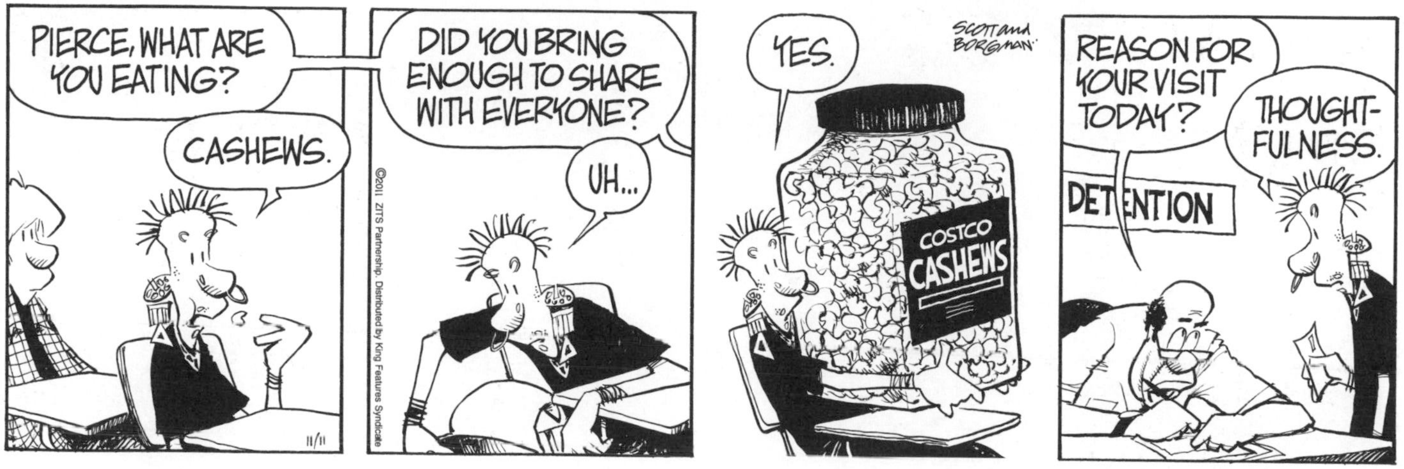

PIERCE, WHAT ARE YOU EATING?
CASHEWS.
11/11
DID YOU BRING ENOUGH TO SHARE WITH EVERYONE?
UH...
©2011 ZITS Partnership. Distributed by King Features Syndicate
YES.
SCOTT and BORGMAN
COSTCO CASHEWS
REASON FOR YOUR VISIT TODAY?
THOUGHT-FULNESS.
DETENTION

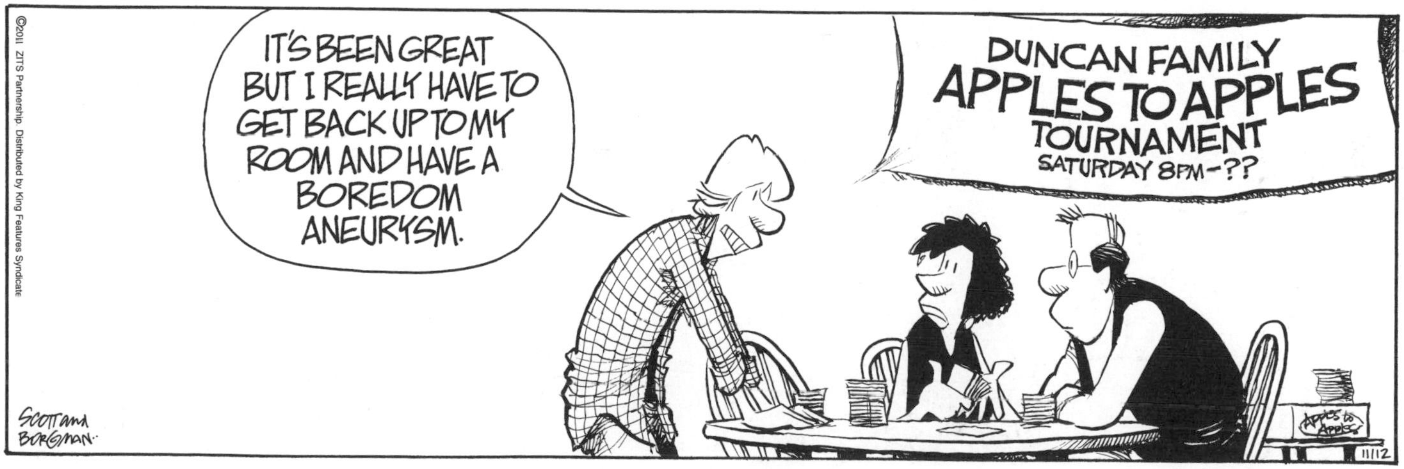

©2011 ZITS Partnership. Distributed by King Features Syndicate
IT'S BEEN GREAT BUT I REALLY HAVE TO GET BACK UP TO MY ROOM AND HAVE A BOREDOM ANEURYSM.
DUNCAN FAMILY
APPLES TO APPLES
TOURNAMENT
SATURDAY 8PM-??
SCOTT and BORGMAN
11/12

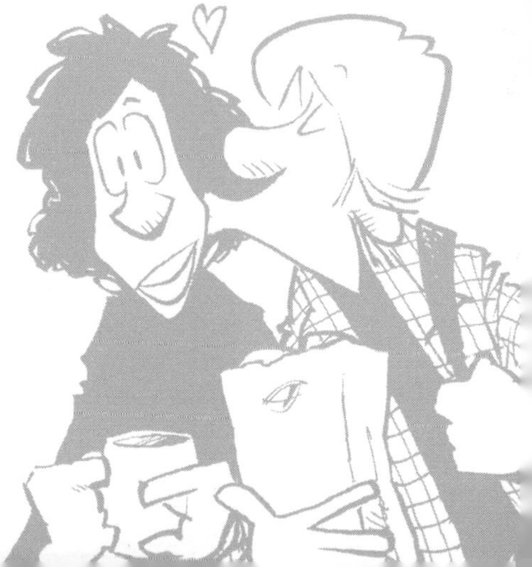

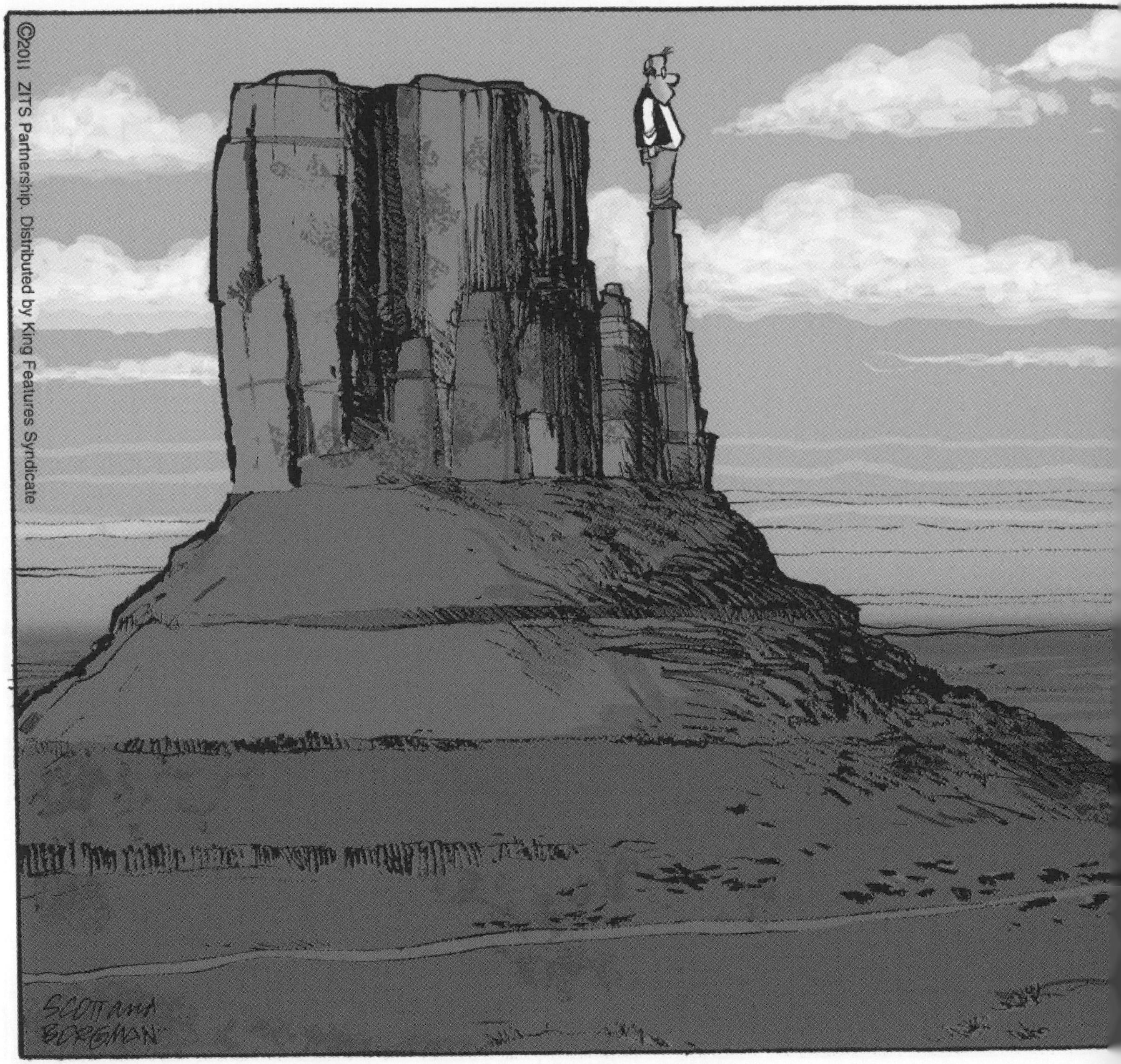
©2011 ZITS Partnership. Distributed by King Features Syndicate
SCOTT AND
BORGMAN

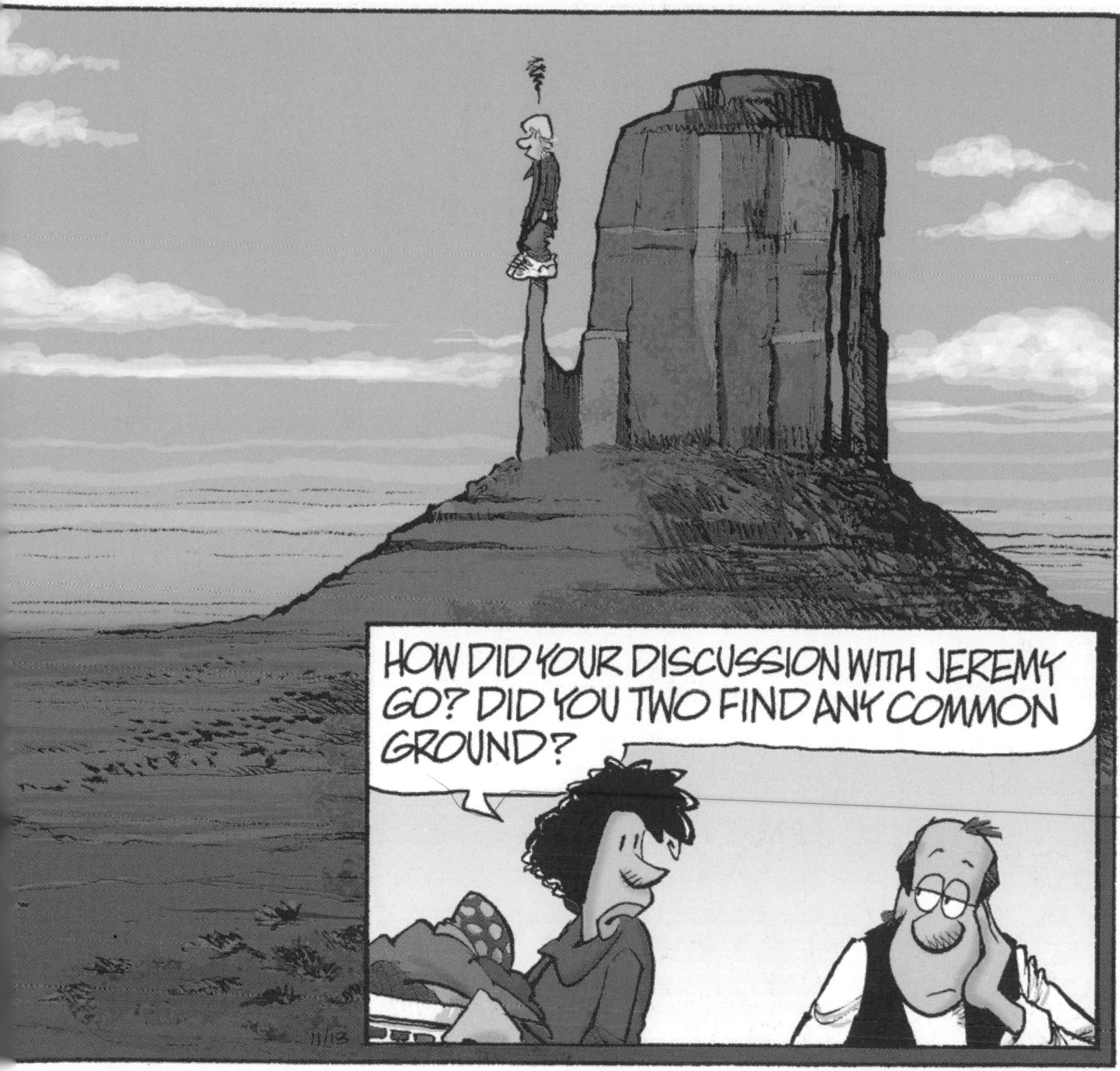
HOW DID YOUR DISCUSSION WITH JEREMY GO? DID YOU TWO FIND ANY COMMON GROUND?
11/13

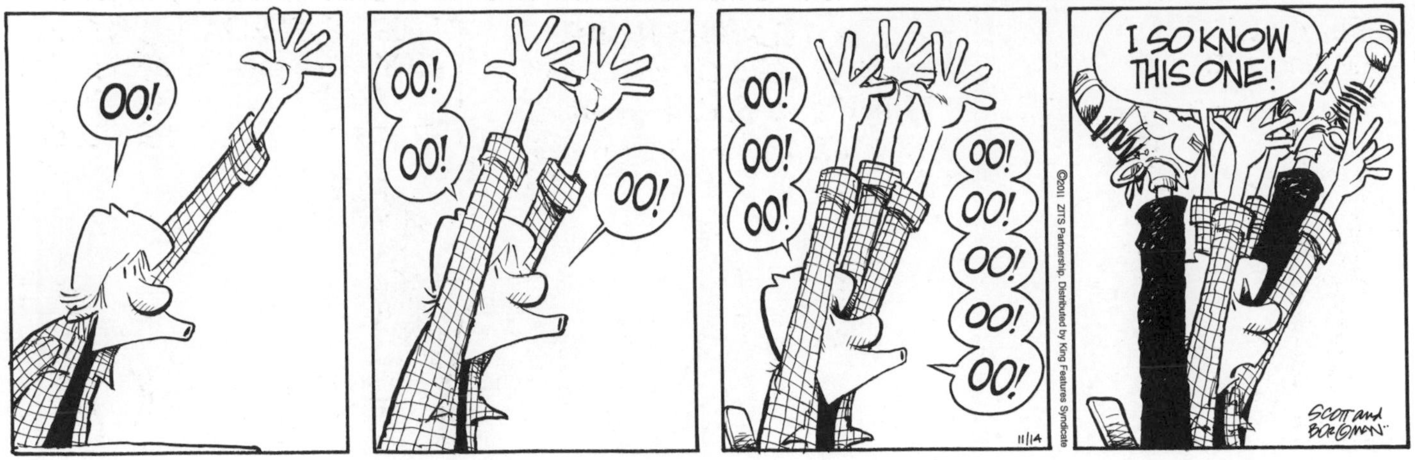
OO!
OO!
OO!
OO!
OO!
OO!
OO!
OO!
OO!
OO!
OO!
OO!
11/14
I SO KNOW THIS ONE!
©2011 ZITS Partnership. Distributed by King Features Syndicate
SCOTT AND BORGMAN

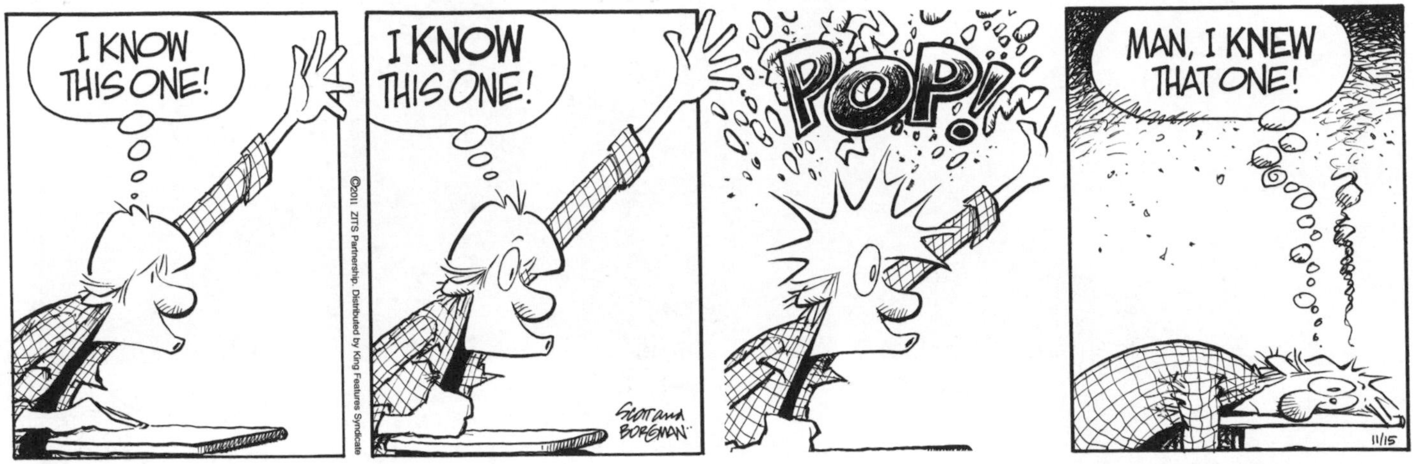
I KNOW THIS ONE!
©2011 ZITS Partnership. Distributed by King Features Syndicate
I KNOW THIS ONE!
SCOTT AND BORGMAN
POP!
MAN, I KNEW THAT ONE!
11/15

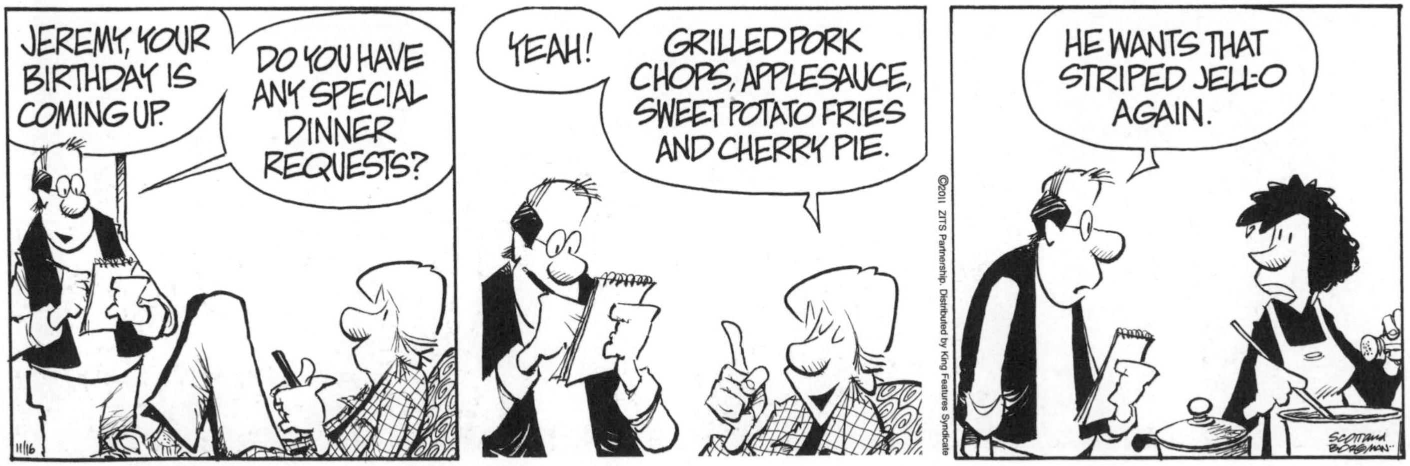
JEREMY, YOUR BIRTHDAY IS COMING UP.
DO YOU HAVE ANY SPECIAL DINNER REQUESTS?
11/16
YEAH!
GRILLED PORK CHOPS, APPLESAUCE, SWEET POTATO FRIES AND CHERRY PIE.
©2011 ZITS Partnership. Distributed by King Features Syndicate
HE WANTS THAT STRIPED JELL-O AGAIN.
SCOTT AND BORGMAN

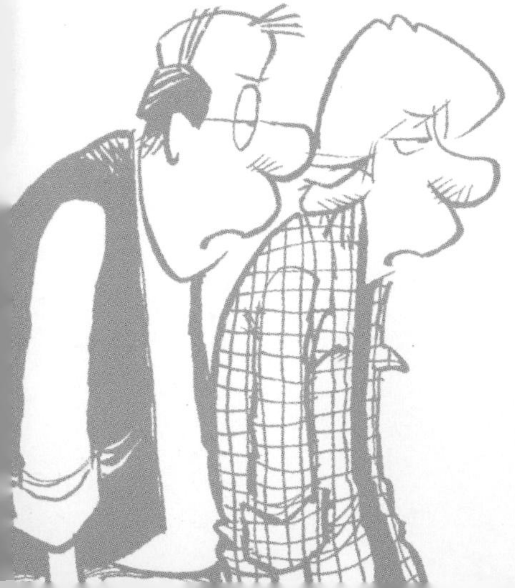

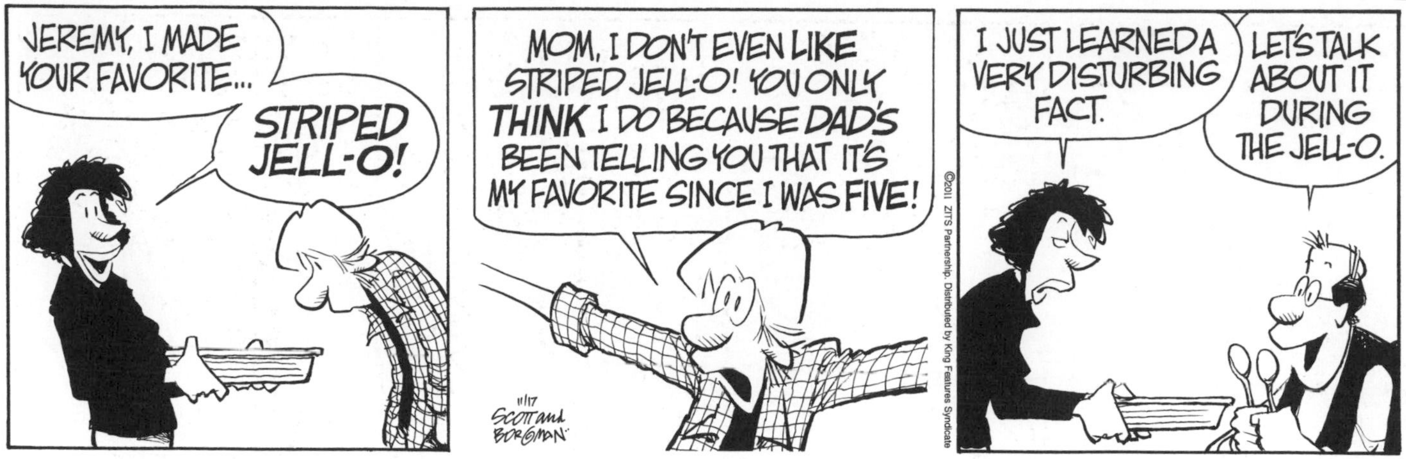
JEREMY, I MADE YOUR FAVORITE...
STRIPED JELL-O!
MOM, I DON'T EVEN LIKE STRIPED JELL-O! YOU ONLY THINK I DO BECAUSE DAD'S BEEN TELLING YOU THAT IT'S MY FAVORITE SINCE I WAS FIVE!
11/17
SCOTT and BORGMAN
I JUST LEARNED A VERY DISTURBING FACT.
LET'S TALK ABOUT IT DURING THE JELL-O.

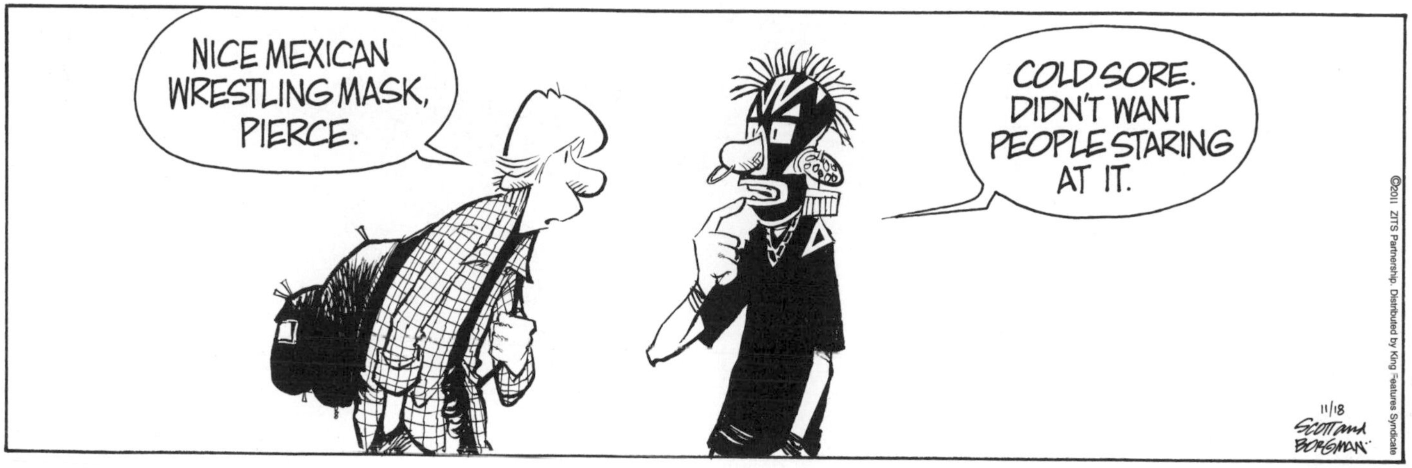
NICE MEXICAN WRESTLING MASK, PIERCE.
COLD SORE. DIDN'T WANT PEOPLE STARING AT IT.
11/18
SCOTT and BORGMAN

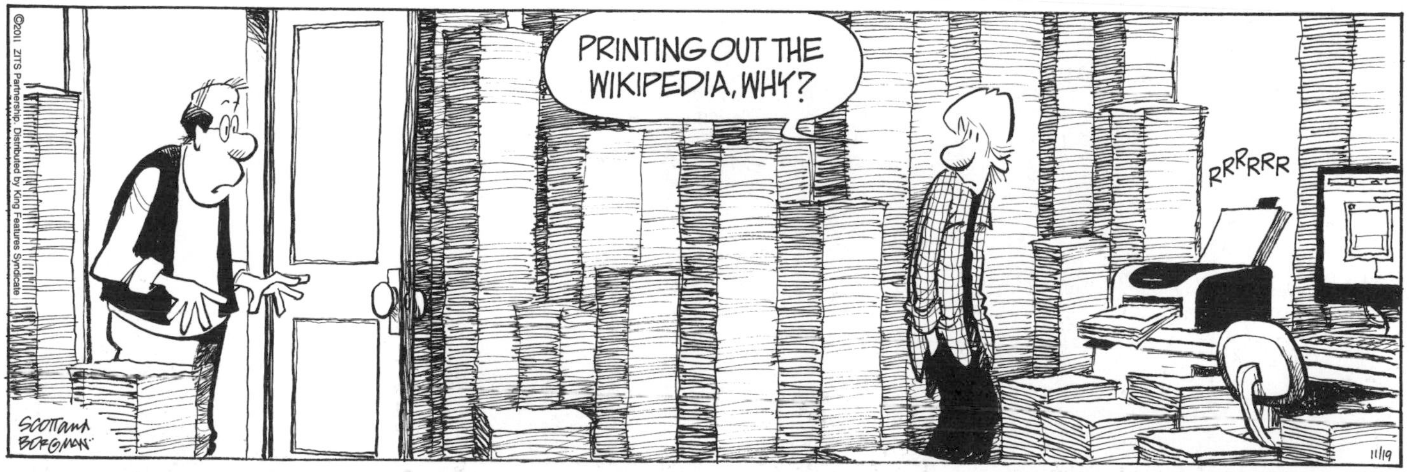
PRINTING OUT THE WIKIPEDIA, WHY?
RRRRRR
SCOTT and BORGMAN
11/19

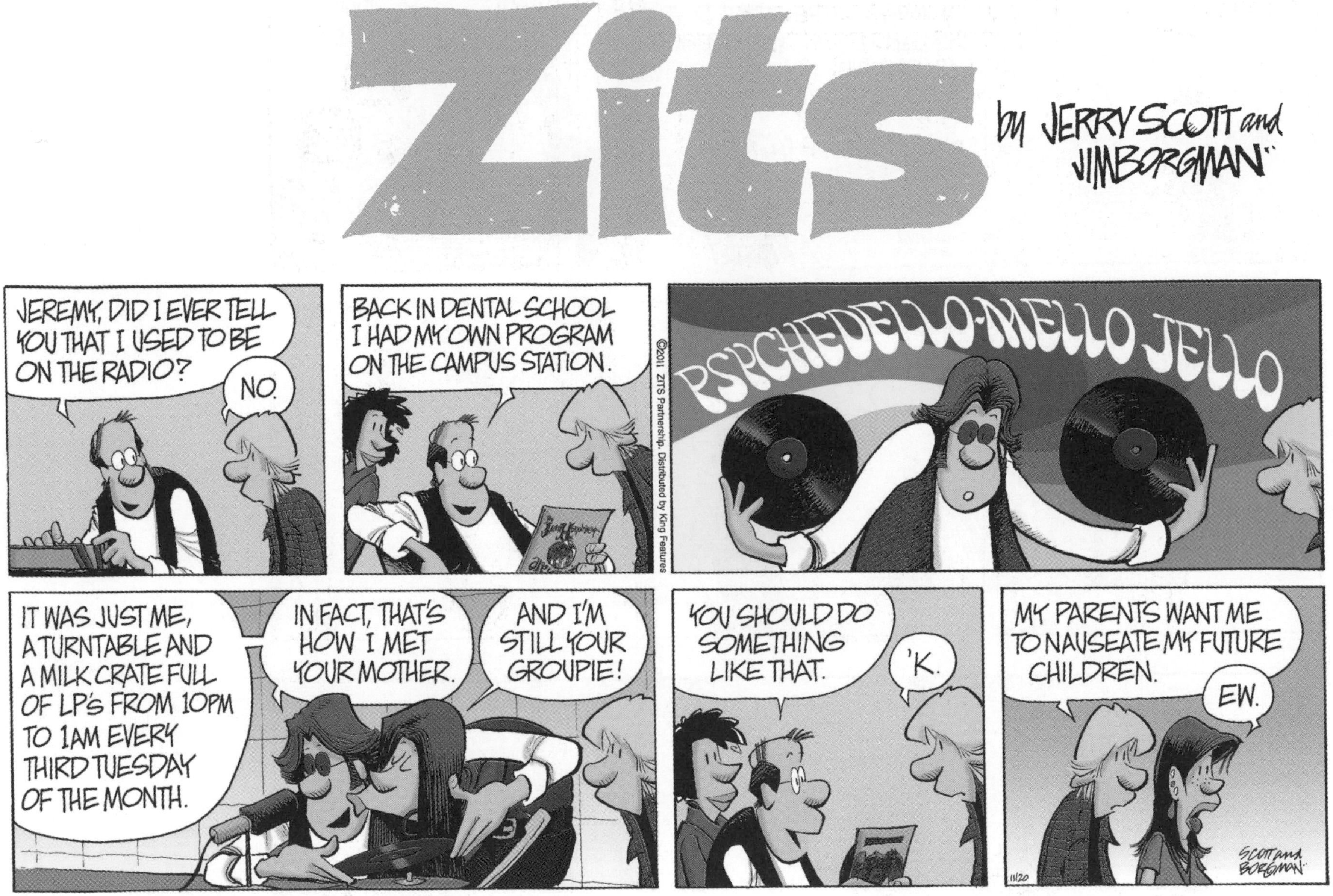

ZITS
by JERRY SCOTT and JIM BORGMAN
JEREMY, DID I EVER TELL YOU THAT I USED TO BE ON THE RADIO?
NO.
BACK IN DENTAL SCHOOL I HAD MY OWN PROGRAM ON THE CAMPUS STATION.
©2011 ZITS Partnership. Distributed by King Features
PSYCHEDELLO-MELLO JELLO
IT WAS JUST ME, A TURNTABLE AND A MILK CRATE FULL OF LP'S FROM 10PM TO 1AM EVERY THIRD TUESDAY OF THE MONTH.
IN FACT, THAT'S HOW I MET YOUR MOTHER.
AND I'M STILL YOUR GROUPIE!
YOU SHOULD DO SOMETHING LIKE THAT.
'K.
MY PARENTS WANT ME TO NAUSEATE MY FUTURE CHILDREN.
EW.
SCOTT and BORGMAN
11/20

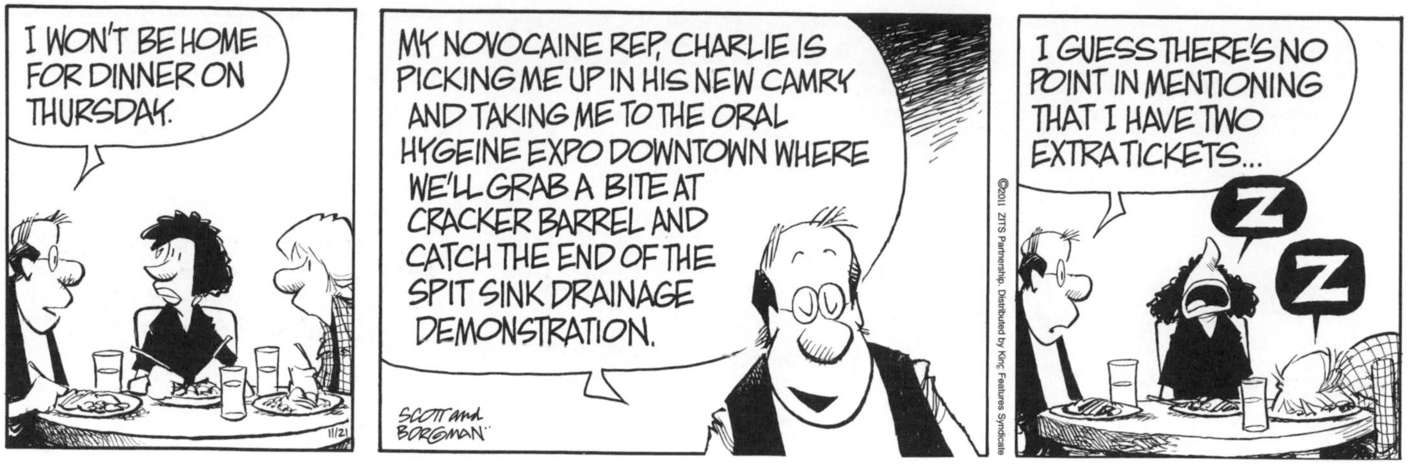
I WON'T BE HOME FOR DINNER ON THURSDAY.
MY NOVOCAINE REP, CHARLIE IS PICKING ME UP IN HIS NEW CAMRY AND TAKING ME TO THE ORAL HYGEINE EXPO DOWNTOWN WHERE WE'LL GRAB A BITE AT CRACKER BARREL AND CATCH THE END OF THE SPIT SINK DRAINAGE DEMONSTRATION.
I GUESS THERE'S NO POINT IN MENTIONING THAT I HAVE TWO EXTRA TICKETS...
Z
Z
©2011 ZITS Partnership. Distributed by King Features Syndicate
SCOTT AND BORGMAN
11/21

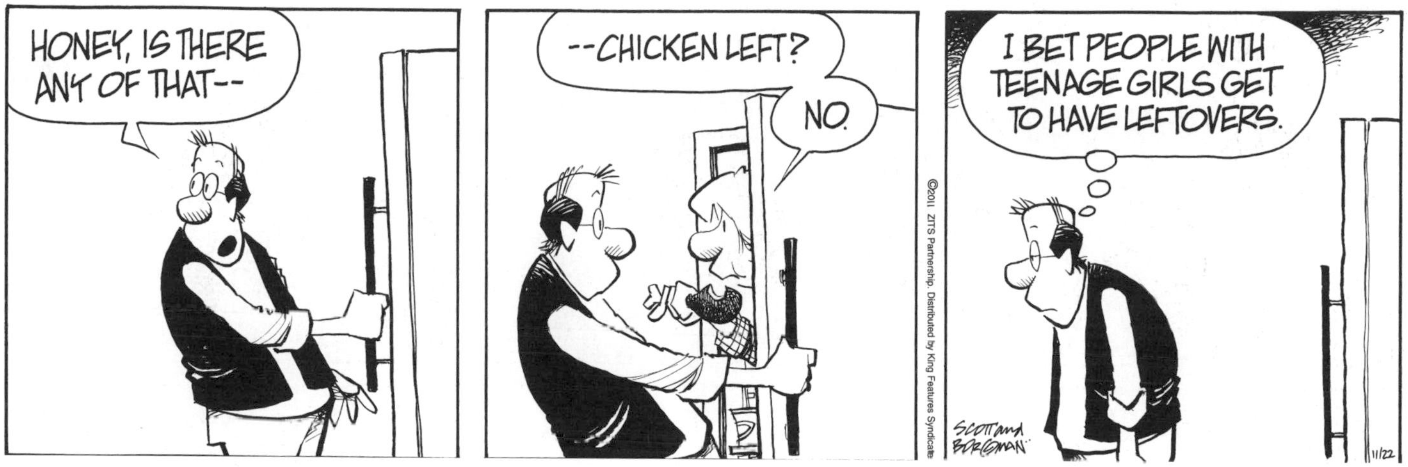
HONEY, IS THERE ANY OF THAT--
--CHICKEN LEFT?
NO.
I BET PEOPLE WITH TEENAGE GIRLS GET TO HAVE LEFTOVERS.
©2011 ZITS Partnership. Distributed by King Features Syndicate
SCOTT AND BORGMAN
11/22

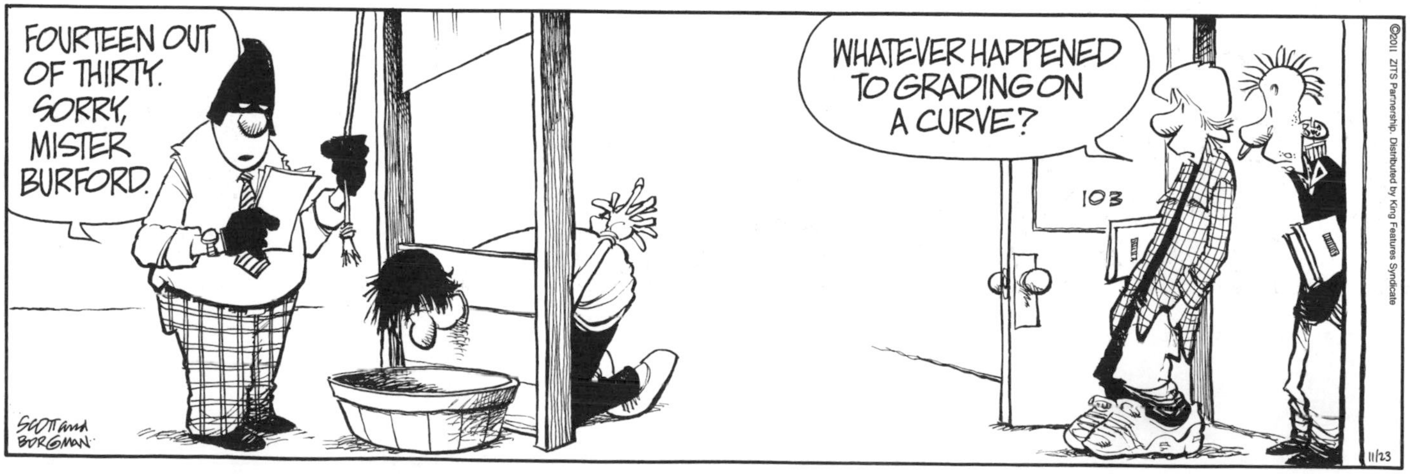
FOURTEEN OUT OF THIRTY. SORRY, MISTER BURFORD.
WHATEVER HAPPENED TO GRADING ON A CURVE?
103
©2011 ZITS Partnership. Distributed by King Features Syndicate
SCOTT AND BORGMAN
11/23

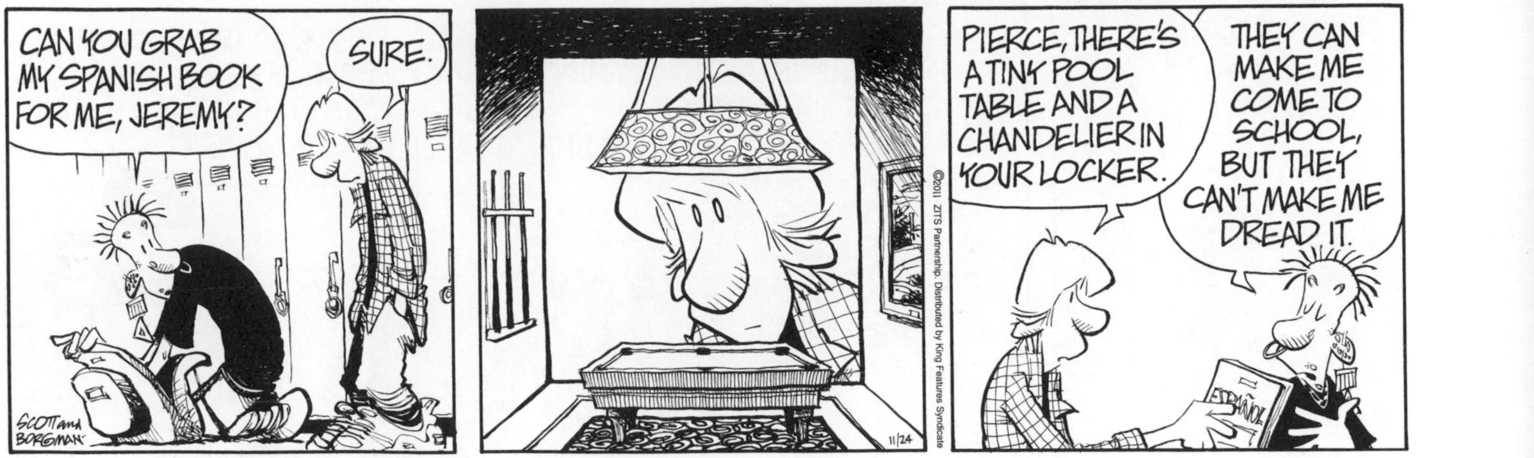
CAN YOU GRAB MY SPANISH BOOK FOR ME, JEREMY?
SURE.
SCOTT and BORGMAN
11/24
©2011 ZITS Partnership. Distributed by King Features Syndicate
PIERCE, THERE'S A TINY POOL TABLE AND A CHANDELIER IN YOUR LOCKER.
THEY CAN MAKE ME COME TO SCHOOL, BUT THEY CAN'T MAKE ME DREAD IT.
ESPAÑOL

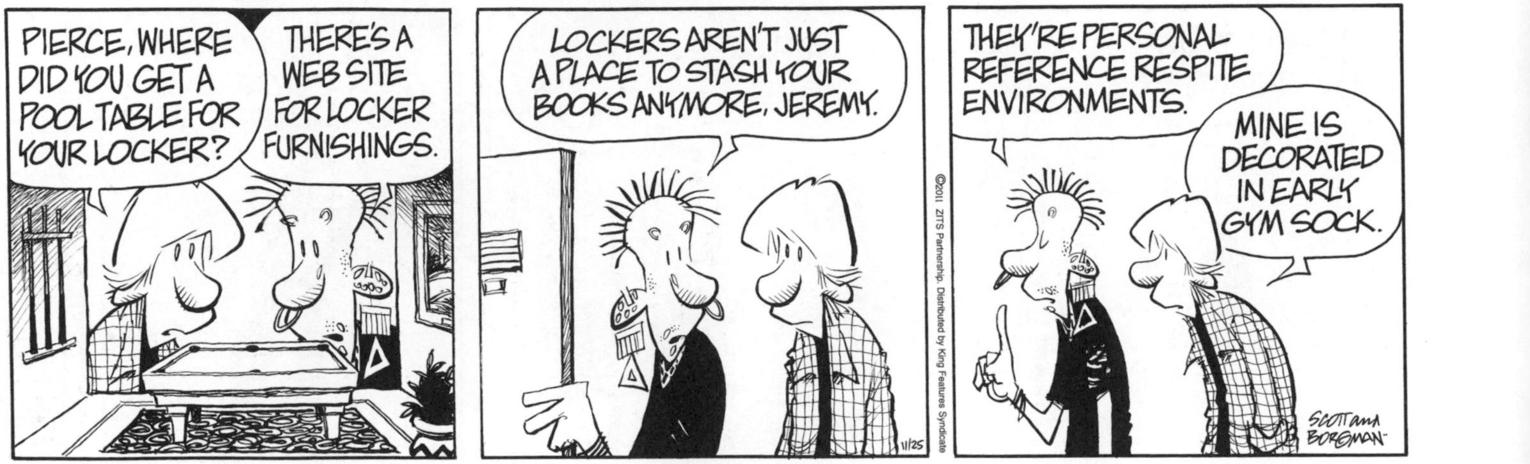
PIERCE, WHERE DID YOU GET A POOL TABLE FOR YOUR LOCKER?
THERE'S A WEB SITE FOR LOCKER FURNISHINGS.
LOCKERS AREN'T JUST A PLACE TO STASH YOUR BOOKS ANYMORE, JEREMY.
11/25
©2011 ZITS Partnership. Distributed by King Features Syndicate
THEY'RE PERSONAL REFERENCE RESPITE ENVIRONMENTS.
MINE IS DECORATED IN EARLY GYM SOCK.
SCOTT and BORGMAN

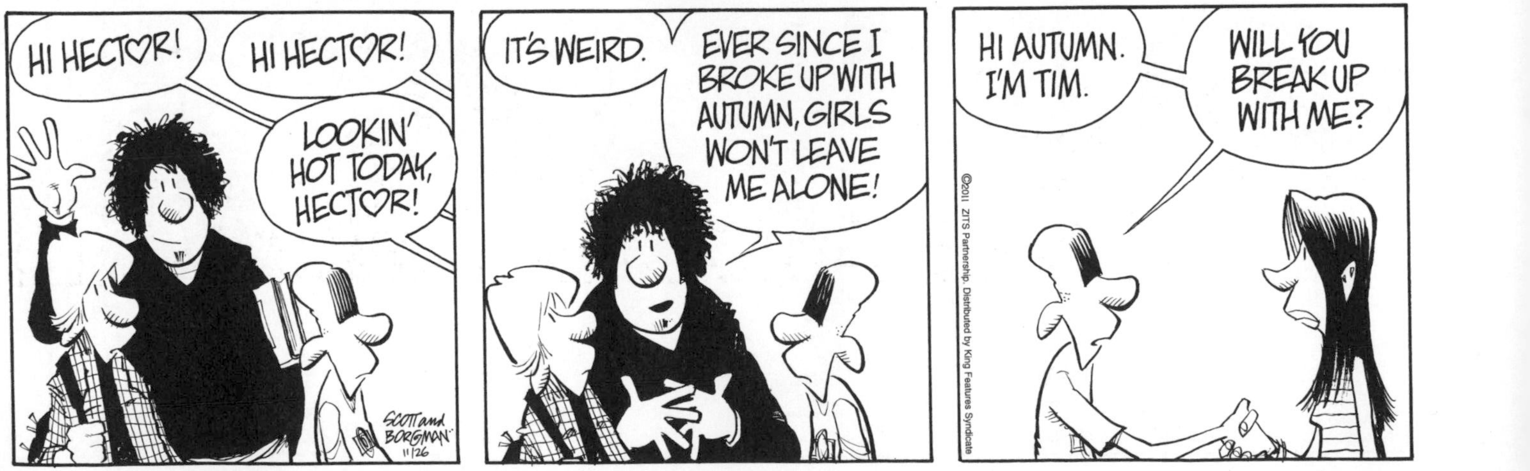
HI HECTOR!
HI HECTOR!
LOOKIN' HOT TODAY, HECTOR!
SCOTT and BORGMAN
11/26
IT'S WEIRD.
EVER SINCE I BROKE UP WITH AUTUMN, GIRLS WON'T LEAVE ME ALONE!
©2011 ZITS Partnership. Distributed by King Features Syndicate
HI AUTUMN. I'M TIM.
WILL YOU BREAK UP WITH ME?

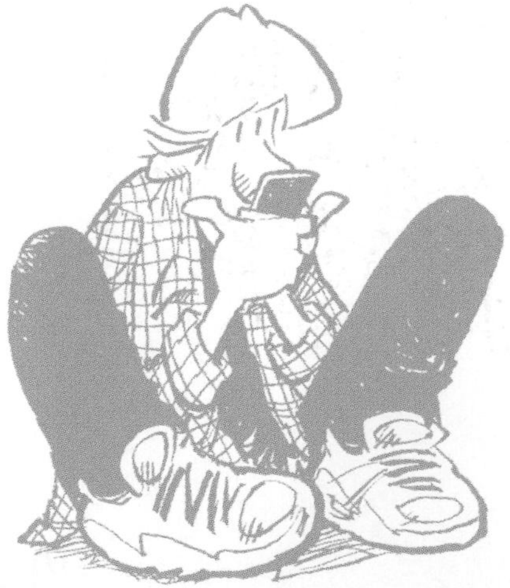

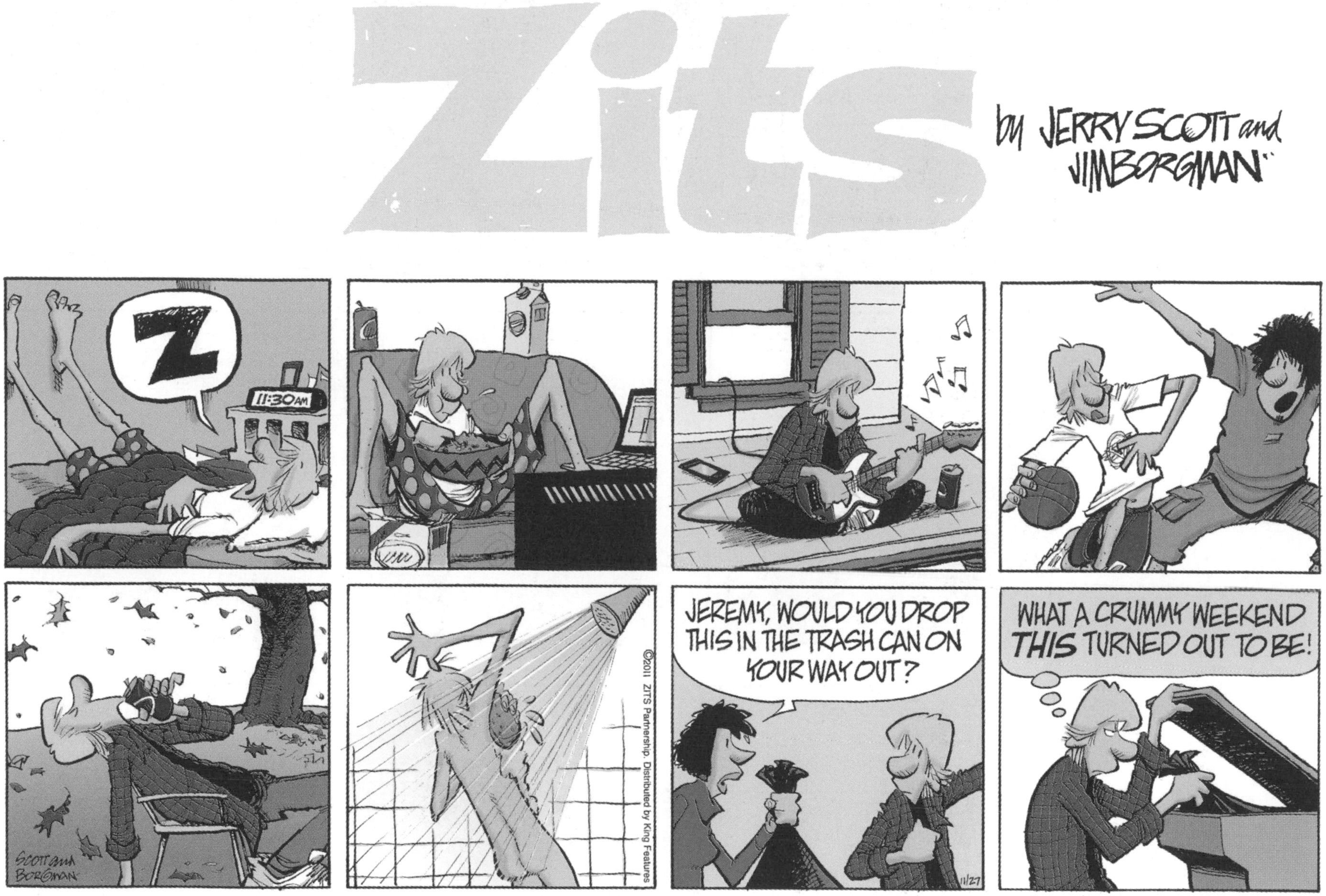
Zits
by JERRY SCOTT and JIM BORGMAN
Z
11:30 AM
SCOTT and BORGMAN
©2011 ZITS Partnership. Distributed by King Features
JEREMY, WOULD YOU DROP THIS IN THE TRASH CAN ON YOUR WAY OUT?
11/27
WHAT A CRUMMY WEEKEND THIS TURNED OUT TO BE!

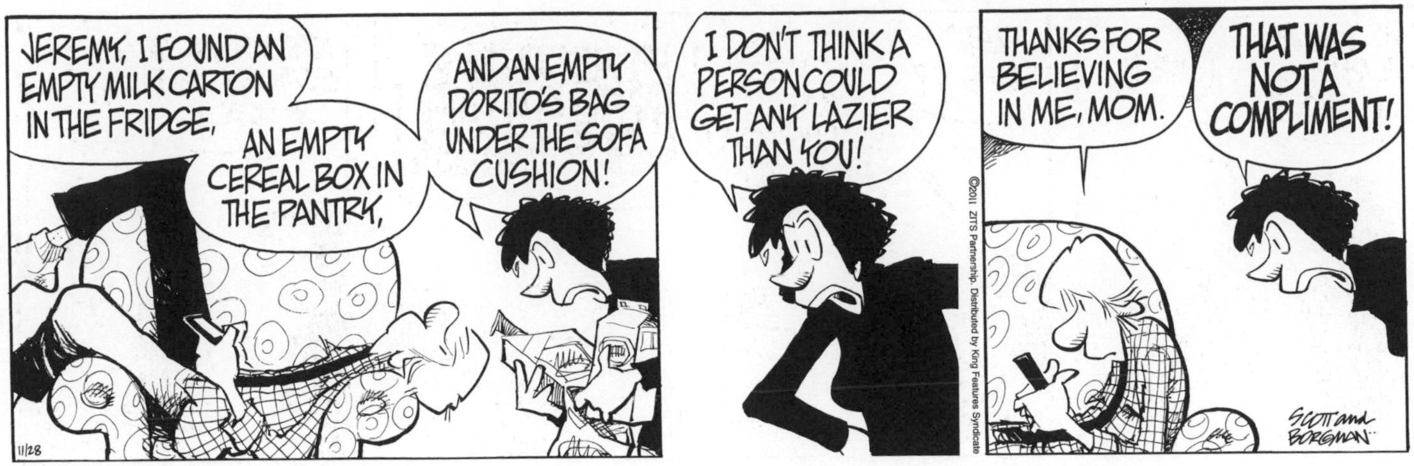
JEREMY, I FOUND AN EMPTY MILK CARTON IN THE FRIDGE,
AN EMPTY CEREAL BOX IN THE PANTRY,
AND AN EMPTY DORITO'S BAG UNDER THE SOFA CUSHION!
I DON'T THINK A PERSON COULD GET ANY LAZIER THAN YOU!
THANKS FOR BELIEVING IN ME, MOM.
THAT WAS NOT A COMPLIMENT!
11/28
©2011 ZITS Partnership. Distributed by King Features Syndicate
SCOTT and BORGMAN

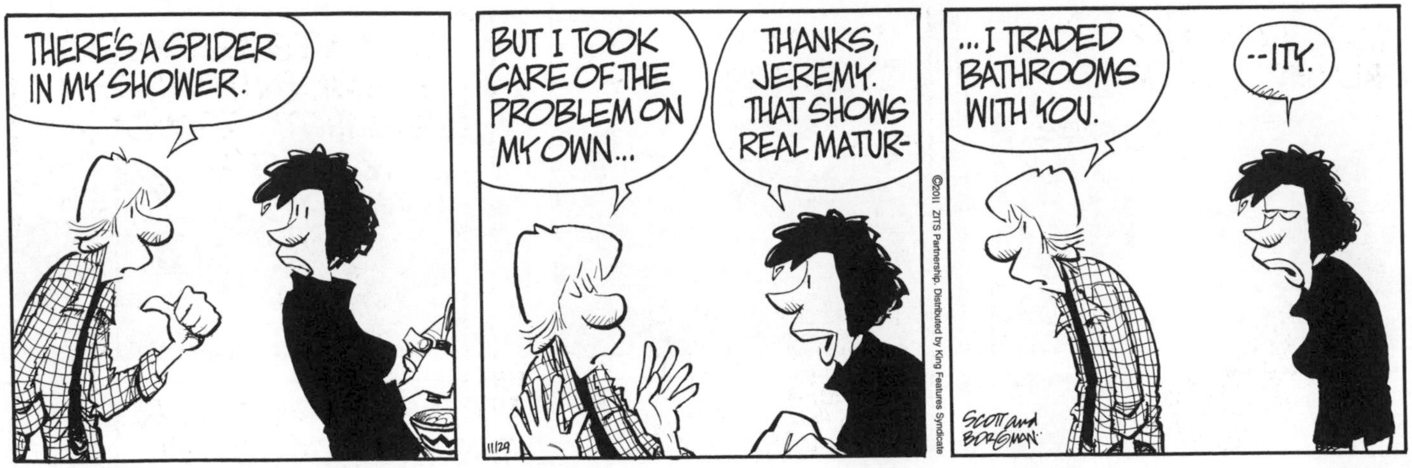
THERE'S A SPIDER IN MY SHOWER.
BUT I TOOK CARE OF THE PROBLEM ON MY OWN...
THANKS, JEREMY. THAT SHOWS REAL MATUR-
...I TRADED BATHROOMS WITH YOU.
--ITY.
11/29
©2011 ZITS Partnership. Distributed by King Features Syndicate
SCOTT and BORGMAN

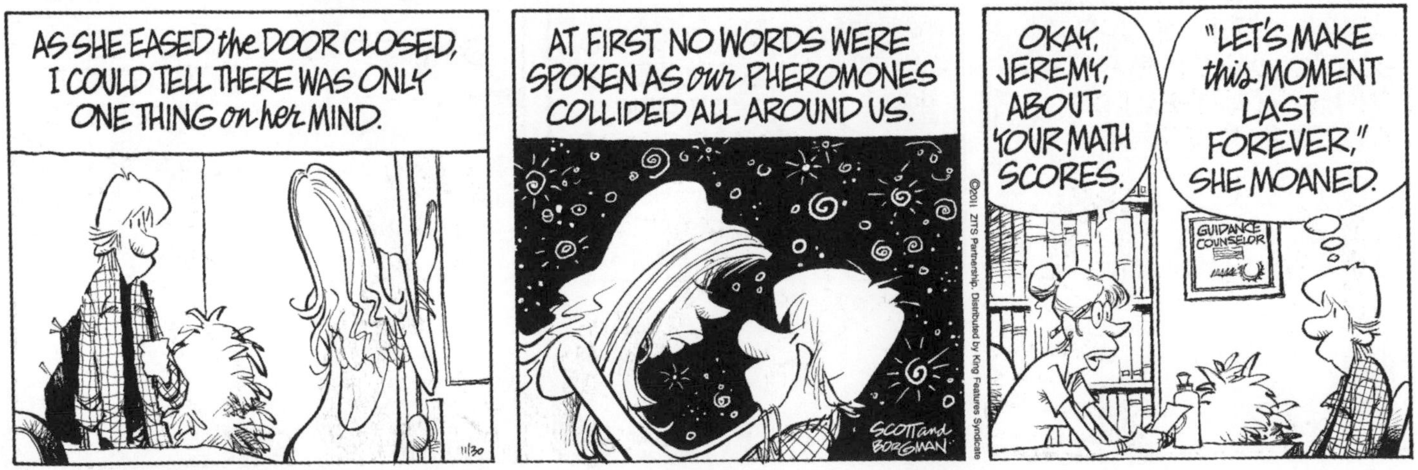
AS SHE EASED the DOOR CLOSED, I COULD TELL THERE WAS ONLY ONE THING on her MIND.
11/30
AT FIRST NO WORDS WERE SPOKEN AS our PHEROMONES COLLIDED ALL AROUND US.
SCOTT and BORGMAN
OKAY, JEREMY, ABOUT YOUR MATH SCORES.
"LET'S MAKE this MOMENT LAST FOREVER," SHE MOANED.
GUIDANCE COUNSELOR
©2011 ZITS Partnership. Distributed by King Features Syndicate

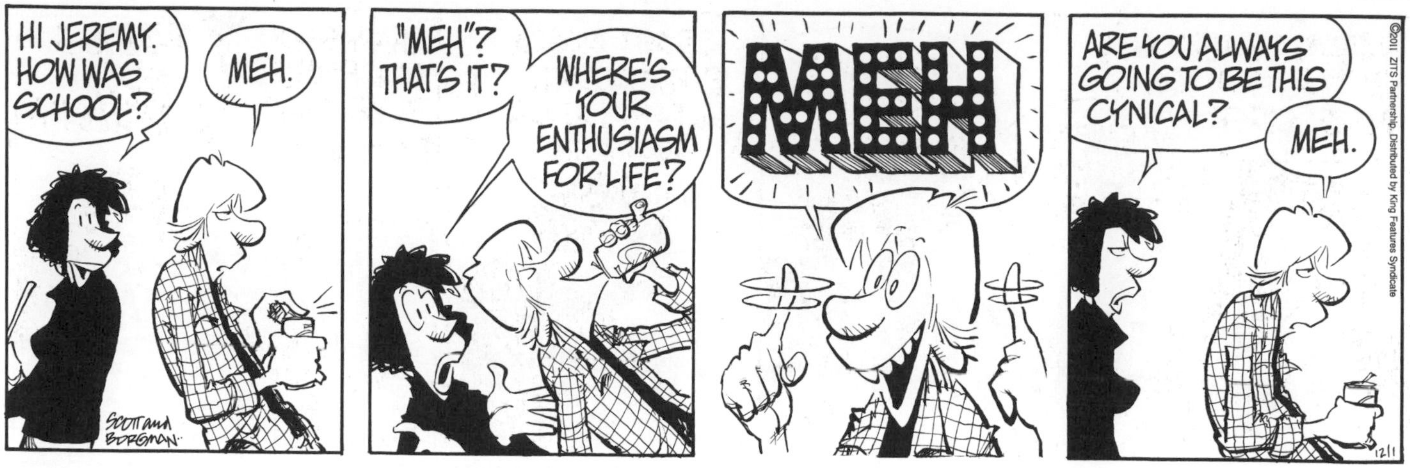
HI JEREMY. HOW WAS SCHOOL?
MEH.
SCOTT and BORGMAN
"MEH"? THAT'S IT?
WHERE'S YOUR ENTHUSIASM FOR LIFE?
MEH
ARE YOU ALWAYS GOING TO BE THIS CYNICAL?
MEH.
©2011 ZITS Partnership. Distributed by King Features Syndicate
12/1

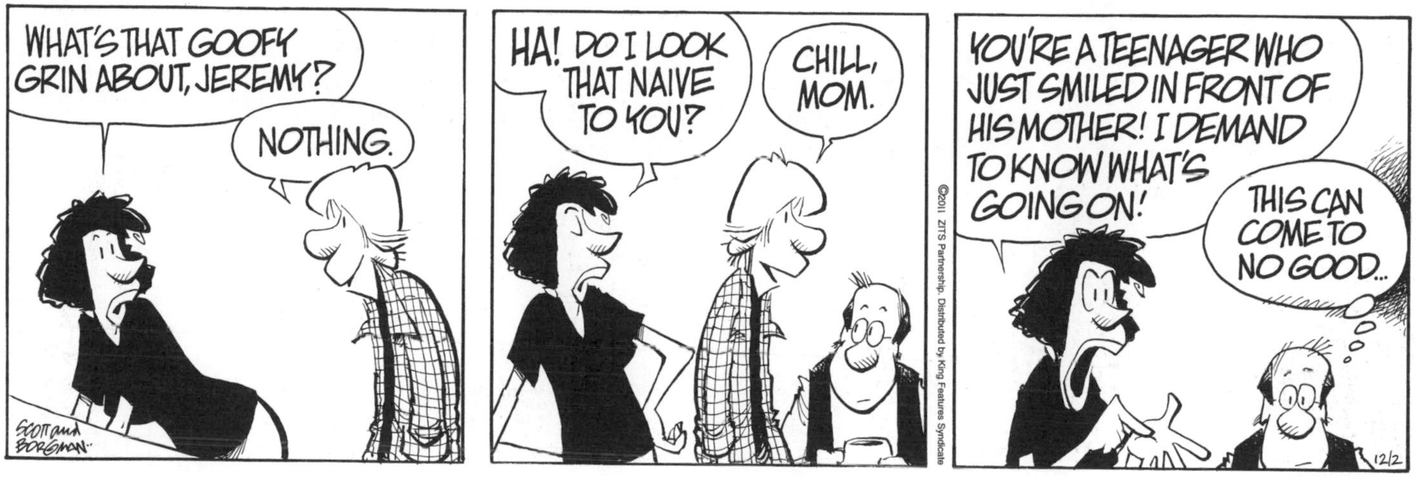
WHAT'S THAT GOOFY GRIN ABOUT, JEREMY?
NOTHING.
SCOTT and BORGMAN
HA! DO I LOOK THAT NAIVE TO YOU?
CHILL, MOM.
©2011 ZITS Partnership. Distributed by King Features Syndicate
YOU'RE A TEENAGER WHO JUST SMILED IN FRONT OF HIS MOTHER! I DEMAND TO KNOW WHAT'S GOING ON!
THIS CAN COME TO NO GOOD...
12/2

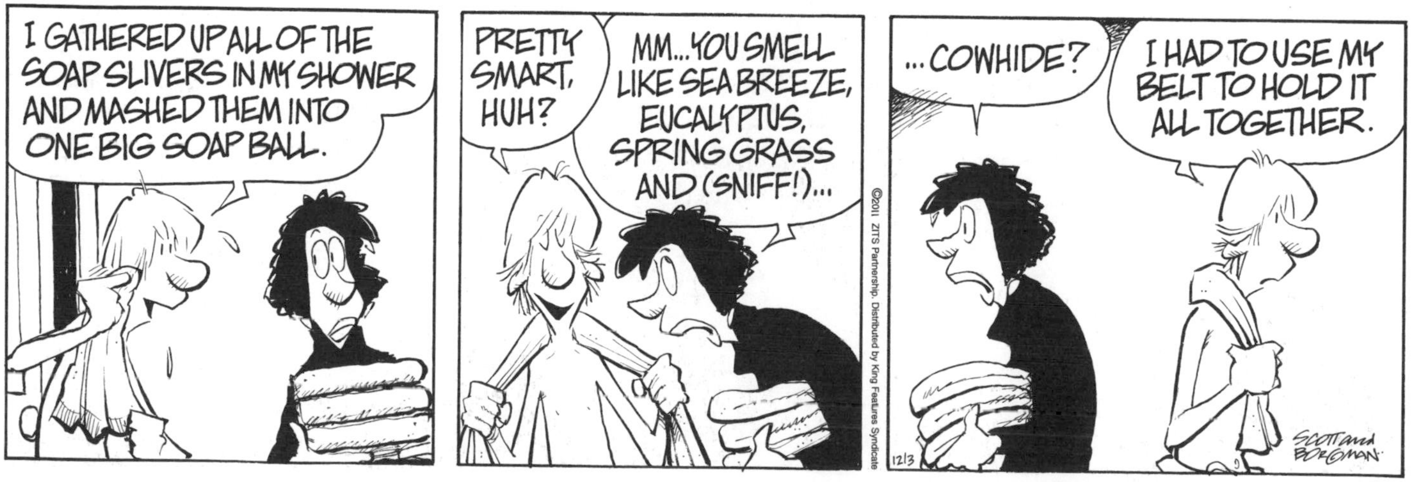
I GATHERED UP ALL OF THE SOAP SLIVERS IN MY SHOWER AND MASHED THEM INTO ONE BIG SOAP BALL.
PRETTY SMART, HUH?
MM... YOU SMELL LIKE SEA BREEZE, EUCALYPTUS, SPRING GRASS AND (SNIFF!)...
©2011 ZITS Partnership. Distributed by King Features Syndicate
12/3
...COWHIDE?
I HAD TO USE MY BELT TO HOLD IT ALL TOGETHER.
SCOTT and BORGMAN

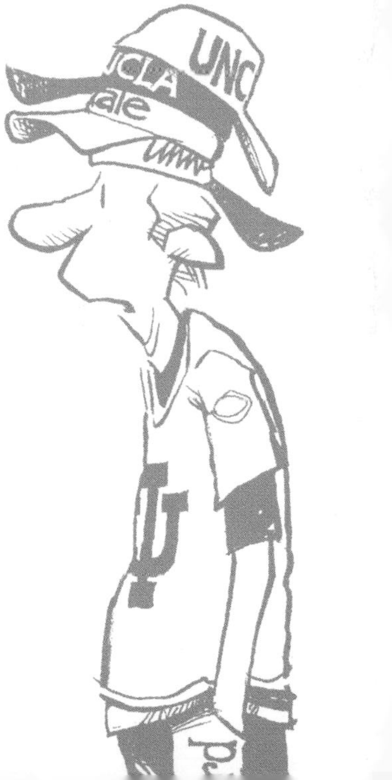
UNC
UCLA
Yale

Zits

by JERRY SCOTT and JIM BORGMAN

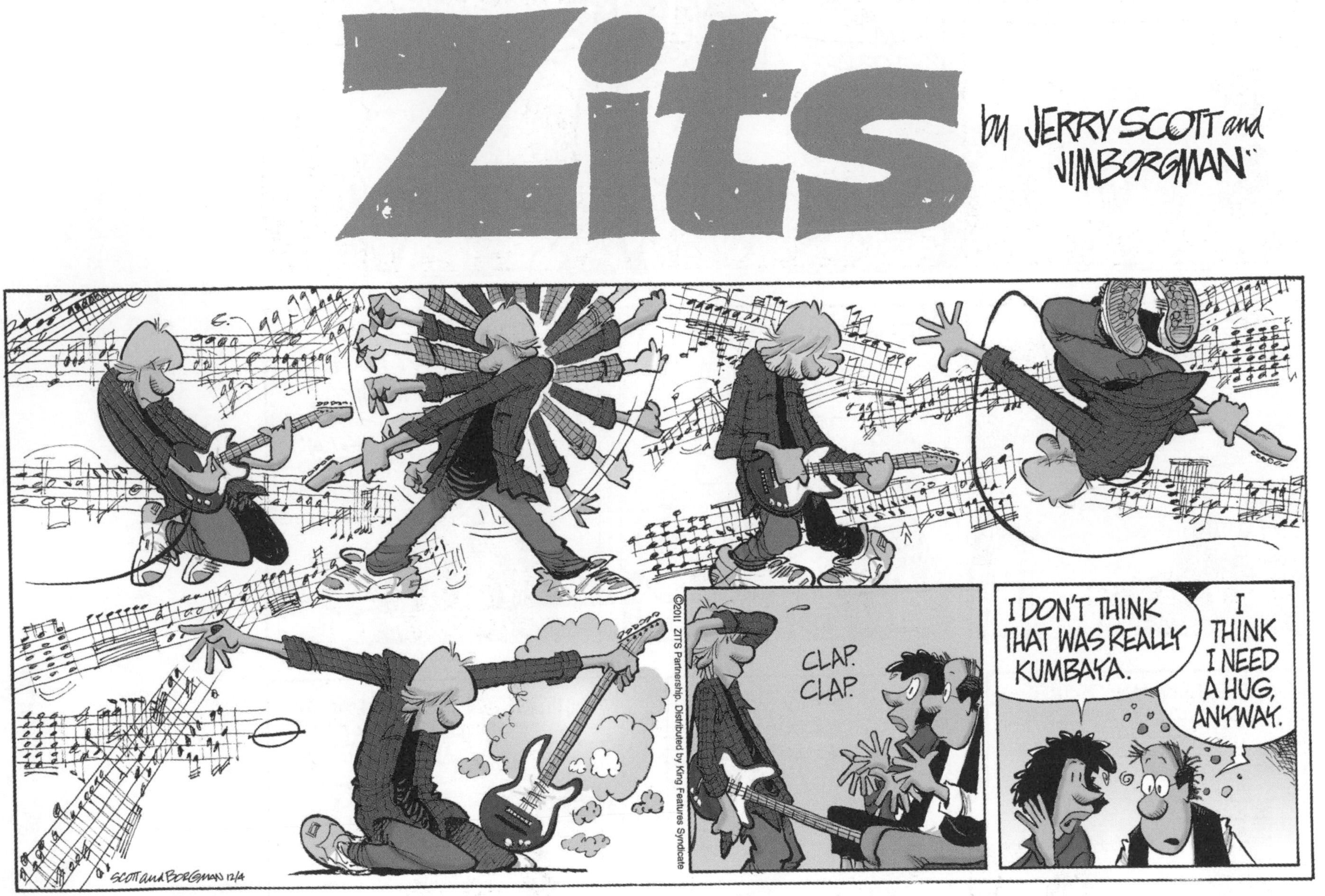

SCOTT and BORGMAN 12/4
©2011 ZITS Partnership. Distributed by King Features Syndicate
CLAP. CLAP.
I DON'T THINK THAT WAS REALLY KUMBAYA.
I THINK I NEED A HUG, ANYWAY.

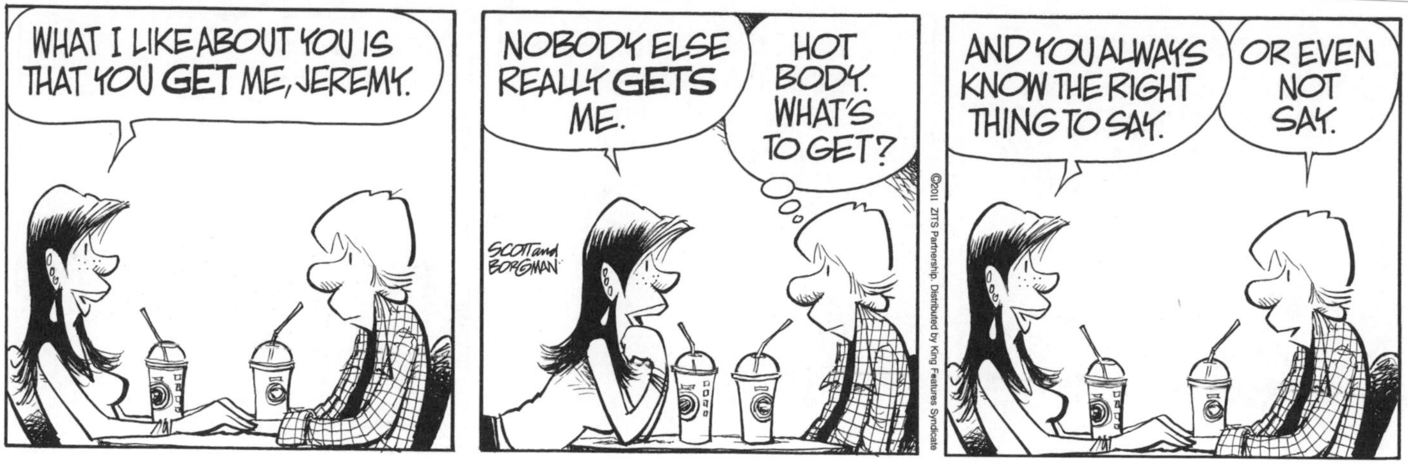
WHAT I LIKE ABOUT YOU IS THAT YOU **GET** ME, JEREMY.
NOBODY ELSE REALLY **GETS** ME.
HOT BODY. WHAT'S TO GET?
SCOTT and BORGMAN
©2011 ZITS Partnership. Distributed by King Features Syndicate
AND YOU ALWAYS KNOW THE RIGHT THING TO SAY.
OR EVEN NOT SAY.

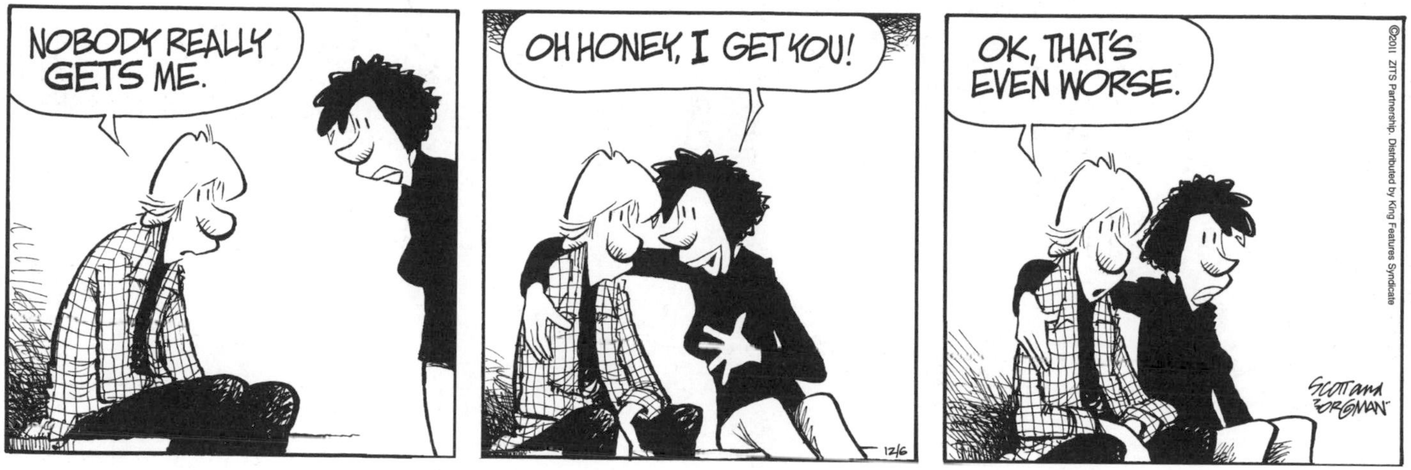
NOBODY REALLY **GETS** ME.
OH HONEY, **I** GET YOU!
12/6
OK, THAT'S EVEN WORSE.
©2011 ZITS Partnership. Distributed by King Features Syndicate
SCOTT and BORGMAN

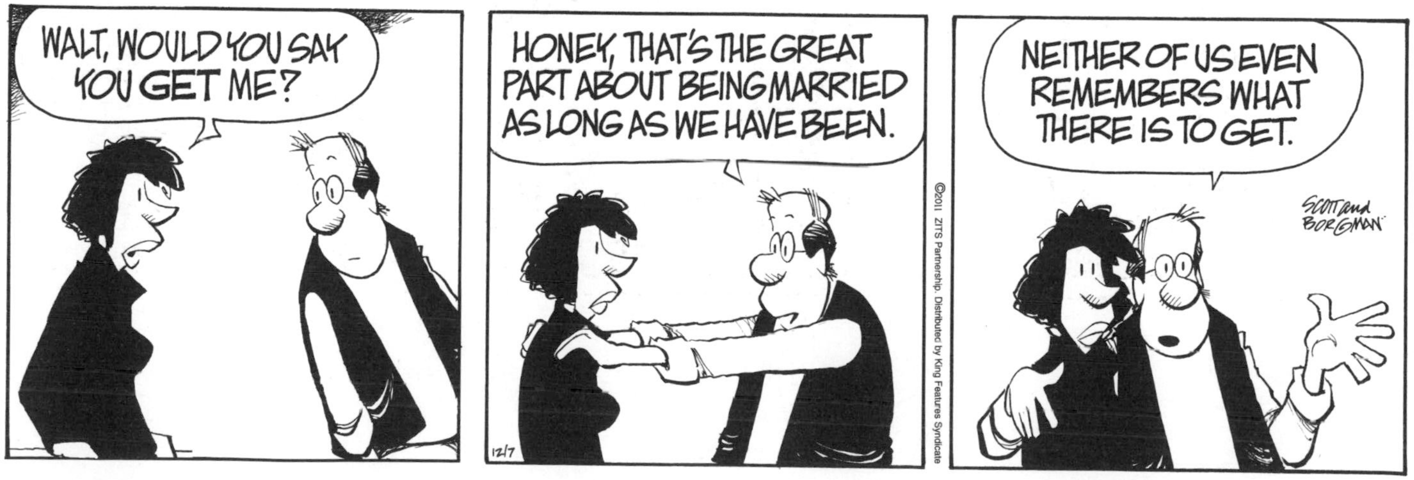
WALT, WOULD YOU SAY YOU **GET** ME?
HONEY, THAT'S THE GREAT PART ABOUT BEING MARRIED AS LONG AS WE HAVE BEEN.
12/7
©2011 ZITS Partnership. Distributed by King Features Syndicate
NEITHER OF US EVEN REMEMBERS WHAT THERE IS TO GET.
SCOTT and BORGMAN

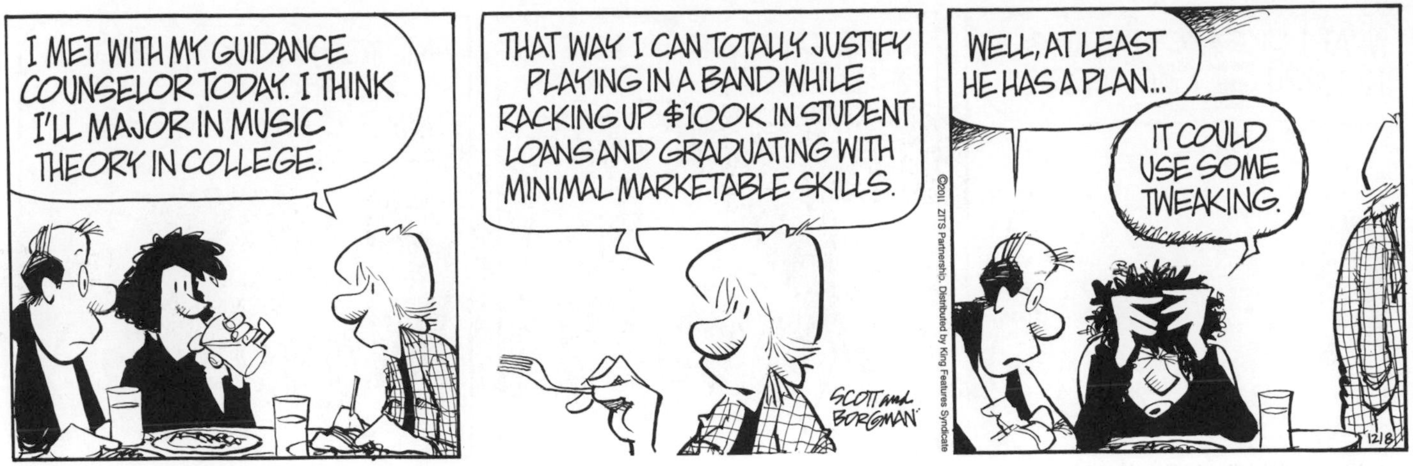
I MET WITH MY GUIDANCE COUNSELOR TODAY. I THINK I'LL MAJOR IN MUSIC THEORY IN COLLEGE.
THAT WAY I CAN TOTALLY JUSTIFY PLAYING IN A BAND WHILE RACKING UP $100K IN STUDENT LOANS AND GRADUATING WITH MINIMAL MARKETABLE SKILLS.
SCOTT and BORGMAN
©2011 ZITS Partnership. Distributed by King Features Syndicate
WELL, AT LEAST HE HAS A PLAN...
IT COULD USE SOME TWEAKING.
12/8

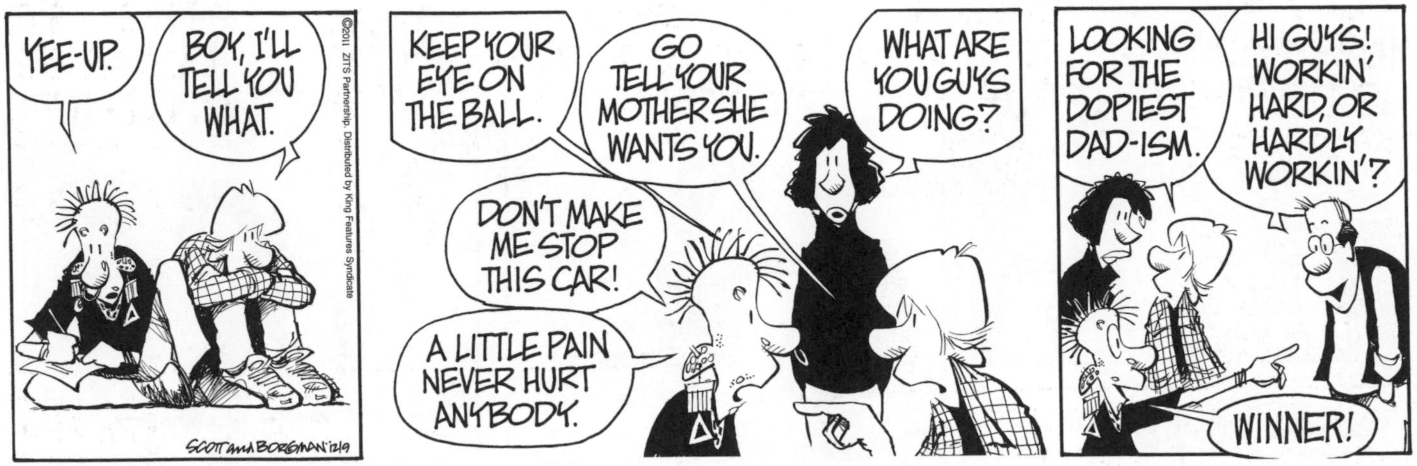
YEE-UP.
BOY, I'LL TELL YOU WHAT.
SCOTT and BORGMAN 12/9
©2011 ZITS Partnership. Distributed by King Features Syndicate
KEEP YOUR EYE ON THE BALL.
GO TELL YOUR MOTHER SHE WANTS YOU.
WHAT ARE YOU GUYS DOING?
DON'T MAKE ME STOP THIS CAR!
A LITTLE PAIN NEVER HURT ANYBODY.
LOOKING FOR THE DOPIEST DAD-ISM.
HI GUYS! WORKIN' HARD, OR HARDLY WORKIN'?
WINNER!

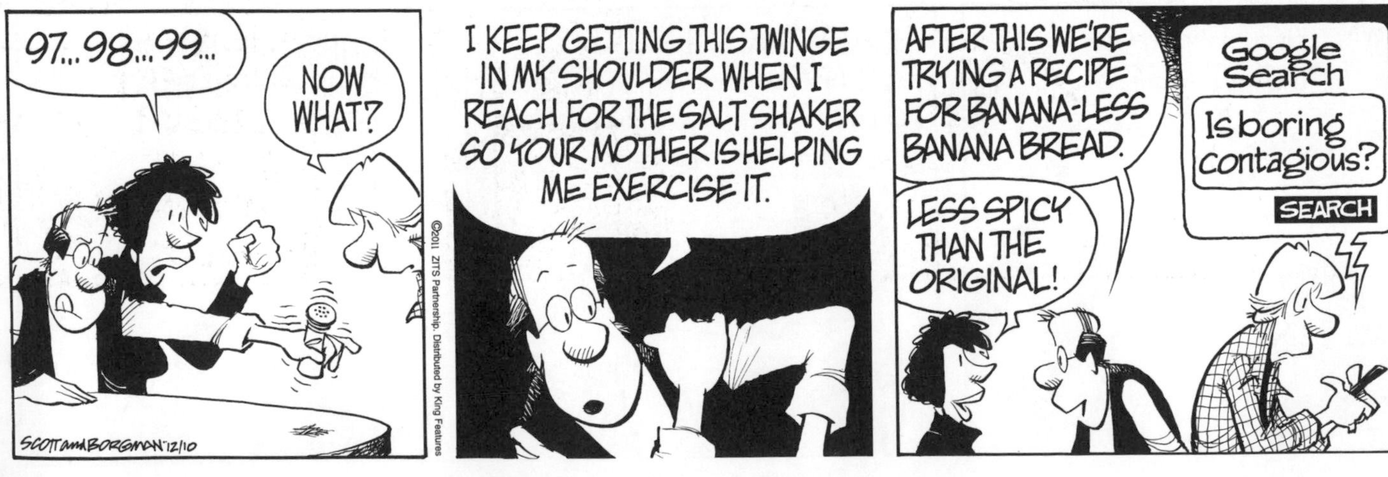
97...98...99...
NOW WHAT?
SCOTT and BORGMAN 12/10
©2011 ZITS Partnership. Distributed by King Features
I KEEP GETTING THIS TWINGE IN MY SHOULDER WHEN I REACH FOR THE SALT SHAKER SO YOUR MOTHER IS HELPING ME EXERCISE IT.
AFTER THIS WE'RE TRYING A RECIPE FOR BANANA-LESS BANANA BREAD.
LESS SPICY THAN THE ORIGINAL!
Google Search
Is boring contagious?
SEARCH

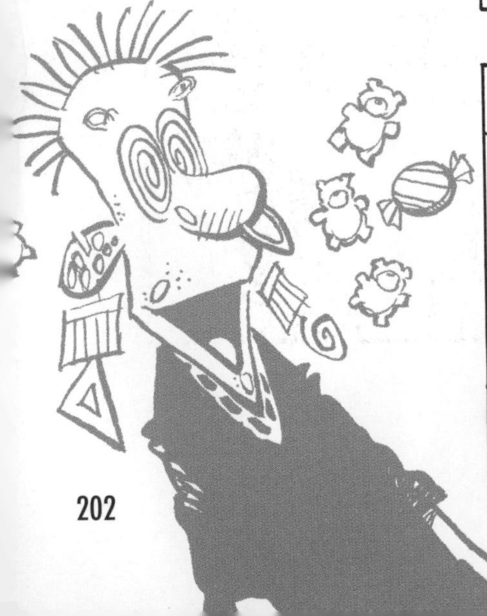

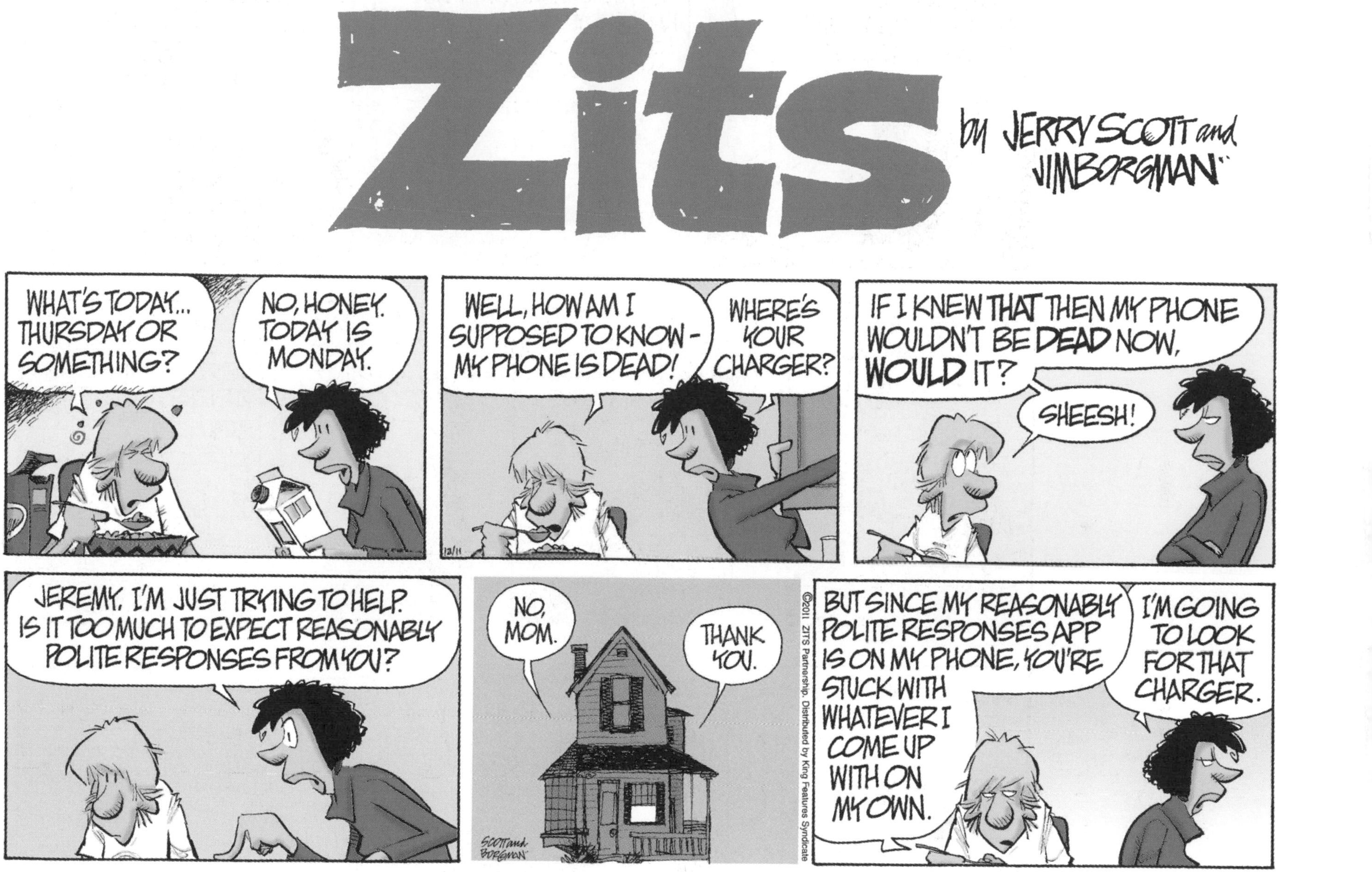
Zits
by JERRY SCOTT and JIM BORGMAN
WHAT'S TODAY... THURSDAY OR SOMETHING?
NO, HONEY. TODAY IS MONDAY.
WELL, HOW AM I SUPPOSED TO KNOW - MY PHONE IS DEAD!
WHERE'S YOUR CHARGER?
12/11
IF I KNEW THAT THEN MY PHONE WOULDN'T BE DEAD NOW, WOULD IT?
SHEESH!
JEREMY, I'M JUST TRYING TO HELP. IS IT TOO MUCH TO EXPECT REASONABLY POLITE RESPONSES FROM YOU?
NO, MOM.
THANK YOU.
SCOTT and BORGMAN
©2011 ZITS Partnership. Distributed by King Features Syndicate
BUT SINCE MY REASONABLY POLITE RESPONSES APP IS ON MY PHONE, YOU'RE STUCK WITH WHATEVER I COME UP WITH ON MY OWN.
I'M GOING TO LOOK FOR THAT CHARGER.

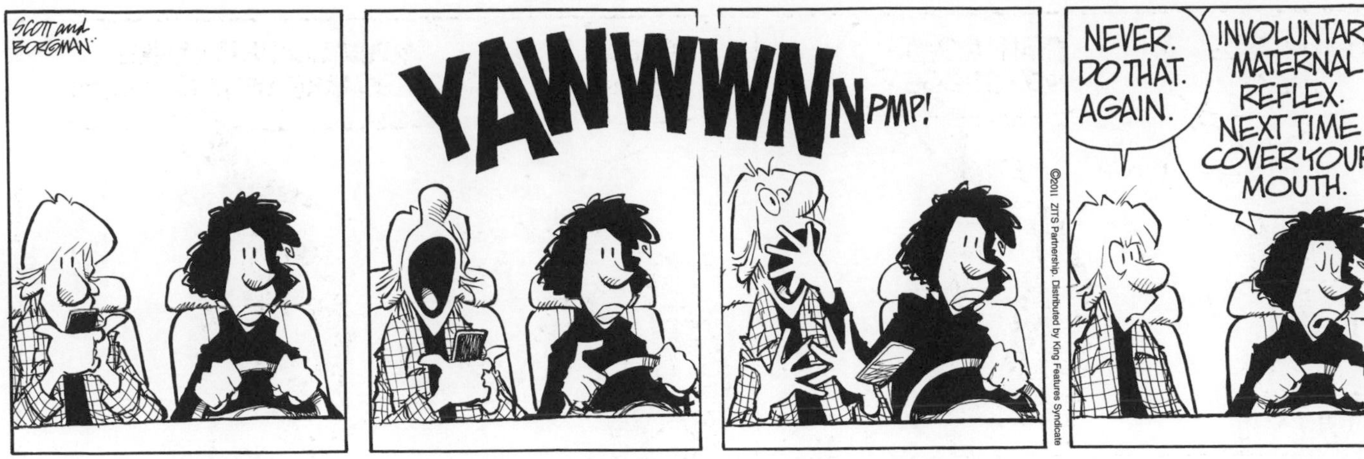
SCOTT and BORGMAN
YAWWWNN PMP!
NEVER. DO THAT. AGAIN.
INVOLUNTARY MATERNAL REFLEX. NEXT TIME COVER YOUR MOUTH.
©2011 ZITS Partnership. Distributed by King Features Syndicate

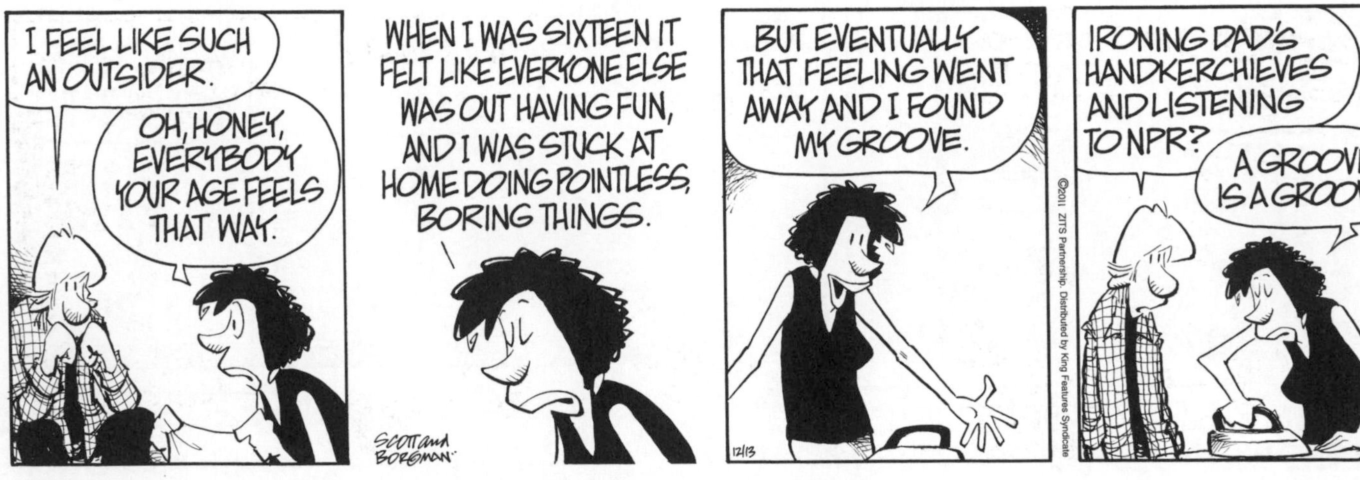
I FEEL LIKE SUCH AN OUTSIDER.
OH, HONEY, EVERYBODY YOUR AGE FEELS THAT WAY.
WHEN I WAS SIXTEEN IT FELT LIKE EVERYONE ELSE WAS OUT HAVING FUN, AND I WAS STUCK AT HOME DOING POINTLESS, BORING THINGS.
SCOTT and BORGMAN
BUT EVENTUALLY THAT FEELING WENT AWAY AND I FOUND MY GROOVE.
12/13
IRONING DAD'S HANDKERCHIEVES AND LISTENING TO NPR?
A GROOVE IS A GROOVE.
©2011 ZITS Partnership. Distributed by King Features Syndicate

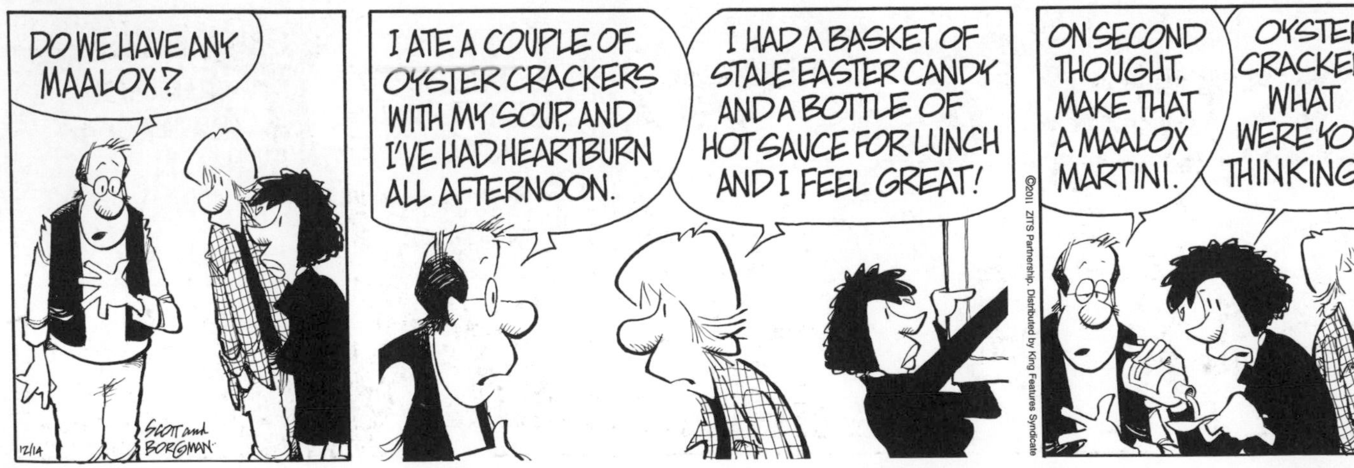
DO WE HAVE ANY MAALOX?
12/14
SCOTT and BORGMAN
I ATE A COUPLE OF OYSTER CRACKERS WITH MY SOUP, AND I'VE HAD HEARTBURN ALL AFTERNOON.
I HAD A BASKET OF STALE EASTER CANDY AND A BOTTLE OF HOT SAUCE FOR LUNCH AND I FEEL GREAT!
ON SECOND THOUGHT, MAKE THAT A MAALOX MARTINI.
OYSTER CRACKERS! WHAT WERE YOU THINKING??
©2011 ZITS Partnership. Distributed by King Features Syndicate

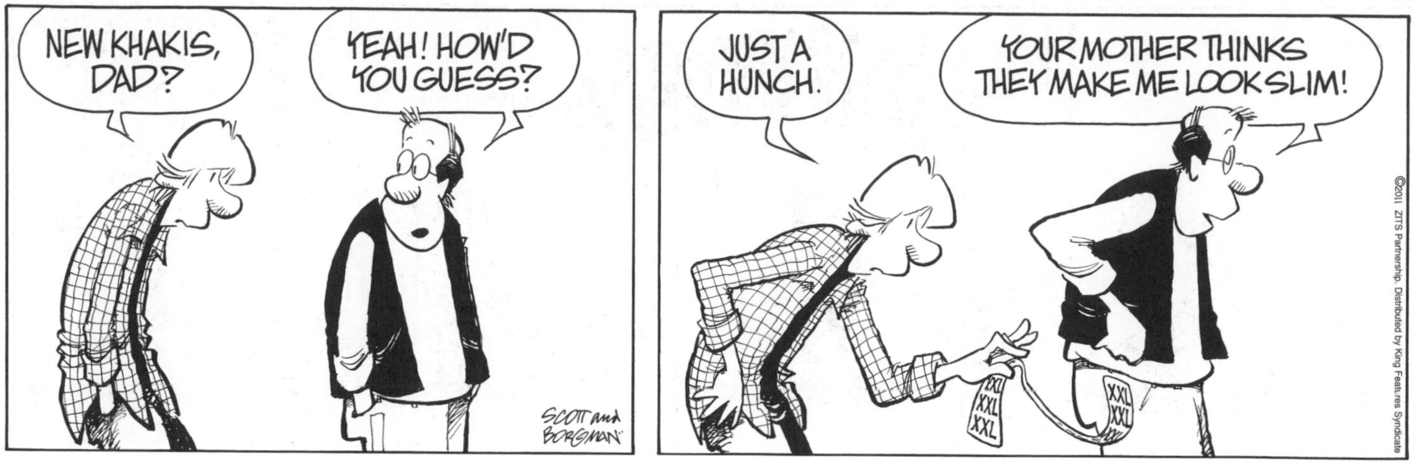
NEW KHAKIS, DAD?
YEAH! HOW'D YOU GUESS?
JUST A HUNCH.
YOUR MOTHER THINKS THEY MAKE ME LOOK SLIM!
XXL XXL XXL
XXL XXL XXL
SCOTT and BORGMAN
©2011 ZITS Partnership. Distributed by King Features Syndicate

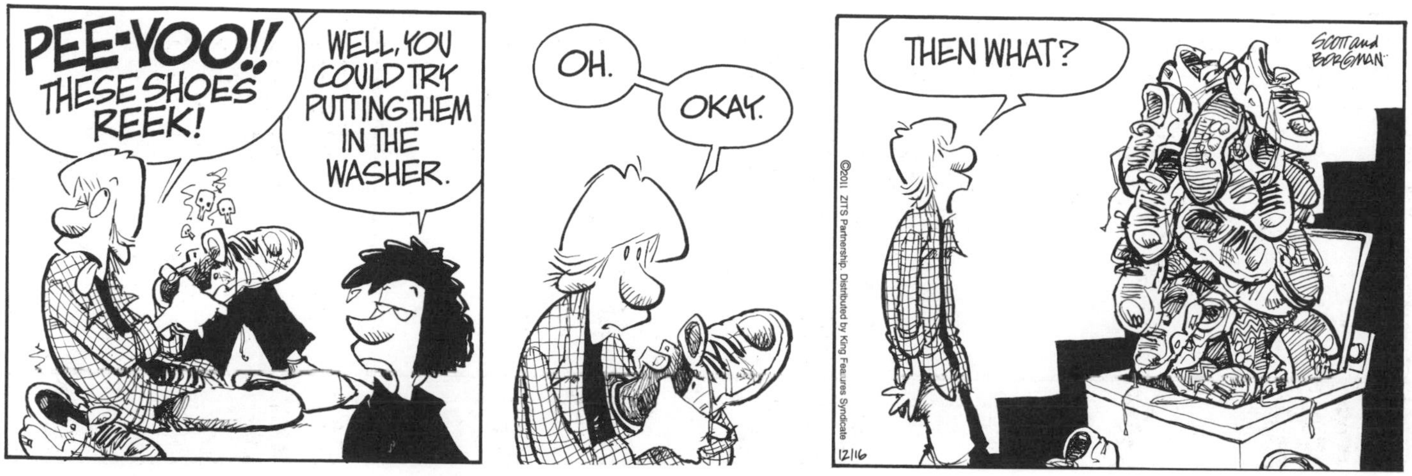
PEE-YOO!! THESE SHOES REEK!
WELL, YOU COULD TRY PUTTING THEM IN THE WASHER.
OH.
OKAY.
THEN WHAT?
SCOTT and BORGMAN
©2011 ZITS Partnership. Distributed by King Features Syndicate
12/16

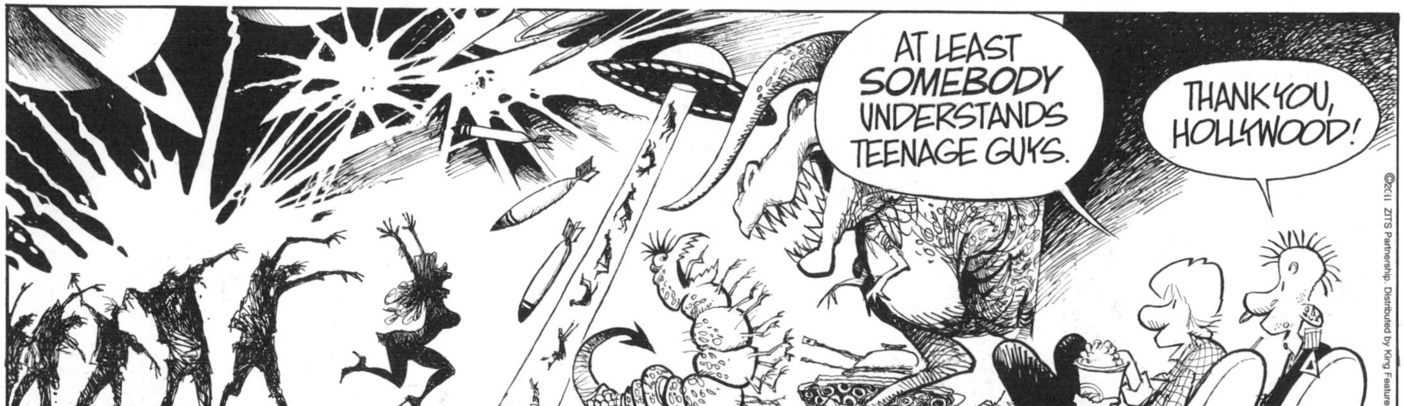
AT LEAST SOMEBODY UNDERSTANDS TEENAGE GUYS.
THANK YOU, HOLLYWOOD!
SCOTT and BORGMAN
©2011 ZITS Partnership. Distributed by King Features Syndicate

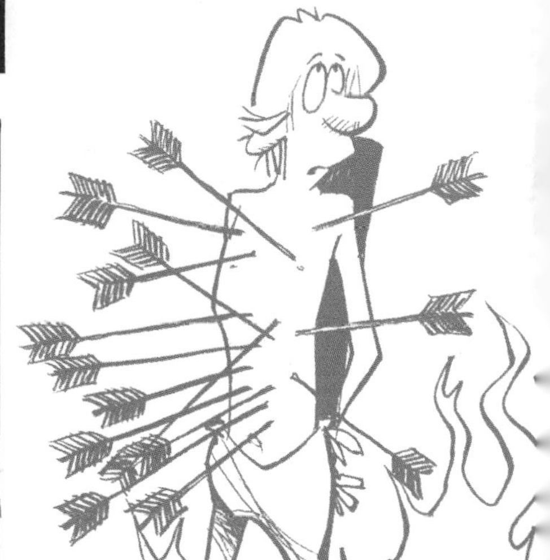

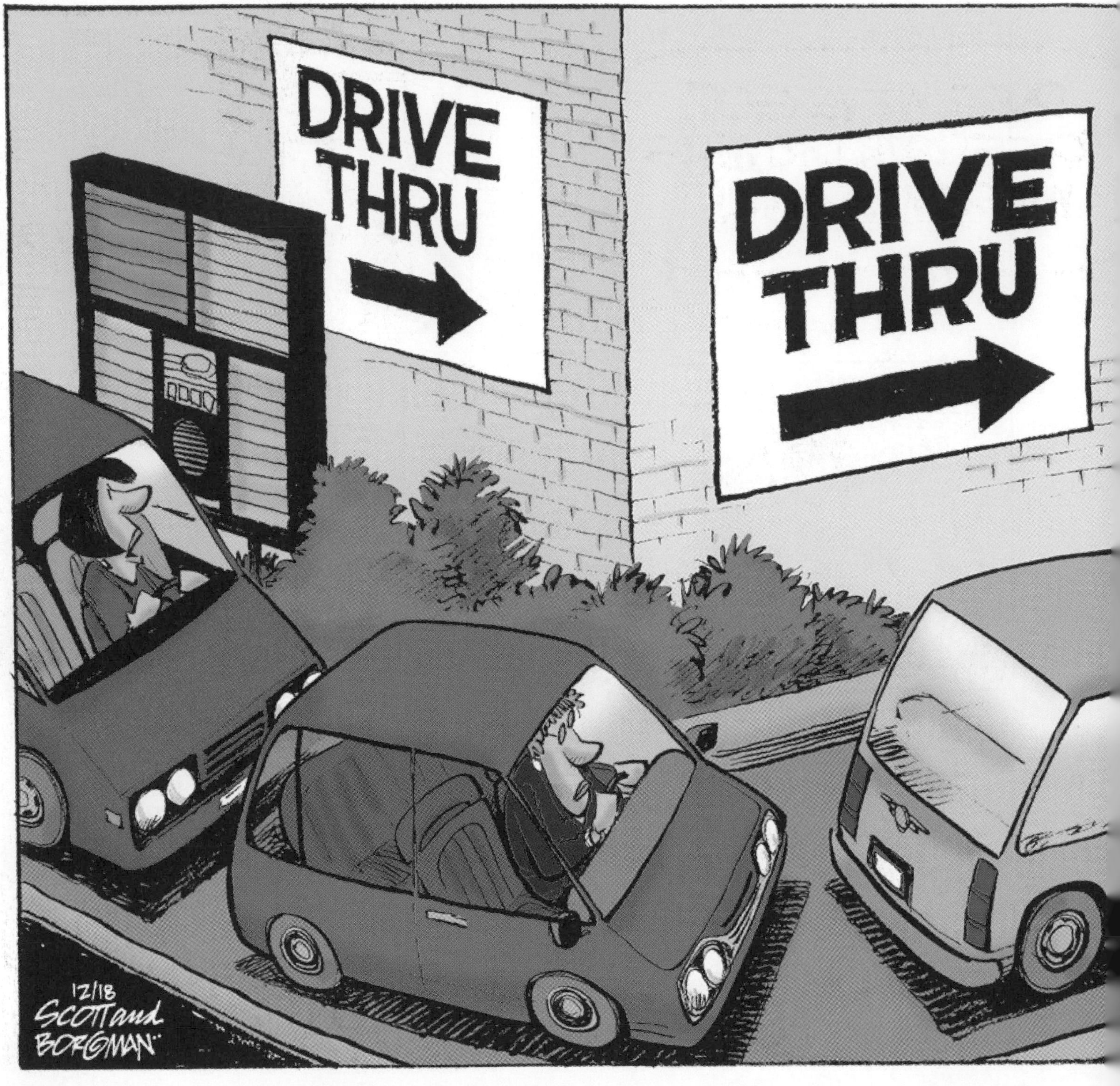
DRIVE
THRU
DRIVE
THRU
12/18
SCOTT and
BORGMAN

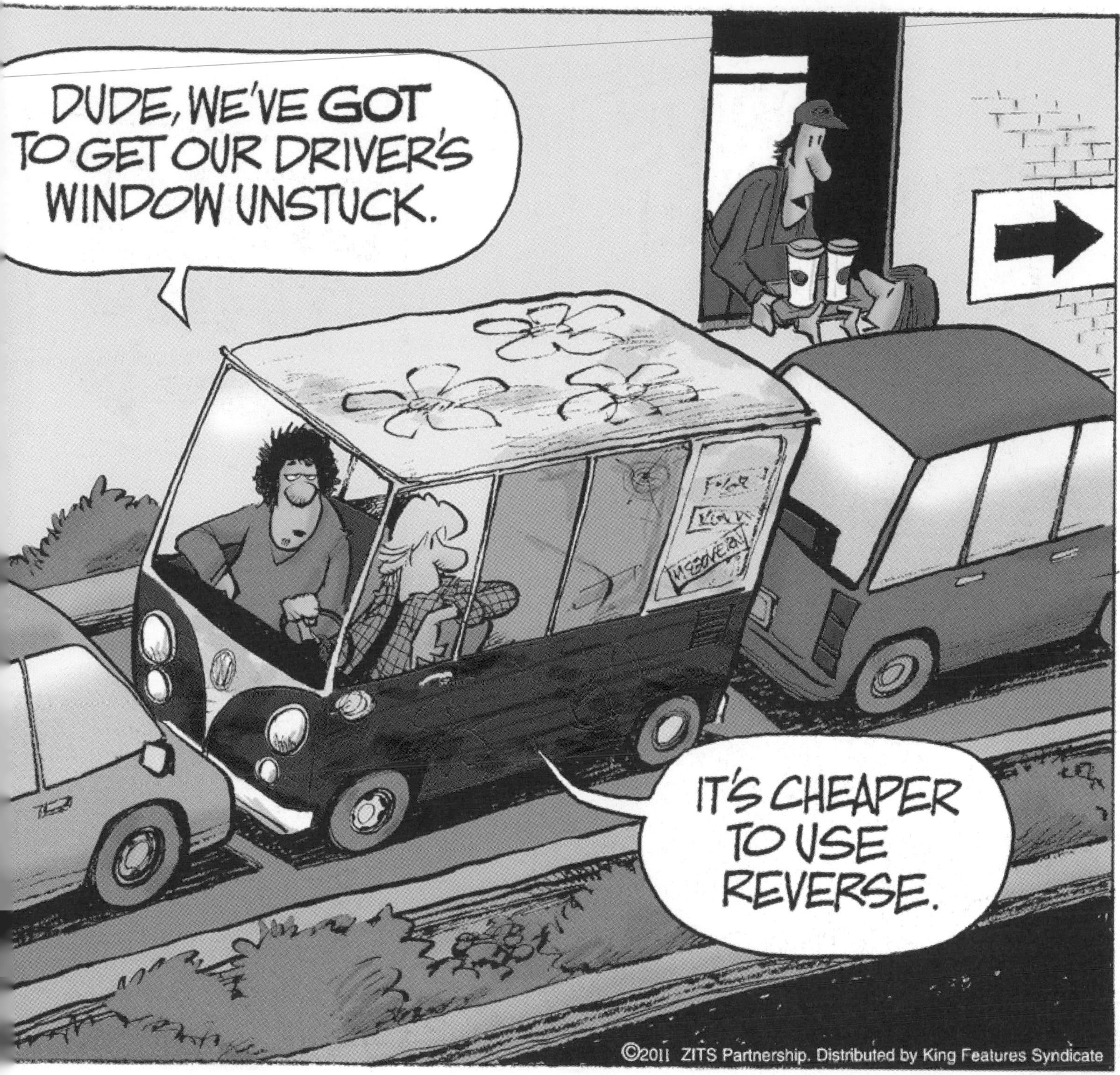
DUDE, WE'VE GOT TO GET OUR DRIVER'S WINDOW UNSTUCK.
IT'S CHEAPER TO USE REVERSE.